STRUCTURES

STRUCTURES

Fourth Edition

Daniel L. Schodek

Harvard University

Upper Saddle River, New Jersey
Columbus, Ohio

Library of Congress Cataloging-in-Publication Data

Schodek, Daniel L.
   Structures / Daniel L. Schodek.—4th ed.
      p. cm.
   Includes index.
   ISBN 0-13-027821-1
    1. Structural analysis (Engineering)   2. Structural design.   I. Title.
TA645.S37 2001
624.1′7—dc21   00-037358

Vice President and Publisher: Dave Garza
Editor in Chief: Stephen Helba
Executive Editor: Ed Francis
Production Editor: Christine M. Buckendahl
Production Coordinator: Mary Verrill, Clarinda Publication Services
Design Coordinator: Robin G. Chukes
Cover Designer: Thomas Borah
Cover Photo: SuperStock
Production Manager: Matthew Ottenweller
Marketing Manager: Jamie Van Voorhis

This book was set in Times Roman by The Clarinda Company, and was printed and bound by R. R. Donnelley & Sons Company. The cover was printed by Phoenix Color Corp.

10 9 8 7 6 5 4 3

ISBN: 0-13-027821-1

Preface

There exists an invariant set of physical principles founded in the field of mechanics that can be used by designers as aids to understanding the behavior of existing structural forms and in devising new approaches. The development of these principles has flowered during the past three centuries to the extent that they are amazingly well established and documented. Some new understandings, of course, are continuing to occur and will hopefully always occur. Still, the analytical tools already available to the designer are extensive and enormously powerful. This is true to the extent that the real challenge in the field of structures lies not so much in developing new analytical tools but in bringing those currently in existence to bear in the designing and formulation of creative structural solutions with the intent of making better buildings.

In this book we discuss in an introductory way the nature of the invariant physical principles that underlie the behavior of structures under load. The primary goal of the book, however, is not simply to teach analytical techniques but, more generally, to explore their role in the design of structures in a building context. Because of this larger goal, the book covers material discussed not only in specialized engineering curricula but also, to some extent, that covered in architecture curricula as well. The traditional hard boundaries between subdisciplines in engineering (e.g., statics and strength of materials) have also been deliberately softened and a more integrative approach taken.

The book is divided into three major parts. Part I is an introduction to the subject and to fundamental concepts of analysis and design. Part II introduces the reader to most of the primary structural elements used in buildings and discusses their analysis and design. Each of the chapters in this part is divided into sections that (1) introduce the element considered and explain its role in building, (2) discuss its behavior under load in qualitative terms (an "intuitive" approach), (3) examine its behavior under load in quantitative terms, and (4) discuss methods for designing (rather than just analyzing) the element. Part III contains a unique discussion of the logic of structural design, as it is a part of the larger building design process. The Appendices generally discuss more advanced principles of structural analysis.

The book is intended largely as a resource for students and instructors wishing to design their own curriculum. For those wanting to adopt a strictly qualitative approach to the subject, for example, it is possible to read only Chapter 1 in Part I, the sections entitled "Introduction" and "General Principles" in each of the chapters in Part II, and all of Part III. This coverage will provide a brief qualitative overview of the field with a special emphasis on design rather than analysis. For those students who already have a background in the analytical aspects of structures, Part III contains summary information useful in a design context. Part III can be read independently by such students.

Within Parts I, II, and III there is a certain redundancy in the way analytical topics are covered so that students or instructors can integrate the material in the order they see fit. Shear and moment diagrams, for example, are first introduced in an abstract way in Chapter 2. They are reintroduced in connection with the analysis of a specific structural element—the truss. *Where* the different presentations are introduced, if at all, may be varied by the instructor. The author, for example, typically chooses to introduce shear and moment diagrams initially as a part of truss analysis and then follow up with the more abstract development of shear and moment diagrams in Chapter 2 before going into beam analysis and design. Other instructors may choose to approach the subject material differently. The book is designed to have sufficient flexibility to support different approaches. In any event, the material is presented in such a way that a direct cover-to-cover reading is also appropriate.

The author is, of course, indebted to a vast number of people in either a direct or an indirect way for the approach taken in this book. Professor Spiro Pollalis contributed his time and help in revising the manuscript and in preparing the accompanying student CD which contains examples and case studies. The endless patience and contributions of several years of students in the Graduate School of Design at Harvard who have taken courses involving the material contained herein are also greatly appreciated. Especially important are Kay, Ned, and Ben Schodek, who provided their own special form of support. Thanks also to the reviewers of this edition for their helpful comments and suggestions: James W. Axley, Yale University; and Kurt G. Benedict, Wentworth Institute of Technology.

Daniel L. Schodek

Cambridge, Massachusetts

Contents

PART I

INTRODUCTORY CONCEPTS

The three chapters in Part I provide an overview and introduction to structures and their use in buildings. The first chapter is a self-contained overview of the field and discusses different ways of classifying structural elements and systems. The second chapter reviews certain fundamental principles of mechanics that are generally applicable to the analysis of any structure. The third chapter considers the loads that structures must be designed to carry and generally discusses the structural analysis and design process as it occurs in a building context.

CHAPTER 1

Structures: An Overview

1–1 INTRODUCTION

Definitions are a time-honored way of opening any book. A simple definition of a *structure* in a building context is that a structure is a device for channeling loads that result from the use and/or presence of the building to the ground. Important in the study of structures are many widely varying concerns. The study of structures certainly involves coming to understand the basic principles that define and characterize the behavior of physical objects subjected to forces. More fundamentally, it even involves defining what a force itself is, since this familiar term represents a fairly abstract concept. The study of structures in a building context also involves dealing with much broader issues of space and dimensionality. The words size, scale, form, proportion, and morphology are all terms commonly found in the vocabulary of a structural designer.

As a way of getting into the study of structures, it is useful to reconsider the first definition of a structure given here. Although valuable in the sense that it defines the purpose of a structure, the original definition unfortunately provides no insight into the makeup or characteristics of a structure: What *is* this device that channels loads to the ground? To adopt the complex and exacting style of a dictionary writer, a *structure* could be defined as a physical entity having a unitary character that can be conceived of as an organization of positioned constituent elements in space in which the character of the whole dominates the interrelationship of the parts. Its purpose would be defined as before.

Although it might be very hard to believe, a contorted and relatively abstract definition of this type which is almost laughably academic in tone actually has some merit. It first states that a

2

structure is a *real* physical object, not an abstract idea or interesting issue. A structure is not a matter of debate, it is something that is built. The implication is that a structure must be dealt with accordingly. Merely verbally postulating that a structure can carry a certain type of load or function in a certain way, for example, is inadequate. A physical device must be provided for accomplishing the desired ends that conforms to basic principles governing the behavior of physical objects. Devising such a structure is the role of the designer.

The expanded definition also makes the point that a structure functions as a whole. This is a point of fundamental importance and one easily forgotten when confronted with a typical building composed of a seemingly endless array of individual beams and columns. There is in such cases an immediate tendency to think of the structure only as an assembly of individual small elements in which each element performs a separate function. In actuality, all structures are, and must be, primarily designed to function as a whole unit and only secondarily as an array of discrete elements. In line with the latter part of the expanded definition, these elements are invariably so positioned and interrelated as to enable the overall structure to function as a whole in carrying either vertically or horizontally acting loads to the ground. No matter how some individual elements are located and attached to one another, if the resultant configuration and interrelation of all elements does not function as a whole unit in channeling loads of all anticipated types to the ground, the configuration cannot be said to be a structure. The reference to anticipated types of loads in the previous statement is included to bring up the important fact that structures are normally devised in response to a specific set of loading conditions and function as structures only with respect to these conditions. They are often relatively fragile with respect to unanticipated loads. A typical building having a structure capable of carrying normally encountered occupancy and environmental loads cannot, for example, be simply picked up by a corner and transported through space. It would simply fall apart, since its structure would not have been designed to carry the unique loadings involved. So much for Superman carrying buildings around.

While on the subject of formal definitions, the act of designing a structure can be defined in language at least as complex as that used previously to define a structure, but again the result is of some value. Designing a structure is the act of positioning constituent elements and formulating interrelations with the objective of imparting a desired character to the resultant structural entity. The notions that elements are positioned and that relationships exist among these elements are basic to the concept of designing a structure.

There are many ways that elements can be positioned to carry loads and there are many relationships that may exist. For example, a block arch is made of carefully positioned elements. A beam may be related to a column either by simply resting on top of it, or it may be rigidly attached to it, with radically different structural actions ensuing. These issues are explored in the remainder of the book.

1-2 GENERAL TYPES OF STRUCTURES

1-2-1 Primary Classifications

Introduction. Fundamental to an understanding of any field is a knowledge of the way type groups within the field are systematically distinguished, ordered, and named. A knowledge of the criteria or presumed relationships that form the basis for classifications of this type is similarly important. This section introduces one method for classifying structural elements and systems, which is simply according to their shape and basic physical properties of construction (see Figure 1–1). Since this classification scheme implies that complex structures are the result only of additive aggregations of elements, it is inherently simplistic. Of significance in aggregations is only the additive nature of the elements. Of significance in structures is that the elements are also positioned and related with the intent of giving the structure certain load-carrying attributes. Still, the simpler classification approach illustrated in Figure 1–1 is useful as an introduction.

Geometry.   In terms of their basic geometries, the structural forms indicated to the left in Figure 1–1 can generally be classified either as *line-forming elements* (or composed of line elements) or as *surface-forming elements*. Line-forming elements can be further distinguished as straight or curved. Surface-forming elements are either planar or curved. Curved-surface elements can be of either single or double curvature.

Strictly speaking, there is, of course, no such thing as a line or surface element, since all structural elements have thicknesses. For classification purposes, however, it is still useful to classify any long, slender element (such as a column whose cross-sectional dimensions are small with respect to its length) as a line element. Similarly, surface elements also have thicknesses, but this thickness is again small with respect to length dimensions.

Closely coupled with whether an element is linear or surface-forming is the material and/or method of construction used. Many materials are naturally line-forming. Timber, for example, is inherently line-forming simply because of the way in which timber is grown. It is possible, however, to make minor surface-forming elements directly from timber (as is evidenced by common plywood) or larger surface-forming structures by aggregating more elemental pieces. Other materials, such as concrete, can be line-forming or surface-forming with equal ease. Steel is primarily line-forming, but it is also possible to make directly minor surface-forming elements (e.g., steel decking).

Stiffness.   Figure 1–1 also illustrates a second fundamental classification, which is according to the stiffness characteristics of the structural element. The primary distinction here is whether the element is rigid or flexible. *Rigid elements,* such as typical beams, are those that do not undergo *appreciable* shape changes under the action of a load or changing loads [see Figure 1–2(a)]. They are, however, usually bent or bowed to a small degree by the action of the load.

Flexible elements, such as cables, are those in which the element assumes one shape under one loading condition and changes shape drastically when the nature of the loading changes [see Figure 1–2(b)]. Flexible structures maintain their physical integrity, however, no matter what shape they assume.*

Often associated with whether an element is rigid or flexible is the material of construction used. Many materials, such as timber, are inherently rigid. Other materials, such as steel, can be used to make either rigid or flexible members. A good example of a rigid steel member is the typical beam (an element that does not undergo appreciable change in shape under changing loads). A steel cable or chain, however, is clearly a flexible member since the shape that such elements

---

*The common English-language connotations of the terms "rigid" and "flexible" are evoked here. In some more advanced structural theory applications, these terms are not used in their literal sense. Rather, distinctions are made between stiffness, strength, and stability.

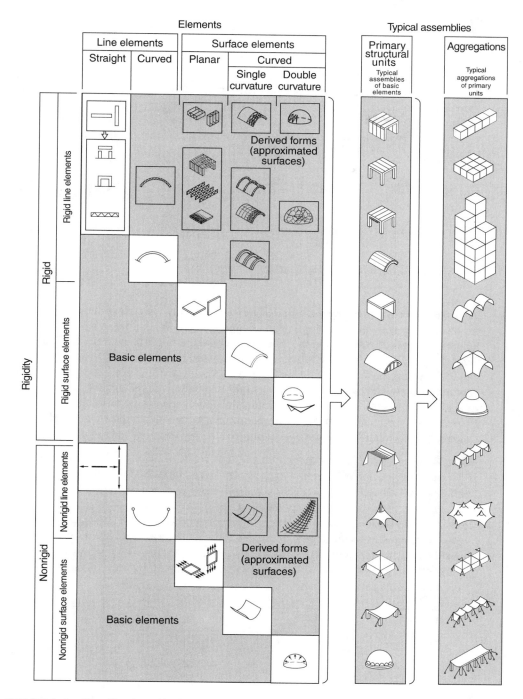

FIGURE 1–1 Classification of basic structural elements according to geometry and primary physical characteristics. Typical primary structural units and other aggregations are also illustrated. The schema is limited and suggests nothing about the importance of properly positioning constituent elements to make feasible structural assemblies.

5

(a) Rigid structure (e.g., a beam). The structure is stiff and does not undergo appreciable changes in shape with changes in the loading condition.

(b) Nonrigid or flexible structure (e.g., a cable). The shape of the structure changes with changes in the loading condition.

FIGURE 1–2 Nonrigid and rigid structures.

assume under loading is a function of the exact pattern and magnitudes of the load carried. A steel cable thus changes shape with changing loads. Whether a structure is rigid or flexible therefore depends *either* upon the inherent characteristics of the material used or on the amount and microorganization of the material in the element.

Many specific structures that are usually classified as rigid are in actuality rigid only under certain given loading conditions or under minor variations of the given loading condition. When the loading changes dramatically, structures of this type become unstable and tend to collapse. Structures such as arches made by aggregating smaller rigid elements (e.g., blocks) into larger shapes are often in this category.

One-Way and Two-Way Systems. A very basic way of distinguishing among structures is according to the spatial organization of the system of support used and the relation of the structure to the points of support available. The two primary cases of importance here are one- and two-way systems. In a *one-way system* the basic load-transfer mechanism of the structure for channeling external loads to the ground acts in one direction only. In a *two-way system* the direction of the load-transfer mechanism is more complex but always involves at least two directions. A linear beam spanning between two support points is an example of a one-way system (see the top of Figure 1–3). A system of two crossed elements resting on two sets of support points not lying

One-way Structures		Two-way Structures	
One-way beam	One-way plate	Two-way beams	Two-way plate

FIGURE 1–3 Types of structural elements. (continued)

Typical Rigid Structures

Post & beam

Simple truss

Load-bearing walls

Block dome

Frame

Trussed frame

Plate or slab

Rigid shell

Block arch

Three-hinged arch

Folded plate

Geodesic dome

Rigid fixed arch

Two-hinged arch

Cylindrical shell

Ribbed dome

Arch with tie-rod

Arch with buttresses

Block vault

Hyperbolic paraboloid

Typical Flexible Structures

Suspended cable

Double cable

Suspended cables

Pneumatic membrane

Suspended cable

Cable-stayed

Tent

Stretched net

FIGURE 1–3 (continued)

on the same line and in which both elements share in carrying any external load is an example of a two-way system. A square, flat rigid plate resting on four continuous edge supports is also a two-way system. An external load cannot be simplistically assumed to travel to a pair of the supports in one direction only.

The distinction between one- and two-way structural action is of primary importance in a design context. As will be discussed in more detail later, there are situations typically involving certain patterns in the support system used that often lead to certain advantages (in terms of the efficient use of materials) in using a two-way system as compared to a one-way system. Other patterns in the support system, however, often lead to the converse result. For this reason it is useful even at this early stage to begin distinguishing between one- and two-way systems.

Materials.   A very common classification approach to structures is simply by the type of material used (e.g., wood, steel, or reinforced concrete structures). A strict classification by materials, however, is somewhat misleading and is not adopted here since the principles governing the behavior of similar elements composed of different materials (e.g., a timber and steel beam) are invariant, and the actual differences present are superficial. More general descriptions are of more intrinsic value at this stage.

As one begins taking a more detailed look at structures, however, the importance of materials will increase. One reason for this is that there is a close relationship between the nature of the deformations induced in a structure by the action of the external loading and the material and method of construction that is most appropriate for use in the structure. Steel can be used under virtually all conditions. Plain concrete can be used only in situations where the structure is only compressed or shortened under the action of the load. Concrete will crack and fail when subjected to forces that tend to elongate the material. Concrete reinforced with steel, however, can be used in situations where elongating forces are present, since the steel can be designed to carry these forces. These and other considerations will be studied in more detail later in this book.

1–2–2   Primary Structural Elements

Elements.   Common rigid elements include beams, columns or struts, arches, flat plates, singly curved plates, and shells having a variety of different curvatures. Flexible elements include cables (straight and draped) and membranes (planar, singly curved, and doubly curved). In addition, there are a number of other types of structures that are derived from these elements (e.g., frames, trusses, geodesic domes, nets, etc.). Assigning a specific name to refer to an element having certain geometrical and rigidity characteristics is done as a matter of convenience only and has its basis in historical tradition. Naming elements in this way can, however, be misleading, since it is too easy to fall into believing that if two elements have different names, the way they carry loads must also be different. This is not necessarily so. Indeed, one of the basic principles of structures that later portions of this book will clarify and elaborate on is that the fundamental load-carrying mechanism for all structures is the same. At this point, however, it is still useful to retain and use the traditional names as a way of gaining familiarity with the subject.

Beams and Columns.   Structures formed by resting rigid horizontal elements on top of rigid vertical elements are commonplace. Often called post-and-beam structures, the horizontal elements *(beams)* pick up loads that are applied transversely to their lengths and transfer them to the supporting vertical columns or posts. The *columns,* loaded axially by the beams, transfer the loads to the ground. Since the beams are bowed or bent as a consequence of the transverse loading carried (see Figure 1–3), they are often said to carry loads by *bending.* The columns in a beam-and-column assembly are not bent or bowed, since they are subjected to axial compressive forces only. In a building, the absolute length of individual beams and columns that is possible is rather limited as compared to some other structural elements (e.g., cables). Beams and columns are therefore typically used in a repetitive pattern. Simple single-span beams and columns are discussed more extensively in Chapters 6 and 7, respectively. Continuous beams that bear on multiple support points are discussed in Chapter 8. Continuous beams often exhibit more advantageous structural properties than simpler single-span beams supported only at two points.

Frames.   The *frame,* illustrated in Figure 1–3, is similar in appearance to the post-and-beam type of structure but has a different structural action because of the rigid joints that are made between vertical and horizontal members. This joint rigidity imparts a measure of stability against lateral forces that is not present in the post-and-beam system. In a framed system both beams and columns are bent or bowed as a consequence of the action of the load on the structure. As with the post-and-beam structure, the lengths of individual elements in a frame structure that are possible are limited. Consequently, members are typically formed into a repetitive pattern when used in a building. In Chapter 9 we discuss frames in detail.

Trusses.   *Trusses* are structural members made by assembling short, straight members into triangulated patterns. The resultant structure is rigid as a result of the exact way the individual line elements are positioned relative to one another. Some patterns (e.g., a pattern of squares rather than triangles) do not necessarily yield a structure that is rigid (unless joints are treated in the same way as in framed structures). A truss composed of discrete elements is bent or bowed in an overall way under the action of an applied transverse loading in much the same way that a beam is bent or bowed. Individual truss members, however, are not subject to bending but are only either compressed or pulled upon. Trusses are explored in depth in Chapter 4.

Arches.   An *arch* is a curved, line-forming structural member that spans between two points. The common image of an arch is that of a structure composed of separate wedge-shaped pieces that retain their position by mutual pressure induced by the load. The exact shape of the curve and the nature of the loading are critical determinants as to whether the resultant assembly is stable. When shapes are formed by simply stacking rigid block elements, the resultant structure is functional and stable only when the action of the load is to induce in-plane forces that cause the structure to compress uniformly. Structures of this type cannot carry loads that induce elongations or any pronounced type of bowing in the member (the blocks simply pull apart and failure occurs). Block structures can be very strong, however, when used properly, as their extensive historical usage attests. The strength of a block structure is due exclusively to the *positioning* of individual elements, since blocks are typically either simply rested one on another or mortared together (the mortar does not appreciably increase the strength of the structure). The positioning is, in turn, dependent on the exact type of loading involved. The resultant structure is thus rigid only under very particular circumstances. These issues are discussed more extensively in Chapter 5.

   The *rigid arch* is frequently used in modern buildings. It is curved similarly to block arches but is made of one continuous piece of deformed rigid material (Figure 1–3). If rigid arches are properly shaped, they can carry a load to supports while being subject only to axial compression, and no bowing or bending occurs. The rigid arch is better able to carry variations in the design loading than is its block counterpart made of individual pieces. Many types of rigid arches exist and are often characterized by their support conditions (fixed, two-hinged, three-hinged). Arches of this type are discussed in more detail in Chapter 5.

Walls and Plates. Walls and flat plates are rigid surface-forming structures. A load-bearing wall can typically carry both vertically acting loads and laterally acting loads (wind, earthquake) along its length. Resistance to out-of-plane forces in block walls is marginal. A flat plate is typically used horizontally and carries loads by bending to its supports. Plate structures are normally made of reinforced concrete or steel.

Horizontal plates can also be made by assembling patterns of short, rigid line elements. Three-dimensional triangulation schemes are used to impart stiffness to the resultant assembly. Plate structures are explored in more detail in Chapter 10.

Long, narrow rigid plates can also be joined along their long edges and used to span horizontally in beamlike fashion. These structures, called *folded plates,* have the potential for spanning fairly large distances. Folded plates are explored in detail in Chapter 10.

Cylindrical Shells and Vaults. Cylindrical barrel shells and vaults are examples of *singly curved-plate* structures. A barrel shell spans longitudinally such that the curve is perpendicular to the direction of the span. When fairly long, a barrel shell behaves much like a beam with a curved cross section. Barrell shells are invariably made of rigid materials (e.g., reinforced concrete or steel). A *vault,* by contrast, is a singly curved structure that spans transversely. A vault can be conceived of as basically a continuous arch.

Spherical Shells and Domes. A wide variety of doubly curved surface structures are in use. These include structures that are portions of spheres and those that form warped surfaces (e.g., the hyperbolic paraboloid). The number of shapes possible is actually boundless. Probably the most common doubly curved structure is the spherical shell. It is convenient to think of this structure as a rotated arch. This analogy, however, is actually misleading with respect to how the structure actually carries loads because of the fact that loadings induce circumferential forces in spherical shells which do not exist in arches. Exact differences are discussed in Chapter 12. Domed structures can be made of stacked blocks or a continuous rigid material (reinforced concrete). Shells and domes are very efficient structures capable of spanning large distances using a minimum of material. Dome-shaped structures can also be made by forming short rigid line elements into repetitive patterns. The *geodesic dome* is a structure of this type.

Cables. *Cables* are flexible structural elements. The shape they assume under a loading depends on the nature and magnitude of the load. When a cable is simply pulled on at either end, it assumes a straight shape. This type of cable is often called a *tie-rod.* When a cable is used to span between two points and carry an external point load or series of point loads, it deforms into a shape made up of a series of straight-line segments. When a continuous load is carried, the cable deforms into a continuously curving shape. The self-weight of the cable itself produces such a *catenary curve.* Other continuous loads produce curves that are similar in appearance but not exactly the same as the catenary curve.

Suspension cables can be used to span extremely large distances. They are quite often used for bridges, where they support a road deck, which in turn carries the traffic loading. Since moving traffic loads would ordinarily cause the primary support cable to undergo shape changes as load positions changed, and with this changes in the shape of the road surface would occur, the horizontal bridge deck is made into a continuous rigid structure so that the road surface remains essentially flat and the load transferred to the primary support cables remains essentially constant. Cable-stayed structures are used to support roof surfaces in buildings, particularly in long-span situations. Cable structures are discussed more extensively in Chapter 5.

Membranes, Tents, and Nets.   A *membrane* is a thin, flexible sheet. A common *tent* is made of membrane surfaces. Both simple and complex forms can be created using membranes. For surfaces of double curvature, such as a spherical surface, however, the actual surface would have to be made as an assembly of much smaller segments, since most membranes are typically available only in flat sheets (a spherical surface is, of course, not developable). A further implication of using a flexible membrane to create the surface is that it either has to be suspended with the convex side pointing downward or, if used with the convex side pointed upward, supplemented by some mechanism to maintain its shape. Pneumatic, or air-inflated, structures are of the latter type. The shape of the membrane is maintained by the internal air pressure inside the structure. Another mechanism is to apply external jacking forces that stretch the membrane into the desired shape. Various stressed-skin structures are of this general type. The need to pretension the skin, however, imposes various limitations on the shape that can be formed. Spherical surfaces, for example, are very difficult to pretension by external jacking forces, while others, such as the hyperbolic paraboloid, can be handled with comparative ease.

    Nets are three-dimensional surfaces made up of a series of crossed curved cables. Nets are very analogous to membrane skins. By allowing the mesh opening to vary as needed, a wide variety of surface shapes can be formed. An advantage of using crossed cables is that the positioning of the cables mitigates fluttering due to wind suctions and pressures. In addition, tension forces are typically induced into the cables by jacking devices, so that the whole surface is turned into a type of stretched skin. This also gives the roof stability and resistance to flutter. Membranes and nets are discussed more extensively in Chapter 11.

1–2–3   Primary Structural Units and Aggregations

Introduction.   While many of the basic elements discussed in the preceding section can indeed function in isolation as load-carrying structures, it is evident that some of them must be combined with others if the intent is to create a structure that encloses or forms a volume. It is in this respect that structures used in buildings are often distinct from those used for other purposes. Building structures are typically volume-forming in nature; others are not necessarily so. Bridge structures, for example, are typically used to form or support linear surfaces.

    In this context it is useful to introduce for building design the general notion of a *primary structural unit,* which is simply a discrete volume-forming structural element or assembly of structural elements. Four columns supporting a rigid planar surface at its corners, for example, form a primary unit. Units of this type can be stacked and/or placed side by side to form a connected series of volumetric units. When placed side by side, columns are typically shared between units. Primary units are often an intermediate step between a series of discrete elements (e.g., beams and columns) and an entire building complex. The way discrete elements can be conceptually assembled into units and then aggregated often, but certainly not always, reflects the way building complexes are actually constructed.

The importance of thinking about structures in terms of units of this type is most apparent in preliminary design stages. The usefulness of the idea stems from the fact that the dimensions of a unit must invariably be related to the programmatic requirements of the building considered. Many buildings, for example, can be considered to be made up of a cellular aggregation of volumetric units of sizes related to the intended occupancy. Housing is an illustration of such a building type. In this case the dimensions of the primary structural unit would be directly related to the functional dimensions of the housing units themselves. The primary structural unit, however, could be larger and encompass several functional units. It could not be smaller than the minimum functional subdivision of a unit. The point herein is simply that the dimensions of the primary structural unit are either the same as, or a multiple of, the critical functional dimensions associated with the building occupancy. In some cases, it should be noted, the building can be defined as essentially consisting of one large functional unit (e.g., a skating rink) and not consisting of an aggregation of cellular volumes. These are simple but immensely valuable concepts useful in early design stages that are explored in more detail in Part III of the book.

Structural Units.   Primary structural units may be made using different combinations of the elements discussed previously (see Figure 1–4). For common cellular units, it is pedagogically useful to distinguish among the *horizontal spanning* system, the *vertical support* system, and the *lateral support* system. For planar surfaces, horizontal spanning systems may be made up of one- or two-way spanning elements. For systems made of one-way spanning elements, there is often a hierarchy present. For example, short-span surface-forming plank or decking elements are periodically supported by a series of closely spaced secondary beams, which in turn may be supported themselves by other beams. Loads acting on the surface, such as snow, are first picked up by the decking and are then transferred to the secondary beams. The secondary beams in turn transfer the loads to the vertical support system. Forces are transferred from one member to another via the development of *reactive* forces at member supports. Loads and related internal forces consequently tend to build up in members in lower layers of the hierarchy, which thus often need to be made larger and stiffer than others.

Hierarchies of virtually any number of layers may be used, but one, two, and three layers are most common. In short-span situations, beam and decking systems are common. As spans increase, trusses or cables might be used for secondary and primary spanning elements. Obviously, other spanning systems, such as arches and barrel shells, could be used as well.

Plate-and-grid systems may also be used for spanning horizontally. For short spans, there is often only one layer present when plates are used. As spans increase, a hierarchic system of plates and beams may be used.

For common cellular assemblies, vertical support systems are typically composed of load-bearing walls or columns. Load-bearing walls may be used to receive loads along their length (e.g., from a horizontal plate). Columns receive concentrated forces, typically from the ends of beams. There is thus a close relation between the pattern of the vertical support system and the nature of the horizontal spanning system.

Horizontally acting forces (wind, earthquake) tend to cause structures to collapse laterally. Wall structures are inherently resistant to these forces. Beam and column systems, however, typically need cross bracing. Rigid-frame systems that are also resistant to lateral forces provide an alternative to beam-and-column assemblies. Stability responses of this type are explored more in a following section.

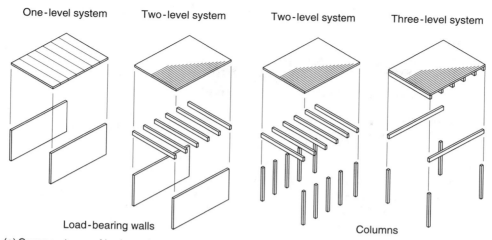

One-level system Two-level system Two-level system Three-level system

Load-bearing walls   Columns

(a) Common types of horizontal spanning systems (one, two, and three level systems) used in relation to different types of load-bearing wall and columnar vertical support systems.

Horizontal spanning system

Vertical support system

Lateral support system

Roof loads

Decking carries roof loads by bending.

Decking reactions become forces on beams (which carry loads by bending).

Beam reactions become forces on trusses.

Truss reactions cause compressive forces to develop in columns.

Columns are in compression. →

Column reactions become forces on foundations (which distribute the forces into the earth).

(b) Common assembly of elements. The surface-forming decking is supported by a secondary framing system consisting of closely spaced beams, which is in turn supported by a primary system of more widely spaced trusses. A one-on-one fit exists between the trusses and the supporting columns.

(c) The decking transfers roof loads to the secondary beams. The beams transfer the loads to the trusses, which in turn carry them to the columns. The columns transmit the loads to the foundations. These force transfers occur through the development of reactive forces between members and typically get progressively larger at lower levels.

FIGURE 1–4 Typical structural units.

13

1–3   BASIC ISSUES IN THE ANALYSIS AND DESIGN OF STRUCTURES

1–3–1   Fundamental Structural Phenomena

In the preceding section we discussed the nature of structural forms in broad terms. The specific forms noted experience applied forces that potentially cause the form to slide or overturn as a whole, or to collapse internally. Alternatively, components could break apart or deform badly. The forces causing overturning or collapse come from the specific environmental or use context present (e.g., wind, earthquakes, occupancies) or from the self-weight of the form itself. These same applied loadings produce internal forces in a structure that stress the material used and may cause it to fail or deform. There are several fundamental ways in which failure can occur. In the following we describe these phenomena briefly (see Figure 1–5). In subsequent chapters we explore them in greater detail.

A *first* set of concerns deals with the *overall stability* of a work. As a whole unit, a structure might overturn, slide, or twist about its base—particularly when subjected to horizontally acting

FIGURE 1–5   Structural phenomena and general design responses.

wind or earthquake forces. Structures that are relatively tall and/or have small bases are particularly prone to overturning effects. Forces induced by earthquakes tend to cause overturning or sliding actions, but they are dependent in magnitude on the weight of the structure because of the inertial character of earthquake forces. Overturning or twisting need not be caused only by horizontally acting forces. A work might simply be out of balance under its own self-weight and overturn. The use of wide, rigid foundations helps prevent overturning, as does the use of special foundation elements such as piles capable of carrying tension forces.

A *second* set of concerns deals with *internal,* or *relational, stability.* If the parts of a structure are not properly arranged in space or interconnected appropriately, an entire assembly can collapse internally. Collapses of this type invariably involve large relative movements within the structure itself. Assemblies may be internally stable under one loading condition and unstable under another. Horizontally acting wind or earthquake forces, in particular, cause collapses of this kind. There are several basic mechanisms—walls, frame action, cross bracing—for making an assembly internally stable. In the following section we explore the issue of stability in greater detail.

A *third* set of concerns deals with the *strength* and *stiffness* of constituent elements. There are many structural issues that revolve around the strength of component parts of a structure. These failures, which may or may not lead to total collapse, may be caused by excessive tension, compression, bending, shear, torsional, bearing forces, or deformations that are developed internally in the structure as a consequence of the applied loadings. Associated with each force state are internal stresses that actually exist within the fabric of the material itself. By carefully designing components in response to the force state present, the actual stresses developed in the components can be controlled to safe levels.

1–3–2   Structural Stability

A fundamental consideration in designing a structure is that of assuring its *stability* under any type of possible loading condition. All structures undergo some shape changes under load. In a stable structure the deformations induced by the load are typically small, and internal forces are generated in the structure by the action of the load that tend to restore the structure to its original shape after the load has been removed. In an unstable structure, the deformations induced by a load are typically massive and often tend to continue to increase as long as the load is applied. An unstable structure does not generate internal forces that tend to restore the structure to its original configuration. Unstable structures quite often collapse completely and instantaneously as a load is applied to them. It is the fundamental responsibility of the structural designer to assure that a proposed structure does indeed form a stable configuration.

Stability is a crucial issue in the design of structures that are assemblies of discrete elements. For example, the post-and-beam structure illustrated in Figure 1–6(a) is apparently stable. Any horizontal force, however, tends to cause deformations of the type indicated in Figure 1–6(b). Clearly, the structure has no capacity to resist horizontal loads, nor does it have any mechanism that tends to restore it to its initial shape after the horizontal load is removed. The large changes in angle that occur between members characterize an unstable structure that is beginning to collapse. This particular structure will collapse almost instantaneously under load. Consequently, this particular pattern of members is referred to as a *collapse mechanism.*

There are really only a few fundamental ways of converting a self-standing structure of the general type shown in Figure 1–6(b) from an unstable to a stable configuration. These are illustrated in Figure 1–6(d). The first is to add a *diagonal member* to the structure. The structure cannot now undergo the parallelograming indicated in Figure 1–6(b) without a dramatic release in the length of the diagonal member (this would not occur if the diagonal were adequately sized to take the forces involved). Another method used to assure stability is through *shear walls*. These are rigid planar surface elements that inherently resist shape changes of the type illustrated. A reinforced concrete or masonry wall can be used as a shear wall. Either a full or a partial wall can be used (the required extent of a partial wall depends on the magnitudes of the forces involved). A final method used to achieve stability is through stopping the large angular changes between members that is associated with collapse by assuring that the nature of the connections between

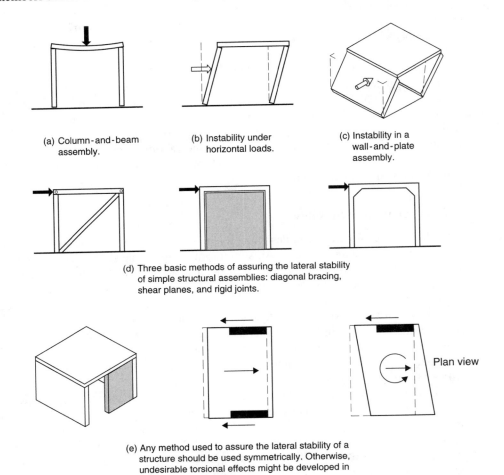

(a) Column-and-beam assembly.

(b) Instability under horizontal loads.

(c) Instability in a wall-and-plate assembly.

(d) Three basic methods of assuring the lateral stability of simple structural assemblies: diagonal bracing, shear planes, and rigid joints.

Plan view

(e) Any method used to assure the lateral stability of a structure should be used symmetrically. Otherwise, undesirable torsional effects might be developed in the structure.

FIGURE 1–6 Stability of structures.

members is such that their angular relationship remains a constant value under any loading. This is done by making a *rigid joint* between members. This is a very common form of joint. A typical table, for example, is a stable structure because there is a rigid joint between each table leg and the top that maintains a constant angular relationship between the elements. Structures using rigid joints to assure stability are referred to as *frames*.

There are, of course, variants on these basic methods of assuring stability. Still most structures composed of discrete elements rely on one or the other of these basic approaches for stability. More than one approach can be used in a structure (e.g., a structure having both rigid joints and a diagonal), but a measure of redundancy is obviously involved.

Referring to the assemblies diagrammed in Figure 1–7, one or another of the lateral-stability devices must be used to ensure that the structures do not collapse laterally. A single volumetric element may be designed with one stability device in one direction and another in the other. A larger aggregation of volumetric units might have stability devices along the external periphery only (instead of around each unit) or at a few locations internally.

FIGURE 1–7   Common structural options for a typical volumetric unit.

1-3-3 Members in Tension, Compression, Bending, Shear, Torsion, and Bearing: An Introduction

The action of an external force on a structure due to its environment or use produces internal forces within a structure. The most common internal force states are those of tension, compression, bending, shear, torsion, and bearing (Figure 1-8). Associated with each of these force states are related internal stresses and strains. *Stress* is a measure of internal force intensity per unit area [typically measured in lb/in.^{2} or N/mm^2 (MPa)], and *strain* is a measure of deformation (typically measured in in./in. or mm/mm).

   Tension forces tend to pull an element apart. The strength of a tension member depends on the cross-sectional area of a member and the material of which it is made. Members in tension can be quite strong, as attested to by the many cables in use in long-span structures. The strength of a tension member is generally independent of its length. Tension stresses are uniformly distributed across the cross section of the member (stress = force/area).

   Compression forces tend to crush or buckle an element. Short members tend to crush and have high strengths comparable to members in tension. The load-carrying capacity of a long compression member, however, tends to decrease with increasing lengths. Long compression members may become unstable and may suddenly snap out from beneath a load at certain critical load levels. This sudden inability to carry additional load typically occurs without evident

FIGURE 1-8 Compression, tension, bending, shear, bearing, torsion, and deflections.

material distress. The phenomenon is called *buckling*. Because of the buckling phenomenon, long compression members are not capable of carrying very high loads.

Bending is a complex force state associated with the bowing of a member (typically, a beam) under a transversely applied loading. The bending action causes fibers on one face of the member to elongate, and hence be in tension, and fibers on the opposing face to compress. Thus both tension and compression stresses are developed at the same cross section (this complex force state is *not* given simply by stress = force/area). These stresses act perpendicular to the face of the section. A member subject to bending can carry only a surprisingly small amount of load relative to the size of the member and in comparison to a member carrying purely tensile forces. The strength of a member in bending is highly dependent on the amount and distribution of material in a cross section, as well as its type. Special responses to carrying bending forces include the ubiquitous wide-flange shape in steel or the common reinforced concrete beam (where the steel is used to carry the tension forces involved).

Shear is a force state associated with the action of opposing forces that tend to cause one part of a structure to slide with respect to an adjacent part. Stresses that act tangential to the sliding surface are developed. Shear stresses are common in beams.

Torsion is a twisting. Both tension and compression stresses are normally developed in a member subjected to torsion.

Bearing stresses exist at the interface between two members when forces are transferred from one member to another. Bearing stresses are developed, for example, at the ends of beams where they rest on walls or column tops. The stresses act perpendicular to the faces of the members.

Deflections caused by loads on members must be limited to allowable values. Other, more complex stresses and stress interactions are also developed in members. In subsequent chapters we discuss these phenomena in detail.

1–4 FUNICULAR STRUCTURES: ARCHES, CABLES, AND RELATED FORMS

1–4–1 Basic Characteristics

Many whole structures can be characterized as being primarily in a state of pure tension or compression. These are interesting structures deserving special treatment. Consider a simple flexible cable spanning between two points and carrying a load. This structure must be exclusively in a state of tension, since a flexible cable can withstand neither compression nor bending. A cable carrying a concentrated load at midspan would deform as indicated in Figure 1–9. The whole structure is in tension. If this exact shape were simply inverted and loaded precisely in the same way, it is evident by analogy that the resultant structure would be in a state of pure compression. If the loading condition is changed to a continuous load, a flexible cable carrying this load would naturally deform into the parabolic shape indicated in Figure 1–9. Again, the whole structure is in tension. If this exact shape were inverted and loaded with the same continuous load, the resultant structure would be in a state of compression. The common arch is predominantly a structure of this type. Structures with shapes derived in this way, wherein only a state of tension or compression is induced by the loading, are referred to as *funicular structures*.

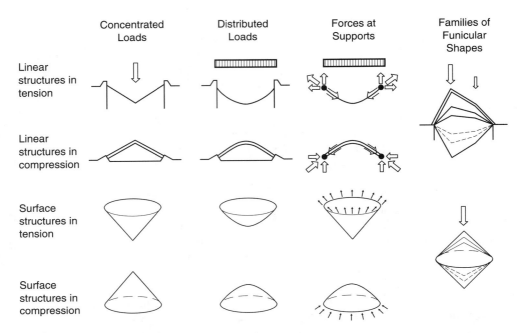

FIGURE 1–9 Typical funicular structures.

The easiest way to determine the funicular response for a particular loading condition is by determining the exact shape a flexible string would deform to under the load. This is the tension funicular. Inverting this shape exactly yields a compression funicular. There is only one funicular shape for a given loading condition. Bending would develop in any structure whose shape deviates from the funicular one for the given loading. Figure 1–10 illustrates an early, but nonetheless latter-day, analysis of a well-known structure that is based on the idea that an arch can be conceived of as an inverted catenary.

Funiculars need not be only two-dimensional structures, but can be three-dimensional as well (see Figure 1–9). The shape a flexible membrane assumes under a uniformly distributed load is of special interest. Since the funicular response is clearly not spherical, but rather parabolic, it follows that the ubiquitous spherical shell often commonly thought ideal as a structural form for this type of loading is, in fact, not exactly a funicular response for the vertical loads which commonly act on buildings (it is, however, for a radial loading). This does not, however, limit its usefulness, since there are other mechanisms at work (circumferential forces) in a shell structure of this type that still cause the structure to be highly efficient. These mechanisms are discussed in Chapter 12. Figure 1–11 illustrates a well-known example of the application of the idea of three-dimensional funicular shapes as the basis for determining the form of a structure.

1–4–2 Structural Behavior

There are many variants possible in the way funicular structures are used in actual practice. Clearly, they can be used in their pure forms as arches or cables. More generally, however, the

FIGURE 1–10   St. Peter's Dome, Rome. Construction of the thrust line as an inverted catenary. (From Poleni, *Memorie istoriche della Gran Cupola del Tempio Vaticano,* 1748.)

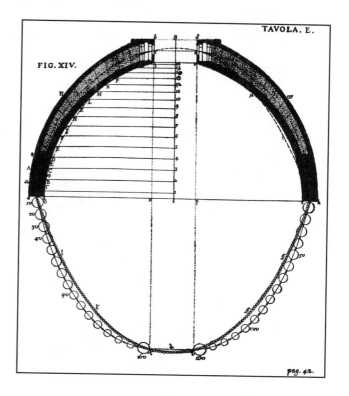

basic behavior of many different structural forms can be described in terms of funicular action. These structures can consequently be viewed as special forms of funicular structures. Some basic transformations of simple funicular shapes into other structural types are illustrated in Figure 1–12.

Figure 1–12(a) illustrates basic funicular responses for a concentrated load and a uniformly distributed loading. Figure 1–12(b) illustrates the type of movement that can be expected at the support points if the structure were not constrained at these points. A tension funicular typically wants to pull inward and downward. The support or foundation system must apply an outward and upward force on the structure at each end to maintain its shape and to keep it from collapsing. These forces are reactive in nature and are thus commonly referred to simply as *reactions* [see Figure 1–12(c)]. Note that the reactions exert an equal and opposite pull on the structure. The applied forces are thus balanced by equal and opposite reactive forces. A compression funicular produces a converse effect. The structure wants to move outward and downward. There is thus an outward and downward force exerted on the foundation which must in turn exert an equal and opposite set of forces on the structure if the shape of a structure is to be maintained. The combinations of applied forces acting on the foundation are commonly called thrusts. The foundation must contain these thrusts.

The final or resultant direction of the thrusts associated with a funicular structure can be shown to be along the tangent to the slope of the structure at the point where the structure meets the support. This follows from the fact that since bending is not present in the structure, all

(a) Inverted photo of the funicular model for the Colonia Guel chapel by Antonio Gaudi

(b) Sketch of the exterior of the chapel drawn from an inverted photo of the model.

(c) Inverted photo of the interior of the model

(d) Companion sketch for the interior of the chapel

FIGURE 1–11   Use of three-dimensional funicular models. The suspended weights are carefully modeled to represent the actual weights involved.

internal forces are directed axially along the length of the member. As Figure 1–12(d) indicates, this can have important bearings on the design and shaping of the foundation structure.

The use of built-in massive foundations is not the only way of handling the thrusts developed in a funicular structure. Part of the thrusts can be absorbed into the structure itself by adding an additional member. Figure 1–12(e) illustrates doing this for several structures. In tension funiculars, the tendency of the two ends to move inward can be restrained by simply introducing a linear member capable of carrying a compressive force (a strut) between the two points. This would have the net result of relieving the foundation of the necessity of providing restraint to the inward pulling forces of the structure. Hence, the foundation could be designed to carry only vertical forces. The same is true for compressive funicular structures (e.g., arches). By simply tying the two ends of an arch together, the outward-spreading tendency of the structure is eliminated and the foundation can be designed to carry vertical forces only. A tension force would develop in the tie-rod connecting the ends of the arch.

There are several points of interest in connection with the preceding discussion. One is that the force that must be carried by the compressive strut or tension tie-rod is exactly equal to the horizontal component of the total force developed by the structure at the foundation. Using struts or ties does not eliminate this force but merely handles it in a different way. In some circumstances it might be preferable to use a strut or tie rather than absorbing the horizontal thrust by means of a massive foundation. Designing and building foundations capable of handling horizontal forces is no easy matter. It is relatively easy, however, to design and build a foundation capable of carrying vertical forces only. For this reason ties or struts are frequently used. Ties, in particular, are quite an efficient way of taking up the horizontal component of the thrust in a compression funicular, since they can be simply long tension members. Struts for cable structures are less desirable, since the element is a long member in compression and thus potentially susceptible to buckling.

The remaining illustrations in Figure 1–12 indicate further evolution of the basic funicular shapes considered into other forms. While it is not the intent to explore these transformations in detail, some general observations will be made.

In some triangulated configurations of linear members (i.e., trusses), the primary action of the structure can also be discussed in terms of funicular shapes. In the truss shown to the left in Figure 1–12(f), a close inspection reveals that the center diagonals function exactly like a cable carrying a concentrated load, and the member across the top as a compression element serving the function previously described. The two end verticals simply translate the whole assembly vertically upward and are thus in compression. Other truss configurations can be discussed in similar ways. The analogy, however, does not extend to all conceivable shapes of triangulated bar networks. More sophisticated methods of analysis for any type of truss are discussed in Chapter 4.

Figure 1–12(h), (i), and (j) illustrates other transformations of the basic funicular structure into forms that could be aggregated to enclose volumes. Obviously, the method of taking up the horizontal thrusts generated by the structure is a crucial determinant of the exact characteristics of the structures developed. The assembly shown in Figure 1–12(i), which carries a uniformly distributed load and is arch-shaped, is a time-honored way of taking care of horizontal thrusts by simply adding buttressing elements. More preferable than the case shown would be lining up the buttressing elements with the slope of primary structure at the point of connection.

There is thus a wide variety of structures that are apparently different but are actually related in terms of their internal structural behavior.

Concentrated Loading
Uniformly Distributed Loading

(a) Loading and support condition.

(b) Horizontal movement tendencies at supports if not restrained.

(c) Type of forces developed at supports—reactions and thrusts.

(d) Use of foundations to contain thrusts. Foundations must be designed to carry both vertical and horizontal components of thrusts.

(e) Use of tension ties or compression struts. These elements absorb the horizontal components of the thrusts. Foundations need only be designed to carry vertical forces.

FIGURE 1-12   Funicular structures: transformations derived from basic shapes.

24

Uniformly Distributed Loading

Concentrated Loading

(f) Simple truss shapes based on funicular considerations.

(g) Internal force distribution in simple trusses. Internal action is similar to that of corresponding structures illustrated in (e).

(h) Profiles for use in volume-enclosing aggregations, potential movement and collapse tendencies.

(i) Use of tie or buttressing elements to assure stability. These elements are in a state of tension or compression only.

(j) Use of vertical elements in bending to assure stability.

FIGURE 1–12 (continued)

25

FIGURE 1–13 Classification of typical structures according to their basic load-carrying actions.

1–5 OTHER CLASSIFICATIONS

As a way of summarizing some of the concepts previously discussed, a classification of structures that tends to reflect their internal structural behavior is illustrated in Figure 1–13. The nature of the loading and boundary conditions are clearly important, whereas they were not at all reflected in the classification previously discussed and illustrated in Figure 1–1. There are other differences, but also overlaps, as a close comparison of the two schemes will indicate.

The level of detail associated with the classification scheme presented in Figure 1–13 is clearly limited. Many of the entries could be expanded into a categorization of their possible transformations of the general type previously discussed and illustrated in Figure 1–13. Still, it is useful as a conceptual device.

The two methods of classification thus far discussed are not the only ways structures could be classified. Other classification schemes could be developed on the basis of span or load-carrying capabilities. Those factors will be considered later in this text and comparisons drawn in the final chapters. A highly interesting way of classifying structures would be according to energy considerations. Although a topic not yet discussed, energy is stored in a structure as work is done on it (in the form of applied loads). Considerations of this type would be used to characterize structures into categories such as low-energy structures or high-energy structures.

These and other classification schemes are well worth reviewing or delving into as a way of developing a general appreciation for both the wide variety of structures in use and the ways in which they are interrelated.

QUESTIONS

1–1 Determine how the load-carrying capacity of a long slender column varies with length; for example, as the length of a column is doubled, what happens to its load-carrying capacity? Do this by measuring the load required to buckle a series of slender compression elements of similar cross sections but varying lengths. A simple bathroom scale can be used to measure loads. Square basswood pieces ($\frac{1}{8}$ in. $\times$ $\frac{1}{8}$ in.) are recommended. Simply support the ends without restraining rotations. Concentrate on long pieces only (as pieces get shorter, the failure load is more difficult to measure). Graphically plot your results (buckling load versus column length).

1–2 Take a thin sheet of rubber and inscribe a grid on it. Subject the sheet to different loading conditions and support types. Minimally, do the following:
A. Take a square sheet, continuously support its edges, and pile sand on it.
B. Repeat, except support the sheet at corners only.
C. Repeat (A) and (B), using a concentrated load at midspan instead.
Note how the surface deforms in each case by studying how elemental parts of the grid deform. Identify the most highly deformed areas in each case (regions of highest stress). Sketch the deflected shapes obtained.

1–3 Consider Figure 1–11, which illustrates the hanging-weight model used by Gaudi for the Colonia Gell chapel. Were similar model analyses used for other Gaudi works? Was the structure actually built? Is the chapel illustrated a singular example of Gaudi's concern for structure, or are there other examples? Consult your library.

CHAPTER 2

Principles of Mechanics

2-1 INTRODUCTION

Mechanics is the branch of applied science dealing with forces and motions. Fundamental to the field is the notion of *equilibrium,* the condition existing when a system of forces acting on a body is in a state of balance. The term *statics* is used to describe the part of mechanics specifically concerned with relations between forces acting on rigid bodies that are in equilibrium and at rest. The term *dynamics* refers to the part of mechanics dealing with rigid bodies in motion. If correctly placed inertial forces are taken into account, bodies in motion can also be considered to be in equilibrium. The field of study usually referred to as *strength of materials* is an extension of mechanics that addresses the relationship between applied or external forces acting on a body and the internal effects produced by these forces in the body. The study of the deformations produced in a body by a set of external forces is an integral part of the field of strength of materials.

The distinctions made here reflect the way the study of the general subject area has evolved in the engineering disciplines. In most engineering curricula, statics, dynamics, and strength of materials are normally treated as separate topics presented sequentially under the general umbrella of mechanics. During the process of analyzing and designing structures in buildings, however, professionals freely use as tools ideas and elements from each of these basic fields (as well as others) in a nonsequential manner. The chapters in Part II adopt this more integrative approach. At this point, however, it is pedagogically useful to retain the traditional engineering distinctions.

In the first part of this chapter we introduce certain fundamental ideas in statics. In the second part we focus on basic elements of strength of materials. The field of dynamics is outside the scope of the book and is not addressed. The following presentation is intended to provide only an overview of the basic issues involved in statics and strength of materials. Topics are therefore presented succinctly. The reader is referred to any of a number of basic texts that treat the subject matter more elaborately.[1]

2-2 FORCES AND MOMENTS

2-2-1 Analysis Objectives and Processes

Section 2–2 explores forces, moments, and equilibrium concepts. Before developing these concepts in a formal way, however, it is useful to look more directly at a simple example to show where the discussion will lead.

Concepts of force, moment, and equilibrium are given visual expression in the mobile by Alexander Calder illustrated in Figure 2–1.[2] Clearly the mobile as a whole is in careful balance, as is each of its parts. Any typical arm of the mobile experiences a set of forces acting upon it. These forces consist of both *external,* or *applied, forces*—e.g., one of the weights—and *internal forces,* or *reactions,* that are developed within the structure at connection points. The arm itself must be in *equilibrium* with respect to these forces (assuming that it is not sliding in space or spinning madly about). The net translational effect of all forces or force components acting on an object must have a sum of zero along any axis or in any direction. As developed in Section 2–3, this fundamental requirement will be formally expressed in the following way: $\Sigma F = 0$ (a symbolic notation read as "the sum of forces equals zero"). Likewise, there must be no net rotational effects of the forces about the point of suspension. Note that the rotational effects of the forces about the suspension point can be quantified as a product of the magnitude of the force times its distance from the point of suspension ($F \times d$). This rotational effect is called a *moment* ($M = F \times d$). Moments can act in clockwise or counterclockwise directions. For the arm to be in rotational equilibrium, the net total of these rotational moments acting on the arm must be zero, or $\Sigma M = 0$. In the mobile, a clockwise-acting moment acting on an arm is invariably exactly balanced by one that acts in a counterclockwise direction. Note that a small force acting a long distance away from the suspension point can have the same rotational effect as a large force acting over a short distance.

The analytical drawings that illustrate the force systems that act on an object are called *equilibrium diagrams* (sometimes called *free-body diagrams;* see Section 2–3–3). Constructing these kinds of diagrams is a first step in making a static analysis of a structure. Using equilibrium concepts, it is then possible to determine numerical values for the *reactions* (force interactions generated by the action of one object on another; see Section 2–3–3) that occur at supports or connections. Subsequently, internal forces (*shears* and *bending moments;* see Section 2–4–3), *stresses* (internal forces per unit area), and *strains* (deformations caused by stresses) can be determined (see Section 2–6).

---

[1]Students wishing a more extensive coverage of the application of structural principles to sculpture should see Schodek, *Structure in Sculpture,* M.I.T. Press, Cambridge, Massachusetts, 1993.

[2]For example, F. P. Beer and E. R. Johnston, *Vector Mechanics for Engineers: Statics,* McGraw-Hill Book Company, New York, 1972.

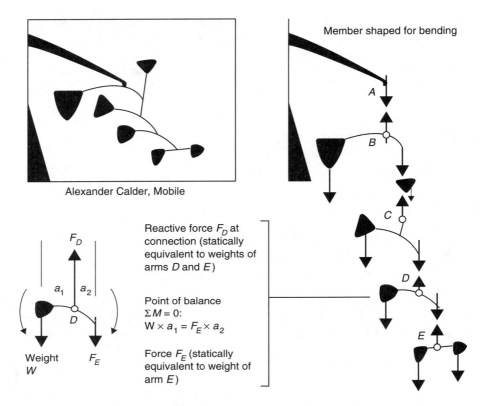

FIGURE 2–1 Basic equilibrium diagrams for each arm of the mobile are shown to the right. The diagram for arm D is shown in more detail.

The following sections explore these concepts in greater detail. What happens, for example, if the forces applied to an object are inclined? What if the forces are distributed over a surface rather than acting at a point?

2–2–2 Forces

Fundamental to the field of mechanics is the concept of force and the composition and resolution of forces. A *force* is a directed interaction between bodies. Force interactions have the effect of causing changes in the shape or motion, or both, of the bodies involved. The basic concept of force is undoubtedly familiar to the reader and is probably felt to be intuitively obvious. But viewed from a historical perspective, there was originally nothing obvious about the idea of force and the characterization of a force in terms of magnitude, sense, and direction. The precise formulation of these concepts is really quite a remarkable accomplishment in view of the degree of abstraction involved. Indeed, distinctions between force and weight as a special form of force and the notion of nonvertical forces were only just beginning to be appreciated by scholars in the Middle Ages. The name of Jordanus de Nemore is recurrently connected to the emergence of these concepts. Once force was conceived in vectorial (directional) terms, the problem of force components and the general composition and resolution of forces was addressed by a variety of individuals, including Leonardo da Vinci, Stevin, Roberval, and Galilei. This problem, often termed *the* basic problem in statics, was finally solved by Varginon and Newton.

2-2-3 Scalar and Vector Quantities

A distinction is invariably made in the study of mechanics between scalar and vector quantities. *Scalar* quantities can be adequately characterized by magnitude alone. *Vector* quantities must be characterized in terms of both magnitude and direction. Forces are typically vector quantities. Any vector quantity can be represented by a line. The direction of the line with respect to a fixed axis denotes the direction of the quantity. The length of the line, if drawn to scale, represents the magnitude of the quantity [see Figure 2-2(a)].

The line of action of a force is a line of indefinite length of which the force vector is a segment. Since most structures that will be dealt with in this text are essentially rigid bodies that deform only slightly under the application of a force, it can be assumed that the point of application of a given force may be transferred to any other point on the line of action without altering the translatory or rotational effects of the force on the body. Thus a force applied to a rigid body may be regarded as acting *anywhere* along its line of action.

2-2-4 Parallelogram of Forces

Essential to a study of structural behavior is knowing the net result of the interaction of several vector forces acting on a body. This interaction can be studied in terms of the laws of vector addition. These laws and fundamental postulates are based on experimental observation. Historically, the first method of adding vector quantities was based on the *parallelogram law*. In terms of force vectors, this proposition states that when the lines of action of two forces intersect, there is a single force, or *resultant,* exactly equivalent to these two forces, which can be represented by the diagonal of the parallelogram formed by using the force vectors as sides of the parallelogram [see Figure 2-2(b)-(d)]. In general, a resultant force is the simplest force system to which a more complex set of forces may be reduced and still produce the same effect on the body acted upon. Figure 2-3 illustrates a numerical example.

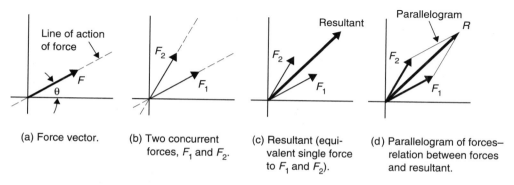

(a) Force vector. (b) Two concurrent forces, F_1 and F_2. (c) Resultant (equivalent single force to F_1 and F_2). (d) Parallelogram of forces–relation between forces and resultant.

FIGURE 2-2 Free vectors, force interactions, resultant forces, and the parallelogram of forces.

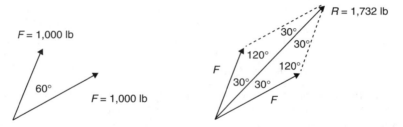

FIGURE 2-3 Parallelogram methods of finding the resultant force R of two concurrent forces. R can be found algebraically or graphically.

A graphic technique for finding the resultant force of several force vectors whose lines of action intersect is illustrated in Figure 2–4. The individual vectors, drawn to scale, are joined in tip-to-tail fashion. The order of combination is not important. Unless the resultant force is zero, the force polygon thus formed does not form a closed figure. The closure line is identical to the resultant force of the several individual vectors (i.e., the resultant is that vector which would extend from the tail of the first vector to the tip of the last vector in the group). The resultant closes the force polygon. This general technique follows from the parallelogram law. An algebraic method for finding the resultant of several forces acting through a point is discussed in Section 2–2–6.

Although conceptually very simple, graphical approaches to finding the resultants of force systems are extremely powerful as structural analysis aids. Historically, they found wide application because of the ease of their application. Graphical techniques were used extensively by early investigators in their attempts to understand the behavior of complex structures. Figure 2–5 illustrates a latter-day analysis of a gothic structure by graphic techniques. Figure 2–6 illustrates the *sphere model* of an arch that utilizes graphic techniques. The model, based simply on the parallelogram law, is still a very elegant way of looking at arches. Although

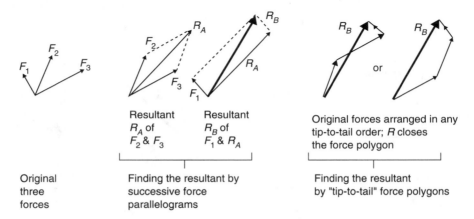

FIGURE 2-4 Graphical methods of finding the final resultant force R_B of a concurrent force system.

(a) Upper portion of buttress.

(b) Diagram showing typical lines of thrust in a cross section.

FIGURE 2–5   Application of graphic methods to the analysis of a gothic structure (Amiens). The dead weights of the vertical buttresses and pinnacle help turn the thrusts of the flying buttresses downward through the middle portion of the buttresses themselves. The vertical buttresses are stable and not prone to overturning or cracking when the force resultants pass through the middle portions of these buttresses.

going into either of these analyses in detail is beyond the scope of this book, it can be noted that the techniques used are extremely simple and based on the concepts discussed in this chapter. Graphical techniques are no longer extensively used but remain a very elegant way of looking at structures and are very useful in developing an intuitive feeling for the flow of forces in a structure.

2–2–5   Resolution and Composition of Forces

A process that follows directly from the fundamental proposition of the parallelogram of forces is that of breaking up a single force into two or more separate forces that form a force system equivalent to the initial force. This process is usually referred to as *resolving a force into components*. The number of components that a single force can be resolved into is limitless (see Figure 2–7). In structural analysis it is often most convenient to resolve a force into rectangular, or cartesian, components. By utilizing right angles, components can be found by using simple trigonometric functions. When a force F is resolved into components on the x and y axes, the components become $F_x = F(\cos \theta)$ and $F_y = F(\sin \theta)$. The process can be reversed if F_x and F_y are given and it is desired to know the resultant force F: $F = \sqrt{F_x^2 + F_y^2}$ and $\theta = \tan^{-1}(F_y/F_x)$.

It should be stressed that using cartesian components is a matter of convenience only. A right angle is nothing more than a special form of a parallelogram. Figure 2–7 illustrates

TAVOLA.D.

FIG.XI.

FIG.X.

FIG.XIII

FIG.XII.

Internal forces developed between spheres (the "line of thrust")

W

Weight of sphere

W   W

Equilibrium diagrams of upper spheres

(a) From Poleni, *Memorie istoriche della Gran Cupola del Tempio Valicano, 1748:* The spheres are arranged in accordance with the line of thrust.

Resultant force due to weights of upper spheres

The next lower sphere must be aligned with the upper resultant for the structure to be stable.

(b) The line of thrust is the locus of the internal force resultant developed in the structure.

FIGURE 2-6 Early "sphere model" of an arch: If a series of spheres is stacked as illustrated, the assembly is stable. Note that the shape is the inversion of a freely hanging chain made of similar spheres. The assembly will collapse if either the loading or the positioning of the spheres is changed.

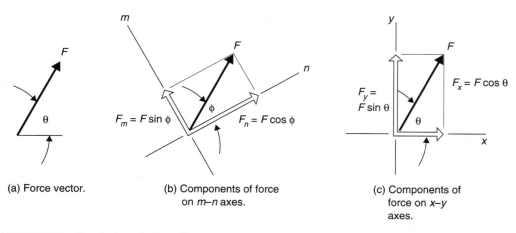

(a) Force vector.

(b) Components of force on *m–n* axes.

$F_m = F \sin \phi$ $F_n = F \cos \phi$

(c) Components of force on *x–y* axes.

$F_y = F \sin \theta$ $F_x = F \cos \theta$

FIGURE 2-7   Resolution of a force into components.

several manipulations with components. For example, a force of $F = 500$ lb that acts $30°$ to the horizontal has components of $F_x = 500 \cos 30° = 433$ lb and $F_y = 500 \sin 30° = 250$ lb. Or, assume that two forces acting orthogonally to one another have values of 100 and 200 lb, respectively. The resultant of these two forces is given by $R = \sqrt{F_x^2 + F_y^2} = \sqrt{(100)^2 + (200)^2} = 223.6$ lb. $\theta = \tan^{-1}(100/200) = 26.6°$. Components obviously could be found in three dimensions as well as two.

◆ ◆   **EXAMPLE**

Determine the components on the x and y axes of a force F of 1000 lb that acts at an angle of $\phi = 60°$ to the x axis.

Solution:

$$F_x = F \cos \phi = 1000 \cos 60° = 866.6 \text{ lb}$$
$$F_y = F \sin \phi = 1000 \sin 60° = 500 \text{ lb}$$

Alternatively, if the components of a force F were known to be orthogonal and have values of 866.6 lb and 500 lb on the x and y axes, respectively, how would you find the magnitude and direction of F?

$$F = \sqrt{F_x^2 + F_y^2} = \sqrt{(866.6)^2 + (500)^2} = 1000 \text{ lb}$$
$$\tan \phi_x = 500/866.6 = 0.92 \quad \therefore \quad \phi_x = 60°$$

or:

$$\phi_x = \tan^{-1} 500/866.6 = 60°$$
$$F = F_x/\cos \phi = 866.6/\cos 60° = 1000 \text{ lb}$$

◆

2–2–6   Statically Equivalent Systems

Implicit in the discussion in the previous section is the notion of static equivalency. When a system of forces applied to a body can be replaced by another system of forces applied to the same body without causing any net change in translational or rotational effects on the body, the two force systems are said to be *statically equivalent.* A resultant force, for example, is statically equivalent to the force system from which it was derived. The series of diagrams in Figure 2–8 illustrate one process for determining the statically equivalent single resultant force for a series of coplanar concurrent forces. *Concurrent forces* act through the same point and thus do not tend to produce rotational effects about that point (the moment arms are zero). The algebraic process illustrated depends on resolving each force into components (F_x and F_y forces) and summing components acting in similar directions. The resultant force is then given by $R = \sqrt{(\Sigma F_x)^2 + (\Sigma F_y)^2}$ and its orientation by $\theta_x = \tan^{-1}(\Sigma F_y/\Sigma F_x)$.

A single statically equivalent force for a *nonconcurrent* force system (in which forces do not intersect at a common point) can also be found. This process is illustrated in Appendix 2.

2–2–7   Moments

Moment of a Force.   A force applied to a body tends to cause the body to translate in the direction of the force. Depending on the point of application of the force on the body, the force may also tend to cause the body to rotate. This tendency to produce rotation is called the *moment* of the force (see Figure 2–9). With respect to a point or line, the magnitude of this turning or

Determination of resultant
forces: graphical method

Force polygon: force
system is in equilibrium.

Resultants of concurrent force systems: graphical methods

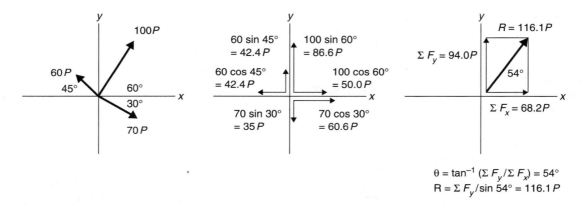

$\theta = \tan^{-1} (\Sigma F_y / \Sigma F_x) = 54°$
$R = \Sigma F_y / \sin 54° = 116.1P$

Resultants of concurrent force systems: algebraic method

FIGURE 2–8   Concurrent force systems.

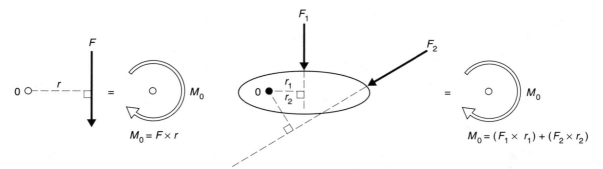

(a) Moment of a force about a point
(moment = force × distance).

(b) Rotational moment of several forces about a point.

FIGURE 2–9   Moments.

rotational tendency is equal to the product of the magnitude of the force and the perpendicular distance from the *line of action* of the force to the point or line under consideration. The moment M of a force F about a point O is thus simply $M_0 = F \times r$, where r is the perpendicular distance from the line of action of F to point O. r is often called the *moment arm of the force*. A moment has the units of force times distance (e.g., ft-lb or $N \cdot m$). A force of 1000 lb acting 5 ft away from a point produces a moment of $M = F \times r = 1000$ lb $\times$ 5 ft $= 5000$ ft-lb.

◆ ◆ **EXAMPLE**

The concept of a moment can be used to understand the behavior of many familiar objects. In the Calder mobile (Figure 2–1), the moments on each side of the point of suspension must be identical for balance to occur. Assume that $W = 100$ lb, F_E (the weight of the lower arm) $= 150$ lb, $a_1 = 4.5$ ft, and $a_2 = 3$ ft. Demonstrate that the arm is in balance about the point of suspension. See Figure 2–10.

FIGURE 2–10

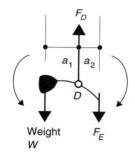

Solution:

The rotational moment of W about the point of suspension is given by

$$M_1 = W \times a_1 = 100 \text{ lb} \times 4.5 \text{ ft} = 450 \text{ ft-lb}$$

This rotational effect must be balanced by the moment produced by the other force:

$$M_2 = 150 \text{ lb} \times 3 \text{ ft-lb} = 450 \text{ ft-lb}$$

Since $W \times a_1 = F_E \times a_2$, the arm is in rotational balance ($\Sigma M = 0$). ◆

Moment of a Distributed Load. In structural analysis it is quite often necessary to determine the moment of some sort of continuous or distributed load acting on a body. Consider the continuous load that has a constant magnitude of w lb/ft or kN/m that is illustrated in Figure 2–11. An elemental portion of the load, $w\, dx$, produces a moment about point 0 of $(x)w\, dx$. The total moment of the entire load about point 0 is thus $M_0 = \int_0^L wx\, dx = wL^2/2$. Note that the same moment is obtained by imagining that the continuous load is replaced by an equivalent concentrated load acting at the center of mass of the load. For the case shown the equivalent concentrated load is wL [i.e., $(w$ lb/ft$)(L$ ft$) = wL$ lb], which can be considered to act at $L/2$. The moment of this equivalent force system is $M_0 = (wL)(L/2) = wL^2/2$, which is the same moment obtained from $M_0 = \int_0^L wx\, dx$. For example, for the member shown in Figure 2–11, a uniform loading

Equivalent concentrated load

(a) Uniformly distributed load:

$$M_0 = \int_0^L wx\,dx = \frac{wL^2}{2}$$

(b) This model produces the same rotational moment about point 0 as the uniformly distributed load shown in (a): $M_0 = wL \times L/2 = \dfrac{wL^2}{2}$

FIGURE 2–11   Moments of a distributed load.

of 100 lb/ft on a 20-ft-long member produces a moment about point O of the following: $M_0 = wL^2/2 = (100 \text{ lb/ft})(20 \text{ ft})^2/2 = 20{,}000 \text{ ft-lb}$. Or, $M_0 = (wL)(L/2) = (100 \text{ lb/ft})(20\,ft)(10\,ft) = 20{,}000 \text{ ft-lb}$.

◆ ◆ **EXAMPLE**

The member shown in Figure 2–12 is in balance, much like the ancient see-saw. The left part ($L_t = 10$ feet) is made of timber with a weight of $w_t = 5$ lb/ft and the other half of aluminum with a weight of $w_a = 15$ lb/ft. What length L_a must the aluminum part have for the member to be in exact balance?

(a) A balanced beam made of two materials. The length of one piece is known. The length of the other piece is to be found.

(b) Loading model that shows structure in rotational equilibrium. The rotational moment of the load to the left exactly equals that of the load to the right. To find L_a, equate the rotational moments and solve for L_a:

$$w_t\,L_t^2/2 = w_a\,L_a^2/2$$

(c) The uniform loads may be converted for visualization and computational convenience into equivalent concentrated loads which produce the same moment about the balance point.

FIGURE 2–12   A balanced beam with uniformly distributed loads.

Solution: The rotational moments of each part about the fulcrum must exactly balance each other. Thus:

$$\underbrace{w_t L_t^2/2}_{\substack{\text{Rotational moment} \\ \text{of timber part}}} = \underbrace{w_a L_a^2/2}_{\substack{\text{Rotational moment} \\ \text{of aluminum part}}}$$

$$(5 \text{ lb/ft})(10 \text{ ft})^2/2 = (15 \text{ lb/ft})(L_a^2)/2$$

$$\therefore L_a = 5.77 \text{ ft} \qquad \blacklozenge$$

Moments Due to Multiple Forces.   The total rotational effect produced by several forces about the same point or line is merely the algebraic sum of their individual moments about that point or line. Thus, $M_0 = (F_1 \times r_1) + (F_2 \times r_2) + \cdots + (F_n \times r_n)$.

Moments About a Line.   The rotational effect on a rigid body caused by multiple forces acting about a line, but not in the same plane, is the same as that which would result if all of the forces were acting in the same plane.

Moment of a Couple.   A *couple* is a force system made up of two forces equal in magnitude but opposite in sense and having parallel lines of action that are not on the same straight line ($\rightleftarrows$). A couple tends to cause only rotational effects on bodies and does not cause translation. The moment of a couple is simply the product of one of the forces times the perpendicular distance between the two forces. It can be shown, however, that the moment of a couple is actually independent of the reference point selected as a moment center. The magnitude of the rotational effect produced by a couple on a body is also independent of the point of application of the couple on the body.

2–3   EQUILIBRIUM

2–3–1   Equilibrium of a Particle

A body is in equilibrium when the force system acting on the body tends to produce no net translation or rotation of the body. It is in a state of balance. Equilibrium exists in *concurrent* force systems (where all forces act through a single point) when the resultant of the force system equals zero. A concurrent force system having a resultant force may be put in equilibrium by applying another force (typically called an *equilibrant*) equal in magnitude, of the same line of action, but of opposite sense.

If a force system is in equilibrium, its net resultant must be zero, and it follows that $\Sigma F_x = 0$ and $\Sigma F_y = 0$. Thus, the algebraic sum of all the components of the forces applied to a particle in the x direction must be zero. Likewise for the y direction, x and y need not be horizontal and vertical. The statement is true for any orthogonal set of axes, no matter what their orientation.

More generally, the conditions $\Sigma F_x = 0$, $\Sigma F_y = 0$, and $\Sigma F_z = 0$ are necessary and sufficient to ensure equilibrium in a concurrent force system. A force system satisfying these conditions will not cause the particle to translate (rotation is not a problem, since all forces act through the same point in concurrent force systems).

2–3–2   Equilibrium of a Rigid Body

General Equilibrium Conditions.   When a nonconcurrent-force system acts on a rigid body, the potential for both translation and rotation is present. For the rigid body to be in equilibrium, neither may occur. With respect to translation, this implies that, as in the case of concurrent-force systems, the resultant of the force system must be zero. With respect to rotation, the net rotational moment of all forces must be zero. The conditions for equilibrium of a rigid body are, therefore, $\Sigma F_x = 0$, $\Sigma F_y = 0$, $\Sigma F_z = 0$ and $\Sigma M_x = 0$, $\Sigma M_y = 0$, $\Sigma M_z = 0$.

Sign Conventions. When working with general force systems, sign conventions are always problematic. One classic approach for length measurements is to use x, y, and z values measured from a reference point on the extreme left of the structure. Thus, distances measured from this point to the right are always positive $(+x)$. For forces, a similar convention can be used. A force acting vertically upward would be positive $(+F)$ and one acting downward would be negative $(-F)$. Components of forces would be similarly designated. For rotational moments, note that with respect to a reference point on the extreme left of the structure, an upward force $(+F\uparrow)$ located to the right a positive distance $(+d)$ would cause a positive moment about the point that acts in a counterclockwise direction, or: $M = (+F)(+d) = +Fd$. A downward force would be negative $(-F)$ and cause a negative moment that acts in the clockwise direction, or: $M = (-F)(+d) = -Fd$. While useful, this convention can get cumbersome and confusing (particularly for rotational moments) when nonvertical forces are present. Most individuals simply use a convention directly relating to the rotational sense of the moment effect. Thus, moments that tend to produce *counterclockwise* rotations are considered positive $\oplus M$) and those that tend to produce *clockwise* rotations are considered negative $(\ominus M)$. These conventions are for equilibrium calculations involving external forces only. Other conventions will be developed later for describing internal forces and moments that act within the structure.

◆ ◆ **EXAMPLE**

Determine the unknown forces F_A and F_B in the structure shown in Figure 2–13 so that it is in a state of static equilibrium.

FIGURE 2–13

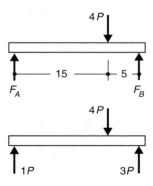

Solution:

Force equilibrium in the vertical direction, $\Sigma F_y = 0$: $F_A + F_B - 4P = 0$.
    This expression cannot yet be solved, since there is only one equation and two unknown force values.

Force equilibrium in the horizontal direction, $\Sigma F_x = 0$:
No forces act in the horizontal (or x) direction.

Moment equilibrium about point A

$$\Sigma M_A = 0$$

$$(+F_A)\,(0) + (-4P)(+15) + (+F_B)(+20) = 0$$

$$F_A(0) - (4P)(15) + F_B(20) = 0 \qquad \therefore \quad F_B = 3P\uparrow$$

From $\Sigma F_y = 0$: $F_A + F_B - 4P = 0$:

$$F_A + 3P = 0 \qquad \therefore \quad F_A = 1P\uparrow \qquad\qquad \blacklozenge$$

In the following section, we will see that the forces F_A and F_B in situations similar to that shown typically occur at structural supports and are reactive in nature. On the other hand, there might be situations where the forces are applied. Here the point is that no matter what their origin, they *must* have the numerical values noted for the structure to be in equilibrium.

Two-Force Members.   Several special equilibrium cases exist. When a rigid member is subjected to only two forces, the forces cannot have arbitrary magnitudes and lines of action if the member is to be in equilibrium. Consider the member shown in Figure 2–14. By summing moments about point A it can be seen that there is no way that the structure can be in rotational equilibrium *unless* the line of action of the force at B passes through point A. In a similar way, it is necessary that the line of action of the force at A must pass through point B if the structure is to be in rotational equilibrium about point B. Thus, the two forces *must* be collinear. They must also be equal in magnitude but opposite in sense. This result is particularly important in the analysis of trusses.

Three-Force Members.   As with two-force members, three forces acting on a member cannot have random orientations and magnitudes if the member is to be in equilibrium. This can be seen with reference to Figure 2–14. For the member to be in rotational equilibrium,

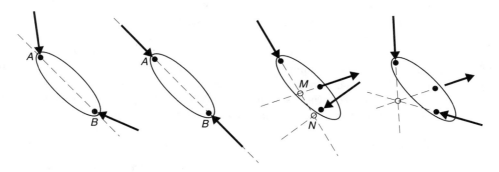

(a) Two-force members: when only two forces act on a rigid body, they must be collinear.

(b) Three-force members: when three forces act on a rigid body, their lines of action must intersect at a point.

FIGURE 2–14   Two- and three-force members.

FIGURE 2–15 Application of graphical methods to the analysis of a gothic structure. The weight of the buttress and its reactions form a three-force system. Consequently, all forces meet at a single point.

(*from Mohrmann*)

it is evident that the lines of action of all three forces must pass through a common point.

Figure 2–15 shows a latter-day analysis of a gothic structure that illustrates the principle that the lines of action of three-force members must pass through the same point.

2–3–3   Applied and Reactive Forces

Forces and moments that act on a rigid body can be divided into two primary types: applied and reactive. In common engineering usage, *applied forces* are those that act directly on a structure (e.g., snow). *Reactive forces* are those generated by the action of one body on another and hence typically occur at connections or supports. The existence of reactive forces follows from *Newton's third law,* which generally states that to every action there is an equal and opposite reaction. More precisely, the law states that whenever one body exerts a force on another, the second always exerts on the first a force which is equal in magnitude, opposite in direction, and has the same line of action. In Figure 2–16(b), the force on the beam causes downward forces on the foundation and upward reactive forces are consequently developed. A pair of action and reaction forces thus exist at each interface between the beam and its foundations. In some cases, moments form part of the reaction system as well [see Figure 2–16(c)].

The diagrams in Figure 2–16, which show the complete system of applied and reactive forces acting on a body, are called *free-body diagrams.*

If a body (such as any of those illustrated) is indeed in a state of equilibrium, it is clear that the general conditions of equilibrium for a rigid body that were stated in the previous section must be satisfied. The magnitude and direction of any reactive forces developed must be such that equilibrium is maintained and are thus necessarily dependent on the characteristics of the applied force system. The whole system of applied and reactive forces acting on a body (as represented by the free-body diagram) must be in a state of equilibrium. Free-body diagrams are consequently often called *equilibrium diagrams.* Drawing equilibrium diagrams and finding reactions for loaded structural members is a common first step in a complete structural analysis.

Support Conditions.   The nature of the reactive forces developed on a loaded body depends on the exact way in which the body is either supported or connected to other bodies. Figure 2–17 illustrates relations between the type of support condition present and the type of reactive forces developed. Several basic types of support conditions are indicated; others are possible. Of primary importance are pinned connections, roller connections, and fixed connections. In *pinned connections,* the joint allows attached members to rotate freely but does not allow translations to occur in any direction. Consequently, the joint cannot provide moment resistance but can provide

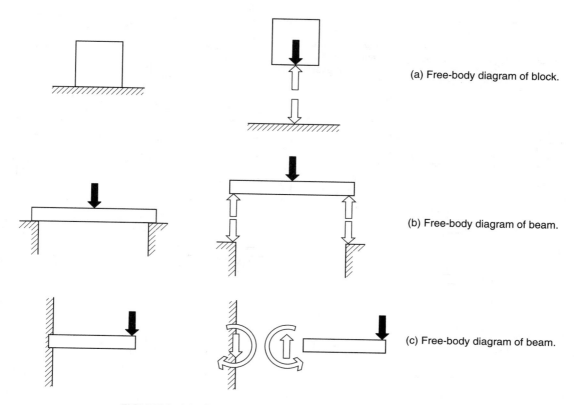

(a) Free-body diagram of block.

(b) Free-body diagram of beam.

(c) Free-body diagram of beam.

FIGURE 2–16 Reactions and free-body (or equilibrium) diagrams.

force resistance in any direction. A *roller connection* also allows rotations to occur freely. It resists translations, however, only in the direction perpendicular to the face of the support (either into *or* away from the surface). It does not provide any force resistance parallel to the surface of the support. A *fixed joint* completely restrains rotations and translations in any direction. Consequently, it can provide moment resistance and force resistance in any direction. Other types of supports include a *cable support* and a *simple support.* These are similar to the roller connection except that they can provide force resistance in one direction only. The connections shown are, of course, idealized. *The relation between these idealized connections and those actually present in building structures is discussed in Section 3–3–2. Ideally, the reader should study Section 3–3–2 in parallel with the calculation principles presented below.*

For a structure to be stable there must be a specific minimum number of force restraints provided by the supports. For a simple beam loaded with both downward and horizontal forces there must be three (this corresponds to the fact that there are three conditions of equilibrium for this type of structure: $\Sigma F_x = 0$, $\Sigma F_y = 0$, and $\Sigma M = 0$). One way of meeting this requirement is to use a fixed connection. Another is to use a pinned connection on one end and a roller connection on the other. It is, of course, possible to use connections that offer more degrees of restraint than the minimum required.

FIGURE 2–17 Types of support conditions: idealized models.

Structures having connections or supports that provide more than the minimum needed for stability are referred to as *statically indeterminate externally*. Since there are more unknown constraining forces than there are equations of equilibrium for solution, it is not possible to solve for the magnitudes of these constraining forces by statics alone. Other techniques must be used. These are discussed in succeeding chapters.

Reactions for Typical Load and Support Conditions. The following examples illustrate how reactions are calculated for common situations. In the first example, the applied loads act vertically downward, and the structure has pin and roller support conditions. In the preceding discussion, it was argued that a reactive force can develop in any direction at a pinned connection, but only perpendicular to the plane of support in a roller joint. Common sense correctly suggests, however, that when all applied loads act vertically, all reactive forces will also act vertically, including the one at the pin. From a calculation perspective, it is still necessary to assume initially that the reaction at the pin is inclined. The reaction analysis should then predict that the force is indeed vertical (the horizontal component should turn out to be zero, meaning that the force actually acts vertically). This is the case in the first example. In the second example, the applied force is inclined. An inclined reactive force is found to develop at the pin. This is a common result—when a structure carries any applied force with a horizontal component, the reactive force at the pin will also be inclined so that necessary equilibrium balances can be obtained. The following examples include cantilever structures which illustrate that roller conditions can develop either compressive or tension (tie-down) reactions.

◆ ◆   EXAMPLE

Determine the unknown reaction forces R_A and R_B in the structure shown in Figure 2–18. Use x and y components of R_B in the equilibrium analysis.

FIGURE 2–18   Reactions for a simple beam with vertical loads.

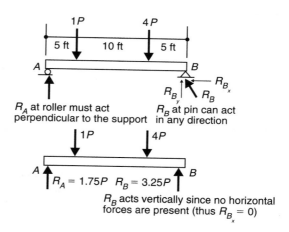

Solution: The reactive force roller R_A at the left must by definition act perpendicularly to the support plane. The pinned condition on the right can potentially provide a reactive force resistance R_B in any direction, so it is shown acting at an angle and broken into x and y components. By inspection, however, and noting that the external forces act only in the vertical direction, it can be simply surmised that the actual direction of the reactive force at the pin is in the vertical direction only. If there were a horizontal force component present, the structure could not be in equilibrium in the vertical direction. Use force components for R_B in the following.

Force equilibrium of all the forces acting in the vertical direction, $\Sigma F_y = 0$ $\uparrow +$:

$$R_A + R_{B_y} - 1P - 4P = 0 \qquad \text{or} \qquad R_A + R_{B_y} = 5P$$

While valid, this equation cannot yet be solved due to the presence of two unknowns.

Force equilibrium in the horizontal direction, $\Sigma F_x = 0$ $\overset{+}{\rightarrow}$:

$$0 + R_{B_x} = 0$$

Since there are no forces acting in the horizontal direction, R_{B_x} must obviously be zero, which in turn implies that the resultant R_B acts vertically and is identically equal to R_{B_y}.

Moment equilibrium about point A, $\Sigma M_A = 0$:
Algebraic signs for forces and distances can be used to determine the rotational sense, or the common convention that moments that act in the counterclockwise direction are positive can be used.

$$R_A(0) + (-1P)(+5) + (-4P)(+15) + R_{B_y}(+20) + R_{B_x}(0) = 0$$
$$\text{or } -5P - 60P + 20R_{B_y} = 0 \quad \therefore \quad R_{B_y} = 3.25P \uparrow$$

Note that since $R_{B_x} = 0$, $R_B = R_{B_y}$.

$$R_A + 3.25P = 5P \quad \therefore \quad R_A = 1.75P \uparrow \qquad \blacklozenge$$

◆ ◆   **EXAMPLE**

Determine the reactions to the structure in Figure 2–19, which has an inclined applied force.

FIGURE 2–19

Solution: For convenience, the applied load is broken up into horizontal and vertical components. These components are then considered as applied loads. The vertical reactions are first found. Since $\Sigma F_y = 0$ can rarely be solved first directly, use $\Sigma M_A = 0$ since this will immediately yield the vertical component of the reactive force at *B*.

Moment equilibrium about point A, $\Sigma M_A = 0$ ⊕:

$$R_A(0) - 4P \sin 60° (5) + R_{B_y}(10) + R_{B_x}(0) = 0$$
$$\text{or } -3.46P(5) + 10R_{B_y} = 0 \quad \therefore \quad R_{B_y} = 1.73P$$

R_{By} is the component of the reactive force at *B* in the vertical direction. To find the reactive force at *A* that acts in the vertical direction—which must act vertically because of the roller condition—sum forces in the vertical direction.

Force equilibrium of all the forces acting in the vertical direction, $\Sigma F_y = 0$ $\uparrow +$:

$$-4P \sin 60° + R_{A_y} + R_{B_y} = 0$$
$$-3.46P + R_{A_y} + 1.73P = 0 \qquad \therefore \quad R_A = 1.73P$$

Force equilibrium in the horizontal direction, $\Sigma F_x = 0$ $\overrightarrow{\ }$:

$$4P \cos 60° - R_{B_x} = 0$$
$$2.0P - R_{B_x} = 0 \qquad \therefore \quad R_{B_x} = 2.0P$$

Resultant reactive force R_B at B:

To find the resultant force at B, use the two known components, R_{B_x} and R_{B_y}.

$$\tan^{-1} \theta_B = 1.73/2.0 \qquad \therefore \quad \theta_B = 40.85°$$
$$R_B = 1.73P/\sin\theta = 2.64P \quad \text{or} \quad = 2.0P/\cos\theta = 2.64P$$

Thus, $R_B = 2.64P$ at $40.85°$ to the horizontal. All reactions are now known. Observe that the reaction at B must be inclined so that it provides a resistive force to balance the horizontal component of the applied load. If it simply acted vertically as in the previous example, the structure would not be in equilibrium. Also note that if there were two rollers present, instead of a pin and a roller, it would be impossible for the reactions to provide equilibrium restraints and the structure would slide to the right.

In the moment calculations, several forces went through the moment center. Moment arms were thus of zero length, indicating that the forces produced no rotational effects about the point considered. In the future, forces having zero-length moment arms will not be included in the equilibrium calculations. ◆

◆ ◆   **EXAMPLE**

Determine the unknown reaction forces R_A and R_B in the structure shown in Figure 2–20.

FIGURE 2–20

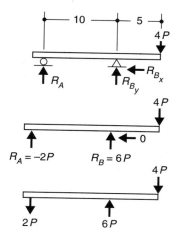

Solution: The pinned connection on the right can potentially provide a force R_B that can act in any direction. Since there are no external forces acting horizontally, however, it is evident that the force must necessarily act only vertically. (If it had a component in the x direction, $\Sigma F_x = 0$ could not be satisfied.) The roller on the left can transmit a force R_A in the vertical direction only, but this force may be upwardly or downwardly directed. Assume that it acts upwardly.

Moment equilibrium about A, $\Sigma M_A = 0$ ⊕:

$$(R_B \times 10) - (4P \times 15) = 0 \qquad \therefore \quad R_B = 6P$$

Find R_A from $\Sigma F_y = 0$ ↑+:

$$R_A + R_B - 4P = 0$$
$$R_A + 6P - 4P = 0$$
$$R_A = -2P\uparrow \quad \text{or} \quad +2P\downarrow$$

The negative sign in the solution indicates that the direction assumed for R_A was incorrect and that it actually acts in the direction shown (as a "tie-down" force). Rollers can be designed to act as tie-downs. ◆

◆ ◆ **EXAMPLE**

Determine the unknown reaction forces R_A and R_B in the structure shown in Figure 2–21.

FIGURE 2–21

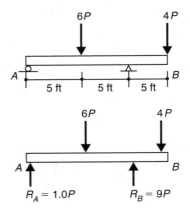

Solution: This problem is similar to the last, but shows that the direction of the force at the roller is dependent on the magnitudes and locations of the loadings present.

Moment equilibrium about point A, $\Sigma M_A = 0$ ⊕:

$$-6P(5) - 4P(15) + 10R_B = 0 \qquad \therefore \quad R_B = 9P\uparrow$$

Force equilibrium of all the forces acting in the vertical direction, $\Sigma F_y = 0$: +↑

$$R_A + R_{B_y} - 6P - 4P = 0 \qquad \therefore \quad R_A = 1.0P\uparrow \qquad\qquad ◆$$

◆ ◆ EXAMPLE

Determine the unknown reaction forces R_A and R_B in the structure shown in Figure 2–22.

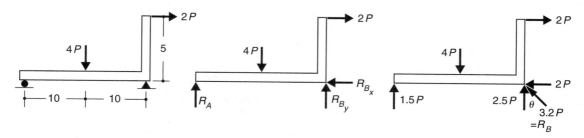

FIGURE 2–22

Solution: The pinned connection on the right can potentially provide a force resistance in any direction, as is reflected in Figure 2–22 by an unknown force R_B acting at the connection at an arbitrary angle. The roller on the left can transmit forces in the vertical direction only. Components of R_B are initially used.

Force equilibrium of all the forces acting in the vertical direction, $\Sigma F_y = 0$ ↑+:

$$R_A + R_{B_y} - 4P = 0 \text{ or } R_A + R_{B_y} = 4P$$

Force equilibrium in the horizontal direction, $\Sigma F_x = 0$ $\overset{+}{\rightarrow}$:

$$2P - R_{B_x} = 0 \qquad \therefore \quad R_{B_x} = 2P$$

Moment equilibrium about point A, $\Sigma M_A = 0$ ⊕:

$$R_A(0) - (4P)(10) + R_{B_y}(20) + R_{B_x}(0) - (2P)(5) = 0 \qquad \therefore \quad R_{B_y} = 2.5P \uparrow$$

Find R_A from $\Sigma F_y = 0$: $R_A + R_{B_y} = 4P$:

$$R_A + 2.5P = 4P \qquad \therefore \quad R_A = 1.5P \uparrow$$

Find the resultant force R_B from R_{B_x} and R_{B_y}:

$$R_B = \sqrt{R_{B_x}^2 + R_{By}^2} = 3.2P$$
$$\tan^{-1}\theta = 2.5/2.0 \qquad \therefore \quad \theta = 51.3°$$

◆

◆ ◆ EXAMPLE

Determine the unknown forces R_A and R_B in Figure 2–23. The uniformly distributed load is first converted into an equivalent concentrated load for equilibrium calculations.

Solution:

Moment equilibrium about A: $\Sigma M_A = 0$ ⊕:

$$\Sigma M = 0: \quad R_A L - (wL)(L/2) = 0$$
$$R_A = wL/2 = (50 \text{ lb/ft})(20 \text{ ft})/2 = 500 \text{ lb}$$

FIGURE 2–23

Force equilibrium in the vertical direction: $\Sigma F_y = 0 \quad +\uparrow$:

$$\Sigma F = 0: \quad R_A + R_B - wL = 0 \quad \therefore \quad R_B = 500 \text{ lb}$$

Note that by symmetry, $R_A = R_B$. Thus, it is possible to solve for the unknown forces by considering equilibrium in the vertical direction only: $\Sigma F = 0; R_A + R_B =$ total downward load $= wL$. Thus, $R_A = R_B = wL/2 = 500$ lb. ◆

◆ ◆ **EXAMPLE**

Determine the reactions for the structure shown in Figure 2–24. Note that 1 kip $= 1000$ lb.

FIGURE 2–24

Solution: For the purposes of determining the reactions, the uniformly distributed load that acts over part of the structure is modeled as a statically equivalent concentrated load.

Moment equilibrium about point A, $\Sigma M_A = 0$:

$$\underbrace{[(2 \text{ kips/ft})(10 \text{ ft})]}_{\substack{\text{equivalent} \\ \text{concentrated load}}} \underbrace{(15 \text{ ft})}_{\substack{\text{moment arm} \\ \text{(to loading center)}}} - 20R_B \qquad \therefore \quad R_B = 15 \text{ kips}$$

where $1 \text{ kip} = 1000 \text{ lb}$.

Force equilibrium in the vertical direction, $\Sigma F_y = 0$:

$$R_A + R_B - [(2 \text{ kips/ft})(10 \text{ ft})] = 0 \qquad \therefore \quad R_A = 5 \text{ kips} \qquad\blacklozenge$$

◆ ◆ EXAMPLE

Determine the reactions for the structure shown in Figure 2–25. Use components.

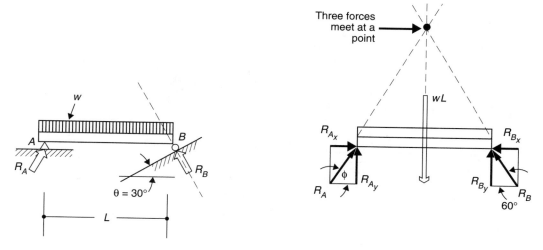

FIGURE 2–25   Beam with roller resting on a sloped support.

Solution

Equilibrium in the vertical direction: $\qquad \Sigma F_y = 0: R_{A_y} + R_{B_y} - wL = 0.$

The total load acting downward due to the distributed loading is simply the load per unit length multiplied by the length over which the load acts. Note that the direction of the unknown reaction R_B is initially known because roller joints can transmit loads only perpendicular to the surfaces on which they roll. Hence, R_{B_y} must be $R_B \sin 60°$. The direction of R_A is not known a priori.

Moment equilibrium about point A, $\Sigma M_A = 0$:

$$+R_{B_y}(L) - (wL)\left(\frac{L}{2}\right) = 0 \quad \text{or} \quad R_{B_y} = \frac{wL}{2}$$

Hence, $R_{A_y} = wL/2$ from $\Sigma F_y = 0$. All other unknown components of the two reactive forces pass through the moment center and consequently have zero moment arms and drop out of the equation. The moment produced by the uniformly distributed load was found by imagining it to be concentrated at its center of mass and finding the moment produced by this concentrated load about point A (see Section 2–2–7). Modeling uniform loads in this way is frequently done for the purpose of finding reactions. It is not a valid technique, however, for other purposes such as finding beam sizes.

Final reactions:
Since R_{B_y} is now known, R_B can be calculated next. Thus, $R_{B_y} = R_B \sin 60°$ or $R_B = R_{B_y}/\sin 60° = (wL/2)/\sin 60° = 0.58wL$. R_{B_x} is simply $R_B \cos 60°$, or $0.29wL$. From $\Sigma F_x = 0$, it can be seen that $R_{B_x} = R_{A_x}$. Hence, $R_{A_x} = 0.29wL$. Since $R_{A_y} = wL/2$, it follows that $R_A = 0.58wL$.   ◆

Principle of Superposition.   For typical rigid structures that carry multiple loadings, it is possible to determine the reactions for each individual load and then to add all of the obtained results together. This approach is often very useful for conceptualizing the behavior of structures under different loading conditions.

◆ ◆   **EXAMPLE**

Determine the reactions to the structure in Figure 2–26 using a superposition technique.

FIGURE 2–26   Principle of superposition.

Solution: The reactions for each individual loading are first determined (as shown to the right in Figure 2–26) and then simply added.   ◆

Forces and Reactions Associated with Overturning.   In many situations when applied forces act horizontally or have significant horizontal components, they tend to cause a structure to overturn. Determining reactions for these situations is straightforward and no different in principle than any previous example. Care must simply be taken to use the correct moment arms associated with the overturning and reactive forces. The first example below illustrates how a rigid structure resists overturning via the use of tie-down supports. The second example illustrates how a structure with no tie-down supports can resist overturning via its own dead weight.

◆ ◆   **EXAMPLE**

Determine the reactions for the structure shown in Figure 2–27.

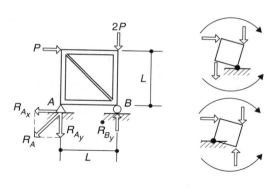

Moment about B produced by external forces

Resisting moment that must be developed by the reaction

Moment about A produced by external forces

Resisting moment that must be developed by the reaction

The directions of the reactions can be determined by inspecting how the external forces tend to rotate the body

FIGURE 2–27

Solution

Moment equilibrium about point A, $\Sigma M = 0$ ↻:

$$-P(L) - 2P(L) + R_{B_y}(L) = 0, \quad \text{or} \quad R_{B_y} = 3P \uparrow$$

Equilibrium in the vertical direction, $\Sigma F_y = 0$ ↑+:

$$-R_{A_y} + R_{B_y} - 2P = 0; \quad \text{hence,} \quad R_{A_y} = P \downarrow$$

Equilibrium in the horizontal direction, $\Sigma F_x = 0$ →+:

$$-R_{A_x} + P = 0, \quad \text{or} \quad R_{A_x} = P \leftarrow$$

Resultant force at A:

$$R_A = 1.4P @ 45° \qquad \blacklozenge$$

Figure 2.28 illustrates a rotational stability analysis of a block with a large dead weight that is subjected to an overturning force. In this case, there are no active mechanisms such as pins to prevent overturning. As will be seen, when the dead weight is high, the applied overturning moment is less than the moment available to resist overturning (which is associated with the dead weight of the structure) and the structure is stable. If the applied moment is greater that the resisting moment, the structure overturns. If the applied and resisting moments are exactly equal, the structure is in neutral equilibrium. The example is a simplification of the buttress analysis shown in Figure 2–5(b). Many high-rise buildings, however, that have no tie-down piles but which rely on their own dead weights and proportions to resist overturning due to wind or earthquake forces, can be analyzed similarly.

General equilibrium conditions based on a moment analysis are shown at the top of the figure. If the overturning moment of the horizontal load exceeds the resisting moment associated with the weight and size of the block, then the block will overturn. If not, then the block is either

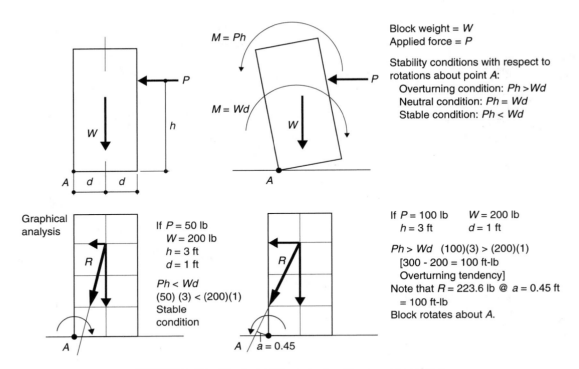

FIGURE 2–28 Block stability analysis with respect to point A.

in neutral equilibrium or stable. The lower part of the figure uses both an algebraic procedure and a graphically oriented approach similar to that shown in Figure 2–5. As long as the inclined force (statically equivalent to the horizontal and vertical forces combined) passes through the point of tipping, or to its right, the block will not overturn. (Note that block could be stable, but cracking could still occur in a masonry structure; see Section 7–3–1).

The example demonstrates that increasing resistance to overturning can be accomplished by either increasing the dead weight of the structure, increasing the width of the base footing, decreasing the height at which the applied horizontal force acts, or some combination thereof.

Special Types of Reactions: Fixed-End Moments. Many typical structures, especially cantilevered beams, have their ends rigidly attached to walls or other supports. The nature of this connection is such that it completely restrains the end of the member from either rotating or translating. Thus, a member can simply project from a wall or column face. Reactive forces that are developed at the support include the usual vertical and horizontal forces that prevent the member from translating, but also developed are *restraining moments* that prevent the end of the member from rotating. These restraining moments balance the external applied moments at the same point. These restraining moments are typically called *fixed-end moments,* and are a special form of reaction. A version can be felt by simply ending one's arm and feeling what happens at the shoulder joint. Typically, these restraining moments are provided for by physical mechanisms that depend on the type of structure used. In a wide-flange beam cantilevered from a column, for example, the top and bottom flanges of the member are welded to the column face. Force couples are developed in the welds that provide the restraining fixed end moment (see Figure 16–3 in Chapter 16). If a structure has multiple fixed ends (e.g., fixed on both ends) and/or many other reaction points, it becomes *statically indeterminate* and values cannot be found by techniques presented in Chapter 2 (see Chapters 8 and 9 for solution techniques).

◆ ◆ **EXAMPLE**

Determine the fixed-end moments for the two beams in Figure 2–29.

FIGURE 2–29   Fixed-end moments.

Solution: For the beam to the left with the concentrated load P, the rotational moment at support A that is associated with the applied load is simply given by $M_{\text{applied}} = PL$. The balancing fixed-end moment is equal in value but of opposite sense, thus: $M_A^F = PL$. For the beam to the right with the uniformly distributed loading, the rotational moment at support A that is associated with the applied load is simply given by $M_{\text{applied}} = (wL)(L/2) = wL^2/2$. The balancing fixed-end moment is equal in value but of opposite sense, thus: $M_A^F = wL^2/2$.   ◆

Cables.   Many structures are supported on one end or the other by cables. Reactive forces are developed within the cables that provide equilibrium forces for the supported structure. As noted in Figure 2–17, the forces developed in a cable are in tension (cables cannot provide compressive force resistance) and inherently directed along the length of the cable. Thus, the direction of a cable defines the direction of the reaction it provides. The reactive force developed is equivalent to the internal tension force in the cable.

◆ ◆ **EXAMPLE**

Determine the reactions to the cable-supported structure shown in Figure 2–30.

Solution: The steps in the determination of forces are shown in Figure 2–30. An equilibrium diagram is first drawn in which the direction of the reaction provided by the cable is shown as coincident with the location and direction of the cable. The internal force in the cable, T_{BC}, is treated as an external reaction for calculating the equilibrium of the beam AB. Moments are summed about point A to obtain T_{BC}. Note that the moment arm of T_{BC} is perpendicular to the line of action of T_{BC}. Once T_{BC} is determined, forces are

Cantilever beam supported by a cable. An internal force T_{BC} is developed within the cable.

$\Sigma M_A = 0$
$T_{BC} (0.5L) - P(0.5L) = 0$
$T_{BC} = P$ (Tension)

$\Sigma R_X = 0$
$T_{BC} \cos 30 + R_{A_x} = 0$
$R_{A_x} = 0.866P$

$\Sigma F_y = 0$
$T_{BC} \sin 30 + R_{A_y} - P = 0$
$R_{A_y} = 0.5P$

$R_A = P$ @ $\theta = 30$

Note that the lines of action of the three forces meet at a point

Final equilibrium diagram showing final forces

FIGURE 2–30 Cable-supported structure.

summed in the horizontal direction to obtain the horizontal component of the left reactive force R_A (the horizontal component of the cable force is equal to the horizontal component of the left reaction). Summing forces in the vertical direction yields the vertical component of R_A. R_A can then be found from its components. A final equilibrium diagram is drawn. The three forces acting on the structure meet at a point (see Section 2–3–2 on three-force members). Note that the use of a cable induces a compressive force in beam AB equivalent to the horizontal component of the cable force. Also observe that the reactive force at C is equal and opposite to the force in the cable. ◆

◆ ◆ **EXAMPLE**

A stayed-cable mast is shown in Figure 2–31 with two different loading conditions. Determine the forces present in the cable and at the support points.

Solution: The steps of the solution are shown in Figure 2–31. In the case of the first loading condition where the force is applied at the top of the mast, the load P tends to produce a clockwise overturning moment that is balanced by a resisting moment associated with force T_{BC} developed in cable BC. The cable force is assumed to be in tension, as it must be, and acts in the counterclockwise direction. The moment arm for the cable force is the perpendicular distance from the base pin A to the cable BC. The cable force T_{BC} is found by summing moments about A. Thus,

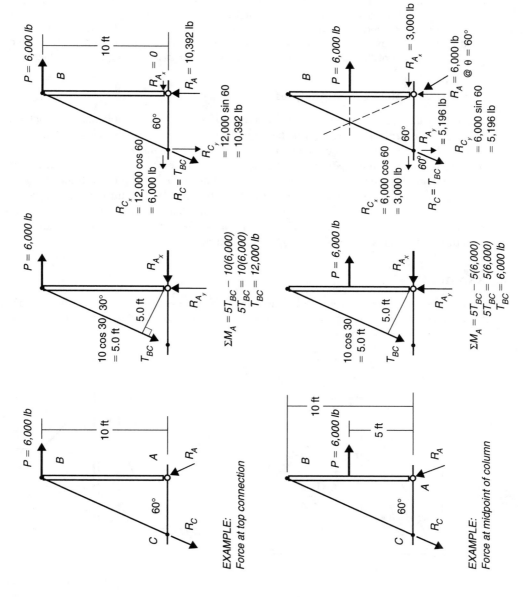

FIGURE 2-31 Cable-stayed column with two loading conditions.

57

$5T_{BC} = 10(6000)$, or $T_{BC} = 12,000$ lb. Note that the reaction at C is numerically equal to the force T_{BC} developed in the cable. Equilibrium in the vertical and horizontal directions considered next to find the reactive force at A. The reactive force at A, which was initially assumed to be inclined, turns out to act only vertically. Since the reaction acts vertically (in this specific case), the compressive force developed in the mast has an equivalent numerical value. In the lower example, the location of the applied horizontal force has been lowered and the same kind of analysis repeated. In this case, the reaction at A was found to have a horizontal component. The reactive force at A cannot be simply assumed to be oriented in the same way as is the mast. In this case the force in the mast is numerically equivalent to the vertical component of the inclined reactive force at A. The mast is also subject to bending by force P.

2-3-4 Complete Static Analyses

The following example illustrates a complete static analysis for a cable-stayed structure. Reactions for the overall structure are first determined. The structure is then decomposed into its fundamental components. Each component is shown with the complete set of external and internal or reactive forces acting upon it. Reactions for one member become applied forces to the adjacent member, e.g., the reactions to the beam become equal and opposite forces applied to the mast. The equilibrium of different components can be considered in turn until all of the unknown forces at connections have been found. Note the way that forces at connections are shown as equal and opposite, a necessary condition that follows from the fact that these forces are reactive in nature and actually internal to the overall structure.

◆ ◆ **EXAMPLE**

For the structure shown in Figure 2–32(a), determine the reactions at the base of the structure, the internal force present in the stabilizing cable CA, and the internal force in cable CE that supports the projecting member.

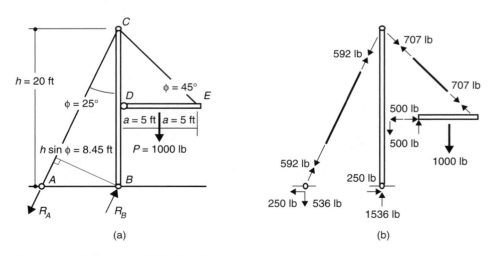

(a)   (b)

FIGURE 2-32 (a) Structure; (b) final analysis results.

For Whole Structure

Find T_{CA} and R_A (Figure 2–33):

FIGURE 2–33

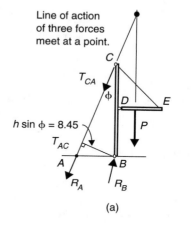

Line of action
of three forces
meet at a point.

$h \sin \phi = 8.45$

$1556 \text{ lb} = R_B$

$80.7 = \theta$

(b)

(a)

$\Sigma M_B = 0$:

$$T_{CA} (h \sin \theta) - Pa = 0$$
$$T_{CA} (h \sin \theta) = Pa$$
$$T_{CA} (20 \sin 25°) = 5(1000)$$
$$T_{CA} (8.45) = 5(1000)$$
$$T_{CA} = 592 \text{ lb @ } 75° \text{ to horizontal}$$

Note that $R_A = T_{CA}$

$\Sigma F_x = 0$:

$$-R_A \sin 25° + R_{B_x} = 0 \qquad \theta = \tan^{-1}(1536/250)$$
$$R_{B_x} = 250 \text{ lb} \qquad\qquad = 80.7° \text{ to horiz.}$$

$\Sigma F_y = 0$:

$$-R_A \cos 25° + R_{B_y} - 1000 = 0 \qquad R_B = 1536/\sin \theta$$
$$R_{B_y} = 1536 \text{ lb} \qquad\qquad = 1556 \text{ lb}$$

For the Beam:

Find cable force T_{EC} and R_D (Figure 2–34):

$$\Sigma M_D = 0: \quad T_{EC} [7.07] - 5(1000) = 0$$
$$T_{EC} = 707 \text{ lb}$$

Find R_{D_x} and R_{D_y}:

$$\Sigma Fx = 0: \quad -707.2 \cos 45° + R_{D_x} = 0, \quad \text{or} \quad R_{D_x} = 500 \text{ lb}$$
$$\Sigma Fy = 0: \quad -707.2 \sin 45° + R_{D_y} = 0 \quad \text{or} \quad R_{D_y} = 500 \text{ lb}$$

Thus, $R_D = 500/\sin 45° = 707 \text{ lb at } 45°$

FIGURE 2–34

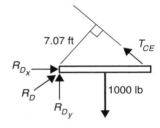

Final equilibrium diagrams are shown in Figure 2–32(b). All members should be in equilibrium (check by $\Sigma F_x = 0$ and $\Sigma F_y = 0$). ◆

2–4 INTERNAL FORCES AND MOMENTS

Forces and moments can be either external or internal. Forces or moments that are applied to a structure are described as *external* (e.g., a weight attached to the end of a rope). Forces and moments that are developed within a structure in response to the external force system present in the structure are described as *internal* (e.g., the tension in a rope resulting from the pull of an attached weight). Internal forces and moments are developed within a structure due to the action of the external force system acting on the structure and serve to hold together, or maintain the equilibrium of, the constituent particles or elements of the structure.

These internal forces or moments that are developed within a member are in direct response to externally applied forces and are typically in tension, compression, shear, or bending. They are rarely constant throughout a specific structure, but vary from point to point. Only in a simple structure, such as a rope with a weight on the end, are the forces constant within the structure. In a typical beam, however, the external forces acting on the structure generate internal forces that vary from point to point. This section begins a general study of these internal forces and their distributions by first considering simple members in a state of pure tension or compression, in which the external forces are applied along the length of the structure (so-called *axial forces*). Following this treatment is a series of sections on *shear forces* and *bending moments* that are developed within a structure. An ability to determine their magnitudes and distributions is fundamental to analyzing and designing structures. These axial forces, shear forces, and bending moments in turn produce stresses and corresponding deformations within the material fabric of the structure. Section 2–5 will introduce the concept of *stress*. For now, we will focus on how to determine internal force and moment states in structures.

2–4–1 Axial Forces (Tension and Compression)

Consider the system shown in Figure 2–35. It is obvious that a tension force has developed in the cable supporting the block which has a magnitude equal to the weight of the block. More formally, equilibrium diagrams can be drawn as illustrated. As the diagram illustrates, the equilibrium of the block is maintained by the development of an internal force, F_t, in the cable, which in this case is simply equal to the weight of the block.

Internal compressive forces are obviously similar in character but opposite in sense. Figure 2–35 illustrates a member in which the internal compressive force varies due to the character of

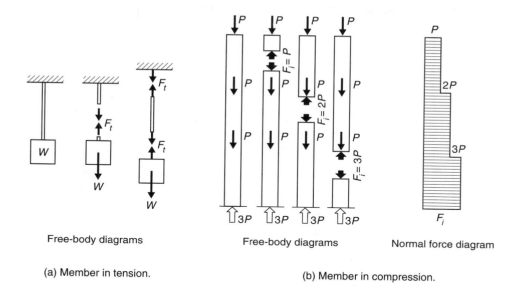

Free-body diagrams

(a) Member in tension.

Free-body diagrams

(b) Member in compression.

Normal force diagram

FIGURE 2–35 Internal tension and compression forces in members.

the external force system present. The magnitude and direction of the internal forces developed are such that *all parts* of the structure are in a state of equilibrium, as they must be no matter what part of the structure is considered.

2-4-2   Shear and Moment

Basic Phenomena.   This section begins a study of the type of internal forces and moments generated in a member carrying an external force system that acts transversely to the axis of the member. The concepts of shear and moment in structures introduced here are of fundamental importance to an understanding of the behavior of structures under load. They also provide the basis for developing tools for designing structures. These same concepts are later developed in the context of looking at a particular structural type (trusses, see Section 4–3–5). In succeeding chapters we draw out and elaborate on the theme of shear and moment in connection with other structural elements. One reason why the material is presented here at this time is that the concepts of shear and moment apply to all specific structural elements (e.g., beams, trusses, cables) presented in subsequent chapters of the book. *Nonetheless, given the somewhat abstract nature of the material, readers may find it better to skip this section for the time being and pick it up again at a later point. A useful point to pick up the material is directly after "the equilibrium of sections" approach to truss analysis, which intrinsically deals with the same phenomena (see Sections 4–3–4 and 4–3–5 in Chapter 4) or as part of beam analysis (Chapter 6).*

Consider the loaded cantilever member illustrated in Figure 2–36. There are two primary ways in which the member might fail as a result of the applied load. One potential type of failure is for the load to cause two contiguous parts of the member to slide relative to each other in a direction parallel to their plane of contact. This is called a *shear failure.* The internal force

(a) Cantilever structure.

(b) Internal forces and moments are generated in the beam which serve to maintain the equilibrium of portions of the structure.

(c) Possible failure modes: when the structure cannot provide these internal forces or moments, failure of the type indicated can occur.

FIGURE 2–36 Shear and moment in structures.

developed in the member that is associated with this phenomenon is called an *internal shear force*. This internal shear force is developed in response to the components of the external force system that act transversely to the long axis of the member and tend to cause the type of transverse sliding indicated in Figure 2–36(c). These internal shear forces resist or balance the net external shearing force tending to cause the sliding. Failure of the type illustrated occurs when the member can no longer provide an equilibrating internal force of this type.

The second possible mode of failure is that illustrated in Figure 2–36(b). This type of failure is obviously associated with the tendency of the transverse external forces to cause part of the structure to rotate, or *bend*. Since free rotation cannot occur in a rigid body (unless a pin connection is present), an internal resisting or balancing moment equal and opposite to the applied moment (the moment associated with the rotational tendencies of the external forces) must be developed within the structure. Failure of the type shown occurs when the structure can no longer provide a resisting moment equal to the applied moment.

At any section of the loaded member, internal shear forces and moments are developed simultaneously. If the member is decomposed at this point into two parts, the forces and moments developed internally serve to maintain the translational and rotational equilibrium of each part. They also represent the internal actions and reactions of one part of the member on the other part. As will be seen later, one of the objectives of the structural design process is to create a structural configuration capable of providing these internal shears and moments in an efficient way and with factors of safety sufficient to prevent shear and moment failures.

Internal shear forces and moments of this type described above are developed in *any* structure carrying transverse loads. Determining the magnitude of these quantities is a straightforward process based on the fundamental proposition that any structure, or any part of any structure, must be in a state of equilibrium under the action of the complete force system (including internal as well as external forces and moments) acting on it. The external force system is typically known. Parts of the force system not initially known, such as reactions at supports, can be readily calculated by methods previously discussed. If the equilibrium of an isolated portion of a structure is considered, the unknown internal shears and moments that must be present at the point of decomposition can be determined through equilibrium considerations involving known parts of the external force system.

2–4–3 Distribution of Shears and Moments

Shear and Moment Diagrams.   There is commonly a variation in the magnitude (and often the sense) of the shears and moments present at different sections in a structure. The distribution of these shears and moments in a structure can be found by considering in turn the equilibrium of different elemental portions of the structure and calculating the shear and moment sets for each elemental portion. As an aid in visualizing the distribution of these shears and moments, the values thus found can be plotted graphically to produce what are called *shear and moment diagrams*. Shear and moment diagrams are invaluable aids in the analysis and design of structures, and a working knowledge of what they mean and how to draw them quickly is of permanent importance. It should be emphasized that their use is not solely restricted to beams. They represent a graphic way of looking at the effects of an external force system acting on any type of structure.

The following text sections will discuss in detail how to construct shear and moment diagrams for any loading condition. It is useful, however, to simply talk through the general nature and uses of these diagrams first. Figure 2–37 illustrates shear and moment diagrams for a simple beam structure carrying a concentrated loading. At any section in the structure, the external force system causes shearing and bending actions to develop throughout the structure. For vertically acting forces, at any specific section of the structure along its length there is a *net external shear force* present that is the algebraic sum of all upwardly and downwardly acting forces (applied forces, loads, and reactions) that exist. This external shear force is balanced by an *internal resisting shear force* that serves to maintain the translational equilibrium of the section. In the upper part of Figure 2–37 note that the directional sense of the internal shear forces varies depending on the location considered. The shaded diagram shown immediately below is a graphical depiction of the magnitude of the external shear force present at each section of the structure along its length. The diagrammatic convention, based on the potential relative movements of adjacent parts of the structure at a section, will be discussed in detail subsequently (see Figure 2–39). The resulting diagram suggests that there are different shear magnitudes and different relative movement tendencies in different parts of the structure. Figure 2–37 also indicates the tendency of the structure to bend underneath the load. In this case it bows into a concave curve. At any specific section of the structure there is a *net external bending moment* that causes a certain amount of bowing at the section. The external bending moment is the algebraic sum of the rotational effects produced by all external forces (applied forces, loads, and reactions) to the left (or right) of the section considered. This external bending moment is balanced by an *internal resisting bending moment* that serves to maintain the rotational equilibrium of each part of the structure. The shaded diagram shown below the bending diagram is a graphical depiction of the magnitude of the external bending moment present at each section of the structure along its length. The fact that the diagram varies from zero to some maximum value and then decreases indicates that the external bending moment (and balancing internal resisting moment) varies in exactly the same way. Thus the maximum tendency of the structure to fail in bending typically occurs where the diagram peaks. The specific sign convention used is shown later in Figure 2–39, where it is noted that a value is considered positive when compression exists on the top face of the structure and tension exists on the bottom—a condition associated with a concave shape—and is considered negative when reverse bending occurs.

EXTERNAL AND INTERNAL SHEAR FORCES

Deformation tendencies due to shear force

Internal or resisting shear forces

Internal or resisting shear forces balance external shear forces at any point x: V_{R_x}

External forces

Each beam section is in equilibrium under internal & external shear forces

Shear forces at a specific section of the structure: V_{E_x}

"Positive" shear

"Negative" shear

┌─ RESISTING SHEAR FORCES IN SPECIFIC STRUCTURES
(see Chapters 6-12 for further discussions and calculation methods)

Trusses: Resisting shear forces are provided by vertical components of internal forces developed in members

Beams: Resisting shear forces are provided by vertically acting shear stressess

Cables: Resisting shear forces are provided by vertical components of internal cable forces

Diagram or graph showing the distribution and magnitude of shear forces along the length of a structure. The sign convention reflects the different deformation tendencies present. See the following sections of this text.

EXTERNAL AND INTERNAL BENDING MOMENTS

Deformation tendencies due to bending moments

Internal or resisting bending moments balance external bending moments at any point x: M_{R_x}

Each beam section is in equilibrium under internal & external moments

Bending Moments at a specific section of the structure: M_{E_x}

+ "Positive" moment

┌─ RESISTING BENDING IN SPECIFIC STRUCTURES
(see Chapters 6-12 for further discussions and calculation methods)

Trusses: A moment couple formed by horizontal components of internal forces in members balances external moments

Beams: Bending stresses acting over the face of a beam form a resisting moment couple

Cables: Horizontal components of cable and reactive forces form a resisting moment couple that balances the external bending moment

Diagram or graph showing the distribution and magnitude of bending moments along the length of a structure. The varying height of the diagram reflects the intensity of the bending present at each section along its length. The positive sign in the diagram reflects the sign convention that concave bending is positive. See the following sections of this text.

FIGURE 2–37 General nature of externally applied and internally resisting shear forces and bending moments in structures, and illustrations of how different types of structural configurations actually provide the resisting or balancing shears and moments via forces or stresses developed within members.

Figure 2–37 also suggests that the specific mechanism by which a structure provides the necessary internal resisting shear and moment values to balance the externally applied shear forces and bending moments at a point varies with the type of structure used. In a typical truss structure, internal resisting shear forces are provided by components of internal forces developed in specific members (often the diagonals—particularly when upper and lower chords are parallel and horizontal). The resistance to external bending moments is provided by a force couple (oppositely acting force pairs that are separated by a moment arm corresponding to the depth of the structure at the point considered) generated by internal forces developed in truss members (particularly the upper and lower chords, but normally involving horizontal components in the diagonals). Chapter 4 discusses these mechanisms in more detail. In a beam structure, internal resisting shear forces are provided by tangentially acting shear stresses acting over the face of the section (stresses acting over an area produce a force). Bending-moment resistance is provided via both tensile and compressive bending stresses that act perpendicularly to the face of the structure. These stresses act over the upper and lower faces of the beam to produce a resisting moment couple. (Note, however, that these stresses are not uniformly distributed but vary in intensity across the face.) In a reinforced concrete beam, the tensile force part of the force couple would be carried by the reinforcing steel. Chapter 6 discusses these mechanisms in more detail. Figure 2–37 also suggests how a cable structure provides internal resisting shear and moment values, as discussed more extensively in Chapter 5. Figure 13–10 presents similar analyses for other structural configurations.

The variations in sense and intensity of shear and moment values along the length of a structure have profound design implications. Magnitudes of shears and moments as represented in the diagrams are used to determine the required size of a beam or to determine the appropriate depth and member sizes in a truss. Using a constant-cross-section and/or constant-depth structure in connection with a loading condition with a set of shear and moment diagrams that vary in intensity usually means that the structure has been sized for peak values at specific points and is oversized elsewhere (a condition indicating that some material is not structurally utilized to its fullest potential). Alternatively, the shapes of the diagrams can be used to fashion a structure whose cross-sectional size and/or depth varies along its length in such a way that material is used to a high level of efficiency. Many designers shape trusses or beams along their lengths in a way that reflects the external force distributions shown in the diagrams. These are but a few of the uses of shear and moment diagrams. Subsequent chapters will draw out these uses in greater detail. Here the next objective is to learn how to draw these diagrams.

Determination of Shears and Moments at a Cross Section. The member shown in Figure 2–38 is in equilibrium. Reactions have been determined. Assume that we want to know the nature of the internal forces at some arbitrary location, such as section x–x located at midspan. To find these internal forces, the structure is decomposed into two parts at this location. Consider the left portion of the structure [Figure 2–38(b)]. This part of the structure is not in equilibrium if only the effects of the external force system acting on this part are considered. The net effect of the portion of the external force system acting on this part of the structure is to cause it to translate vertically downward and rotate in a clockwise direction. The net downward force is called the *external shear force* (V_E) present at the section. In this case, at $x = L/2$, it is given by $V_E = +3P/4 - P = P/4\downarrow$. For this part of the structure to be in equilibrium, it is evident that the

(a) Loaded structure and deflected shape. The loading causes shears and bending moments to develop in the structure.

(b) Separating the beam into two parts. Only the external force system is shown. The parts are not in equilibrium since no internal forces are shown.

(c) Net effects of the external force system on each part of the beam about the section at $L/2$:

Left part: $V_E = +3P/4 - P = P/4\downarrow$
$M_E = (3P/4)(L/2) - P(L/4) = PL/8$

Right part: $V_E = P/4\uparrow$
$M_E = (P/4)(L/2) = PL/8$

(d) For each part of the beam to be in equilibrium, an internal resisting shear force, V_R, and internal resisting moment, M_R, must be provided by the structure. For equilibrium, $V_R = V_E$ and $M_R = M_E$. These internal shears and moments represent the actions and reactions of one part of the beam on the other part.

(e) Summary — loading and reactions.

(f) Diagram showing the distribution of all shear forces present throughout the structure. The shear force found above at section x–x is shown as a negative value. (See discussion on sign contentions.)

(g) Diagram showing the distribution of all bending moments present throughout the structure. The bending moment found above at section x–x is shown as a positive value according to the graphic sign convention that convex curvatures are positive.

FIGURE 2-38 Shear forces and bending moments in a beam. Values are calculated at section x–x in (a) to (d). Figures (f) and (g) are diagramatic representations of values throughout the beam as calculated according to the methods presented in the following section.

structure must somehow provide an *internal resisting shear force* (V_R) equal in magnitude but opposite in sense. Thus, $V_E = V_R$. Hence, $V_R = P/4\uparrow$.

The net rotational effect associated with the portion of the external force system acting on the part of the structure considered (in this case the portion to the left of midspan) is called the *external bending moment* (M_E). If sign conventions are temporarily ignored (a new convention to be described in the next section is used), the external bending moment at $x = L/2$ is simply given by $M_E = (3P/4)(L/2) - (P)(L/4) = PL/8$. For equilibrium to be maintained, it is evident that the structure must provide an *internal resisting moment* (M_R) equal in magnitude but opposite in sense at this location. Since $M_R = M_E$, $M_R = PL/8$.

A more direct approach is to write immediately the equations of equilibrium for the complete free-body diagram of the part of the structure considered [see Figure 2–38(d)]. Thus, at $x = L/2$,

$$\Sigma F_y = 0: \qquad +3P/4 - P + V_R = 0 \qquad \therefore \quad V_R = P/4\uparrow$$

$$\Sigma M_x = 0: \qquad +(3P/4)(L/2) - (P)(L/4) - M_R = 0 \qquad \therefore \quad M = PL/8$$

Obviously, this is not a conceptually different approach. It does not, however, stress that the external force system creates a net translatory force and applied moment at the section which must be balanced by numerically similar internal forces and moments acting in the opposite senses.

These internal shear and moment values could have also been found by considering the equilibrium of the right rather than left portion of the structure. The external shear force V_E for this part is given by $V_E = P/4\uparrow$. Since $V_E = V_R$, $V_R = P/4\downarrow$. Numerically, this is the same result as found previously. The sense of the force, however, is opposite.

In a like vein, the external moment on the right part is given by $M_E = (P/4)(L/2) = PL/8$; since $M_E = M_R$, $M_R = PL/8$. This is numerically equal to the moment found previously, but again of opposite sense.

Note that these shear and moment values are valid only for the specific section considered. Values for other points are shown graphically in Figure 2–38(f) and (g).

Sign Conventions.   That the shears and bending moments found by considering alternate parts of the structure should be numerically equal but opposite in sense is reasonable in view of the fact that the forces found are actually internal to the structure and represent the *action and reaction* of one part of the structure on the other. This does bring up a difficulty, however, in terms of sign conventions. Designating the internal shear or moment as either positive or negative by its direction only, as was done for calculating reactions, is misleading because of the fact that with reference to one part of the structure a value would be positive and with reference to the other part the value would be negative. The same shear forces and moments, however, are involved. A different convention is therefore adopted. The general convention usually employed is based on the physical effects of forces and moments or structures. With respect to bending moments, note that the tendency of either the external force system acting on the left part or the external force system acting on the right part is to cause the structure to deform or bend, as illustrated to the left in Figure 2–39(a). When the external force system causes this type of *concave* curvature to develop at a section in the member, the bending moment present at the section is said to be *positive*. An equivalent convention is to say that upward-acting external forces tend to cause positive moments to develop at a section. If the external force system tends to produce a *convex* curvature (concave downward) at a section, the moment present is said to be *negative*. Equivalently, downward-acting forces tend to produce negative bending moments at a section.

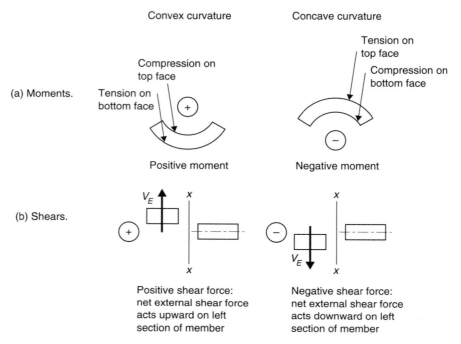

FIGURE 2–39   Sign convention used for shear and moment diagrams.

Yet another way of visualizing positive moments is to say that positive moment diagrams are plotted on the compression face of the structure. Conventions of this type give the same sign to the moment developed at a section regardless of whether the right or left part of a structure is considered. The convention described is used in the United States. Just the opposite convention is commonly used in Europe and elsewhere, where moments are plotted on the tension face of the structure. Diagrams resulting from the two conventions are similar in shape and mean the same thing, but look like inversions of one another.

For shear, the convention typically used is that when the external forces acting on the left part of a structure have a net resultant that acts vertically upward, the shear is said to be positive. Positive shear is associated with the tendency of the external forces to produce relative movements of a section of the type illustrated to the left in Figure 2–39(b). An "up-down" relative movement is considered positive.

Distribution of Shears and Moments.   This section discusses how to construct diagrams that illustrate the magnitudes and distributions of shears and moments along the length of a structure. As will be seen, these diagrams are essentially graphs of the algebraic expressions for how external shear forces and bending moments vary along the length of a structure. Formally, expressions are written for the variation of the external shear force V_E and the external bending moment M_E as a function of a variable distance x along the length of the member, with the left end of the member typically being chosen as a reference point. The sign conventions discussed in the previous section are used. For simple legibility purposes, the areas beneath the plotted graphs are often shaded. Once familiarity is gained with the formal methods of constructing shear and moment diagrams, the reader will rapidly find that a series of "shortcuts"—notably finding values that are critical points—will facilitate the rapid construction of these diagrams.

◆ ◆   **EXAMPLE**

Draw shear and moment diagrams for the beam shown in Figure 2–40(a).

(a) Loaded beam.

(b) External and internal shears and moments:

For $0 \le x \le 2L/3$: $V_x = P/3$
$M_x = (P/3)x$

For $2L/3 \le x \le L$: $V_x = P/3 - P = -2P/3$
$M_x = (P/3)x - P(x - 2L/3)$

At $x = 2L/3$: $M_{max} = 2PL/9$

Shear

Moments

(c) Graphical depiction of V_x and M_x.   (d) Shear and moment diagrams.

FIGURE 2–40   Shear and moment diagrams for a simply supported beam carrying a concentrated load.

Solution: Vertical reactions are first calculated. $\Sigma M = 0$: $P(2L/3) - L(R_B) = 0$; $\therefore$ $R_B = 2P/3$. $\Sigma F = 0$: $R_A + R_B = P$; $\therefore$ $R_A = P/3$. Next, consider the free-body diagram of an elemental portion of the beam (having a length x) to the left of the load. As shown in the figure, the rotational effect of the set of external forces acting on the left portion of the beam about the cross section defined by the distance x is simply given by $M_E = (P/3)(x)$. The net translatory effect is given by $V_E = P/3$. Thus, if $x = 0$, $M_E = 0$ and $V_E = P/3$. If $x = 2L/3$, $M_E = 2PL/9$ and $V_E = P/3$ (if the section is infinitesimally to the left of the load). Once x moves to the right of the load, new equations for shears and moments are needed, since a new force now acts on the elemental portion of the beam considered. Thus, $M_E = (P/3)(x) - P[x - \frac{2}{3}(L)]$ and $V_E = +(P/3) - P = (-\frac{2}{3})P$. Graphically, these shears and moments can be plotted as illustrated in Figure 2–40(c). ◆

◆ ◆ **EXAMPLE**

Draw shear and moment diagrams for the structure illustrated in Figure 2–41.

FIGURE 2–41

Solution: Reactions are first calculated as before. Next, equations for shear and moment at a distance of x from the left reaction are determined by considering the equilibrium of the portion of the structure to the left of x.

For $0 < x < L/3$:

$$V_E = \frac{4P}{3}$$

$$M_E = \left(\frac{4P}{3}\right)x$$

For $L/3 < x < 2L/3$:

$$V_E = \frac{4P}{3} - P = \frac{P}{3}$$

$$M_E = \left(\frac{4P}{3}\right)x - P\left(x - \frac{L}{3}\right)$$

For $2L/3 < x < L$:

$$V_E = \frac{4P}{3} - P - 2P = -\frac{5P}{3}$$

$$M_E = \left(\frac{4P}{3}\right)x - P\left(x - \frac{L}{3}\right)$$
$$- 2P\left(x - \frac{2L}{3}\right)$$

These expressions can be plotted to obtain shear and moment diagrams, as illustrated in Figure 2–41. The shear forces are constant between loads, whereas the moments vary linearly. Note that critical values of the moment occur at $x = L/3$, where $M = 4PL/9$, and $x = 2L/3$, where $M = 5PL/9$. Major changes in the shear present also occur at these points. It is also interesting to note that the maximum value of the moment does not occur at midspan but at a point where the shear diagram passes through zero. ◆

In structures carrying concentrated loads, critical moment and shear values invariably occur directly beneath the concentrated load application points. By utilizing this observation, the moment diagram can be drawn more easily by simply considering sections beneath the load points. Thus, the moment at $x = L/3$ (the first load point) is simply given by $M_E = (4P/3)(L/3) = 4PL/9$. That at $x = 2L/3$ (the second load point) is given by $M_E = (4P/3)(2L/3) - (P)(L/3) = 5PL/9$. The latter is even easier to find if the equilibrium of a portion of the structure to the right instead of left of the section studied is considered. Thus, $M_E = (5P/3)(L/3) = 5PL/9$. The values of $4PL/9$ and $5PL/9$ define critical points on the moment diagram. Straight lines can be drawn between them, since by inspection it is evident that the moments vary linearly between critical points.

Two sign conventions for the moment diagram are shown. The upper one is used in the U.S. The lower one is widely used elsewhere.

◆ ◆ **EXAMPLE**

Draw shear and moment diagrams for the two cantilevered beams shown in Figure 2–42. Do not write formal equations but determine values as directly as possible. Observe that the structures are mirror images of one another.

Solution: Once the reactions are determined, the shear diagrams can be quickly drawn by noting that applied forces "push" the shear diagram up and down (see Figure 2–42). Since there is no load variation between vertical forces, the shear diagram is constant and horizontal between load points. The moment diagram for the structure to the left can be quickly drawn by noting that bending moments must inherently be zero at member ends and that the peak value must be at the interior support. Values can be found by simply multiplying a single force times a distance on either the left or right side of the support. The moment diagrams must vary linearly between zero and the maximum values calculated since there are no intervening forces. In the two cases shown, observe that the moment diagrams are similar in algebraic sign since the deformed shape is the same in both cases. The shear diagrams of the mirror image structures have similar numerical values, but with opposite algebraic signs. This is because the sense of shear deformation differs in each case. This would have absolutely no effect on sizing a beam to carry the loads or any other application. ◆

◆ ◆ **EXAMPLE**

Draw shear and moment diagrams for the cantilever structure shown in Figure 2–43.

Solution: Shears and moments at any section defined by a distance x from the left end of the member are determined through considering the equilibrium of the structure to the left of x. The moment of the uniform load to the left of the section considered is found by replacing the uniformly distributed load by a statically

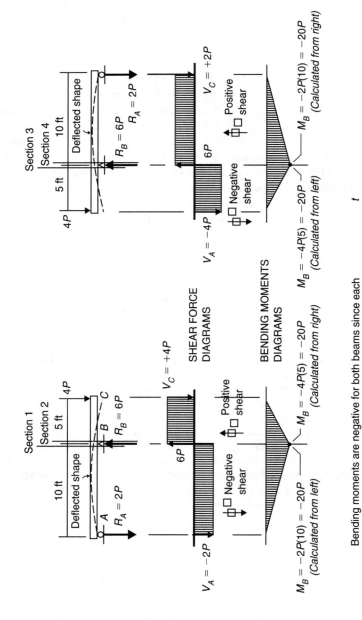

FIGURE 2–42 Shears and moments in similar cantilever structures oriented differently.

(a) Loading.

(b) Free-body diagram of portion of beam showing modeling of distributed load.

(c) Shear diagram.

(d) Moment diagram.

FIGURE 2–43

equivalent concentrated load acting at the center of mass of the portion of the load considered (see Section 2–2–5). For $0 < x < L$:

$$V_E = -wx$$

$$M_E = -wx\left(\frac{x}{2}\right) = -\frac{wx^2}{2}$$

Critical values occur at $x = L$, where $V_E = -wL$ and $M_E = -wL^2/2$. Note that the shear forces vary linearly according to the first power of x and that the moments vary according to the second power of x.

◆

◆ ◆ **EXAMPLE**

Draw shear and moment diagrams for the uniformly loaded simply supported structure shown in Figure 2–44.

Solution: As before, the net effect of the external force system acting on an elemental portion of the structure is to produce at the section considered a translational shear force, V_E, and rotational moment, M_E. These external shears and moments must be balanced by an internal resisting shear force, V_R, and internal resisting moment, M_R, provided by (or developed in) the structure if equilibrium is to be maintained.

(a) Loading.

(b) Segment of structure of length x: external force system and equivalent external shear force and bending moment.

$V_{E_x} = wL/2 - wx$

$M_{E_x} = (wL/2)x - wx(x/2)$

At $x = 0$:

$V_{E_x} = wL/2, \ M_{E_x} = 0$

At $x = L/2$:

$V_{E_x} = 0, \ M_{E_x} = wL^2/8$

(c) Equilibrium diagrams: an internal resisting shear force and bending moment is developed in the structure to maintain the equilibrium of the segment.

(d) Expressions for the shear and moment as a function of x and their graphical depictions.

FIGURE 2-44

For $0 \lessgtr x \lessgtr L$:

$$V_E = \frac{wL}{2} - wx$$

$$M_E = \left(\frac{wL}{2}\right)x - (wx)\left(\frac{x}{2}\right)$$

Note that the shear diagram varies linearly and has maximum values at $x = 0$ and $x = L$, where $V_E = wL/2$ and $V_E = -wL/2$, respectively. The moment diagram varies according to the second power of x and reaches a maximum at midspan (where the shear is zero). The maximum moment present is $M = wL^2/8$. This is one of the most frequently encountered expressions in structural theory. It is commonly used in the analysis and design of simple beams but crops up in other, less expected places as well.   ◆

◆ ◆   **EXAMPLE**

Draw shear and moment diagrams for the partially loaded beam shown in Figure 2–45.

FIGURE 2–45

Solution: Reactions are first calculated as before. Next, equations for shear and moment are determined and plotted as before.

For $0 \geqslant x \geqslant 12$:

$$V_E = 15 - 2x$$

$$M_E = 15x - 2x\left(\frac{x}{2}\right)$$

For $12 \geqslant x \geqslant 16$:

$$V_E = 15 - 2(12)$$

$$M_E = 15x - 2(12)(x - 6)$$

Note that where uniform loads are actually on the member, the shear diagram varies linearly and the moment diagram parabolically. Determining the maximum moment present in the structure could be a tedious job since it is *not* necessarily obvious where this maximum moment occurs. A trial-and-error process of assuming different values of x would work, but a more direct approach making use of the fact that the moment has a critical value where the shear is zero is much easier.

   If a correct but less rigorous approach to constructing the shear diagram is adopted, it can be seen that the shear diagram can be easily drawn by noting that the left reaction, so to speak, pushes the shear diagram initially up to a level corresponding to the left reaction (indicating that a shear force exists in the beam immediately to the right of the reaction of a value equal to that of the reaction—a result that would have been found by passing a section through that point). The effect of the uniform load is to cause the shear diagram to decrease at a rate per unit length equal to the load per unit length (this is also evident by looking at the shear equation noted above). The shear diagram thus has a slope equal to the uniform load itself. This information can then be used to find where the shear diagram passes through zero. Hence, $15 = 2x$, or $x = 7.5$. This is equivalent to setting $V_E = 0$ in the original shear equation (i.e., $0 = 15 - 2x$). By noting that the moment is generally a critical value at points of zero shear, the moment can be calculated at $x = 7.5$ to yield the maximum moment present. Thus, $M_E = 15(7.5) - 2(7.5)(7.5/2) = 56.25$.   ◆

Principle of Superposition.   Complex loading conditions can be separated into simpler loading cases (see Figure 2–46). Individual shear and moment diagrams can then be constructed and algebraically combined to create a composite diagram of the original complex loading. Superposition principles are generally valid for common rigid structures where the deformation of the structure does not significantly affect load location.

Shapes of Diagrams.   Some summary observations can be made about the shapes of shear and moment diagrams (see Figure 2–47). Concentrated loads generally produce shears that are constant in magnitude along sections of a structure between concentrated loads, and the shear diagram consequently consists of a series of horizontal lines. Moments in such structures vary linearly (according to the first power of x) between concentrated loads. Moment diagrams are consequently composed of sloped lines. Uniformly distributed loads tend to produce linearly varying shear forces. Shear diagrams correspondingly consist of a sloped line or a series of sloped lines. Uniformly distributed loads produce parabolically varying moments. Moment diagrams are correspondingly curved. Combined loads produce combined shapes. While not rigorously provable at this point, it is also generally true that a point of zero shear corresponds to a location of a maximum or minimum moment. This latter observation is particularly valuable for locating critical design moments in structures having unusual loading conditions.

Relation of Moment Diagram to Deflected Shape of Structure.   As previously discussed, transverse loads produce a bowing in the structure. Depending on the way the loads act, the bowing produced can be either concave upward or the reverse. The overall deflected shape of the structure is intimately related to the nature of the bowing present and, consequently, to the moments present.

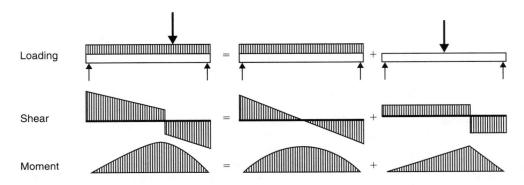

FIGURE 2–46   Principle of superposition.

Beam with double canti-lever — uniform loading ($M_1 = M_2 = 0.021wL^2$ when $a = 0.21L$)

$$V_1 = wa$$
$$V_2 = \frac{wL}{2} - wa$$
$$M_1 = \frac{wa^2}{2}$$
$$M_2 = w\left[\frac{L^2}{8} - \frac{La}{2}\right]$$

Beam with single canti-lever — uniform loading ($M_1 = M_2 = 0.043wL^2$ when $a = 0.29L$)

$$R_1 = V_1 = \frac{w}{2L}(L^2 - a^2)$$
$$V_2 = wa$$
$$V_3 = \frac{w}{2L}(L^2 + a^2)$$
$$M_1 = \frac{w}{8L^2}(L + a)^2(L - a)^2$$
$$M_2 = \frac{wa^2}{8}$$

Simple beam — uniform loading partially distributed

$$R_1 = V_{1max} = \frac{wa}{2L}(2L - a)$$
$$R_2 = V_2 = \frac{wa^2}{2L}$$
$$M_{max} = \frac{R_1^2}{2w}$$

Cantilever beam — concentrated load at free end

$$R = V = P$$
$$M_{max} = PL$$

Simple beam — concentrated load at midspan

$$R = V = \frac{P}{2}$$
$$M_{max} = \frac{PL}{4}$$

Beam overhanging at one support — concentrated load

$$R_1 = V_1 = \frac{Pb}{L} \qquad R_2 = V_2 = \frac{Pa}{L}$$
$$M_{max} = \frac{Pab}{L}$$

Simple beam — two equal concentrated loads symmetrically placed

$$R = V = P$$
$$M_{max} = Pa$$

Beam overhanging at one support — concentrated load

$$R_1 = V_1 = \frac{Pa}{L} \qquad M_{max} = Pa$$
$$R_2 = V_1 + V_2 = \frac{P}{L}(L + a)$$

Simple beam — linearly increasing uniform loading

$$R_1 = V_1 = \frac{wL}{6} \qquad R_2 = V_2 = \frac{wL}{3}$$
$$M_{max} = \frac{wL^2}{9\sqrt{3}}$$

FIGURE 2–47 Shear and moment diagrams for typical structures.

Consider the member shown in Figure 2–48. The loads on the ends of the projecting cantilevers produce a bowing that is concave downward in the left and right regions of the member. The moment diagram is negative in these zones, which are commonly called *negative moment regions* in U.S. practice. Associated with the concave downward bowing is a stretching of the upper fibers of the structure, which puts them in a state of tension, and a shortening of the lower fibers, which are consequently put in a state of compression. Converse phenomena occur in the middle portion of the member, in the *positive moment region.* Between positive and negative moment regions transition points must obviously occur. Because of the reversal of curvature that takes place, it is evident that no bowing or bending is present at the transition points. Consequently, they are points of zero moment. These points are typically called *points of inflection.*

A numerical example showing a cantilevered beam is illustrated in Figure 2–49. As is evident, the point of inflection indicating a point of reverse curvature corresponds to a point of zero moment, but not necessarily to a point of zero shear. The point of zero moment could be found by writing an equation for the moment values present in terms of some variable x and equating the expression to zero.

2–4–4 Relations among Load, Shear, and Moment in Structures

Although a topic generally outside the scope of this book, it can be shown that relationships of the following type exist among the load, shear, and moment in a structure: $w = dV/dx$, $V = dM/dx$, $V_B - V_A = \int_A^B w\, dx$, and $M_B - M_A = \int_A^B V\, dx$.

Briefly, these relationships can be found by looking at the equilibrium of an infinitesimal length of a structure and considering translatory and rotational equilibrium (see Figure 2–50). Shear forces V and M, and their incremental changes dV and dM, are considered. Thus, from $\Sigma F_y = 0$ we obtain $+V - (V + dV) + w\, dx = 0$, or $w = dV/dx$; and from $\Sigma M_x = 0$ we obtain

FIGURE 2–48 Relationship between the moment diagram and the deflected shape of a structure.

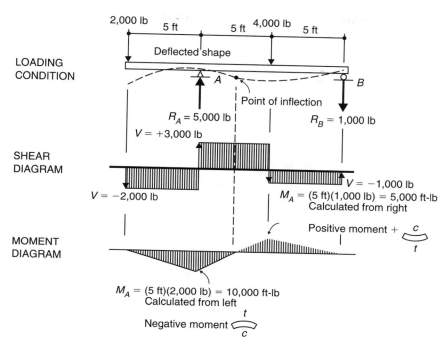

FIGURE 2–49   Deflected shape, shear, and moment diagrams for a cantilevered beam.

$+M + V\,dx + (w\,dx)(dx/2) - (M + dM) = 0$, or $V = dM/dx$ (when terms of negligible magnitude are dropped during the solution).

Applications of these principles are many. The value of the distributed load at a point is equal to the slope of the shear diagram at the same point. The value of the shear at a point is equal to the slope of the moment diagram at the same point. The *change* in moment between points on a structure is represented by the area under the shear diagram between the same two points (points of reference and boundary conditions must be carefully considered). Techniques of this kind are highly useful in checking the accuracy of shear and moment diagrams (Figure 2–50). They clearly point out that the maximum/minimum value of the moment in a structure occurs when the shear diagram passes through zero (since $dM/dx = 0$ at this point).

2–5   INTRODUCTION TO STRESSES

Associated with each of the states of tension, compression, shear, or bending moments within a structure are corresponding internal *stresses*. Stress, or *force intensity per unit area,* is a measure of how a force is distributed over an area. A force acting over a small area produces higher unit stresses than does the same force acting over a larger area. These stresses tend to cause a material to fail in tension or compression or via a shearing action. Different materials have different capacities that can be experimentally determined for carrying different types of stresses. Thus, by

BASIC PRINCIPLES

$$w = dV/dx$$
$$V_B - V_A = \int_A^B w\, dx$$
$$V = dM/dx$$
$$M_B - M_A = \int_A^B V\, dx$$

APPLICATIONS

FIGURE 2-50 Relations between loads, shears, and moments.

80

knowing the stress level present, a member can be determined to be safe or adequately or inadequately sized. Corresponding to these stresses are related *strains,* or deformations per unit length of material. Strains contribute to the overall deformed shape of a structure, including its total deflections.

Tension and Compression Stress.   This section considers the internal forces and corresponding stresses in simple tension and compression members. As will be seen, these stresses are easy to determine because they are uniform across the cross-sectional surface of a member. *More complex stress states associated with shear and bending will be discussed in Chapter 6.* These latter stresses are nonuniformly distributed across a cross section and their determination is correspondingly more complex. Following the discussion of simple tension and compression stresses will be an introduction to material properties.

Consider a simple tension member of the type illustrated in Figure 2–51. It is evident that the internal tension present is not actually concentrated at a specific spot [as the arrows symbolizing internal force in Figure 2–51(b) would seem to indicate] within the cross section of the member,

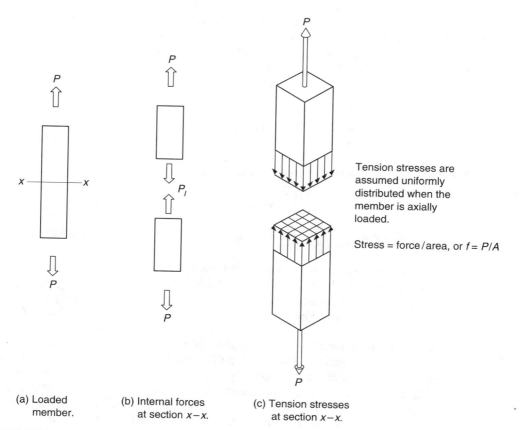

Tension stresses are assumed uniformly distributed when the member is axially loaded.

Stress = force/area, or $f = P/A$

(a) Loaded member.

(b) Internal forces at section $x-x$.

(c) Tension stresses at section $x-x$.

FIGURE 2–51   Tension members.

but is rather distributed over the entire cross section. The total internal force necessary to equilibrate the external force acting on the member is in actuality the resultant of all distributed forces, or stresses, acting at the cross section.

With respect to a simple element carrying a tension force, it is reasonable to assume that if the external force acts along the axis of the member and at the centroid, or point of symmetry of the cross section, the stresses developed at the cross section are of uniform intensity. Their resultant would have the same line of action as the external force present. When stresses are uniformly distributed, their magnitude is given by

$$\text{stress} = \frac{\text{force}}{\text{area}} \quad \text{or} \quad f = \frac{P}{A}$$

where f is the stress (force intensity per unit area), P is the axial force present, and A is the area of the cross section considered. Stresses of this type are often called *axial,* or *normal,* stresses. The stresses developed in a member loaded in direct compression can be similarly described.

The assumption that stresses associated with axial loads are uniformly distributed across a cross section is a reasonable one when the load is applied in a purely axial way and the member involved is straight and of uniform cross section. At unique points, such as where the external load is applied or at discontinuities in the member, more complex stress patterns may occur. The assumption, however, is generally quite good and perfectly acceptable as a working hypothesis for preliminary design purposes. This approach is not valid for beams and other members in bending which have more complex stress distributions (see Chapter 6).

◆ ◆ **EXAMPLE**

A member having a square cross section that measures 2 in. × 2 in. (50.8 × 50.8 mm) carries a tension load of 24,000 lb (106.75 kN). What is the stress level present at a typical cross section?

Solution: Assuming that the internal stress is uniformly distributed:

$$\text{stress} = \frac{\text{force}}{\text{area}} \quad \text{or} \quad f = \frac{P}{A} = \frac{24,000 \text{ lb}}{2 \text{ in.} \times 2 \text{ in.}} = 6000 \text{ lb/in.}^2$$

$$f = \frac{106.75 \text{ kN}}{50.8 \times 50.8 \text{ mm}} = 0.0414 \text{ kN/mm}^2 = 41.4 \text{ N/mm}^2 = 41.4 \text{ MPa}$$

Note that the axial or normal stress in a member depends only on the force applied and cross-sectional area involved. The actual stress developed does *not* depend on the type of material of which the member is made. Bending, shear, and other types of stresses are nonuniformly distributed and *not* described by $f = P/A$. These stresses are considered in Chapter 6. ◆

Strength of Tension Members.   The strength of a tension member depends on a number of factors. The probable mode of failure is a pulling apart of the member at the weakest location along its length. The load-carrying capacity of a member subjected to pure tension is independent of the length of the member if the member has a uniform cross section throughout (in terms of both area and material). The presence of a single weak spot, such as a point of reduced cross-sectional area, determines the capacity of the whole member (at such locations the actual stress level as given by $f = P/A$ is higher than elsewhere because of the smaller value of A).

When a member is axially loaded, stress levels defined by $f = P/A$ develop. If the material used can sustain this stress intensity, the member will carry the load. As stress levels increase, due to increasing loads, for example, there comes a point where the stress intensity present exceeds the capability of the material used to withstand the pulling apart. This is the *failure stress level* of the material. It is a property of the material used. Failure stress levels are experimentally determined for various materials. When the *actual* stress level, given by $f = P/A$, in a member exceeds the failure stress level for the material used, the member will pull apart.

For steel, experiments have shown that the apparent tension stress level associated with the *beginning* of the material pulling apart or *yielding* is approximately $F_{yield} = 36{,}000$ lb/in.^{2} (248 N/mm^2 or 248 MPa). In Section 2.6 we explore material properties in greater detail.

Allowable Stresses.   From the point of view of determining if a member is of adequate size to support a given tension load, it is necessary first to determine the actual stress level in the member ($f = P/A$). If this actual stress level is less than the experimentally determined failure stress level for the material, the member can support the loading involved. From a design point of view, however, it is desirable that a statement that a member is adequately sized involve a factor of safety of some type. Loads and failure stresses can never be predicted with absolute certainty and a conservative note should be introduced when designing members.

One way of introducing a factor of safety into the design process is to use an *allowable stress* (F_t) rather than failure or yield stresses as the measure against which actual stresses are compared. Thus,

$$F_{t_{allowable}} = \frac{F_{yield}}{\text{factor of safety}}$$

For steel, for example, a factor of safety of 1.5 is often used. Thus, the allowable stress level in tension for a steel member is given by $F_t = (36{,}000 \text{ lb/in.}^2)/1.5 = 24{,}000$ lb/in.^{2} or $F_t = (248 \text{ N/mm}^2)/1.5 = 165$ N/mm^2. This value can be used in evaluating the acceptability of a given member or as a tool for determining the required size of a new member, given the load it must carry. In sizing a new member, the required cross-sectional area for a member in tension carrying a load P is given by

$$A_{required} = \frac{\text{force}}{\text{allowable stress}} = \frac{P}{F_t}$$

◆ ◆   **EXAMPLE**

What diameter of steel rod is required to support a tension load of 10,000 lb (44.5 kN)? Assume that the allowable stress for the steel is $F_t = 24{,}000$ lb/in.^{2} (165 MPa or 165 N/mm^2).

Solution:

Area required

$$A = \frac{P}{F_t} = \frac{10{,}000 \text{ lb}}{24{,}000 \text{ lb/in.}^2} = 0.416 \text{ in.}^2 \quad \text{or} \quad A = \frac{44{,}500 \text{ N}}{165 \text{ N/mm}^2} = 270 \text{ mm}^2$$

Diameter

$$\frac{\pi d^2}{4} = 0.416 \text{ in.}^2 \quad \text{or} \quad d = 0.73 \text{ in.}$$

$$= 270 \text{ mm}^2 \quad \text{or} \quad d = 18.5 \text{ mm}$$

◆

2-6   MECHANICAL PROPERTIES OF MATERIALS

2-6-1   Introduction

In this section we present a brief coverage of the various properties of materials that are of interest from a structural design viewpoint. Of primary interest are the strength and load-deformation properties of a material. In the final analysis, these properties are really explicable only in terms of the internal forces that act between the constituent parts of the material (i.e., the molecules or, in some cases, the atoms). This extent of investigation is, however, beyond the scope of this book. Instead, the coverage will be primarily descriptive in tone and will not dwell on the reasons underlying particular material behavior. *Readers new to the subject material may find it better to omit this section temporarily and return to it later (e.g., as part of beam analysis in Chapter 6).*

2-6-2   General Load-Deformation Properties of Materials

The application of a load to a member invariably produces dimensional changes in the member. The member under load undergoes changes in size or shape or both. For many common materials, such as steel, the dimensional changes produced can be roughly categorized into one of two general types, elastic and plastic deformations, that occur sequentially with increasing loads. When a member is first loaded, deformations are in the *elastic range* of the material. In the elastic range, the member generally returns to its original dimensions if the applied loads are removed (the behavior is similar to that of a spring). Deformations in the elastic range depend directly on the magnitude of the stress level present in the member. As loads increase, deformations in many materials move into the *plastic range.* This occurs when the stress in the material reaches a sufficiently high level to cause a permanent change (i.e., a breaking down) in the internal structure of the material. Once these internal changes have occurred, the original state cannot be exactly regained, even if the load is removed completely. Consequently, when a material moves into the plastic range, it undergoes irreversible dimensional changes and a permanent set exists even if all external loads are completely removed. The load or stress levels associated with the plastic range are invariably higher than those associated with the elastic range. In the plastic range, deformations are nonlinearly dependent on the load or stress level present. Deformations in the plastic range are very large relative to those in the elastic range. Quite often material in the plastic range simply pulls apart (i.e., undergoes massive deformations) under a relatively constant load.

As will be discussed in more detail later, not all materials demonstrate both elastic and plastic behavior under increasing loads. Steel does; plain concrete does not.

2-6-3   Elasticity

Elastic Behavior.   The primary way of describing elastic changes in size or shape is through the concept of *strain* (ϵ). Strain is generally defined as the ratio of the change in size or shape of an element subjected to stress to the original size or shape (S) of the element (i.e., $\epsilon = [\Delta S/(S + \Delta S)] \doteq \Delta S/S)$. As a ratio, it has no physical dimensions. There is a general relationship between stress and strain in elastic materials that was first postulated by Robert Hooke (1635–1703) and is known as *Hooke's law.* Hooke's law states that for an elastic body, the ratio of the stress present on an element to the strain produced is a constant. Thus,

$$\frac{\text{stress}}{\text{strain}} = \text{constant for a material} = \text{modulus of elasticity} = E$$

The magnitude of the constant is a property of the material involved and is referred to as the *modulus of elasticity.* The units for this constant are the same as those for stress (i.e., force per unit area) since strain is a dimensionless quantity. The relationship between stress and strain shown above implies that strain in a member is linearly dependent on the stress level present. The constant relating stresses and strains (the modulus of elasticity) is determined experimentally.

When a member is subjected to a simple tensile force, it will elongate a certain amount (Figure 2–52). If L is the original length of the member and ΔL is the change in length, the strain, ϵ, present in the member is

$$\text{strain} = \frac{\text{increase in length}}{\text{original length}} \quad \text{or} \quad \epsilon = \frac{\Delta L}{L}$$

Strain is actually dimensionless. It may be useful, however, to think of strain as the amount of deformation per unit of length. In these terms, the dimensions of strain would be millimeters/ millimeter or inches/inch.

A typical way of determining the modulus of elasticity (E) of a material is to take a member of known length and cross-sectional area, subject it to a known load, and measure the amount of elongation (ΔL). Since the stress present can be readily calculated by using the relation $f = P/A$ and the strain found from the relation $\epsilon = \Delta L/L$, the modulus of elasticity can be determined, or $E = f/\epsilon$. Moduli of elasticity (E) of many different materials can be found by a general procedure of this type. For steel, $E_s = 29.6 \times 10^6$ lb/in.^{2} (204,000 N/mm^2 or 204,000 MPa), and for aluminum, $E_A = 11.3 \times 10^6$ lb/in.^{2} (77,900 N/mm^2). A typical value for concrete is $E_c = 3 \times 10^6$ lb/in.^{2} (20,700 N/mm^2) and for timber is $E_T = 1.6 \times 10^6$ lb/in.^{2} (11,000 N/mm^2). The values for concrete and timber vary widely according to the precise characteristics of the concrete mix tested or the grade and species of wood used (Appendix 15).

Once the value of E for a material is known, it can be used as a constant to predict deformations in the material under different conditions of stress.

With respect to Figure 2–53, the modulus of elasticity is nothing more than the *slope* of the stress-strain curve within the elastic range of the material. As the stress level present in a member continues to increase, a point is reached where the strains developed are no longer linearly dependent on the stress. This point is termed the *proportional limit* of the material. After this point is passed, the concept of a constant modulus of elasticity is not valid. For some materials, such as steel, the magnitude of the deformations that occur in the plastic range are literally enormous as compared to those in the elastic range.

It should be noted that some materials, such as aluminum, do not have pronounced proportional limits (see Figure 2–54). Other materials, such as cast iron, exhibit virtually no

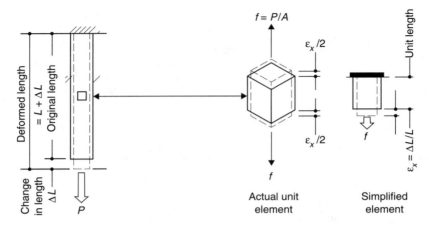

(a) Axially loaded tension member: an applied tension force produces a longitudinal elongation whose magitude depends on the cross-sectional area of the member, the length of the member, the material the member is made of, and the magnitude of the applied force.

(c) "Strain" in a tension member: strain is the amount of deformation per unit length that occurs in a loaded member.

(b) Elastic behavior: for members of a given size made of "linearly elastic materials" (e.g., steel), the amount of deformation that takes place is proportional to the magnitude of the applied load. This elastic relationship holds true until the load is of sufficient magnitude to cause a breakdown to occur in the material.

(d) Relation between stress and strain: in linearly elastic materials there is a constant relationship between the magnitude of the stress present and the resultant strain, i.e., stress/strain = constant = modulus of elasticity (E).

FIGURE 2–52   Stresses, strains, and elongations in a simple tension element.

plastic deformations at all. Different materials thus behave in widely differing ways under load.

Lateral Deformations in the Elastic Range.   As illustrated in Figure 2–52, a member subjected to an axial force undergoes elastic changes in its lateral dimensions as well as in the direction of the applied load. Lateral dimensions in a member decrease when the member is subjected to a tensile force and increase when the member is subjected to a compressive load. A constant relation exists between these lateral changes and those that occur in the longitudinal direction.

(a) Stress–strain diagram.

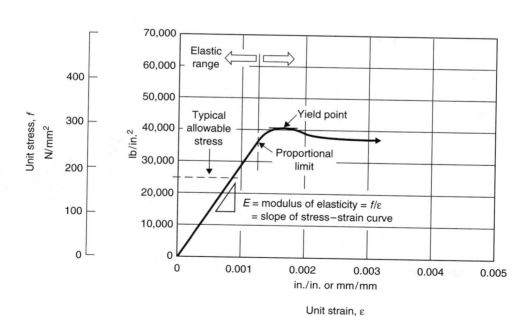

(b) Enlarged portion of elastic range.

FIGURE 2–53 Typical stress-strain diagrams for structural steel tested in tension.

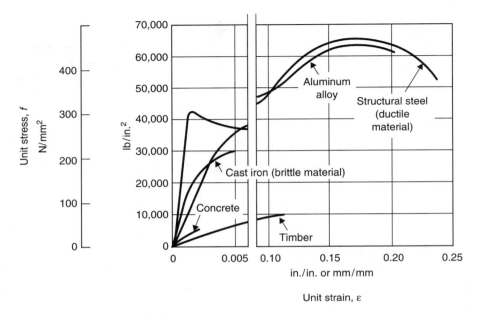

FIGURE 2–54 Typical stress-strain diagrams for different materials.

This relation is usually called *Poisson's ratio* (v) and is defined by $v = -\epsilon_y/\epsilon_x$. For steel, Poisson's ratio is about 0.3.

2–6–4 Strength

The term *strength* is often used with reference to the load-carrying capacity of a material. Materials often exhibit relatively complex behaviors under load, which necessitates a more precise definition of the term strength. Steel, for example, continues to be able to carry increasing stress levels past the proportional limit, but it does so with greater amounts of deformation for given increases in unit stress than occur within the elastic range. A critical point, termed the *yield point,* is reached when the steel deforms without any increase in stress at all. In fact, when steel is being experimentally studied in a load-testing machine (which typically applies deformations and measures stresses or loads rather than vice versa), an actual decrease in the stress level appears to occur (see Figure 2–53). When a load is directly applied (instead of deformations), the yield point simply marks a sudden increase in deformations. The material then undergoes massive deformations (in the plastic range) at a relatively constant stress level. As deformations increase, however, the steel begins to be able to carry small additional loads and the stress level present increases again. A level is reached that marks the maximum stress the steel can carry. This is called the *ultimate strength* of the material. After this level is reached, the steel deforms extremely rapidly, reduces in cross-sectional area (i.e., *necks*), and finally pulls apart *(ruptures).*

2-6-5   Other Material Properties

Ductile and Brittle Behavior.   Materials that undergo large plastic deformations of the type described above before rupture occurs are generally referred to as *ductile* materials. Steel is a classic example of a ductile material. Conversely, if a material does not exhibit plastic behavior under load but rather ruptures under load with little evident deformation, the material is said to be *brittle*. Cast iron is a brittle material, as is plain concrete. The stress-strain curves shown in Figure 2–54 illustrate the differences in behavior under load between the two general types of material.

The amount of ductility or brittleness present in materials such as steel can actually be controlled by altering their constituency or method of processing. Increasing the carbon content of steel, for example, reduces ductility. Alternatively, a steel exhibiting little ductility can be made more ductile by annealing it (heating it to a high temperature and allowing it to cool slowly).

Implications of Ductility for Structural Design.   From a structural design viewpoint, materials such as steel that exhibit the ductile or plastic behavior described before are very desirable, since the plastic region (with its slightly increased load-carrying capacity after the yield point) represents a measure of reserve strength. Design stress levels, or *allowable* stress levels, are invariably set below the yield stress of the material and are well within the elastic range of the material. A steel beam, for example, would be designed to have its actual stress level equal to or less than the allowable stress value. A certain level of elastic beam deflection corresponds to this stress level and its associated elastic strain. If loads on the beam increase beyond the anticipated design levels, bending stress levels and strains also increase until the yield point of the material is reached. At this point, the steel yields, but does not physically rupture, and the beam begins undergoing the massive deflections associated with the move of the material into the plastic range. These deflections are very visibly evident compared to design deflections, and can serve as a visual warning of impending failure. Because of the increase in stress required to reach the ultimate strength of the material, the beam can still carry slightly increased loads even when these massive deflections are evident. Only after the ultimate strength of the material is reached does the member fail. Since this phenomenon is coupled with an increased load-carrying capacity in the beam due to the plastic stress redistribution that occurs (see Section 6–4–3), the beam has a significant reserve load-carrying capacity. The plasticity of a material is consequently a very useful and desirable property.

Brittle materials do not exhibit plastic behavior. Structural members using brittle materials, such as cast iron beams, do not visibly deflect to any great degree prior to failure and thus give no advance warning of impending collapse. Such members are dangerous and are not used. Concrete is also a brittle material, but when used in conjunction with ductile steel the overall member can be designed to have a measure of ductility (see Section 6–4–4).

Strain Rate Effects.   As the rate of load application on a structure increases, many normally ductile materials begin behaving in a brittle manner (less plastic deformation is present). Proportional limits and yield points often increase with increasing strain rates.

Temperature Effects.   Low temperatures often cause many materials that are normally ductile, such as steel, to begin to exhibit brittle behavior. In many senses, the effects of low temperatures on materials are equivalent to those of high strain rates.

Creep Effects.   The term *creep* refers to the continued deformation with time of a material under a constant stress level. Plastics and plain concrete, for example, tend to creep greatly under load. Steel does not. Long-term deflections in structures due to creep effects can be significant. Creep can also cause unfavorable stress redistributions to occur in reinforced concrete members.

Fatigue Effects.   A material subjected to alternating stress cycles may fail at a relatively low stress level (even less than the elastic strength of the material). The endurance limit of a material is the maximum unit stress that the material can withstand for an indefinite number of cycles without failure. Most ferrous materials, such as steel, have well-defined endurance limits. Nonferrous materials (e.g., aluminum) do not. Fatigue is not generally a problem in buildings because of the absence of continuing sources of fatigue. Most vibrations simply do not last long enough to be a problem.

Effects of Localized Stresses, Cracks, and Flaws.   In any structure it is likely that microcracks or flaws exist. At these points stresses often develop that are very high over a small area. These are called *stress concentrations.* When brittle materials are used, it is likely that at these stress concentrations cracks will develop and continue to propagate until the member fails. When ductile materials are used, the material deforms locally a slight amount at these stress concentrations, allowing a relieving redistribution in stresses to occur (the tip of the crack becomes, so to speak, blunted). Cracks are less likely to propagate than in brittle materials. Consequently, minor cracks or flaws in a structure such as a typical wide-flange steel beam are not particularly serious and do not significantly affect the load-carrying capacity of the member. This is not true with brittle members.

2–7   DEFORMATIONS IN TENSION AND COMPRESSION MEMBERS

For axially loaded tension or compression members in which internal stresses are uniformly distributed at a cross section, the elongation or shortening that occurs depends on the magnitude of the applied load, the cross-sectional area of the member, the length of the member, and the type of material of which the member is made.

The deformations present in an axially loaded member can be evaluated by using the fact that for any elastic material the ratio of the stress (f) present to the strain (ϵ) caused is a constant value [i.e., stress/strain = constant = modulus of elasticity (E)]. The elongation in a tension member can be found by determining the strain associated with the stress level present ($\epsilon = f/E$) and then using this ratio to find the total deformation present ($\Delta L = \epsilon L$).

◆ ◆   **EXAMPLE**

Consider a simple tension member that carries an axial load of $P = 5000$ lb (22,240 N). Find the total elongation in the member due to the load shown. Assume that the member is made of steel which has a modulus of elasticity of $E = 29.6 \times 10^6$ lb/in.^{2} (204,000 N/mm^2). Also, assume that the member is 120 in. (3048 mm) long and has a cross-sectional area of 2 in.^{2} (1290 mm^2).

Solution:

$$\text{load} = P = 5000 \text{ lb} = 22{,}240 \text{ N}$$

$$\text{area} = 2.0 \text{ in.}^2 = 1290 \text{ mm}^2$$

$$\text{stress} = f = \frac{P}{A} = \frac{5000 \text{ lb}}{2.0 \text{ in.}^2} = 2500 \text{ lb/in.}^2$$

$$= \frac{22{,}240 \text{ N}}{1290 \text{ mm}^2} = 17.24 \text{ N/mm}^2$$

$$\text{strain} = \epsilon = \frac{f}{E} = \frac{2500 \text{ lb/in.}^2}{29.6 \times 10^6 \text{ lb/in.}^2} = 0.0000845 \text{ in./in.}$$

$$= \frac{17.24 \text{ N/mm}^2}{204{,}000 \text{ N/mm}^2} = 0.0000845 \text{ mm/mm}$$

$$\text{elongation} = \Delta L = \epsilon L = 0.0000845(120 \text{ in.}) = 0.0101 \text{ in.}$$

$$= 0.0000845(3048 \text{ mm}) = 0.257 \text{ mm}$$

Note that the magnitude of both the strain and the total elongation are relatively small numbers. If the same member were made of aluminum having a modulus of elasticity of $E = 11.3 \times 10^6$ lb/in.^{2} (77,900 N/mm^2), the strains and elongations would be increased. Thus,

$$\text{strain} = \epsilon = \frac{f}{E} = \frac{2500 \text{ lb/in.}^2}{11.3 \times 10^6 \text{ lb/in.}^2} = 0.000221 \text{ in./in.}$$

$$= \frac{17.24 \text{ N/mm}^2}{77{,}900 \text{ N/mm}^2} = 0.000221 \text{ mm/mm}$$

$$\text{elongation} = \Delta L = \epsilon L = 0.000221(120 \text{ in.}) = 0.0265 \text{ in.}$$

$$= 0.000221(3048 \text{ mm}) = 0.67 \text{ mm} \qquad \blacklozenge$$

Instead of finding stresses and strains first and then calculating elongations, it is possible to determine a single expression for the elongation in a member in terms of the load *P*, member length *L*, cross-sectional area *A*, and modulus of elasticity *E*:

$$\Delta L = \epsilon L = \left(\frac{f}{E}\right)L = \left(\frac{P/A}{E}\right)L = \frac{PL}{AE}$$

This is an often-used expression in structural analysis and design. It clearly shows that elongations in an axially loaded member are linearly dependent on the load present and the length of the member, and inversely dependent on the cross-sectional area and modulus of elasticity.

◆ ◆   **EXAMPLE**

Find the elongation caused by a tensile force of 7500 lb (33,360 N) in a steel member 144 in. (3658 mm) long having a cross-sectional area of 0.785 in.^{2} (506.5 mm^2). Note that $E = 29.6 \times 10^6$ lb/in.^{2} (204,000 N/mm^2).

Solution:

$$\Delta L = \frac{PL}{AE} = \frac{(7500 \text{ lb})(144 \text{ in.})}{(0.785 \text{ in.}^2)(29.6 \times 10^6 \text{ lb})} = 0.046 \text{ in}$$

$$= \frac{(33,360 \text{ N})(3658 \text{ mm})}{(506.5 \text{ mm}^2)(204,000 \text{ N/mm}^2)} = 1.18 \text{ mm}$$

◆ ◆ **EXAMPLE**

Assume that a 10-in.-long piece of steel ¼ in. × 2 in. ($A = 0.5$ in.^{2}) is bonded parallel to a piece of aluminum of the same dimensions. Both carry a compressive load of 5000 lb. What are the stresses in each material, and how much does the bonded assembly deform?

Solution: Note that $P = A_s f_s + A_a f_a$, but it is not known how the stresses are distributed between the two materials. This can be found by noting that the strains in steel and aluminum must be identical due to the bonding; thus, $\epsilon_s = \epsilon_a$. Since $\epsilon = f/E$, $f_s/E_s = f_a/E_a$, or $f_s = (E_s/E_a)f_a$. Sometimes this is written $f_s = nf_a$, where $n = E_s/E_a$. For this case, $n = (29,300,000/11,300,000) = 2.6$. The stress developed in the stiffer steel is thus 2.6 times that developed in the aluminum: $f_s = 2.6f_a$. Since $P = A_s f_s + A_a f_a = nA_s f_a + A_a f_a = (2.6)(0.5)(f_a) + (0.5)(f_a) = 5000$, thus $f_a = 2777$ lb/in.^{2} and $f_s = 7220$ lb/in.^{2} (The nA_s value is often called a *transformed area;* the steel is considered to have been transformed into a modified area of aluminum that is structurally equivalent.) To find final deformations, $\epsilon_a = f_a/E_a = 2777/11,300,000 = 0.000246$. $\Delta L = \epsilon_a L = 0.00245$ in. ◆

QUESTIONS

See Figure 2–55.

2–1 A force of P defined by the angle $\theta_x = 75°$ to the horizontal acts through a point. What are the components of this force on the x and y axes? See Figure 2–55(Q1).
Answer: $P_x = 0.26P$, $P_y = 0.97P$.

2–2 The components of a force on the x and y axes are $0.50P$ and $1.50P$, respectively. What are the magnitude and direction of the force? See Figure 2–55(Q2).
Answer: $1.58P$ at $\theta_x = 71.5°$.

2–3 The following three forces act concurrently through a point: a force P acting to the right at $\theta_x = 30°$ to the horizontal, a force P acting to the right at $\theta_x = 45°$ to the horizontal, and a force P acting to the right at $\theta_x = 60°$ to the horizontal. Find the single resultant force that is equivalent to this three-force system. See Figure 2–55(Q3).
Answer: $2.93P$ at $45°$.

2–4 The following three forces act through a point: P at $\theta_x = 45°$, $2P$ at $\theta_x = 180°$, and P at $\theta_x = 270°$. Find the equivalent resultant force. See Figure 2–55(Q4).
Answer: $1.33P$ at $192.8°$.

2–5 Determine the reactions for the structure shown in Figure 2–55(Q5).
Answer: $R_A = 600$ lb ↑ and $R_B = 400$ lb ↑.

2–6 Determine the reactions for the structure shown in Figure 2–55(Q6).
Answer: $R_{A_v} = P/2$ ↑, $R_{B_v} = 5P/2$ ↑.

2–7   Determine the reactions for the structure shown in Figure 2–55(Q7).
Answer: $R_A = 2667$ lb ↑ and $R_B = 667$ lb ↓.

2–8   Determine the reactions for the structure shown in Figure 2–55(Q8).
Answer: $R_{A_v} = 10P/3$ ↑, $R_{B_v} = 8P/3$ ↑.

2–9   Determine the reactions for the structure shown in Figure 2–55(Q9).
Answer: $R_A = 10$ k ↑ and $R_B = 10$ k ↑ (1 k = 1000 lb).

2–10   Determine the reactions for the structure shown in Figure 2–55(Q10).
Answer: $R_{A_v} = 5wL/18$ ↑, $R_{B_v} = wL/18$ ↑.

2–11   Determine the reactions for the structure shown in Figure 2–55(Q11).
Answer: $R_A = 11.2$ k and $R_B = 17.8$ k (1 k = 1000 lb).

2–12   Determine the reactions for the structure shown in Figure 2–55(Q12).
Answer: $R_{A_v} = wL/2$ ↑, $R_{A_H} = wL/2$ →, $R_{B_v} = wL/2$ ↑, $R_{B_H} = wL/2$ ←, $R_B = 0.71\ wL$.

2–13   Determine the reactions for the four beams shown in Figure 2–55(Q13). Notice that the three inclined members are identical except for the type of end conditions present.
Answer: $R_A = P/2$ ↑, $R_B = P/2$ ↑; $R_{A_v} = P/2$ ↑, $R_{A_H} = 0$, $R_{B_v} = P/2$ ↑, $R_{B_H} = 0$; $R_{A_v} = 0$, $R_{A_H} = P/2$ →, $R_{B_v} = P$ ↑, $R_{B_H} = P/2$ ←; $R_{A_v} = P/2$ ↑, $R_{A_H} = 0$, $R_{Bv} = P/2$ ↑, $R_{B_H} = 0$.

2–14   What is the maximum shear force present in the beam analyzed in Question 2–5 [Figure 2–55(Q5)]? The maximum bending moment? Draw shear and moment diagrams for this same beam.
Answer: $V_{max} = 600$ lb and $M_{max} = 4800$ ft-lb.

2–15   Draw shear and moment diagrams for the beam analyzed in Question 2–6 [Figure 2–55(Q6)]. What is the maximum shear force present? What is the maximum bending moment present?
Answer: $V = -3P/2$, $M = -PL$.

2–16   Draw shear and moment diagrams for the beam analyzed in Question 2–7 [Figure 2–55(Q7)].
Answer: $V_{max} = -2000$ lb and $M_{max} = -10{,}000$ ft-lb.

2–17   Draw shear and moment diagrams for the beam analyzed in Question 2–8 [Figure 2–55(Q8)]. What is the maximum shear force present? What is the maximum bending moment present?
Answer: $V = +10P/3$, $M = 10PL/9$.

2–18   Draw shear and moment diagrams for the beam analyzed in Question 2–9 [Figure 2–55(Q9)].
Answer: $V_{max} = 1000$ lb and $M_{max} = 7500$ ft-lb.

2–19   Draw shear and moment diagrams for the beam analyzed in Question 2–10 [Figure 2–55(Q10)]. What is the maximum shear force present? What is the maximum bending moment present?
Answer: $V = +5wL/18$, $M = 25wL^2/648$.

2–20   Draw shear and moment diagrams for the beam analyzed in Question 2–11 [Figure 2–55(Q11)].
Answer: $V_{max} = 11.2$ k and $M_{max} = 88.1$ ft-k.

2–21   Draw shear and moment diagrams for the beam analyzed in Question 2–12 [Figure 2–55(Q12)]. What is the maximum shear force present? What is the maximum bending moment present?
Answer: $V = \pm wL/2$, $M = wL^2/8$.

2–22   Draw shear and moment diagrams for the four beams analyzed in Question 2–21. For the inclined members, the shear and moment diagrams should be drawn with respect to the longitudinal axes of the members. Transverse components of the applied and reactive forces should thus be considered in determining shears and moments. Compare the maximum moments developed in all four beams. Discuss.

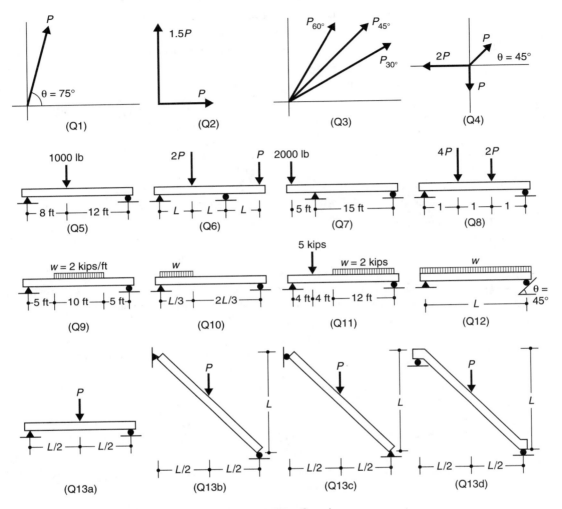

FIGURE 2-55 Questions.

2-23 Determine by reviewing manufacturers' literature or other sources the moduli of elasticity for at least two different types of plastics (e.g., plexiglass and polyvinyl chloride). Consult your library.

2-24 What is the unit strain present in an aluminum specimen loaded to 10,000 lb/in.²? Assume that $E_a = 11.3 \times 10^6$ lb/in.²

Answer: 0.000885 in./in.

2-25 What is the unit strain present in a steel specimen loaded to 24,000 lb/in.²? Assume that $E_s = 29.6 \times 10^6$ lb/in.²

Answer: 0.000811 in./in.

2–26 A steel bar that has a cross-sectional area of 2.0 in.^{2} is 20 ft long and carries a tension force of 16,000 lb. How much does the bar elongate? Assume that $E_s = 29.6 \times 10^6$ lb/in.^{2}
Answer: 0.032 in.

2–27 A steel bar that is 20 mm in diameter is 5 m long and carries a tension force of 20 kN. How much does the bar elongate? Assume that $E_s = 0.204 \times 10^6$ N/mm^2.
Answer: 1.56 mm.

2–28 Conduct a detailed study of how the technique of graphic statics can be used to analyze the forces in a gothic structure. Consult your library. See, for example, the following references: Jacques Heyman, "The Stone Skeleton," *International Journal of Solids and Structures,* Vol. 2, 1966, 249–279; and William Wolfe, *Graphical Analysis, A Text Book on Graphic Statics,* 1st ed., McGraw-Hill Book Company, Inc., New York, 1921. Also see W. Zalewski, and E. Allen, *Shaping Structures: Statics*, John Wiley, New York, 1995.

CHAPTER 3

Introduction to Structural Analysis and Design

3–1 ANALYSIS AND DESIGN CRITERIA

Introduction. This chapter provides an introduction to the analysis and design of structures in a building context. In order to analyze or design a structure, it is necessary to establish criteria that can be used as either measures for determining whether a given structure is acceptable for use in a specified circumstance or for use directly as design objectives that must be met. The more important criteria are discussed next.

Serviceability. The structure must be able to carry the design load safely—without excessive material distress and with deformations within an acceptable range. The ability of a structure to carry loads safely and without material distress is achieved by using safety factors in the design of the element. By altering the size, shape, and choice of materials, stress levels in a structure can be maintained at a level considered acceptable for life safety and such that material distress (e.g., cracking) does not occur. This is basically a *strength* criterion and is of fundamental importance.

Another aspect of the serviceability of the structure is the nature and extent of the deformations caused by the load and whether these deformations are acceptable or not. Excessive deformations could result in the structure's interfering with or causing distress to some other building element. They could also simply be visually undesirable. It should be noted that because a structure appears to be deforming excessively does not necessarily mean that the structure is unsafe. Large deflections or deformations may be associated with an unsafe structure, but not necessarily (consider the large deflections associated with diving boards). Deformations are controlled by varying the *stiffness* of a structure. Stiffness depends largely on the type, amount, and distribution of material in a structure. Often it is necessary to use a larger member to achieve necessary stiffness than is required to achieve the necessary structural strength.

Associated with deformations, but not the same phenomena, are *movements* in structures. In some situations, the actual accelerations and velocities of structures carrying dynamic loads are perceptible to building occupants and can cause discomfort. The movements associated with multistory buildings under the action of wind are a case in point. Criteria thus relate to limiting accelerations and velocities. Control is achieved through manipulations involving the stiffness of the structure and its damping characteristics.

Efficiency.   This criterion involves the relative economy with which a structure achieves its design objective. A measure often used is the amount of material required to support a given loading in space under the conditions and constraints specified. It is quite possible that several different alternative structural responses to a given loading situation will be equally serviceable. This does not mean, however, that each will require exactly the same amount of structural material to achieve the same level of serviceability. Some solutions may require less material than others. The use of minimum volume as a criterion is one that has intrinsic conceptual appeal to a large number of architects and engineers and is one that will be extensively used throughout this text.

Construction.   Construction considerations are often influential in choosing a structural response. It is entirely possible that a structural assembly that is highly efficient in terms of the way material is used will not be easy to fabricate and assemble. Construction criteria are diverse and include such considerations as the amount and type of effort or human power required to construct a given facility, the type and extent of equipment required, and the total amount of time necessary to complete construction.

A general factor influencing the ease of construction of a facility is the complexity of the facility as reflected in the number of different pieces involved and the relative degree of effort necessary to assemble the pieces into a whole. The size, shape, and weight of the pieces are also important since the type of equipment necessary for construction is often dictated by these factors. In general, an assembly consisting of pieces of a size and shape manageable with easily available construction equipment and that can be assembled with either few or highly repetitive operations will be relatively easy to construct. Although highly important, construction ease will not be dealt with extensively in this book.

Costs.   Costs are invariably an influential factor in the choice of most structures. The concept of cost cannot be dissociated from the two considerations discussed immediately above, material economy and ease of construction. Total costs of a structure are dependent primarily on the amount and cost of material used, the amount and cost of labor required to construct the facility, and the cost of equipment needed during construction. Obviously, a highly efficient structure that is not difficult to construct will probably be an economical one. In this book, however, we do not deal with costs in a comprehensive way.

Other.   There are, of course, a host of other factors that are influential in selecting a structure. In contrast to the relatively objective and measurable criteria discussed above, many of these additional factors are subjective in nature. Not the least of these is the role of structure as it forms a part of the larger image of the building as envisioned by the architect (e.g., the role of structure as a space definer, etc.). Although obviously a subject of interest and depth, these considerations are largely beyond the scope of this book.

3–2 LOADS ON STRUCTURES

3–2–1 Introduction

In analyzing or designing a structure, it is necessary to have a clear picture of the nature and magnitude of the loads applied to the structure. Figure 3–1 illustrates in a diagrammatic way the primary loads that must be considered and ways of describing and characterizing them.

Of fundamental importance is the distinction between static and dynamic loads. *Static* forces are those that are slowly applied to a structure and are steady-state in character. Resultant deformations in the structure associated with these forces also slowly develop, are steady-state in character, and reach a peak when the static force is maximum. *Dynamic* forces are those that are suddenly applied to a structure. Often they are not steady-state forces and are characterized by rapid changes in magnitude and location. Associated structural deformations also vary rapidly. Dynamic forces can cause oscillations to occur in structures such that peak deformations do not necessarily occur when the applied forces are maximum.

3–2–2 Static Forces

Dead Loads. Static forces are typically subclassified into dead loads, live loads, and forces due to settlements or thermal effects.

Dead loads are those forces acting vertically downward on a structure that are relatively fixed in character. The self-weight of the structure itself is a dead load. The weights of any permanent building elements, such as floor surfaces, mechanical equipment, nonmoveable partitions, and so on, are also dead loads. The exact weights of these elements are typically known (or can be easily determined) to a high degree of accuracy. All methods for calculating the dead load

FIGURE 3–1 Typical types of loading conditions.

of an element are based on a consideration of the unit weight of the material involved and on the volume of the element. Unit weights are empirically determined and tabulated for easy use in a number of sources. Determining volumes is a straightforward but occasionally tedious process. Tabular information of the type illustrated in Tables 3–1 and 3–2 is available to facilitate the process of obtaining dead loads for common building elements.

Live Loads.   Live loads are those forces that may or may not be present and acting upon a structure at any given point in time. Although movable, live loads are still typically applied slowly to a structure. Use or occupancy loads are live loads. Occupancy loads include personnel, furniture, stored materials, and other similar items. Snow loads are also live loads. All live loads are characterized by their movability. They typically act vertically downward but occasionally can act horizontally as well.

Wind loads and earthquake forces, considered later, are special forms of live loads typically considered separately because of their dynamic aspects. Predicting what magnitudes and distributions characterize live loads is a highly difficult task. An empirical approach is consequently taken in which measurements have been made of the nature and magnitudes of the loads associated with different occupancy types. From these statistical data, equivalent loads typically expressed in terms of a load per unit area have been derived for design purposes. Concentrated loads are occasionally used also. These equivalent loads generally reflect in one figure the net effects of all live loads associated with a particular occupancy type. They generally represent the maximum expected combination of occupancy-related forces that the structure would possibly have to carry in its lifetime. As such they are founded on certain assumptions about what loads can be reasonably expected on a structure and the frequency of their occurrence. No safety factors are included.

The actual live loads on a structure at any particular point in time are typically less than the loads a structure actually must be designed to carry. At some point, however, there is a high probability that the structure will indeed have to carry the design loading. It should also be evident that a structure initially designed to carry loads derived from one occupancy type should be

Table 3–1   AVERAGE DENSITIES OF MATERIALS

Material	lb/ft^3	kg/m^3
Metals		
Aluminum, cast	165	2643
Copper, cast	556	8907
Steel, rolled	490	7849
Concrete		
Plain	144	2307
Lightweight	75–110	1201–1762
Reinforced	150	2402
Brick	100–130	1602–2083
Glass, plate	161	2579
Earth		
Clay, dry	63	1009
Clay, damp	110	1762
Earth, dry	75–95	1201–1521
Earth, damp	80–100	1281–1602

Table 3-2 AVERAGE LOADS OF CONSTRUCTION COMPONENTS

Component	lb/ft^2	kg/m^{2a}	N/m^{2b}
Roofs			
Asphalt shingles	2.0	9.8	95.8
Cement asbestos shingles	4.0	19.5	191.5
Composition roofing			
3-ply and gravel	5.5	26.8	263.3
5-ply and gravel	6.5	31.8	311.2
Corrugated metal			
20 U.S. std. gage	1.7	8.3	81.4
28 U.S. std. gage	0.8	3.9	38.4
Concrete plank decking	6.5	31.8	311.2
(per inch of thickness)			
Insulation, rigid fiberglass	1.5	7.3	71.8
Lumber sheathing (1 in., 2.54 cm)	2.5	12.2	119.7
Plywood sheathing (1 in., 2.54 cm)	3.0	14.6	143.6
Floors			
Concrete slab, stone aggregate	12.0	58.6	574.6
(per inch of thickness)			
Hollow-core concrete planks	45–50.0	220–244.0	2155–2394.0
(6 in., 15.2 cm, thick)			
Plywood (1 in., 2.54 cm)	3.0	14.6	143.6
Steel decking	2–10.0	10–49.0	96–480.0
Walls			
Brick			
4 in., 10.2 cm	40.0	195.3	1915.2
8 in., 20.4 cm	80.0	390.6	3830.4
Hollow concrete block, heavy			
Heavy aggregate			
4 in., 10.2 cm	30.0	146.5	1436.4
8 in., 20.4 cm	55.0	268.5	2633.4
Light aggregate			
8 in., 20.4 cm	38.0	185.5	1819.4
Wood studs (2 × 4, 16 in. oc)			
Window assembly	8.0	39.1	383.0

[a]Conventional metric system.
[b]SI system.

carefully checked before being subjected to loads from other occupancy types. A structure initially designed to carry loads derived for apartment houses would be inadequate, for example, if the building were converted into use as an office building or storage warehouse.

Table 3-3 illustrates equivalent live loads recommended for several different occupancy types. Provisions in building regulations typically require that structures be designed according to loadings of this general type. The loadings shown are illustrative only and should not be used for design purposes (local building code recommendations should be used instead).

Table 3-3   TYPICAL UNIFORMLY DISTRIBUTED LIVE LOADS

Occupancy or Use	lb/ft^2	N/m^2	Occupancy or Use	lb/ft^2	N/m^2
Apartments			Office buildings		
Corridors	80	3830	Offices	60	2873
Private apartments	40	1915	Lobbies	100	4788
Public rooms	100	4788	Residential dwellings		
Assembly halls			First floors	40	1915
Fixed seats	60	2873	Second floors	30	1436
Movable seats	100	4788	Schools		
Dance halls	100	4788	Classrooms	40	1915
Garages, public	100	4788	Corridors	80	3830
Gymnasiums	100	4788	Stairs	100	4788
Hotels			Stores, retail		
Corridors	100	4788	First floor	100	4788
Guest rooms	40	1915	Upper floors	75	3591
Public rooms	100	4788	Theaters		
Libraries			Aisles, corridors	100	4788
Reading rooms	60	2873	Balconies	60	2873
Stacks	150	7182	Floors	60	2873
Manufacturing	125	5985	Stage floors	150	7182

Snow Loads.   Snow loads on roofs vary very widely and depend on such factors as elevation, latitude, wind frequency, duration of snow fall, site exposure, roof size, geometry, and inclination. As a rule of thumb, the weight of snow is about 0.5 to 0.6 lb/ft^2 per inch of snow depth.

These figures vary widely, however, depending on snow density. Most design snow loads for typical urban areas range from 20 to 60 lb/ft^2 (958 to 2873 N/m^2) (see Table 3-4). Local experience should always be checked, however, since in particular areas loads can be much higher than these figures indicate. This is particularly true in mountainous regions. Snow loads in some inhabited areas have been as high as 250 to 300 lb/ft^2 and even higher in uninhabited areas.

3-2-3   Wind Loads

Static Effects of Wind.   A structure in the path of wind causes wind to be deflected or, in some cases, stopped. As a consequence, the kinetic energy of the wind is transformed into the potential energy of pressure or suction. The magnitude of the pressure or suction caused by the wind at a

Table 3-4   TYPICAL SNOW LOADS

Region	lb/ft^2	N/m^2
Southern states	0–15	0–718
Central states	25–35	1197–1676
Northern states	30–50	1436–2394
Great Lakes, New England, and mountain areas	30–80	1436–3830

point on a structure depends on the velocity of the wind, the mass density of the air, the geometrical shape, dimensions, and orientation of the structure, the exact location of the point considered on the structure, the nature of the surface that the wind acts on, and the overall stiffness of the structure.

As any fluid such as air flows around an immersed object, a complex flow pattern is generated around the object. The nature and complexity of the flow pattern depend upon the shape of the object. Flows can be either smooth or turbulent. The forces acting on the object as a result of the impinging air flow can be either pressure forces or suction forces. The more an object is streamlined, the less is the total reactive force exerted by the structure in opposing the motion of the air. Figure 3–2 illustrates air flows around some typical shapes in a diagrammatic way.

The magnitude of the forces involved as air moves around a shape is dependent on the velocity of the wind, among other factors. Design wind velocities for different geographical locations are determined from empirical observations. They range from lows of 60 mi/h (96 km/h) in some inland regions to highs of 100 mi/h (161 km/h) in other inland regions and 120 mi/h (193 km/h) in some coastal zones. Design velocities are usually based on a 50-year mean recurrence interval. Since wind velocities increase with height above ground, design values are accordingly increased. Allowance is also made for whether the building site is in an urban or rural setting. More sophisticated analyses also include gust-response factors, which are a function of the size and height of the structure, the surface roughness, and the obstacles present in the surrounding terrain. Local building codes should be consulted for exact design loadings or velocities.

Once the design wind velocity is known, it is possible to determine the dynamic pressure arising from wind action and to express it as an equivalent static force. The dynamic pressure of wind can be determined by application of the well-documented *Bernoulli equation* for fluid flow, which yields the expression $q = \frac{1}{2}\rho V^2$, where q is the dynamic pressure, ρ is the mass density of air, and V is the velocity of wind. For standard air (usually defined as 0.0765 lb/ft^3), the velocity pressure in pounds per square foot at a height h is given by $q_h = 0.00256V_h^2$, where V_h is

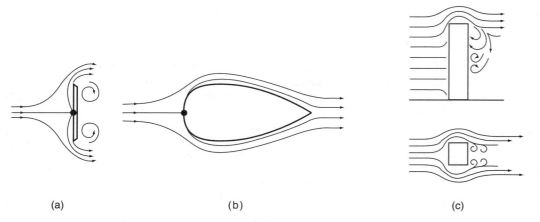

| (a) | (b) | (c) |

FIGURE 3–2 Wind flow about different shapes.

expressed in miles per hour. The conversion of this force into an equivalent static force involves the use of a pressure coefficient, C_D, that depends on the geometry of the body that the wind impinges upon. The reactive force, F_D, exerted by the structure in opposing the motion of the wind can be found by using this pressure coefficient and the dynamic pressure expression. Thus, $F_D = C_D q_h A$, where C_D is the pressure coefficient for the shape involved, q_h is the velocity pressure at height h, and A is the exposed area of the building surface normal to the wind. A more exact expression would also involve the use of a gust factor, G_F. Thus, $F_D = C_D q_h A G_F$. Using the simpler expression, the *average* static pressure, p, is given by $p = F_D/A$ or $p = C_D q_h$. The latter expression is frequently used.

The *pressure coefficient, C_D,* depends on the building form. C_D is also often referred to as the *shape coefficient.* Pressure coefficients for different shapes generally reflect the relative amount of obstruction caused by the shape to an impinging air flow. Streamlined shapes have pressure coefficients smaller than nonstreamlined shapes. When the flow of air is completely stopped by the shape, the pressure coefficient is equal to unity ($C_D = 1$). In actual building shapes, the flow of air is never actually stopped, but is deflected. Flow patterns around actual buildings are extremely complex. For this reason, pressure coefficients for a number of different building shapes and configurations have been developed and tabulated. Since on any given building the wind produces both pressure and suction (depending on the location of the point considered), there are specific pressure coefficients tabulated for different locations on a building. Typical coefficients are shown in Figure 3–3 (see ASCE Standard-7-95).

For $h/b/L = 1{:}8{:}16$

Wind force $= C_d q_h A$

C_d = pressure coefficient
 (+ pressure − suction)

qh = velocity pressure $= \frac{1}{2}\rho v^2$

A = exposed surface area

FIGURE 3–3 Typical wind-force coefficients (C_D) for a gabled building. (Pressure coefficients actually depend on exact dimensions of building.)

These coefficients are a sampling only. The literature contains detailed information for a wide variety of situations and building configurations.[1] Typical resultant design wind loads are on the order of 20 to 40 lb/ft^2 (960 to 1920 N/m^2).

Dynamic Effects of Wind. In our previous discussion, the static nature of wind forces was stressed. The dynamic nature of wind forces, however, is also extremely important. Dynamic effects can arise in several ways. One is simply that wind is rarely a steady-state phenomenon. Buildings are therefore subjected to alternating forces. This is particularly true for buildings in an urban setting. As is evident in Figure 3–2(c), the flow pattern of air around a building is not smooth. If there is a group of closely spaced buildings, the wind pattern is even more complex, since some buildings are in the turbulent wake of others. The action of the wind becomes that of a buffeting. The result is that buildings can begin swaying to and fro due to these alternating load effects.

Winds can produce a dynamic response in buildings even when the wind is at a relatively steady-state velocity. This is particularly true in structures that are relatively flexible, as is the case in many cable-supported roof structures. The wind causes varying force distributions on the roof surface, which in turn cause shape changes, either major or minor, to occur. The new shape causes different pressure or suction distributions, which again lead to new shape changes. The result is a constant movement or flutter in the roof. The problem of roof flutter is a major one in the design of flexible structures. Techniques for controlling roof flutter invariably have major design implications. The phenomenon of dynamic movement in flexible structures is discussed in much greater detail in connection with cable design. The effects can be disastrous, as illustrated by the dramatic failure of the Tacoma Narrows Bridge in Washington State in 1940. A wind caused an initial twisting to develop in the structure, which then began to oscillate in a twisting motion of increasing amplitude (the deck was at one time 45° to the horizontal) until the 2800-ft (840-m) structure collapsed. (See Figure 5–4.)

Wind phenomena can be very complex. Under some conditions, a severe problem called "vortex shedding" can occur. This effect causes fluctuating forces on the side of a building and occurs under steady windstreams. It is associated with the clustering of swirling vortices. Various kinds of perforated shrouds or strakes can be used to mitigate the problem.[2]

The dynamic effects of wind can be very problematic in high-rise structures by causing undesirable swaying (see Chapter 14). The phenomenon of *resonance,* described in the next section, can also occur.

3–2–4 Earthquake Forces

Earthquakes are vibratory phenomena associated with shock loadings on the earth's crust. While these shock loads can result from a number of causes, one of the primary reasons is the sudden slippage that frequently occurs between adjacent crust plates that make up the earth's surface. Locations where this slippage occurs are called *fault zones.* The shock associated with this slippage is propagated in the form of waves. These waves cause the earth's surface and any buildings resting on it to vibrate. As the building is vibrated, forces are developed in the structure of the building because of the tendency of the mass of the building to resist the motion. The forces

---

[1]International Conference of Building Code Officials, *Uniform Building Code.*

[2]See T.V. Lawson, *Wind Effects on Buildings, Vol. 1,* Applied Science Publishers, Ltd., London, 1980.

developed are consequently inertial in character. The magnitude of these forces depends on many factors. The mass of the building is clearly important, since the forces involved are inertial. The larger the mass present, the greater are the forces developed. Other factors include the way the mass is distributed, the stiffness of the structure, the stiffness of the soil, the type of foundation, the presence of damping mechanisms in the building, and, of course, the nature and magnitude of the vibratory motions themselves. The last are difficult to describe precisely since they can be almost random in nature. Some discernible patterns are present, however. The motions generated are three-dimensional in nature. The horizontal ground movements are usually the most important from a structural design viewpoint.

The mass and rigidity of a structure, and its related natural period of vibration, are the most important of all the factors that affect the overall response of a structure to motion and the specific nature and magnitude of the forces developed as a consequence of the motion. The following generally discusses some fundamental issues of static and dynamic behavior as a prelude to a discussion of a commonly used static method of analysis. It is useful to consider first how a completely rigid structure responds to a simple vibratory motion. Structures having flexibility, as is common in all building structures, will be considered next. *The reader may wish to also read Section 14–2 simultaneously. Section 14–2 discusses the basic phenomena of earthquakes in greater detail than herein.*

Basic Phenomena.   When a completely rigid structure, such as a solid block, is subjected to base vibrations, the structure simply moves as a unit along with the forcing motions. Since there is a natural physical tendency for any mass initially at rest to remain at rest, there are internal forces set up in the rigid body due to the ground motion that are inertial in character (Figure 3–4). The upper mass of the body tends to remain at rest while the base tends to be translated due to the ground motion. These different tendencies result in the development of internal forces. For a simple rigid block of weight W subjected to a horizontal ground motion characterized by an acceleration a, the inertial force F_i that is developed is simply $F_i = (W/g)a$, where g is the acceleration due to gravity. This expression follows directly from Newton's first law, discussed earlier. For equilibrium, a shearing force (V) is developed at the base of the structure such that $V = F_i = (a/g)W$. This is also the force that the structure must be capable of withstanding. Quite simply, then, when ground accelerations are known or can be estimated, the shear force that a totally rigid structure must resist at its base can be found as a percentage of the weight of the building (say, 5 to 20%). Structural elements would have to be designed to carry this total shearing force.

FIGURE 3–4   Inertial forces due to ground motion in a rigid body.

Forces generated in a body are very sensitive to the magnitudes of the accelerations involved. If a body is very slowly displaced so that the accelerations involved are essentially zero or if it is moved at a constant velocity (again a case of zero accelerations), then there are no inertial forces generated in the body at all (happily, the earth spins and moves through space at a constant velocity or we would all be in what could only be described as deep trouble). Consequently, the aspects of earthquake motions that are of most importance are the magnitudes of the accelerations involved.

Although the concepts described here formed the basis for many of the earliest approaches to earthquake design, the model is undoubtedly simplistic. If the actual flexibility that a structure possesses is taken into account, a more sophisticated model is needed to predict the exact forces generated in a structure due to ground accelerations. One very important reason for going to a more complex model is that the forces generated in a flexible structure depend not only on the magnitude of the ground accelerations involved but on the relative stiffness and vibratory-motion characteristics of the structure itself. An interaction can take place which can lead to forces much higher than those predicted by the simpler static model.

An aspect of primary importance in considering the behavior of flexible structures subjected to ground accelerations is the *natural period of vibration* of the structure. Consider the simple structure illustrated in Figure 3–5. If the top of the structure is horizontally displaced and then released, the top of the structure would oscillate back and forth with slowly decreasing amplitudes until the structure finally came to rest. These free vibratory movements are not random at all but vary in precise ways. The vibrations are said to be harmonic, since the displacement varies in a sinusoidal way with the time after release. The time required for the motion to go through one complete back-and-forth cycle is termed the natural period of vibration T. The frequency f of this vibration is defined as the number of cycles that occur per unit time. Note that $f = 1/T$.

The frequency of free vibration that occurs in a structure of the type described depends directly on the mass of the structure and the relative stiffness of the columns with respect to horizontal forces. If the columns were of low stiffness, they would provide relatively little in the way of restoring forces which would tend to cause the deflected structure to resume its original shape after release. Consequently, the top of the structure would lumber back and forth at a relatively slow pace until the oscillations died down. A structure of this type is said to have a long natural period of vibration. If, on the other hand, the columns were very rigid, they would provide

(a) Basic structure.

(b) If the top of the structure is displaced and released, the structure will freely vibrate.

(c) The amplitudes of the free vibrations that occur generally vary sinusoidally with time and eventually tend to damp out.

FIGURE 3–5   Free vibration in a simple structure.

significant restoring forces, tending to cause the structure to resume its original shape after release. Consequently, the structure would still oscillate back and forth, but this time would do so quite rapidly. A structure of this type is said to have a short natural period of vibration.

The fact that the oscillations in a structure of either long or short natural periods die out with time is due to the presence of damping mechanisms in the structure. Damping mechanisms that absorb energy are present in all building structures. In the structure shown in Figure 3–5, frictional forces that are bound to exist in the pinned connections between the beam and columns, for example, would cause damping to occur. In larger structures other damping mechanisms, such as cracking of partitions, also exist.

The situation described here is one where free vibrations occur due to a release of an imposed displacement at the top of the structure. If the base of the structure is instead suddenly translated a short distance horizontally, the mass of the structure (particularly the beam) would initially tend to resist translation because of inertial tendencies. The structure would consequently be set in vibration (a situation converse to the initial one would be created). If the base of the structure were translated back and forth continuously, as would be the case in an earthquake, the structure would obviously continue to vibrate as long as the ground motion is present. In this case, however, the actual vibratory motion that occurs can potentially be strongly influenced by the precise characteristics of the ground motions and is not simply a free vibration. In cases when the frequency of the ground movements is completely different from that of the natural frequency of free vibration associated with the structure, the consequence is that no real interactive effect occurs. In cases when the frequency of the ground movement is approximately the same as that of the natural frequency of vibration of the structure, however, an interactive effect can occur which tends to cause the amplitudes of the vibrations to increase above the magnitudes associated with the imposed ground displacements.

This phenomenon, called *resonance,* is a crucial one in structural design. One way of visualizing the phenomenon is to think in terms of how a weight suspended from a simple spring behaves (see Figure 3–6). There are some very direct analogies, as will be discussed shortly, between a spring system of this type and the frame discussed above. If the suspended weight is displaced and released, a free vibration similar to that described for the frame will occur. The natural period of this vibration is given by the familiar $T = 2\pi\sqrt{W/gk}$, where W is the weight involved, g is the acceleration due to gravity, and k is the spring constant defining the load-deformation characteristics of the spring (this expression is discussed in any basic physics textbook). If, on the other hand, the weight were simply suspended from the spring and the end of the spring itself moved up and down, then one of the following phenomena would occur. If the applied oscillatory movement were very slow (i.e., a long period), the suspended weight would simply translate along with the spring at the same rate. The spring would not be elongated but would also simply ride along. On the other hand, if the applied oscillatory motion were extremely rapid, the suspended weight would merely stay relatively stationary in space since the inertial tendency of the weight would prevent it from following the imposed rapid movements. Rapid elongations and relaxations would occur in the spring (which means internal forces develop and relax), but these are not necessarily large and no greater than the amplitude of the applied oscillations.

The critical case arises when the period of the applied oscillations is exactly equal to the natural period of vibration of the spring-weight system. In this event the initial applied oscillations cause the weight to begin vibrating up and down. If the applied oscillations continue, the amplitude of the vibratory movements in the spring-weight system will continue to increase. The

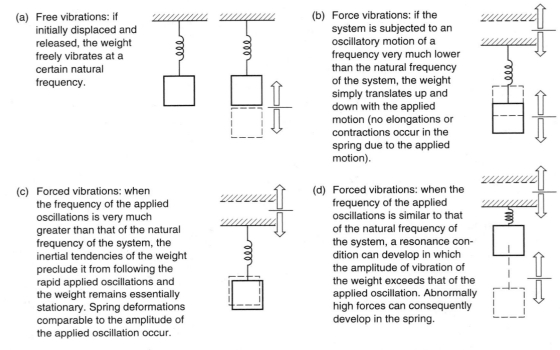

(a) Free vibrations: if initially displaced and released, the weight freely vibrates at a certain natural frequency.

(b) Force vibrations: if the system is subjected to an oscillatory motion of a frequency very much lower than the natural frequency of the system, the weight simply translates up and down with the applied motion (no elongations or contractions occur in the spring due to the applied motion).

(c) Forced vibrations: when the frequency of the applied oscillations is very much greater than that of the natural frequency of the system, the inertial tendencies of the weight preclude it from following the rapid applied oscillations and the weight remains essentially stationary. Spring deformations comparable to the amplitude of the applied oscillation occur.

(d) Forced vibrations: when the frequency of the applied oscillations is similar to that of the natural frequency of the system, a resonance condition can develop in which the amplitude of vibration of the weight exceeds that of the applied oscillation. Abnormally high forces can consequently develop in the spring.

FIGURE 3–6 Free and forced vibrations in a simple spring-weight system.

relative elongations and contractions of the spring would hence also continue to increase, and along with this so would the magnitude of the force developed in the spring. The amplitudes could easily increase far beyond those of the original applied oscillations. The result can be that the system approaches a point of resonance wherein the relative movements tend to become indefinitely large (and, consequently, so do internal forces in the spring), so that eventually the system self-destructs. All the phenomena described above can be demonstrated by suspending a weight from a rubber band and vibrating it at different speeds.

Real structures can and do behave in much the same way that the simpler system described above does. When the natural frequency of the applied movements exactly equals the natural period of vibration of the system itself, the phenomenon of resonance (and accompanying ever-increasing and uncontrollable deformations) can occur. Fortunately, most buildings inherently possess sufficient damping mechanisms so that dramatic resonances of this type rarely occur in buildings. Still the phenomenon does cause abnormally high displacement amplitudes to occur, which correspond to abnormally high force intensities in structural members. Failure to take into account the dynamic action of an earthquake loading can thus potentially lead to highly undesirable consequences.

The dynamic analysis of a structure more complex than the simple ones discussed can be very involved due to the many modes of vibration that are possible. As will be described in more detail later, a multistory building can vibrate in different modes, which can cause floors on different levels to accelerate in different directions at the same time (see Section 14–2). Predicting how a multistory structure will vibrate can be very complex. Analytical predictions, however, are possible by modeling the structure as a complex system of point masses (representing building weights), springs (representing the stiffnesses of the structural members), and damping devices (representing the energy-absorbing mechanisms present in a building, such as those formed when partitions crack because of vibratory movements).

Static Models.   Because of the complex dynamic action described, a static model for assessing earthquake forces of the type initially described can be highly misleading. For initial design purposes, however, a variation of the static model is still often used despite known inadequacies, owing simply to the complexity of the dynamic analyses required. An expression in a common building code for determining earthquake design forces, for example, is of the form $V = ZICW/R_W$. In this expression, V is the total static shear at the base of the structure, W is the total dead load of the building, C is a coefficient that depends on the fundamental period of vibration (T) of the building, Z is a factor depending on the geographical location of the building and the probable seismic activity and intensity of the location, I is an importance factor depending on the building type (e.g., hospitals), and R_w is a factor that reflects the building's type of construction, materials, and bracing system. S is a coefficient that depends on the fundamental period of the site. The coefficient C is given by expressions such as $C = 1.25S/T^{2/3} < 2.75$. The building period T is estimated through expressions of the form $T = C_t(h_n)^{3/4}$, where h_n is the building height, and C_t is a coefficient that depends on the type of structural system and number of stories present in the building. All these expressions and factors are largely empirically determined and formulations and specific numerical values frequently change with changing building codes. The base shear V obtained through the evaluation of these factors is then distributed at the various story levels through prescribed methods to act as applied lateral loads.

An implication of the static equation is that for a given building, the design force V is greater when a relatively "stiff" bracing system is used than it is when a more "flexible" one is adopted. This result is important from a design viewpoint (see Section 14–2).

The empirical approach briefly outlined here is described in detail in the *Uniform Building Code*.[3] Another approach has recently been developed by the Applied Technology Council, which uses a different formulation.

Dynamic rather than static analyses are now common due to the availability of computer-based programs. Chapter 14 discusses these issues in greater detail.

3–2–5   Load Combinations

A great number of different types of loadings act on a structure. Of critical importance in determining design loads is the question of whether or not all of these loadings act on the structure simultaneously. Dead loads by definition always act on a structure. The variability is in the live load or combination of live loads. Is it reasonable, for example, to design a structure to sustain at the same time the maximum loads that might result from an earthquake and those associated with a maximum wind force, and a full-occupancy loading condition? The probability that all these loadings will occur with maximum intensity at the same point in time is remote.

The structure *could* be designed to carry the simultaneous maximums of all possible loadings, but the resultant structure would, in all probability, be greatly oversized for the load

---

[3]International Conference of Building Officials, *Uniform Building Code*.

combinations that would actually occur during the lifetime of the structure. In recognition of this, many codes or regulations allow specific reductions in design loadings when certain load combinations are present.

With respect to occupancy loads in a multistory building, it is extremely unlikely that all floors of the building will simultaneously carry maximum occupancy loads. For this reason, a reduction is allowed in the design loading for members carrying the contributory effects of live loadings from many floors. A typical recommendation is as follows: (1) No reduction shall be applied to the roof live load. (2) For live loads of 100 lb or less per square foot, the design live load on any member supporting 150 ft^2 or more may be reduced at the rate of 0.08%/ft^2 of area supported by the member, except that no reduction shall be made for garages or for areas to be occupied as places of public assembly. The reduction shall exceed neither R, as determined by the following, nor 60%: $R = 23(1 + D/L)$, in which R = reduction, percent; D = dead load per square foot of the area supported by the member; and L = design live load per square foot of the area supported by the member. For storage live loads exceeding 100 lb/ft^2 no reduction shall be made except that the design live loads on columns may be reduced 20%.

For combinations of different types of loadings, it is often (but not always) permissible to reduce the total design force by some specified factor. For example, rather than designing for 1.00[dead load + live load + wind load + earthquake load], many codes allow you to design for 0.75[dead load + live load + (wind load or earthquake load)]. The expectation is clearly that not all loads will act on the structure at their full value simultaneously. On the other hand, it is usual that the structure is designed for the full dead and live load considered acting simultaneously, or 1.00[dead load + live load]. Usually multiple types of possible loading conditions must be considered and the structure designed to carry the worst possible combination.

3–3 THE GENERAL ANALYSIS PROCESS

3–3–1 Basic Steps

This section explores the basic steps in analyzing a given structure with the intent of determining its adequacy for a given situation. The general process of analysis typically includes the following steps:

1. The nature and extent of the structure to be analyzed must first be determined. If a structure is decomposed into its more basic elements, it is necessary to *model* the boundary conditions of the element so that its true context is correctly represented. This modeling often assumes the form of forces and moments at the ends of the member. In many cases, this modeling is simple (e.g., in a simply supported beam system). This modeling will be briefly explored in the following section. In other cases, it is more difficult (e.g., a beam in a framed structure having rigid joints), and it may be mandatory to increase the extent of the structure studied. This is often a more complicated analysis process, as will be seen later.

While in some cases the extent of the structure to be considered is obvious, in many cases it is not at all apparent what constitutes the full extent of the structure to be considered. This situation usually arises when the entire structure in a building is considered as a whole as a device for channeling loads to the ground. It is often unclear, for example, whether certain building elements serve a structural function in addition to other functions. An exterior enclosure wall, for example, may serve not only as a weather-control device, but also as a mechanism for assuring the lateral stability of the whole structure. Whether it does or not depends on its characteristics and the relation of the element to the other building elements, particularly to those carrying vertical loads, as typically manifested in the way the elements are joined or connected. The detailing of the connection might be the determinant of whether the enclosure wall serves a structural function or not. Alternatively, the obvious existence of other mechanisms for ensuring lateral stability (e.g., cross bracing) may be an indicator of whether or not the element must serve in this capacity. Each element in the building must be reviewed with respect to its potential contribution as a constituent part of the whole structure. This often cannot be done, however, without a simultaneous consideration of the nature of the loadings associated with the building as a whole.

2. Another basic step in the analysis process that is generally done concurrently with the first described is determining the nature of the external force system acting on the structure considered. This often involves such activities as determining how distributed occupancy loads that act on a surface are picked up by supporting structural elements. This would need to be established to determine what portion of the total load is carried by each constituent element. The adequacy of each specific element can then be investigated.

3. Once the external force system acting on the structure considered is defined, the next step in the analysis process is typically to determine through application of equilibrium principles the set of reactive forces and moments that are developed at the boundaries of the structure as a consequence of the external loading present. This is often a straightforward process if the structure considered is not extensive, but can be extremely difficult in more involved structures. For *statically determinate structures,* where there are typically no more than three unknown reactions, the reactions can be found through simple application of the basic equations of statics ($\Sigma F_x = 0$, $\Sigma F_y = 0$, and $\Sigma M_0 = 0$). A beam simply resting on two supports is a statically determinate structure. In more complex structures there are often more than three unknown reactive forces. These forces cannot be solved for directly by use of the equations of statics, since (1) there are more unknown forces than there are equations for solution, and (2) the reactive forces are dependent on the physical properties of the member (including its shape and material of construction). More involved methods of analysis are thus required. Methods suitable for this type of structure will be discussed in following chapters. Simpler structures whose reactions can be found by statics alone will be considered in the latter part of this chapter.

4. After establishing the nature of the complete force system consisting of both applied and reactive forces acting on the structure, the next step in the general analysis is to determine the nature of the internal forces and moments developed in the structure as a consequence of the action of the external forces. For linear rigid elements such as beams, this typically involves determining the magnitude and distribution of internal resisting shears and moments in the structure. For other structures, more specific measures (e.g., the axial forces in truss members) may alternatively be found. Specific techniques for determining internal force states are developed in the chapters in Part II that deal with specific structural elements.

5. By knowing the internal force states present in the structure, one can next determine whether the actual member used is adequate to carry these forces without material distress or excessive deformations. Determining this typically involves predicting the internal stress levels associated with the internal force states present and then comparing these stress levels with stress levels known to be safe for the material involved. Predicting actual stress levels involves considerations of the amount and distribution of material in a structure. The allowable stress levels to which these are compared are based on empirical findings for the material involved (see Section 2–4–2). Predicting deformations involves consideration not only of the amount and distribution of material, but also of the basic load-deformation characteristics of the material. Criteria for what constitutes an acceptable deformation are also empirically based. Techniques for making predictions of this type are discussed in succeeding chapters.

The preceding steps more or less describe the process common to analyzing any type of structure.

3–3–2   Modeling the Structure

This section briefly explores how to isolate an elemental part of a whole structure and to model it in a way useful for analysis purposes. Structures are decomposed into more basic elements by conceptually taking them apart, typically at connections between members, and by replacing the action of the adjacent elements acting on them with a set of forces and moments having an equivalent effect. This is often trivially easy, as in the simple structure illustrated in Figure 3–7(a). In this case, the modeling forces are simply reactive forces. At each point of connection, a set of equal and opposite forces exists. On column B, for example, the force R_B acts downward, is equivalent to, and replaces the effect of the entire loaded horizontal beam system acting on the column. The modeling in this case is simple. Note, however, that an assumption has been made. This is that the beams are simply resting one on top of the other and on the column. The joint is assumed to transmit vertical forces only. This is true only under certain conditions, notably when the connection between members is not rigid. Thus, the column does not restrain the free rotation of the end of the beam. If it did, the modeling shown would be incorrect, and a more complex model of the type generally illustrated in Figure 3–7(b) is necessary. This type of structure, a *frame,* is studied in more detail in Chapter 9.

As is evident from the preceding discussion, effective modeling depends on identifying the exact structural nature of the joints between members. For analytical convenience, connections are modeled as one of the basic types discussed in Section 2–3–3 (e.g., pins, rollers, and rigid joints). Determining what model is most appropriate for an actual connection in practice is no easy matter and involves judgment. Several actual connections and their equivalent models are illustrated in Figure 3–8.

(a) Post-and-beam assembly: since the beam simply rests on top of the columns, the joint does not restrain rotation. Vertical forces can be transmitted only by the joint.

(b) Frame: since the beam is rigidly attached to the columns, the columns tend to restrain the rotation of the ends of the beam. Hence both forces and moments can be transmitted by the rigid connection.

FIGURE 3–7   Isolating structural elements.

FIGURE 3–8 Types of connections and idealized models.

The first step in analyzing a joint is to determine whether the nature of the joint is such that the rotations induced by a load acting on one member are transmitted to the other through the joint. If the joint does *not* transmit rotations, it is usually modeled as a pin or roller. The choice between the two depends on whether the joint can transmit forces in only one direction or in any direction. If forces can be transmitted in any direction, the joint is considered pinned. Pinned joints allow relative rotations to occur between members, but not translations, and can transmit forces in any direction. If forces can be transmitted in one direction only, the joint is considered as a roller. The latter allows not only rotations to occur between members, but also translations in the direction perpendicular to the transmitted force. In many situations, it should be noted, pinned points are literally made with a pin connecting two members, and a roller connection with actual rollers. Older bridges and buildings were often done this way—hence, the names of the joints (Figure 3–9). Such literal connections are occasionally still made in very large building structures.

If the joint does indeed transmit rotations, hence moments, between members, it is typically considered a *rigid* joint. A rigid joint always maintains a fixed angle between two members. When a rigid joint of the type shown in Figure 3–8(f) is part of a frame, however, it can translate and rotate as a whole unit (see Chapter 9). When a member joins a firm foundation with a connection that does not allow any rotation or translation to occur between the member end and the foundation, the resulting joint is called a *fixed-ended* connection [see Figure 3–8(o)]. Forces of any direction can be transmitted by this type of joint.

Quite often the difference between a pinned joint and a rigid one is difficult to determine immediately. Usually, if one member is connected to another at only one point, the joint is pinned. If the member is connected at two widely separated points, the joint is typically rigid. It is virtually impossible for rotations in one member to be transmitted to another through a connection

(a) Early "lenticular" bridge located in Lowell, Massachusetts. (b) Typical "pinned" connection.

FIGURE 3–9 Many early structures used connections that were quite literally "pinned." The term is still used to describe conceptually similar connections in modern structures (1882 lenticular truss bridge in Lowell, Massachusetts).

that can be idealized as a point, as long as the member is large with respect to the size of this point. Figure 3–8(e) and (f) illustrate two steel wide-flange members connected in these two different ways. Figure 3–8(e) represents a pin connection, since the members are joined essentially at only one point. In Figure 3–8(f), the welding that joins the top and bottom flanges of one member to the other causes this connection to be rigid.

In real structures, roller joints may or may not resist uplift forces. As Figure 3–8(g) illustrates, however, they can be designed to do so. When loadings are known to be only downward, actual joints are sometimes not designed to resist uplifting. In this text it will be assumed, however, that a roller joint can resist either downward or uplifting forces, since if they must resist upward forces, they can be designed to do so.

The previous discussion focused on the nature of various joints. It should also be noted that there are minimum requirements with regard to the number and type of joints connecting the structure to the ground. Sufficient restraints must be provided by the joints so that the basic equations of equilibrium, $\Sigma F_x = 0$, $\Sigma F_y = 0$, and $\Sigma M_0 = 0$, can be satisfied. As illustrated in Figure 3–10(c), for example, a simple beam cannot simply rest on two rollers, since if a horizontal force were applied, the structure would translate horizontally. An alternative way of looking at this is to say that $\Sigma F_x = 0$ could never be satisfied. Thus, at least one of the two joints must be pinned. Both joints could be pinned as well. Typically, one of the joints is not restrained horizontally, however, since making it into a roller serves the very useful function of allowing expansions and contractions due to thermal effects to occur unrestrained. Pinning both ends would cause a very large buildup of forces to occur as the structure tried to change length with a change in temperature. The forces potentially involved are enormous and can lead to serious failures. Thus, the support condition illustrated in Figure 3–10(b) is typical.

3–3–3   Modeling the External Loads

Loadings in a building are typically either concentrated or uniformly distributed over an area. The former need no modeling other than as necessary to characterize them as a force

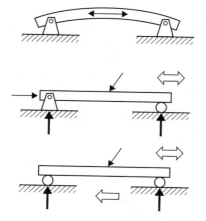

(a) When both ends of a member are pinned, temperature changes can induce large internal forces in the member since it cannot freely expand or contract.

(b) Replacing one pin with a roller allows expansion and contraction to occur freely. The structure is, however, still stable.

(c) If roller connections are used at both ends, the structure would slide under the action of horizontal loads. Hence, at least one connection must be pinned.

FIGURE 3–10   Use of roller connections.

vector. In the latter, however, some modeling is needed when the area considered is actually made up of an assembly of one-way line and surface elements. These elements would pick up different portions of the total load acting over the surface depending on their arrangement.

Consider the simple structural assembly shown in Figure 3–11(a). Since all connections in this illustration are simply supported, the structure can be decomposed as indicated. For the wide plank elements, the reactions are better characterized as *line* reactions [as illustrated in Figure 3–11(b)] than as point reactions. The reactions from all the planks supported by a beam then become loads acting on the beam. Note that these loads form a continuous line load. Loads of this type are expressed in terms of a load or force per unit length (e.g., lb/ft or N/m) and are commonly encountered in the structural analysis process. These loads can be calculated by first determining the reactions of the planks and then considering them as loads on the supporting beam [see Figure 3–11(c)].

Another way of looking at this same loading is to think in terms of *contributory areas*. By a symmetry argument, each of the beams can be considered as supporting an area of the extent indicated in Figure 3–11(d). The width of each area is often called the *load strip*. When the member is looked at in elevation, the load acting over the width of the load strip is considered transferred to the support beam. If the uniformly distributed load is constant and the load strip is of a constant width, the amount of load carried *per unit length* by the support beam is simply the load per unit area multiplied by the width of the load strip. This process is illustrated in Figure 3–11(e). The result is again a continuous line load describable in terms of a load per unit length. This process is valid for symmetrical loads only.

Both of the methods described above should yield the same load on the supporting beams [see Figure 3–11(f)]. Of the two, the former is a more correct model of how the structure works and how loads are carried to the ground. The latter is, however, often more convenient to use and is consequently utilized as a shorthand way of determining loads.

The model used can be as simple or as sophisticated as the analyst deems necessary. In early design stages, the type of approximation previously discussed is adequate for most purposes. The loading considered should, of course, include both live- and dead-load components. The exact value of the latter can be found only through a detailed consideration of the size and unit weights of the various elements that constitute the whole assembly. Determining these values can be tedious. An alternative is to use an approximate equivalent weight, typically expressed as a force per unit area, to represent the weight of an entire assembly of some complexity. Thus, in Figure 3–12 the average dead load of the complete deck, joist, and beam system can be expressed as (w_2) lb/ft^2 or (w_1) N/m^2, where the value of w is estimated or found from empirical data. Since live loads are also expressed in terms of a force per unit area, the calculation process is facilitated, since both loads can be considered simultaneously. Procedures of this type are alright for preliminary purposes, but more detailed takeoffs should be made at later stages in the complete analysis process.

◆ ◆ **EXAMPLE**

Assume that the combined average live and dead load of the floor system shown in Figure 3–12 is 50 lb/ft^2. Determine the load strip widths and associated loading models for beams 1, 2, and 3.

(a) Structure assembly: planks resting on beams.

Load = w lb/ft^2 (N/m^2)

(b) Typical plank element: loads and reactions become loads on the beams.

w lb/ft or N/m

Unit width

a

$R = w(a/2)$

$R = w(a/2)$

w lb/ft

$wa/2$ $wa/2$ $wa/2$ $wa/2$

wa

(c) Loads carried by beams.

$wa/2$

wa

$wa/2$

The center beam picks up the reactions from planks on two sides.

(d) Contributory areas: each beam is assumed to support an area of the surface as indicated.

Loaded area assumed carried by beam B

Loaded area assumed carried by beam A

Load = w lb/ft^2 (N/m^2)

Loaded area assumed carried by beam C

(e) Load strips:
Load unit length = (width of load strip) × (load unit area)

$w_A = w(a/2)$
$w_B = w(a)$
$w_C = w(a/2)$

w_A w_B w_C

$a/2$ a $a/2$

(f) Diagrammatic representation of beams and loads. The load/unit length, or wa, in lb/ft or N/m, is often denoted simply as w.

$wa/2$ wa $wa/2$

$waL/4$ $waL/4$ $waL/2$ $waL/2$ $waL/4$ $waL/4$

A B C

FIGURE 3–11 Two approaches to modeling loading conditions. The model shown on the left most correctly reflects how surface loads are picked up by a beam system. The model on the right, which is based on the concept of contributory areas, is often used for convenience. Both approaches yield the same loading on the beams.

FIGURE 3–12 Load modeling.

Solution:

Reactions: beam 1
From Section 2–3–2:

$$R_A = R_B = wL/2 = (125 \text{ lb/ft})(18 \text{ ft})/2$$
$$= 1125 \text{ lb (by symmetry)}$$

Or, directly:
$$\Sigma M_A = 0$$

$$+R_B (18 \text{ ft}) - \underbrace{(125 \text{ lb/ft})(18 \text{ ft})}_{\substack{\text{equivalent} \\ \text{total load}}} \underbrace{(9 \text{ ft})}_{\substack{\text{moment arm} \\ \text{to equivalent} \\ \text{total load}}} = 0 \qquad \therefore \quad R_B = 1125 \text{ lb}$$

$$\Sigma F_y = 0$$

$$R_A + R_B = 0 \qquad \therefore \quad R_B = 1125 \text{ lb}$$

Reactions: beam 2

$$R_A = R_B = wL/2 = (250 \text{ lb/ft})(18 \text{ ft})/2$$
$$= 2250 \text{ lb (by symmetry)}$$

Reactions: beam 3

Use equivalent concentrated loads and argue that by symmetry $R_A = R_B$:

$$R_A = R_B = [\underbrace{(250 \text{ lb/ft})(6 \text{ ft})}_{\substack{\text{equivalent} \\ \text{concentrated} \\ \text{load}}} + \underbrace{(125 \text{ lb/ft})(6 \text{ ft})}_{\substack{\text{equivalent} \\ \text{concentrated} \\ \text{load}}} + \underbrace{(250 \text{ lb/ft})(6 \text{ ft})]/2}_{\substack{\text{equivalent} \\ \text{concentrated} \\ \text{load}}}$$

$$R_A = R_B = 1875 \text{ lb}$$

Note that the load per unit length carried by an end beam is typically one-half that of an interior beam and that the presence of a hole in the deck has a significant effect on the type of loading model developed.

◆

◆ ◆   **EXAMPLE**

Determine the reactions for a typical interior joist in the floor framing system shown in Figure 3–13(a). Assume that the spans and loads are as shown.

(a) Basic joist system.

(b) Joist system supporting
a partition.

FIGURE 3–13   Example of floor framing system.

Solution:

Typical joist span $= L = 16.0$ ft $= 4.88$ m
Typical center-to-center spacing $= a = 16$ in. (1.33 ft) $= 0.406$ m
Live load $= w_L = 40$ lb/ft$^2 = 1915$ N/m^2
Dead load $= w_D$:

$$
\begin{array}{llll}
\text{finished flooring} & = & 2.5 \text{ lb/ft}^2 & = & 119.7 \text{ N/m}^2 \\
\text{rough flooring} & = & 2.5 \text{ lb/ft}^2 & = & 119.7 \text{ N/m}^2 \\
\text{sheet rock ceiling} & = & 10.0 \text{ lb/ft}^2 & = & 478.8 \text{ N/m}^2 \\
\text{joists (estimated)} & = & \underline{9.0 \text{ lb/ft}^2} & = & \underline{430.9 \text{ N/m}^2} \\
\text{total dead load} & = & 24.0 \text{ lb/ft}^2 & = & 1149.1 \text{ N/m}^2 \\
\end{array}
$$

total load $= w_D + w_L = (24.0 + 40.0) = 64.0$ lb/ft^2
$= (1915 + 1149.1) = 3064.1$ N/m^2

Reactions:

$$\Sigma F_Y = 0: \qquad R_A + R_B - \underbrace{(w_D + w_L)}_{\substack{\text{force per} \\ \text{unit length}}}\underbrace{(a)(L)}_{\substack{\text{joist} \\ \text{length}}} = 0$$

$$\underbrace{}_{\substack{\text{total downward} \\ \text{force}}}$$

$$\Sigma M_A = 0:$$

$$0(R_A) + L(R_B) - \underbrace{(w_D + w_L)(a)(L)}_{\substack{\text{total downward} \\ \text{force}}}\underbrace{(L/2)}_{\substack{\text{moment} \\ \text{arm}}} = 0 \qquad R_B = \frac{(w_D + w_L)(a)(L)}{2}$$

From $\Sigma F_Y = 0$:

$$R_A = (w_D + w_L)(a)(L)/2$$

$$R_A = R_B = \frac{(64.0 \text{ lb/ft}^2)(1.33 \text{ ft})(16.0 \text{ ft})}{2} = 682 \text{ lb}$$

$$= \frac{(3064.1 \text{ N/m}^2)(0.406 \text{ m})(4.88 \text{ m})}{2} = 3035 \text{ N}$$

A typical joist reaction is therefore 682 lb (3035 N). ◆

◆ ◆ **EXAMPLE**

Determine the reactions for a typical interior joist in the floor framing system that supports a partition wall as shown in Figure 3–13(b). Assume that all the loads and spans are the same as those used in the preceding example and that the only difference is the addition of the partition wall.

Solution:

Partition:

Assume that the partition is 8.0 ft (2.44 m) high and weighs 20 lb/ft^2 (958 N/m^2). The concentrated force on a joist exerted by the partition is computed as follows. The joists are spaced 1.33 ft (0.406 m) on centers, and, as the partition is 8.0 ft (2.44 m) high, the area of the partition that bears on one joist is $8.0 \times 1.33 = 10.67$ ft^2 (or $0.406 \times 2.44 = 0.99$ m^2). The concentrated force on a single joist is therefore 10.67 ft$^2 \times 20$ lb/ft$^2 = 213.4$ lb (or 0.99 m$^2 \times 958$ N/m$^2 = 950$ N). This force is located as shown in Figure 3–13(b). All other loads (i.e., $w_D + w_L$) are as in the preceding example.

Reactions:

$$\Sigma M_A = 0: \qquad 0(R_A) + L(R_B) - [(w_D + w_L)(a)(L)]\frac{L}{2} - \frac{L}{3}(P) = 0$$

$$16.0(R_B) - [(64.0 \text{ lb/ft}^2)(1.33 \text{ ft})(16.0 \text{ ft})](8.0 \text{ ft}) - (16.0/3 \text{ ft})(213.4 \text{ lb}) = 0$$

$$R_B = 753 \text{ lb}$$

$$4.88(R_B) - [(3064.1 \text{ N/m}^2)(0.406 \text{ m})(4.88 \text{ m})](2.44 \text{ m}) - (4.88 \text{ m}/3)(950 \text{ N}) = 0$$

$$R_B = 3352 \text{ N}$$

$$\Sigma F_y = 0: \qquad R_A + R_B - (w_D + w_L)(a)(L) - P = 0 \qquad R_A = 824 \text{ lb} = 3668 \text{ N} \qquad \blacklozenge$$

When a beam is supporting a series of closely spaced joists that in turn support a plank deck, it is evident that each joist carries a uniform load per unit length. Figure 3–14 illustrates the process. This load can be found by multiplying the width of the load strip carried (i.e., the joist spacing) by the load per unit area. This method is typically used whether the planks over the joists are continuous over several joists or simply span from joist to joist. Theoretically, there is some difference in the two cases, but it is not of sufficient consequence to change the model for a simple joist system. Joist reactions can next be found. The collector, in turn, carries the reactions of the joists. The collector thus actually carries a series of closely spaced concentrated loads. For calculation convenience, however, these loads on the collector beam are often re-

(a)   (b)

FIGURE 3–14   An equivalent uniformly distributed load can be used to approximate a series of closely spaced concentrated loads.

placed with a uniformly distributed load per unit length found by considering the load strip width of the contributory area of the surface supported by the member—a reasonable modeling *if* the concentrated loads are closely spaced.

◆ ◆ **EXAMPLE**

Determine the loads on columns M and N in the structure shown in Figure 3–15. Assume that the loading is given by w_T lb/ft^2 and that this value reflects both live and dead loads. Assume $L = 20$ ft, $a = 6$ ft, and $w_T = 50$ lb/ft^2.

Load acts over whole surface.

Roof deck reaction become loads on joists.

Joist reactions become loads on beams.

Beam reactions become loads on columns.

Column reactions become loads on foundations.

(a) Structure

(b) Free-body diagrams.

FIGURE 3–15 Example structure.

(c) Free-body diagrams of
joists, beams, and columns.

FIGURE 3–15   (continued)

Solution: The first step is to determine how the surface load is channeled to the columns. This is best done by drawing free-body diagrams for each element in the structure (see Figure 3–15). To determine the magnitudes of the column loads it is necessary first to calculate the load carried by each joist, then to calculate the reactions for each joist, and finally to calculate the reactions of the beams that carry the joists. These reactions are the column loads. This process of starting with an analysis of the smallest members actually picking up the loading and tracing it through by considering each collecting member is common in most problems of analysis.

Basic behavior

The decking transfers loads to the joists. The reactions of the joists become forces applied on the two transverse collector beams. The reactions of the two transverse beams become the forces exerted on the columns, which in turn become forces on the foundations.

Joist reactions: members A and D

The load/unit length carried by each joist is found by considering the width of the load strip carried by each joist. The end joists, A and D, carry load strips ($a/2$) in width. If the total load per unit area is w_T, the load per unit length carried by joists A and D is simply $w_T(a/2)$.

By symmetry:

$$R_{A1} = R_{A2} = w_T(a/2)(L) \div 2 \quad \therefore \quad R_{A1} = R_{A2} = 0.25\, w_T a L$$
$$R_{A1} = R_{A2} = 0.25(50)(6)(20) = 1500\ \text{lb}$$

Or, by summing moments:
$\Sigma M_{RA1} = 0$:

$$-[w_T(a/2)(L)](L/2) + 1.0L(R_{A2}) = 0 \qquad R_{A2} = 0.25w_TaL$$

$\underbrace{\text{total load}}\quad\underbrace{\text{moment}}\quad\underbrace{\text{moment}}\quad\underbrace{\text{unknown}}$
arm   arm   reaction

$$-[(50)(6/2)(20)](20/2) + 1.0(20)R_{A2} = 0 \qquad R_{A2} = 1500 \text{ lb}$$

$\Sigma F_y = 0$:

$$+R_{A1} + R_{A2} - w_T(a/2)(L) = 0 \qquad R_{A1} = 0.25w_TaL$$

$\underbrace{\text{unknown}}_{\text{reaction}}\quad\underbrace{\text{calculated}}_{\text{above}}\quad\underbrace{\text{total}}_{\substack{\text{downward}\\\text{load}}}$

$$R_{A1} + 1500 - 50(6/2)(20) = 0 \qquad R_{A1} = 1500 \text{ lb}$$

Similarly,

$$R_{D1} = 0.25w_TaL = 1500 \text{ lb} \quad \text{and} \quad R_{D2} = 0.25w_TaL = 1500 \text{ lb}$$

Joist reactions: members B and C
The load/unit length carried by joists B and C is not a constant due to the presence of the opening. In sections where the decking is continuous, the width of the load strip is (a). The load/unit length is consequently $w_T(a)$. In sections where the hole is present, each joist carries a load strip of one-half that in continuous sections, or $(a/2)$. The load/unit length on these sections is $w_T(a/2)$.
$\Sigma M_{RB_1} = 0$:

$$-[w_T(a)(0.7L)](0.7L/2) - [w_T(a/2)(0.3L)](0.7L + 0.3L/2) + R_{B_2}(1.0L) = 0$$

$\underbrace{\text{load}}\quad\underbrace{\text{moment}}_{\text{arm}}\quad\underbrace{\text{partial load}}\quad\underbrace{\text{moment arm}}\quad\underbrace{\text{reaction moment}}_{\text{arm}}$

$$-[50(6)(0.7)(20)](0.7)(20/2) - [50(6/2)(0.3)(20)][0.7(20) + 0.3(20/2)] + R_{B_2}(20) = 0$$
$$R_{B_2} = 0.3725w_TaL = 2235 \text{ lb}$$

$\Sigma F_y = 0$:

$$R_{B1} + R_{B2} - [w_T(a)(0.7L)] - [w_T(a/2)(0.3L)] = 0 \qquad R_{B1} = 0.4775w_TaL$$

$\underbrace{\text{reaction}}\quad\underbrace{\text{reaction}}\quad\underbrace{\text{load}}\quad\underbrace{\text{partial load}}$

$$R_{B1} + 2235 - [50(6)(0.7)(20)] - [(50)(6/2)(0.3)(20)] = 0 \qquad R_{B1} = 2865 \text{ lb}$$

Similarly,

$$R_{C1} = 0.4775w_TaL = 2865 \text{ lb} \quad \text{and} \quad R_{C2} = 0.3725w_TaL = 2235 \text{ lb}$$

Column forces:
The forces on columns M and N are the reactions of the transverse beam-carrying joist loads (reactions) $R_{A1}, R_{B1}, R_{C1},$ and R_{D1}.

By symmetry:

$$R_M = R_N = (R_{A1} + R_{B1} + R_{C1} + R_{D1}) \div 2$$
$$= (1500 + 2865 + 2865 + 1500)/2$$
$$= 4365 \text{ lb}$$

Or, by summing moments:
  Beam $MN \ \Sigma M_{R_M} = 0$:

$$-R_{A1}(0) - R_{B1}(a) - R_{C1}(2a) - R_{D1}(3a) + R_M(0) + R_N(3a) = 0$$
$$-1500(0) - (2865)(6) - 2865(2)(6) - 1500(3)(6) + R_M(0) + R_N(3)(6) = 0$$
$$R_N = 0.7275 w_T aL = 4365 \text{ lb} \quad \text{and}$$
$$\Sigma F_y = 0: \qquad -R_{A1} - R_{B1} - R_{C1} - R_{D1} + R_M + R_N = 0$$
$$R_M = 0.7275 w_T aL = 4365 \text{ lb}$$

The forces on columns O and P are the reactions of the second transverse beam.
  By symmetry:

$$R_O = R_P = (R_{A2} + R_{B2} + R_{C2} + R_{D2}) \div 2$$
$$= (1500 + 2235 + 2235 + 1500) \div 2$$
$$= 3735 \text{ lb}$$

Equilibrium checks:
The total load that acts downward on the structure is $w_T \times A$, where A is the area of the surface. The forces developed on the four foundation points must total to this same value (which provides a good overall check on your results):

$$R_M + R_N + R_O + R_P = w_T \times A$$
$$4365 + 4365 + 3735 + 3735 = 50 \text{ lb/ft}^2 (324 \text{ ft}^2)$$
$$16,200 \text{ lb} = 16,200 \text{ lb}$$

Alternatively, using SI units, assume that $L = 6.1$ m, $a = 1.83$ m, and $w_T = 244.1$ kg/m^2. The first step is to convert the distributed load into a force measure; thus, $(244.1 \times 9.807) = 2393.9$ N/m$^2 = 2.39$ kN/m^2. The force on column M is then given by $0.7275(2.39$ kN/m$^2)(1.83$ m$)(6.1$ m$) = 19.41$ kN .   ◆

◆ ◆   **EXAMPLE**

Determine the forces on a typical interior truss in the structure illustrated in Figure 3–16. Also determine the reactions for the truss analyzed. Assume $L_1 = 60$ ft $= 18.3$ m and $L_2 = 25$ *ft* $= 7.6$ *m* and that the loads are as shown in the following solution.

Roof loading–uniformly distributed: w

Typical truss spacing

Load area carried by typical transverse beam

L_2

L_2

$L_1/4$

Typical transverse beam spacing

$L_1/4$

$L_1/4$

$L_1/4$

Load area carried by typical truss

$L_1/4$

Built-up roofing

Sheathing

Truss

Transverse beam

Joists

(a) Structure.

$w(L_1/4)$

L_2

$L_1/4$

R_B R_B

L_2

R_B

R_B R_B

R_B

Load area carried by interior panel point of truss

$R_p/2$

$R_p = R_p + R_p$
$= w L_1 L_1/4$

R_p

R_p

R_p

$R_p/2$

$R_p/2$ R_p R_p R_p $R_p/2$

R_T R_T

Free-body diagram of truss

(c) Models for determining forces on truss panel points.

(b) Actual free-body diagrams.

Load area carried by typical truss

(d) Model for finding truss reactions directly.

FIGURE 3–16 Loading models.

126

Solution:

Loads:

Assume that the live load is 35 lb/ft^2 (1676 N/m^2). Assume the following dead loads:

Roofing	7.0 lb/ft^2 =	335 N/m^2
Sheathing	2.5 =	120
Joists and beams	8.0 =	383
Truss	4.0 =	191
Total	21.5 lb/ft^2 =	1029 N/m^2

Here the dead weights of the joists, beams, and trusses were estimated in terms of an approximate equivalent distributed load. This is often done in preliminary design stages. More detailed takeoffs are made in successive stages. Using the equivalent distributed load figures and the assumed live loading, the total distributed load (live plus dead) is given by

$$35 + 21.5 = 56.5 \text{ lb/ft}^2 \qquad \text{or} \qquad 1676 + 1029 = 2705 \text{ N/m}^2.$$

Forces on truss:

The way a unit area of distributed live load is eventually carried to the supports is illustrated in the series of free-body diagrams shown in Figure 3–16(b). The load is first picked up by the roof decking, which carries it to adjacent joists. The reactions of the decking become forces on the joists. The reactions of the joists in turn become forces on the transverse beams. The reactions of the transverse beams become forces on the panel points of the trusses. The magnitudes of these forces could be determined by calculating each of the reactions involved in turn. This precise method, which accurately reflects how the structure carries loads, is, however, cumbersome. Forces on the panel points of the truss can be determined more quickly by an alternative approach, which involves the models illustrated in Figure 3–16(c). These models are based on the concept of contributory areas. As the illustration suggests, it is possible to determine the force present at a truss panel point by finding the relative portion of the roof which serves as the contributory area for the panel point and then simply multiplying this area by the magnitude of the distributed uniform loading.

contributory area for a typical interior panel point

$$= \left(\frac{L_1}{4}\right)(L_2) = \frac{L_1 L_2}{4}$$

interior-panel-point force $= R_P = \dfrac{w_T L_1 L_2}{4} = \dfrac{(56.5 \text{ lb/ft}^2)(60 \text{ ft})(25 \text{ ft})}{4} = 21{,}187.5 \text{ lb}$

$$= \frac{(2705 \text{ N/m}^2)(18.3 \text{ m})(7.6 \text{ m})}{4} = 94{,}053 \text{ N}$$

contributory area for a typical exterior panel point

$$= \left(\frac{L_1}{8}\right)(L_2) = \frac{L_1 L_2}{8}$$

exterior-panel-point force $= \dfrac{w_T L_1 L_2}{8} = \dfrac{R_p}{2}$

$$= 10{,}593.75 \text{ lb} = 47{,}026.5 \text{ N}$$

The final free-body diagram for the truss is shown in Figure 3–16(c).

Reactions:

The reactions of the truss can be obtained by using the free-body diagram shown in Figure 3–16(c) with the forces found above. Because of symmetry, a typical reaction is evidently given by $(R_p/2 + R_p + R_p + R_p + R_p/2)/2 = 42,375$ lb $= 188,106$ N. Alternatively, it is possible to find the reactions of the truss directly (without going through the step of finding the panel-point forces) by considering the loading model illustrated in Figure 3–16(d). Figure 3–16(d) illustrates the relative portion of the total roof surface carried by a typical interior truss. This is the contributory load area for the truss. This area can be used to find the total load carried by the truss and then the reactions. The figure illustrates that each reaction picks up one-half of the total contributory load area.

$$\text{contributory area for a typical truss} = L_1 L_2$$
$$\text{total downward force on truss} = w_T L_1 L_2 = (56.5 \text{ lb/ft}^2)(60 \text{ ft})(25 \text{ ft})$$
$$= 84,750 \text{ lb}$$
$$= (2705 \text{ N/m}^2)(18.3 \text{ m})(7.6 \text{ m}) = 376,212 \text{ N}$$

Since each truss has two reactions that are symmetrically placed with respect to the load, each reaction is simply one-half the total load, or $84,750/2 = 42,375$ lb or $376,212/2 = 188,106$ N. These are the same values that were noted before. For finding truss reactions it is evident that this procedure saves time.

It should be emphasized that the use of loading models based on the notion of contributory areas is valid only when there is not any extreme asymmetry in either the loading condition or structure. For partial loading conditions it is necessary to calculate the reactions for each individual element and consider them as forces acting on the elements supporting it. This process then needs to be repeated until the reactions of the final collecting element on the foundation are found. ◆

◆ ◆ **EXAMPLE**

Determine the forces on the structural frames shown in Figure 3–17 due to the action of wind impinging upon the face of the building. Assume that $w = 20$ lb/ft^2, $h = 15$ ft, and $L = 25$ ft.

Solution: The forces can be determined either by tracing through the way specific elements such as girts are loaded and the way their reactions become loads on the frames or by using a contributory-area concept. Both methods are illustrated in Figure 3–16. Numerical values can be found by substitution; e.g., $whL/4$: 1875 lb. ◆

(a) Diagram of basic structural and enclosure system.

The reactions of G_1 and G_2 become loads on the rigid frames.

$$P_1 = whL/4$$
$$P_2 = whL/2$$
$$P_3 = whL/4 + whL/4$$
$$P_4 = whL/2 + whL/2$$

(b) Model of how wind loads are transferred to rigid frames, the siding first picks up the distributed wind forces and transfers them to the horizontal girts (G_1 and G_2), which in turn transfer them to the frames.

(c) Simplified model for directly determining loads on the frames. The loads on the rigid frames can be determined directly by considering the contributory are carried by each load point on the rigid frames. If the enclosure framing were different, the way the load areas are assigned might also be different.

FIGURE 3–17 Modeling wind loads on rigid frames.

QUESTIONS

3–1 Find two bridges in your local area and identify the type of support conditions present (e.g., hinged, roller). Draw a sketch of the actual supports and a diagram of the symbol used to represent the support.

3–2 Find two different types of trusses used in buildings in your local area and identify the type of support condition present. Draw a sketch of the actual end condition and a diagram of the symbol used to represent the support.

3–3 Consider a typical corridor in the building that you are in or in one nearby. What do you estimate the *actual* live load to be during normal traffic conditions? During fire conditions?

3–4 What are the snow loads and wind loads specifically recommended for buildings in your local area? Consult a copy of the local building code in force.

3–5 For the floor system shown in Figure 3–12, assume that the combined live and dead load present is equal to 80 lb/ft^2. Determine reactions present for beams 1, 2, and 3 in the floor system (first determine load strip widths, then determine the appropriate loading model for each beam, and finally determine reactions for each beam by a statics analysis).

Answer: Beam 1: 1800 lb each end; beam 2: 3600 lb each end; beam 3: 2400 lb each end.

3–6 For the beam shown in Figure 3–13(a), determine the reactions if the live load is changed to 30 lb/ft^2.

3–7 Repeat the example analyzed in Figure 3–17 assuming that $w = 25$ lb/ft^2, $h = 12$ ft, and $L = 28$ ft. Show how loadings are traced through.

PART II

ANALYSIS AND DESIGN OF STRUCTURAL ELEMENTS

In the nine chapters in Part II we systematically treat all the major structural elements used in a building context. Each chapter contains initial sections that define the element and discuss its attributes in a qualitative way. The following sections present more detailed analysis of the structural characteristics of the element and discuss principles that are useful in a design context.

As discussed in more detail in Part III, design endeavors may be classified into *first-, second-,* and *third-order* activities, generally characterizing the sequence in which design decisions are encountered and must be made. First- and second-order activities deal with establishing relations between broader design intents, specific morphological characteristics of the building, and the type and attributes of different structural systems (materials, systems, structural hierarchies, bay geometries). Third-order activities focus on member and connection design within the constraints previously established by earlier decisions. It is in the latter sense that the term *design* is used in Part II. A thorough knowledge of the analysis and design of such members as arches, cables, beams, columns, trusses, frames, plates, shells, and membranes is a necessary precursor to understanding first- and second-order design activities, and for this reason the analysis and design of elements are discussed first, even though the design process does not proceed in this sequence.

CHAPTER 4

Trusses

4-1 INTRODUCTION

Although structures made of jointed members have been constructed throughout history, the conscious exploitation of structural advantages inherent when individual linear members are formed into triangulated patterns is of relatively recent origin. Structures of this type, commonly called *trusses,* were indeed built quite early. Simple trusses using relatively few members often appeared in common pitched roofs. More complex trusses were used in isolated instances. A bridge using a form of timber truss, for example, was built across the Danube River by the Romans as early as 500 B.C. Such examples, however, had little significant impact on the methods of building of the time. The Italian architect Andrea Palladio (1518–1580) gave an illustration of a correctly triangulated truss structure and indicated that he had some knowledge of its potential and the way it carried forces. Trusses were occasionally used afterward in large public buildings such as Independence Hall, Philadelphia, but again without having much impact as a structural innovation. It was the bridge builders of the early nineteenth century who first began systematically to explore and experiment with the potential of the truss. This was in response to the demands of rapidly expanding transportation systems of the time. Emiland Gauthey's *Traité de la Construction des Ponts* (posthumously published between 1809 and 1813 by his nephew, the famous mathematician Louis Navier of the Ecole Polytechnic in Paris) provided a foundation for many subsequent theoretical works in the area. Gauthey's treatise included a discussion of what he termed the principles of *equilibrium of position* and *equilibrium of resistance*. The former was an initial attempt to resolve bridge loads into components in individual members. The latter dealt with material properties and the sizing of truss members. Later important contributions include Squire Whipple's classic of structural engineering, *A Work on Bridge Building,* published in 1847. The development of the truss was thus fostered by a tentative but rapidly expanding body of theoretical knowledge. This contrasts with other structural forms which typically developed slowly over time in a strictly empirical way. The truss soon became a common structural form used in civil engineering structures spanning long distances. The use of trusses in buildings also increased, although more slowly due to different traditions and needs, until they became a common element in modern architecture.

The emergence of the truss as a major structural form has been rapid and its impact significant. The remainder of this chapter explores what a truss is, how it works, and why it is an important structural form. The presentation is an inquiry into a specific structural element. On a more general level, the methods of analysis and design presented for trusses are used to demonstrate principles that are broadly applicable to the analysis and design of a wide range of other structural forms.

4-2   GENERAL PRINCIPLES

4-2-1   Triangulation

A truss is an assemblage of individual linear elements arranged in a triangle or combination of triangles to form a rigid framework that cannot be deformed by the application of external forces without deformation of one or more of its members. The individual elements are typically assumed to be joined at their intersections with *pinned* connections (see Sections 2–4–1 and 3–3–2). Members are customarily arranged so that all loads and reactions occur only at these intersections.

The primary principle underlying the use of the truss as a load-carrying structure is that arranging elements into a triangular configuration results in a stable shape. Consider the two pin-connected structures shown in Figure 4–1(b) and (c). Application of a load to the structure shown in Figure 4–1(b) will cause the massive deformation indicated. This is an unstable structure, which forms a *collapse mechanism* under external loading. A structure of this type may be deformed without a change in length of any individual member. The triangulated configuration of members shown in Figure 4–1(c) clearly could not deform or collapse in a similar manner. This configuration is thus *stable.* Any deformations that occur in this stable structure are relatively minor and are associated with small changes in member length caused by forces generated in the members by the external load. Similarly, the angle formed between any two members remains relatively unchanged under load in a stable configuration of this type. This is in marked contrast to the large angle changes which occur between members in an unstable configuration of elements [see Figure 4–1(b)]. The external force causes forces to be developed in members of the stable triangulated structure. As will be explained in detail in Section 4–3–2, the forces developed are either purely tensile or purely compressive. Bending is not present, nor can it be developed as long as external loads are applied at nodal points.

Since a basic triangle of members is a stable form, it follows that any structure made of an assembly of triangulated members is also a rigid, stable structure. This idea is the principle underlying the viability and usefulness of the truss in building, since larger rigid forms of any geometry can be created by the aggregation of smaller triangular units. Again, the effect of

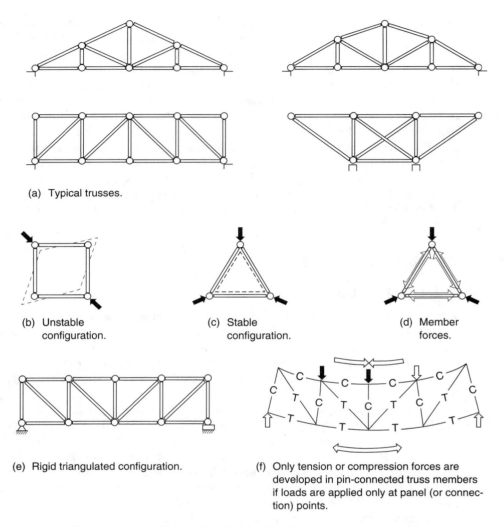

(a) Typical trusses.

(b) Unstable configuration.

(c) Stable configuration.

(d) Member forces.

(e) Rigid triangulated configuration.

(f) Only tension or compression forces are developed in pin-connected truss members if loads are applied only at panel (or connection) points.

FIGURE 4–1 Typical trusses and basic triangulation principles.

external loads is to produce a state of either pure tension or compression in the individual members of the assembly. For common trusses with vertically acting loads, compressive forces are usually developed in upper chord members and tensile forces in lower chord members. Either type of force may develop in an interstitial member, although there is often an alternating pattern of tensile and compressive forces present.

It is extremely important that trusses be loaded only with concentrated loads that act at joints for truss members to develop only tensile or compressive members. If loads are applied directly onto truss members themselves, bending stresses will also develop in the loaded members in addition to the basic tensile or compressive stresses already present, with the consequence that member design is greatly complicated and the overall efficiency of the truss is reduced.

4-2-2   Member Forces: Qualitative Analyses

As discussed in following sections, the nature of the forces in the members of any truss can be determined through application of the basic equations of equilibrium. For some simple truss configurations, however, the basic sense (tension, compression, zero) of the forces in many members can be determined by less involved techniques which may prove useful in visualizing how certain trusses carry external loads.

One way of determining the sense of the force in a truss member is to visualize the probable deformed shape of the structure as it would develop if the member considered were *imagined* to be removed. The nature of the force in the member can then be predicted on the basis of an analysis of its role in *preventing* the deformation visualized.

Consider the diagonals shown in truss A in Figure 4–2(a). If the diagonals were imagined removed, the assembly would dramatically deform, as illustrated in Figure 4–2(b), since it is a non-triangulated configuration. In order for the diagonals to keep the type of deformation shown from occurring, it is evident that the left and right diagonals must prevent points *B–F* and points *B–D,*

(a) Basic truss assemblies.

(b) The senses of the forces in the diagonals can be determined by first imagining them to be removed and then ascertaining their role in preventing the probable type of truss deformation that would occur. Thus, a diagonal placed between *B* and *F* in truss A would have to be in tension because its role is to prevent *B* and *D* from drawing apart in the manner indicated.

(c) Final force distribution in trusses: *C*, compression: *T*, tension.

(d) A "cable" or "arch" analogy can also be used to determine the senses of the forces in different members. In the truss to the left, member *FBD is* imagined to be a "cable" and is obviously in tension. Other members serve roles related to maintaining the equilibrium of this basic "cable" configuration.

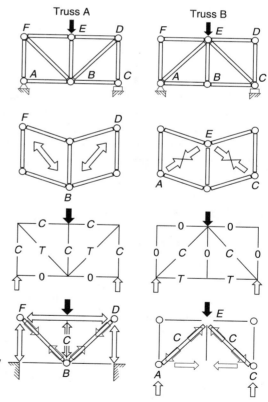

FIGURE 4-2   Forces in truss members: the senses of the forces in some simple truss configurations can be determined through intuitive approaches. More complex trusses require quantitative approaches.

respectively, from drawing apart. Consequently diagonals placed between these points would be pulled upon. Hence, tension forces would develop in the diagonal members. The diagonals shown in truss B in Figure 4–2 must be in a state of compression since their function is to keep points *A–E* and *C–E* from drawing closer together.

With respect to member *BE* in both trusses, it is fairly easy to imagine what would happen to points *B* and *E* if member *BE* were removed. In truss A, points *B* and *E* would have a tendency to draw together, hence compressive forces develop in any member placed between these two points. In truss B, however, removal of member *BE* leads to *no change* in the gross shape of the structure (since it remains a stable triangulated configuration); hence the member serves no direct role for this loading. It is a *zero-force member.* Note that members *AF, FE, ED,* and *DC* in truss B could also be removed without altering the basic stability of the remainder of the configuration, and hence are also zero-force members. This is obviously not true for the same members in truss A. Final forces in both truss A and truss B are illustrated in Figure 4–2(c).

Another completely different way of visualizing the forces developed in a truss is to use an *arch* and *cable* analogy. It is evident, for example, that truss A can be conceived of as a cable with supplementary members [see Figure 4–2(d)]. Truss B can be conceived of as a simple linear arch with supplementary members. Diagonals in truss A are consequently in tension while diagonals in truss B must be in compression. The forces in other members can be determined by analyzing their respective roles in relation to containing arch or cable thrusts or providing load transfer or reactive functions. As Figure 4–3 indicates, special forms of more complex trusses can also be visualized in this same general way.

Obviously, both of the methods discussed above for visualizing forces in trusses become exceedingly difficult or even impossible to apply when more complex triangulation patterns are present. A method of visualizing forces in such trusses on the basis of joint equilibrium considerations is considered in the next section. In general, however, complex truss forms must be mathematically analyzed according to methods to be discussed for correct results to be obtained.

4–3 ANALYSIS OF TRUSSES

4–3–1 Stability

The first step in the analysis of a truss is always to determine whether the truss studied is indeed a stable configuration of members. It is usually possible to tell by inspection whether or not a truss is stable under external loads by considering each joint in turn to determine if the joint will always maintain a fixed relation to other joints under any loading condition applied to the truss. In general, any truss composed of an aggregation of basic triangular shapes will be a stable structure.

The appearance of nontriangular shapes in a bar pattern is an obvious sign that the truss should be looked at carefully. The truss indicated in Figure 4–4(a) is unstable and would collapse under load in the manner illustrated. This truss clearly does not have a sufficient number of bars to maintain a fixed geometrical relationship between joints. Assuming that the remaining truss members are adequately designed for the loads they carry, the addition of a member from *B* to *E*, as indicated in Figure 4–4(b), would make this into a stable configuration.

(a) Basic "cable" unit: the diagonal members are obviously in tension.

(b) A simple truss configuration can be formed by placing a horizontal member between the ends of the cable. The horizontal member is in compression since it resists the inwardly directed cable thrusts.

(c) The same configuration can be raised vertically by end compression members.

(d) A more complex truss form can be generated by imaging the entire assembly shown in (c) to be carried by another cable member. Another horizontal compression element is then needed to resist the cable thrusts.

(e) The same process can be repeated to form even more complex trusses. Note that the forces in the vertical and diagonal members increase away from the middle of the truss since increased portions of the external loading are carried. Member sizes could be designed to increase accordingly.

(f) The total force present in the upper chord is greatest at midspan, where the "individual" top chords are actually combined into one member. Chord forces decrease toward either end of the truss. The same is true for the lower tension chord.

FIGURE 4–3 Cable analogy in truss analysis: many complex truss forms can be imagined to be composed of a series of simpler basic cable units. If the directions of the diagonals were all reversed, an arch analogy could be used to analyze the structure. This analogy approach, however, is useful for only a few limited truss forms.

137

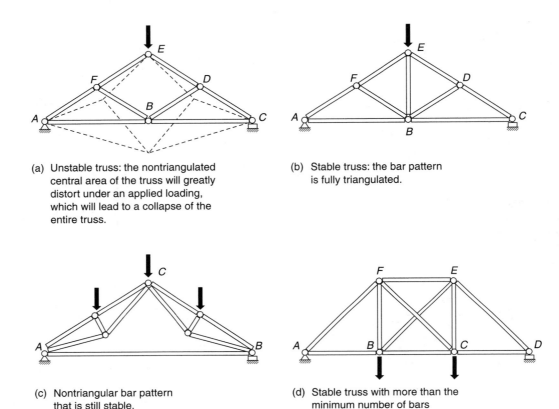

(a) Unstable truss: the nontriangulated central area of the truss will greatly distort under an applied loading, which will lead to a collapse of the entire truss.

(b) Stable truss: the bar pattern is fully triangulated.

(c) Nontriangular bar pattern that is still stable.

(d) Stable truss with more than the minimum number of bars necessary for stability.

FIGURE 4–4 Internal stability. Nontriangulated forms may collapse.

It is possible for a truss to include one or more figures that are not triangles and still be stable. Study Figure 4–4(c), which illustrates a truss of this type. It is made up of groups of rigid triangulated bar patterns connected to form nontriangular, but still stable, figures. The group of triangles between *A* and *C* form a rigid shape, as do those between *B* and *C*. Joint *C* is thus held fixed in relation to joints *A* and *B* in much the same way as occurs in a simpler triangular figure. The group of triangles between *A* and *C* can be thought of as a "member," as can those between *B* and *C*.

In a single truss it is quite possible to have more than the minimum number of bars necessary to achieve a stable structure. One of the two middle diagonal members of the truss shown in Figure 4–4(d) could be considered redundant. *Either* member *BE* or member *CF* could be removed and the resultant configuration would still be stable. Obviously, removing both would cause the structure to become a collapse mechanism.

The importance of determining whether a configuration of bars is stable or unstable cannot be overestimated, since there are few errors more dangerous. Total collapse occurs immediately after an unstable configuration is loaded. As an aid to ascertaining the stability of configurations, expressions have been developed which relate the number of joints present in a truss to the number of bars necessary for stability. A simple basic planar triangle has three bars ($n = 3$) and three joints ($j = 3$). Adding a single new connection beyond the original three requires the addition of two new bars or members. Hence the total number of members *(n)* in a truss having a number of connections *(j)* is given by the following: $n = 3 + 2(j - 3)$. [Three members (3) are originally present and for each new joint ($j - 3$) two new members are added.] This same expression can be rewritten more simply as $n = 2j - 3$. A similar expression can be found for three-dimensional bar networks. A simple tetrahedron is known to be a stable structure. Three bars are required to form each additional new node added to this basic form. There are six bars to begin with and new bars are added at the rate of three for each node beyond the original four. Thus, $n = 6 + 3 (j - 4) = 3j - 6$.

Consider the planar truss shown in Figure 4–4(b). In this case, $j = 6$, so n must be $2(6) - 3$, or 9. This is the minimum number of bars required for stability. Since the truss actually has this number of bars, it is a stable configuration. Generally speaking, fewer bars than are given by this expression will result in an unstable structure; more may indicate a structure with redundant members. The expression, however, is not foolproof and should not be used as a replacement for a careful visual inspection of the truss. The expression is more correctly an indicator of whether or not the internal forces in a structure can be calculated by the equations of statics alone than a predictor of stability. However, it is a useful tool for stability assessments, since it is not possible to calculate the forces in an unstable structure by the equations of statics.

Another aspect of stability is illustrated in Figure 4–5. Truss configurations may be used to stabilize structures with respect to laterally acting loads. Doing so via the use of rigid members is straightforward. In certain cases, however, cables may be used in lieu of rigid members when the cables are subjected to tension forces only. The stability considerations thus far have assumed that all truss members can carry both tension and compression forces equally well. Cable members do not meet this assumption, since they buckle out of the way when subjected to compressive forces. As illustrated, whether tension or compression is developed in a diagonal depends on its orientation. When the loading comes from either direction, either tension or compression may be developed in a diagonal. A structure with a single diagonal cable could be unstable, a fact not predicted by the previous expressions relating the number of joints and members. If cables were to be used, a cross-cable system would be required wherein one cable takes up the horizontal force while the other buckles harmlessly out of the way.

4–3–2   Member Forces: General

This section considers classical analytical methods for determining the nature and distribution of forces in the members of a truss that has known geometrical characteristics and carries known loads. The principle underlying the analytical techniques to be developed is that any structure, *or any elemental portion of any structure,* must be in a state of equilibrium. This principle is the key to common truss analysis techniques. The first step in analyzing a truss of many members is to isolate an elemental portion of the structure and consider the system of forces acting on the element. If some of these forces are known, it is usually possible to calculate the others by use of the basic equations of statics, since it is known that the element must be in equilibrium. These equations are merely formal statements of the notion that any set of forces, including both those that are externally applied and those internally developed, must form a system whose net result is zero.

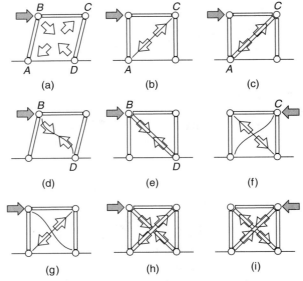

(a) Deformed shape of a simple pin-connected structure without
diagonals. The original distance between points *A* and *C* tends
to be increased and that between *B* and *D* tends to be decreased.

(b) A cable placed between points *A* and *C* will have tension forces
developed in it because it resists the tendency of the two points
to separate. The cable will stabilize the structure and keep it
from collapsing.

(c) A rigid element placed between *A* and *C* will serve the same
function as a cable. Tension forces will be developed in the member.

(d) Placing a cable between points *B* and *D* is useless in keeping the
structure from collapsing. The points move toward one another.
A cable placed between these two points would simply buckle
out of the way. The same thing would happen to the cable in
(b) if the direction of the load were reversed.

(e) Placing a rigid element between points *B* and *D* can stabilize
the structure. Compressive forces would be developed in
the member.

(f) In order to completely stabilize the structure with respect to loads
(g) from either direction, by using cables, it is necessary to use a
crossed-cable system. Under a specific loading, one cable
will operate effectively in stabilizing the structure, while the other
simply buckles out of the way. Reversing the loading causes a
reversal in which member operates effectively.

(h) Crossed rigid elements can also be used, but a certain degree of
(i) redundancy is involved, since a single diagonal is capable of
stabilizing the structure alone with respect to loads in either direction.

FIGURE 4–5 Diagonal bracing.

The extent of the portion of the structure selected for study is not restricted. A whole segment consisting of several members and joints could be considered, or attention could be limited to a single joint or member. To find the internal forces present at a particular location in a structure, it is necessary that the structure be decomposed at least at that point. Figure 4–6(b)–(e) illustrates free-body diagrams for typical elemental pieces of the truss shown in Figure 4–6(a). Each of the pieces shown must be in a state of equilibrium under the action of the force system present on the piece. The force system considered consists of not only any external loads applied to the piece, but also those which are internal to the structure as a whole. The latter are forces developed in members in response to the external loading on the whole truss, which are necessary to maintain the equilibrium of elemental portions of the truss. In considering the equilibrium of an element, it is often useful to think of these as applied forces. At points where the truss is decomposed, internal forces are shown to be equal in magnitude but opposite in sense in adjacent elements. This follows from the discussion in Chapter 2, where we considered Newton's third law: that the forces of action and reaction between elements in contact with each other have the same magnitude and line of action, but are of opposite sense. Since the members of a truss are pin-connected and their ends are free to rotate, only forces, and not moments, can be transmitted from one member to another at the point of connection. Thus, only vector forces are indicated in the free-body diagrams shown. Since only forces and not moments can be transmitted at the connections, the forces at either end of a member must act collinearly (assuming that the member itself is not subjected to external loads) if the member is indeed to be in a state of equilibrium. (See the discussion in Section 2–3–2 on two-force members.) If the member itself is aligned with these forces, it follows that the member is only axially loaded and not subject to bending moments.

4–3–3 Equilibrium of Joints

Equilibrium of Joints within Trusses.   The fact that any portion of any structure must be in a state of equilibrium forms the basis for all truss-analysis techniques directed toward finding forces in truss members. In analyzing a truss by the classical *method of joints,* the truss is considered to be composed of a series of members and joints. Member forces are found by considering the equilibrium of the various joints which are idealized as points. Each of these joints or points must be in a state of equilibrium.

Figure 4–6(e) illustrates a typical truss that has been decomposed into a set of individual linear elements and a set of idealized joints. Free-body diagrams for all the individual members and joints are shown.

By looking at the joints themselves, it can be seen that the system of forces acting on a joint is defined by the bars attached to it and by any external loads that might occur at the location of the joint. As shown in Figure 4–6(e), the forces on a joint are equal and opposite to those on the connecting members. Each joint must be in a state of equilibrium. The system of forces applied to the joint all act through the same point. From an analytical perspective, we are therefore interested in the equilibrium of a point. This requires consideration of translational equilibrium only. Rotational equilibrium is not a concern, since all forces act through a common point and thus produce no rotational effects. This is the key to analysis of trusses by the method of joints. For planar structures, two independent equations of statics exist for a concurrent force system ($\Sigma F_x = 0$ and $\Sigma F_y = 0$). Thus, two unknown forces can be found by application of these

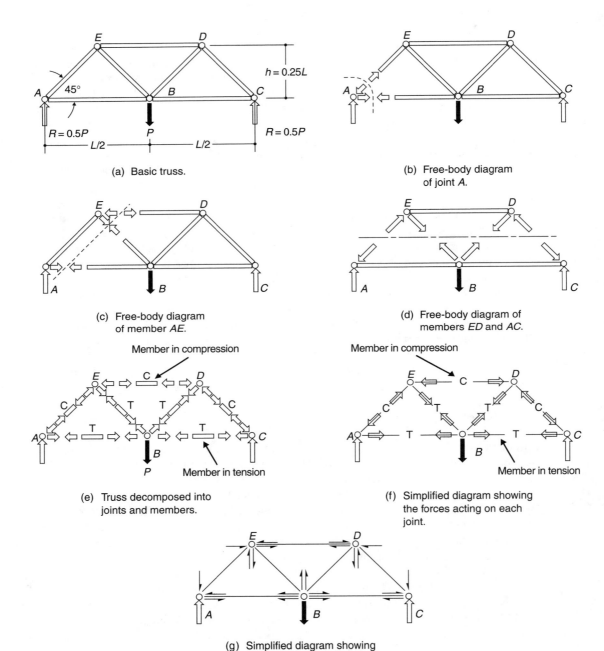

(a) Basic truss.

(b) Free-body diagram of joint A.

(c) Free-body diagram of member AE.

(d) Free-body diagram of members ED and AC.

Member in compression

Member in tension

(e) Truss decomposed into joints and members.

Member in compression

Member in tension

(f) Simplified diagram showing the forces acting on each joint.

(g) Simplified diagram showing the components of the forces acting on the joints.

FIGURE 4–6 Typical free-body diagrams for elemental truss pieces. These diagrams are based on the fundamental principle that any structure, or any portion of any structure, must be in a state of equilibrium. The free-body diagrams in (e), (f), and (g) are used for solution of bar forces by the method of joints.

equations to the complete system of forces represented in the free-body diagram of a joint. If a joint with a maximum of two unknown forces is considered first, it is possible to calculate these forces. The starting point for an analysis of the forces in a truss is often at a support where the reaction has been determined by considering the rigid-body equilibrium of the whole structure. Once all the forces acting on the initial joint have been found (and thus also the forces in the bars attached to the joint), it is possible to proceed to another joint. Since the bar forces previously found can now be treated as known forces, it is convenient to next consider an adjacent joint. The next illustrated example will clarify the process.

A few words should be said about the *arrow convention* used. The arrows illustrate graphically the nature and direction of the forces developed on an element. Thus, the arrows shown on member DE in Figure 4–6(e) are used to indicate that forces causing the element to be in a state of compression are developed as a consequence of the loads on the larger structure. Note that the arrows seemingly subject the member to a compressive force. Conversely, the arrows shown on member BC in Figure 4–6(e) are used to indicate that a state of tension exists in the element. With respect to the joints, these arrows are shown to be equal and opposite. Thus, the action of member DE (in a state of compression) on joint E apparently is one of pushing against the joint. In actuality, a reaction is developed. In an analogous way, the action of member BC (in a state of tension) is seemingly to pull on joint C. It is quite useful to visualize a joint as being in a state of equilibrium when the "pushes" and "pulls" of the members framing into the joint balance each other.

Analysis of bar forces in a truss by the method of joints using hand-calculation techniques is generally straightforward for trusses with few members. For the truss shown in Figure 4–6, the first step is preferably to draw a set of free-body diagrams of the type shown in Figure 4–6(e). Alternatively, simplified diagrams of only the forces on the joints themselves may be drawn [see Figure 4–6(f)]. The equations of translational equilibrium ($\Sigma F_x = 0$ and $\Sigma F_y = 0$) are then applied in turn to each joint. In drawing the free-body diagrams and writing equilibrium equations, it is necessary to assume that an unknown bar force is in a state of either tension or compression. The state of stress assumed can be arbitrary. Whether or not the force is in the state of stress assumed will be evident from the algebraic sign of the force that is found after equilibrium calculations have been made. A positive sign means that the initial assumption was correct, while a negative sign means the converse.

To develop a more intuitive feeling for the force distribution in a structure, it is useful to try to determine correctly whether a member is in tension or compression by a careful qualitative inspection of each joint's equilibrium. Consider joint A in Figure 4–6(e)–(g), where it can be seen qualitatively that the directions assumed are intrinsically reasonable. The reaction is known to act upward. For equilibrium in the vertical direction to obtain, there *must* be a force acting downward. Only force F_{AE} of the two unknown member forces has a component in the vertical direction and would be capable of providing the downward force necessary to balance the upward reaction. Member AB is horizontal and thus has no component in the vertical direction. Force F_{AE} must therefore act in the downward direction shown. Thus, member AE must be in a state of compression. If force F_{AE} acts in the direction shown, it is evident that it has a horizontal component acting toward the left. For the joint to be in horizontal equilibrium, there must be some other force with a horizontal component acting to the right. The reaction acts only vertically and so does not enter into consideration. Force F_{AB} must therefore act to the right if equilibrium in the horizontal direction is to obtain. Member AB is hence in a state of tension. Looking next at joint E and noting that member AE is in compression, it is evident that member EB must be in tension to provide a downward component necessary to balance the upward one of the force in member AE. Member ED is horizontal and thus can contribute no component in the vertical direction. If forces F_{AE} and F_{EB} act in the directions shown, both have a component in the horizontal direction acting to the right. The force in member ED must therefore act to the left to balance the sum of horizontal components of the forces in the two diagonals. Member ED is thus in compression. Since the truss is symmetrical, the state of stress in the remaining members can be found by inspection (member DC must be in compression, BC in tension, and DB in tension). Note that joint B is also apparently in a state of equilibrium. Thus, the state of stress in all the members can be qualitatively determined without resort to calculation. This process is not possible with all trusses, but success is frequent enough to make the attempt worthwhile. This qualitative approach clearly does not yield numerical magnitudes of bar forces. These can be found only by formally writing the equations of equilibrium and solving for the unknown forces. The mathematical process, however, is conceptually similar to the qualitative one described before. Both are based on the principle that any element of a structure must be in equilibrium. To solve for numerical magnitudes, each joint is considered in turn. In the following, the reference axes used are vertical and horizontal.

◆ ◆ **EXAMPLE**

Determine all the member forces in the truss shown in Figure 4–6.

Solution: Draw joint equilibrium diagrams for the whole structure and then consider the equilibrium of each joint in turn. See Figure 4–7.

FIGURE 4–7

Member in compression

P Member in tension

Joint A

Equilibrium in the vertical direction:

$$\Sigma F_y = 0 \uparrow +:$$

$$\underbrace{+ 0.5P}_{\substack{\text{reaction } R_{A_v} \\ \text{in vertical} \\ \text{direction}}} - \underbrace{F_{AE}\sin 45°}_{\substack{\text{vertical component of} \\ \text{force in member } AE; \\ \text{the member is assumed to} \\ \text{be in compression}}} = 0$$

$$F_{AE} = +0.707P \quad \text{(compression)}$$

$R_{A_v} = 0.5P$

Joint A

FIGURE 4–8(a)

Member AE is in compression as assumed, since the sign is positive. See Figure 4–8(a).

Equilibrium in the horizontal direction:
$\Sigma F_x = 0 \rightarrow +:$

$$\underbrace{-F_{AE}\cos 45°}_{\substack{\text{horizontal component}\\\text{of force in member } AE}} + \underbrace{F_{AB}}_{\substack{\text{force in member } AB,\\\text{assumed to be in}\\\text{tension}}} = 0 \quad \therefore \quad F_{AB} = +0.5P \quad \text{(tension)}$$

Member *AB* is in tension as assumed, since the sign is positive. The next step is to proceed to an adjacent joint. Joint *B* involves three unknown forces for which only two independent equations are available for solution. Joint *E*, however, involves only two unknown forces. So go to this joint next.

Joint E

Equilibrium in the vertical direction:
$\Sigma F_y = 0 \uparrow +:$

$$+ F_{AE}\sin 45° - F_{EB}\sin 45° = 0$$

Since F_{AE} is known, F_{BE} can be solved for:

$$F_{EB} = +0.707P \quad \text{(tension)}$$

Since these are the only two forces at this joint having components in the vertical direction, the components must be equal. Since the member angles are the same, the member forces must also be the same. Thus, the force in member *EB* could have been found by inspection. See Figure 4–8(b).

Joint *E*

FIGURE 4–8(b)

Equilibrium in the horizontal direction:
$\Sigma F_x = 0 \rightarrow +:$

$$+ F_{AE}\cos 45° + F_{EB}\cos 45° - F_{ED} = 0$$
$$F_{ED} = 1.0P \quad \text{(compression)}$$

F_{ED} is merely the sum of the horizontal components in the two diagonals. Next proceed to an adjacent joint (either *B* or *D*).

Joint B

Equilibrium in the vertical direction:
$\Sigma F_y = 0 \uparrow +:$

$$F_{EB}\sin 45° + F_{BD}\sin 45° - P = 0$$

Since F_{EB} is known, F_{BD} can be solved for:

$$F_{BD} = 0.707P \quad \text{(tension)}$$

Joint *B*

FIGURE 4–8(c)

A symmetry argument would yield the same result, that is, F_{BD} must be similar to F_{EB} since the truss is geometrically symmetrical and is symmetrically loaded. Otherwise, there is no a priori reason to believe the forces to be the same. See Figure 4–8(c).

Equilibrium in the horizontal direction:
$$\Sigma F_x = 0 \rightarrow +:$$

$$-F_{AB} + F_{BC} - F_{EB}\cos 45° + F_{BD}\cos 45° = 0 \quad \text{or} \quad F_{BC} = 0.5P \quad \text{(tension)}$$

Joint D

Joint D

FIGURE 4–8(d)

Equilibrium in the vertical direction:
$$\Sigma F_y = 0 \uparrow +:$$

$$-F_{BD}\sin 45° + F_{DC}\sin 45° = 0$$
$$F_{DC} = 0.707P \quad \text{(compression)}$$

Equilibrium in the horizontal direction:
$$\Sigma F_x = 0 \rightarrow +:$$

$$+F_{DE} - F_{DB}\cos 45° - F_{DC}\cos 45° = 0$$
$$1.0P - 0.707P \cos 45° - 0.707P \cos 45° = 0$$

All forces are known. The equation sums to zero. This is a good check on the accuracy of calculations. See Figure 4–8(d).

Joint C

Equilibrium in the vertical direction:
$$\Sigma F_y = 0 \uparrow +:$$

$$-F_{DC}\sin 45° + 0.5P = 0 \quad \text{or}$$
$$-0.707P \sin 45° + 0.5P = 0$$

Again, this is a check, since all forces are known. See Figure 4–8(e).

Joint C

FIGURE 4–8(e)

Equilibrium in the horizontal direction:
$$\Sigma F_x = 0 \rightarrow +:$$

$$-F_{BC} + F_{DC}\cos 45° = 0 \quad \text{or}$$
$$0.5P + 0.707P \cos 45° = 0$$

Again this is a check. All member forces are already known. ◆

Analysis Steps.   The following example emphasizes the general sequence of steps in analyzing a truss using the joint equilibrium approach more so than the actual numerical analyses. The analyst should be able to "think through" sequences of this kind before starting the analysis of any kind of truss.

◆ ◆   **EXAMPLE**

Determine the member forces in the cantilevered truss shown in Figure 4–9, using a joint equilibrium approach.

Determine Reactions:

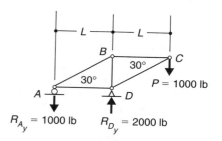

$\Sigma M_A = 0 \quad -(1000)(2L) + R_{D_y}(L) \therefore R_{D_y} = 2000$ lb

$\Sigma F_y = 0 \quad -1000 + R_{A_y} + R_{D_y} = 0 \therefore R_{A_y} = 1000$ lb

$\Sigma F_x = 0 \quad R_{D_x} = 0$

Find Member Forces: Use $\Sigma F_y = 0$ & $\Sigma F_x = 0$ at Each Node:

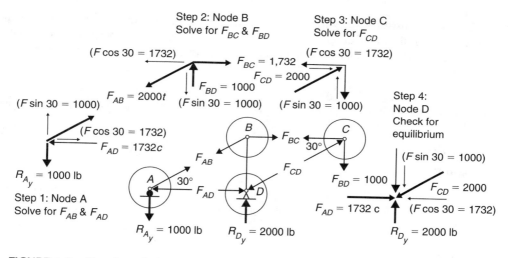

FIGURE 4–9 Steps in analyzing a truss by joint equilibrium methods.

Solution:

As illustrated in Figure 4–9, reactions must first be determined using the techniques presented in Chapter 2. Next, the analyst identifies a node where there are no more than two unknown forces present—typically a support connection where there is a known reaction and two unknown member forces. (If more than three unknowns are present, member forces cannot be found directly by this method.) In the case shown, the starting node connection is A. One then proceeds to an adjacent node with no more than two unknown forces and repeats the process.

Step 1—Node A:

The sense of the forces (tension, compression) in members F_{AB} and F_{AD} are assumed. The force F_{AB} in the diagonal is assumed to be in tension so that it has an upward component to balance the downward reaction. This implies that the force F_{AD} in the lower chord should be in compression so that it has a leftward component to balance the rightward horizontal component of the diagonal force in F_{AB}. The analyst then sums forces in the vertical direction to find F_{AB}. Note that the vertical component of F_{AB} equals the vertical reaction, or $\Sigma F_y = 0: -1000 + F_{AB}\sin 30 = 0$, or $F_{AB} = 2000$ in tension. F_{AD} can be found next since it is equal to the horizontal component of F_{AB}, or $\Sigma F_x = 0: -2000 \cos 30 + F_{AD} = 0$, or $F_{AD} = 1732$ in compression.

Step 2—Node B:
Since F_{AB} is known, forces can be summed in the vertical direction to obtain F_{BD} and in the horizontal direction to obtain F_{BC} (using approaches similar to that described in Step 1).

Step 3—Node C:
Since F_{BC} is known, forces can be summed in the vertical direction to obtain F_{CD}. All member forces are now known.

Step 4—Node D:
Since all member forces are known, summing forces in the vertical and horizontal directions provides a good calculation check. If balances are not obtained, an error has been made during earlier steps. ◆

Complex Trusses. Many trusses have geometries that render the analysis procedure more difficult. The following example involves solving simultaneous equations since individual equilibrium expressions cannot be solved directly. A way around this complexity is then presented.

◆ ◆ **EXAMPLE**

Determine the forces in members F_{FC} and F_{FG} in the truss shown in Figure 4–10. Start at the right support, where the reaction is known.

Solution:

Joint E

$$\Sigma F_y = 0 \qquad -F_{EF}\sin 30° + 3P/4 = 0 \quad \text{or} \quad F_{EF} = 1.5P \qquad \text{(compression)}$$
$$\Sigma F_y = 0 \qquad F_{EF}\cos 30° - F_{DE} = 0 \quad \text{or} \quad F_{DE} = 1.3P \qquad \text{(tension)}$$

Joint D

$$\Sigma F_x = 0 \qquad F_{DE} - F_{CD} = 0 \quad \text{or} \quad F_{CD} = 1.3P \qquad \text{(tension)}$$
$$\Sigma F_y = 0 \qquad -P + F_{FD} = 0 \quad \text{or} \quad F_{FD} = 1.0P \qquad \text{(tension)}$$

Joint F

$$\Sigma F_y = 0 \qquad -F_{FD} + F_{EF}\sin 30° - F_{FG}\sin 30° + F_{FC}\sin 30° = 0$$
$$\Sigma F_x = 0 \qquad -F_{EF}\cos 30° + F_{FG}\cos 30° + F_{FC}\cos 30° = 0$$

F_{FD} and F_{EF} are known. Each equation still involves two unknown forces (F_{FG} and F_{FC}). Solving the equations simultaneously yields

$$F_{FG} = 0.5P \qquad \text{(compression)}$$
$$F_{FC} = 1.0P \qquad \text{(tension)}$$

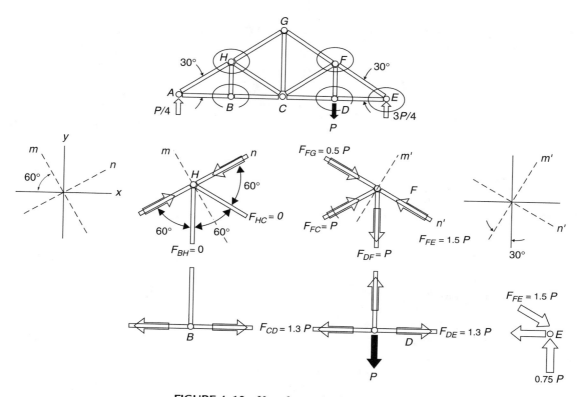

FIGURE 4–10   Use of rotated reference axes.

The need to solve two equations simultaneously can be obviated by using a rotated reference axis system $(m'n')$ rather than the traditional vertical and horizontal (xy) system. Thus, with respect to $m'n'$:

$$\Sigma F_{m'} = 0 \qquad\qquad -F_{FD}\cos 30° + F_{FC}\cos 30° = 0 \qquad F_{FC} = 1.0P$$
$$\Sigma F_{n'} = 0 \qquad F_{FD}\sin 30° + F_{FC}\sin 30° - F_{EF} + F_{FG} = 0 \qquad F_{FG} = 0.5P$$

An easier method of analysis for this kind of problem is discussed in a subsequent example using the equilibrium of sections approach (see Section 4–3–4).   ◆

Simplifying Conditions.   Occasionally, truss analysis by the method of joints can be facilitated by paying attention to some special conditions that frequently arise. One of these is the appearance of *zero-force* members. Consider the truss shown in Figure 4–11 and refer directly to joint B. By inspecting the equilibrium of this joint in the vertical direction, it is possible to determine by observation that there is no internal force at all developed in member BI. There is no applied external load and members BC and BA are horizontal, having no component in the vertical direction. If there were any force in member BI, the joint would not be in equilibrium; hence, there can be no force present in member BI. It is a zero-force member. The same is true for the force in member HC. By isolating joint J and considering equilibrium in both the horizontal and vertical directions, it can be seen that both members framing

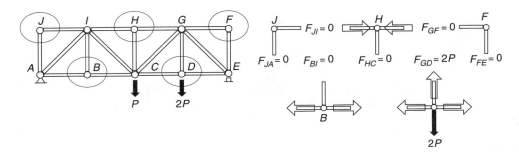

FIGURE 4–11   Simplifying conditions in truss analysis.

into it (*JA* and *JI*) are also zero-force members. The same is true of the members framing into joint *F*.

This approach of picking out selected members and joints for quick determination of forces also can be applied to some joints with external loads applied. Isolating joint *D* (see Figure 4–11), inspection of equilibrium in the vertical direction indicates that the force developed in member *DG* must be equal and opposite to the applied load. Thus, member *DG* carries a force of 2*P* and is in tension.

As a further example of simplifying conditions, consider the truss shown in Figure 4–10 that was analyzed previously. Inspection of joint *B* indicates that member *BH* must be a zero-force member. This implies that member *HC* is also a zero-force member. This can most easily be seen by thinking in terms of the rotated axis system shown in Figure 4–10 and considering equilibrium in the *m* direction. Member *HC* cannot have any force in it if joint *H* is to be in equilibrium in this direction (as it must be in any direction). Inspection of joint *D* indicates that *DF* must carry a tension force of *P*. This implies that member *FC* carries a compressive force of *P*. Again, this is most easily seen by thinking in terms of a rotated axis system, as indicated in Figure 4–10. Since F_{DF} is shown to be equal to *P* in tension, the component of this force in the *m'* direction must be balanced by a similar component in member *FC*. The members make a similar angle to the *m'* axis, so it follows that the forces must be numerically the same if the components are the same; thus, $F_{FC} = P$.

Simplifying conditions of the type described facilitates calculations enormously. But the technique is most valuable in the development of a more intuitive understanding of the force distributions present in a truss.

Graphic Statics.   The truss in Figure 4–6 can be also analyzed in an alternative way by using graphic statics techniques based on joint equilibrium. These approaches are based on the tip-to-tail graphic techniques discussed in Section 2–2–4 where reactions and member forces are graphically depicted to scale. These approaches were once the basic method used for truss analysis prior to the advent of computers, and are still favored by many because of their basic elegance and visualization advantages. Nonetheless, keep in mind that these kinds of graphic approaches are often difficult to apply to highly complex trusses and are of limited usefulness for indeterminate trusses (see Section 4–3–6). Graphical solutions techniques are illustrated in Figure 4–12. Keep in mind that a closed tip-to-tail polygon drawn for any particular node means that it is in translatory equilibrium in the *x* and *y* directions.

Typical "tip-to-tail" diagrams

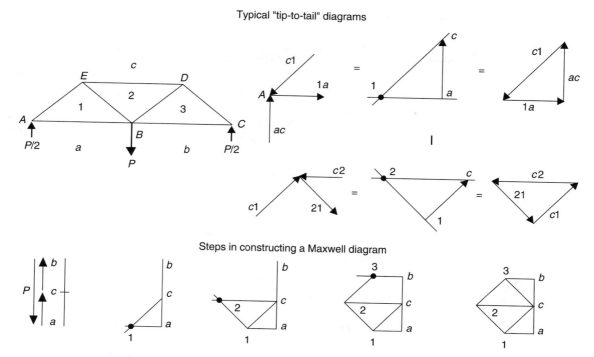

FIGURE 4–12   Graphical method of analysis.

In using this approach, it is best to first redefine members and loads in terms of adjacent spaces, as shown in Figure 4–12. Only spaces separated by forces are designated. The load P becomes ba, the reaction R_{A_v} becomes ac, the force F_{AE} becomes $c1$, and so forth. Using this nomenclature, typical underlying polygons for the tip-to-tail approach are illustrated in Figure 4–9 on the upper-right side. For joint A, the known reaction ac is laid off to scale. Proceeding clockwise around the joint, the directions of the unknown forces in $c1$ and $a1$ are drawn through c and a, respectively. The location of point 1 is necessarily defined at the intersection of the lines of action of these two forces so that a closed polygon (necessary for equilibrium) is formed. Unknown forces in $c1$ and $1a$ can be measured directly. With $c1$ known, a similar process can be repeated at joint E and other joints.

As shown in the lower half of Figure 4–12, this whole process can be streamlined in a composite diagram by first drawing a force polygon for the reactions and loading (simply a vertical line) and drawing the diagram for A. Since $c1$ is common in the solution of both joints A and E, a composite diagram for A and E may next be drawn, as illustrated. Proceeding to joint B on the composite diagram, point 3 is located by extending lines of action of 23 and $b3$ from known points. Proceeding to joint D, the process is repeated to form the final diagram. With practice, diagrams of this type may be drawn directly without the intermediate steps shown at the top in Figure 4–12 to obtain the last diagram in the series, which is often called a *Maxwell diagram* after its developer, the English engineer James Maxwell. Forces may be measured directly from this scaled drawing. The sense of each of the forces may be determined by looking at the forces in sequence around any particular node, observing the same sequence of letters on the Maxwell diagram, and keeping in mind the tip-to-tail graphic convention that underlies these diagrams. On the last diagram, force *ac* is the left upward reaction (at node A). The top of line *ac* is thus the head of the force arrow representing the reaction. Line *c*1 on the last diagram represents the force in the left diagonal and its tail is connected to the head of *ac*. Thus, it is acting downward and to the left. Looking at node A on the truss diagram, this means it is pushing on the joint and is thus in compression. On the Maxwell diagram, line 1*a* represents the force on the lower left chord member. Its tail is connected to the head of the force in member AE (*c*1). Looking at node A on the truss diagram, this means it is pulling on the joint and is thus in tension. Note that *ca, c*1, and 1*a* thus form a closed tip-to-tail polygon, which means that the joint is in equilibrium. The sense of the member forces at other joints could be similarly determined.

4-3-4 Equilibrium of Sections

In our discussion of the equilibrium of joints, the elemental portions of the truss defined for equilibrium considerations were the joints themselves but *any* portion of a structure must be in a state of equilibrium. It follows that the limits of the portion considered can be extended to a complete subassembly consisting of several joints and members. Consideration of the equilibrium of a larger subassembly can then be the vehicle used for finding unknown bar forces. This concept of considering the equilibrium of a portion of a structure larger than a point is a very powerful one and will form the basis for the analysis and design of many structures other than the truss forms currently under discussion.

Solution of bar forces by this approach is best illustrated by example. Again consider the truss shown in Figures 4–6 and 4–13. Assume that you wish to know the forces in members *ED, BD,* and *BC.* The truss is first considered to consist of two subassemblies. Free-body diagrams for these subassemblies are shown in Figure 4–13. The internal set of forces shown is developed as a consequence of the external loading of the whole structure and serves to maintain the equilibrium of the elemental subassemblies of the truss. The complete force system acting on a subassembly, consisting of internal forces and any external forces present, must form a system whose net result is zero. Both translational equilibrium and rotational equilibrium must be considered, since the forces acting on the body form a coplanar, but nonconcurrent and nonparallel, force system (see Section 2–3).

Before solving mathematically for the bar forces in the example, by formal application of the equations of statics, it is useful to try to determine by qualitative inspection the senses of the member forces. Study equilibrium requirements in the subassembly shown to the left in Figure 4–13, for example. It can be seen that the force in member *BD* must act upward as shown to supply the vertical component necessary for balancing the difference between the upward reaction of 0.5*P* and the downward force of *P* acting on the subassembly (a net of 0.5*P* acting downward). Thus, the member must be in a state of tension. Since the subassembly to the left must be in rotational equilibrium also, the moment produced by the external forces must be exactly balanced by the moment developed by the internal forces (see Figure 4–13). By summing moments about point *B*, it can be seen that the sense of the force in member *DE* must be in the direction shown if moment equilibrium is to occur about point *B*. Remember that the sum of the moments produced by *all* forces must be zero about *any* point. Hence,

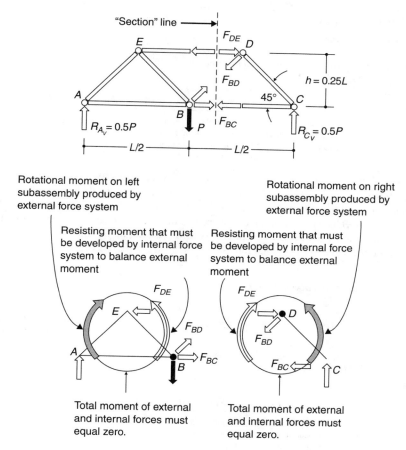

FIGURE 4–13 Free-body diagrams for solution of forces in members F_{ED}, F_{BD}, and F_{BC} by the method of sections.

member DE must be in a state of compression. The forces shown on the left subassembly are equal and opposite on the right subassembly. Since the right subassembly must also be in translatory and rotational equilibrium, the sense of the force in member BC can be found by summing moments about point D. For moment equilibrium to obtain about this point, force F_{BC} must act in the direction shown and so be in a state of tension. Thus, the states of stress in the unknown bar forces can be qualitatively determined. The mathematical process for determining the numerical magnitudes of the forces is conceptually similar to the process just described.

◆ ◆ **EXAMPLE**

Determine the forces in members DE, BD, and BC of the truss shown in Figure 4–13.

Solution:

Left Subassembly

Translatory equilibrium in the vertical direction:
$$\Sigma F_y = 0 + \uparrow:$$

$$+0.5P \underbrace{\quad}_{} - \underbrace{P}_{} + \underbrace{F_{BD}\sin 45°}_{} = 0 \quad \therefore \quad F_{BD} = 0.707P \qquad \text{(tension)}$$

$$\begin{array}{ccc}
\text{reaction } R_{A_v} & \text{external} & \text{vertical component of} \\
\text{in vertical} & \text{load} & \text{force in member } BD; \text{ the} \\
\text{direction} & & \text{member is assumed to be} \\
& & \text{in tension}
\end{array}$$

Member *BD* is in tension, as assumed, since the sign is positive. We could next try $\Sigma F_x = 0$, but this would involve two unknown forces (F_{ED} and F_{BC}), and the equation could not be solved directly. Try to find an equation involving only a single unknown force by considering moment equilibrium about a point. By selecting point *B*, one unknown force, F_{BC}, acts through the moment center and consequently falls out of the moment equation (since its moment arm is zero), leaving an equation involving only the remaining unknown force and known external forces.

Moment equilibrium about point B:
$$\Sigma M_B = 0: \oplus$$

$$-\underbrace{(0.5P}_{} \times \underbrace{0.5L)}_{} + \underbrace{(F_{ED}}_{} \times \underbrace{h)}_{} = 0 \quad \text{or} \quad -0.25PL + F_{ED}(0.25L) = 0$$

$$\begin{array}{cccc}
\text{reaction} & \text{moment} & \text{member} & \text{moment} \\
R_{A_v} & \text{arm} & \text{force} & \text{arm}
\end{array}$$

or

$$\underbrace{0.25PL}_{} = \underbrace{F_{ED}(0.25L)}_{} \quad \therefore \quad F_{ED} = +P \qquad \text{(compression)}$$

$$\begin{array}{cc}
\text{"applied" moment} & \text{"resisting" moment} \\
\text{produced by ex-} & \text{developed by in-} \\
\text{ternal forces} & \text{ternal forces}
\end{array}$$

The member is in compression, as assumed. The step where the moment developed by the internal forces is shown equal to that produced by the external forces is not actually necessary. It does, however, represent a fundamentally important way of looking at structural behavior and is important for design purposes. This way of looking at structures will be discussed further in Section 4–3–8. Now that two of the forces acting on the subassembly are known, the remaining unknown force can readily be found by application of the last unused equation of statics: $\Sigma F_x = 0$.

Translatory equilibrium in the horizontal direction:
$$\Sigma F_x = 0 \mp:$$

$$-F_{ED} + F_{BD}\cos 45° + F_{BC} = 0 \quad \text{or} \quad -P + (0.707P)\cos 45° + F_{BC} = 0$$
$$\therefore \quad F_{BC} = +0.5P \qquad \text{(tension)}$$

Member *BC* is in tension, as assumed. All unknown forces acting on the left subassembly have now been found. These forces act in an equal and opposite way on the right subassembly. As is obvious, it should also be in equilibrium. It is good to check this.

Right Subassembly

Moment equilibrium about point D:
  $\Sigma M_D = 0 \oplus$:

$$-(F_{BC} \times 0.25L) + (0.5P \times 0.25L) = 0$$
$$-(0.5P \times 0.25L) + (0.5P \times 0.25L) = 0 \qquad \text{Check!}$$

Translatory equilibrium in the vertical direction:
  $\Sigma F_y = 0 + \uparrow$:

$$-F_{BD}\sin 45° + 0.5P = 0$$
$$-0.707P \sin 45° + 0.5P = 0 \qquad \text{Check!}$$

Translatory equilibrium in the horizontal direction:
  $\Sigma F_x = 0 \mp$:

$$-F_{BC} - F_{BD}\cos 45° + F_{ED} = 0$$
$$-0.5P - 0.707P \sin 45° + 1.0P = 0 \qquad \text{Check!}$$

The right-hand subassembly is in a state of translational and rotational equilibrium.   ◆

The approach just illustrated can be used to find member forces in planar trusses when no more than three unknowns are involved, since there are only three independent equations of statics available for analyzing the equilibrium of planar rigid bodies. Care must be taken in isolating subassemblies so that only three unknowns are present. The decomposition shown in Figure 4–6(d), for example, is perfectly valid, and each subassembly is indeed in a state of translatory and rotational equilibrium. However, the decomposition is not useful from an analytical viewpoint, since there are more unknown forces acting on each segment than could be solved for by using the basic equations of statics.

The descriptive name associated with this approach, the *method of sections,* stems from one particular way of looking at how subassemblies are separated from the remainder of the truss. An imaginary section line is passed through the truss, dividing it into two segments. It actuality there is no implication that the section line must be straight. The method of joints could quite easily be thought of in terms of passing a section line around each joint [see Figure 4–6(b)]. Both can be interchangeably used in analyzing trusses. The method of joints is often considered preferable for use when all the bar forces in a truss must be determined. The method of sections is particularly useful when only a limited number of forces must be found.

◆ ◆   **EXAMPLE**

Determine the forces in members *FG* and *FC* in the truss shown in Figure 4–14 (the same truss previously analyzed by the method of joints).

Solution: For determination of the force in member *FC*, the truss is decomposed as shown in Figure 4–14(b). Point *E* is selected as the moment center as a matter of convenience, since the unknown forces

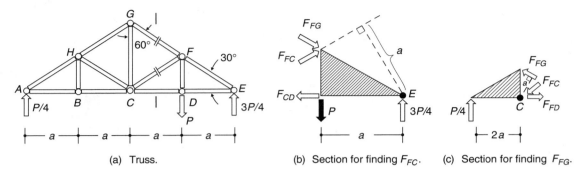

(a) Truss.   (b) Section for finding F_{FC}.   (c) Section for finding F_{FG}.

FIGURE 4–14 Truss analysis by the method of sections.

F_{FG} and F_{CD} pass through the point and hence would not enter into the moment equation because their moment arms are zero.

$\Sigma M_E = 0$:

$$-F_{FC}(a) + P(a) = 0 \quad \text{or} \quad F_{FC} = 1.0P \quad \text{(compression)}$$

To find the force in member *FG*, it is more convenient to decompose the structure as shown in Figure 4–14(c) and use point *C* as a moment center.

$\Sigma M_c = 0$:

$$+ F_{FG}(a) - \left(\frac{P}{4}\right)(2a) = 0 \quad \text{or} \quad F_{FG} = 0.5P \quad \text{(compression)}$$

The results are obviously the same as obtained by the method of joints but are found in a considerably more direct way. ◆

◆ ◆ **EXAMPLE**

Determine the forces in members *MN, ML,* and *KL* of the truss shown in Figure 4–15(a).

Solution: A section line is first passed through these three members and the truss is decomposed into subassemblies. The left subassembly is shown in Figure 4–15(a).

Left Subassembly

$\Sigma F_y = 0 + \uparrow$:

$$+ 3.5P - P - P - P - F_{ML}\sin 45° = 0 \qquad \therefore \ F_{ML} = 0.707P \quad \text{(compression)}$$

$\Sigma M_m = 0$:

$$-(3.5P \times 3a) + P(2a) + (Pa) + F_{KL}(a) = 0 \qquad \therefore \ F_{KL} = 7.5P \quad \text{(compression)}$$

$\Sigma F_x = 0 \ \mp$:

$$-F_{KL} + F_{MN} - F_{ML}\cos 45° = 0$$
$$-7.5P + F_{MN} - 0.707P \cos 45° = 0 \qquad \therefore \ F_{MN} = 8.0P \quad \text{(tension)} \qquad ◆$$

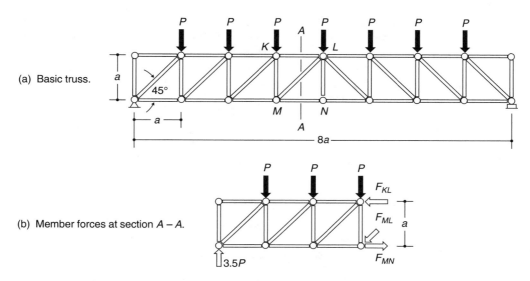

FIGURE 4-15   Solution of bar forces by the method of sections.

Finding the same forces in the last example by the method of joints would be a long and tedious process, since each joint would have to be considered in turn from one of the ends. The example also illustrates some very important points about forces in a truss. The three member forces found are clearly dependent on the overall geometry and dimensions of the truss and loading condition, and on the local geometry of the three members themselves. Thus, the force in the top chord (member *KL*) is directly related to the height of the truss. If the height were doubled, the member force would be halved, or vice versa. The force in the diagonal is also related to the height. Increasing the truss height would decrease the force in the diagonal, since the sine of the angle involved is increased. The force in the lower chord would also decrease as the truss height is increased. It is very important to note that these forces, which are sensitive to the local geometry at the section considered, are *independent* of many other physical aspects of the truss. Insofar as these three forces are concerned, it makes no difference whether the remainder of the diagonals have the original orientation or an alternative orientation. Indeed, the geometry of the truss at other sections could be drastically altered, and the three forces would not be affected as long as *their* local geometry remained constant.

The discussion above illustrates the power of the method of sections as a conceptual tool. The observations presented could have been made through analysis by the method of joints, but doing so would have been very cumbersome.

4-3-5   Shears and Moments in Trusses

At this point it is useful to introduce a particular way of looking at how trusses carry loads, which is of fundamental importance and will prove useful in designing them. This involves studying a truss in terms of sets of externally applied forces and moments and responding sets of internal resisting forces and moments. *A general study of shears and moments has already been presented in Section 2–4–2. The following section focuses on applications of these concepts to truss analysis.*

Consider the truss shown in Figure 4–16 and the diagram of the portions of the structure to the left of section *A–A*. Note that as yet the diagram in Figure 4–16(b) is *not* an equilibrium diagram, since only the set of *external* forces, consisting of applied loads and the reaction at the support, are shown. Study of this diagram indicates that insofar as translation in the vertical direction is concerned, the *net* effect of this set of forces is to produce an *upward* acting force of 0.5*P* [see Figure 4–16(c)]. This net force is often referred to as the *external shear force* (V_E). A study of the rotational effects about *A–A* produced by this set of forces reveals that the net effect is a rotational moment of 4*Pa* [see Figure 4–16(c)]. This net moment is often referred to as the *external bending moment* (M_E) present at the section. The descriptive term *bending* comes from the tendency of this net external moment to produce bowing in the whole truss.

The function of the set of forces developed internally in members of the truss can now be discussed in terms of the external shear force and bending moment present at the section. For vertical equilibrium to obtain in the portion of the structure shown, a set of internal forces must be developed in the structure whose net effect is a resisting force of an equal magnitude but opposite sense to the applied external shear force. This net force is referred to as the *internal resisting shear force* (V_R) [see Figure 4–16(d)]. In a like manner, the net rotational effect of this set of internal forces must be to provide *an internal resisting moment* (M_R) equal in magnitude but opposite in sense to the external bending moment (or applied moment) present on the portion of the structure considered, so that the *total* rotational moment is zero, as it must be for equilibrium [see Figure 4–16(d)]. Thus, $M_E = M_R$, or $M_E - M_R = 0$.

In the structure shown (with respect to equilibrium in the vertical direction), the top and bottom chords cannot provide any of the internal resisting shear force necessary to balance the external shear force because they are horizontal and can have no force components in the vertical direction. The entire resisting shear force must be provided by the vertical component of the force in the diagonal member. This way of looking at the structure could also be used as either a way of calculating the force in the member or checking the force found by some other method. With respect to moment equilibrium, there must be a couple ($\leftrightarrows$) developed by the set of internal forces to provide an equilibrating moment to the applied external bending moment. As indicated in Figure 4–16(e), the horizontal forces in the chord members act with the horizontal component of the force in the diagonal to provide the couple which balances the external bending moment.

Looking at the behavior of structures this way, it is easier to see that the basic structural function of *any* configuration of bars used in a truss is to provide a resistance to the external shears and moments present. This, then, is the *thread of similarity* which conceptually ties structures together. The exact way different structures respond to the same loading may vary, but each provides (and *must* provide) the same internal resisting shears and moments no matter what truss configuration is used. This way of thinking about the behavior of trusses is also important in a design situation. One must determine the structural configuration which most efficiently provides the necessary set of internal resisting shears and moments for given external shear forces and bending moments.

4–3–6 Statically Indeterminate Trusses

In all the trusses previously discussed, it was possible to calculate member forces by application of the equations of statics. Trusses of this type are often referred to as being *statically determinate*. There exist other truss structures where this is not possible because of the number of

(a) Truss.

(b) External force system acting on left subassembly.

(c) External bending moment and shearing force equivalent to the external force system acting on left subassembly.

$\Sigma F_y: -P - P + 2.5P = 0.5P$

External shear (V_E)

$\Sigma M_x: +2a(2.5P) - a(P) = 4Pa$

External moment (M_E)

(d) Equilibrium diagram for left subassembly: an internal resisting shear force (V_R) and internal resisting moment (M_R) is developed in the structure for equilibrium.

(e) The internal resisting shear force (V_R) and internal resisting moment (M_R) are developed through the action of the forces in the bars.

(f) Equilibrium diagrams of left and right subassemblies in terms of internal and external force systems.

(g) Equilibrium diagrams of left subassembly in terms of equivalent internal and external shears and moments. The sum of shear and moment sets on each subassembly must be zero.

$M_E = 4Pa \qquad M_R = 4Pa$

$V_E = 0.5P \quad V_R = 0.5P$

FIGURE 4–16 Shear and moment in trusses. These diagrams illustrate the development of shearing forces and moments at a section in a truss through the action of the external force system acting on the truss. A resisting set of shears and moments is developed at the same section through the action of the internal forces developed in the bars.

external supports or number of truss bars. Consider the planar truss shown in Figure 4–17. It is not possible to calculate the forces in the middle members by the equations of statics alone, since there are four unknown bar forces and only three equations of statics available to use in solving for these unknowns. The calculation difficulties are evident when one considers equilibrium in the vertical direction for the left subassembly. Thus:

$$\Sigma F_y = 0 + \uparrow:$$

$$+ (P/3) - F_{BE}\sin \theta - F_{FC}\sin \theta = 0 \quad \text{or} \quad F_{BE}\sin \theta + F_{FC}\sin \theta = P/3$$

Clearly, this equation cannot be solved. Applying the other equations of equilibrium for a planar rigid body, $\Sigma F_x = 0$, $\Sigma M_0 = 0$, will not yield equations that could be solved, either alone or simultaneously. Structures of this type are referred to as being *statically indeterminate internally*. It should be emphasized that all the principles of statics discussed are still valid and applicable in structures of this type. It is still true that any elemental portion of the truss is in translational and rotational equilibrium ($\Sigma F_x = 0$, $\Sigma F_y = 0$, and $\Sigma M_0 = 0$ still apply) but some other method must be used to calculate member forces. One way to interpret the physical meaning of a structure being statically indeterminate, however, is that the senses and magnitudes of the internal forces present in members of the structure are dependent on the actual physical properties of the members themselves. Stiffer members generally carry greater internal forces than do less stiff members. The matrix analysis procedures discussed in Section 4–3–10 and Appendix 12 are frequently used to analyze trusses of this type. The truss can still be simply analyzed, however, if the crossed diagonals are made using cables (see the following discussion).

4–3–7 Use of Special Tensile Members: Cables

In all the trusses discussed previously it was tacitly assumed that an individual truss member was capable of carrying the tensile or compressive force generated in the member. Other types of members, however, can be useful. One such member is commonly referred to as a *cable,* which is capable of resisting tensile forces only. Physically, members of this type are typically thin steel rods or actual wound cables. Such members cannot resist compressive forces but are often used when a truss member is known from analysis to always be in a state of tension and need never carry compressive forces. Members carrying only tension forces can have much smaller cross sections than those carrying compressive forces and are often considered desirable. A cable

FIGURE 4–17 Truss that is statically indeterminate internally. The magnitudes of the forces present depend on the physical properties of the members.

could potentially be used wherever analysis has demonstrated that a tension force is present in a member.

One of the crucial issues in using cables as elements in a truss is the question of *stability*. The repetitive element in the truss is no longer a basic triangular shape composed of rigid members, inherently stable under any loading condition, but is a special shape, stable only under particular loading conditions. Care must be taken to assure that the cable member, intended to carry tensile forces only, is never expected to carry compressive forces. *Stress reversals* of this type would usually cause the whole truss to become unstable. Stress reversals in members are often caused by a change in the location of the external loads applied to the whole structure. With respect to the truss shown in Figure 4–18(a–1), note that if the load were applied at joint *E* rather than joint *F*, the force distribution in the truss would be as shown in Figure 4–18(b–1). If an attempt were made to use the cable arrangement shown in Figure 4–18(a–2) to carry a force at *E* as indicated, the truss would become unstable and collapse under the second loading condition. This is because member *BE*, previously in tension and thus designed as a cable, would have to be capable of resisting a compressive force when the truss is subjected to its new loading. Clearly, it cannot, and the member would "buckle" out of the way. The truss would consequently become unstable and begin collapsing, as indicated in Figure 4–18(b–2). Potential instability due to stress reversals is thus a critical issue in using cables in trusses. If cables are used, it is mandatory to review every possible way that the truss could be loaded, to determine if a cable member is potentially subjected to compressive forces. If it is, a cable cannot be used at this location and a member capable of carrying compressive loads must be used.

In some specific situations, however, an alternative to designing a member capable of carrying either tension or compressive loads is to use additional cables. In the set of diagrams shown in Figure 4–18 it is evident that if a *crossed-cable* system is used in the middle [see Figure 4–18(e)], the truss illustrated is stable under varying load conditions. When the external load is at joint *F*, the cable between *B* and *E* acts in tension and makes the truss stable, while the cable between *F* and *C* merely buckles (harmlessly) out of the way and carries no load. The converse is true when the external load is at *E*. Thus, crossed cables are useful in assuring the stability of trusses under varying load conditions. The same truss appears to be statically indeterminate (as described earlier in this section), but in this case it can still be simply analyzed via basic statics. Any cable is assumed to buckle harmlessly out of the way when subjected to compressive tendencies and is thus known a priori to be a zero-force member. Hence, the truss reverts back to a statically determinate form.

4–3–8   Space Trusses

The stability inherent in triangulated patterns of bars is also present when extended into the third dimension. Whereas the simple triangle is the basic repetitive element in planar trusses, the tetrahedron is the basic repetitive element in three-dimensional trusses.

The principles developed for analyzing planar trusses are generally applicable to space trusses. Again, stability is a primary consideration. The presence of nontriangulated patterns is a sign that each joint in turn should be looked at closely to see if it will always maintain the same fixed geometric relationship to other joints when a load is applied to any point on the structure.

The forces developed in the members of a space truss can be found by consideration of the equilibrium in space of elemental portions of the space truss. Obviously, the equations of

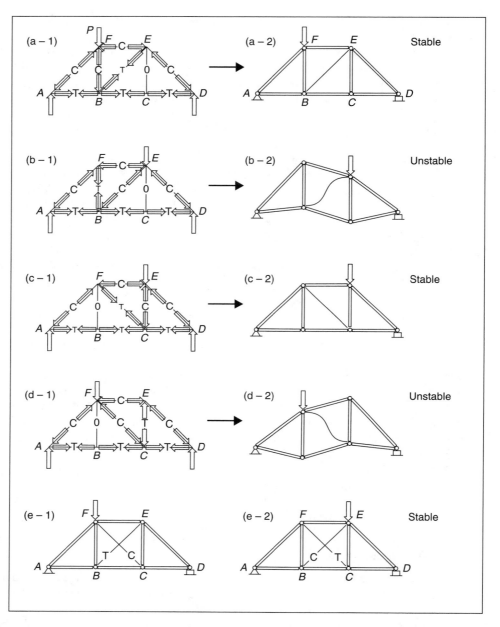

FIGURE 4–18 Cables in trusses: effect of changing load conditions and the use of crossed cables. Parts (a) and (c) illustrate trusses stable under a particular loading condition. Parts (b) and (d) illustrate the instability that could occur if loading conditions are changed. Part (e) illustrates the use of crossed cables as a device for making a truss using cables stable under several loading conditions.

statics used must be the *full* set of equations developed in Section 2–3 for the equilibrium of a rigid body in three dimensions, rather than the simplified set for the equilibrium of a rigid body in two dimensions used in the previous section on planar truss analysis. The relevant equations are

$$\Sigma F_x = 0, \quad \Sigma F_y = 0, \quad \Sigma F_z = 0 \quad \text{and} \quad \Sigma M_x = 0, \quad \Sigma M_y = 0, \quad \Sigma M_z = 0$$

While straightforward, application of these equations by hand is usually tedious due to the large number of joints and members typically present in a large three-dimensional truss and will not be undertaken in this text. Figure 4–19, however, illustrates the results of such an analysis for

(a) Typical three-dimensional configuration.

(b) Any joint must be in a state of translatory and rotational equilibrium. Thus, $\Sigma F_x = 0$, $\Sigma F_y = 0$, and $\Sigma F_z = 0$.

Tension ————
Compression ————
Zero force – – – – –

(c) Any larger segment must be in a state of translatory and rotational equilibrium. With respect to moment equilibrium, for example, the external moment (M_E) generated at a section must be exactly balanced by an internal resisting moment (M_R) provided by member forces.

(d) Force distribution in truss.

FIGURE 4–19   Three-dimensional bar configurations.

a simple configuration. Computer formulations are usually used to analyze more complex configurations (see Section 4–3–10).

4–3–9 Joint Rigidity

In all the previous discussions it has been assumed that the trusses studied were modeled according to the assumptions stated in the opening sections of this chapter. All joints between bars have been considered to be idealized pin connections. In many cases, actually making a connection may be neither possible nor desirable. If the actual joint conditions are such that the ends of the bars are not free to rotate, local bending moments may develop in the bars in addition to any axial loads present. If these bending moments were too large, the member would have to be designed so that it would still be safe under the action of the combined axial and bending stresses. The magnitudes of bending stresses typically induced by rigid joints are rarely more than 10 to 20% of the axial stresses normally developed. For preliminary design purposes these secondary bending stresses are often simply ignored, but at some later point in the design process they would be reconsidered. One positive effect of increasing joint rigidity is to increase the overall resistance of the truss to deflections. Making joints rigid is rarely an influential factor affecting the general shaping of the final truss.

4–3–10 Computer-Aided Methods of Analysis

The numerical analysis of multimember trusses by hand calculation can be tedious. In recent years, there have been a number of analytical methods developed for truss analysis that are particularly suitable for use with a computer. Currently, many formulations exist wherein a user can input the geometry of a truss structure (often using a graphical interface), specify loads on nodes, and quickly get a range of analytical results, including forces in all members and nodal displacements. The latter can be used to create overall deflection patterns. Both statically determinate and indeterminate trusses can be analyzed. Typically, the user must clearly specify node locations, the geometry of how members connect to nodes, and types and directions of loading conditions. Normally, an initial estimate must be made of member sizes and materials (this information is obviously necessary for indeterminate structures and for calculating truss deflections).

The analytical approaches that underlie these computer-based formulations are discussed extensively in Appendix 12. Briefly, there are two primary approaches used. One approach uses what are typically called *force methods*. In force methods, member forces are treated as primary unknown values. A brief inspection of the method of joints, for example, reveals that a set of equations could be written for the vertical and horizontal equilibrium of each node of a truss under the action of impinging member forces. This complete set of equations could be solved to find forces in individual members. Force methods, however, have been largely replaced by what are typically called *displacement* or *stiffness* methods. In displacement or stiffness methods, the actual displacements of the nodes are treated as the primary unknowns. Displacement approaches tend to be more powerful and robust than force approaches. They can be used indistinguishably for determinate and indeterminate trusses. In particular, *matrix displacement methods* are in wide use and underlie many commonly used analysis programs. Appendix 12 discusses matrix displacement methods in more detail. The reader should keep in mind that most of these formulations are analytical only. They do not tell a user how to design a truss, but rather analyze a given configuration.

Partial listing of
tabulated results

Member	$P_x{}'$
1	−0.433
2	0.500
3	0.500
4	−0.433
5	−1.300
6	−1.300
7	0.500
8	0.000
9	0.000
10	−0.500
11	1.500
12	−1.000
13	1.000

Input geometry (see Figure 4-14)

Graphical plot of axial forces. The width of the plot represents
the magnitude of the force present.

Graphical plot of axial nodal deflections
(scale exaggerated)

FIGURE 4–20   Analysis results obtained using a computer-based structural analysis program.

In addition to the particular method of analysis noted above, many other analytical approaches are available, including finite-element techniques (Appendix 13). There are many implementations as well, each with differing ways of specifying input and output parameters. Figure 4–20 shows the same truss previously analyzed in Figure 4–14. A widely available analysis program has been used to create the analytical results shown.[1] Input geometry for nodes can be specified by coordinate data or by an interactive graphic interface. Support conditions were defined via various joint restraint options. Member end conditions were specified as pinned. As with most programs, it is then necessary to specify "member sizes" before an analysis can take place. While forces in this particular structure do not depend upon initial size estimates, forces in *indeterminate* trusses (or any other type of indeterminate structure) do depend upon initial member size estimates. In this simple case, virtually any default size can be specified. In more complex cases, it would be necessary to guess at sizes, analyze the structure, improve size estimates,

---

[1]*Multiframe* by Formation Design Systems.

and repeat. In any event, starting from any default estimate will point the user in the right direction. Analytical results typically include force distributions and deflected shape information (via numerical tabulations and often graphical plots). Different loading cases can be quickly analyzed. Influences of shape variations can also be quickly analyzed by changing the input geometry.

4-4 DESIGN OF TRUSSES

4-4-1 Objectives

There are many aspects to the design of trusses. Broad issues include the overall external configuration of a truss, the pattern of its internal triangulation, and attitudes toward material choice and member design. Important dimensional variables include the spans and depths of the trusses, lengths of specific truss members (particularly compression members), spacing of trusses, and transverse beam spacing (which in turn dictates the way loads are brought onto trusses and, frequently, the placement of nodes within a truss). Broad contextual issues or other design objectives may well dictate many of these parameters, while others may be directly manipulated.

Criteria used to develop designs vary. *Structural efficiency* objectives are common and are reflected in design procedures that seek to minimize the total amount of material used in a truss to support a given loading over a given span while providing adequate safety and stiffness. Overall external configurations and related internal triangulation patterns are manipulated with this objective in view. Internal triangulation patterns are similarly affected. Truss depths are surely an important variable in minimizing volume requirements. Member design attitudes are also affected. Each individual truss member might be sized precisely to carry its internal force. Since forces vary among members, so will member sizes. Rods or cables might well be used. Member design attitudes might also affect overall configurations and internal patterns (e.g., efficient patterns may be developed that minimize the length of long compression members and maximize the length of tension elements).

Alternatively, design criteria might be based on *construction efficiency* considerations related to the fabrication and making of a truss. Responding to these objectives often leads to trusses with simple external configurations (often parallel upper and lower chords or simple gabled forms). Equally simple internal triangulation patterns are often used as well with the objective of making all members the same lengths. Member design attitudes are affected as well. Instead of making different truss members different sizes in response to the varying forces present, the maximum force present anywhere might be identified and used as a basis for sizing all members throughout the structure (even when forces present are less than the size can carry), simply because it might be easier to fabricate a truss in this way. Making all members identical surely makes making joint connections easier than when adjacent members are differently sized and shaped. Common variants of this attitude include using three different sizes, one for the upper chord, another for the lower chord, and a third for interstitial members.

Although other design objectives could be noted as well and the characterization just presented is somewhat simplistic, *structural efficiency* versus *constructional efficiency* objectives provide a useful point of comparison in subsequent discussions. Often, these objectives are conflicting in the sense that they lead to quite different design responses.

4–4–2   Configurations

Probably the single question most asked in a design context is: What shape should it be? Unfortunately, there is no easy answer to this question. Several common configurations are shown in Figure 4–21. External configurations vary, as do internal patterns. Configurations are influenced by both broad external factors and direct structural or construction considerations. Different configurations are useful for different purposes and may be suitable for different span lengths and/or loading conditions.

External Factors.   External factors are not immediately a concern of this book but should still be noted since they often are primary influences on truss configurations. For example, the shapes shown in (c) and (d) are largely responses to external factors. The common pitched roof is ingrained in our building traditions for a number of very good reasons and roof trusses are shaped accordingly. The northlight truss shown in (y) is commonly configured so that light may be admitted through upper zones into spaces below. The scissors truss shown in (w) is often used to open up space beneath. Trusses of many different shapes may be made to work, but this does not mean that they are particularly efficient or attractive from a structural or constructional point of view. The scissors truss noted, for example, is quite susceptible to large deflections (its actual structural depth is quite shallow), and member sizes must be quite large if the truss is to work for anything other than minor spans.

Basic Forms.   From both structural and constructional perspectives, the parabolically shaped truss and the parallel chord truss shown in Figure 4–21 provide useful discussion referents. Assume that they are subjected to a series of identical point loads across their tops. A useful way of discussing these two configurations is through a consideration of the external shears and moments that are developed in the truss structures in response to external loadings (see Sections 4–3–5 and 2–4–2). Internal forces in truss members are developed in response to these external shears and moments as shown in Figure 4–22. Maximum bending typically occurs at the center of a simply supported truss with uniform loads and decreases toward the ends, whereas maximum shears occur at either end and decrease toward the center. Upper and lower chord members often primarily (but not exclusively) carry moments, and forces are developed within them in direct proportion to the moment present and the height of the structure (for a given moment, a shallow structure will experience high forces, and vice versa). Typically, $M_{\text{external}} = Cd = Td$, where C and T are the gross horizontal internal forces present and d is the depth of the truss. External shears are resisted by vertical components in inclined members.

Parallel Chord Trusses.   In a parallel chord truss, external moments are largely resisted by couples directly formed by the forces in the upper and lower chords: $M_{\text{external}} = Cd = Td$. Since the truss depth d is constant, C and T must vary with varying values of M_{external}, as shown in Figure 4–23. Thus, the forces in chord members generally vary as shown. The external shear forces are carried exclusively by the diagonals since the chords are horizontal and can contribute no vertically acting resisting forces. The forces in the diagonals then must generally vary as the external shear force varies. Member forces consequently vary widely. This influences member design attitudes, since members must either be designed in response to specific force levels present or designed on the basis of maximum values (see Section 4–4–4).

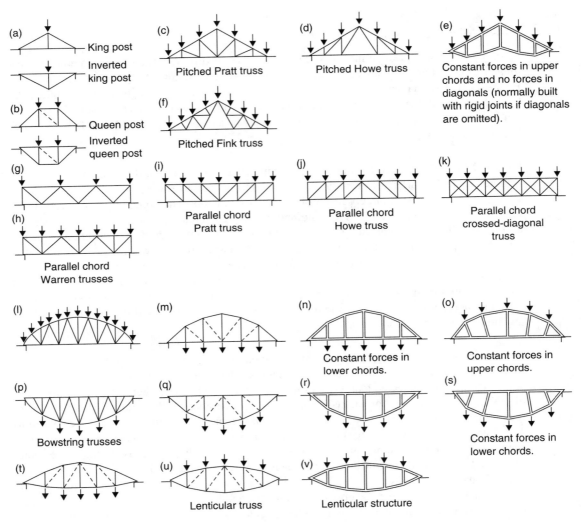

(a) King post
Inverted king post

(b) Queen post
Inverted queen post

(c) Pitched Pratt truss

(d) Pitched Howe truss

(e) Constant forces in upper chords and no forces in diagonals (normally built with rigid joints if diagonals are omitted).

(f) Pitched Fink truss

(g)

(h) Parallel chord Warren trusses

(i) Parallel chord Pratt truss

(j) Parallel chord Howe truss

(k) Parallel chord crossed-diagonal truss

(l)

(m)

(n) Constant forces in lower chords.

(o) Constant forces in upper chords.

(p) Bowstring trusses

(q)

(r)

(s) Constant forces in lower chords.

(t)

(u) Lenticular truss

(v) Lenticular structure

Funicularly shaped trusses: depths vary with bending moment (horizontal components of chord forces are equal and diagonals are zero-force members under design loadings). Shaped trusses with no diagonals are built with rigid joints to handle varying loadings (see Chapter 9 on rigid-frame structures).

(w) "Scissors" truss

(x) Cantilevered truss (funicularly shaped)

(y) Northlight trusses

(z) Monitors with clerestories

FIGURE 4–21 Common types of trusses.

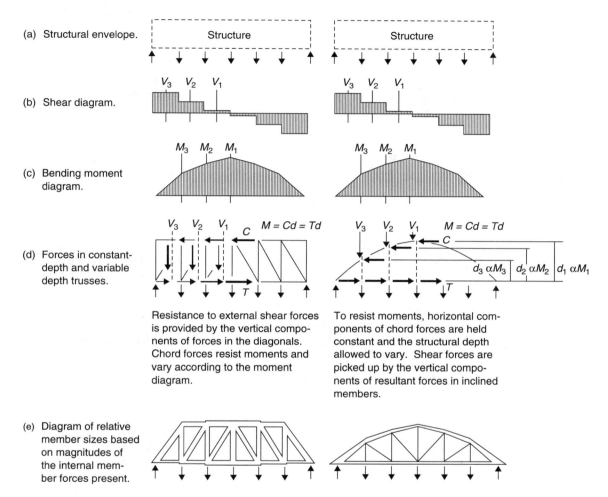

(a) Structural envelope.

(b) Shear diagram.

(c) Bending moment diagram.

(d) Forces in constant-depth and variable depth trusses.

Resistance to external shear forces is provided by the vertical components of forces in the diagonals. Chord forces resist moments and vary according to the moment diagram.

To resist moments, horizontal components of chord forces are held constant and the structural depth allowed to vary. Shear forces are picked up by the vertical components of resultant forces in inclined members.

(e) Diagram of relative member sizes based on magnitudes of the internal member forces present.

FIGURE 4-22   Shaping of trusses based on internal shears and moments.

Different diagonal organizations are possible, with different sloping patterns yielding different force states within them. In order to make the most efficient use of tension or compression elements, a typical objective might be to try to cause as many as possible of the longest members of a truss to be in tension rather than compression. This can often be done by paying careful attention to how certain members are oriented in the truss.

Parallel-chord trusses having bar patterns of the type illustrated in Figure 4–23(a) invariably have all diagonals in tension (for the loading shown), whereas trusses having patterns of the type illustrated in Figure 4–23(f) have all interior vertical members in tension while diagonals are in compression. The reversal of the direction of diagonals at midspan in such trusses is characteristic of designs for symmetrical loadings. Pratt and Howe were nineteenth-century bridge designers who developed and popularized the forms shown.

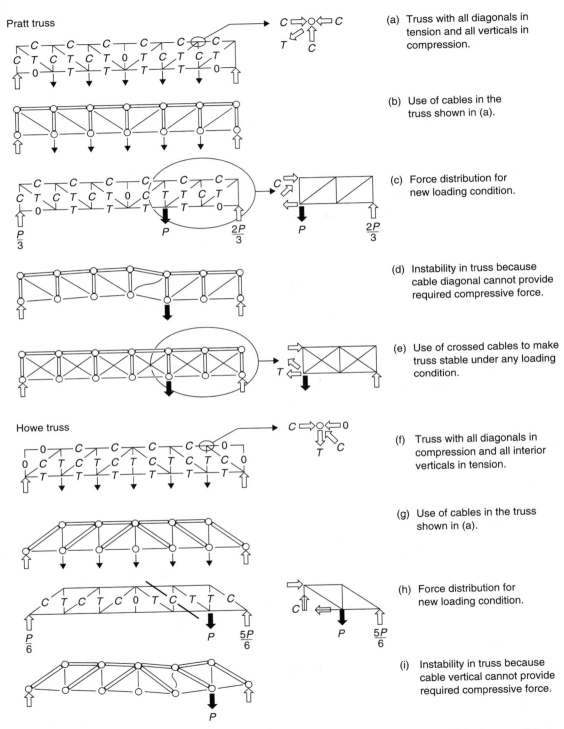

FIGURE 4–23 Parallel chord trusses: force distributions, use of cables, effects of changing load conditions.

170

Whether cables can be used for tension elements in these trusses depends largely on whether or not the loading condition on the truss is invariant. In the diagrams shown it is obviously suggested that cables could be suitable for use as tension elements. If members of this type are used, extreme care should be taken to assure that these tensile members are never expected to carry compressive forces. As previously noted, stress reversals of this type could cause the truss to become unstable. Stress reversals are usually associated with a change in the pattern of external loads carried by the truss. Consider what would happen to the same two trusses under discussion if they were expected to carry the single load shown, a case that might occur if the other loads were *simply removed*. Analysis of the member forces due to these loads results in the distributions shown. Clearly, some of the members previously in tension are now in compression. If a cable were used in members previously in tension but now in compression, the trusses would become unstable and collapse as indicated. This illustrates a fundamental design consideration. Each element in a structure must be designed to carry adequately the forces which might develop in it under *any* possible loading condition that *might* occur. This could involve a large number of different load combinations.

The trusses shown can be made stable for the new loading condition by using members capable of carrying the compressive forces indicated rather than using cables. Alternatively, for the truss shown in Figure 4–23(b), the addition of crossed cables would cause this truss to be stable. The reader should carefully inspect the truss shown in Figure 4–23(g) to see if the addition of a crossed cable leads to stability. Clearly, it does not. For this reason trusses having this bar pattern rarely use cables, or they are used only when the nature of the external loads are so predictable that stress reversals need not be feared. This is sometimes the case when the dead load carried by a truss significantly exceeds the live load or if there is no live load at all, since the former is usually fixed and precisely determinable while live loads are not.

It is useful to highlight briefly two other general types of bar configuration often encountered in a constant-depth truss. The first is a statically indeterminate (internally) configu-

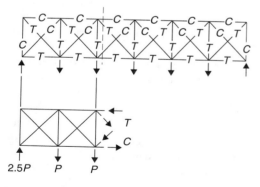

(a) Statically indeterminate (internally) truss using crossed diagonals.

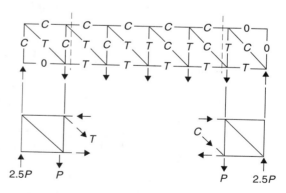

(b) Statically determinate truss with similarly sloped diagonals (note that force states vary).

FIGURE 4–24   Force distributions in parallel chord trusses using rigid diagonals that are capable of carrying either tension or compression forces.

ration, shown in Figure 4–24(a). An approximate force distribution for the loading indicated, based on the assumption that the diagonals are of similar stiffnesses and equally share in carrying the shear forces present is also shown. The reader should study this truss closely and determine if it is indeed stable under loading conditions other than the one illustrated. (It is, but being able to explain *why* is of crucial importance in gaining a thorough understanding of the structural behavior of trusses.) A second typical type of parallel chord truss has all the diagonals oriented in one direction [Figure 4–24(b)]. From a study of the previous diagonal organizations, it can be seen that in such cases diagonals on one half of the structure are in compression and the other half are in tension. It makes little sense to use cables for diagonals in such a situation.

Funicularly Shaped Trusses.   Shaped trusses of the type shown to the right in Figure 4–22 are often quite efficient in a structural sense. Note that the truss shown is funicularly shaped for the loading, since it reflects the shape assumed by a flexible cable under the same loading (albeit inversely). The configuration responds to the magnitudes of the shears and moments present. As the bending moment varies from a maximum at the center to a minimum at the ends, the depth of the structure varies as well (see Figure 4–24). Nodes are consequently at varying heights and connecting members are sloped. This shaping leads to forces of more or less similar magnitude being developed in upper and lower chord members (forces in upper members are slightly higher and not quite constant due to their sloping). Interestingly, if the structure is precisely shaped, the sloped chord members may also carry the shear forces involved via their vertical components. Note that the slope of the chord members increases toward the ends of the structure, where the shear forces are highest. Vertical resisting components in sloped members are thus highest as well at these points. Interstitial members carry only small forces. In fact, if precisely shaped, all interior members turn out to be zero-force members, no matter what specific internal triangulation pattern is used.

Figure 4–25 illustrates variations on the truss discussed. Conceptually the zero-force members could simply be removed to form a nontriangulated configuration without changing the ability of the structure to carry design loads to the ground. Pinned structures without diagonals are, however, of dubious practicality, since they are stable *only* under the exact loading patterns shown. If the loading pattern were changed in *any* way (e.g., if even one of the loads were removed or its magnitude altered), the configurations would no longer be stable and would collapse. This is because the required shear and moment resistance at the different locations is now no longer the same as that for which the structure was originally designed and the structure cannot intrinsically satisfy these new requirements as it did for the design loading. The same overall configuration with diagonals, however, is stable under not only the design loading but any other loading condition. A function of the interstitial members is to carry forces generated by other nonuniform loads the structure must occasionally bear. If the loads were suspended from the lower-chord panel points instead of being applied to the upper chord, the vertical interior members would serve as suspension rods transferring the applied loads to the upper chord members.

One final transformation of the truss shown in Figure 4–25(a) is of interest. The *lens*-shaped structure shown in Figure 4–25(c) has the same structural depth at all sections as the original structure. Its outer configuration is clearly part of the same family of shapes as that present in the

$R_V = 2.5P$ $R_V = 2.5P$

(a) Funicularly shaped truss for a series of identical and equally spaced concentrated loads. Interstitial members are zero-force members under the primary loading condition shown but carry forces when the loading changes. This is a common type of bridge structure.

Arch

(b) Transformation of the truss shown in (a) in which the non-load-carrying interstitial members are eliminated and the function of the lower chord (which acts as a tension tie) is replaced by buttresses. An arch structure results. If the linear segments of the structure shown are pin-connected, the assembly is stable only under the loading condition shown. Joints are thus often made rigid.

Arch

Cable

(c) A further transformation of the assemblies shown in (a) and (b) into a lens-shaped structure. The depth of the structure at any section is the same as before. One way of conceiving of the structural action of the assembly is to think of it as a combination arch and cable in which the horizontal thrusts of the arch are exactly balanced by those of the cable. Hence, no net horizontal forces develop at the foundation, only vertical forces. The structure is stable only under the loading condition shown.

FIGURE 4–25 Funicular trusses: transformations of a funicular truss into related forms.

original truss. An analysis of this truss would reveal that the interstitial diagonals are zero-force members and thus serve only the function of stabilizing the assembly under variant loading conditions. The verticals transfer loads such that the upper and lower chord members are similarly loaded (a condition that must be met for the shape similarity to be correct).

Instead of conceiving of this lens-shaped structure as a special form of truss, it could equally well be conceived of as a combination *arch-cable* structure. In this conception the outward thrusts of the upper arch are identically balanced by the inward pulls of the cable, with the consequence that there is no net lateral force present at the reaction, a result long acknowledged to be advantageous in foundation design (See Chapter 5 on arches and cables).

The lens-shaped form was commonly used in many *lenticular* trusses built in the last century for use as bridges (see Figures 4–26 and 3–9). Additional diagonal bracing was typically used to allow the structures to carry nonuniform loading patterns.

Funicularly shaped trusses are interesting. Obviously, what is happening in these trusses is that the specific members organized along the lines of the funicular shape for the loading involved have become the dominant, actually only, mechanism for transferring the external loads to the supports. Other members are zero-force members serving a bracing function at most. A remarkably simple load-carrying action is thus displayed by these trusses.

FIGURE 4–26 Lenticular truss: the Smithfield Street Bridge across the Monongahela River in Pittsburgh, Pennsylvania (circa 1883). (Courtesy of the American Society of Civil Engineers.)

For the rather remarkable load-carrying actions described to occur, it is necessary that the basic shape of the structure correspond *exactly* to the funicular shape. Relative heights of the interior points on the trusses shown in Figures 4–25, 4–26, and 4–27, for example, must be exactly determined. The relative heights are clearly a function of the loads and their locations. In general, the external moments present at different sections are first calculated. A maximum depth d_{max} is selected and corresponding maximum forces in chords are calculated: $T_{max} = C_{max} = M_{max}/d_{max}$. The depth d_x of the structure at other sections is then varied directly in response to the moment M_x present on the assumption that the horizontal components of the chord forces are maintained constant: $d_x = M_x/T_{max} = M_x/C_{max}$. By knowing the different structural depths, member slopes can be found and final resultant forces in members calculated on the basis of known slopes and horizontal components. The vertical components of these forces will be found to balance the external shear forces present at the sections. This process is described in more detail in Chapter 5.

Since different loading conditions lead to different overall configurations (as can be appreciated from the deflected string method of arriving at funicular shapes), a shape funicular for one loading will not be funicular for any other. This implies that forces are developed in interior members of trusses designed to be funicular for one loading when nondesign loads are present. The load-carrying action would again be more complex in such a case.

Comparing a truss not having an overall funicular shape for the loading involved with a funicularly shaped one (see Figure 4–27) reveals that deviating from the funicular shape not only serves to make the total member length involved longer but more members are subjected to primary forces (and would thus have to be designed as load-carrying rather than zero-force members). The consequence is that it can be expected that a strategy of using a funicular shape for the overall envelope of a truss may be more likely to lead to a lighter-weight or minimum-volume solution than a nonfunicular shape.

Other Special Shapes.   Other truss configurations that have been specially shaped to carry loads in basically a funicular way are illustrated in Figure 4–21. Under primary design loadings, the diagonals in these forms are zero-force members, but are obviously needed for stability under varying loading conditions if joints are pin connected. Some actual structures reflecting these forms have been made without the aid of diagonals by using rigid rather than pinned connections, and can carry off-balanced loads via bending in members. (Strictly speaking, these then become *rigid-frame* structures rather than trusses; see Chapter 9.)

Figure 4–21(r) is funicularly shaped in response to the moment diagram, but the forces naturally vary slightly along the lower chord. Figure 4–21(s) seeks constant forces along the lower chord, which can be accomplished by inclining the uprights in a precise way. For sloped roofs, the shape shown in Figure 4–21(e) seeks to maintain similar forces in upper and lower chords (Robert Maillart used a shape such as this in his building at Chiasso in 1924). The cantilevered form shown in Figure 4–21(x) seeks to maintain similar and nearly constant forces in opposing chords (it is obviously reminiscent of the Eiffel Tower, which is subject to wind loads).

4–4–3   Depths of Trusses

One of the most frequently encountered questions during the design of a truss is that of how deep it should be or whether there is an optimal depth for a truss. It would seem that this should be a relatively easy design question to answer, but it is, on the contrary, one of the more difficult. As

Loading

A cable allowed to deform freely assumes the funicular shape for the loading

Funicularly shaped structures

Arbitrary truss shape: for comparable portions, the funicularly shaped truss uses less total member length and involves fewer loaded members. Deviating from the funicular shape also induces forces in additional members.

(a) Funicularly shaped trusses carry loads to supports in a very direct way. No forces are generated in internal members. Only those aligned with the funicular shape carry loads. If the loading changed from that shown, the shapes illustrated would no longer be funicular and forces would be induced in more members.

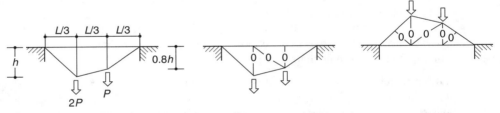

(b) There is only one general funicular shape for a given loading. When designing a funicularly shaped truss, care must be taken to assure that the slopes of members correspond exactly to the funicular shape (see Chapter 5).

FIGURE 4–27 Funicular trusses: trusses based on the funicular shape for the applied loading demonstrate a uniquely simple load-carrying action.

already noted in Section 4–3–4, the member forces, hence volumes, generated in a truss by an external load are invariably dependent on the dimensions, including the height (*d*) of the truss.

As can be appreciated, determining an optimum height which minimizes the total volume of a truss is no easy matter, but the process is conceptually straightforward. For each truss member, a volume expression based on the member forces written as a function of the variable height *d* is first determined and a total volume expression for the entire set of members obtained. This expression is then minimized with respect to the variable height (see Section 5–4–1).

In general, the optimization process will reveal that trusses that are relatively deep in relation to their span are most efficient and shallow trusses, less so. Angles formed by the diagonals with respect to the horizontal are typically from 30 to 60°, with 45° often a good choice for determining triangulization geometries.

Over the years, rules of thumb have evolved that help estimate what the depth of a truss should be. Trusses that carry relatively light loads and are closely spaced often have depths approximately $\frac{1}{20}$ of their span (e.g., roof load-transfer members). Secondary collector trusses that carry reactions produced by load-transfer members are usually deeper, since the loads carried are larger, and can be on the order of $\frac{1}{10}$ of their span. Primary collector trusses, which support huge loads (e.g., a truss carrying the column loads from a multistory building over a clear span on the ground floor), are usually very deep and are often made equal to the depth of a story, say $\frac{1}{4}$ or $\frac{1}{5}$ of the span of the truss. Rules of thumb of this nature should not be taken as final truths. Some of the best and most efficient uses of trusses in building contexts have occurred when heights varied drastically from what the ratios above suggest. Still, when in doubt, they are a place to start. In Chapter 15 we discuss rule-of-thumb applications in greater detail.

4-4-4   Member Design Issues

Critical Loadings.   The selection of physical members for use in a given truss configuration is one of the more straightforward aspects of truss design. The crucial issue is predicting what force a member should be designed to carry. In earlier sections it was shown that the nature and magnitude of the force present in a particular member are dependent on the specific loading condition on the whole truss. It is thus necessary to consider the whole spectrum of possible loading conditions and analyze the forces present in each of the members under each of these conditions. A particular member would then be designed in response to the maximum (critical) force possible. Consequently, individual members quite often are designed in response to *different* loading conditions (e.g., the diagonals of a truss may be designed for one external loading condition and the chord members for another). Only in instances where the loading condition is invariant are all truss members designed in response to the forces generated by the same load.

Member Design.   Once the critical force in a member has been found, the problem becomes one of choosing an appropriate material and a set of cross-sectional dimensions for a member of known length having simple pin-ended connections and subjected to a known tension or compressive force. There is usually no great difficulty in designing the member. Quantitative techniques for designing members of this type are discussed in greater detail in Section 2-4 and Chapter 7. Of primary importance is that members carrying only tension forces can usually be designed to have much smaller cross sections than those carrying compressive forces of a similar magnitude. The cross-sectional area of a tension member is directly dependent on the magnitude of the force present and the allowable stress of the material used and is independent of member length. Thus: *area required = tension force/allowable stress*. For members in compression it is necessary to take into account the possibility of a buckling failure, which can occur in long members subjected to compressive forces. The load-carrying capacity of the compressive member is inversely proportional to the square of the member's length for long members. If compressive members are relatively short and below a certain maximum length, buckling is not a problem and the cross-sectional area is then directly dependent only on the magnitude of the force involved and the allowable crushing stress of the material and is again independent of the specific length of the element. The general implication of this is that long compression members (possibly subject to buckling) require a *greater cross-sectional area* to support a given compressive load than would a short member (not subject to buckling). Exactly what defines a long or short member is discussed extensively in Section 7–3. In truss design, either members in tension or short compressive members are considered more desirable than long compressive members, since less material is required to carry a given force. A *truss design objective* is often to create a situation where as many members as possible carry only tension forces or are short compressive members, because this often means less total material is required to support the given external loads. Techniques for doing this will be discussed shortly.

Constant- Versus Variable-Size Members. The relative sizes of members, designed in response to the forces actually present, in two typical trusses are shown diagrammatically in Figure 4–22. Obviously, the illustration is not meant to represent real members but is intended to convey a graphic sense of material distribution.

Instead of varying the size of each individual member in response to specific forces present, it may be more convenient or less costly to make several pieces (e.g., the entire top or bottom chord) out of constant-cross-section continuous members. Whether or not to do so is a design decision that must be evaluated in light of other factors. When the top chord is designed to be a continuous member of a constant cross section, for example, the cross section used must be designed to carry the maximum force present in the top chord. Since this would usually occur only in one segmental portion of the entire top chord, this same cross section would be excessively large for the remaining segments and so potentially inefficient from a material's use viewpoint.

Whether or not to size each truss member in exact response to the forces present or to base all member sizes on certain critical elements is not an easy choice to make. The latter is often done when a large number of trusses are used repetitively, spaced closely together, and designed to carry relatively light loads (e.g., mass-produced bar joists). The members of major trusses carrying large dead loads are often designed more in response to the actual forces carried.

Buckling Considerations: Effects on Patterns. The dependency of the load-carrying capacity of a compressive member on its length and the associated design objective of trying to make such members relatively short often influence the pattern of triangulation used: Consider the truss shown in Figure 4–28(a) and the force distribution in its members shown in Figure 4–28(b). Assuming that the members shown in compression are relatively long members, Figure 4–28(a) also indicates how the compression members might buckle (the directions of buckle shown are arbitrary, since there is no way of predicting in which direction the member would actually buckle). The tension members would exhibit no such tendency to buckle. Note that the top chord members are the longest in the truss and carry relatively high compressive forces. Members could undoubtedly be sized to carry these forces, but with a few relatively minor alterations to the bar pattern, it is possible to reduce the total amount of material required in the top chord below what would be required for the configuration shown in Figure 4–28(a). This can be done by locating members to serve as bracing for these top chords. There are four zero-force members in the original configuration. A close look at the truss reveals that these members are not necessary to the stability of the truss (as some zero-force members occasionally are) and could be removed. Or they could be relocated as shown in Figure 4–28(c). These members would now serve as midpoint bracings, thereby effectively halving the effective lengths of top chord members.

This type of bracing has an enormous influence on the load-carrying capacity of the top chord members. Recall that halving the length of a compressive member increases the load

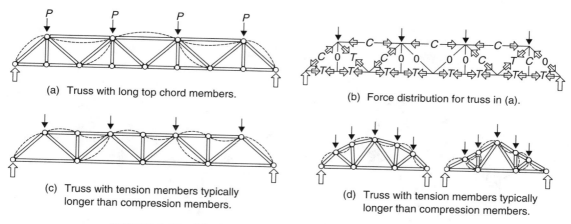

(a) Truss with long top chord members.

(b) Force distribution for truss in (a).

(c) Truss with tension members typically longer than compression members.

(d) Truss with tension members typically longer than compression members.

FIGURE 4–28   Member buckling: relation to triangularization pattern.

required to cause buckling by a factor of 4 (see Section 7–3). A much smaller member could be used to support the axial load shown than would be the case in the original configuration. This is satisfactory, since the cross-sectional areas of tension members required to carry given loads are not dependent on member length. Short compression members and longer tension members often characterize trusses that have been designed with care. This principle is often the design determinant underlying configurations of many trusses commonly found in use.

It might be thought that with the preceding approach the bracing members would have to be very large to serve their function. Usually this is not so, since there is relatively little force exerted on a brace member, so they can be quite small. Sizing these members exactly is a difficult problem beyond the scope of this book. Often they are simply given a certain minimum size empirically known to be adequate or, more likely, those same members carry some relatively large load when the external loading pattern on the truss changes. Sizes for other loads are usually more than adequate when the member serves only a bracing function.

Effect of Lateral Buckling on Member Design.   The preceding discussion treated only the behavior of a truss in its own plane. Even in a planar structure, however, the *out-of-plane* direction is extremely important. Consider the planar truss shown in Figure 4–29 and assume that the top chords were made of members symmetrical about both the y and z axes. A square or round member (including a pipe) would exhibit a symmetry of this type. More precisely, the members of interest are those having equal *moments of inertia* about both axes and they need not necessarily be geometrically symmetrical (see Appendix 3). If a top chord of this type carries an axial compressive load, it is equally apt to buckle in the horizontal xz plane. This implies that a crucial design issue is to assure that this mode of buckling does not adversely affect the load-carrying capacity of the truss.

Assume that transverse beams were used to carry the loads from the decking to the truss as shown in Figure 4–29(b). These beams inherently brace the top chord in the horizontal plane at the points of attachment. Since the chords are braced only at these points, it is still possible for the top chords to buckle in the horizontal plane, as shown in Figure 4–29(b). The effective lengths of the top chord members, insofar as their resistance to buckling is concerned, is $2a$, not

(a) Possible directions of member buckling when top chord is braced at each panel point. Use of a symmetrical member with equal stiffnesses about the *x* and *y* axes is appropriate.

(b) Possible directions of member buckling when top chord is not symmetrically braced. Top chord members may be made stiffer about one axis than the other to mitigate out-of-plane buckling tendencies.

FIGURE 4–29   Lateral buckling of truss members: use of transverse members for bracing.

just *a*. Without transverse bracings in the horizontal plane at other points, minimizing top chord length in the vertical plane to gain design advantages is an exercise in futility, as the members will merely buckle in the horizontal plane. Members in the vertical plane do nothing to prevent this type of buckling. From a design point of view, it is necessary to brace the truss as shown in Figure 4–29(a). This makes the effective length of the top chords the same in both directions. An alternative would be to change the cross-sectional geometry of the top chord members, making them more inherently resistive to buckling in the horizontal plane. This is diagrammatically illustrated in Figure 4–29(b), in which the member is made stiffer in the horizontal (*xz*) plane. Using techniques discussed in detail in Section 7–4 it is possible to design member characteristics so that the potential for buckling in the vertical plane (about the weak axis of the member shown, but with an effective member length of *a*) is exactly identical to that for buckling in the horizontal plane (about the stronger axis of the member but with an effective member length of 2*a*). Such a member is diagrammatically illustrated. Many member configurations could provide the necessary balance in stiffnesses.

Which of the two approaches just discussed is preferable for controlling the potential for member buckling in the horizontal plane depends on many other design considerations. Of primary concern would be the effect of the transverse beam spacing in the design of the roof decking. One spacing or the other might prove to be more desirable in this respect. A detailed look at the design of the decking is necessary to answer this question.

Effects of Lateral Buckling of Bar Assemblies.   While usually there is the possibility for bracing the top chord in the horizontal plane, it is possible to have a truss that is essentially freestanding

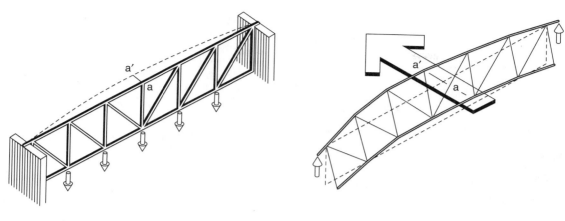

(a) Truss before lateral buckling.

(b) Lateral buckling of truss.

FIGURE 4–30   Lateral buckling of planar truss without any bracing.

(Figure 4–30). In structures of this type, there is, in *addition* to the possibility of individual member buckling of the type discussed previously, the possibility that very large portions of the structure may buckle *laterally.* This type of buckling, which often makes the use of freestanding trusses undesirable, is illustrated in Figure 4–30. In the truss shown, the entire set of top chord members is in a state of compression, so the *entire* top of the truss can buckle as indicated. Preventing this phenomenon is no small design task. The whole length of the top of the truss can be thought of as the effective length of a long composite compression member. The type of bracing provided when transverse beams are attached to the top chord, however, generally prevents this type of buckling.

When trusses must be free-standing and hence cannot be braced by transverse members, it is necessary to make the top chord of the structure sufficiently stiff in the transverse direction to resist lateral buckling. This can be done by increasing the lateral dimension of the top chord or by adopting a three-dimensional triangular pattern (Figure 4–31).

4–4–5   Planar Versus Three-Dimensional Trusses

There are a number of issues that should be considered in making a decision to use either a planar or a three-dimensional structure. Which uses a greater amount of material to support a given load in space, or are planar and three-dimensional structures similar in this respect? Quantitative resolution of this very complex question is unfortunately beyond the scope of this book. It should be noted, however, that nothing a priori suggests that three-dimensional trusses necessarily use less material for equivalent loads and spans than planar trusses. In fact, it can be demonstrated that when trusses are used as one-way spanning elements, a planar truss usually requires less volume of truss material than does a comparable three-dimensional truss serving the same function. Thus, when trusses are used as one-way spanning elements a series of planar trusses is often preferable to a series of three-dimensional trusses, particularly when they are used on the interior of a building and lateral bracing is intrinsically provided by the roof framing system or some other mechanism.

(a) Planar truss with stiffened top chord to provide resistance to lateral buckling.

(b) Three-dimensional truss: width of top plane provides resistance to lateral buckling.

(c) Three-dimensional truss: sloped side members provide resistance to lateral buckling.

FIGURE 4–31   Preventing lateral buckling of bar assemblies in free-standing trusses.

Three-dimensional configurations often prove more efficient when trusses are used to form two-way systems (see Chapter 10). Three-dimensional trusses also prove efficient when the trusses are used in a free-standing way (without transverse beams framing into their top chords). In these cases, the forms are inherently resistant to simple overturning laterally. Their compression zones are also naturally resistant to lateral buckling of whole bar assemblies.

The top plane of the three-dimensional truss shown in Figure 4–31(b) inherently provides a strong resistance to lateral buckling and is one of the primary reasons why such configurations are often used. A truss of the type shown in Figure 4–31(c) also inherently provides a measure of bracing against this phenomenon, owing to the orientation of the diagonals. In these two cases the resistance to lateral buckling provided by three-dimensional structures is largely dependent on the spacing of members in the third dimension, with a larger spacing more desirable than a very small one. The determination of an optimum separation is a difficult problem beyond the scope of this book. The spacings illustrated are, however, quite reasonable.

QUESTIONS

See Figure 4–32.

4–1 Discuss in detail the historical development of quantitative methods of analyzing truss structures. Consult your library.

4–2 For the truss shown in Figure 4–32(Q2), quantitatively determine the magnitudes of the forces present in all of the truss members. A method-of-joints approach is suggested.

Answer: $F_{AH} = F_{FE} = 70.7$ compression, $F_{AB} = F_{BC} = F_{CD} = F_{DE} = F_{FD} = F_{HB} = 50$ tension, $F_{HC} = F_{GC} = F_{FC} = 0$, and $F_{FG} = F_{GH} = 50$ compression.

4–3 For the truss shown in Figure 4–32(Q3), qualitatively determine the nature of the force present in each of the members. Numerical values are not required.

4–4 For the truss shown in Figure 4–32(Q3), quantitatively determine the magnitudes of the forces present in all the truss members. A method-of-joints approach is suggested.

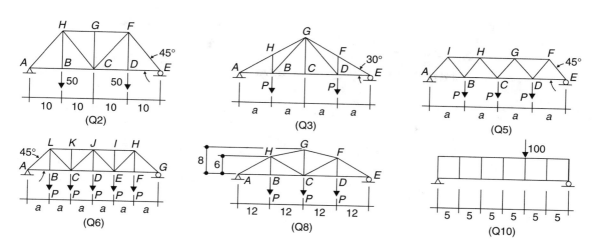

FIGURE 4–32   Problems.

4–5 For the truss shown in Figure 4–32(Q5), quantitatively determine the magnitudes of the forces present in all the truss members. Use a method-of-joints approach.

4–6 For the truss shown in Figure 4–32(Q6), quantitatively determine the magnitudes of the forces present in all the truss members. A method-of-joints approach is suggested.

4–7 Determine the force in member *GH* in the truss shown in Figure 4–32(Q5) by using a method-of-sections approach.

 Answer: $F_{GH} = 4P$.

4–8 For the truss shown in Figure 4–32(Q8), quantitatively determine the magnitudes of the forces present in all the truss members. A method-of-joints approach is suggested.

4–9 Quantitatively determine the forces in members *JI, JE,* and *ED* in the truss shown in Figure 4–32(Q6) by a method-of-sections approach. How would the force in member *JI* be affected if the overall depth of the structure was doubled? How would the forces in members *JI* and *JE* be affected if the depth of the truss were continually decreased until it approached zero?

4–10 Consider the parallel chord truss shown in Figure 4–32(Q10). Obviously, the truss needs diagonal elements for stability. Add the diagonal elements in an arrangement such that *all* the diagonals are in a state of tension under the loading condition indicated.

4–11 Draw a diagram of the relative sizes of the individual members of the truss shown in Figure 4–32(Q6). Assume that cables are used for tension elements.

CHAPTER 5

Funicular Structures: Cables and Arches

5–1 INTRODUCTION TO FUNICULAR STRUCTURES

Few types of structures have so consistently appealed to the imagination of builders as either the hanging cable or the arch. These two apparently different types of structures share some fundamental characteristics that cause them to be more closely related than might initially appear, particularly in terms of their basic structural behavior.

A cable subjected to external loads will obviously deform in a way dependent on the magnitude and location of the external forces. The form acquired is often called the *funicular* shape of the cable (the term *funicular* is derived from the Latin word for "rope"). Only tension forces will be developed in the cable. Inverting the structural form obtained will yield a new structure that is exactly analogous to the cable structure except that compression rather than tension forces are developed. Theoretically, the shape found could be constructed of simply stacked elements that are nonrigidly connected (a "compression chain") and the resultant structure would be stable. Any slight variation in the nature of the applied loading, however, would mean that the structure would cease to be funicular in shape and bending would develop under the new loading, with the result that complete collapse could occur since the nonrigidly connected blocks cannot resist this bending. Since the forms of both the tensile and compressive structures that are derived in the manner described above are related to the notion of a loaded hanging rope, they are collectively referred to as *funicular structures*.

5-2   GENERAL PRINCIPLES OF FUNICULAR SHAPES

Of fundamental importance in the study of arches and cables is a knowledge of what exact curve or series of straight-line segments defines the funicular shape for a given loading. The funicular shape is that naturally assumed by a freely deforming cable subjected to the loading. A cable of constant cross section carrying only its own dead weight will naturally deform into a *catenary* shape (Figure 5–1). A cable carrying a load that is uniformly distributed along the horizontal projection of the cable, as is the primary loading in a suspension bridge supporting a horizontal bridge deck, will deform into a parabola. Cables carrying concentrated point loads will (ignoring the dead weight of the cable itself) deform into a series of straight-line segments.

While there is only one general shape of structure that is funicular for a given loading, there is invariably a family of structures having the same general shape for any given condition. All the structures illustrated in Figure 5–1, (e) and (f) for example, are funicular for the loadings indicated. Clearly, all structures in a group have the same shape, but the physical dimensions are different. Within a family, the relative proportions of all the shapes are identical. It is obvious that such a family could be obtained simply by using a series of flexible cables of different lengths. All would deform in a similar way under the action of the load, but the actual amount that the structure would sag would be different.

The magnitude of the forces developed in the arch or cable, however, *are* dependent on the relative height or depth of the funicular shape in relation to its length as well as the magnitude and location of the applied loads. The greater the rise of an arch or the sag of a cable, the smaller are the internal forces developed in the structure, and vice versa. Reactive forces developed at the arch or cable ends also depend on these parameters. End reactions have both vertical and horizontal thrusts which must be resisted by the foundations or some other element such as a compressive strut or tie rod.

Note that in a funicular structure, the shape of the funicular structure *always changes beneath an external load.* Where the structure is not loaded, the structure remains straight. The funicular shape appropriate for a continuous load must therefore change continuously. By a similar token, if the shape of the structure changes when there is no load change present, bending will be present. The presence of bending may or may not be problematic, depending on the way the structure is built. A masonry structure subject to bending might develop cracks and collapse (see Section 5–5–1). A steel structure, however, could be designed to accommodate both the axial forces and the bending present (see Chapter 6). It would have larger dimensions, however, than a pure funicularly shaped form with only axial forces present. It is also interesting to note that if the shape of a funicular structure is simply imagined and superimposed on the actual structure considered, the amount of deviation of the actual structure from the funicular shape generally reflects the severity of the bending present in the actual structure [see Figures 5–2(g) and (h)]. These points will be returned to and elaborated upon in later sections.

5-3   ANALYSIS AND DESIGN OF CABLE STRUCTURES

5-3-1   Introduction

The flexible suspension bridge, which was initially developed in China, India, and South America, is of great antiquity. While most early bridges used rope, often made from bamboo, there is

(a) Uniformly distributed load
along length of cable
(e.g., self-weight of cable).

(b) Uniformly distributed load
on horizontal projection.

(c) Cable forces. Only tension forces
are developed in a cable. Maximum
forces occur at the reactions.

(d) Arch forces. Only compression
forces are developed in an ideal
arch. Maximum forces occur at
reactions.

(e) Concentrated loads: family of
funicular shapes for a typical
loading. As the structural depth
of a funicular structure decreases,
internal forces increase, and vice
versa.

(f) Uniformly distributed loads:
family of funicular shapes for
a horizontally distributed
uniform loading.

FIGURE 5–1 Funicular structures.

186

(a) Structure in tension: the shape assumed by a flexible cable under an applied loading is called the funicular shape for that loading.

(c) Structure in compression: inverting the shape assumed by a flexible cable under an applied loading yields a shape that carries the load by axial compression only.

(e) Structure in bending: a structure that is shaped to be funicular for a concentrated load at midspan becomes subject to bending when the loading changes.

(g) Structure in bending: when the shape of the structure does not correspond to the funicular shape for the loading, bending invariably develops.

(b) Structure in tension: Funicular shape for a uniformly distributed loading.

(d) Structure in compression: inverting the tension funicular yields a shape that carries loads by axial compression. The common arch shown above is thus one type of funicular structure.

(f) Structure in bending: a funicular structure for a uniformly distributed load becomes subject to bending when the loading changes.

(h) Structure in bending: the deviation at any point between the structure and the funicular line for the loading generally reflects the amount of bending present in the structure at that point.

FIGURE 5–2 Funicular and nonfunicular structural shapes.

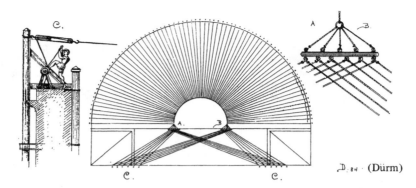

FIGURE 5–3 Cable roof structure over Roman Colosseum, circa A.D. 70. Rope cables anchored to masts spanned in a radial fashion across the open structure supported a movable sunshade that could be drawn across to cover the arena. The span of the structure was 620 ft (188 m) along the major axis and 513 ft (156 m) along the minor axis. (From Dürm.)

recorded evidence of bridges made using chains in China as early as the first century A.D. In addition to the varieties of tents that used ropes, cable structures also found application in some major buildings. A rope cable structure, for example, was used in about A.D. 70 to roof a Roman amphitheater (Figure 5–3). Still it was in connection with suspension bridges that the use of cables as theoretically understood structural elements was developed. This theoretical understanding is actually rather recent, since the suspension bridge remained relatively unknown in Europe (although a type of chain-suspended structure was built in the Swiss Alps in 1218), where most developments in structural theory were occurring, until the sixteenth century, when, in 1595, Fausto Veranzio published a drawing of a suspension bridge. It was not until 1741 that a permanent iron chain footbridge, located in Durham County, England, was finally built. This bridge was probably the first significant suspension bridge in Europe. It failed, however, to establish a precedent.

A major turning point in the evolution of the suspension bridge occurred in the early part of the nineteenth century in America, when James Findley developed a suspension bridge capable of carrying vehicular traffic. His initial bridge, built in 1801 over Jacobs Creek in Uniontown, Pennsylvania, used a flexible chain of wrought-iron links. Findley's real innovation was not the cable itself, however, but the introduction of a *stiffened bridge deck* in which the stiffening was achieved by longitudinal trusses made of wood. The use of a stiffened deck kept the supporting cable from changing shape, and consequently changing the shape of the road surface it supported, by distributing concentrated vehicular loads over a larger portion of the cable. With this innovation the modern suspension bridge was born. The work of Findley became known to others, possibly even to the great builder Thomas Telford in England, who designed the bridge over the Menai Strait in Wales (1818–1826). Louis Navier, the great French mathematician, discussed Findley's work in his classic book on suspension bridges, *Rapport et Mémoire sur les Ponts Suspendus,* published in 1823, in which he gave Findley credit for the introduction of the stiffened bridge deck and provided a way for other bridge builders to become aware of his work.

Other great suspension bridges were built in rapid succession, including the beautiful Clifton Bridge in England by Isombard Brunel, John Roebling's Brooklyn Bridge in 1883, and a

(a) Twisting oscillations in the Tacoma Bridge immediately before total collapse in 1940. The deck initially began heaving in vertical wave motions in winds of 25 to 40 mph. Rhythmic twisting of increasing amplitudes followed until a 600-foot section collapsed into the Narrows. The failure was due to vortex shedding associated with wind action. The shape of the deck and its extreme flexibility contributed to the collapse (the depth of its plate girder stiffening was only 8 feet or 1/350 of the span).

(b) The new Tacoma bridge completed in 1950. The narrow deck and thin plate girder section was changed into a more rigid stiffened truss.

(c) Main structural elements. Diagram of primary forces in cables and masts due to vertical dead and live loads on bridge deck. Under normal vertical loading conditions, deck loads are transferred to the supporting suspension cables. The vertical masts not only support the cables but provide resistance to lateral forces.

FIGURE 5–4 Suspension bridge structure. [(a) Courtesy of Special Collections Division University of Washington Libraries; (b) Courtesy of the Department of Transportation, State of Washington.]

(a) The vertical dead load of the supported roadway is uniformly distributed. The cable assumes a parabolic shape and the bridge deck is level.

(b) Live loads are movable. With a nonrigid bridge deck, the cable and deck would naturally change shape as a load moves across the length of the span.

(c) By making the bridge deck rigid in the longitudinal direction, the forces caused by a concentrated load are more uniformly distributed on the cable. The cable shape and deck shape remain relatively constant.

FIGURE 5–5 Importance of rigid bridge decks.

host of other major bridges. Two significant modern bridges are the Verrazano-Narrows Bridge, with a middle span of 4260 ft (1300 m), and the new Kobe bridge in Japan. The basic structural issues in designing a suspension bridge are illustrated in Figures 5–4 and 5–5.

The application of cables to buildings other than tents developed more slowly because of the lesser need to span large distances and the intrinsic problems of using cables when they were applied. Although James Bogardus submitted a proposal for the Crystal Palace of the New York Exhibition of 1853 in which the roof of a circular cast iron building, 700 ft (213 m) in diameter, was to be suspended from radiating chains anchored to a central tower, the pavilion structures of the Nijny-Novgorod exhibition that were designed by V. Shookhov in 1896 marked the actual beginning of modern applications. Subsequent significant structures include the locomotive roundhouse pavilion at the Chicago World's Fair in 1933 and the Livestock Judging Pavilion built at Raleigh, North Carolina, in the early 1950s. Since then, a number of other significant cable-supported buildings have been constructed.

5–3–2   Suspended Cable Structures: Concentrated Loads

Reactions are developed at cable supports such that the overall cable is in a state of equilibrium. The cable itself normally exerts a force on the supports that acts inwardly and downwardly. Reactive forces provided by the foundation are equal in magnitude and opposite in sense. It is usually not possible to calculate these reactions directly by considering the equilibrium of the whole cable only. Reactive forces are normally considered in terms of their components in the horizontal and vertical directions. Since each reactive force has two components, a total of four unknown components is present; but only three independent equations of statics are available to aid in their determination. As will be shown below, it is necessary to consider the equilibrium of an isolated portion of the structure in order to find reactive forces.

An accompanying task is normally to determine the precise geometry of the cable. The exact shape of a loaded cable depends on the loading conditions present and may not be arbitrarily defined a priori by the designer. A maximum sag or some other value may be specified beforehand, but not the exact shape of the cable itself. Finding the exact shape of the cable is a fundamental objective of analysis procedures.

Internal forces in cable members are invariably in a state of pure tension. A cable can be conceived of as a continuous series of discrete elements connected to one another by hinged connections—a chain is an obvious image. Hence, each discrete element is free to rotate as it will under the action of a load. The connections are such that local internal bending moments cannot be transmitted from one element to another. It then follows that the sum of all rotational effects produced about *any* such location by the external and internal forces must be zero (this is the principle underlying approaches described below for calculating cable geometries and reactive forces). All internal forces that exist in a cable, therefore, must be in a state of pure tension. *If* the exact geometry of the cable were known or somehow established, then the magnitudes of internal forces could be calculated via an approach similar to the joint equilibrium approach described for trusses (any point on a cable must necessarily be in a state of vertical and horizontal translatory equilibrium under the action of all of the internal and external forces acting on the point).

It has been stressed in Chapters 2 and 4 that the function of any structure can be defined as that of carrying the external shears and moments generated by the effects of applied loads. In a cable or funicular-shaped arch, the external shear at a section is balanced by an internal resisting shear force that is provided by the vertical component of the internal axial force developed in the cable or arch member. The overall external bending moment at the same section is balanced by an internal resisting moment that is provided by the couple formed by the horizontal component of the axial force in the funicular member and the horizontal force acting through the end support of the structure. This latter force may be either the horizontal thrust developed at the foundation or the internal force present in a tie-rod or compression strut used between end points of an arch or cable structure, respectively.

The following example illustrates how cable geometries, reactions, and internal forces can be determined through application of the principles described.

◆   ◆   **EXAMPLE**

Figure 5–6 illustrates a cable structure carrying two loads. Assume that the deformed structure has the maximum depth shown under the first load. The deformed structure has another critical depth under the second load. The latter depth is not precisely known beforehand, but it must be a value that is directly dependent on the maximum depth of the other point, which is a given.

Solution: The first step in the analysis process is to determine the reactions at the ends of the member. Vertical components can be found in a straightforward manner by considering moment equilibrium of the whole structure about one or the other reaction. Horizontal components can be found by passing a section through the structure at a location of known structural depth and considering the equilibrium of either the right or left portion of the structure. Thus:

Vertical reactions:

$$\Sigma M_A = 0 \ \oplus: \qquad -15(10) - 30(5) + 45R_{B_v} = 0 \qquad \therefore \quad R_{B_v} = 6.7$$

$$\Sigma F_Y = 0 + \uparrow: \qquad -10 - 5 + R_{A_v} + R_{B_v} = 0 \qquad \therefore \quad R_{A_v} = 8.3$$

Horizontal reactions:

Pass a vertical section through the structure immediately to the right of the location of the maximum depth and consider the equilibrium of the left portion of the structure:

$$\Sigma M_C = 0 \ \oplus: \qquad -15(8.3) + 10(R_{A_H}) = 0 \qquad \therefore \quad R_{A_H} = 12.5$$

For the whole structure:

$$\Sigma F_X = 0 \overset{+}{\rightarrow}: \qquad -R_{A_H} + R_{B_H} = 0 \qquad \therefore \quad R_{B_H} = 12.5$$

Depth of structure at point D:

Pass a vertical section immediately to the left of point D and consider the equilibrium of the right portion of the structure. Let h_D equal the height of the structure at this point. Thus,

$$\Sigma M_D = 0 \ \oplus: \qquad -h_D(12.5) + 15(6.7) = 0 \qquad \therefore \quad h_D = 8.3$$

Note that no other structural depth would satisfy rotational equilibrium considerations at this point.

Cable forces:

Forces in individual segments in the cable can now be found by using the method of joints (see Chapter 4). The results of this process are illustrated in Figure 5–6(c). It should be noted that the absolute magnitude of the forces in different segments vary. Cables are *not* constant-force structures.   ◆

(a) Cable structure and loading. The structure deforms into a shape responsive to the relative magnitudes of the loads applied. The sag at only one point can be specified since the magnitudes of the relative deformations are interdependent.

(b) The cable sag at points other than the sag specified can be calculated by considering the equilibrium of different pieces of the structure. For the structure shown, the first step is to determine the left horizontal reaction (R_{A_H}) by considering the equilibrium of the left portion of the structure ($\Sigma M_C = 0$).

The unknown sag at point D can then be calculated by considering the equilibrium of the right-hand portion by noting that $R_{A_H} = R_{B_H}$ and summing moments about point D ($\Sigma M_D = 0$), treating h_D as an unknown.

(c) Once the geometry of the structure is completely specified, internal forces in various segments of the cable can be determined through joint equilibrium considerations.

(d) An alternative analytical process is to first draw shear and moment diagrams for the basic loading condition and then use a method of sections approach to find vertical and horizontal components of cable forces.

(e) The internal shear and moment provided by the structure at any section must balance the external shear and moment present at that section. The internal shear is provided by the vertical component of the force in the cable. The internal moment is provided by the couple formed between the horizontal reaction and the horizontal component of the force in cable. Note that the horizontal component of the force in the cable is always equal to the horizontal thrust because of translatory equilibrium in the horizontal direction. The force in a cable segment is found by resolving vertical and horizontal components into a single resultant force.

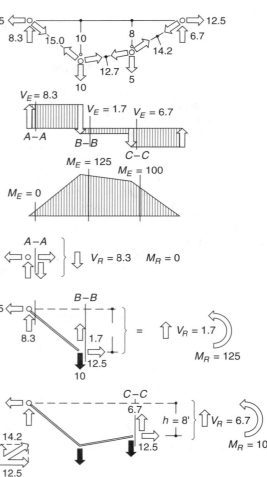

FIGURE 5-6 Analysis of a cable supporting concentrated loads.

◆ ◆   **EXAMPLE**

An *alternative* method of analysis for the same structure (Figure 5–6) is to first draw shear and moment diagrams for the external loading condition and then use what is basically a *method-of-sections* approach. Vertical reactions are first found as before.

Solution: The horizontal reactions can be found by observing that the structure must provide an internal moment resistance equal and opposite in sense to the external moment at every point. The internal moment is provided by a couple formed between the end horizontal reaction and the horizontal component of the cable force. Considering the structure at point C:

$$\underbrace{10R_{A_H}}_{\substack{\text{internal} \\ \text{resisting} \\ \text{moment}}} = \underbrace{125}_{\substack{\text{external applied} \\ \text{moment (see moment} \\ \text{diagram)}}} \quad \text{or} \quad R_{A_H} = 12.5$$

This is obviously essentially the same process as described before but is a conceptually different way of thinking about it.

Depth of structure at point D:
As before:

$$\underbrace{h_D(12.5)}_{\substack{\text{internal} \\ \text{resisting} \\ \text{moment}}} = \underbrace{100}_{\substack{\text{external} \\ \text{moment}}} \quad \text{or} \quad h_D = 8.3$$

Cable forces:
Sections are passed through points immediately to the right of each critical point and equilibrium of the left portion considered [see Figure 5–6(e)]. Note that in each case the internal shear resistance that balances the external shear force is provided by the vertical component of the force in the cable. The vertical and horizontal forces are components of the actual forces in the cables and can be used to calculate these forces.

The second method presented is extremely useful for conceptualizing how cable or arch structures provide a mechanism for carrying the shear and moment associated with the external load. It also shows particularly well how the reactions and internal forces depend on the height of the structure. Doubling the initial maximum depth would decrease horizontal thrusts, for example, by a factor of 2. Cable forces would thus be reduced. Still the new combination of cable height and force would still yield the same internal balancing shear and moments discussed above.   ◆

◆ ◆   **EXAMPLE**

Alternatively, a *graphical technique* may also be used to analyze the same cable (Figure 5–7). While seemingly simple, graphic techniques are quite subtle and must be used with care. The process is only briefly described herein.

Solution: First redefine members and loads in terms of adjacent spaces as shown. A force polygon is first constructed as shown. The total downward force present is equal to the line connecting the starting and ending points. If the vertical reactions are first calculated via statics, they are marked on the line as well. To find the shape of the structure, the individual forces P_1 and P_2 are replaced by component pairs since graphic

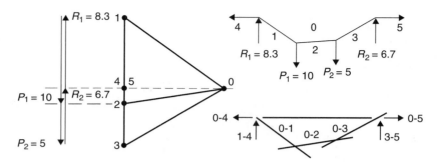

FIGURE 5–7 Use of graphic statics in determining cable forces and stresses.

statics work best with inclined forces. As shown, a "pole" point 0 on the horizontal with the reaction point is arbitrarily chosen to the right and lines connected to P_1 and P_2 to create force polygons equivalent to the original loads (e.g., Forces 0–1 and 0–2 are components of P_1). Forces in cable members 0–1 and 0–2 necessarily balance P_1 (from joint equilibrium considerations) while 0–2 and 0–3 balance P_2. Forces 0–4 and 4–1 must necessarily be equal to the horizontal and vertical components of the final force in cable member 1–0 (so that the left node point is in translatory equilibrium). Forces 0–5 and 5–3 must be components of the final force in cable member 0–3. For the whole structure to be in horizontal equilibrium, 0–5 and 0–4 must be identical in magnitude (as shown on the diagram) but opposite in sense. Forces are then drawn through known points on their respective lines of action as shown to determine the cable shape. Force magnitudes in the segments may be scaled directly. Changing the position of the pole point 0 would obviously change the height of the structure, but not its shape. Initially establishing the location of the pole point 0 is equivalent to a design decision establishing cable slopes. In this technique it is very difficult to stipulate a maximum cable sag first. Instead of finding vertical reactions first through statics, they may be found by arbitrarily choosing any pole location, drawing the components of P_1 and P_2 as before, and then drawing a "closing line" to determine the directions of the components of the reactions. This closing line is then drawn on the polygon to determine the reactions. A new polygon with a horizontal closing line is then drawn and the process proceeds as before. Techniques of this type may be used with any number of loadings acting in any direction and with supports on different levels. ◆

5–3–3 Suspended Cables: Uniformly Distributed Loads

Cables or arches carrying uniformly distributed loads can be analyzed in much the same way as described for concentrated loads. Since the funicular shape is a constantly curving one, however, a variant of the method of sections is the exclusive analytical technique used.

◆ ◆ **EXAMPLE**

Consider the cable shown in Figure 5–8. Assume the maximum cable sag to be $h_{\max}$. The first step is to calculate vertical reactions which are formed through considering the equilibrium of the overall structure. The following steps are to calculate horizontal reactions, find the shape of funicular curve, and then determine the internal forces in the cable.

(a) Cable structure and loading.

(b) Shear and moment diagrams for loading condition.

(c) The first step in the analysis process is to find the reactions. Horizontal reactions can be found by passing a section through a point where the cable sag is known or specified and considering moment equilibrium about that point. Thus,

$$R_{A_H}(h) = wL^2/8$$

or $R_{A_H} = wL^2/8h$

(d) The equation of the deflected shape of the cable is found by considering the equilibrium of different sections of the cable. Thus,

$$(wL^2/8h)y - wLx/2 + wx^2/2 = 0$$

or $y = 4h(Lx - x^2)/L^2$

(e) The slope of the cable at any point can be evaluated by considering the deflected shape. At the ends of the cable, the slope is also given by the ratio of the vertical and horizontal components of the end reactions. The maximum cable force is merely the resultant of these two forces. The cable force at midspan is less and is numerically equal to the horizontal thrust: $T_{L/2} = wL^2/8h$.

FIGURE 5–8 Analysis of a cable supporting a horizontally distributed load.

195

Solution:

Vertical reactions:

$$R_{A_v} = R_{B_v} = \frac{wL}{2} \qquad \text{by inspection}$$

Horizontal reactions:

Pass a section through the structure at midspan (the location of known sag) and consider the equilibrium of the left portion of the structure to find R_{A_H}:

$$\Sigma M_{L/2} = 0: \quad -R_{A_H}h_{max} - \left(\frac{wL}{2}\right)\left(\frac{L}{2}\right) + \left(\frac{wL}{2}\right)\left(\frac{L}{4}\right) = 0 \quad \therefore \quad R_{A_H} = \frac{wL^2}{8h_{max}}$$

Alternatively, using shear and moment diagrams directly:

$$\underbrace{R_{A_H}h_{max}}_{\substack{\text{internal} \\ \text{resisting} \\ \text{moment}}} = \underbrace{\frac{wL^2}{8}}_{\substack{\text{external} \\ \text{applied} \\ \text{moment}}} \quad \therefore \quad R_{A_H} = \frac{wL^2}{8h_{max}}$$

Shape of cable:

The shape of the cable can be found by considering the equilibrium of different sections of the structure. Consider a section of the structure defined by a distance x from the left connections. Let y be the depth of the cable at that point.

$$\Sigma M_x = 0: \quad \left(\frac{wL^2}{8h_{max}}\right)(y) - \left(\frac{wL}{2}\right)(x) + wx\left(\frac{x}{2}\right) = 0 \quad \therefore \quad y = \frac{4h_{max}(Lx - x^2)}{L^2}$$

Alternatively, equating the internal resisting moment to the external applied moment:

$$\left(\frac{wL^2}{8h_{max}}\right)y = \left(\frac{wL}{2}\right)x - (wx)\left(\frac{x}{2}\right) \quad \therefore \quad y = \frac{4h_{max}(Lx - x^2)}{L^2}$$

The equation found is obviously that of a parabola. The absolute value of the slope at either end is given by $(dy/dx)_{x=0,x=L} = \theta_{x,L} = 4h_{max}/L$. This slope could have also been found by considering the ratio of the horizontal and vertical reactions: $\theta = (wL/2)(wL^2/8h_{max}) = 4h_{max}/L$.

Cable forces:

Since the slope of the cable is zero at midspan, where both the external and internal shear forces are also zero, the cable force can be seen to identically equal the horizontal reaction by considering the horizontal equilibrium of the section to the left or right of midspan. Thus, the cable force at midspan becomes $T_{L/2} = wL^2/8h_{max}$. The cable force in the cable at either end connection is found by simple joint equilibrium considerations: $\Sigma F_x = 0$: $T_{0,L}\cos\theta = wL^2/8h_{max}$, where θ is given by $4h_{max}/L$ and $\cos\theta$ by $1/\sqrt{1 + 16h_{max}^2/L^2}$. Thus, $T_{0,L} = (wL^2/8h_{max})\sqrt{1 + 16h_{max}^2/L^2}$.

Alternatively, $T_{0,L} = \sqrt{(R_{A_H})^2 + (R_{A_v})^2} = R_{A_H}\sqrt{1 + (R_{A_v}/R_{A_H})^2} = (wL^2/8h_{max})\sqrt{1 + 16h_{max}^2/L^2}$. The force in the cable at the ends thus exceeds that at midspan. ◆

◆ ◆   **EXAMPLE**

A series of cables spaced at 15 ft (4.6 m) on center span 100 ft (30.5 m) between abutments and carry a live load of 50 lb/ft^2 (2394 N/m^2). Each cable has a maximum sag of 20 ft (6.1 m). Assume that the dead load of the whole structure is 50 lb/ft^2 (2394 N/m^2). Also, assume both the live load and dead load to be horizontally projected. Find the minimum required cable diameter assuming the allowable cable stress is 75,000 lb/in.^{2} (517 N/mm^2).

Solution:

Reactions:

$$\text{vertical} = R_{A_v} = \frac{wL}{2} = \frac{[(50 + 50)\ \text{lb/ft}^2](15\ \text{ft})(100\ \text{ft})}{2} = 75,000\ \text{lb}$$

$$= \frac{[(2394 + 2394)\ \text{N/m}^2](4.6\ \text{m})(30.5\ \text{m})}{2} = 334\ \text{kN}$$

$$\text{horizontal} = R_{A_H} = \frac{wL^2}{8h} = \frac{[(50 + 50)\ \text{lb/ft}^2](15\ \text{ft})(100\ \text{ft})^2}{8(20\ \text{ft})} = 93,750\ \text{lb}$$

$$= \frac{[(2394 + 2394)\ \text{N/m}^2](4.6\ \text{m})(30.5\ \text{m})^2}{8(6.1\ \text{m})} = 417\ \text{kN}$$

Maximum cable force (at ends):

$$T = \sqrt{R_{A_v}^2 + R_{A_H}^2} = (75,000^2 + 93,750^2)^{1/2} = 120,000\ \text{lb}$$

$$= (334^2 + 417^2)^{1/2} = 534\ \text{kN}$$

Alternatively,

$$T = R_{A_H} \sqrt{1 + 16h^2/L^2} = 93,750\ \text{lb}\left[1 + 16\left(\frac{20^2}{100^2}\right)\right]^{1/2} = 120,000\ \text{lb}$$

$$= 417\ \text{kN}\left[1 + 16\left(\frac{6.1^2}{30.5^2}\right)\right]^{1/2} = 534\ \text{kN}$$

Cable diameter:

$$A = \frac{T}{f_{\text{allowable}}} = \frac{120,000}{75,000} = 1.60\ \text{in.}^2 = \frac{534,000\ \text{N}}{517\ \text{N/mm}^2} = 1033\ \text{mm}^2$$

Twisted-strand cable would probably be used, in which the total diameter is made up of a series of individual wire strands of smaller diameters. The gross area of the total diameter therefore does not equal the net area of the cross sections of individual strands. The resisting area of the whole cable is about two-thirds of its gross area. Thus, the gross area of the cable needed for this example is (3/2)(1.60) = 2.4 in.^{2} or (3/2)(1033) = 1550 mm^2. This leads to a cable diameter of 1¾ in. or 45 mm.   ◆

5–3–4   General Funicular Equation

A more general approach can be taken to the analysis of cables than previously discussed, which is very useful in treating more complicated structures that are not symmetrically loaded or which have cable supports at different levels.

FIGURE 5-9 Cable with supports at different levels.

Consider the cable shown in Figure 5–9. As before, the first step in the analysis process is to find the reactions. If ΣM_{B_E} is used to designate the sum of all the rotational moments about point B of all the external loads [e.g., $P_n(L - x_n) + P_{n-1}(L - x_{n-1}) + \cdots$], the total moment equilibrium expression for the entire cable about point B becomes $\Sigma M_B = 0$: $-R_{A_H}(h) - R_{A_v}(L) + \Sigma M_{B_E} = 0$; $R_{A_v} = (\Sigma M_{B_E}/L) - R_{A_H}(h)/L$.

This expression cannot be directly solved because both R_{A_v} and R_{A_H} are unknown values. The next step is to pass a section through a point x on the cable *where the cable sag is known* and consider the moment equilibrium of the left portion of the cable. Let ΣM_{x_E} be used to designate the sum of the external moments of the loads on the left portion about this point. Noting that the moment arm of R_{A_H} at this point is given by $(hx/L - y_x)$, where y_x is the cable sag from a line connecting the two end points of the cable, the moment expression about x becomes $\Sigma M_x = 0$: $-R_{A_H}(hx/L - y_x) - R_{A_v}x + \Sigma M_{x_E} = 0$. Substituting R_{A_v} from above yields $R_{A_H}(y_x) = (x/L)\Sigma M_{B_E} - \Sigma M_{x_E}$.

If y_x is specified at a point, then R_{A_H} can be evaluated. Once R_{A_H} is known, it can be used to find unknown cable sags at points other than x. Cable forces can be found by equilibrium considerations in a manner similar to that described previously.

5-3-5 Cable Lengths

The length of a cable can be evaluated from considering the basic expression for the deformed shape of a cable. For a *uniformly loaded* cable with a horizontal chord (both supports on the same level), let L_{total} be the total length of the cable, L_h the span, and h the maximum sag. The total cable length can be shown to be approximately $L_{\text{total}} = L_h(1 + \frac{8}{3}h^2/L_h^2 - \frac{32}{5}h^4/L_h^4)$.

For the derivation for this and other important expressions defining the elongation of a cable, the reader is referred to other references.[1]

---

[1]See, for example, C. H. Norris and J. B. Wilbur, *Elementary Structural Analysis,* 2nd ed., McGraw-Hill Book Company, New York, 1960; or J. Scalzi, W. Poddorny, and W. Teng, *Design Fundamentals of Cable Roof Structures.* U.S. Steel Corporation, Pittsburgh, Pa., 1969.

(a) Winds blowing over roof surface in its naturally deflected shape cause suction forces to develop. These suction forces cause the flexible roof to begin rising.

(b) As the roof changes shape due to the suction forces, the effect of the wind on the new shape becomes one of pressure rather than suction. This causes the roof to move downward again.

(c) As the roof moves up and down, the effect of the wind alternately produces suctions and pressures causing further movements. A constant fluttering of the roof results.

FIGURE 5–10   Dynamic effects of wind on flexible roof structure.

5–3–6   Wind Effects

A critical problem in the design of any cable roof structure is the dynamic effect of wind, something that does not significantly affect an arch structure. Consider the simple roof structure supported by cables in Figure 5–10. As the wind blows over the top of the roof, a suction will be created. If the magnitude of the suction force due to the wind exceeds the dead weight of the roof structure itself, the roof surface will begin to rise. As it begins rising and dramatically changing shape, the forces on the roof begin to change, since the magnitude and distribution of wind forces on a body are dependent on the exact shape of the body. Since the wind forces change due to the changing shape of the roof, the flexible structure itself again changes shape in response to the new loading. The process is cyclical. The roof will not remain in any one shape, but will move, or flutter, as long as the wind is present.

While the description of wind effects presented above is useful, a more rigorous way of understanding wind effects is via a study of vibratory phenomena in cables. Although a full treatment of such phenomena is beyond the scope of this book, some observations can be made.

A vibration in a structure that is induced by wind (or earthquake) effects is a reciprocating or oscillating motion which repeats itself after an interval of time. This interval of time is called the *period* of vibration. The *frequency* of vibration is numerically equal to the reciprocal of the period.

All suspension structures (and other structures as well) have a *natural frequency* of vibration when acted on by an externally applied force. When an external dynamic force acting on the structure comes within the natural frequency range, a state of vibration may be reached where the driving-force frequency and the body's natural frequency are in tune, a condition referred to as *resonance*. At resonance the structure undergoes violent vibration, resulting in structural damage (see Section 3–2–4).

The natural frequency of a suspended cable is given by $f_n = (N\pi/L)\sqrt{T/(w/g)}$, where L is the cable length, N is any integer, w is the applied load per unit length, T is the cable tension, and g is the acceleration due to gravity. The first three modes of vibration are shown in Figure 5–10.

The cable could vibrate in these and other modes, depending on the frequency of the exciting force.

Resonance in a cable would occur when the external exciting force has a frequency exactly equal to the first natural frequency of the cable or any of its higher frequencies. Unfortunately, for many cable structures, the frequency of wind forces is often close to the natural frequency of the cable structure. Major cable structures have been destroyed because of this phenomenon, as witnessed by the well-known Tacoma Narrows failure [See Figure 5–4(a)].

There are only several fundamental ways to combat flutter due to wind forces. One is to simply increase the dead load on the roof, thereby also increasing cable tensions and changing natural frequencies. Another is to provide anchoring guy cables to the cable at periodic points to tie the structure to the ground. A related method is to use some sort of crossed-cable or double-cable system. The latter method is extremely interesting, since it is possible to create an internally self-damping system. This approach is discussed in more detail in Section 5–4.

5–4   DESIGN OF CABLE STRUCTURES

Although most of the discussions thus far have focused on the cable as a simple, singly curved or draped suspension element, cables are used in a great variety of ways. Cable structures are more correctly categorized into either suspension structures or cable-stayed structures. *Suspension structures* can be typically subclassified into the following: (1) single-curvature structures, in which roofs are made by placing cables parallel to one another and using a surface formed by beams or plates to span between cables; (2) double-cable structures, in which interconnected double cables of different curvatures are used in the same vertical plane; and (3) double-curvature structures, in which a field of crossed cables of different and often reverse curvatures make up the primary roof surface. (These structures are discussed in Chapter 11.) *Cable-stayed structures* typically use vertical or sloping compression masts, from which straight cables run to critical points or horizontally spanning members.

5–4–1   Simple Suspension Cables

General Principles.   Suspended cable systems are capable of great spans. For given spans and loading conditions, primary design issues hinge on the decision of how to proportion the geometry of a cable in terms of its sag-to-span ratio. Cable forces, lengths, and diameters all depend on this ratio. Forces in supporting masts or tie-back cables, hence their sizes, are influenced by this ratio as well. These issues are discussed below. Simply suspended cable systems are particularly sensitive to vibratory wind effects (see Section 5–3–5), which have caused the destruction of major cable structures in the past. Special precautions must be taken to prevent wind-induced instability. For example, cable tensions can be controlled, which in turn affect the natural period of vibration of a cable and hence its susceptibility to vibratory phenomena. Various tie-downs or stiffening devices provided by the enclosure surface can be used as well.

Cable Sags.   The forces in cable structures, hence their size, are critically dependent on the amount of sag or rise relative to the span of the structure. The horizontal component of the force in a uniformly loaded level-ended cable, for example, is given by $T_h = wL^2/8h_{max}$, where h_{max} is the maximum sag present. Obviously, doubling the maximum sag decreases T_h by a factor of 2.

FIGURE 5–11   Methods for determining optimal cable sags.

In general, as the sag h_{max} is made smaller, the cable force becomes larger, and vice versa. Clearly, it is not possible to have a zero-sag cable, since this would imply indefinitely large cable forces and consequently indefinitely large cable cross sections.

Given this sensitivity to structural depth, finding the most appropriate sag or rise becomes an optimization problem. As h_{max} increases, the force in the cable decreases and thus the related cross-sectional area required also decreases. The cable length, however, simultaneously increases. Clearly, an indefinitely long cable requires an indefinitely large volume. Conversely, as h_{max} decreases, cable forces and required cross-sectional areas increase, but the cable length decreases. An optimum value of h_{max} must exist. This optimum value can be determined simply by developing an expression for the cable volume in terms of h_{max}, using the analytical expressions developed in Section 5–3–4, and minimizing the value of the expression with reference to the critical variable h_{max}.

This process can be illustrated for a simple cable with a point load (Figure 5–11). The force in either cable AC or BC is $T_{AC} = T_{BC} = P/2 \sin \phi$. For a material with an allowable stress of F, the required cross-sectional area of either cable is $A = P/2F \sin \phi$. The length of either cable is $L_\phi = (L/2)/\cos \phi$. The volume of either cable becomes $V = AL_\phi = [P/2F \sin \phi][(L/2)/\cos \phi]$. The total volume of the cable system becomes $V_{total} = 2[P/2F \sin \phi][(L/2)/\cos \phi]$. This expression can be minimized ($dV/d\phi = 0$) to obtain the minimum volume of material required, or a graph may be plotted. The minimum volume occurs when $\phi = 45°$ or h or L equals a $1:2$ ratio ($h/L = 0.5$). In this case $V_{min} = PL/F$. Note on the graph, however, that there is actually a large range for ϕ where the volume is a near minimum. A similar process for a cable with a uniform loading will result in a depth equal to approximately one-third the span of the structure ($1:3$).

The exact sag or rise chosen for use, however, is invariably dependent on the overall context in which the cable is used (including the design of supporting masts). Most cable structures used in buildings have sag/span ratios between $1:8$ and $1:10$.

Supporting Elements.   In addition to the actual roof cables, other structural elements (e.g., masts, guy cables) are needed to make a building structure. The elements typically support the cable in space and provide a means for transferring its vertical and horizontal thrusts to the ground. The design of these elements is as crucial as is the design of the cable.

A basic design issue is whether to absorb the horizontal thrusts involved directly through the foundations or by using a supplementary horizontal compression strut. While designing foundations to absorb both vertical and horizontal thrusts is difficult, doing so is entirely feasible, depending on soil or other foundation conditions that are existent. The use of horizontal compression struts is much less frequent because of the long unbraced length of such members, which makes them highly susceptible to possible buckling since they are in compression. Required sizes for the struts would be very large and tend to offset any efficiencies gained by using a cable to span a long distance.

Figure 5–12 illustrates several types of common support elements found in buildings using cables to make a volume-forming enclosure. Figure 5–12(a) shows a cable supported by end piers. In this case the entire horizontal thrust of the cable must be resisted by the vertical pier acting like a cantilever beam. Owing to the very large horizontal thrusts, significant bending is induced in the pier and it must be made quite large. (The sizing of members that are in bending is discussed in Chapter 6.) The foundation of the pier must also be designed to resist the overturning moment. By and large, this approach is economically viable only in lightly loaded cables of relatively short span.

Figure 5–12(b) shows a cable supported by guyed masts. When the masts are vertical, the horizontal cable thrust is taken up completely by the guy cable, which transfers the force to the ground. The mast itself picks up only axial compression forces. No bending is present. The mast is designed as a column (see Chapter 7), which picks up the sum of the vertical force components in both the primary and guy cables. Since mast foundations need only carry vertical loads, they are fairly easy to design and construct. The foundation for the guy cable, however, is more complex, since it needs to withstand not only lateral forces but uplift forces as well. By and large, however, this use of guyed masts is a fairly efficient type of cable-support system.

A variant of the approach described here is shown in Figure 5–12(c), in which the masts are tilted. In this case part of the horizontal thrusts are picked up by the inclined masts acting in compression and the remainder by the attached guy cables. While this increases the axial force in the masts and their lengths as well, and thus increases their size, this tilting reduces the forces in the guy cables and their ground attachments. Since uplift forces in the guy cable ground attachments are reduced, foundations can be more easily made.

In all the above, the sag chosen for the cable is a significant variable since pier or mast lengths are directly related to this value for a given functional enclosed cable height above ground. The deeper the sag, the more substantial support members become because of the need to control buckling in long columns (see Chapter 7). Sags smaller than the one-third depth/span value discussed in the preceding section are thus often used to achieve a more optimum overall solution. Sag/span ratios of around 1:8 to 1:10 are often used.

5–4–2 Double-Cable Systems

Double-cable systems are interesting design responses to the difficult task of controlling wind-induced vibratory *flutter* that makes the use of simple suspended cable systems problematic (see Section 5–3–6). A double-cable structure typically consists of two coupled pretensioned cables and related struts or ties that function together in carrying an external force. Two types are illustrated in Figure 5–13. In the double concave system, pretensioning is obtained by jacking forces

(a) Pier supports: the vertical piers supporting the ends of the cables carry the vertical components of the cable reactions by axial compression and the horizontal component by bending. This system is good for cables of relatively short span only.

Pier supports

The greater the span L or the height H, the larger must be the supporting piers.

Basic force system. Note that the foundation must prevent the piers from overturning.

(b) Guyed mast supports: the horizontal components of the cable thrusts are absorbed by diagonal guy cables and transferred to the ground. The vertical masts act in axial compression only. This system is good for relatively long span cables.

Guyed mast supports

$$T_{G_H} = T_{G_H}$$
$$C_M = T_{G_V} + T_{C_V}$$

Increasing forces

T_C T_C

Free-body diagram of top of cable mast

As the guy cable angle changes as shown, the forces in the guy cable tend to increase. Mast forces also increase accordingly.

Basic force system. The masts carry axial forces. The guyed cable foundations must prevent guy uplift and sliding.

(c) Inclined guyed masts: inclining the masts causes them to pick up some of the horizontal cable thrusts, thus reducing the forces in the diagonal guy cables. This system is good for long-span cables.

Inclined guyed masts

$$T_{G_H} + C_{M_H} = T_{C_H}$$
$$T_{G_V} + T_{C_V} = C_{M_V}$$
$$C_M = C_{M_V}/\cos\phi$$

Free-body diagram of top of cable mast

Basic force system. The masts carry only downward forces. Guy cable foundations must prevent guy uplift and sliding.

FIGURE 5–12   Different types of cable-support systems.

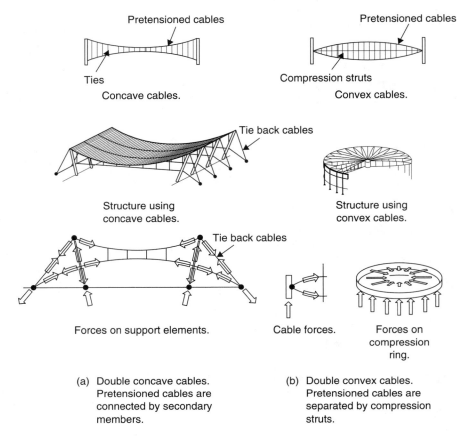

Pretensioned cables

Ties

Concave cables.

Pretensioned cables

Compression struts

Convex cables.

Tie back cables

Structure using concave cables.

Structure using convex cables.

Tie back cables

Forces on support elements.

Cable forces.

Forces on compression ring.

(a) Double concave cables. Pretensioned cables are connected by secondary members.

(b) Double convex cables. Pretensioned cables are separated by compression struts.

FIGURE 5–13 Use of double-cable systems to prevent roof flutter due to wind effects. In both cases shown, the cable force in the upper member is slightly different from that in the lower member. Therefore, each member has a different natural frequency of vibration, which causes the whole assembly to be a self-damping mechanism, since neither cable can freely vibrate in its natural mode because of the other cable.

applied via the tie-back cables (the interior cables are literally stretched). In the convex system, the upper and lower cables are pretensioned internally.

When the convex assembly shown in Figure 5–13(b) is put in place, it essentially acts much like a truss in that the top member tends to compress while the bottom member tends to elongate. Since both cables have already been pretensioned, these tendencies cause a reduction in the tension force in the top cable and an increase in the force on the bottom cable. The top cable must be designed and prestressed so that under full loading the change in force in the top cable is not large enough to cause the cable to lose all its initial prestressing and go slack. The bottom cable must be sufficiently sized to carry both the initial pretensioning and the added tension that develops under loading. The structure shown in Figure 5–13(a) behaves differently under loading in that the pretensioned upper cable is subject to further tension while the pretensioning in the lower cable is reduced.

In both structures, the external loads and the pretensioning forces cause large horizontal forces to be developed on the supporting elements. A series of tie-back cables are used to take care of these forces in the structure shown in Figure 5–12(a). A large continuous compression ring, typically made out of steel, is used to take care of these forces in the structure shown in Figure 5–13(b) (since the ring takes up the horizontal forces, the columns carry only vertical loads).

The dynamic behavior of the roof types just described is interesting. As mentioned in Section 5–3–6, the natural frequency of vibration of a tight cable depends on the tension present in the cable. Since both cables are, as discussed here, at different tensions, it is evident that each has a slightly different natural frequency of vibration. The natural frequency of vibration of the lower cable will thus always tend to be slightly different from the upper cable. As an external exciting force tends to cause either cable to vibrate in one of its fundamental modes, the other cable will tend to damp out the vibrations in the cable, since it has a different natural frequency of vibration. The result is that any oscillations are damped out since neither cable can go into resonance because of the damping effect of the other attached cable with a different natural frequency.

It is possible, however, that the whole assembly (which must have its own natural frequency, which is distinct from those of either of its constituents) could go into resonance. The natural frequency of the whole system is related to the combination of individual cable frequencies and is higher than either. If this combined frequency can be made sufficiently high by careful design, the danger of there being a wind with a sufficiently high critical velocity to cause the whole system to resonate can be minimized to the point where no danger exists.

5–4–3   Cable-Stayed Structures

Many common cable structures for both buildings and bridges incorporate rigid beam elements as well as rigid column elements. Figure 5–14 illustrates an extremely simple version of an

In this configuration, the forces in the cable tie-back and mast are highly sensitive to the distance between them. As the distance decreases toward zero, forces tend to become indefinitely large.

FIGURE 5–14   Forces in the tie-backs of a simple cable-stayed building structure.

assembly of rigid elements and cables. The parallel cable and mast system is frequently used in buildings to reduce the amount of space occupied by more normal tie-back cables that would simply extend diagonally directly to the ground. In this particular structure, forces in individual cables and rigid elements can be calculated directly by the basic methods of statics discussed in Chapter 2. As can be seen from the simple reaction analyses shown in Figure 5–14, the forces developed in the tie-back cable are extremely sensitive to the distance separating the vertical cable and mast. Increasing this distance decreases forces and vice versa. As the distance between them gets very small, internal forces can become extremely large. One job of the designer is to balance structural imperatives dictated by high internal forces versus the spatial advantages of having a reduced distance between the cable and mast. The designer must also ensure that the structure is stable under all loading conditions. In the case shown, the structure must obviously be stabilized in the out-of-plane direction. Unfortunately, it is also prone to collapse if large earthquake or wind forces act in particular directions (see Figure 5–14). Tie-down cables at the ends could remedy the latter problem but are spatially awkward.

Figure 5–15 shows several other types of structures. These are typically called *cable-stayed* structures. They are designed to have the necessary stability under all anticipated types of loading conditions. A cable-stayed structure (Figure 5–16) is one in which a series of linear cables periodically support a rigid horizontal member (such as a beam or truss). The cables typically radiate or otherwise spring from one or more compression masts. The whole system is capable of large spans without the complexity of using curved cables. Many bridge structures have recently been constructed in this way, as have a number of buildings.

In a typical structure, the external loading is shared between the cable system and the primary spanning element functioning in its own right as a beam or truss. The number of cables used depends on the size and stiffness of the spanning element. Cables may be closely spaced and a relatively small beam or truss used, or widely spaced and a bigger and stiffer beam or truss

(a) Cable-stayed bridge with asymmetrical mast and radiating cables.

(b) Cable-stayed bridge with central mast and parallel cables.

(c) Cable-stayed roof structure with central mast and non-load-bearing side enclosure walls.

(d) Cable-stayed rigid roof with stabilizing tie-back cables.

FIGURE 5–15 Typical cable-stayed structures.

Cable-stayed building structure

The beam would have to be modeled as a
continuous structure with four supports
(2 end pins, 2 elastic cable supports) in order
to both determine exactly the forces carried
by the center diagonal cables and
subsequently design the beam (see
Chapter 8).

Bending moments developed in
the beam (see Chapter 8)

FIGURE 5–16   Forces in the tie-backs of a simple cable-stayed building structure.

used. In general, the approach is most useful when spans are beyond those normally possible for rigid beams or trusses spanning in their own right (see Part III).

The cables themselves are invariably in tension. Determining cable forces can be simple or highly complex, depending on the number of cables in the system and the relative stiffness of the beam or truss. A useful first approximation for designing the cable and mast system is to ignore the stiffness of the beam or truss and to assume that the cable system carries all of the loads.

The angles formed by the supporting cable to the suspended load are critical. Shallow angles are to be avoided since attached cables would not provide the stiff support necessary to the supported beam, and forces developed in the cables would become extremely high.

Forces in masts and tie-backs that stabilize masts may be determined fairly readily through basic equilibrium considerations. Masts can become quite tall in cable-stayed structures and pose their own design difficulties, due to the buckling phenomena in long members (see Chapter 7).

Supported beams or trusses are designed much like continuous beams over several supports (in this case the cable attachments), as described in Chapter 8. When only one set of cables in a plane is used, as is the case in many bridges, the cross section must be designed to carry the significantly large torsional forces involved from imbalanced loadings (see Chapter 6).

Figure 5–16 suggests some of the issues involved in analyzing a cable-stayed roof structure for a building. By and large, these analyses when exactly done are highly complex and beyond the scope of this text.

5–5 ANALYSIS AND DESIGN OF ARCHES

5–5–1 Masonry Arches

The arch has its roots in antiquity. Masonry arches derive their load-carrying capability from their curved geometry, which causes only compressive forces to be developed between adjacent blocks. Masonry is naturally unable to resist tension stresses, which would lead to immediate cracking and potential instability of the whole structure. For a masonry arch to collapse, however, it is necessary for a failure mechanism consisting of more than one crack to develop (Figure 5–17). Significant shape changes accompany the development of such a failure mechanism. Analyses of these shape changes were used by early investigators seeking to understand the behavior of masonry arches. Many failures were caused by lateral movements at the base of arches which were induced by the horizontal components of the arch thrusts.

The general analogy of an arch as an inverted cable, and hence a structure subject to only compressive forces, has already been discussed. Strictly speaking, however, the shapes of masonry arches rarely exactly follow the funicular shapings, which are parabolic in nature for uniformly distributed loadings, suggested by the inverted-cable analogy. Certainly, the common semicircular masonry arch is not parabolic. This would tend to suggest that some bending and associated shape changes are induced in the structure which could lead to the development of tension stresses, hence cracks. Such deviations are typically not problematic, however, because of the large dimensions of the blocks in common masonry arches and the normal presence of surrounding masonry wall enclosures that contain the arch and help keep it from changing shape. The funicular line itself can be contained within the dimensions of a large block structure. If it were contained within the middle third of the masonry, no tension stresses and associated cracks would develop at all (see Section 7–3–1).

The primary loading on masonry arches is normally their own distributed self-weight. Unusual loadings on normally curved arches, such as high concentrated point forces, can cause severe bending and possible failure to occur (it may be noted that the funicular line for the loading cannot be contained easily within the dimensions of the structure). Such loadings are to be avoided unless the arch is specially shaped to receive them. When curved arches are surrounded by masonry walls, however, point forces are less problematic since the corbelling action of the walls tends to distribute the applied point force more uniformly as well as help restrain shape changes. Note that since some tension can occur on the inside face of an arch, failure could still occur even if walls surround the arch. In most cases, however, dead loads far exceed live loads and the compressive forces associated with the dead weight of a curve-shaped masonry arch typically dominate the possible tension forces that could result from live-load variations, with the consequence that such structures can usually withstand a reasonably diverse group of loading patterns without collapsing. The keystone does not play a key structural role in terms of force carrying. Depending on its design, it can usefully tie the arch into the surrounding masonry.

5–5–2 Parabolic Rigid Arches: Uniformly Distributed Loadings

With the advent of steel and reinforced concrete, the inherent member rigidity possible with the new materials made the arch a more versatile form, since the material rigidity allowed the arch to maintain its basic shape and not collapse when subjected to unanticipated loads. A modern rigid arch is often shaped in response to a primary loading condition and carries loads in axial compression when this loading is actually present but is also designed to have sufficient bending resistance to carry load variations. The structure, however, cannot be funicular for the new loading. It is in this way that a rigid arch is fundamentally different from a flexible cable. A flexible cable must always change shape under changes in loading and is thus essentially momentless under all loadings (localized bending effects cannot be resisted), whereas a rigid arch is momentless only

Uniformly distributed loading

Free-standing parabolic arch (stable)

Line of action of internal force in structure (funicular line)

Free-standing circular arch with narrow voussoirs

Uniformly distributed plus concentrated loading

Free-standing circular arch with added concentrated load

Uniformly distributed plus concentrated loading

Free-standing arch with no horizontal restraint

Tension causes cracks to open

Collapse mechanism (minimum of four hinges)

Collapse mechanism (rotational)

Collapse mechanism (sliding)

Uniform compression

Nonuniform compression

Tension develops on one face (thus possible cracking)

Tension

Middle third

Force

Force

Force

See Chapter 7 for a discussion of the middle-third concept

Free-standing arch on blocks

Free-standing arch partly braced by blocks or part of wall

Walls distribute concentrated forces

Walls prevent cracks from opening

Free-standing arch (stable due to width of vossoirs)

Arch stabilized by surrounding masonry wall (also makes carrying moving loads feasible)

Loading

Collapse tendency

Loads reduced at haunches

Varying the dead weight to control the location of the line of force and reduce collapse tendencies

FIGURE 5–17 Masonry arches.

under one loading condition but is capable of carrying some localized bending due to load variations. Thus it can retain its original shape under varying loading conditions.

For a primary uniformly distributed loading condition, the shape of a rigid arch is ideally parabolic. When parabolic, compressive forces are consequently developed within the structure that are described by the same equations as developed for the forces in a uniformly loaded cable in tension (Section 5–3–3). Maximum arch forces are developed at the springing: $C_{max} = \sqrt{R_{A_v}^2 + R_{A_H}} = (wL^2/8h_{max})\sqrt{(1 + 16h_{max}^2/L^2)}$. Minimum forces are at the crown: $C_{max} = wL^2/8h_{max}$. The vertical component of the inclined arch thrust (given by C_{max} above) is simply $R_{A_v} = wL/2$, while the horizontal component of the thrust is $R_{A_H} = wL^2/8h_{max}$. The angle formed by the tangent to the arch at its springing is also like that of a parabolic cable: $\theta = \tan^{-1}4h_{max}/L$.

Analyzing parabolic or semicircular arches for point loads is difficult and beyond the scope of this book. Such loadings do induce undesirable bending. Closely spaced point loads may begin to approximate a uniform loading and bending may be a minimum in such cases. The types of support conditions present (hinged or fixed) also strongly influence the amount of bending developed. Fixed arches develop bending moments near supports which are difficult to calculate.

◆ ◆ **EXAMPLE**

A parabolically shaped arch has a span $L = 150$ ft and a maximum height $h_{max} = 75$ ft. Assume $w_{dead+live} = 2000$ lb/ft [Figure 5–18(a)]. Determine the maximum force in the arch, the thrust it exerts on its foundations if buttresses are used, and, alternatively, the forces that would be developed if a tie-rod system were used. A second structure carrying point loads is shown analyzed in Figure 5–18 using techniques discussed in Section 5–3–2.

Solution:

Vertical reactions:
$$R_{A_v} = wL/2 = (2000)(150)/2 = 150,000 \text{ lb}$$

Horizontal reaction:
$$R_{A_H} = wL^2/8h_{max} = (2000)(150^2)/8(75) = 75,000 \text{ lb}$$

Maximum internal arch force and thrust exerted on foundations [Figure 5–18(a)]:
$$C_{max} = \sqrt{R_{A_v}^2 + R_{A_H}^2} = \sqrt{150,000^2 + 75,000^2} = 167,500 \text{ lb}$$

If a tie-rod system were used:

force in tie-rod = 75,000 lb   vertical force on foundation = 150,000 lb   ◆

5–5–3 Funicular Arches: Point Loadings

Exact shapes that carry all applied loads by axial compression only may be determined for other loading conditions as well. For a series of point loads, the shape of the structure may be determined by the methods discussed for finding the shape of cables in Section 5–3–2. A maximum height is assumed and compatible heights under remaining loads are calculated on the basis that the sum of the rotational effects on an isolated section about any point on the arch is zero (since no bending is present).

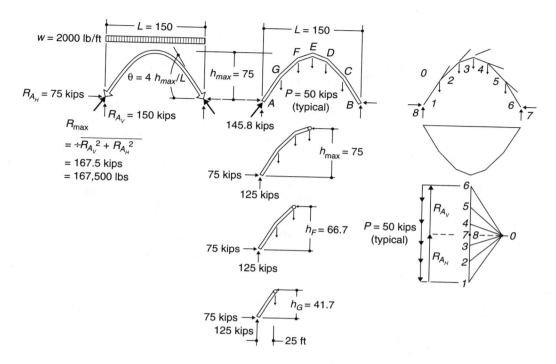

(a) Structure A:
Funicular shape for
uniformly distributed
loading condition.

(b) Structure B:
Funicular shape for a
series of point loads
(analysis of geometry).

(c) Structure B:
Funicular shapes for
point loadings as deter-
mined by graphic statics.

FIGURE 5–18   Analysis of two funicularly shaped arch structures. The structure in (a) carries a uniformly distributed load. The structure in (b) carries a series of concentrated loads.

◆ ◆ EXAMPLE

Determine the funicular shape of an arch for the five-point loads shown in Figure 5–18(b). Assume that $P = 50,000$ lb, $L = 150$ ft, and $h_{max} = 75$ ft. Find the force in AG and the inclined thrust exerted on the foundation.

Solution:

Reactions:

$$\Sigma F_V = 0: \qquad R_{A_v} = 5P/2 = 125,000 \text{ lb}$$

$$\Sigma M_E = 0: \qquad 75R_{A_H} = 75(125,000) - 50(50,000) - 25(50,000)$$

$$\therefore \quad R_{A_H} = 75,000 \text{ lb}$$

Height at F:

$$M_F = 0: \qquad h_F(75,000) = 50(125,000) - 25(50,000) \qquad \therefore \quad h_F = 66.7 \text{ ft}$$

Height at G:

$$M_G = 0: \quad h_F(75,000) = 25(125,000) \quad \therefore \quad h_F = 41.7 \text{ ft}$$

Force in member Ag by joint equilibrium:
$$F_{AG} = \sqrt{75,000^2 + 125,000^2} = 145,800 \text{ lb}$$

This same force is exerted on the foundation.

Graphical techniques may also be used to find the appropriate shape of a funicular arch for point loadings. The technique is the same as was discussed in Section 5–3–2 for finding the shapes of cables. Vertical reactions are determined, a force polygon with an arbitrarily selected pole point 0 is determined, and a force polygon is drawn through known points of action. Force magnitudes may be scaled off the original polygon. Varying the pole location along the horizontal would change the height of the structure, but not its shape. Selecting a maximum height and matching a shape to it is difficult using this technique. ◆

5–5–4   Design of Arch Structures

General Shape Issues.   As already noted, there is a close relation between the shape of a structure and the loading and support conditions present if the structure is to behave in a funicular manner (i.e., carry forces by the development of only internal tension or compression forces). When the shape of the structure corresponds with the funicular shape for the loading present, no significant undesirable bending is present in the member and efficient use of material occurs. An arch carrying a uniformly distributed loading must be parabolically shaped for the structure to be funicularly shaped. Other shapes are appropriate for different loadings. This does not mean that nonfunicular shapes cannot be used, merely that bending develops within them and that sizes and shapes of members must be increased and altered accordingly. The following chapters on beams and frames detail how this is done.

Support Elements.   As with cables, a basic issue in arch design is whether or not to absorb the horizontal thrusts by some interior element, in this case a tie-rod, or by the foundations. When it is functionally possible to do so, tie-rods are very frequently used (far more so than their counterpart struts in cable structures). Since the tie-rod is a tension element, it is a highly efficient way to take up the outward arch thrusts. The foundation then need only be designed to provide a vertical reaction and thus can be considerably less complex or substantial than one designed for both horizontal and vertical forces.

With regard to using vertical elements beneath arches, many of the same observations made in connection with designing support elements for cables are appropriate. Usually, there is less need, however, to support an arch on top of vertical elements because of the amount of head room naturally provided by the arch shape. When it is possible to place an arch directly on the ground, it should be done. Tie-rods that can be buried in the ground can then be used, which facilitates the foundation design. If arches must be used on top of vertical elements, the use of buttressing elements is generally preferable to attempting to design the verticals to act as vertical beams which carry the horizontal thrusts by bending.

The rise of most arches is made fairly deep, since there is no need to reduce the structural depth as was the case in cable design due to the natural headroom provided by the arch shape.

Lateral Behavior of Arches.   A primary design consideration is how to cope with the behavior of an arch in the *lateral* direction. It is obvious that a typical arch, which lies in one vertical

(a) Lateral stability can be a problem.

(b) Lateral buckling due to high internal forces can be a problem.

(c) The lateral buckling problem can be solved by laterally bracing arches with other elements, such as those from the roof structure. Cross bracing or some other mechanism is needed to assure lateral stability.

FIGURE 5–19   Arch design considerations.

plane, must be prevented from simply toppling over sideways. There are two mechanisms commonly used to prevent this. One is to use fixed-base connections. As was previously mentioned, however, there are certain disadvantages to using fixed connections, which have to do more with the in-plane rather than out-of-plane behavior of an arch. For very large structures, the use of fixed-base connections for lateral stability also requires massive foundations to prevent overturning. Another more commonly used method for achieving lateral stability is by relying on members that are transversely placed to the arch. The approach diagrammed in Figure 5–19(c) is fairly commonly used. A pair of arches at either end of a complete structure are stabilized through the use of diagonal elements. Interior arches are stabilized by being connected to the end arches by connecting transverse members.

The second major problem with respect to the behavior of trusses in the lateral direction is that of lateral buckling. Since internal forces are often fairly low, arches designed with high-strength materials (e.g., steel) can be fairly slender elements. An out-of-plane buckling of the type illustrated in Figure 5–19(b) can consequently potentially occur. As with trusses, one solution to the lateral buckling problem is to increase the stiffness of the arch in the lateral direction by increasing its lateral dimensions. Another solution is to laterally brace the arch periodically along its length with transverse members (Figure 5–20). Fairly slender arches can then be used. It should be noted that the same system used to stabilize arches from overturning laterally also provides lateral bracing for arch members and prevents lateral buckling from occurring.

Designing for Load Variations.   As mentioned earlier, one of the most significant aspects of the modern arch is that it can be designed to sustain some amount of variation in load without

(a) Rigid arches used in bridges. The bridge deck is suspended from the arch. The transverse members stabilize the structure with respect to lateral forces through frame action.

(b) The rigidity of the arches makes it possible for concentrated loads on the bridge deck to be carried. In the structure shown, rigidity is achieved through triangularization of discrete elements.

(c) Rigid arches used in buildings. Roof decks are usually placed directly on transverse members, which are, in turn, supported by the arches. Lateral stability is usually achieved through diagonal bracing elements.

(d) The rigidity of the arches makes it possible to carry nonuniform roof loadings. Either deformed rigid members can be used, or, in larger buildings, a triangulated built-up member of the type illustrated in (b).

FIGURE 5–20 Use of arches in bridges and buildings.

either changing shape or experiencing damage. Only arches designed and constructed using rigid materials, such as steel or reinforced concrete, have this capability (Figure 5–20).

The shape of an arch is usually initially determined as a response to its primary loading condition (e.g., parabolic for uniformly distributed loads). If a load of a different type comes to bear on the arch, bending is developed in arch members in addition to axial compressive stresses. For the arch to be able to carry this load variation it must be sufficiently large to handle both the bending and axial forces. Techniques for doing this are described in Chapter 6, which discusses members in bending. At this point, the aspects of primary importance are that designing a rigid member to carry bending is usually quite possible and that the size of the member is very sensitive to the amount of bending present. The higher the bending, the larger must be the member used. If bending is very large, the design is not feasible. A primary design issue faced, therefore, is to determine an arch shape in which a minimum of bending is present under any possible loading condition. Some bending, however, must invariably be present, since a single shape cannot be funicular for multiple loading conditions.

5-5-5   Three-Hinged Arches

As a way of developing a better feel for the analysis and design of arches, and because of the importance of the type of structure in its own right, it is useful to consider a very special form of structure—the *three-hinged arch*—which may or may not be a funicular structure, depending on its exact shape. The arches and cables examined previously were all assumed to be funicularly shaped. Since no internal bending moments exist, the sum of the rotational moments produced by externally acting forces and reactions for *any* elemental part of the funicularly shaped structure consequently had to total zero. *If* the structure is not funicularly shaped, this condition of moment equilibrium under the action of externally acting forces and reactions exists only at pins or hinges where free rotation is allowed to occur. Such is the case with the three-hinged arch.

The three-hinged arch is a structural assembly consisting of two rigid sections that are connected to each other and ground foundations by hinged or pinned connections. Unless the two segments form a funicular shape for the loading involved, and they need not, the term three-hinged "arch" can be somewhat misleading. The term arch is, however, still commonly used to describe such structures, whether they are exactly funicularly shaped or not.

Three-hinged arch structures were developed by French and German engineers in the mid-nineteenth century, partly as a way of overcoming calculation difficulties with older forms of fixed arches. The introduction of hinges at the crown and foundation connections of the structure allowed horizontal thrusts and internal forces to be precisely calculated and exact funicular shapes determined for each of the two rigid segments. Large structures could then be built with greater confidence. With improved calculation techniques, their use fell out of favor because of unfavorable rigidity characteristics and construction difficulties (see Section 5–5–4).

The famous *Galérie des Machines,* actually named *Palais des Machines,* of the Paris Exposition in 1889 was composed of a series of three-hinged arches, as were many other notable buildings (see Figure 5–21). It is possible to tell by inspection (with reference to the deflected string analogy) that the structure is not funicularly shaped. At this point this is of no consequence. Note that the nature of the connection at *B* is such that the end of member *AB* is free to rotate under the action of the load (Figure 5–22). The joint offers no potential restraint. This implies that member *BC* in no way participates in restraining the rotation of the end of *AB*. Ends of attached members can rotate freely and independently. The connection cannot transmit internal moments from one member to the other or provide any sort of rotational resistance (consequently, no internal moments are shown at connections in free-body diagrams). Hence, the sum of all the rotational effects produced about this point by the external and internal forces must be zero.

Since the external load acts directly and transversely to the left member, the direction of the force transmitted through a pinned connection is not necessarily collinear with the member. As the following example indicates, however, the magnitudes and directions of the forces at each of the connections can be found by considering the equilibrium of the whole structure first and then of each piece in turn.

◆   ◆   **EXAMPLE**

Figure 5–22 shows the three-hinged arch structure of the famous *Galérie des Machines. Estimating* that the span is 377 ft, the height to the crown 154 ft, the bay spacing 70.5 ft, and further estimating the dead load at 50 lb/ft² and the live load at 40 lb/ft², a loading model with full dead load and full live load is illustrated in

FIGURE 5–21 *Galérie des Machines,* International Exhibition, Paris, 1889. Base of three-hinged arch. The structure spanned 377 ft (111 m). (Reprinted from *Universal Exposition Paris, 1889.* Volume III, Report of the United States Commissioners.)

Figure 5–22(a). The roof area supported by one rib is (377 ft/2)(70.5 ft) = 13,289 ft^2. Determine the forces at the three connections, R_A, R_B, and R_C. These forces are considered next in terms of their components.

Solution:

Loads:
The uniformly distributed loads are first converted into equivalent concentrated loads for the purpose of finding reactions:

$$P_1 = P_2 = (40 + 50 \text{ lb/ft}^2)(13,289 \text{ ft}^2) = 1,196,000 \text{ lb, or } 1196 \text{ kips}$$

(a) Analysis of forces for full dead load and full live load.

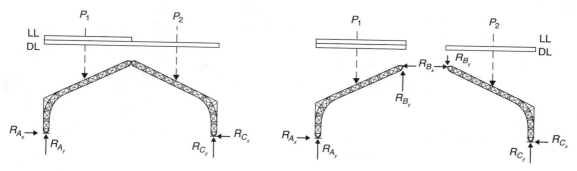

(b) Analysis of forces for full dead load and partial live load.

(c) Typical pinned base connection and
foundation detail. Horizontal thrusts
are resisted by the pile foundations
rather than by tie-rods or other devices.

FIGURE 5–22   Three-hinged arch connection forces in the *Galérie des Machines*.

Whole assembly:
First consider the equilibrium of the *whole* structure.

$$\Sigma F_y = 0: \quad R_{A_y} + R_{C_y} = P_1 + P_2 = 1196 + 1196 = 2392 \text{ kips}$$

$$\Sigma F_x = 0: \quad R_{A_x} + R_{C_x} = 0 \quad \text{or} \quad R_{A_x} = R_{C_x}$$

$$\Sigma M_A = 0: \quad 377R_{C_y} - (94.25)(1196) - (282.75)(1196) + 0R_{A_y} + 0R_{A_x} + 0R_{C_x} = 0$$

$$R_{C_y} = 1196 \text{ kips} \quad \therefore \quad R_{A_y} = 1196 \text{ kips}$$

Note that the values of the horizontal components cannot yet be found. It is necessary to consider the equilibrium of parts of the structure.

Left assembly:
Directions of the forces at the crown connection are assumed. Since the connection is pinned, no internal resisting moments are present at the pin (only forces). But the entire left assembly must be in translatory and rotational equilibrium as a unit.

$$\Sigma F_y = 0: \quad R_{A_y} + R_{B_y} = P_1 \quad \therefore \quad R_{B_y} = 1196 - 1196 = 0$$

$$\Sigma M_B = 0: \quad -188.5R_{A_y} + (94.25)(1196) + (154R_{A_x} + 0R_{B_y} + 0R_{B_x} = 0$$

$$\text{Since } R_{A_y} = 1196 \text{ kips}, \quad R_{A_x} = 732 \text{ kips}$$

$$\Sigma F_x = 0: \quad R_{B_x} + 0 \quad \text{or} \quad R_{A_x} = R_{B_x} \quad \therefore \quad R_{B_x} = 732 \text{ kips}$$

Also, from $\Sigma F_x = 0$ for the whole assembly, $R_{C_x} = R_{A_x} = 732$ kips.

Right assembly:
As a check, note that $\Sigma F_y = 0$ or $R_{C_y} + R_{B_y} = P_2$. Also note that $\Sigma M_B = 0$, or $-94.25P_2 + 188.5R_{C_y} - 154R_{C_x} = 0$.

Final forces:
All components of the connection forces are now known. Note that the vertical component of the force at the crown connection is zero, indicating that the two assemblies do not tend to slip vertically with respect to one another. This is not always true but is a consequence in this instance of both the loading and structural symmetries. Resultant forces R_A, R_B, and R_C can be found from their components ($R_A = R_C = 1402$ kips, $R_B = 732$ kips). The reactive forces at the base connections are inclined, so the foundations must resist outward thrusts. Note that each assembly can be considered as a "three-force" member (see Section 2–3), so lines of action meet at a point. The same is true for the structure as a whole. For finding member sizes and shapes, however, it is necessary to consider the actual distributed nature of the loadings (see Chapters 6 and 9). The final horizontal forces at the base connections could have been restrained by a tie-rod but were actually carried by pile foundations in the real structure. Use of a tie-rod would have made the forces exerted on the foundation act vertically. ◆

◆ ◆ **EXAMPLE**

Repeat the preceding analysis assuming that the 40-lb/ft^2 live loading acts only on one-half of the structure. A loading model with full dead load and a partial live load is illustrated in Figure 5–22(b). Determine the forces at the three connections, R_A, R_B, and R_C.

Solution:

Loads:

The uniformly distributed loads are first converted into equivalent concentrated loads for purpose of finding reactions:

$$P_1 = 1196 \text{ kips (as before)} \quad \text{and} \quad P_2 = (50 \text{ lb/ft}^2)(13{,}289 \text{ ft}^2) = 664 \text{ kips}$$

Whole assembly:

First consider the equilibrium of the *whole* structure.

$$\Sigma F_y = 0: \qquad R_{A_y} + R_{C_y} = P_1 + P_2 = 1860 \text{ kips}$$
$$\Sigma F_x = 0: \qquad R_{A_x} + R_{C_x} = 0 \quad \text{or} \quad R_{A_x} = R_{C_x}$$
$$\Sigma M_A = 0: \qquad 377 R_{C_y} - (94.25)(1196) - (282.75)(664) + 0R_{A_y} + 0R_{A_x} + 0R_{C_x} = 0$$
$$R_{C_y} = 797 \text{ kips} \qquad R_{A_y} = 1063 \text{ kips from } \Sigma F_y = 0$$

Left assembly:

Directions of the forces at the crown connection are assumed.

$$\Sigma F_y = 0: \qquad R_{A_y} + R_{B_y} = P_1 \quad \therefore \quad R_{B_y} = 1196 - 1063 = 133 \text{ kips}$$
$$\Sigma M_B = 0: \qquad -188.5 R_{A_y} + (94.25)(1196) + 154 R_{A_x} = 0$$
$$\text{Since } R_{A_y} = 1063 \text{ kips}, \quad R_{A_x} = 569 \text{ kips}$$
$$\Sigma F_x = 0: \qquad R_{A_x} + R_{B_x} = 0 \quad \text{or} \quad R_{A_x} = R_{B_x} \quad \therefore \quad R_{B_x} = 569 \text{ kips}$$

Right assembly:

A check of $\Sigma F = 0$ and $\Sigma M = 0$ reveals that this assembly is in balance.

Final forces:

All components of the connection forces are now known. Note that the crown connection now provides a reactive shear force that keeps the two assemblies from slipping apart in the vertical direction. The pin at the top is subjected to a shearing force of this magnitude and must be designed to carry it (see Chapter 16). ◆

◆ ◆ EXAMPLE

The famous AEG factory by Peter Behrens shown in Figure 5–23 is a three-hinged arch structure. We *estimate* the dead load at 50 lb/ft^2 and the live load at 40 lb/ft^2; and $L = 128$ ft, $h_1 = 146$ ft $h_2 = 123$ ft, bay spacing $= 84$ ft. A rib supports an area of $(128)(84/2) = 5376$ ft^2. Determine the forces at the three connections, R_A, R_B, and R_C. This problem is more complicated because the support conditions are at different levels.

Solution:

Loads:

The uniformly distributed loads are first converted into equivalent concentrated loads for the purpose of finding reactions:

$$P_1 = (40 + 50)(5376) = 484{,}000 \text{ lb} = 484 \text{ kips} \quad \text{and} \quad P_2 = 484 \text{ kips}$$

(a) Peter Behrens and Karl Bernhard, AEG Turbine Factory, Berlin, 1908–1910.

(b) Section. The main structure can be modeled as a three-hinged arch.

(c) Reactions.

(d) Analysis model.

FIGURE 5–23 AEG Turbine Factory by Peter Behrens, 1908–1909. This simplified analysis ignores the contribution of ties extending from A to the right part of the structure in partially resisting the outward thrusts. (Courtesy of SASKIA Ltd., Cultural Documentation.)

Whole assembly:
First consider the equilibrium of the *whole* structure.

$$\Sigma F_y = 0: \quad R_{A_y} + R_{C_y} = P_1 + P_2 = 968$$
$$\Sigma F_x = 0: \quad R_{A_x} + R_{C_x} = 0 \quad \text{or} \quad R_{A_x} = R_{C_x}$$
$$\Sigma M_A = 0: \quad 128R_{C_y} - 123R_{C_x} + 0R_{A_y} + 0R_{A_x} - 32(494) - 96(484) = 0$$
$$128R_{C_y} - 123R_{C_x} - 61{,}952 = 0$$

These equations cannot be solved directly as they were before.

Right assembly:

$$\Sigma M_B = 0: \quad 64R_{C_y} - 146R_{C_x} + 0R_{B_y} + 0R_{B_x} - (32)(484)$$
$$= 64R_{C_y} - 146R_{C_x} - 15{,}488 = 0$$

This equation and that from $\Sigma M_A = 0$ above can be solved simultaneously for R_{C_y} and R_{C_x}: $R_{C_y} = 659$ kips and $R_{C_x} = 183$ kips.

$$\Sigma F_y = 0: \qquad -R_{B_y} + R_{C_y} = 484 \qquad \therefore \quad R_{B_y} = 175 \text{ kips}$$
$$\Sigma F_x = 0: \qquad R_{B_x} = R_{C_x} = 183 \text{ kips}$$

The remaining forces can be found from the original equations: $R_{A_x} = R_{C_x}$ and $R_{A_y} + R_{C_y} = P_1 + P_2 = 968$. Thus, $R_{A_x} = 183$ kips and $R_{A_y} = 309$ kips. All components are now known.

Final forces:

Final forces are illustrated in Figure 5–23. Note that the horizontal reaction components are still equal, as they must be, even though the structure is not symmetrical. Only when a horizontal force (e.g., wind) acts on the structure are these forces unequal. ◆

It should be noted that the forces found at the base and crown hinges for both structures analyzed were influenced only by the location in space of the three hinges and the magnitude and line of action of the external load. *Nowhere* did the specific shape of the individual rigid segments from *A* to *C* and from *B* to *C* ever enter into or affect the calculations. As long as they are rigid and their end point locations defined, any segmented shape (e.g., linear, arbitrarily curved, exact funicular shapes) could have been used and the magnitude of the forces developed at the hinged connections would not have been affected (assuming dead load differences are ignored).

The independence of connection forces in three-hinged assemblies from the specific shape of the segmented pieces is an important concept, since it forms the basis for some useful design approaches, as shown next.

Shaping of Three-Hinged Arches.   As noted, three-hinged arches may assume any shape. The logic of structural design, however, leads back to a funicular shape. For example, we noted that the forces developed at the connections do not depend directly on the shape of the two subassemblies (except for dead-weight considerations) but on the loading conditions and geometry present. Thus connection forces may be approximately determined in the abstract (before assembly shapes are specified). These forces may then be used to help infer an appropriate shape.

Consider Figure 5–24. Assume that it is desired to determine appropriate structural shapes for the segmental pieces to be used for members *AC* and *BC* in the structure such that bending is minimized or eliminated.

Since the structure is statically determinate, it is possible to determine by the methods just described the connection forces for each structure *without* knowing their precise shapes (assuming that the dead loads of the structure are ignored). Rigid segments of unspecified shape are assumed. Vertical and horizontal forces determined through equilibrium calculations for each of the structures are shown.

By analyzing the complete force system acting on each segment of each structure, it is possible to shape each segment so that bending is minimized. Consider the right segment from *B* to *C*. Note that if the uniform load is considered to be replaced by a statically equivalent concentrated load, it is a three-force member in which the lines of action of all forces again meet at a point. At the base connection it is evident that the structure must be aligned with the direction of the resultant reaction for the structure to be in compression. The same is true for the crown connection (point *B*). The directions of the reactions determine the alignment of the structure at each of these points. From previous work, it is obvious that the structure would form a continuous parabolic curve between the two known alignments.

The inverted-string analogy is again a quite useful tool in imagining the appropriate shape for the member. The shape is parabolic, with the tangents to the curve defined at the supports by

(a) Loading and assumed location of hinges.

(b) Forces at connections.

(c) Funicular shape.

(d) Line of action of forces for the right member.

(e) Aligning structure with line of action of forces causes only compressive forces to be developed in the structure.

(f) Bending will develop in any other shape that is used.

FIGURE 5–24   Shaping three-hinged arches for full loadings.

the direction of the reactions and the tangent at the supports by the direction of the reactions and the tangent at the crown connection (point B) horizontal. The shape is clearly that associated with the common *arch* discussed previously.

Consider another example, the three-hinged arch shown in Figure 5–25(a) (which is actually shaped in response to an inwardly directed radial load) under the action of a concentrated load. Since the structure has three hinges, it can be analyzed as discussed in Section 5–5–4. Note that the pin is shown independently, but it could be considered attached to either the left or right member. The base reactions and crown connection forces can be envisioned as external forces acting on the member. In this specific case the forces are collinear. This set of forces tends to cause bending to develop along the length of the member. The greatest bending would occur at the point labeled M. This is the location where, if the member were not designed to withstand the bending, cracks would first develop and the member would initially fail. The greater the

(a) Semicircular three-ringed arch with concentrated load.

(b) Analysis of structure.

(c) Reactive forces at member connections cause bending to develop. The maximum bending occurs at point M, i.e., $M_{max} = [P\sqrt{2}/2]d_{max}$.

(d) If a member aligned with the line of action of the moment inducing forces is used, no bending will be developed in the member. Doing this is equivalent to aligning the structure with the funicular shape.

Bending is present.

No bending is present.

(e) The moment present in the structure is proportional to the deviation of the structure from the funicular or pressure line.

FIGURE 5–25   Bending is developed in arch structures not funicularly shaped for the applied load.

magnitude and moment arm of the external forces about a point on the structure, the greater is the bending developed at that point, and vice versa.

Depending on the loads involved, the structure could be designed to withstand the bending developed. From a design point of view, however, it is preferable to attempt finding a shape that reduces or eliminates this bending altogether. For this particular example, finding such a shape is easy. If a linear element were simply placed in line with the line of action of the collinear applied forces, the member would be subjected only to axial forces. No bending would be present (the moment arm of the applied forces is zero). For the loading indicated, it is therefore structurally preferable to use the shape indicated in Figure 5–25(d) than the one in Figure 5–25(a). Member sizes required would be considerably smaller. Functional requirements may dictate the use of the original shape, but this is not a point of concern in this discussion.

It should be noted that the shape found above that carries the load without bending is nothing more than the funicular shape for the loading as envisioned by imagining the deflected shape of a cable and inverting it. It should also be noted that the amount of bending developed at a point on the original structure is directly proportional to the deviation of that point from the funicular line [see Figure 5–25(e)]. This is a generalizable result of usefulness in a design context.

Although it is not possible to devise a single shape that is funicular for *all* different multiple loading conditions, the effects of bending can be minimized by careful design. Consider the situation shown in Figure 5–26, in which it is desired to design an arch structure having three

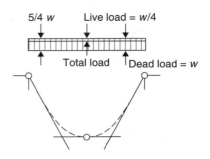

(a) Assume that the location of three hinges is given. A structure is to be designed to carry a full dead and live load and a full dead load and partial live load.

(b) Funicular shape for full-loading conditions.

(c) Funicular shape for full dead load and partial live load (left segment carries live load).

(d) Funicular shape for full dead load and partial live load (right segment carries live load).

(e) Superimposed funicular shapes.

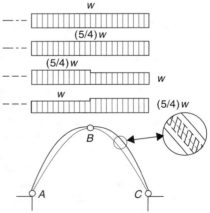

(f) A more rigorous analysis can be used to identify more accurately critical slopes for the structure. Analyses other than that shown are also needed.

(g) If a structure is designed to contain the full spread of funicular lines for all possible load variations, then blending is minimized. If the lines are contained within the middle third of the cross-section, then only compressive stresses are developed in the structure.

FIGURE 5–26 Designing to minimize the effects of load variations. The famous Salginatobel bridge, designed by Robert Maillart and constructed between 1929 and 1930, reflects the same general shaping shown in (g) but is more sophisticated in structural concept. Several steel railroad bridges, such as one in Roxbury, MA, which were conceived by anonymous designers and built around the turn of the twentieth century, also had the same general shape.

hinges located in space as shown to carry any of the following loading conditions: (1) dead load only, (2) full dead load plus full live load, and (3) full dead load plus a live load over either the left or right segment of the structure. Figures 5–26(b)–(d) shows the funicular shapes for the different loading conditions. The middle hinge defines the height of the structure at midspan, since the funicular line must pass through the hinge (the hinge is a point at which the rotational and bending moments of the forces about that point are zero—the condition defining any point on a funicular curve). Superimposing the funicular shapes obtained yields the result shown in Figure 5–26(e). If the effects of the off-balanced live loads are small, the curves will be very close together. When the curves are close together, a structure can be sized so that the whole family of curves is contained within its cross section. If this is done, bending will be minimal in the structure under any of the possible load variations. If the funicular lines can all be contained within the middle of the cross section of the member used, the structure will still carry loads primarily by axial compression without any tension stresses being developed (see Section 7–2–1 for a discussion of why forces acting within the middle third of a cross section produce compressive stresses only). Figure 5–26(f) illustrates a more quantitative analysis of the same structure. A resultant structural form is shown in Figure 5–26(g).

5–5–6 Comparisons between Fixed Two-Hinged and Three-Hinged Arches

There are three primary types of arches used that are normally described in terms of their end conditions: the three-hinged arch, the two-hinged arch, and the fixed-ended arch (see Figure 5–27). For arches shaped funicularly for the loading present, basic reactions, connection faces, internal shears, and moments can be found by direct application of the basic equations of statics. The two-hinged arch and fixed-ended arch are more complicated to analyze when subjected to unusual loading conditions and bending is present, and rigorous analysis techniques are not treated in this text. Three-hinged arches are statically determinate structures and can easily be analyzed.

The structural behavior of the three arch forms that are comparable in every way (and carrying identical loads) except in the type of end condition used is not appreciably different *when* each is shaped as a funicular response to the applied loading. Internal compressive forces are similar. Significant differences arise, however, when other factors are considered. Important factors include the effects of possible support settlements, the effects of member expansion and contraction due to changing temperatures, and the relative amount of deflection induced by an applied load. Figure 5–27 illustrates how the different arches behave with respect to these factors.

In general, it is evident that different end conditions are preferable with respect to different phenomena. The presence of hinges is very useful when supports settlements and thermal effects are considered, since they allow the structure to flex freely. Undesirable bending moments can be generated by similar phenomena in fixed-ended arches. The fixed-ended arch is far less likely to deflect excessively, however, under load than is the three-hinged or two-hinged arch and is thus preferable in this respect. Three-hinged arches tend to be flexible under load, to the point of being potentially problematical.

The choice of which end conditions should be used depends on the exact design conditions present and if one or the other is of dominant importance. The two-hinged arch is frequently used because it combines some of the advantages of the other two types of arches while not comparably sharing their disadvantages.

Three-hinged arch

w

Primary forces

Two-hinged arch

w

Primary forces

Fixed-ended arch

w

Primary forces

(a) If each structure is funicularly shaped, the primary internal forces present in each type of arch will be similar.

(b) Support settlements. The three-hinged arch is least affected by support settlements, whereas the fixed-ended arch is most affected.

The three-hinged arch is relatively unaffected by support settlements since the two arch segments merely rotate with respect to one another (the hinges allow the structure to flex freely).

The two-hinged arch is relatively unaffected by vertical settlements since the hinges allow the structure to simply rotate as a unit. Horizontal spreading of the foundations, however, induces destructive bending at the crown of the arch.

The fixed-ended arch is severely affected by any type of foundation settlement. The absence of hinges does not allow the structure to flex freely, and destructive bending moments are consequently induced in the structure.

The three hinges allow relative rotations to occur between members, which reduces the stresses associated with temperature expansions and contractions.

The presence of the hinges reduces the overall stiffness of the three-hinged arch and increases its sensitivity to deflections.

(c) Temperature expansions and contraction. The three-hinged arch is least affected, and the fixed-ended arch is the most affected.

While unable to flex as freely as the three-hinged arch, the pins present in the two-hinged arch allow some flexing to occur, which reduces the effects of temperature movements. Some undesirable bending moments, however, are still generated in the structure.

The fixed-ended arch is severely affected by temperature expansions and contractions since no relief mechanism is present. Undesirable bending moments are created.

(d) Stiffness: the fixed-ended arch is the most preferable for deflection control, followed by the two-hinged arch. The three-hinged arch follows a poor third. For structure similar in all respects except for the joint conditions:

$$\Delta_F < \Delta_{2H} < \Delta_{3H}$$

The two-hinged arch is stiffer than the three-hinged arch but less rigid than the fixed-ended arch.

The fixed-ended arch is very stiff and highly resistant to deflections.

FIGURE 5-27 Effects of different types of arch end conditions. Since there are relative advantages and disadvantages for each type of arch, the choice of which type of end conditions should be used depends on the specific design context involved. The two-hinged arch is often used because of its compromise nature (in that it possesses some of the advantages of both the three-hinged arch and fixed-ended types of arches while not possessing extreme disadvantages).

QUESTIONS

5–1 What is the maximum force developed in a cable that carries a single concentrated load of P at midspan and which spans a total distance of L? Assume that the cable has a maximum sag of $h = L/5$.

5–2 What is the maximum force developed in a cable carrying a uniform load of 500 lb/ft that spans 200 ft? Assume that the cable has a maximum midspan sag of 20 ft.
    Answer: 135,000 lb.

5–3 What is the maximum force developed in a funicularly shaped arch that carries a uniformly distributed load of 800 lb/ft and spans 120 ft? Where does this force occur?

5–4 What is the maximum force developed in a funicularly shaped arch that carries a uniformly distributed load of 10,000 N/m and spans 35 m? Assume that the rise of the arch is 8 m. What is the force in the arch at midspan?
    Answer: 191.4 kN.

5–5 Determine the exact shape of a cable that spans 100 ft, has a maximum sag of 10 ft, and supports three concentrated loads of 5000 lb apiece, which are located at quarter-points along the span (i.e., at 25, 50, and 75 ft from the left support point). Determine the force present in each segment of the cable.

5–6 Draw shear and moment diagrams for the loading condition described in Question 5–5 and demonstrate how the cable structure supporting the loadings develops internal resisting shear forces and moments that equilibrate the externally applied shear forces and bending moments.

5–7 How would the maximum force developed in the cable described in Question 5–1 be affected if the left end support were elevated a distance $h = L/10$ above the right support? Again assume that the cable sag is a maximum of $L/5$, but assume that this distance is measured with respect to a line connecting the two end supports.

5–8 Determine the funicular shape for a structure that carries a uniform load of w from $x = 0$ to $x = L/3$ and is unloaded elsewhere. First sketch the probable shape of the structure and then determine appropriate algebraic expressions that precisely define the shape.

5–9 Determine the funicular shape for a structure that carries a uniform load of w across its entire span and a concentrated load of P at midspan. Sketch the probable shape of the structure first and then determine appropriate algebraic expressions that precisely define the shape.

5–10 Is there any maximum to the distance that a cable can span? Discuss.

5–11 If your answer to Question 5–10 is essentially affirmative, find what the maximum span would be. Make *any* assumptions you need to but clearly specify them.

5–12 What is the force required to pull a cable to zero sag?

CHAPTER 6

Members in Bending: Simple Beams

6–1   INTRODUCTION

Few structural elements are as ubiquitous as the common beam. Post-and-beam systems, in which a horizontal member is simply rested on two vertical supports, have formed the basic construction approach for much of the architecture of both early and recent civilizations. This is at least partly attributable to the convenience and simplicity of the beam as an element of construction. This simplicity with respect to construction, however, belies the fact that internally beams have a far more complex load-carrying action than do many other structural members (e.g., trusses or cables). Indeed, little was known about the exact mechanisms by which beams carry loads until very recently, relative to the length of time such elements have been used. A sketch by Leonardo da Vinci indicates that he tried to describe beam action in a rational way.

Another product of the Renaissance, however, is more responsible not only for laying the groundwork for our current understanding of beam theory, but also for founding, in Hans Straub's words, ". . . an entirely new branch of science: the theory of the strength of materials." The man is Galileo Galilei. Galilei was the first to begin investigating the bending problem in a systematic way (see Figure 6–1). The term *bending problem* refers to the study of stresses and deformations generated in an element bowed by the action of forces (typically perpendicular to the axis of the element) so that the fibers on one face of the element are elongated and those on the opposite face contracted.

Although Galileo was not completely successful in solving the problem, his initial formulation laid the foundation for future investigators. The names of Hooke, Mariotte, Parent, Leibnitz,

(a) Cantilever beam.

(b) Bending-stress distribution according to Galilei, later demonstrated to be incorrect.

FIGURE 6-1 Early beam theory. (From Galileo Galilei, *Discorsi e dimostrazioni matematiche,* 1638.)

Navier, and Coulomb are all linked with this problem. Auguste Coulomb (1736–1806) is generally credited with the final solution of the bending problem. Investigators in the rapidly expanding field of *strength of materials* soon tackled other problems commonly associated with beams, such as the effects of torsion, until by now the field is amazingly well developed.

6-2 GENERAL PRINCIPLES

6-2-1 Beams in Buildings

Few buildings are constructed that do not make use of beams. In addition to the more evident beam assemblies that often serve as primary structural systems, many other common building components (such as parts of some stairways or large window mullions) are, from a structural viewpoint, beams.

When used to form the primary structural system in a building, beam elements are most typically used in a repetitive, pattern-forming way. Most often the pattern comprises a hierarchical arrangement of beams. Planar surface load-transfer members (e.g., decking or planks) usually have limited span capabilities and are therefore typically supported periodically by larger-span secondary members to form a two-level system. These members are, in turn, sometimes supported by collector beams to form a three-level system. Loads acting on the surface are first picked up by the surface members, then transferred to the secondary members, which in turn transfer them to the collectors or supports. The amount of load carried by each member thus progressively increases. This increase in loading, coupled with an increase in length, typically leads to a progressive increase in member size or depth (Figure 6–2).

There can obviously be any number of levels in such a hierarchical arrangement. A three-level arrangement is typically the maximum used. One- and two-level arrangements are also

(a) Hierachical arrangements in one-way structural systems. One-, two-, and three-level systems. Member sizes vary in proportion to the span and amount of loading carried.

One-level arrangement

Two-level arrangement

Three-level arrangement

Concrete wearing surface

Primary beam span

Secondary beam span

Decking beam span

Decking

Primary wide-flange beam

Secondary wide-flange beam

(b) Typical steel system: three-level arrangement.

FIGURE 6–2 Beams in buildings.

231

quite common. For spanning any given space, it is obvious that, in general, a system of any level can be used. Simply because any arrangement could be made to be serviceable, however, does not imply that all possible arrangements are equally desirable based on considerations of efficiency, construction ease, costs, or other criteria.

The actual stresses developed in a beam depend on the amount and distribution of material in the cross section of the member. Basically, the larger the beam, the smaller the stresses. The way this material is organized in space, however, is important. A thin rectangular member that is placed on its side cannot carry anywhere near the same amount of load as an equivalently sized member placed so that its maximum depth is in line with the applied loads. It is thus not just the area of the member that is important, but its distribution as well. Generally, the deeper a member is, the stronger it is vis-à-vis bending.

Important basic design variables include the magnitudes of the loads present, the distances between the loads, and the nature of the support conditions of the beam (Figure 6–3). Support conditions are particularly important. A member that has its ends restrained is much stiffer than one whose ends are free to rotate. A beam with fixed ends, for example, can carry a concentrated load at midspan twice that of a similarly sized beam with unrestrained ends. A beam that is *continuous* over several supports also offers some advantages as compared to a series of simply supported ones, although there are some trade-offs involved (see Chapter 8).

6–2–2 Basic Stress Distributions

External loadings on a beam produce a set of internal forces and related stresses and deformations. As discussed in Section 2–4–2, the externally produced actions can be described in terms of *bending moments* and *shear forces*. For equilibrium to obtain for the portion of the structure shown, a set of internal forces must be developed in the structure whose net effect is to produce a rotational moment equal in magnitude but opposite in sense to the external bending moment and a vertical force equal and opposite to the external shear force. These internal resisting forces are generated through the development of internal bending and shear stresses (see Figures 6–4 and 6–5).

At any one cross section of the beam, fibers in the upper portion of the beam are shortened and those in the lower portion elongated by the action of the external bending moment. The deformations vary in a linear or near-linear way from a maximum elongation on one face to a maximum shortening at the other. There must exist a layer somewhere near the middle of the beam where the beam fibers are neither shortened nor elongated. This layer is of particular importance in the study of beams and is called the *neutral axis* of a beam. For a symmetrical cross section, as in a rectangular beam, it can be correctly expected that this plane is at the midheight of the beam. This need not be so if the section is not symmetrical. It will be shown later that the neutral axis corresponds with the *centroid* (see Appendix 3) of the cross section.

If the beam is constructed of a material that is *linearly elastic,* the stresses produced by bending are directly proportional to the deformations present. Thus, in the beam under consideration, the stresses induced by the load are maximum at the outer fibers of the beam and decrease linearly to zero at the neutral axis. Tensile stresses are associated with elongations in beam fibers, and compressive stresses with contractions. Together these stresses are typically referred to as *bending stresses.*

(a) Typical beams

Transversely applied loads cause internal bending stresses, shear stresses, bearing stresses, and accompanying deflections to develop. Other phenomena (torsion) may also occur. Making the beam deeper rather than shallower generally improves its load-carrying capabilities. Either making a beam continuous over several supports or restraining its ends greatly increases both the rigidity and load-carrying capacity of the member.

(b) General behavior of beams.

FIGURE 6-3   Typical types of beams and important factors in beam design.

Bending stresses produce an internal resisting moment (M_R) that balances the externally applied bending moment (M_E). The action is not unlike that discussed for trusses, in which the internal resisting moment at a section was provided by a couple ($\leftrightarrows$) produced by member forces separated by a known distance. In beams, the internal moment resistance is still provided by a couple, but one whose forces are produced by tensile and compressive stress fields acting over portions of the face of the cross section. The effect of compressive stresses in the upper zone acting over the area can be equivalently described by a single resultant compressive force acting at a particular location. The same is true for the tensile stresses. The internal resisting

(a) Loads applied transverse to the axis of a member cause the member to bow.

(b) The amount of curvature (1/R) developed in a beam at a cross section depends directly on the magnitude of the external moment present at the section. The actual deformations in the beam associated with this curvature vary linearly from a maximum tensile elongation on one face of the beam to a maximum compressive deformation on the other face.

Compressive stresses

No deformations

Tensile strains

(c) The stresses developed because of bending are, in a linearly elastic material, directly proportional to the magnitude of the deformations present. The plane of zero stress is called the neutral axis of the section.

Compressive stresses

Neutral axis

Tensile stresses

FIGURE 6–4 Bending stresses in a beam. Parts (a) and (b) illustrate the general type of deformations produced by the external loading. Part (b) illustrates the deformations present at a cross section and (c) illustrates the bending stress at the same cross section.

234

(a) Loaded beam.

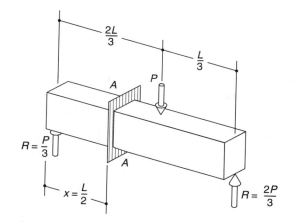

(b) The net effect of the external force
system acting on a portion of the
beam is to produce an upward shear
force, V_E, and a rotational moment,
M_E. An equilibrating set of resisting
shears and moments, V_R and M_R
are devloped in the beam.

$$\Sigma F_y \quad V_E = P/3$$
$$\Sigma M_x \quad M_E = (P/3)x$$
$$\text{at } x = L/2$$
$$M_E = PL/6$$

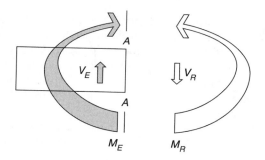

(c) Vertical shear stresses developed
at the section and acting over the
face of the section provide the
internal resisting shear, V_R.

(d) Bending stresses developed at the
section act over the face of the
section to produce a couple which
provides the internal resisting
moment, M_R .

FIGURE 6–5 Basic load-carrying mechanisms in a beam.

235

couple (M_R), therefore, can be thought of as being provided by these two resultant forces separated by the moment arm indicated [see Figure 6–5(d)]. Unlike trusses, the moment arm is not a distance known a priori, since it depends on the locations of the resultant tension and compression forces, which in turn depend upon the nature of the way stresses are distributed and on the shape of the cross section on which they act. Techniques for finding what this moment arm and related stresses should be are discussed in detail in Section 6–3–1. It is shown there that bending stresses at a cross section depend on the moment (M) that is present, the location (y) up or down at the section, and a measure of the amount and distribution of material present [the *moment of inertia* (I)], such that $f = My/I$ (see the *General Theory* section that follows on page 241).

The bending stresses just discussed are developed in response to the applied external moment and, in the examples discussed, act horizontally and consequently do nothing to balance the external shear forces. The external shear force is balanced by *shear stresses* which act on the face of the section [see Figure 6–5(c)]. The question of how these stresses are distributed is complex and is covered later in this chapter, where it will be demonstrated that they are maximum at the neutral axis of the cross section and decrease nonlinearly toward the outer faces. The important point, however, is that the resultant effect of these stresses acting over the face of the cross section is to produce a resultant vertical shear force which equilibrates the applied external shear force. Shear stresses of another type are also developed in beams. These stresses act horizontally rather than vertically (see Section 6–3–3).

A knowledge of how bending and shear stresses vary along the length of the beam is important. Since the stresses at a cross section depend on the magnitude and sense of the external shears and moments at that cross section, the distribution of stresses along the length of the beam can be found by studying the distribution of shears and moments in a beam.

The basic principles for finding the distribution of shears and moments in a member have already been covered in Section 2–4–2. There it was noted that when the equilibrium of an elementary portion of a member is considered, the effect of the set of external forces (including reactions) is to produce a net rotational effect (the external moment, M_E) about the cut section considered and a net vertical translatory force (the external shear force, V_E) and that these quantities are balanced by an equilibrating set of shears and moments (V_R and M_R) developed internally in the structure (i.e., $V_R = V_E$ and $M_R = M_E$). Clearly, the magnitudes of these shears and moments depend on the extent of the elemental section considered and the set of forces acting on it. Thus, the distribution of these shears and moments can be found by considering in turn the equilibrium of different elemental portions of the structure and calculating the shear and moment sets for each elemental portion. As an aid in visualizing the distribution of these shears and moments, the values thus found can be plotted graphically to produce *shear and moment diagrams*. These diagrams were discussed previously in Section 2–4–2.

Figure 6–6 shows the general relationship between the shear and moment distribution in a structure and the shear and bending stresses developed. Figure 6–7 shows the relationship between the moment distribution present and the bending stresses developed in a beam having an inflection point.

In addition to bending stresses and horizontal and vertical shear stresses, other considerations of importance in beam analysis include bearing stresses, torsional stresses, combined stresses, the shear center of a beam, principal stresses, and the deflection characteristics of a beam. These topics are discussed later in this chapter.

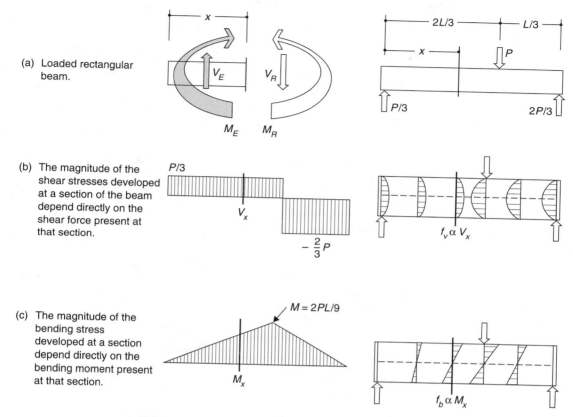

(a) Loaded rectangular beam.

(b) The magnitude of the shear stresses developed at a section of the beam depend directly on the shear force present at that section.

(c) The magnitude of the bending stress developed at a section depend directly on the bending moment present at that section.

FIGURE 6–6   Distribution of forces and stresses in a beam.

6–3   ANALYSIS OF BEAMS

In this section we review briefly topics normally addressed in detail in textbooks devoted more exclusively to a study of the strength of materials.[1] The following topics, which generally comprise the basic issues involved in the analysis of beams made of linearly elastic materials, are addressed: (1) bending stresses, (2) shearing stresses, (3) bearing stresses, (4) combined stresses, (5) torsional stresses, (6) shear centers, (7) principal stresses, and (8) deflections.

6–3–1   Bending Stresses

Introduction.   As noted in the introductory discussion on the general behavior of beams, bending stresses that vary linearly at a cross section are developed in response to the action of the external bending moment existing in the beam at that point.

Before looking at how to determine these bending stresses in a quantitative way, it is useful to review the general factors on which the bending stresses in a beam depend. Consider the beam

---

[1]See, for example, Ferdinand L. Singer, *Strength of Materials,* 2d ed., Harper & Row, New York, 1962.

FIGURE 6–7 Positive and negative moment regions in a beam.

illustrated in Figure 6–8. The stress distribution depicted is based on the assumption that stresses are linearly dependent on deformations. The magnitude of the bending stresses (f_y) present at a point is directly dependent on the magnitude of the external moment (M) present at the section. The magnitude of f_y must also directly depend on the distance (y), which defines the location of the point considered with respect to the neutral axis of the beam. It is also quite reasonable to expect that the stress (f_y) will be inversely dependent on some measure defining the size and shape of the beam itself. Increasing the size of the beam should decrease the stress level in the beam for a given moment. Let us temporarily simply designate this measure as I (typically called the *moment of inertia*) without as yet defining it further. There are no other parameters on which the bending stress can be dependent. The actual stresses developed, for example, are *not* influenced by the type of material used, in the same way that the forces in a truss member were not dependent on the material of which the member was made. Ascertaining whether a member is safe under a given loading does require consideration of the strength characteristics of the material, but this is a different problem than the one addressed here.

Since the bending stress (f_y) directly depends on the moment (M) and the locational parameter (y), and inversely on the measure of the properties of the beam section (I), the variables generally relate in the following way:

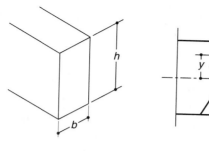

(a) Loaded beam of width b and depth h.

(b) Strain distribution at cross section x–x.

(c) Stress distribution at cross section x–x.

(d) Stress field [$f = MC/I$].

$\frac{1}{3}(h/2) = h/6$

(e) For a rectangular beam, bending stresses acting over the face of the cross section:

$$T = C = (1/2)(f_b)(b \times h/2)$$

M_R

Face of beam

(f) Equivalent force couple in a rectangular beam:

$$M_R = C \times d_1 = T \times d_1$$
$$M_R = f_b \, (bh^2/6) \text{ or}$$
$$f_b = M_R/(bh^2/6)$$

FIGURE 6–8   The bending stresses at any point in a beam of any cross section are given by $f_y = My/I$. For the *special case* of a rectangular beam, the maximum bending stress is given by: $f_b = Mc/I = M/(bh^2/6)$.

$$f_y \Rightarrow \left(M, y, \frac{1}{I} \right) \qquad \text{As} \quad \begin{cases} M \text{ increases} & f_y \text{ increases} \\ y \text{ increases} & f_y \text{ increases} \\ I \text{ increases} & f_y \text{ decreases} \end{cases} \qquad \text{Thus,} \quad f_y \Rightarrow \frac{My}{I}$$

It is interesting to note that if the units of the stress f_y are lb/in.², the units of M are in.-lb, and the units of y are in., then the units of I (the term characterizing the nature of the cross section) must be the rather unique unit of in.⁴, so that the expression My/I is dimensionally correct [i.e., lb/in.² = (in.-lb)(in.)/in.⁴]. Alternatively, in the SI system of units, the units of the stress f are (N/mm²), or MPa, the units of M are N·mm, and the units of y are mm. The units of I must, therefore, be mm⁴. Thus, N/mm² = (N·mm)(mm)/mm⁴.

There is nothing in this discussion that will allow us to make any further statement about what the term I actually is. This must be done through equilibrium calculations. The following illustrates the procedure for finding the bending stresses at any point in a rectangular beam and clarifies what the term I actually represents.

Rectangular Beams. The tensile and compressive components of the stress field present in a rectangular beam, or any other shape of beam for that matter, generate a force couple ($\leftrightarrows$) that provides an internal resisting moment (M_R) that equilibrates the rotational effect of the external moment (M_E) present at the section. An expression for this internal resisting moment can be found in terms of the unknown bending stresses developed at the section. The unknown internal stresses associated with the internal force couple can then be solved for by setting the expression equal to the known external moment present at a section ($M_R = M_E$). This procedure is demonstrated for the specific case of a rectangular beam in this section and for a general shape in Appendix 5.

Consider the beam shown in Figure 6–8 of width b and depth h (sometimes d is used for the beam depth). The compressive stresses acting over the upper half of the beam are statically equivalent to a single force, C, acting as indicated in Figure 6–8(b). The magnitude of this force is simply the *average* compressive stress times the area over which it acts (i.e., force = average stress × area). Its location is determined by considering the way the stresses are distributed. For a triangular stress distribution, this location is at the third point from the base of the triangle, as illustrated in Figure 6–8(e). (See the discussion on the *centroids* of figures in Appendix 3.) The tension stress field can be similarly described in terms of an equivalent static force, T, acting as illustrated in Figure 6–8(f). The internal resisting moment in the beam is the couple formed by these two forces. By equating this resisting moment to the external moment, the stress at the outer fibers can be explicitly determined: $f_b = M/(bh^2/6)$.

A general expression for the bending stress, f_y, at a point defined by a distance y from the neutral axis, can also be found. By similar triangles, note that $f_y/y = f_b/c$ (see Figure 6–8). Thus, $f_b = f_y(c/y)$ or $f_y = f_b(y/c)$. Noting that $c = h/2$, the expression for f_b becomes $f_y = My/(bh^3/12)$. If the quantity $bh^3/12$ is defined as the moment of inertia (I) for a rectangular beam, we have

$$f_y = \frac{My}{I}$$

This is the same general expression discussed before. The value of $I = bh^3/12$ found here is valid *only* for rectangular beams. Note that it has the units of in.^{4} or mm^4.

An examination of these results indicates that the bending stresses developed in a beam are extremely sensitive to the depth of the beam. For a given applied moment, doubling the depth of a beam while holding its width constant would reduce bending stresses by a factor of 4. Alternatively, doubling the width of a beam while holding its depth constant would only reduce bending stresses by a factor of 2. These observations follow from manipulations with the expression $f = M/(bh^2/6)$.

◆ ◆ **EXAMPLE**

A cantilever beam that is rectangular in cross section and of length L carries a concentrated load of P at its free end. Determine the maximum bending stress present in the member. Assume that the dimensions of the beam are as follows: $b = 4$ in. (101.6 mm), $h = 6$ in. (152.4 mm), $L = 8$ ft (2.44 m). Assume that

$P = 500$ lb (2224 N). It is evident that the maximum bending stress occurs where the moment is a maximum and on the outer fibers of the beam at the same section.

Solution:

Maximum bending moment:

$$PL = 500 \text{ lb} \times 8 \text{ ft} = 4000 \text{ ft-lb} = 48,000 \text{ in.-lb}$$
$$= 2224 \text{ N} \times 2.44 \text{ m} = 5426.6 \text{ N·m} = 5.426 \times 10^6 \text{ N·mm}$$

Maximum bending stress $= f_b$ *at* $y = c$:

$$f_b = \frac{M}{bh^2/6} = \frac{48,000 \text{ in.-lb}}{4 \text{ in.} \times (6 \text{ in.})^2/6} = 2000 \text{ lb/in.}^2$$

$$= \frac{5.426 \times 10^6 \text{ N·mm}}{101.6 \text{ mm} \times (152.4 \text{ mm})^2/6} = 13.79 \text{ N/mm}^2 = 13.79 \text{ MPa}$$

Alternatively, the maximum bending stress can be found by using the more general expression for bending stresses ($f_y = My/I$):

Moment of inertia:

$$I = \frac{bh^3}{12} \text{ (for a rectangular section)}$$

$$= \frac{4 \text{ in} \times (6 \text{ in.})^3}{12} = 72 \text{ in.}^4 = \frac{101.6 \text{ mm} \times (152.4 \text{ mm})^3}{12} = 30.0 \times 10^6 \text{ mm}^4$$

Maximum bending stress $= f_b$ *at* $y = c$:

$$f_b = \frac{My}{I} = \frac{Mc}{I} = \frac{(48,000 \text{ in.-lb})(6 \text{ in.}/2)}{72 \text{ in.}^4} = 2000 \text{ lb/in.}^2$$

$$= \frac{(5.426 \times 10^6 \text{ N·mm})(152.4 \text{ m}/2)}{30.0 \times 10^6 \text{ mm}^4} = 13.79 \text{ N/mm}^2$$

The stresses are predicted to exist within the cross section of the beam regardless of what material is present and say nothing directly about whether the member is safe or unsafe in bending. *If* the material used has a low allowable stress level, say, 1200 lb/in.^{2} as might exist for timber, the member is unsafe in bending and could conceivably actually fail before the predicted stress level of 2000 lb/in.^{2} is reached. *If* the material used has a higher allowable stress level, say, 24,000 lb/in.^{2} as might exist for steel, then the member is safe in bending and the predicted stress level would be reached.   ◆

General Theory.   The basic method described here for finding the stresses in a beam is of general applicability. When the shape of the cross section is complex, however, finding statically equivalent forces and their locations for the stress fields present is very involved. To simplify calculations, the problem has been solved for in general terms and the results presented in the form $f_y = My/I$. In this formulation, a general expression for I appears that can be evaluated for any different shape of cross section. This general formulation is presented in detail in Appendix 4, to which the reader is referred. In general, the procedure used in deriving this expression is quite similar to that demonstrated for the rectangular beam, except that the shape of the member is not specified and operations are made with respect to an elemental area within the cross section.

Thus, the moment resistance in a beam of any cross-sectional shape is generated by stresses acting over areas to produce forces, which in turn act through a moment arm to produce a resisting moment. In the case of an elementary area, dA, the force on the element is directly proportional to y [i.e., force $= f_y \, dA = f_b(y/c) \, dA$] and its moment is the force acting over the distance y [i.e., moment $= yf_y \, dA = (f_b/c)y^2 dA$]. Thus, the term $y^2 \, dA$ represents the *resistance to bending* associated with the elemental area dA and its location, defined by y, in the beam. The total moment resistance of the beam is the sum of the contributions of all elemental areas, or $M = \int_A (f_b/c)(y^2 \, dA)$. If I is defined as $\int_A y^2 \, dA$, then $M = f_b I/c$, or $f_b = Mc/I$, as before. The term $\int_A y^2 \, dA$ represents the total resistance to bending associated with the sum of all elemental areas in the beam. This expression is commonly encountered as the *second moment* of an area in mathematics and is discussed in basic calculus textbooks, where the term is evaluated for different shapes. The expression is usually called the *moment of inertia* in the structural engineering field. Appendix 4 contains an extensive discussion of this term, including exactly what it means, and illustrates its application to several typical beam shapes. The moment of inertia for a rectangular beam of width b and depth h, for example, is demonstrated to be $I = bh^3/12$ (as found before from equilibrium considerations). For a triangular shape, $I = bh^3/36$. For a circular shape, $I = \pi d^4/64$.

The expression $f_b = Mc/I$ is applicable for finding the stresses at the extreme fiber of the beam, located by the distance c. For the stresses at any point located by the distance y, the expression becomes $f_y = My/I$. The distance y, like the distance c, is measured from the neutral axis of the member. It is thus necessary to know exactly where this axis lies. In Appendix 5 it is demonstrated that the neutral axis usually coincides with the *centroid* of the section of the beam. (For prestressed or post-tensioned beams, this is not the case; nor is it the case with sections made of multiple materials). The centroid of a cross-sectional area, actually defined by $\int_A y \, dA = 0$, can be visualized as that point at which the geometric figure defining the area would balance.

The location of the centroid of a figure also determines the location of the plane of zero deformations and bending stresses in the figure. In cross sections that are symmetrical about their horizontal axes, such as a rectangle, square, or circular shape, the centroid (and hence neutral axis) is invariably at the midheight of the section. Deformations and bending stresses vary linearly in the member and are proportional to the distance from the neutral axis of the member [see Figures 6–4 and 6–8(c)].

◆ ◆ **EXAMPLE**

A cantilever beam that is 10 ft long with a 5-in. by 10-in. rectangular cross section carries a concentrated load of $P = 10,000$ lb at its end. What are the maximum bending stresses developed at the base of the cantilever? Is the beam safe if the allowable stress in bending is $F_b = 1200$ lb/lb/in.^{2}? What would happen to the stresses if the width of the section were doubled and the depth held constant? If the depth were doubled and the width held constant?

Solution:

The maximum bending moment is given by $M = PL$ or $M = 5000$ lb (10 ft) $= 10,000$ ft-lb $= 120,000$ in.-lb. The moment of inertia defined by $I = \int_A y^2 dA$. For a *rectangular* section, this expression evaluates to $I = bh^3/12$ (see Appendix 4), or $I = (5)(10)^3/12 = 416.6$ in.^{4}. The maximum bending stresses at the extreme outer fibers of the beam (top and bottom faces) are given by $f = Mc/I$. The distance c is measured from the centroid to the outer fibers, or, in this case, $c = h/2 = 10/2 = 5$. Thus, $f = Mc/I = (120,000$ in.-lb)(5 in.)/(416.7 in.^{4}) $= 1440$ lb/in.^{2}. This is the actual maximum bending stress that exists anywhere in the beam. Since the actual stress of 1440 lb/in.^{2} exceeds the allowable stress of 1200 lb/in.^{2}, the beam is not safe in bending.

If the width of the beam were doubled to $b = 10$ in. and the depth held constant, I changes. Thus, $I = bh^3/12 = (10)(10)^3/12 = 833.3$ in.^{4}. Thus, $f = Mc/I = (120{,}000$ in.-lb$)(5$ in.$)/(833$ in.$^4) = 720$ lb/in.^{2}. Since this value is less than the allowable stress, the beam is safe in bending. If the depth of the beam were doubled to $d = 20$ in. and the width held constant, $I = bh^3/12 = (5)(20)^3/12 = 3333$ in.^{4}. The distance c also changes to $c = h/2 = 20/2 = 10$ in. Thus, $f = Mc/I = (120{,}000$ in.-lb$)$ $(10$ in.$)/(833$ in.$^4) = 360$ lb/in.^{2}. Since this value is less than the allowable stress, the beam is safe in bending. Note that doubling the beam depth is far more effective in reducing stresses than is doubling the beam's width (even though each has the same cross-sectional area). ◆

◆ ◆ **EXAMPLE**

A simply supported beam spans 25 ft and carries a uniform loading of $w = 600$ lb/ft (Figure 6–9). As shown, a maximum bending moment of $M = wL^2/8 = (600$ lb/ft$)(25$ ft$)^2/8 = 46{,}875$ ft-lb $= 562{,}500$ in.-lb is developed at midspan (see Section 2–4–3). Three beams of equal cross-sectional area but different shapes are considered for use. In which beam are the maximum bending stresses the lowest? [See Appendix 4 for derivation of the moment of inertia (I) values for rectangular, circular, and triangular cross sections.] Note that it is critical to use the correct c distance in calculating bending stress. The triangular cross section has a different c distance for its upper and lower extremities, thus implying that stress magnitudes vary accordingly.

FIGURE 6–9 Beam using either a rectangular, circular, or triangular section. Maximum moment present is $M = 562{,}500$ in.-lb.

Solution:

Rectangular Beam:

Section properties:

$$I = bh^3/12 = (8 \text{ in.})(15 \text{ in.})^3/12 = 2250 \text{ in.}^4$$

$$c_{max} = 7.5 \text{ in.}$$

Maximum bending stresses:

$$f_{max} = Mc/I = (562{,}500 \text{ in.-lb})(7.5 \text{ in.})/2250 \text{ in.}^4$$
$$= 1875 \text{ lb/in.}^2 \quad \text{(top or bottom)}$$

Circular Beam:

Section properties:

$$I = \pi r^4/64 = (6.7 \text{ in.})^4/64 = 1160 \text{ in.}^4$$

$$c_{max} = 6.7 \text{ in.}$$

Maximum bending stresses:

$$f_{max} = Mc/I = (562{,}500 \text{ in.-lb})(6.7 \text{ in.})/1160 \text{ in.}^4$$
$$= 3006 \text{ lb/in.}^2 \quad \text{(top or bottom)}$$

Triangular Beam:

Section properties:

$$I = bd^3/36 = (12 \text{ in.})(20 \text{ in.})^3/36 = 2667 \text{ in.}^4$$
$$c_{top} = 13.3 \text{ in.} \quad \text{and} \quad c_{bot} = 6.7 \text{ in.}$$

Maximum bending stresses:

$$f_{top} = Mc/I = (562,500 \text{ in.-lb})(13.3 \text{ in.})/2667 \text{ in.}^4$$
$$= 2805 \text{ lb/in.}^2 \quad \text{(top)}$$
$$f_{bot} = Mc/I = (562,500 \text{ in.-lb})(6.7 \text{ in.})/2667 \text{ in.}^4$$
$$= 1403 \text{ lb/in.}^2 \quad \text{(bot)}$$

Comparison:

The smallest stresses are developed in the rectangular beam (it could thus carry the greatest external loading before becoming overstressed). Note that the triangular section has a higher I value than any of the sections but develops higher stresses than the rectangular beam because of its larger c distance. The circular cross section has a lower I value than the other two because more material is nearer the neutral axis (Figure 6–10).

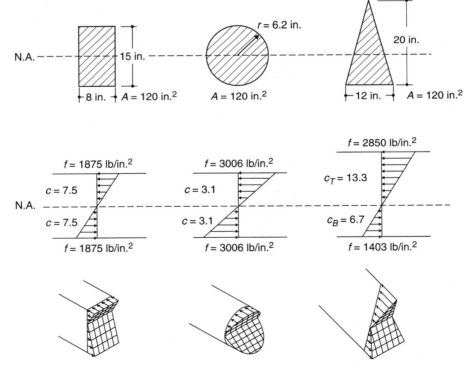

FIGURE 6–10 Comparison of bending stresses in different beam sections with identical areas subjected to the same bending moment of 562,500 in./lb. ◆

◆ ◆   **EXAMPLE**

For the same loading condition shown in the previous example ($M = 562{,}500$ in.-lb), assume that a symmetrical box section was used (Figure 6–11). What is the maximum bending stress present? [The crux of this problem is calculating the I value for the section. In this example, the hole is treated as a "negative" area (see Appendix 4).] The approach shown is valid *only* for symmetric cross sections. Otherwise, the location of the centroid would need to be found and I calculated by $I = \int_{A} y^2 dA$.

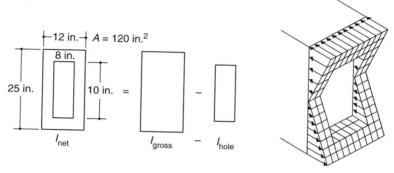

FIGURE 6–11   Box beam.

Solution:

Section properties:

$$I_{net} = I_{gross} - I_{hole} = b_1 h_1^3/12 - b_2 h_2^3/12$$
$$= (12)(25)^3/12 - (8)(10)^3/12 = 14{,}958 \text{ in.}^4$$
$$c_{max} = 12.5 \text{ in.}$$

Maximum bending stress:

$$f = Mc/I_{net} = (562{,}500)(12.5)/14{,}958$$
$$= 470 \text{ lb/in.}^2$$

The maximum stress present is thus lower than in any other of the three sections shown in the previous example. Box beam shapes are extremely efficient because they move material away from the neutral axis and toward the outer fibers of the beam (see Section 6–4–1).   ◆

Symmetrical Sections.   The following example further illustrates the procedure used in determining if a beam constructed of a given material carrying a certain load is adequately sized with respect to bending. This simply involves calculating the maximum critical bending stress actually developed in the beam (which occurs at the section of maximum moment along the length of the beam and at the fiber of the beam farthest removed from the neutral axis of the beam) and comparing this actual stress to a stress level predetermined as being acceptable for the material used (the *allowable* stress for the material). As discussed in Section 2–6, this allowable stress contains a specified factor of safety. Obviously, if the actual stress present at a point exceeds the allowable stress, the beam is considered *overstressed* at that point and is not considered acceptable.

◆ ◆ **EXAMPLE**

A simply supported beam carries a concentrated load of P at midspan. Assume that the dimensions of the beam are as follows: $b = 5$ in. (127 mm), $h = 10$ in. (254 mm), and $L = 10$ ft (3.048 m). Also assume that $P = 4000$ lb (17.792 kN). If the allowable stress in bending for the specific type of timber used is $F_b = 1500$ lb/in.^{2} (10.34 N/mm^2 or 10.34 MPa), is the beam adequately sized with respect to bending?

Solution:

Maximum bending moment:

$$M = \frac{PL}{4} = \frac{(4000 \text{ lb})(10 \text{ ft})}{4} = 10,000 \text{ ft-lb} = 120,000 \text{ in.-lb}$$

$$= \frac{(17.792 \text{ kN})(3.048 \text{ m})}{4} = 13.56 \text{ kN·m} = 13.56 \times 10^6 \text{ N·mm}$$

Moment of inertia:

$$I = \frac{bh^3}{12} = \frac{(5 \text{ in.})(10 \text{ in.})^3}{12} = 416.7 \text{ in.}^4 = \frac{(127 \text{ mm})(254 \text{ mm})^3}{12} = 173.4 \times 10^6 \text{ mm}^4$$

Maximum bending stress $= f_b$ *at* $y = c$:

$$f_b = \frac{Mc}{I} = \frac{(120,000 \text{ in.-lb})(10 \text{ in.}/2)}{416.7 \text{ in.}^4} = 1440 \text{ lb/in.}^2$$

$$= \frac{(13.56 \times 10^6 \text{ N·mm})(254 \text{ mm}/2)}{(173.4 \times 10^6 \text{ mm}^4)} = 9.93 \text{ N/mm}^2$$

Note that the stress level calculated is independent of the type of material used in the beam (i.e., the same stress would be present no matter whether the beam was made of timber, steel, or plastic). If the material used has the allowable stress value originally noted, however, the beam is adequately sized with respect to bending since the actual stress developed is less than this allowable stress [i.e., $(f_b = 1440 \text{ lb/in.}^2) \leq (F_b = 1500 \text{ lb/in.}^2)$ or $(9.93 \text{ N/mm}^2) \leq (10.34 \text{ N/mm}^2)$].   ◆

Symmetrical Beam Sizing.   The process for determining the required cross-sectional dimensions of a simple symmetrical beam to carry safely a given bending moment is straightforward. A material is first selected and *allowable stresses* in bending are defined. Required section properties are next found on the basis of making the actual bending stress level in the beam equal to, or less than, the allowable stress level in bending. This process is based on the use of the bending stress relationship $f_y = M_y/I$. The maximum stress occurs when y is maximum (or $y_{max} = c$). Thus, in order to make the actual bending stress at $y_{max} = c$ equal to the allowable stress, we simply substitute F_b (the allowable stress for the material) for f_y, c for y_{max}, and solve for the other terms in the relationship $f_y = My/I$. Hence, for *any* beam shape,

$$S_{\text{required}} = \left(\frac{I}{c}\right)_{\text{req'd}} = \frac{M}{F_b}$$

The I/c measure is termed the section modulus, S, of a beam. The problem is then to find an S or I/c value for a beam equal to, or greater than, the value of M/F_b.

For a *rectangular* beam (b = width, h = depth), $S_{\text{req'd}} = I/c = (bh^3/12)/(h/2) = bh^2/6$. Thus, $(bh^2/6)_{\text{req'd}} = M/F_b$, or $(bh^2)_{\text{req'd}} = 6 M/F_b$.

Any rectangular beam with a combination of b and h dimensions that yields $bh^2 = 6M/F_b$ will be acceptable with respect to bending. Further beam design considerations are discussed in Section 6–4.

◆ ◆   **EXAMPLE**

A simply supported rectangular timber beam that is 12 ft long carries a concentrated load of 4000 lb at midspan. What would the required depth of the member be if the width b is 2.0 in.? If b is 4.0 in.? Assume that the allowable stress in bending is $F_B = 1600$ lb/in.^{2}

Solution:

Bending moment at midspan: $M = PL/4 = (4000 \text{ lb})(12 \text{ ft})/4 = 12{,}000 \text{ ft-lb} = 144{,}000 \text{ in.-lb}$
Required section modulus: $S = M/F_B$; $\therefore bh^2/6 = 144{,}000 \text{ in.-lb}/1600 \text{ lb/in.}^2$
Section size: $bh^2_{\text{req'd}} = 540 \text{ in.}^3$
Depth: If $b = 2$ in., $h = 16.4$ in.; if $b = 4$ in., $h = 11.6$ in. Other dimensions could also provide a section modulus of 540 in.^{3}.
◆

Nonsymmetrical Sections.   The general principles discussed previously are applicable to nonsymmetrical as well as symmetrical sections. The critical difference is that in a nonsymmetrical section, such as a T beam or triangular shape, the location of the centroid is no longer obvious and is usually never at the midheight of the section. Its location must be calculated along the lines discussed in Appendix 3. Calculating the moment of inertia I for a section built up of simpler shapes presents special issues. The *parallel-axis theorem* must be used to find moment of inertia values. Appendix 4 discusses such procedures for nonsymmetrical beams.

In the T beam illustrated in Figure 6–12, the centroid is located near the top flange of the member. Deformations and bending stresses in the member still vary linearly in the member and are proportional to the distance from the neutral axis of the member. This implies that the stress levels at the top and bottom of the beam are no longer equal as they typically are in symmetrical sections. The stresses are greater at the bottom of the beam than they are at the top because of the larger y distance. A difference in stress levels between the top and bottom surfaces is characteristic of nonsymmetrical sections. This point has enormous design implications, as discussed in Section 6–4.

◆ ◆   **EXAMPLE**

Determine if the T beam illustrated in Figure 6–12 is adequately sized to carry an external bending moment of 120,000 in.-lb. Assume that the allowable stress in bending of the material used is $F_b = 1200$ lb/in.

Solution: To find the actual bending stresses developed in the T beam, use can be made of $f_y = My/I$, as before. The real task in this problem is to evaluate I and y_{max}, a task more complicated than before because of the nonsymmetrical nature of the cross section. The procedure is to first locate the centroid of the cross section and then to use the parallel-axis theorem to evaluate the moment of inertia about the centroidal axis. Appendix 4 explains the general process for doing this calculation and its underlying rationale in greater detail.

Location of centroid:

Consider the shape to be made up of two rectangular figures ($A_1 = b_1 \times h_1$ and $A_2 = b_2 \times h_2$), as illustrated in Figure 6–12(c). Assume a reference axis as illustrated. Let $\bar{y}_T$ represent the distance from the base

(a) Loaded T beam.

(b) Bending-stress distribution in T beam.

(c) T beam analyzed in example problem.

FIGURE 6–12 Bending stress distribution in a T beam. Since the cross section is nonsymmetric, the centroid of the section is also nonsymmetrically located. The bending-stress distribution is still linear and passes through zero at the centroid (or neutral axis). This results in a difference in stress levels on the upper and lower faces of the beam.

of the figure to the centroid of the whole figure, and $\bar{y}_1$ and $\bar{y}_2$ be the distances to the centroids of the two rectangular figures from this same base. Thus,

$$\bar{y}_T = \frac{\sum_i A_i \bar{y}_i}{\sum_i A_i} = (A_1 \bar{y}_1 + A_2 \bar{y}_2)/(A_1 + A_2)$$

$$= \frac{(2 \text{ in.} \times 10 \text{ in.})(13 \text{ in.}) + (2 \text{ in.} \times 12 \text{ in.})(6 \text{ in.})}{(2 \text{ in.} \times 10 \text{ in.}) + (2 \text{ in.} \times 12 \text{ in.})} = 9.18 \text{ in.}$$

Moment of inertia:

Let $\bar{I}_T$ represent the moment of inertia of the whole figure about its centroidal axis. Let I_1 and I_2 represent the moments of inertias of the two rectangular figures about their own centroidal axes and d_1 and d_2 be the locations of these axes with respect to the centroidal axis of the whole figure. As explained in detail in Appendix 4, $\bar{I}_T$ can be found by using the parallel-axis theorem; thus,

$$\bar{I}_T = \sum_i (\bar{I}_i + A_i d_i^2) = \left[\left(\frac{b_1 h_1^3}{12}\right) + (b_1 h_1)(d_1)^2\right] + \left[\left(\frac{b_2 h_2^3}{12}\right) + (b_2 h_2)(d_2)^2\right]$$

$$= \left[\frac{(10 \text{ in.})(2 \text{ in.})^3}{12} + (10 \text{ in.})(2 \text{ in.})(3.82)^2\right]$$

$$+ \left[\frac{(2 \text{ in.})(12 \text{ in.})^3}{12} + (2 \text{ in.})(12 \text{ in.})(3.18)^2\right]$$

$$= (6.7 + 291.9) \text{ in.}^4 + (288.0 + 242.7) \text{ in.}^4$$

$$= 829.3 \text{ in.}^4$$

Bending stresses:

The general type of bending stress distribution present is the T beam, as illustrated in Figure 6–12(a) and (b). The stresses that occur at the top face of the beam are defined by $f_b = My/I$, where $y = 4.82$ in. (the distance from the top face to the centroidal axis of the figure). Thus,

$$f_b = \frac{My}{I} = \frac{(120{,}000 \text{ in.-lb})(4.82 \text{ in.})}{829.3 \text{ in.}^4} = 697.5 \text{ lb/in.}^2$$

The stresses that occur at the bottom face of the beam are found similarly except that $y = 9.18$ in. Hence,

$$f_b = \frac{My}{I} = \frac{(120{,}000 \text{ in.-lb})(9.18 \text{ in.})}{829.3 \text{ in.}^4} = 1328.3 \text{ lb/in.}^2$$

The stresses at the bottom face of the beam are clearly much larger than those at the top face of the beam. This is due to the nonsymmetrical nature of the cross section. If the allowable stress of the material used in the beam is given by $F_b = 1200$ lb/in.^{2}, then the beam is overstressed on its lower face (i.e., 1328.3 lb/in.^{2} > 1200 lb/in.^{2}). Note that stresses on the upper face are within the acceptable range. The beam is still considered inadequately sized, however, because of the overstress occurring on the lower face.

$$\bar{y}_T = 233.17 \text{ mm} \qquad \bar{I}_T = 345.15 \times 10^6 \text{ mm}^4 \qquad f_b = 4.82 \text{ N/mm}^2 \qquad f_b = 9.16 \text{ N/mm}^2 \qquad \blacklozenge$$

Top region of beam is in compression.
A beam not rigid in the lateral direction
can buckle laterally because of the
compressive force present.

FIGURE 6–13 Lateral buckling in beams. The top region of the beam is in compression. A beam not rigid in the lateral direction can buckle laterally because of the compressive force present.

6–3–2 Lateral Buckling of Beams

Consider the thin, deep beam illustrated in Figure 6–13. Application of a load may cause *lateral buckling* in the beam, and failure will occur before the strength of the section can be utilized. The phenomenon of lateral buckling in beams is similar to that found in trusses. An instability in the lateral direction occurs because of the compressive forces developed in the upper region of the beam coupled with insufficient rigidity of the beam in this direction. In the examples discussed thus far it was assumed that this type of failure does not occur. Depending upon the proportions of the beam cross section, lateral buckling can occur at relatively low stress levels.

Prevention of lateral buckling can be provided in two primary ways: (1) by using transverse bracing, or (2) by making the beam stiff in the lateral direction. When a beam is used to support a roof deck or a secondary framing system, transverse bracing is automatically provided by these elements. If a beam is used in a situation where this type of bracing is not possible, the beam can be made sufficiently stiff in the lateral direction by increasing the transverse dimension of the top of the beam. In a rectangular beam, the basic proportions of the cross section can be controlled to accomplish the same end. The exact determination of these dimensions is beyond the scope of this book, but Figure 6–14 illustrates when lateral bracing is not required for timber beams and recommends types of bracing when it is. Different rules apply for steel plates.

◆ ◆ **EXAMPLE**

A cantilever beam 10 ft in length supports a concentrated load of 1000 lb at its free end. The maximum moment developed in the beam is, therefore, $M = PL = (10 \text{ ft} \times 12 \text{ in./ft})(1000 \text{ lb}) = 120{,}000$ in.-lb. Assume that the allowable stress in bending is $F_b = 1200$ lb/in.^{2} Determine the required member size.

Solution:

$$f = \frac{Mc}{I} = \frac{M}{S} \quad \text{or} \quad S_{\text{req'd}} = \frac{M}{F_b}$$

$$\frac{bh^2}{6} = \frac{M}{F_b} = \frac{(120{,}000 \text{ in.-lb})}{1200 \text{ lb/in.}^2} = 100 \quad \therefore \quad bh^2 = 600$$

FIGURE 6–14 Lateral bracing required for timber beams. These proportions are rough guides only.

Depth-to-width Ratio: Type of Lateral Bracing Required

2 to 1   None.

3 to 1   Hold ends of beam in position.

6 to 1   Diagonal bridging should be used.

5 to 1   Hold compression edge in line continuously.

7 to 1   Hold both edges in line continuously.

Any beam with a bh^2 value of 600 will be satisfactory with respect to bending. The following table indicates acceptable beams (in all cases, $bh^2 = 600$).

Trial Beam Size (in.)		Cross-Sectional Area (in.^{2})	Depth/Width Ratio	Lateral Bracing
b	h			
0	5.5	110	0.27:1	None req'd
10	7.7	77	0.77:1	None req'd
5	11.0	55	2.2:1	None req'd
3.5	13.1	46	3.7:1	Bracing req'd
2	17.2	34.4 ·	8.6:1	Bracing req'd

◆

As is evident from the preceding example, there are often many different beam cross sections that could potentially be used in a common situation. Beams that are relatively wide and shallow typically require much more material to support a given load than do beams that are relatively thin and deep. The choice of which type to use is up to the designer. There are invariably design trade-offs involved. If relatively efficient thin deep beams are used, the designer *must* assure that lateral bracing of the appropriate type is provided. Providing such bracing usually requires additional material and is also an added cost item. If there is no way to provide the necessary lateral bracing, or if the designer chooses not to provide it, the proportions of the beam *must* be selected so that the member itself provides sufficient inherent resistance to lateral buckling.

Note that if a beam is used in the common situation of supporting floor decking, an inspection of the bracing requirements indicates that using beams that are relatively shallow (e.g., 2:1 or 3:1 depth/width ratios) is inefficient since the decking inherently provides lateral bracing and it is *not* necessary to have a beam capable of doing so independently. Consequently, much thinner and deeper beams are used in such instances (beams with depth/width ratios of between 5:1 and 7:1 are typically found in common house construction). So much for the exposed beams using 2:1 or 3:1 depth/width ratios that are typically found in brand-new suburban chalets.

6–3–3 Shear Stresses

As noted in the opening section, equilibrium of an elemental portion of a beam with respect to vertical shear forces occurs through the development of vertical shearing stresses developed in the beam. The resultant force, $V_R = \int_A f_v\, dA$, equivalent to these stresses is equal in magnitude but opposite in sense to the external shear force, V_E. To gain an understanding of the magnitude and distribution of these stresses, it is actually more convenient to look first at the horizontal shear stresses also known to exist in the beam.

The presence of horizontal shear stresses may be visualized most easily by considering two beams, one made of a series of unconnected planes (similar to a deck of cards) and the other of a solid piece of material (see Figure 6–15). Under the action of a load, a slippage occurs between each of the planes in the former case as the whole assembly deforms. The structure is essentially behaving as a series of thin superimposed beams. The second structure behaves in a composite way and is much stiffer than the first and able to carry a much higher load. If the surfaces of the planes on the first structure were bonded together, the resulting structure would also behave as a composite whole. If this were done, stresses acting in the bond parallel to the adjacent surfaces would be developed, since the planes would still have a tendency to slide. These stresses are called *horizontal shearing stresses*. As long as the material can carry these stresses, adjacent planes in a beam remain in contact and the structure behaves as a composite whole. When a beam fails due to horizontal shear, slippage between planes occurs. Some materials, such as timber, are particularly weak with respect to stresses of this kind, and failures of this type are not uncommon [see Figure 6–15(d)].

(a) Beam made of unbonded layers. Layers tend to slide horizontally with respect to one another under the action of a load.

(b) In a homogeneous beam, there is a tendency for the same type of relative sliding between adjacent layers to occur.

(c) Horizontal shear stresses are developed in a homogeneous beam as a consequence of this sliding tendency.

(d) Cracks developed in a timber beam as a result of excessively high horizontal shear stresses.

FIGURE 6–15 Horizontal shear stresses in a beam.

(a) Loaded beam.

(b) Diagram of upper-left portion of beam
showing bending stresses and horizontal
shearing stresses. The bending stresses
develop a resultant force acting to the
left. An equilibrating force is developed
by the horizontal shearing stresses acting
over the horizontal plane indicated.

(c) Near the top of the beam, the
horizontal force developed by the
bending stresses is small since they
act over a small area. Horizontal
shearing stresses are also consequently
small.

(d) At the neutral axis of the beam, the
horizontal force developed by the
bending stresses is the maximum
possible. The horizontal shear stresses
which equilibrate this force are consequently maximum.

Equilibrating forces
developed by horizontal
shear stresses

Forces associated with
bending stresses

FIGURE 6–16   Horizontal shear stresses in a beam. In a rectangular beam the horizontal shear stresses
vary parabolically from a maximum at the neutral axis of the member to zero at the top and bottom faces.
The distribution of stresses along the length of a horizontal plane depends directly on the variation in the
external shear force along the same length. Where the external shear force is high, shear stresses will be
high, and vice versa.

In the example illustrated in Figure 6–16, the magnitude of these horizontal shear stresses
can be found by considering the equilibrium, in the horizontal direction, of the upper left portion of the beam (remember that *any* elemental portion of a structure must be in equilibrium so
any portion can be selected for analysis). With respect to equilibrium in the horizontal direction,
it is obvious that the bending stresses acting on the right face of the element produce a horizontal force acting to the left. For equilibrium to obtain, the horizontal force due to bending
must be balanced by other internal forces acting in the opposite direction, which implies the existence of horizontal shear stresses. The equilibrating force is provided by shear stresses acting
in the horizontal direction over the horizontal face of the beam. Other horizontal planes in the
beam also have shearing stresses but of varying magnitudes.

In Figure 6–16(c), a plane near the top of the beam is shown. Again, the bending stresses produce a force in the horizontal direction which causes shearing stresses to develop on the horizontal plane. These forces and stresses, however, are smaller than those at the middle section of the beam, since the bending stresses act over a smaller area and thus produce a smaller horizontal force. Indeed, at the very top layer in the beam there can exist no forces or shear stresses at all. A close look at the magnitudes of these shearing stresses would indicate that they vary parabolically from a maximum at the neutral axis of a beam to zero at free surfaces. The horizontal stresses also vary along the length of the beam in most situations (in particular when the bending stress varies along the length of the beam). An exact expression, based on concepts similar to those discussed above, can be determined for the horizontal shearing stress in a beam. The horizontal shear stress at a layer located a distance y from the neutral axis can be shown to be given by the expression $f_v = VQ/Ib$, where V is the vertical shear force at the vertical section considered, b is the width of the beam at the horizontal layer considered, I is the moment of inertia at the section, and Q is the first moment of the area (about the neutral axis) above the horizontal layer considered ($Q = \int_y dA$). The derivation of this expression and applications of its use is contained in Appendix 6, to which reference is made. There it is also noted that this expression describes not only the horizontal shear stresses at a point, but the vertical shear stresses as well, since it can be demonstrated that the magnitudes of the horizontal and vertical shear stresses acting at a point are always equal (see Figure 6–17). Thus, the vertical shear stresses also vary parabolically with a maximum value occurring at the neutral axis.

The general shear-stress equation $f_v = VQ/Ib$ can be evaluated for the specific case of a rectangular beam (see the following example). In a rectangular beam the maximum shear stresses occur at the neutral axis of the member (at midheight) and are given by $f_v = \frac{3}{2}(V/bh) = \frac{3}{2}(V/A)$, where b and h are the dimensions of the cross section. Thus, the maximum shear stress in a rectangular beam is 1.5 times the value of the average shear stress in a rectangular beam [see Figure 6–18(a)].

In beams constructed of thin-walled sections with a lot of material in flange areas, the shear stresses are more uniform because of the way the material is distributed throughout the cross section. The shear stress in such sections, such as a wide-flange beam, can be reasonably approximated by $f_v = V/A_{web} = V/td$ with relatively little error [see Figure 6–18(b)].

♦ ♦ **EXAMPLE**

Is the timber beam illustrated in Figure 6–19(a) adequately sized with respect to shear? Assume that the allowable shear stress for the material used is $F_v = 150$ lb/in. (1.03 N/mm^2).

Solution: The maximum shear stress occurs at the neutral axis of the beam at the cross section where the shear force, V, is a maximum. The maximum shear stress is given by

$$f_v = \frac{VQ}{Ib} = \frac{V(A'y')}{Ib} = \frac{V(bh/2)(h/4)}{(bh^3/12)b} = \frac{3}{2}\frac{V}{bh} = \frac{3}{2}\frac{2000 \text{ lb}}{(5 \text{ in.})(10 \text{ in.})} = 60 \text{ lb/in.}^2$$

This is the maximum vertical or horizontal shear stress that occurs in the beam. Since 60 lb/in. ≤ 150 lb/in., the beam is adequately sized with respect to shear. Alternatively,

$$f_v = \frac{3}{2}\frac{V}{bh} = \frac{3}{2}\frac{8896 \text{ N}}{(127 \text{ mm})(254 \text{ mm})} = 0.414 \text{ N/mm}^2 < 1.03 \text{ N/mm}^2 \qquad ♦$$

(a) Loaded beam.

(b) Stresses acting on a
portion of the beam.

(c) Horizontal shear stresses
acting on the upper and
lower faces of an elemental
area in the beam. The
stresses produce a rotational
moment.

(d) The rotational moment produced
by the horizontal shear stresses is
exactly balanced by a rotational
moment associated with vertical
shear stresses. The rotational
moments, hence stresses, must be
equal at the point.

(e) Horizontal shear-stress distribution
in a rectangular beam.

(f) Vertical shear-stress distribution
in a rectangular beam.

FIGURE 6–17   The numerical magnitudes of the horizontal and vertical shear stresses at any point in a beam are always equal.

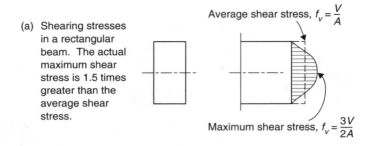

(a) Shearing stresses in a rectangular beam. The actual maximum shear stress is 1.5 times greater than the average shear stress.

Average shear stress, $f_v = \dfrac{V}{A}$

Maximum shear stress, $f_v = \dfrac{3V}{2A}$

(b) Shearing stresses in a wide-flange beam. The actual maximum shear stress is only slightly greater than the average shear stress.

Actual maximum shear stress

Average shear stress, $f_v = \dfrac{V}{A_{web}}$

FIGURE 6–18 Shearing-stress distributions in a rectangular beam and in a wide-flange beam.

◆ ◆ **EXAMPLE**

For the same T beam previously analyzed and again illustrated in Figure 6–19(b), determine the shear stress present at the interface between the top flange element and the web element if $V = 2000$ lb. If glue were used to bond the elements together, what would be the stress on the glue? If nails spaced at 3.0 in. on center were used as connectors, what would be the shear force on each nail? What is the maximum shear stress present in the cross section?

Solution: The expression $f_v = VQ/Ib$ will be used again, with $Q = A'y'$ evaluated for the area of the beam above the interface between the top flange and web element.

$$Q = A'y' = (b_1 \times h_1(y')) = (10 \text{ in.} \times 2 \text{ in.})(3.82 \text{ in.}) = 76.3 \text{ in.}^3$$
$$I = 829.3 \text{ in.} \quad \text{(see previous example)}$$
$$b = 2 \text{ in.}$$
$$V = 2000 \text{ lb}$$
$$f_v = \frac{VQ}{Ib} = (2000 \text{ lb})(76.3 \text{ in.}^3)/(829.3 \text{ in.}^4)(2 \text{ in.}) = 92.0 \text{ lb/in.}^2$$

This is the horizontal or vertical shear stress that occurs at the interface. This implies that if the two rectangular elements were glued together at this interface, the glue would have to be able to withstand this stress. If some other connector, such as nails, were used, the connector would have to be able to carry 2 in. × 92.0 lb/in., or 184 lb/in. If nails were placed 3.0 in. on center, each nail would have to carry 3 in. × 184 lb/in., or 552 lb of shear. This value could be compared to experimentally derived allowable forces on nails to determine if the nail spacing is adequate.

(a) Shear stresses in a rectangular beam.
Shear force: $V = 2000$ lb (8896 N).

(b) Shear stresses in a T beam.
Shear force: $V = 2000$ lb.

FIGURE 6–19   Shearing stresses in beams.

The maximum shear stress in the section occurs at the neutral axis. In evaluating this maximum stress, it is more convenient to consider the area below the neutral axis in evaluating $Q = A'y'$. Thus,

$$Q = A'y' = (2 \text{ in.} \times 9.18 \text{ in.})(9.18 \text{ in.}/2) = 84.3 \text{ in.}$$

$$f_v = \frac{VQ}{Ib} = \frac{(2000 \text{ lb})(84.3 \text{ in.})}{(829.3 \text{ in.}^4)(2 \text{ in.})} = 101.7 \text{ lb/in.}^2$$

The shear-stress distribution for the whole cross section is illustrated in Figure 6–19(b). The discontinuity at the interface occurs because of the change from $b = 2$ in. to $b = 10$ in. Since shear stresses are inversely dependent on the width of the beam, actual shear stresses are significantly reduced in the wide top flange.   ◆

6–3–4 Bearing Stresses

The stresses developed at the point of contact between two loaded members are called *bearing stresses*. Such stresses, for example, are developed at the ends of a simply supported beam where it rests on end supports having certain dimensions. The magnitude of the stresses developed are dependent on the magnitude of the force transmitted through the point of contact and the surface area of the contact between the two elements. The smaller the contact area, the greater the bearing stresses. The stresses produce deformations in both elements at the point of contact. These deformations typically extend into the elements only a small distance.

The magnitude of the bearing stress at a point is simply equal to the load transmitted divided by the area of contact, or $f_{bg} = P/A$. This assumes that the bearing stresses are uniformly distributed over the contact area, an assumption that is not quite correct but reasonably so.

Many materials, such as timber, are particularly susceptible to bearing-stress failures. When a compressive load is transmitted, bearing-stress failures are usually not catastrophic and are typically manifested by an appearance of "crushing" in a material. The failure is generally localized but should be avoided.

◆ ◆ **EXAMPLE**

Assume that the timber beam illustrated in Figure 6–20 carries a uniformly distributed load of 500 lb/ft (7300 N/m) over a span of 16 ft (4.87 m). Also assume that the contact area between the beam and the column it rests on is 4 in. × 4 in. (101.6 mm × 101.6 mm). If the allowable stress in bearing of the timber in

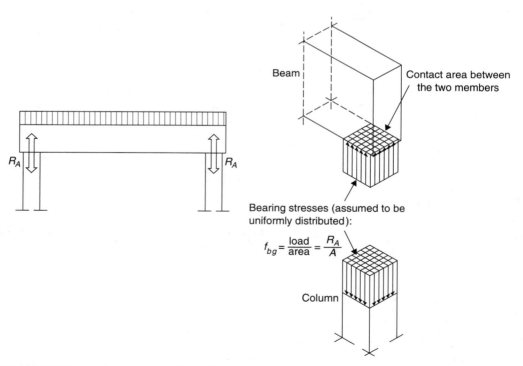

FIGURE 6–20 Bearing stresses at the end of a beam.

the beam is $F_{bg} = 400$ lb/in.^{2} (2.76 N/mm^2), is the area of contact sufficiently large? Determine the actual bearing stress existing at the reaction. The reaction is 4000 lb (17,792 N) and the contact area is 4 in. $\times$ 4 in. $= 16$ in.^{2} (10,322.6 mm^2).

Solution:

$$\text{Actual bearing stress} = f_{bg} = \frac{P}{A} = \frac{4000 \text{ lb}}{16 \text{ in.}^2} = 250 \text{ lb/in.}^2$$

$$= \frac{(17,792 \text{ N})}{(10,322.6 \text{ mm}^2)} = 1.72 \text{ N/mm}^2$$

Since the actual bearing stress is less than the allowable bearing stress (250 lb/in.^{2} < 400 lb/in.^{2}) or (1.72 N/mm^2 < 2.76 N/mm^2), there is sufficient contact area between the two members. ◆

6–3–5   Torsion

Torsion is a *twisting*. Torsional forces develop in a member through the direct application of a torque or twisting moment M_T, or they may develop indirectly because of an off-balanced load or force application. For example, framing one member into the side of another can cause twisting because of the off-balanced load application.

Figure 6–21(a) illustrates a round member subjected to torsion. The analysis of the stresses produced by this type of force is not particularly complex but will not be covered here in detail. Figure 6–21(b) illustrates the type of stresses generated in the member by the applied torque. The force resultants of the stresses developed produce a couple that equilibrates the applied twisting moment. The stress at a point, τ, is dependent on the magnitude of the applied twisting moment, M_T; the location of the point, defined by the distance r from the centroid, and the properties of the cross section, typically designated by the symbol J. The relation between these parameters is given by $\tau = Mr/J$. This expression is clearly analogous to the expression of bending stresses ($f_y = Mc/I$). J is analogous to I and is again given by $\int_A r^2 \, dA$, except that now polar coordinates are used and J becomes the *polar moment of inertia*.

In instances where the section considered is not circular, the analysis of torsional stresses becomes fairly complex. Figure 6–21(c) illustrates a rectangular beam subjected to torsional stresses. Twisting is induced by the beam framing rigidly into the beam. The torsional stresses in such a beam are again dependent on the twisting moment present, M_T, the location of the point considered, and the properties of the rectangular section, and are given by an expression of the form $\tau = \alpha M_T/b^2 d$, where α depends on the relative proportions of b and d. For $d/b = 1$, $\alpha = 0.208$; for $d/b = 3.0$, $\alpha = 0.267$; for $d/b = 10$, $\alpha = 0.312$.

Thin-walled tubes of thickness t may be analyzed simply in terms of shear flows: $q = \tau t$. In general, $M_T = \int rq \, ds$, where ds is along the perimeter and r is the value to the center of twisting. Thus $q \, ds$ gives the contribution of an element to the torque resistance (e.g., for a thin circular tube: $M_T = q(2\pi r)r$, or $q = M_T/2\pi r^2$). More generally, for any thin-walled tube, $M_T = \int rq \, ds$ becomes $M_T = 2Aq$ and $q = M_T/2A$, where A is the area enclosed by the centerline of the tube; then $\tau = q/t$.

When designing, *closed forms* such as tubes, pipes, or box beams are usually better for carrying torsional forces than are *open forms* such as plates or channels. The latter twist badly. Box forms are frequently used for bridge cross sections and other situations where torsion is particularly problematical. (See Figure 6–22.)

(a) Cantilever circular member subjected to a twisting force, M_T.

(b) Torsional stresses developed in the member as a result of the twisting. The torsional stresses may vary from zero at the center of the circular member to a maximum at the surface of the member. These stresses act over the cross-sectional area of the member to produce a resisting torque equal and opposite to the applied torque.

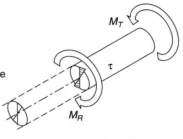

(c) Torsional stresses can be induced in a rectangular member by beams framing into the side of the member.

FIGURE 6–21 Torsion in beams. Torsional stresses are developed in members as a result of the application of a twisting force to the member.

Closed shapes   Open shapes

○ □   [L

Closed shapes have better torsional resistance than do open shapes.

Typical bridge cross sections (closed shapes)

FIGURE 6–22 Closed sections are better for resisting torsion than are open sections. Many bridge configurations are open sections.

6–3–6   Shear Center

Of importance in the use of members that are not symmetrical about the vertical axes and typically composed of thin-walled sections (e.g., a channel section) is the phenomenon of twisting under the action of transverse loads. A symmetrical section, such as a rectangular beam, used as illustrated in Figure 6–23(a), simply deflects downward when loaded. A channel section carrying the same load would twist as indicated in Figure 6–23(b) because the line of action of the load does not pass through what is called the *shear center* of the member. This twisting leads to the development of torsional stresses in the member. The twisting itself can be predicted by a close investigation of the action of the stresses present in the section and can be described in terms of *shear flows,* but this topic is outside the scope of this book. The presence of this twisting does not exclude the use of such members as beam elements, since a section can still be designed to safely carry external forces, but it does complicate their use as well as detract from their efficiency. If it were desired to use such a member to carry transverse forces without twisting, it is possible to do so by locating the load so that it passes through the *shear center* of the beam. In Figure 6–23(c),

(a) A loaded symmetric section will deflect downward without twisting.

(b) Applying the load directly to a nonsymmetric member will cause twisting to develop in the member as it deflects downward.

(c) The direction of twist will depend on the load application point. By applying the load at a special point, called the shear center, the member will deflect without twisting.

FIGURE 6–23   Shear center in beams. In nonsymmetric members, applying a load directly to the member will cause the member to twist. Applying the load at the *shear center* of the beam will cause the member to deflect downward without twisting. The shear center of many nonsymmetric members often lies outside the member.

application of the load as indicated causes the twisting in the directions shown. There must, therefore, exist some point to the right of the section where the load could be applied and cause no twisting. This is the shear center. Other references describe how to locate this point.[2] Note that in the example illustrated, the shear center lies outside the section, thus complicating the use of this location as a point of load application.

6-3-7 Deflections

Consider the beam indicated in the upper left in Figure 6–24(a). The deflection Δ at a particular point in this beam, or in any other, depends on the load P or w, the length L of the beam, inversely on the stiffness of the beam as it depends on the amount and way material is distributed in the cross section (as characterized by the moment of inertia, I), and inversely on the stiffness of the beam as it depends on the stress-deformation characteristics of the material used in the beam (as characterized by the modulus of elasticity, E). Thus, Δ depends on P or w, L, $1/I$, and $1/E$. Note:

$$\text{As} \quad \begin{cases} w \text{ increases, } \Delta \text{ increases} \\ L \text{ increases, } \Delta \text{ increases} \\ I \text{ increases, } \Delta \text{ decreases} \\ E \text{ increases, } \Delta \text{ decreases} \end{cases} \quad \begin{aligned} \Delta &= C_1(wl^4/EI) \\ \Delta &= C_2(PL^3/EI) \end{aligned}$$

The values of L must be raised to the powers noted for the expressions to work out dimensionally. For uniform loads, in. $= (\text{lb/in.})(\text{in.}^a)/(\text{lb/in.}^2)(\text{in.}^4)$, so the exponent a of L must be 4. For point loads: in. $= (\text{lb})(\text{in.}^b)/(\text{lb/in.}^2)(\text{in.}^4)$, so the exponent b of L must be 3. Support conditions also influence the amount of the deflection present. In the above, C_1 and C_2 are constants depending on support conditions. More formal derivations of deflection expressions are contained in Appendices 7, 8, and 9. For a simply supported beam with a uniformly distributed load, C_1 becomes 5/384, so $\Delta = 5wL^4/384EI$.

Evidently, deflections are *highly* sensitive to the length of the beam. It is also interesting to note that for a beam that is exactly similar in all respects except that the ends of the member are fixed rather than simply supported, the deflection is given by: $\Delta = wL^4/384EI$. Thus, fixing the ends of a simply supported beam carrying a uniformly distributed load reduces the midspan deflection by a factor of 5. Note that the form of both expressions is the same, but there is a difference in the modifying constant—which obviously reflects the different boundary conditions. The increased rigidity associated with fixed-ended beams, or also continuous beams, is one of the primary reasons why such members are used extensively in practice.

Deflections for other loading and support conditions are shown in Figure 6–24. Appendices 7, 8, and 9 discuss methods of calculating these expressions.

In designing beams, controlling the magnitude of deflections is always a major problem. It is also difficult to even establish what constitutes an allowable deflection in a beam. Some objective criteria can be established. If a beam deflects such that it interferes with or impairs the functioning of another building element, for example, the allowable deflection could be based on acceptable tolerances for other systems. In many cases, however, the problem is more subjective. Many beams are, for example, perfectly safe from a strength viewpoint but are said to visually

---

[2]Stephen Crandall and Norman Dahl, *An Introduction to the Mechanics of Solids,* McGraw-Hill Book Company, New York, 1959.

(a) Cantilever beam –
      concentrated load at free end

Maximum deflection:

$$\Delta_{max} = \frac{PL^3}{3EI}$$

(b) Cantilever beam –
      uniformly distributed load

Maximum deflection:

$$\Delta_{max} = \frac{wL^4}{8EI}$$

(c) Simple beam –
      uniformly distributed load

Maximum deflection:

$$\Delta_{max} = \frac{5wL^4}{384EI}$$

(d) Simple beam –
      concentrated load at center

Maximum deflection:

$$\Delta_{max} = \frac{PL^3}{48EI}$$

(e) Beam fixed at both ends –
      concentrated load at center

Maximum deflection:

$$\Delta_{max} = \frac{PL^3}{192EI}$$

(f) Beam fixed at both ends –
      uniformly distributed loads

Maximum deflection:

$$\Delta_{max} = \frac{wL^4}{348EI}$$

FIGURE 6–24 Deflections in beams.

"sag" too much. Likewise, when people walk across floors and the floors feel bouncy or springy, the supporting beams are said to deflect too much. With respect to the last point it is true that attempts are made to control floor bounciness by limiting deflections. This is, however, a misconception because people do not feel deflections, they instead sense the accelerations associated with deflections. This is an important point in that there may be other ways to control accelerations than by artificially limiting deflections.

The problem of what determines excessive deflections is tough. Empirical guidelines are often used. A common empirical criterion used to control both the visual sag and bounciness problems is that the deflection of a floor should not exceed $\frac{1}{360}$ of its span (the criterion is usually expressed as $\Delta_{\text{allowable}} = L/360$, where L is the span of the member). Usually, the $L/360$ criterion for floors applies to deflections caused by live loads only. Dead plus live load deflections are typically limited to $L/240$ of the span. Steel members are often upwardly cambered an amount equal to the dead-load deflection, so that the live-load deflection occurs with respect to a horizontal member. Roof deflections are typically limited to $L/240$ for live loads and $L/180$ for live plus dead loads.

If a member deflects more than these guidelines, it is usually considered not acceptable and a member of increased stiffness (i.e., increased I) must be used no matter how low the stress level in the member might be. Evidently, the size of such a member can be found by equating the appropriate deflection expression with the maximum allowable deflection and solving for the required stiffness (e.g., $\Delta_{\text{allowable}} = L/240 = 5wL^4/384EI$, or $I_{\text{req'd}} = 5(240)wL^4/384EL$ for a uniformly loaded beam).

The criteria noted previously and $L/240$ and $L/360$ are felt by many designers to be conservative in view of the origins of these criteria. They have roots in historical building traditions in which the rules were used largely as a measure to prevent plaster affixed to the underside of a floor (or on the ceiling of the room beneath) from cracking. The criteria have since been widely used for many other applications. There is no doubt that floors designed to these limitations are usually perceived by occupants as comfortable and not excessively saggy. It is interesting to note that our perceptions of what constitutes an acceptable level of both visual sag and floor bounciness are probably derived from our cultural conditioning in accepting prior experiences as a measure of correctness. These experiences are in turn based largely on an antiquated plaster-cracking criterion.

◆ ◆ **EXAMPLE**

A simply supported floor beam that is 20 ft (6.1 m) long carries a uniformly distributed live load of 200 lb/ft (2920 N/m). The beam has a rectangular cross section with dimensions $b = 8$ in. (203.2 mm) and $d = 16$ in. (406.4 mm). The modulus of elasticity of the timber is $E = 1.6 \times 10^6$ lb/in.^{2} (11,032N/mm^2). Assume that the beam is initially cambered upward so that it is level under dead loads. What is the maximum live-load deflection at midspan, and is it excessive?

Solution:

Moment of inertia:

$$I = \frac{bd^3}{12} = \frac{(8 \text{ in.})(16 \text{ in.})^3}{12} = 2730 \text{ in.}^4$$

$$= \frac{(203.2 \text{ mm})(406.4 \text{ mm})^3}{12} = 1136.6 \times 10^6 \text{ mm}^4$$

Deflection due to live loading:

$$\Delta = \frac{5wL^4}{384EI}$$

$$= \frac{5(200 \text{ lb/ft}/12 \text{ lb/in.})(20 \text{ ft} \times 12 \text{ in.})^4}{384(1.6 \times 10^6 \text{ lb/in.}^2)(2730 \text{ in.}^4)} = 0.165 \text{ in.}$$

$$= \frac{5(2.920 \text{ N/mm})(6100 \text{ mm})^4}{384(11{,}032 \text{ N/mm}^2)(1136.6 \times 10^6 \text{ mm}^4)} = 4.2 \text{ mm}$$

$$\Delta = 0.165 \text{ in.} < L/360 = 12(20)/360 = 0.67 \text{ in.}$$

Hence, the deflection is not excessive.   ◆

6-3-8   Principal Stresses

One of the most interesting aspects of beam analysis is the way bending and shearing stresses interact. Stresses acting in different directions cannot simply be added algebraically, but their resultant interaction still can be found in much the same way that a resultant force can be found to represent the combined action of several different vector forces acting at a point. In a beam, the result of the interaction between bending and shear stresses is to produce a set of resultant tensile and compressive stresses, typically called *principal stresses,* that act in different directions from either the bending or shear stresses individually.

In a cantilever beam, the stresses acting on several typical elements are illustrated in Figure 6–25. A set of equivalent principal tension and compressive stresses could be found for each of the

Principal stresses in tension

Principal stresses in compression

(a) At the free edge of the beam, only bending stresses are present. Principal compressive and tensile stresses thus act horizontally and vertically at this point.

(b) At intermediate points in the beam both bending stresses and shear stresses are present. The direction of the principal stresses depends on the relative magnitudes of these stresses.

(c) At the neutral axis of the beam, only shear stresses are present. These determine the direction of the principal stresses to be at a 45° angle to the horizontal.

FIGURE 6–25   Principal stresses in a cantilever beam. Principal stresses result from the interaction of bending stresses and shearing stresses. The lines shown are often called stress trajectories and depict the direction of the principal stresses in the member. They are not lines of constant stress.

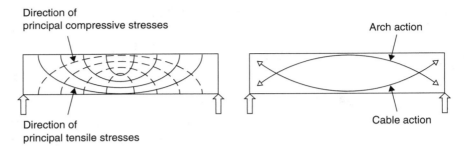

FIGURE 6–26 Lines of principal stresses: implications on general load-carrying mechanisms present in beams.

elements. Note that for an element at the neutral axis of the beam, where bending stresses are zero, only shear stresses exist. As diagrammed in Figure 6–25, these stresses can be resolved into equivalent principal tensile and compressive stresses acting at 45° angles to the neutral axis. At the extreme surfaces of the beam, an element carries only bending stresses, since shear stresses are zero. Thus, the principal stresses in tension become aligned with the bending stresses in tension and have the directions indicated in Figure 6–25. For an intermediate element subject to both shear and bending stresses, the principal stresses have an inclination depending on the relative magnitudes of the shear and bending stresses. By considering elements at other sections in the beam, stress trajectories can be drawn as illustrated. It is important to note that the lines are not lines of constant stress, but are lines of principal stress *direction*. Stress intensity, therefore, can vary depending upon the relative magnitudes and distributions of shear and bending stresses in the beam.

Figure 6–26 illustrates the stress trajectories present in a simply supported beam. Calculation of the magnitudes of principal stresses is a straightforward procedure but beyond the scope of this book. In general, it can be shown that maximum and minimum principal tensile and compressive stresses occur on planes of zero shearing stress and maximum shearing stresses occur on planes at 45° angles to the planes of principal tensile and compressive stresses.

6–3–9 Finite-Element Analyses

The types of stress and deformation analyses presented thus far are the basic tools commonly used for analyzing typical structures. Many structures have complex geometries or loading conditions, however, that demand more sophisticated treatments. One widely used approach is via the use of computer-based *finite-element* methods. A continuous structure is replaced by a conforming meshed network of interconnected discrete pieces of varying shapes and sizes. Forces are applied at nodal points. Energy-based structural analysis techniques and various compatibility requirements are then used to predict forces and displacements. Outputs include various kinds of stress analyses (typically three principal stresses; see Section 6–3–8), strain distributions, and displacement analyses. In a typical complex volumetric solid structure, magnitudes and distributions for three principal stresses are obtained. Problems involving thin-shell structures can be beneficially limited and two principal stress components typically found. Appendix 13 provides some additional information about finite-element methods. Although a valuable approach, finite-element methods are largely outside of the scope of this book.

(a) Cantilevered
    structure

(b) Finite-element
    mesh

Scale for 1st principal stress   (c)

High   Low

The S-shaped deformation indicates
that the structure has a more complex
behavior than that of a simple beam with
an unusual cross section. It is behaving
more like two interconnected small beams
or a rigid frame structure (see Chaper 9)

1st principal stress

FIGURE 6–27   Structure in bending analyzed by finite-element method.

The basic results for a cantilevered structure (a complexly shaped structure with an interior void and rounded edges) analyzed by finite-element methods are shown in Figure 6–27. The finite-element mesh is shown. Many different types of automatic computer-based mesh generators are available. A variety of mesh types and elements are also available. Sizes may be varied as well, with smaller sizes being used where more detailed information is sought. Restraints and external forces are next specified. Solution of the structural analysis algorithms demands the solution of multiple simultaneous equations (hence the need for a computer environment). Detailed results for all stresses and deformations are obtained in tabular form. Selected results can be graphically displayed. One set of results, first principal stresses, are shown in Figure 6–27.

The analysis shown indicates the power of finite-element techniques. A novice analyzing this structure might be tempted to treat it as a single cantilever beam with a unique cross section that has a void along the expected location of the neutral axis and seek to find stresses via $f = My/I$ approaches. The finite-element analysis demonstrates, however, that the structure simply does not behave in a way appropriate to this kind of analysis. Rather it behaves much more like two independent small beams that are interconnected at either end. Stresses and deformation patterns are considerably different for this behavior mode as compared to the first. Stresses are much higher. (Reasons for these differences are many. One point is that an assumption used to obtain normal $f = My/I$ stresses is that plane sections cut through the structure remain plane during force-induced deformations—an assumption clearly not viable here.)

Once principal stresses are found, any of a variety of more complex failure criteria can be used to determine the safety of an element. Rather than using simple allowable stress measures individually associated with just bending or shear, as has previously been done for simple beams, stress interactions are considered. Typical failure criteria include the following: the maximum von Mies stress criterion, the Mohr-Coulomb stress criterion, the maximum normal stress criterion, and the maximum shear stress criterion. The choice of failure criteria depends on many factors, including the loading environment (e.g., rate of load application), material characteristics, and so forth. Appendix 13 discusses these kinds of failure criteria in more detail.

6-4 DESIGN OF BEAMS

6-4-1 General Design Principles

Approaches. Primary variables in designing beams include the following: spans, member spacings, loading types and magnitudes, material type(s), cross-sectional sizing and shaping (including variations along member lengths), and assembly or fabrication techniques. The more a design situation is constrained, the easier it is to design a specific member. The easiest condition is when everything is specified but a member's size, in which case the process can almost be deterministic. As more and more variables are brought into play, as is the normal case in a true design situation, the process becomes considerably more difficult and less deterministic. Iterative approaches are common where several beam designs for different variable sets are developed and compared according to prespecified criteria (e.g., material economy, depth, cost, appearance). This section will focus on design situations with fairly well defined constraints.

Any beam design must meet specified strength and stiffness criteria for safety and serviceability. Design approaches for meeting these criteria are highly dependent on the materials selected for use. Timber, steel, and reinforced concrete beams will be discussed extensively in the following sections. Even within a specified material context, however, broadly differing attitudes may be taken to member design. (1) The size and shape of a member may be determined on the basis of the most critical force state anywhere in the beam, and this same size and shape used throughout the length of the member (even if force levels decrease). The member is thus worked to its maximum capacity at one section only. This strategy is used widely for reasons of ease and construction expediency. (2) An attempt may be made to vary the size and shape of a member along its length in response to the nature and magnitude of the force state present at specific locations, with the intent to have the beam equally stressed along its length and commensurate advantages of material economy. Shaping a beam along its length, however, may prove difficult, depending on the construction approach selected. In the following sections we explore these and other design approaches.

Strength and Stiffness Control. Beams must be sized and shaped so that they are sufficiently strong to carry applied loadings without undue material distress or deformations. When the design act is highly limited to that of finding a beam size and shape for a given span, loading, and material context, the problem reduces to a fairly simple one of finding section properties for a member such that the actual stresses generated in the beam at any point are limited to predetermined safe levels dependent on the properties of the materials used.

Shear and moment diagrams are typically first drawn. The maximum bending moment (M_{max}) is determined. For simple steel or timber members with symmetrical cross sections, initial member size estimates are made using the concept of a "required" section modulus (S) as described in Section 6–3–1. Thus, $S_{req'd} = M_{max}/F_b$. A member with a section modulus equal to, or greater than, this value is selected as a trial size. Remaining stresses and deflections are checked. The procedure described started with a member size based on bending. Depending on the situation, a trial member size may be determined based on deflections or other type of stress. These procedures are illustrated for timber beams in Section 6–4–2 and for steel beams in Section 6–4–3. Reinforced concrete members are considerably more complicated and are treated in Section 6–4–4.

Cross-Sectional Shapes.   The moment of inertia (I) and the section modulus (S) are of primary importance in beam design. A common design objective is to provide the required I or S for a beam carrying a given loading with a cross-sectional configuration that has the smallest possible area. The total volume of material required to support the load in space would then be reduced. Alternatively, the objective could be stated in terms of taking a given cross-sectional area and organizing this material so that the maximum I or S value is obtained, thus allowing the beam to support the maximum possible external moment (hence loading).

The basic principle for maximizing the moment of inertia obtainable from a given area is contained in the definition of the moment of inertia, which is $I = y^2\, dA$. The contribution of a given element of area (dA) to the total moment of inertia of a section depends on the square of the distance of this elemental area from the neutral axis of the section. The sensitivity to the square of the distance is important. This would lead one to expect that for a given amount of material, the best way to organize it in space is to remove it as far as practically possible from the neutral axis of the section (i.e., make the section deep with most of the material at the extremities). Consequently beams with high depth/width ratios are usually more efficient than ones with shallower proportions.

A highly economic cross section also based on the preceding principle is illustrated in Figure 6–28(a), where a thin web member is used to connect two widely separated thick flanges. The question arises of just how thin the web can be. It will be recalled that maximum shearing stresses always occur at the neutral axis of a beam. Thus, it is necessary that the web be of a certain minimum thickness to carry these shear stresses safely. In addition, there are lines of

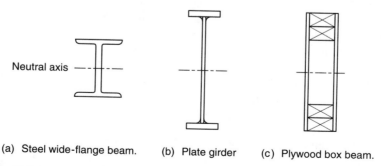

(a) Steel wide-flange beam.   (b) Plate girder   (c) Plywood box beam.

FIGURE 6–28   Efficient beam cross-sectional shapes. Material is removed away from the neutral axis to maximize the moment of inertia of the cross section and hence its resistance to bending.

principal stresses which cross the beam in the middle. The principal compressive stresses could cause the web to buckle locally if it were too thin. Beams of the general proportions indicated in Figure 6–28(a) result after those factors are taken into account. Sections of this type made of steel, called *wide-flange beams,* are commonly used in building construction where bending stresses are typically a more important consideration than shearing stresses. When shear forces are high, it can be expected that beams with thicker webs will be used. An analogous shape in timber is shown in Figure 6–28(b).

The discussion thus far has focused on ways of increasing the moment of inertia (I) of a section. It should be recalled, however, that in design of a beam, the measure that is actually of primary importance is the I/y_{max} value of a section. In cases where the section is symmetric about the neutral axis, increasing the I value automatically increases the section modulus, S. In nonsymmetric sections such as T beams, the design must be based on the condition that the maximum bending stress at any point on the beam is limited to the allowable stresses. At a section this point is defined by y_{max} and occurs on one face of the section. The other face, with a value of y less than y_{max}, is therefore understressed. Hence, the use of such a section is not advantageous in beams made of homogeneous materials such as steel. When a composite material such as reinforced concrete is used, however, T beams can have definite advantageous properties (see Section 6–4–4).

Material Property Variations.   In addition to changing the way material is distributed at a cross section, it is also possible to vary the types of material used within a given cross section so that there is a better matching between the stress state present and the characteristics of the material used. This principle finds its manifestation in beams as diverse as those made of laminated wood (Section 6–4–2) and reinforced concrete (Section 6–4–4).

Shaping a Beam Along Its Length.   The previous section generally considered ways of designing beams of different materials at a single cross section. This section considers the shaping of a beam along its axis as a way of improving the overall efficiency of a beam. The intention behind varying the shape of a member along its axis is to provide a better fit between the characteristics of a beam and the shears and moments which typically vary along the length of a beam.

The subject of shaping beams in response to the shears and moments present has a long history in the field of structures. In the early nineteenth century investigators were already determining appropriate responses for cantilever beams. It is interesting to review this same problem. Consider the cantilever illustrated in Figure 6–29(a), which carries a concentrated load at its end. Let us attempt to find an appropriate beam configuration based on the criterion that the bending stresses developed on the top and bottom surfaces of the beam should be constant along the length of the beam. This is done by setting up an expression for the dimensions of the beam as a function of the external moment present in the beam. An expression for the moment in the beam with respect to an arbitrary reference point is also needed.

For a rectangular section, beam dimensions as a function of M: $S = bd^2/6 = M/F_b$, or $bd^2 = 6M/F_b$. External moment as a function of x: $M = Px$; hence, $bd^2 = 6Px/F_b = x6P/F_b$.

If the beam depth d is assumed constant, and the above expression is rewritten as $b = k_1 x$, then the width b varies directly with x, since the quantity $k_1 = 6P/d^2 F_b$ is a constant. Consequently, a beam shaped as illustrated in Figure 6–29(b) would result. If the width b is assumed constant, the depth d obviously depends on $\sqrt{x}$ [i.e., $d = \sqrt{x}(\sqrt{6P/F_b b}) = k_2 \sqrt{x}$].

(a) Cantilever beam with concentrated load. The bending moment at a point x from the free end is $M_x = Px$. The moment present varies linearly along the length of the beam to a maximum at the base of the cantilever. $M_{Max} = PL$.

(b) Beam shaped along its axis so that constant bending stresses are developed on its upper and lower faces. In this beam, the depth of the beam was assumed to be constant at d and the width b allowed to vary.

(c) Beam shaped along its axis so that constant bending stresses are developed on its upper and lower faces. In this beam, the width of the beam b was assumed constant and the depth d of the beam allowed to vary.

(d) Cantilever beam with uniformly distributed loading. The bending moment at a point x away from the free end is $M_x = wx^2/2$. The moment present varies parabolically to a maximum value at the base of the cantilever of $M_x = wL^2/2$.

(e) Beam shaped along its axis so that constant bending stresses are developed on its upper and lower faces. In this beam, the depth of the beam was assumed to be constant at d and the width b allowed to vary.

(f) Beam shaped along its axis so that constant bending stresses are developed on its upper and lower faces. In this beam, the width of the beam b was assumed constant and the depth d of the beam allowed to vary.

FIGURE 6–29 Shaping a beam in response to the bending moment distribution present.

271

Consequently, a beam shaped as illustrated would result. If it is assumed that the beam section should always be square ($b = d$), then $d^3 = x(6P/F_b)$, or d varies as $\sqrt[3]{x}$.

For comparison purposes, it is useful to repeat this exercise with a cantilever carrying a uniformly distributed load. For a rectangular cross section, beam dimensions as a function of M: $S = bd^2/6 = M/F_b$, or $bd^2 = 6M/F_b$. External moment as a function of x: $M = wx^2/2$; hence, $bd^2 = x^2 6w/2F_b$, or $b = k_3x$ and $d = k_4x$.

If the depth d is assumed constant, then the width b varies with x^2 since $k_3 = 6w/2F_bd^2$ is a constant. If b is assumed constant, then d varies directly with x: $d = x\sqrt{6w/2F_bb} = k_4x$. The shape illustrated in Figure 6–29(f) results.

It should be emphasized that the shapes derived above are not necessarily intended to represent practical structural responses to the loadings indicated. Only bending stresses have been considered at the exclusion of other considerations (e.g., shear stresses, deflections) that might influence the final shapes found for the loadings. They are very much idealized responses to the loadings shown and their value derives largely from this. They are particularly useful as a tool in visualizing whether an actual structural response is appropriate for a given situation.

The shapes found above are not necessarily generalizable to other beams carrying similar loads but supported differently. The moment equations for different types of beams differ, so it can be expected that shapes would also. The student is encouraged to explore types of beams other than the cantilevers illustrated and determine appropriate shapes.

Cross sections other than rectangular can also be used as the basis for determining idealized responses. Figure 6–30 illustrates a steel wide-flange beam designed in response to the moment present for a simply supported beam with a uniformly distributed loading, assuming that the beam should remain of constant depth and that the width of the flange is the only variable. Varying the width of the flange causes the section modulus S to change. This variation could be coupled with the moment distribution present in the beam to obtain a configuration where the bending stress level in the flanges remains constant.

In a wide-flange shape, the beam depth and flange width could be assumed as constant and the flange thickness allowed to vary. Figure 6–29(e) illustrates a beam of this type where, as a matter of construction simplicity, the variation in flange thickness is accomplished by use of horizontal layers of thin steel plates bonded (welded or bolted) together. Again the properties of this beam at each section can be coupled with the amount of moment present to create a situation of essentially constant bending stresses in the beam flanges. Stresses cannot be held purely constant, since discrete changes occur in the flange thickness due to the layering used. Often standard structural steel wide-flange shapes have additional steel plates (commonly called *cover plates*) added at regions of high moment.

Other shapes based on radically different cross sections may also be optimized (see Figure 6–30). Again, dimensions are varied, so that S_x depends on M_x.

Varying Support Locations and Boundary Conditions. Manipulating support conditions can lead to major economies in the use of materials. The immediate intent of such manipulations is usually to reduce the magnitudes of the design moments present or to alter their distribution. A classic way of reducing design moments is to use cantilever overhangs on beams. The effect of cantilevering one end of a simply supported beam with uniform loads is to cause a reduction in the positive moment present while a negative moment develops at the base of the cantilever over the support. The greater the cantilever, the higher the negative moment becomes and the lower

(a) Uniformly distributed loading.

(b) Timber beam shape in which the width was held constant and the depth varied in response to the bending moment present so that bending stresses on upper and lower surfaces are held constant. The depth at the end of the beam was increased because of shear stresses.

(c) Steel beam in which the width was held constant and the depth varied in response to the bending moment present.

(d) Steel beam in which the depth was held constant and the width varied in response to the bending moment present so that bending stresses on upper and lower surfaces are held constant.

(e) Built-up steel plate girder. The section modulus of the beam has been varied to reflect the varying bending moment present by changing the thicknesses of the flange present at a section.

FIGURE 6–30   Varying the sectional properties of beams in response to the bending moment distribution.

the positive moment becomes. The cantilever can be extended until the negative moment even exceeds the positive moment.

Of interest here is that there must exist a certain overhang such that the numerical value of the positive moment is exactly equal to that of the negative moment.

Figure 6–31(b) illustrates a simple beam with variable-length cantilevers on both ends. If no cantilevers were present ($x = 0$), it is evident that the critical design moment would be $M = 0.125wL^2$ (the maximum positive moment at midspan). If the ends were cantilevered to a

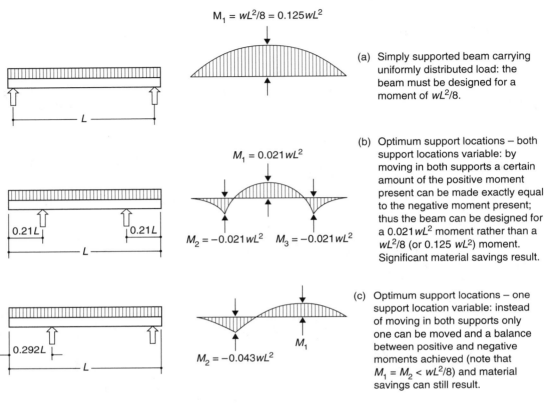

$M_1 = wL^2/8 = 0.125wL^2$

(a) Simply supported beam carrying uniformly distributed load: the beam must be designed for a moment of $wL^2/8$.

$M_1 = 0.021wL^2$

$M_2 = -0.021wL^2 \quad M_3 = -0.021wL^2$

(b) Optimum support locations – both support locations variable: by moving in both supports a certain amount of the positive moment present can be made exactly equal to the negative moment present; thus the beam can be designed for a $0.021wL^2$ moment rather than a $wL^2/8$ (or $0.125\,wL^2$) moment. Significant material savings result.

M_1

$M_2 = -0.043wL^2$

(c) Optimum support locations – one support location variable: instead of moving in both supports only one can be moved and a balance between positive and negative moments achieved (note that $M_1 = M_2 < wL^2/8$) and material savings can still result.

FIGURE 6–31 Locating supports to minimize design moments in beams.

certain specific extent, the structure could be designed for a moment of $M = 0.021wL^2$ at midspan and $M = -0.021wL^2$ at either support. The moment can be reduced no farther than this. Reducing the design moment in this way leads to considerable economies when member sizes are determined. The exact extent of the overhang on either end which results in the positive and negative moments being equal can be found either by a trial-and-error process or by setting up one equation in terms of the variable x for the negative moment at a support and another for the positive moment at midspan and equating them. The optimum overhang is approximately one-fifth of the overall span.

The same approach can be taken when the location of only one instead of both supports can be varied. The optimum overhang is about one-third of the span. Considerations of the type above are one way of answering the question of how far it is possible to cantilever a beam. Rules like the above, however, should be tempered with other considerations. In many cases, for example, the amount of deflection at the end of the cantilever will control how far one can extend the member rather than using criteria based on moment considerations. The type of construction is also important. The measures are not applicable to prestressed or post-tensioned reinforced concrete members, for example, without special considerations. By and large the one-fifth and one-third measures given above are best applied to relatively short or moderate span members made of homogeneous materials.

6–4–2   Design of Timber Beams

The following example illustrates the process used for determining the required size of a simple timber beam within a highly defined span and loading context. Furthermore, a rectangular beam cross section constant throughout the length of the beam is assumed. The only variables are the width and depth of the member. The size of the member is first estimated on the basis of controlling bending stresses, and is then checked for adequacy with respect to shear stresses, bearing stresses, and deflections. Common allowable stress values for timber are listed in Appendix 15.

◆ ◆   **EXAMPLE**

Determine the required size of one of the rectangular floor beams illustrated in Figure 6–32. Assume the following: live load $= 50$ lb/ft^2, dead load $= 15$ lb/ft^2 (includes weight of floor deck, flooring, and estimate of beam weight), allowable stress in bending $= F_b = 1200$ lb/in.^{2}, allowable shear stress $= F_v = 150$ lb/in.^{2}, allowable bearing stress, $F_{bg} = 400$ lb/in.^{2}, and allowable deflection, $\Delta = L/360$ for live loads, and $L/240$ for live plus dead loads. Also assume that $E = 1.6 \times 10^6$ lb/in.^{2}, $L = 16.0$ ft, and $a = 16$ in.

FIGURE 6–32   Floor joist system.

Solution:

Loads:

$$W = \text{load/ft} = \underbrace{(50 \text{ lb/ft}^2 + 15 \text{ lb/ft}^2)}_{\text{distributed load}} \underbrace{(16 \text{ in./12 in./ft})}_{\substack{\text{width of floor deck} \\ \text{carried by one beam}}} = 86.5 \text{ lb/ft}$$

Bending stresses:

$$\left(\frac{I}{c}\right)_{\text{req'd}} = S_{\text{req'd}} = \frac{M}{F_b} \quad \text{or} \quad \left(\frac{bd^2}{6}\right)_{\text{req'd}} = \frac{M}{F_b}$$

$$M = \frac{wL^2}{8} = \frac{(86.5 \text{ lb/ft})(16 \text{ ft})^2}{8} = 2768 \text{ ft-lb} = 33,216 \text{ in.-lb}$$

$$\left(\frac{bd^2}{6}\right)_{\text{req'd}} = \frac{M}{F_b} = \frac{33{,}216 \text{ in.-lb}}{1200 \text{ lb/in.}^2} \quad \text{or} \quad bd^2 = 166.1 \text{ in.}^3$$

Any beam with a value of $bd^2 = 166.1$ in.^{3} will be adequately sized with respect to bending. *Assume that* $b = 1.5$ in. Thus,

$$(1.5 \text{ in.})d^2 = 166.1 \text{ in.}^3 \text{ or } d = 10.5 \text{ in.}$$

A beam 1.5 in. × 10.5 in. would be adequately sized with respect to bending. The nearest stock timber size is a 2 × 12 (actual dimensions are 1½ × 11½). This beam would be slightly oversized but is reasonably close and will be used.

Lateral buckling:
The depth-to-width ratio of the trial beam size is 11.5 : 1.5, or between 7 : 1 and 8 : 1. Deep, narrow beams like this are sensitive to lateral buckling. Bridging should be used or the proportions of the beam must be changed (Section 6–3–2). Assume that bridging is used.

Shear stresses:
The maximum shear force occurs at either end of the beam:

$$V = \frac{wL}{2} = \frac{(86.7 \text{ lb/ft})(16 \text{ ft})}{2} = 694 \text{ lb}$$

$$f_v = \frac{3}{2}\frac{V}{bd} = \frac{3}{2}\left(\frac{694 \text{ lb}}{1.5 \text{ in.} \times 11.5 \text{ in.}}\right) = 60.3 \text{ lb/in.}^2$$

This is the maximum shearing stress in the beam. It occurs at the neutral axis of the member at the reactions. Since the actual shear stress is less than the allowable shear stress (60.3 < 150), the beam is adequately sized with respect to shear stresses.

Bearing stresses:
The force at the ends of the beam is 694 lb. Assume that the area in bearing is 1.5 in. × 2 in.

$$f_{bg} = \frac{P}{A} = \frac{694 \text{ lb}}{1.5 \text{ in.} \times 2 \text{ in.}} = 231 \text{ lb/in.}^2$$

The actual bearing stress is less than the allowable bearing stress (231 < 400), so the beam is not overstressed in bearing at the reactions.

Live-load deflections:
$$\text{Live load} = (50 \text{ lb/ft}^2)(16 \text{ in.}/12 \text{ in./ft}) = 66.5 \text{ lb/ft}$$

$$\Delta = \frac{5wL^4}{384EI}$$

$$= \frac{5[(66.5 \text{ lb/ft})/(12 \text{ in./ft})](16 \text{ ft} \times 12 \text{ in./ft})^4}{384(1.6 \times 10^6 \text{ lb/in.}^2)[1.5 \text{ in.} \times (11.5 \text{ in.})^3/12]} = 0.32 \text{ in.}$$

The actual beam deflection under live loads is 0.32 in. The allowable deflection for the beam under live loads only is given by $\Delta = L/360 = (16 \text{ ft} \times 12 \text{ in./ft})/360 = 0.53$ in. Since 0.32 in. < 0.53 in., the beam does not deflect excessively under design live loads.

Live- and dead-load deflections:

$$\omega = 86.5 \text{ lb/ft} \qquad \therefore \quad \Delta = 0.42 \text{ in.}$$

The actual beam deflection under combined dead and live loads is 0.42 in. The allowable deflection for this combined loading condition is given by $\Delta = L/240 = (16 \text{ ft} \times 12 \text{ in./ft})/240 = 0.80$ in. Since 0.42 in. $<$ 0.80 in., the beam does not deflect excessively under combined dead and live loads. The beam thus meets all deflection criteria.

The same general procedure is followed when SI units are used. For example:

$$\frac{\text{load}}{\text{unit length}} = 86.5 \text{ lb/ft} = 1262.31 \text{ N/m}$$

$$\text{bending moment} = 2768 \text{ ft-lb} = 3753.4 \text{ N·m}$$

$$\text{allowable stress in bending} = F_b = 1200 \text{ lb/in.}^2 = 8.27 \text{ N/mm}^2$$

$$\text{beam size} = S_{\text{req'd}} = \frac{M}{F_b} = \frac{3753.4 \times 10^3 \text{ N·mm}}{8.27 \text{ N/mm}^2}$$

$$\frac{bd^2}{6} = S_{\text{req'd}} = 453{,}857 \text{ mm}^3$$

If $b = 38.1$ mm (1.5 in.), then $d = 267.34$ mm (10.5 in.). Shear stresses, bearing stresses, and deflections would be checked similarly. ◆

Note that constant-depth rectangular beams are not particularly efficient. In the rectilinear beam illustrated in Figure 6–32, there are only *two* spots on the entire beam (points *A* and *B* at section *M–N*) where the beam fibers are stressed to the maximum extent possible. At all other points in the beam the material is understressed. Consequently, the maximum potential of the material is not being fully utilized. The reason for this lies in the nature of bending at a cross section where deformations and bending stresses vary from zero at the neutral axis to a maximum at the extreme fibers. Thus, the stresses doing the most to generate an internal resisting moment to equilibrate the external moment are those near the outer fibers. Those near the neutral axis are of little consequence in this respect. This implies that from a design viewpoint more efficient use of beam material could be made by moving the beam material away from the neutral axis and toward the extremities of the beam.

A second reason why the beam material in the example illustrated in Figure 6–32 is underutilized is that the size of the section was determined in response to the maximum external bending moment present in the beams (at section *M–N*). At other points in the beam, the external bending moment is less (see the moment diagram). Thus, using a section designed in response to the maximum moment will result in inefficiencies at other points. From a theoretical viewpoint, it is possible to vary the size of the beam in response to the internal forces present. A beam with variable dimensions along its length would result (see Section 6–4–1).

Laminated Timber.   A simple rectangular beam shape may also be made out of laminated wood rather than solid-sawn shapes. A laminated beam is one made up of a series of thin layers of wood bonded together to form a composite whole. Large sections are possible. Allowable stress values in bending and shear are normally higher than those for solid-sawn timber sections. For example, an allowable stress in bending for a laminated member might be on the order of $F = 2500$ lb/in. rather than 1200 to 1600 lb/in. common for normal sections. Long-span members are consequently possible (see Appendix 15).

(a) Laminated timber beam. Varying grades of timber to match actual bending stresses.

(b) T beam. Top and bottom sections are made from different grades of timber to match actual stresses.

FIGURE 6–33 Varying the materials in beams to match the bending stresses present.

Most laminated members use high-quality wood throughout. But laminated members do allow for the possibility of varying material properties at a cross section, so that a better match is obtained between actual stress levels and material characteristics. Timber comes in different grades, having different allowable stresses. Grades with high allowable stresses are typically made from high-quality, hence costly, wood. Lower-stress grades are cheaper. This is the basis for achieving an economic section. In the typical bending-stress distribution illustrated in Figure 6–33(a), it is evident that it is not necessary to use wood layers made of the same-quality wood throughout the beam. Layers using wood having high allowable stresses could be used at the extremities of the beam (away from the neutral axis). Successive layers toward the neutral axis could be made of less expensive wood having lower allowable stresses. This technique of putting the stronger material on the outer faces of a beam and weaker material toward the middle can result in economic sections. This same principle can apply to making more effective use of timber in T beams.

The practical design of timber beams is influenced by other factors. Timber has an intrinsic ability to handle very high stresses for short periods of time. Higher allowable stresses are thus permitted for short- as opposed to long-term loadings. Permanent loads require that stresses be reduced by a loading factor of 0.90, while a loading factor of 1.33 may be used for wind loadings. Normal loads have a factor of 1.0 (see Appendix 15).

The modulus of elasticity and permissible stress values used are affected by the type and grade of wood, as well as whether the member is for *dry use* or *wet use*. *Wet use* conditions necessitate the use of reduction factors (see Appendix 14).

When designing large-size beam sections (e.g., in laminated timber) a size factor $C_F = (12/d)^{1/9}$ is used in U.S. practice that applies to bending only and serves to reduce the permissible bending stress.

◆ ◆   **EXAMPLE**

A glued-laminated beam $6\frac{3}{4}$ in. by 21 in. is intended to carry a bending moment of 60,000 ft-lb caused by a short-duration wind load. Assume that $F_b = 2400$ lb/in.^{2} and that dry-use conditions prevail. Is the member adequate in bending?

Solution:

Allowable stresses in bending:

$$\text{shape factor} = C_F = \left(\frac{12}{d}\right)^{1/9} = \left(\frac{12}{21}\right)^{1/9} = 0.94$$

$$\text{load duration factor} = 1.33.$$

$$\text{allowable stress} = 0.94(1.33)(2400) = 3000 \text{ lb/in.}^2$$

Actual stresses:

$$f_b = \frac{M}{S} = \frac{M}{bd^2/6} = \frac{(60,000 \times 12)}{(6.75)(21 \times 21)/6}$$
$$= 1451 \text{ lb/in.}^2 < 3000 \text{ lb/in.}^2$$

The member is adequately sized.   ◆

6–4–3   Steel Beams

Elastic Design.   Steel members are frequently designed on the basis of service loads and allowable stresses. Members used may be either rolled sections (wide flanges, channels) or sections built up of individual elements (plates, angles).

The design of rolled sections is straightforward. Since only a set number of section types and dimensions are rolled, their geometric properties may easily be tabulated and used to facilitate their selection for use in a structural context. A sample listing is shown in Appendix 11. Normally, the bending present is first calculated, a required section modulus value is determined ($S_{\text{req'd}} = M/F_b$), and the least-weight beam with a section modulus value equal to or greater than the required is found. This member is then checked for shear, deflections, and other phenomena.

◆ ◆   **EXAMPLE**

A simply supported steel wide-flange beam that is 25 ft long supports a uniformly distributed live plus dead load of 600 lb/ft. Assume that the allowable stress in bending is $F_b = 24,000$ lb/in.^{2} Determine the required size of the wide flange based on bending stress considerations.

Next check shear stresses and deflections. Assume the allowable stress in shear is $F_v = 14,400$ lb/in.^{2} Since the beam is used for a floor, live-load deflections are limited by $L/360$. Assume that the beam is cambered upward so that it is level under dead-load conditions; hence, deflections need to be checked for live loads only.

Solution:

Maximum bending moment:

$$M = wL^2/8 = (600 \text{ lb/ft})(25 \text{ ft}^2)/8 = 46,875 \text{ ft-lb}$$

Required section modulus:
$$S_{\text{req'd}} = M/F_b = (46{,}875 \text{ ft-lb})(12 \text{ in./ft})/24{,}000 \text{ lb/in.}^2 = 23.4 \text{ in.}^3$$

Beam size based on bending stresses:
By referring to Appendix 14, we can see that either of the following will work: W 8 × 31 ($S = 27.4$ in.^{3}), or W 12 × 27 ($S = 34.1$ in.^{3}). The beam having the least weight is most economical. The W 12 × 27 would therefore be selected even if its S value is considerably higher than needed ($S_{\text{actual}} = 34.1 > S_{\text{req'd}} = 23.4$).

Check shear stresses:

shear force: $V = wL/2 = (600 \text{ lb/ft})(25 \text{ ft})/2 = 7500 \text{ lb}$

shear stress: $f_v = V/td = 7500/(0.24 \text{ in.})(12.0 \text{ in.}) = 2604 \text{ lb/in.}^2$

actual: $f_v = 2604 \text{ lb/in.}^2 <$ allowable $F_v = 14{,}400 \text{ lb/in.}^2$

The value is acceptable.

Check deflections:
Assume that of the 600-lb/ft load, 400 lb/ft is due to the live loads present.

$$\Delta_{\text{actual}} = 5 \, wL^4/384 \, EI = 5(400/12)(25 \times 12)^4/384 \, (29.3 \times 10^6)(204.1) = 0.58 \text{ in.}$$
$$\Delta_{\text{actual}} = 0.58 \text{ in.} < L/360 = (25 \times 12)/360 = 0.83 \text{ in.}$$

The value is acceptable.   ◆

For exceptionally large loads or spans, plate girder sections that are built up with angles and plates are often used. Welding has replaced older riveted joining technology. A trial size is selected, its moment of inertia is calculated via the *parallel-axis theorem* (Appendix 4), and the member is then checked for bending, shear, deflections, and so on.

Practical steel design includes many considerations beyond the scope of this book, including the need to check for compact sections to prevent buckling of flanges and many other phenomena.

Plastic or Ultimate Strength Design of Steel Beams. The analyses presented thus far have been based on the assumption that the beam material is *linearly elastic* (i.e., that stresses are proportional to deformations). Steel is linearly elastic only up to a certain point, when the material begins to deform massively under a relatively constant stress level. Only after significant deformation has occurred does the material actually rupture. These are *plastic deformations*. A simplified stress-strain curve depicting this behavior is shown in Figure 6–34. An appreciation of this behavior is important in understanding how steel beams actually fail. In addition, beams may also be designed on the basis of their ultimate strengths coupled with design failure loads.

Consider the rectangular beam shown in Figure 6–34. When external loads on the beam are low, the material in the beam is in the elastic range and bending stresses are linearly distributed across the cross section. As loads increase, the bending stresses increase until the material at the outer fibers reaches a point, F_y, where it begins to *yield* and enter the plastic range. As indicated in Figure 6–35(d), this corresponds to a resisting moment in the beam of $M_y = F_y(bh^2/6)$ (see Section 6–3–1). Continuing to increase loads causes increased deformations in the beam fibers (a linear variation in strain still occurs, since this is a function of the gross geometry of deformations in bending in the entire beam). There is not, however, a corresponding increase in the stress level in the material in the region where beam fibers are deformed into the plastic region. At this

FIGURE 6-34   Idealized stress-strain curve for ductile material. At a certain stress level, F_y, the material begins to undergo increased deformations without any additional increase in stress level. Actual failure in the material does not occur until relatively large deformations occur.

stage, some fibers near the neutral axis are still below F_y. In the instance shown in Figure 6–35(e), the beam is still capable of carrying load (the outer fibers have yielded but not ruptured). Increasing the external load further causes increased deformations, until all the fibers in the cross section begin to yield. The load that finally causes the fibers nearest the neutral axis to yield is the maximum one the beam can carry. This load corresponds to a maximum resisting moment of $M_p = F_y(bh^2/4)$. Up to this point, the beam has always been able to provide an increased moment resistance capacity to balance the applied moment associated with the external load. After this point, however, the beam has *no* further capacity to resist the external moment and continuing to apply loads would simply cause additional deformations until rupture and collapse finally occur. A *plastic hinge* is said to develop when all fibers are fully yielded at a cross section.

For a rectangular beam, the ratio between the moment associated with the formation of a plastic hinge and that associated with the initial yielding is $M_p/M_y = F_y(bh^2/4)/F_y(bh^2/6) = 1.5$. The term $bh^2/4$ is often called the *plastic section modulus, Z*. In a simple beam, the 1.5 ratio implies that the load, P_f, required to cause the beam to actually fail is 1.5 times the load, P_y, which would cause initial yielding to occur in the member. Other shapes have different ratios of this type. This ratio is often called the *shape factor* for a beam, since it is identical to the ratio of the plastic section modulus (Z) to the elastic section modulus (S) (i.e., shape factor = Z/S). For a wide-flange beam, shape factors vary but average around 1.14. Other factors are 1.7 for a round bar and 2.0 for a diamond.

In statically indeterminate structures, the formation of a single plastic hinge need not lead directly to beam collapse. A number of hinges must form until a collapse mechanism is created. Consider the fixed-ended beam shown in Figure 6–36 and the moments that are developed in the structure. As the load, w, is increased, yielding in the beam first occurs at the ends of the beam where moments are maximum. As load intensity is increased, plastic hinges begin forming at these points. The moment at the center of the structure is also increased. Note that the formation of plastic hinges at the ends of the beam do not cause collapse to occur in the beam, since the structure still has moment-carrying capacity at midspan. Further beam loading would eventually

(a) Strain distribution when outer fibers just begin to yield.

(b) Strain distribution when outer fibers have yielded. Strain distribution is still linear.

(c) Strain distribution when all fibers in cross section have yielded.

(d) Stress distribution when outer fibers just begin to yield.

(e) Stress distribution when the outer, but not the inner, fibers of the beam have yielded. The beam still has a measure of reserve strength at this section.

(f) Stress distribution when all fibers in the cross section have yielded. The beam can support no more moment at this section.

  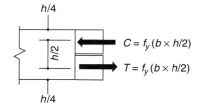

Elastic resisting moment = $F_y(bh^2/6)$

Elastic/plastic resisting moment

Plastic resisting moment = $C(h/2)$
    $= F_y(bh^2/4) = M_P$

FIGURE 6–35 Plastic behavior in beams. As the material in a beam begins to yield under load, the stress distribution present begins to change. The beam can continue to carry moment until all the fibers at a cross section have yielded.

(a) Fixed-end beam. Elastic moment distribution.

(b) As loads on the beam are increased, the beam will begin yielding at the regions of highest moment (at the ends in this case). Plastic hinges begin forming at these points. The beam begins to act like a simply supported beam with a fixed moment resistance at each end. Increases in loads cause a moment redistribution to occur (the moment at midspan begins to increase). Although hinges have formed at two points, the beam can still carry additional load.

(c) Further increases in load will eventually cause the formation of a third plastic hinge at midspan. The beam will collapse when this hinge forms.

FIGURE 6–36   Formation of plastic hinges in a fixed-ended beam. Plastic hinges initially develop where moments are the highest. The beam does not fail, however, until a sufficient number of hinges have formed to cause a collapse mechanism to develop in the beam. Beams of this type have a large measure of reserve strength.

cause a plastic hinge to develop at midspan. A collapse mechanism would then exist and the beam could carry no additional load (total failure is imminent). The failure load, w_u, of the beam is greater than would be implied by a consideration of just the shape factor of the beam alone. It is shown elsewhere that for a restrained rectangular beam the load required to cause failure, w_u, is double that of the load required to initiate yielding, w_y.

Load and Resistance Factor Design Methods.   The approaches described above have been developed into a formal design procedure called the LRFD method based on ultimate or limit state concepts. Load factors are specified to amplify service loads and ultimate yield stresses are used. Typical *load factors* are: limit state design load $= 1.2D + 1.6L$ or $1.4D$. The nominal resistance R_n of a member is determined through plastic design methods as appropriate. A resistance factor ϕ, which is always less than 1, is used as a strength reduction factor to modify the nominal resistance of a member to obtain a usable capacity. (The factor is similar to the capacity-reduction factor in ultimate strength design in concrete.) Thus, $R = \phi R_n$. The values of ϕ are 0.9 for a tension member, 0.85 for a common compression member, 0.9 for flexure, and 0.9 for shear.

The LRFD method is thus based on a consideration of the member at its limiting loads. Deflections, however, must be checked at working loads. Specific LRFD design procedures, however, are beyond the scope of this book.

6-4-4 Reinforced Concrete Beams: General Principles

Basic Behavior. When a beam is made of plain concrete, both tensile and compressive stresses normally associated with bending develop. Concrete is normally capable of carrying appreciable compressive stresses, but cracks tend to develop under very low tensile stress levels. In a plain concrete beam, these cracks would tend to propagate very quickly (see Figure 6–37) and the

Stresses in the concrete above the neutral axis are compressive and nonlinearly distributed. In the tension zone below the neutral axis, the concrete is assumed to be cracked and the tensile force present to be taken up by reinforcing steel.

Typical stress-strain curve for concrete.

Working stress analysis. (Concrete stress distribution is assumed to be linear. Service loads are used in calculations.)

Actual stress distribution near ultimate strength (nonlinear).

Ultimate strength analysis. (A rectangular stress block is used to idealize the actual stress distribution. Calculations are based on ultimate loads and failure stresses.)

FIGURE 6-37 Reinforced concrete beams.

beam would collapse virtually immediately. To make a concrete beam viable, it is therefore necessary to place a reinforcing material (normally steel) that can carry appreciable tension forces in the tension zone to intercept any crack that is tending to propagate through the beam and arrest its development. The tension stresses associated with the crack propagation are then transferred into the reinforcing steel, which in turn develops high tension forces within it. Sufficient steel must be used or it too will pull apart.

Potential cracks can result from either bending stresses, shear stresses, or an interaction of the two stresses and occur throughout the beam, necessitating the use of extensive patterns of steel. Longitudinal reinforcing steel is usually placed to counteract cracks caused by bending, whereas either stirrups (U-shaped bars) or diagonally bent bars are used to provide for cracks developed by shear stresses or principal stresses. Amounts of steel required usually vary in direct proportion to the magnitudes of the bending and shear forces. *Maximum cross-sectional areas of longitudinal steel are necessary where bending moments are highest, and maximum stirrup steel is necessary where shear forces are the highest.*

Steel must be precisely designed. Too little steel will be insufficient to carry the internal forces developed, and the beam will begin yielding too soon and not carry required loads. If too much steel is used, there is a danger that the concrete will prematurely fail in compression long

Beams with compression steel.

Reinforced concrete T beam. The shape of the section causes the stresses in the top flange to be lower than stresses in the web of the member. Concrete is used at the top and steel where the section is assumed to be cracked.

FIGURE 6–37   *(continued)*

before the steel starts yielding in a ductile fashion. A compression failure is dangerous because it occurs without much prior visual warning (the concrete can seemingly suddenly burst). Ideally, sufficient steel is present to carry desired loads, but not so much that it does not yield prior to the concrete failing. Well-designed beams exhibit significant ductility and associated visual deflections prior to actual failure.

6–4–5   Reinforced Concrete Beams: Design and Analysis Principles

Basic Design Approach.   The addition of steel in the tension region to create *reinforced concrete beams* ensures both strength and ductility. Reinforced concrete members inherit the properties of both concrete and steel. Relationships such as $f_y = My/I$ used previously to analyze and design beams are based on the assumption that the material is not cracked and linearly elastic. Neither of these assumptions is valid in the case of reinforced concrete members. Rather, analysis and design procedures are based on a direct consideration of the idea that an internal resisting moment is generated in the member to balance the external moments present.

As loads induce bending in a beam, a deformation pattern of the type illustrated in Figure 6–37 develops. The region below the neutral axis is in tension. The concrete is assumed to be cracked in this region and the forces present completely taken up by the steel. These cracks extend upward until they terminate at the edge of the compressive region. An internal resisting moment is generated in the beam to balance the external moment present at the same section by the couple formed by the tension force in the reinforcing steel and the resultant compressive force (composed of compressive stresses in the concrete acting over the uncracked part of the cross section) in the upper region of the beam. Hence, in a plain reinforced concrete beam only a portion of the concrete is actually participating in carrying the load. The steel and concrete are reasonably assumed to bond to one another and have the same strains at adjacent locations.

For a given structural size, the area of steel required is generally proportional to the magnitude of the bending moment present ($A \propto M$). An increase in the level of the applied bending moment generally demands an increase in the required area of steel. Or, for a given moment, decreasing the depth of a structure also increases required steel areas, and vice-versa. The designer must ensure, however, that the beam remains "ductile," a condition which can result when too much reinforcement is used (see "Ductility" below). Beams must also designed to resist shear stresses, which cause a different kind of cracking. "Stirrups" are often used to carry high shear stresses (see "Shearing Stresses and Diagonal Cracking" on page 294).

Design and Analysis Methods.   For many years an elastic analysis and design procedure based on service loads was used to analyze and design beams. Called *working stress design,* the approach was founded on arguable assumptions and did not adequately address ductility issues, nor did it accurately predict the strength of the member under ultimate loads. This design method is rarely used any longer. A new procedure, called *ultimate strength design,* is now used. It is based on ultimate rather than service loads and better reflects the actual behavior of reinforced concrete members under ultimate loads.

Ultimate Strength Design.   In ultimate strength design (USD), the working loads are amplified to convert them into design failure loads. It is assumed that the reinforced concrete structure starts to fail when these ultimate loads are reached, but not before, and that the member performs adequately until then. The material is controlled for both ductility and a combined concrete-steel failure. For gravity loads, the amplification load factors in the United States are typically of the form of $U = 1.4$(dead load) $+ 1.7$(live load). In the presence of snow loads or lateral loads, a modification of these loads is required and the load factors become $U = 0.75(1.4D + 1.7L + 1.7W)$, $U = 0.75(1.4D + 1.7L + 1.1E)$, or $U = 0.9D + 1.3W$, where D and L are the working dead and live loads and E and W represent earthquake and wind forces, respectively. The various coefficients and combinations clearly reflect varying levels of uncertainty in load estimation or likelihoods of combinations.

In ultimate strength design, safety factors are put on loads rather than on materials. Thus, a typical analysis would use service loads multiplied by some type of factor of safety, and then use actual failure stresses in the analysis.

Ultimate Strength Design: Design for Bending Moments.   In the United States the ultimate strength design (USD) moment-carrying capacities of reinforced concrete beams are given in standards developed by the American Concrete Institute (ACI 318), which have a strong empirical basis. In these expressions, the width of a typical beam with only tension reinforcement is b, and the depth from the extreme compression fiber to the centroid of the reinforcing steel is d (see Figure 6–37—the actual physical depth of the beam is not used since the cover of the steel below does not contribute to its bending strength). M is the ultimate strength bending moment obtained from a moment diagram (with load factors applied).

Moment-carrying values are given by expressions such as $M = T(jd)$ or $C(jd)$, where T is the total tension force developed in the reinforcing steel, C is the total resultant force equivalent to the compression stress field developed in the concrete, and jd is an internal moment arm, which is the distance between C and T (or the distance between the steel and the centroid of the compression stress field). A moment-resisting "couple" is thus formed that balances the applied ultimate bending moment (a behavior rather like a truss, except that the moment arm is not the same as the depth of the structure).

In the diagram shown in Figure 6–37, the internal moment arm is given by $jd = (d - a/2)$, where a is the depth of the compression field stress block (steps for determining the value of a will be discussed shortly).

The total tension force in the steel is given by $T = A \times F$, where A is the cross-sectional area of the steel and F is the yield stress in the steel (recall that ultimate loads and failure stresses are considered in this kind of analysis).

The moment capacity thus *becomes* $M = T(jd) = AF(jd) = AF(d - a/2)$. We see that the required steel area depends directly on the magnitude of the ultimate bending moment (M), or $A_{required} = M/F(d - a/2)$. Note that the actual required steel area A varies with the bending moment present. If M varies, so can the amount of steel A used. Detailed design procedures are presented in Section 6–4–6.

Ductility.   In ultimate strength design (USD), the failure mode of a beam is governed either by an initial failure of concrete or by an initial failure of the reinforcing steel. Depending on the amount of steel present, the failure can be either sudden and brittle, or the member can fail in a ductile mode with the associated positive values of energy absorption and prior visual warning. Too little or too much steel can be problematic.

Since ductility is provided by the reinforcing steel, it is desirable that a failure mode begin with a steel yielding that can be sustained by the concrete until the steel reaches its ultimate strength and fails. Such a controlled failure mode suggests that the amount of reinforcing steel should be within a certain range. If the amount of steel is *very* small, it will yield first but may rapidly reach its ultimate strength with little energy absorption and little warning. This condition can be prevented by positioning more steel than a certain minimum amount. [In the United States, the minimum amount of tension steel is given by the empirical formula $A_{s\text{-min}} = (200/F_y) A_{\text{gross}}$, where F_y is the ultimate strength of the steel in lb/in.^{2} and A_{gross} is the gross cross-sectional area of the beam.] At the other extreme, if more than a certain maximum amount of steel is present, the steel will have an excess capacity for carrying the tension forces involved and will not yield before the concrete reaches its failure levels. In this case the concrete will crush suddenly and in a brittle manner before the steel yields, with little energy absorption and little warning prior to collapse. This state of "overreinforcing" is a dangerous condition and requires special attention, since it is associated with the placement of excessive amounts of steel—a condition that might normally be considered a conservative and safe move. The situation is quite the contrary. This condition is prevented by limiting the amount of steel used so that it yields before the concrete crushes.

For any beam, there is a specific amount of reinforcing steel such that both steel and concrete would start failing at exactly the same time. This is the *balanced steel* condition, and the beam is said to be a *balanced beam* (see below for calculation of the balanced steel). Although an amount of steel equal to the balanced steel is not desirable, the maximum allowed amount of steel is defined as 75% of the balanced steel. Thus, if the amount of tension steel is between the minimum allowed and the maximum allowed, an appropriate ductility level in the beam is ensured.

6-4-6 Reinforced Concrete Beams: Detailed U.S. Design Procedures

Bending Strength. In ultimate strength design, the beam is designed to start failing under the amplified loads. At that level, the steel is expected to have exceeded its yielding point, while the concrete is expected to have entered its nonlinear plastic region. Figure 6–37 illustrates the general stress distribution present prior to failure. The curved stress diagram for the concrete follows from the assumption of a linear strain distribution and the stress-strain diagram for concrete shown in Figure 6–37. An internal resisting moment that balances the externally applied moment is developed by a couple formed by the tension force T (at failure) in the steel and the equivalent compressive force C in the concrete (from equilibrium and in the absence of an axial load, these two forces must be equal). This moment represents the nominal moment capacity of the section. A reduction factor ϕ is applied to the nominal moment capacity to derive the ultimate moment capacity of the section.[3] Thus, the ultimate moment capacity of a beam is $M_u = 0.9M_{un}$, where M_{un} is the nominal strength of the beam. Since the loads have been amplified, no safety factors are placed on materials. Specified yield stresses for steel (F_y) and failure stresses for concrete (f'_c) are used. The steel is assumed to have a bilinear stress-strain curve and be quite ductile. Concrete is assumed to have a nonlinear stress-strain curve that peaks out and then declines before final crushing. Crushing is assumed to occur at a strain level of 0.3% (0.003).

The ultimate moment capacity of a beam is given by the couple formed by the tension and compression forces acting at the cross section, or $M_u = \phi T j_u d = \phi C j_u d$, where d is the effective

---

[3]The reduction factor reflects uncertainties in the actual versus theoretical strength of members. In the United States the reduction factors are as follows: for bending $- \phi = 0.9$; for shear $- \phi = 0.85$; for tied columns (axial compression with lateral ties) $- \phi = 0.7$ and for spiral columns (columns with spiral ties) $- \phi = 0.75$.

depth of the section to the steel and $j_u d$ is the moment arm between T and C. Note that $T = \phi A_s F_y$, where A_s is the cross-sectional area of steel; hence $M_u = \phi A_s F_y j_u d$. The amount of steel present is often expressed in terms of a ratio of the total effective beam area, or $p = A_s/bd$. Since $A_s = pbd$, $M_u = \phi p F_y bd^2 j_u$.

The value of the moment arm j_u remains to be identified. An "equivalent stress block" is typically assumed in order to overcome the complex distribution of stresses in the concrete so that the resultant force C associated with the actual stress distribution and the equivalent stress block are identical. As shown in Figure 6–37 for a rectangular beam, the block is constructed so that it acts over an area ab, where a is the depth of the stress block (a value to be calculated as shown below) and b is the beam width, and has an averaged maximum stress value of $0.85f'_c$. The moment arm thus becomes $j_u d = d - a/2$. The value of a must be calculated. Since $C = T$, it follows that $0.85f'_c ab = A_s F_y$, or $a = A_s F_y/0.85f'_c b$. The ultimate moment capacity of the beam thus becomes $M_u = \phi A_s F_y j_u d = \phi A_s F_y[d - (a/2)]$. Often this expression is rewritten in terms to directly incorporate the value of a and in terms of p (the steel ratio present), or $M_u = \phi p F_y bd^2 ju$, where $j_u = 1 - 0.59p(F_y/f'_c)$.

Balanced Steel. A strain diagram for the balanced beam condition is shown in Figure 6–37. Recall that for steel $\epsilon_y = F_y/E_{steel}$. From the diagram it follows that $c/0.003 = d/(0.003 + F_y/E_s)$. The ratio of steel corresponding to a balanced condition can be found by various substitutions, or $p_b = [0.003/(0.003 + F_y/E_s)] [(\beta_l 0.85f'_c)/F_y]$, where β_l is constant depending on the strength of the concrete ($\beta_l = 0.85$ for lower-strength concretes). To assure that the beam is underreinforced, the steel ratio allowed to be used is taken as 75% of the balanced steel ratio ($p_{max} = 0.75p_b$). Recall that $p = A_s/bd$, so $A_{s\text{-}max} = p_{max}bd$. For given materials, specific allowable steel ratio values can be determined. For $F_y = 40$ ksi, $E_s = 29,000$ kips/in.^{2}, and $f'_c = 3$ kips/in.^{2}, the allowable steel ratio is $p_{max} = 0.75p_b = 0.0278$. For $F_y = 40$ kips/in.^{2} and $f'_c = 5$ kips/in.^{2}, $p_{max} = 0.0437$. For $F_y = 60$ kips/in.^{2} and $f'_c = 5$ kips/in.^{2}, $p_{max} = 0.0252$.

Reinforcing Bars. When designing and analyzing a beam, actual steel rod sizes and areas must be used. The bar sizes available in the United States are from No. 3 to 11 and 14 and 18.

Bar	Diameter (in.)	Area (in.^{2})	Bar	Diameter (in.)	Area (in.^{2})
No. 2	0.250	0.05	No. 8	1.000	0.79
No. 3	0.375	0.11	No. 9	1.128	1.00
No. 4	0.500	0.20	No. 10	1.270	1.27
No. 5	0.625	0.31	No. 11	1.410	1.56
No. 6	0.750	0.44	No. 14	1.693	2.25
No. 7	0.785	0.60	No. 18	2.257	4.00

The spacing between bars should be equal to the diameter of the bars but not less than 1 in. in U.S. practice. A concrete cover is used to protect reinforcing bars, although this concrete cover will inevitably crack if it is in tension. The minimum cover depends on the type of elements, the type of concrete (cast-in-place, precast, prestressed), the size of the bars, and the exposure and varies from 1.5 in. for interior space to 2 in. for exterior space to 3 in. when in permanent contact with the soil. Furthermore, the steel bars should have a minimum development length and possibly anchoring hooks so that stresses are transferred from the steel to concrete. The steel bars should also be designed and placed in concrete members so that distribution requirements are met and the concrete is controlled for excess cracking. These criteria usually require more smaller bars rather than few larger bars and sometimes a lower-strength steel.

Deflections. Calculation of deflections of reinforced concrete members is complicated as a result of the properties of concrete, especially its cracking in the tension zone. According to building codes, the deflections are within limits if the slenderness of the members does not exceed a lower limit, based on the type of the member and the supports, as shown in the table below. If the slenderness criterion is satisfied, further deflection checks are not necessary. Note that these same guidelines are also useful as a starting point for dimensioning beams or slabs or for estimating the efficiency of sections. For computer analysis, the moments of inertia of the reinforced concrete elements must be reduced before they are used to predict their deflections. In the United States a simple approach calls for a reduction of the moment of inertia of members in bending by 60%.

The minimum overall depths of beams or one-way slabs are as shown in the following table.

Member	Simply Supported	One End Continuous	Both Ends Continuous	Cantilever
Solid one-way slabs	$1/20$	$1/24$	$1/28$	$1/10$
Beams	$1/16$	$1/18.5$	$1/21$	$1/8$

◆ ◆ **EXAMPLE**

(a) Determine the ultimate moment capacity of a beam of dimensions $b = 10$ in. and $d_{effective} = 15$ and that has three No. 9 bars (3.0 in.^{2}) of tension reinforcing steel. Assume that $d_{gross} = 18$ in., $F_y = 40$ ksi, and $f'_c = 5$ ksi. (b) Assume that the section is used as a cantilever beam 10 ft long, where the service loads are as follows: dead load = 400 lb/ft and live load = 300 lb/ft. Is the beam adequate in bending? Calculate the ultimate moment capacity of the beam first.

Solution:

(a) $a = A_s F_y / 0.85 f' b = (3)(40,000)/(0.85)(5000)(10) = 2.82$ in.

$\quad M_u = \phi A_s F_y j_u d = \phi A_s F_y [d - a/2] = 0.9(3)(40,000)[15 - (2.82)/(2)] = 1,466,640$ in.-lb

Note that since $p = A_s/bd = 3/(10)(15) = 0.02 < p_{max} = 0.0437$, the beam is indeed adequately below balanced beam conditions and is correctly "underreinforced." Since $A = 3.0 > (200/F_y)A_{gross} = (200/40,000)(10)(18) = 0.9$ in.^{2}, the beam has sufficient steel for minimum ductility.

(b) $U = 1.4D + 1.7L = 1.4(400) + 1.7(300) = 1070$ lb/ft

$\quad M_{u\text{-req'd}} = w_u L^2/2 = (1070)(10^2)/2 = 53,500$ ft-lb = 642,000 in.-lb

Since $M_{u\text{-req'd}} = 642,000 < M_u = 1,466,640$, the beam is adequate in bending.   ◆

◆ ◆ **EXAMPLE**

Determine the ultimate moment capacity of a beam of dimensions $b = 250$ mm and $d = 350$ mm and which has 300 mm^2 of reinforcing steel. Assume that $F_y = 400$ MPa and $f'_c = 25$ MPa.

Solution:

$$a = \frac{A_s F_y}{0.85 f' b} = \frac{(300)(400)}{(0.85)(25)(250)} = 22.6$$

$$M_u = \phi A_s F_y j_u d = \phi A_s F_y \left(d - \frac{a}{2} \right) = 0.9(300)(400)\left(350 - \frac{22.6}{2} \right) = 36.5 \text{ kN·m} \qquad \blacklozenge$$

Designing Beams for Bending.   Initially estimating the size of a beam for a given loading can be difficult. One approach is to assume a size and see if it works. An alternative is to estimate a size based on the expression $M_u = \phi p F_y b d^2 j_u$, where $j_u = 1 - 0.59 p (F_y / f'_c)$. The latter may be expressed directly for real values of F_y and f'_c and an estimated value of p (when p is limited to $0.75 p_b$). For 40-ksi steel and 5-ksi concrete and using $p = 0.0437$ and $j_u = 0.794$, $M_u = \phi p F_y b d^2 j_u$ becomes the following if $\phi = 0.9$: $M_u = 1250 b d^2$. This expression can then be solved for $b d^2$ for any given ultimate load moment to provide an initial size estimate. It is not exact, due to the estimated value of p.

Expressions similar to $M_u = 1250 b d^2$ can be determined for other values of F_y and f'_c and are often written in the form $M_u = R b d^2$. Note that the moment is for ultimate loads. When working with service loads directly, lower R values reflecting the safety factor in the loadings are often used to estimate sizes (e.g., $M_{\text{service}} = R b d^2$ or $M_{\text{service}} = 560 b d^2$). Only approximate sizes are obtained.

$\blacklozenge$ $\blacklozenge$ **EXAMPLE**

A simply supported beam 20 ft long carries a service dead load of 300 lb/ft and a live load of 500 lb/ft. Design an appropriate beam and check that the amount of tension steel is within the limits for ductile beam behavior.

Solution: First, estimate gross beam size: Assume that $F_y = 40$ ksi and $f'_c = 5$ ksi. $U = 1.4D + 1.7L = 1.4(300) + 1.7(500) = 1270$; $M_{u\text{-req'd}} = w_u L^2 / 8 = 1270(20^2)/8 = 63{,}500$ ft-lb. $= 762{,}000$ in.-lb. If $M_u = 1250 b d^2$, then $762{,}000 = 1250 b d^2$, or $b d^2 = 610$. If $b = 8$, then $d = 8.7$. Try an 8-in. by 12-in. beam ($b = 8$, $d_{\text{effective}} = 10.5$).

Next, estimate the area of steel required by first estimating either j_u or p. Note that $M_u = \phi A_s F_y j_u d$. Estimate the moment arm j_u to be around 0.8 (a guess) or calculate $j_u = 1 - 0.59 p (F_y / f'_c) = 0.794$. Then $762{,}000 = 0.9(A_s)(40{,}000)[(0.8)(10.5)]$. A_s becomes approximately 2.5 in.² Alternatively, p could be estimated as somewhat less than $0.75 p_b$ and A_s estimated accordingly [e.g., $0.75 p_b = 0.0278$; $A_s = p b d$; estimating $A_s = 0.025(8)(10.5) = 2.1$ in.²]. Try two No. 10 bars (2×1.27 in.² $= 2.54$ in.²).

Next, check the final trial beam: 8×12 beam (actual size) with two No. 10 bars 1.5 in. from the bottom:

$$a = \frac{A_s F_y}{0.85 f' b} = \frac{(2.54)(40{,}000)}{(0.85)(5000)(8)} = 2.99 \text{ in.}$$

$$M_u = \phi A_s F_y j_u d = \phi A_s F_y \left(d - \frac{a}{2} \right) = 0.9(2.54)(40{,}000)\left(10.5 - \frac{2.99}{2} \right)$$

$$= 823{,}874 \text{ in.-lb} > M_{\text{req'd}} = 762{,}000 \text{ in.-lb} \qquad \text{(acceptable)}$$

Note that since $p = A_s / b d = 2.54/(8)(12) = 0.0264 < p_b = 0.0278$, the beam is correctly "underreinforced." Since $A_{\text{actual}} = 2.54 > A_{s\text{-min}} = (200/F_y) b d = (200/40)(8)(12) = 0.48$ in.², the minimum steel necessary for ductility is present. Since the actual d/L ratio is 1.0/20.0, deflection requirements are satisfied ($d > L/20$). $\qquad \blacklozenge$

Compression Reinforcing Steel.   The bending capacity of a beam is governed by the size of the cross section, the strength of the materials, and the maximum allowable amount of tension steel. The addition of reinforcing steel in the compression zone alone has little effect in the overall bending capacity present. However, the placement of proportional quantities of steel in *both* the tension and compression zones, in addition to the maximum allowable tension steel normally present, increases the bending capacity of the beam without violating the ductility characteristics of the beam. Notice that the compression steel may not reach its yielding stress, since its strain depends on the surrounding concrete, while the tension steel always yields under ultimate loads. The forces in the compression steel are always equal to that in its corresponding tension steel. The additional compression and tension steel behave similarly to a structure with a trusslike action between paired amounts of steel in the compression and tension zones plus a normal reinforced concrete beam utilizing the remaining steel in the tension zone (see Figure 6–37).

T and I Section Beams.   A T configuration beam under gravity loads provides a larger area of concrete in the compression zone, while it removes concrete from the tension zone that is expected to crack. As long as the concrete provides a sufficient cover for the tension reinforcing steel, a T section beam is lighter and can have the same strength with a rectangular beam that its width would be equal to the width of the flange of the T section. However, in areas of negative moment, such as the supports of a continuous beam, the compression zone is at the lower part of the beam and the strength of the beam would be reduced significantly. I beams may be more suitable for such cases.

Design of Slabs.   The design of slabs is similar to that of beams, except that the design is typically done on a unit width basis. In addition, the minimum reinforcement for a slab is governed by shrinkage and temperature requirements and the minimum steel should extend into both directions of a rectangular slab. The required concrete cover for the reinforcing steel in slabs is smaller than the required cover for beams with the same exposure.

Shearing Stresses and Diagonal Cracking.   Unreinforced concrete is a brittle material, and its failure criterion is based on the magnitude of the principal stresses. Thus, the shearing strength of concrete depends on the corresponding principal tensile strength, since the compressive strength of concrete is significantly higher than the tensile strength. The principal stresses in tension result from the interaction of shearing and bending stresses. The lines of principal tensile stresses in a uniformly loaded beam are as illustrated in Figure 6–26. For such a beam, the magnitude of shearing stresses is higher near the supports, with the result that cracks are often generated, as shown in Figure 6–38(a). These cracks are referred to as *diagonal tension* cracks and are quite dangerous, since they can lead to rapid failure of the whole beam. To prevent this, steel reinforcement is used to intersect such cracks. In the past, the steel reinforcement for diagonal tension was provided by bending the tension reinforcement bars toward the supports, as shown in Figure 6–38(a). Recently, the use of stirrups is preferred because of uniformity, ease of construction, and for stresses resulting from horizontal loads, such as earthquakes, that may lead to reversal of shearing stresses.

Design for Shear Stresses.   Shear stresses are usually higher near the supports, but they are checked at a distance *d,* the effective depth, away from the supports. Concrete has a shear strength that may be sufficient to take the shearing stresses without requiring steel reinforcement. The shear strength of concrete for members without axial or torsional loads is given in United

(a) Diagonal tension cracks in a concrete beam. These result from principal tension stresses, which act at 45° to the horizontal. Reinforcing steel must be placed to intersect these cracks. Using diagonal steel (by bending up reinforcing bars) is one way of doing this. Using vertical steel "stirrups" is another way. Care should be taken to provide a sufficient number of stirrups to intersect any possible 45° diagonal tension crack. The amount and placement of stirrup steel depends on the magnitude of the shear force present at a section.

(b) Typical steel placement in reinforced concrete beams. The amount of longitudinal steel required at a section depends on the magnitude of the bending moment present at the section. The amount of vertical steel required depends on the magnitude of the shear force present at the section.

FIGURE 6–38 Shear and diagonal tension in reinforced concrete beams.

States practice by the ACI 318 code expressions, such as $V_c = 2 \sqrt{f'_c} b_w d$, where b_w is the width of the web and d is the effective depth of the section. If the shear strength of the concrete is less than half the shear force at a section of a beam, steel reinforcing stirrups or other forms of reinforcement are required. The yielding strength of reinforcing steel in shear should not exceed 60,000 lb/in.[2] The spacing of the stirrups depends on the magnitude of the shear force and the size of the stirrups but should not exceed $d/2$ (half the effective depth) or 24 in., so that potential cracks will positively cross stirrups. Stirrups provide a shear strength $V_s = A_v f_y d/s$, where A_v is the area of stirrups within a distance s. If the shear strength V_s is more than $4 \sqrt{f'_c} (b_w d)$, the spacing between stirrups should not exceed $d/4$ or 12 in., and if V_s is more than $8 \sqrt{f'_c} b_w d$, the section of the beam should be increased. Thus, for a given size of stirrups, their spacing along the beam may change to provide the required strength. Torsion reinforcement for beams consists of both longitudinal bars and closed stirrups, which are added to the required reinforcement for bending and shear.

6–4–7 Prestressing and Post-Tensioning

A way of making beams more efficient that is particularly suitable for concrete structures is through the use of prestressing or post-tensioning. These are techniques for permanently loading a beam in a controlled way with the intent of building up stresses in the member opposite to those developed by the external service loads.

First consider an ordinary (not reinforced concrete) beam shown in Figure 6–39(a) subjected to both axial forces acting through the centroid of the element and bending forces. The stress

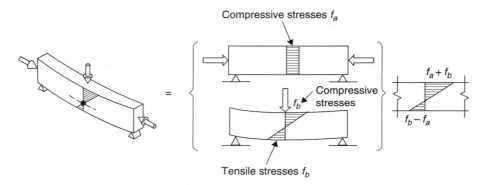

(a) Beam carrying both axial forces and bending moments.

(b) Using the principle of superposition, the stresses associated with each loading condition can be separately determined. The final stress distribution is a combination of these stresses. Similar stresses are additive while unlike stresses tend to counteract each other.

(c) In this example, the compressive stresses caused by the axial forces are sufficiently high to overshadow tensile stresses associated with bending. The entire cross section is thus in compression.

FIGURE 6–39 Combined stresses in beams. The final stress distribution in a beam carrying both axial and bending forces is simply a combination of the stresses associated with the axial forces and those associated with the bending moments.

distribution associated with the axial forces is of uniform intensity and of magnitude $f_a = P/A$. The stress distribution associated with bending is given by $f_y = My/I$. The stress at any point on the cross section of a beam is merely the combination of these two stresses added or subtracted according to whether or not the stresses acting at the point are similar. Thus, either of the stress distributions shown in Figure 6–39(b) or (c) is possible, depending on the relative magnitudes of the axial and bending stresses. In members of this type the neutral axis, or plane of zero stress, no longer corresponds with the centroidal axis of the section.

By applying an axial force sufficiently large to a beam it is possible to develop compressive stresses of a magnitude sufficient to dominate over the tensile bending stresses and thus put the entire cross section in compression. This is particularly important with respect to concrete, which cannot withstand tension stresses and cracks when subjected to them. By putting the entire cross section in compression, more effective use can be made of this material. It is important to note that the compressive stresses from bending and the applied axial force are additive. Thus, the advantages of doing this to a beam made of a material (e.g., steel) inherently capable of withstanding tension stresses is dubious, since the increased level of the combined compressive stresses would govern the amount of load the member could carry.

When the axial load is eccentrically applied, the types of stresses induced are particularly useful for offsetting the bending stresses associated with the service loads (Figure 6–40).

Consider the first of the two most common ways of applying an axial force to a member, that of *prestressing*. In this process, which is typically done in an off-site factory, high-strength steel wires, or tendons, are stretched between two piers so that a predetermined tensile force is developed. Concrete is then cast in formwork placed around these wires and cured. Wires are then cut. The tension force in the wire then in effect becomes equivalent to a compressive force applied to the member (the tension stress in the wires is transferred to the concrete through bond stresses). If the wire is eccentrically placed, the effect of cutting the wires is to induce stresses of the type illustrated in Figure 6–40(c) and to cause the member to bow upward. When upward bowing commences, the dead load of the concrete member itself begins inducing stresses of the type illustrated. Neither of the stress patterns shown in Figure 6–40(d) occurs independently and a combined stress pattern of the type shown to the right of the figure is present after wire cutting. Note that the exact amount of prestress force must be very carefully controlled. Indeed, during this stage of manufacture is when failure often occurs. Turning the beam upside down or on its side would lead to a rather dramatic failure, since dead-load stresses would no longer offset tensile stresses developed by the eccentric load but would accentuate them. When the member is carefully put in place (in this case by supporting it from its ends) the live load can then be applied, which in general results in a final stress distribution of the type illustrated in Figure 6–40(e).

The second most common method of applying a normal force to a member is that of *post-tensioning* (a form of prestressing done at a later construction stage). In this method, which is typically done on-site, a tube, conduit, or equivalent containing unstressed steel tendons is set in place and concrete cast around the tube. After curing, the tendons are clamped on one end and jacked against the concrete on the other end until the required force is developed. The tendons are then anchored on the jacking end and the jacks removed. The tendons are then usually bonded in place by injecting grout into the tube. The net effect is to do the same thing that the prestressing technique accomplishes. Tendons can be draped in a *funicular* manner if desired. Careful design can then yield a member in a state of compression only for the anticipated loading.

(a) Prestressed concrete members. High-strength steel strands are pretensioned between abutments by using jacks.

(b) Concrete is cast around the eccentrically placed pretensioned strands and allowed to cure.

(c) After the concrete has cured, the strands are cut. Since the strands are in the lower part of the beam, cutting of the cables is equivalent to putting a compressive force in the beam at this level. The beam consequently bows upward.

(d) Beam in place. An upward camber is present. Dead load and prestress force stresses are present.

(e) Beam under live load. The live load causes the beam to deflect downwards. The beam thus shows no sag under load. Dead load, live load, and prestress force stresses are present.

(f) Post-tensioned concrete members. Formwork is put in place, a conduit containing an unstressed cable is draped into place, and concrete is cast around the draped conduit.

(g) After the concrete has cured, the cable is tensioned by jacks. This causes the beam to rise upward. The formwork is removed and the cable force is locked in. Grout is inserted into the conduit to cause a bond to develop between the cable and the member.

FIGURE 6–40   Prestressed concrete members.

In both of these approaches, a host of problems exist. An important one is the effect of *creep* in concrete (deformation with time in a constant-stress situation), which has the effect of causing a loss in prestress or post-tension force. These forces must be calculated very carefully so that such losses with time are taken into account. Another consideration is that the stresses due to an eccentric force of the type illustrated are constant along the length of the beam, whereas the stresses associated with live and dead loads vary along the length of the beam. Indeed, with a constant eccentric force, critical prints in the beam are often near the ends and are due to the pre-stress force, since the offsetting effects of stresses due to the live and dead loads are not present. One advantage of post-tensioning over prestressing is that the cable can be draped fairly easily so that the eccentricity of the cable force is a variable which can be adjusted to account for this phe-nomenon. Deforming prestressing steel in this way is more difficult.

In situations where the beam undergoes a reverse curvature, special care must be taken with prestressed or post-tensioned members. In small members (e.g., concrete planks) this is often handled by not placing wires eccentrically but putting them at the centroid of the member. Thus, reliance is placed only on the effect of the uniform stresses produced by the wires. In large struc-tures it is feasible to drape a post-tensioned cable to reflect the anticipated reverse curvature.

A final point is of importance in the ultimate load-carrying capacity of prestressed or post-tensioned members. Usually, the primary criterion in designing such beams is their behavior un-der service or working loads. As loads increase beyond design loads, the beam begins behaving much like a standard reinforced concrete beam (i.e., cracks develop, etc.). The ultimate strength of a prestressed or post-tensioned beam is not overly superior to that of a similarly proportioned plain reinforced concrete beam. The primary value of the tensioning operation is thus to improve the performance of the beam at design or service loads. In particular, a very significant reason for prestressing or post-tensioning is to create a larger effective section for resisting deflections. In plain reinforced concrete beams cracks develop in the tension region and propagate until they reach the compressive zone. This cracked section makes no significant contribution to the stiffness of the section (the magnitude of I would be based only on the extent of the compressive zone and on the amount of steel present). In a prestressed or post-tensioned beam, no tensile stresses are developed and hence no cracks develop. Thus, the entire cross section of a beam con-tributes to the stiffness of the beam. Hence, for two beams of similar gross dimensions, a pre-stressed or post-tensioned one is better able to resist deflections than is its plain reinforced coun-terpart. In addition, the upward camber produced by eccentric prestressing forces is clearly useful in controlling deflections. All members should be carefully designed, however, since pre-stressed members can sometimes exhibit an undesirable "springiness." All in all, however, such members are highly versatile and useful.

QUESTIONS

6–1 Determine the value of the moment of inertia, I, and the section modulus, S, for each of the following cross-sectional shapes:

    A. A 4 in. $\times$ 10 in. rectangle.

    B. A 10 in. $\times$ 20 in. rectangle.

    C. A 10 in. $\times$ 20 in. rectangle with a symmetrically located interior rectangular hole of 8 in. $\times$ 12 in. Consider values about the centroidal strong axis of each section only.

        Answer: (a) 333 in.^{4}, 66.6 in.^{3}; (b) 6666 in.^{4}, 666 in.^{3}; (c) 5514 in.^{4}, 551.4 in.^{3}

6–2 Determine the value of the moment of inertia about the centroidal axis of a triangular cross section having a base dimension of 5 in. and a height of 15 in.

Answer: 468.75 in.^{4}

6–3 Floor joists having cross-sectional dimensions of 1½ in. $\times$ 9½ in. are simply supported, span 12 ft, and carry a floor load of 50 lb/ft^2. Compute the center-to-center spacing between joists to develop a maximum bending stress of 1200 lb/in.^{2} Compute what safe floor load could be carried if the center-line spacing was 16 in. Neglect dead loads.

6–4 Consider a cantilever beam that is 10 ft long and which supports a concentrated load of 833 lb at its free end. Assume that the beam is 2 in. $\times$ 10 in. in cross section and that lateral bracing is present. Draw a diagram of the beam showing the bending-stress distribution present at the base of the cantilever and at every 2.5-ft increment toward the free end of the beam (a total of five locations). Indicate numerical values for the maximum bending stresses at each section. Do a similar exercise for shearing stresses. What generally happens to the magnitudes of the bending and shearing stresses found when the width of the beam is doubled and its depth held constant? What happens when the width of the beam is held constant and its depth doubled?

6–5 Repeat Question 6–4, except assume that the beam is simply supported at either end and carries a uniformly distributed load of 200 lb/ft.

6–6 A simply supported beam 12 ft long carries a uniformly distributed load of 100 lb/ft. Assume that the beam is 1½ in. $\times$ 9½ in. in cross section and is laterally braced. Also assume that the beam is made of timber that has an allowable stress in bending of 1200 lb/in.^{2} and in shear of 150 lb/in.^{2} Is the beam safe with respect to bending and shear stress considerations? What is the maximum deflection of the beam? Assume that $E = 1.6 \times 10^6$ lb/in.^{2} Is this deflection acceptable?

Answer: ($f_b = 959$) < ($F_b = 1200$), $\therefore$ safe in bending; ($f_v = 63.1$) < ($F_v = 150$), $\therefore$ safe in shear; and (0.29) < ($L/240 = 0.6$), $\therefore$ deflections are okay.

6–7 A simply supported steel beam is to be used to span 30 ft and support a uniformly distributed load of 400 lb/ft. Assume that the allowable stress in bending is $F_b = 24,000$ lb/in.^{2} Determine the most efficient wide-flange shape to be used based on a bending stress analysis. Use one of the shapes listed in Appendix 14. Ignore dead loads.

6–8 Assume that a laminated timber beam having cross-sectional dimensions of 8 in. $\times$ 20 in. is available. Based on bending-stress considerations only, how far could this beam span if it carried a uniformly distributed load of 250 lb/ft and were simply supported at either end? How far could it span if it carried the same load but were cantilevered? Assume that the allowable stress in bending is $F_b = 2400$ lb/in.^{2} and that the beams are all adequately laterally braced. Ignore dead loads.

Answer: 58.4 ft if simply supported.

6–9 Assume that a series of laminated timber beams is to be used at 5 ft on center to span 25 ft and carries a uniformly distributed floor live load of 40 lb/ft^2 and dead load of 20 lb/ft^2. Completely design an appropriate prototypical beam. Assume that the allowable stress in bending is $F_b = 2200$ lb/in.^{2}, in shear $F_v = 400$ lb/in.^{2}, in bearing $F_{bg} = 400$ lb/in.^{2}, and that $E = 1.8 \times 10^6$ lb/in.^{2} Make any assumptions that you need to (e.g., about lateral bracing), but clearly state them and/or illustrate with sketches.

6–10 With respect to bending-moment considerations only, draw a sketch of the shape variation present in a beam carrying two equal concentrated loads located at third points in the structure such that a constant bending-stress level is maintained on the top and bottom surfaces of the member. Draw one sketch assuming the width of the beam is held constant and the depth varies, and another assuming that the depth of the beam is held constant and the width allowed to vary.

CHAPTER 7

Members in Compression: Columns

7-1 INTRODUCTION

Along with load-bearing walls, columns are the most common of all vertical support elements. Strictly speaking, columns need not be only vertical. Rather, they are rigid linear elements that can be inclined in any direction, but to which loads are applied only at member ends. They are not normally subject to bending directly induced by loads acting transverse to their axes.

Columns can be usefully categorized in terms of their length. *Short columns* tend to fail by crushing (a strength failure). *Long columns* tend to fail by buckling, which is an instability failure rather than a strength failure. Material rupture occurs only after the member has buckled. Long columns are members in which the length of the element is relatively great as compared to its least lateral dimension. The potential for buckling tends to limit the load-carrying capacity of long members. The buckling phenomenon itself was recognized quite early as being of unique interest. A number of investigators attempted analytical solutions for predicting exactly what load would cause a slender member to buckle. The problem was finally solved by Leonard Euler (1707–1783). Euler was a mathematician born in Switzerland and related through training and association to the celebrated Bernoulli family, long recognized for their contributions to mathematics.

Euler correctly analyzed the action of a long, slender member under an axial load while in St. Petersburg, Russia, in 1759. The form that he gave to the solution is still in use today. It is one of the few early contributions to the structural engineering field that has survived in a virtually unchanged form.

299

7-2 GENERAL PRINCIPLES

Members in which the least cross-sectional dimension present is appreciable relative to the length of the member are short columns. The load-carrying capacity of a short column is *independent* of the length of the member and, when excessively loaded, the short column typically fails by crushing. Consequently, its ultimate load-carrying capacity depends primarily on the strength of the material used and its cross-sectional area. As a compressive member becomes longer and longer, the relative proportions of the member change to the extent that it can be described as a slender element, or long column. The behavior of a slender element under compressive load differs dramatically from that of a short column.

Consider the long compression member illustrated in Figure 7–1 and its behavior under increasing loads. When the applied load is small, the member maintains its linear shape and continues to do so as the load is increased. As a particular load level is reached, the member quite suddenly becomes unstable and deforms into the shape illustrated. This is the *buckling* phenomenon. When the member has buckled, it is no longer capable of carrying any additional load. Added loads will immediately cause added deformation, which will eventually cause the member to snap. This snapping, however, is regarded as a secondary failure, since the maximum load-carrying capacity is that associated with initial buckling. A structure in a buckled mode is *not* serviceable.

The phenomenon of buckling is a curious one. It is a mode of failure that is due to an instability of the member induced through the action of the load. Failures due to instability need not initially involve any kind of material rupture or distress. Indeed, internal force levels can be quite low and buckling can still occur if the member is quite long. The buckling phenomenon is associated with the *stiffness* of the member. A member with low stiffness will buckle before one with high stiffness. Increasing member length causes a reduction in stiffness.

When a member initially becomes unstable, as does a column exactly at the buckling load, the member does not and cannot generate internal forces to restore the structure to its original linear configuration. Such restoring forces are developed below the buckling load. A column exactly at the buckling load is in neutral equilibrium. The system does not have restoring characteristics to reestablish the original configuration of the element once it is displaced.

There are numerous factors that influence the buckling load, denoted P_{cr}, of a long compressive member. *Length,* of course, is a critical factor. In general, the load-carrying capacity of a column varies *inversely* as the square of its length. In addition to the length of the member, the other factors that influence the load necessary to cause a member to buckle are associated with the stiffness characteristics of the member that result from the inherent properties of the specific material used (as reflected by its "modulus of elasticity") and those that result from the amount of material used in a cross section and the way the material is distributed.

The *stiffness* of the member is strongly influenced by the amount and distribution of the material present. In the thin rectangular member illustrated later in Figure 7–4(a), it can be easily experimentally demonstrated, or theoretically proven, that the member will always buckle in the direction indicated. The member is less rigid about this axis than the other. The member has much less of an ability to resist bending about one axis than the other. The member will tend to buckle *about* the weak axis (associated with the lesser ability to resist bending). The same member, however, can be sufficiently stiff about the other axis to resist buckling associated with that axis. The load-carrying capacity of a compressive member is thus not dependent on just the

(a) Short column: the member fails by a crushing action. Its strength depends on the cross-sectional area and crushing strength of the material used.

Stable equilibrium

Initial state

Position after displacing force is applied

Position after displacing force is removed

(b) Long column (load less than the buckling load): the member is in a state of stable equilibrium. If the member is displaced slightly at mid-height it will spring back to its original configuration.

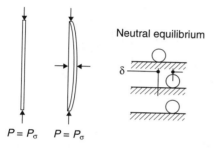

Neutral equilibrium

(c) Long column (load = buckling load): when the load on the column reaches the critical buckling load, the member changes into a state of neutral equilibrium. If the member is displaced from its original linear configuration, it will remain in its new position and not spring back. The buckling load is the maximum load that the column can carry.

Unstable equilibrium

(d) Long column (load greater than the buckling load): if the load on the column is increased beyond the critical buckling load, the member changes into a state of unstable equilibrium. The member will continue to deform under a constant load level until it finally snaps.

(e) General relationship between member length and buckling load. Short members tend to crush while longer ones tend to buckle. The longer the member, the lower its load-carrying capacity (the buckling load of a long member varies inversely with the square of its length).

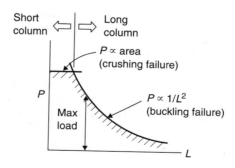

FIGURE 7–1 Behavior of columns under load.

amount of material present in the cross section (as is the case in tension members), but on its distribution as well. A useful measure in this connection is the *moment of inertia, I,* which combines the amount of material present with the way it is distributed into a single stiffness characteristic. Moments of inertia are discussed in Chapter 6 and Appendix 4.

Another factor of extreme importance in influencing the amount of load a member can carry is the nature of the *end conditions* of the member. If the ends of a column are free to rotate, the member is capable of carrying far less load than if the ends are restrained. Restraining the ends of a member increases its stiffness and thus its ability to resist buckling. *Bracing* the element in some direct way also increases stiffness. These important influences are explored in detail in Section 7–3–2.

Figure 7–1(e) summarizes the general relationship between the load-carrying capacity and length of a member in direct compression and with simple pinned ends. As illustrated, the phenomenon of buckling generally causes a reduction in the load-carrying capabilities of compression members. The shape of the buckling curve illustrates that the load-carrying capacity of a long compressive member varies inversely with the square of the length of the member. The maximum load a column can carry, however, is invariably associated with *crushing* (in the short-column range) rather than buckling. Long, slender columns invariably fail at loads less than the crushing load. It follows that the actual stress level present when buckling occurs (the *critical buckling stress*) is invariably less than the crushing or yield stress (i.e., $f_{cr} = P_{cr}/A \leq f_{yield}$). Long columns can fail by buckling at stress levels considerably lower than that associated with yielding in the material.

It should always be remembered that the actual axial stress level present in any symmetrically loaded compressive member, long or short, is always given by $f = P/A$. The stress level at which failure or buckling occurs, however, depends on whether the member is long or short.

7–3   ANALYSIS OF COMPRESSION MEMBERS

7–3–1   Short Columns

Axial Loads.   Compression members that fail primarily by crushing or direct stresses and whose ultimate load-carrying capacity is consequently independent of member lengths are relatively easy to analyze. When the load is applied to the centroid of the cross section of the loaded element, uniform compressive stresses of a magnitude $f = P/A$ are developed. Failure occurs when the actual direct stress exceeds the crushing stress of the material (i.e., $f_a \geq F_y$). The crushing load is given by $P_y = AF_y$, where A is the cross-sectional area of the column and F_y is the yield or crushing stress of the material.

Eccentric Loads.   When loads are eccentrically applied (i.e., not applied at the centroid of the cross section), the resultant stress distribution will not be uniform. The effect of eccentric loads is to produce bending stresses in the member, which in turn interact with direct compressive stresses. If the load is very eccentrically applied, tensile rather than compressive stresses can even be developed at a cross section.

Consider the member shown in Figure 7–2, which is subjected to an eccentric load P acting at a distance e from the centroidal axis of the member. Stresses produced by this load can be found by resolving the eccentric load into a statically equivalent axial force producing only

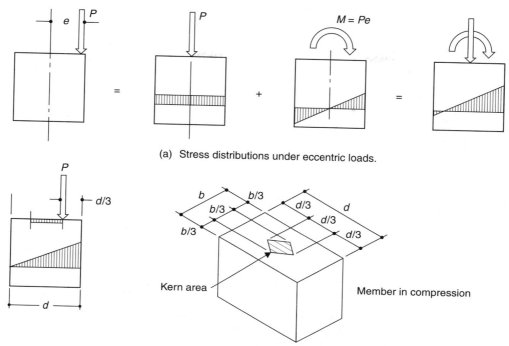

(a) Stress distributions under eccentric loads.

Kern area

Member in compression

(b) Placing a load anywhere within the middle one-third of the section produces only compressive stresses in the cross section. Placing a load outside of the middle one-third leads to the development of tensile stresses on one face of the member.

FIGURE 7–2   Eccentrically loaded columns.

uniform stresses f_a and a couple (moment) which produces only bending stresses f_b. This resolution is illustrated in Figure 7–2. Final stresses are merely the combination of the two stress distributions. Uniform stresses $= f_a = P/A$; bending stresses $= f_b = Mc/I$, where $M = Pe$. Hence, $f_b = (Pe)c/I$. Finally, combined stresses $= f_{\text{actual}} = f_a + f_b = \pm P/A \pm (Pe)c/I$.

An inspection of the stress distributions illustrated in Figure 7–2 reveals that the magnitude of the bending stresses is proportional to the eccentricity e of the load. In a situation of the type indicated, the vertical load P can produce tensile stresses on one face of the element if the eccentricity is large (i.e., bending stresses f_b dominate over axial or normal stresses). When $e = 0$, clearly only compressive stresses f_a exist. There must exist a limit to the eccentricity of the load if the intention is to have only compressive stresses in the member. This point can be found by simply equating the resultant stress to zero ($f_a + f_b = 0$).and solving for the eccentricity; or $P/A = (Pe)c/I$ and $e = I/Ac$. For a rectangular cross section (see Figure 7–2), $P/bd = Pe(d/2)/(bd^3/12)$ and $e = d/6$.

Thus, if the load were placed within this maximum value, the stresses produced would all be compressive. Placing the load exactly at this point ($e = d/6$) produces zero stresses on the opposite face. Exceeding this eccentricity will cause tensile stresses to develop on the opposite face. This location is referred to as the *Kern point*. Note that for a load which can vary in either direction, Kern points exist on either side of the centroidal axis. These locations are at third points on the face of the element. This gives rise to the *middle-third rule,* often referred to in the design of masonry structures (particularly in a historical context), where the design intent is to keep the load inside the middle third to prevent tensile stresses, which masonry cannot withstand, from developing. If the third dimension is considered, a *Kern area* can be found, as indicated in Figure 7–2.

7-3-2 Long Columns

Euler Buckling. As previously mentioned, Leonard Euler was the first investigator to formulate an expression for the critical buckling load of a column. The critical buckling load for a pin-ended column, termed the *Euler buckling load,* is

$$P_{cr} = \frac{\pi^2 EI}{L^2}$$

where E = modulus of elasticity $\quad L$ = length of column between pinned ends

I = moment of inertia $\quad \pi$ = pi (a constant) = 3.1416

The derivation for this expression is contained in Appendix 11. The expression clearly shows that the load-carrying capacity of a column depends inversely on the square of the member's length, directly on the value of the modulus of elasticity of the material used, and directly on the value of the moment of inertia of the cross section. The moment of inertia of concern is the minimum one about any axis for the cross section if the member is not braced.

The Euler buckling expression predicts that when a column becomes indefinitely long, the load required to cause the member to buckle begins to approach zero (see Figure 7–3). Conversely, when the length of a column begins to approach zero, the load required to cause the member to buckle becomes indefinitely large. What actually happens, of course, is that as the member becomes short, the failure mode changes into that of crushing. Consequently, the Euler expression is not valid for short members, since it predicts impossibly high values. The crushing strength becomes a cutoff for the applicability of the Euler expression.

The dependency of the buckling load on the inverse of the square of the length of the column is important. Doubling the length of a column reduces its load-carrying capacity by a factor of 4. Thus, if $P_1 = \pi^2 EI/L_1^2$ and $L_2 = 2L_1$, then $P_2 = \pi^2 EI(L_2)^2$ or $\pi^2 EI/(2L_1)^2 = P_1/4$. Similarly, halving its length increases its load-carrying capacity by a factor of 4 [i.e., $P_2 = \pi^2 EI/(\frac{1}{2}L_1)^2 = 4P_1$]. The buckling load of a column is thus extremely sensitive to changes in the length of the member.

◆ ◆ **EXAMPLE**

Determine the critical buckling load for a 2-in. × 2-in. (50.8-mm × 50.8-mm) steel column that is 180 in. (4572 mm) long and pin-ended. Assume that $E = 29.6 \times 10^6$ lb/in.^{2} (0.204×10^6 N/mm^2).

Solution:

Moment of inertia, I_x or I_y:

$$I = \frac{bh^3}{12} = \frac{2 \text{ in.}(2 \text{ in.})^3}{12} = 1.33 \text{ in.}^4 = \frac{50.8 \text{ mm}(50.8 \text{ mm})^3}{12} = 555 \times 10^3 \text{ mm}^4$$

Since $I_x = I_y$, the column is equally likely to buckle about either axis or about a diagonal, since that I value also is equal to I_x or I_y.

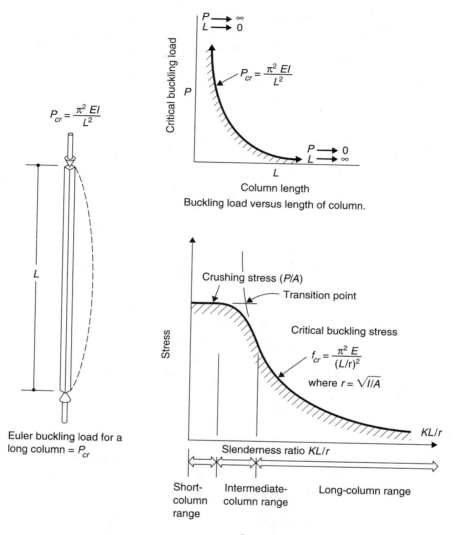

$$P_{cr} = \frac{\pi^2 EI}{L^2}$$

Euler buckling load for a
long column = P_{cr}

FIGURE 7–3   Euler buckling in long columns.

Critical buckling load:

$$P_{cr} = \frac{\pi^2 EI}{L^2} = \frac{\pi^2(29.6 \times 10^6 \text{ lb/in.}^2)(1.33 \text{ in.}^4)}{(180 \text{ in.})^2} = 12,000 \text{ lb}$$

$$= \frac{\pi^2(204,000 \text{ N/mm}^2)(555,000 \text{ mm}^4)}{(4572 \text{ mm})^2} = 53,458 \text{ N}$$

The actual stress level corresponding to this critical buckling load is

$$f_{cr} = \frac{P_{cr}}{A} = \frac{12{,}000 \text{ lb}}{2 \text{ in.} \times 2 \text{ in.}} = 3000 \text{ lb/in.}^2 = \frac{53{,}458 \text{ N}}{50.8 \text{ mm} \times 50.8 \text{ mm}} = 20.7 \text{ N/mm}^2$$

Thus, the column buckles at a relatively low actual stress level, below the crushing stress for steel.   ◆

◆ ◆   **EXAMPLE**

For what length will the square column previously analyzed begin to crush rather than buckle (i.e., what is the transition length between short- and long-column behavior for this specific member)? Assume the yield stress of the steel to be $F_y = 36{,}000 \text{ lb/in.}^2$ (248 N/mm²).

Solution:

For failure by crushing:

$$P_{max} = F_y A = (36{,}000 \text{ lb/in.}^2)(2 \text{ in.} \times 2 \text{ in.}) = 144{,}000 \text{ lb}$$
$$= (248 \text{ N/mm}^2)(50.8 \text{ mm} \times 50.8 \text{ mm}) = 640 \text{ kN}$$

Buckling length for P_{max}:

$$P_{cr} = \frac{\pi^2 EI}{L^2} = P_{max}$$

$$144{,}000 \text{ lb} = \frac{\pi^2(29.6 \times 10^6 \text{ lb/in.}^2)(1.33 \text{ in.}^4)}{L^2} \qquad \therefore \ L = 52 \text{ in.}$$

$$= 640{,}000 \text{ N} = \frac{\pi^2(204{,}000 \text{ N/mm}^2)(555{,}000 \text{ mm}^4)}{L^2}$$

$$\therefore \ L = 1320 \text{ mm}$$

Consequently,

For $L < 52$ in. (1320 mm) the member will crush.

For $L > 52$ in. (1320 mm) the member will buckle.

For $L = 52$ in. (1320 mm) either failure mode is likely.

In actuality, such an exactly defined transition point does not really exist. Rather, a more general transition occurs.   ◆

Shape of Cross Section.   When an unbraced member is nonsymmetrical, it is necessary to take into account the different moments of inertia of the member (Figure 7–4). Members of this type will generally buckle in the direction of their least dimension, or, more precisely, about their weaker axis. A typical rectangular column has two primary moments of inertia, I_x and I_y. Associated with each is a load that will cause the member to buckle about each respective axis, P_{cr_x} and P_{cr_y}. The load that actually causes the whole member to buckle is the smaller of these two values:

$$P_{cr_x} = \frac{\pi^2 EI_x}{L_x^2} \quad \text{and} \quad P_{cr_y} = \frac{\pi^2 EI_y}{L_y^2}$$

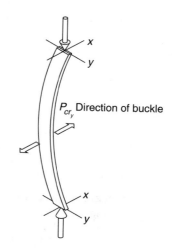

(a) The moment of inertia about one axis is greater than that about the other.

(b) The member can potentially fail by buckling about either axis. The load required to cause it to buckle about the stronger axis, however, exceeds the load which will cause buckling about the weaker axis.

(c) Consequently the member will buckle at $P_{cr_y} = \pi^2 EI_y/L^2$ in the mode shown.

FIGURE 7–4   Buckling of asymmetric cross sections.

◆ ◆   **EXAMPLE**

Determine the critical buckling load for a column with the same cross-sectional area as the column previously analyzed but rectangular: $b = 1$ in., $d = 4$ in. (25.4 mm × 101.6 mm). Assume that $L = 180$ in. (4572 mm). $E = 29.6 \times 10^6$ lb/in.^{2} (204,000 N/mm^2), as before.

Solution:

Moment of inertia:

$$I_x = \frac{bd^3}{12} = \frac{(1)(4^3)}{12} = 5.33 \text{ in.}^4 = \frac{(25.4 \text{ mm})(101.6 \text{ mm})^3}{12} = 2.20 \times 10^6 \text{ mm}^4$$

$$I_y = \frac{db^3}{12} = \frac{(4)(1^3)}{12} = 0.33 \text{ in.}^4 = \frac{(101.6 \text{ mm})(25.4 \text{ mm})^3}{12} = 0.139 \times 10^6 \text{ mm}^4$$

Critical buckling loads:
Load causing buckling about the x axis:

$$P_{cr_x} = \frac{\pi^2 EI_x}{L_x^2} = \frac{\pi^2(29.6 \times 10^6)(5.33)}{(180)^2} = 48,060 \text{ lb}$$

$$= \frac{\pi^2(204,000 \text{ N/mm}^2)(2.20 \times 10^6 \text{ mm}^4)}{(4572 \text{ mm})^2} = 213.8 \text{ kN}$$

Load causing buckling about the y axis:

$$P_{cr_y} = \frac{\pi^2 EI_y}{L_y^2} = \frac{\pi^2 (29.6 \times 10^6)(0.33)}{(180)^2} = 2975.5 \text{ lb}$$

$$= \frac{\pi^2 (204,000 \text{ N/mm}^2)(0.139 \times 10^6 \text{ mm}^4)}{(4572 \text{ mm})^2} = 13.3 \text{ kN}$$

Since the load required to cause the member to buckle about the weaker y axis is much less than the load that is associated with buckling about the stronger x axis, the critical buckling load for the entire column is 2975.5 lb (13.3 kN). The member will buckle in the direction of the least dimension. As compared to the member having an equivalent area but square in shape, the load-carrying capacity of the rectangular member analyzed is greatly reduced. ◆

Critical Buckling Stress.   The Euler expression is often rewritten in a slightly different form that is more useful as a design tool. The critical buckling load for a column can be converted into a *critical buckling stress* f_{cr} simply by dividing both sides of the Euler expression by the area A of the column. Thus, $f_{cr} = P/A = \pi^2 EI/AL^2$. This expression contains two measures related to the dimensional properties of the column, I and A, that can be combined into a single measure. This single measure is called the *radius of gyration r* and is *defined* by $r = \sqrt{I/A}$. Note that $I = Ar^2$. Simply accepting this as a definition, the expression for the critical buckling stress of a column can be rewritten as

$$f_{cr} = \frac{P}{A} = \frac{\pi^2 E}{(L/r)^2}$$

The term L/r is called the *slenderness ratio* of the column. The critical buckling stress depends inversely on the square of the slenderness ratio. The higher the slenderness ratio, the lower is the critical stress that will cause buckling, and vice versa. The slenderness ratio (L/r) is an important way of thinking about columns, since it is the single measurable parameter on which the buckling of a column depends.

The radius of gyration, r, can be interpreted in the following way. The moment of inertia of the cross-sectional area of the column is equal to the product of the area times the square of the distance r by definition (i.e., $I = Ar^2$). Consequently, the radius of gyration of this area with respect to an axis is a distance such that if the total area were conceived of as concentrated at this point, its moment of inertia about the axis would be the same as that of the original distributed area about that axis. The higher the radius of gyration of a section, the more resistant the section is to buckling (although the true measure for resistance to buckling is the L/r ratio). Radius-of-gyration values for different sections are often tabulated in much the same way that moments of inertia are.

◆ ◆   **EXAMPLE**

For the same column previously analyzed ($b = 1$ in., $d = 4$ in., and $L = 180$ in.), what is the critical buckling stress f_{cr_y} that is present? Recall that $I_y = 0.33$ in.[4]

Solution: Determine $r_y = \sqrt{I_y/A} = \sqrt{0.33/4.0} = 0.29$ in. Therefore, $L/r_y = (180/0.29) = 620$. The high L/r_y value indicates that the column is extremely slender and prone to buckling. Determine the critical buckling stress: $f_{cr_y} = \pi^2 E/(L/r_y)^2 = \pi^2 (29.6 \times 10^6)/620^2 = 750$ lb/in.^{2} Note that this buckling stress level is far lower than that associated with material yielding ($F_y = 36,000$ lb/in.^{2}) . ◆

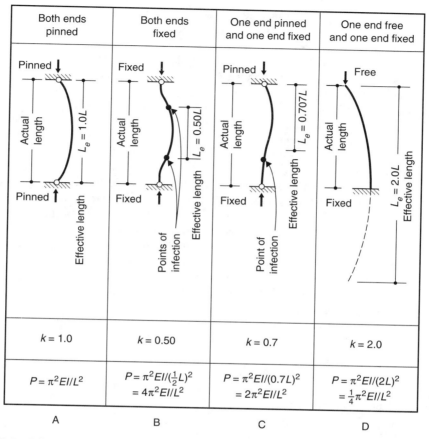

Both ends pinned	Both ends fixed	One end pinned and one end fixed	One end free and one end fixed
$k = 1.0$	$k = 0.50$	$k = 0.7$	$k = 2.0$
$P = \pi^2 EI/L^2$	$P = \pi^2 EI/(\frac{1}{2}L)^2$ $= 4\pi^2 EI/L^2$	$P = \pi^2 EI/(0.7L)^2$ $= 2\pi^2 EI/L^2$	$P = \pi^2 EI/(2L)^2$ $= \frac{1}{4}\pi^2 EI/L^2$
A	B	C	D

FIGURE 7–5   Effects of end conditions on critical buckling loads.

End Conditions and Effective Lengths.   The discussion in the previous section focused on columns having pin-ended connections in which the ends of the members were free to rotate (but not translate) in any direction at their ends. This condition allows the member to deform in the manner illustrated in Figure 7–5(a). Obviously, other end conditions are possible. Restraining the ends of a column from a free-rotation condition generally increases the load-carrying capacity of a column. Allowing translation as well as rotations at the ends of a column generally reduces its load-carrying capacity.

This section considers the relative load-carrying capacity of four columns that are identical in all respects except for their end conditions. The conditions are illustrated in Figure 7–5 and generally represent theoretical extremes, since end conditions in actual practice are often combinations of these primary conditions. Column *A* represents the standard pin-ended column already discussed. Column *B* has both ends fixed (i.e., no rotations can occur). Column *C* has one end fixed and the other pinned. Column *D* has one end fixed and the other completely free to both rotate and translate (and is thus similar to a flagpole).

The theoretical buckling load for each of these columns can be computed in a way similar to that presented in Appendix 11 for the pin-ended column. Different boundary conditions would be used. Another way of finding the load-carrying capacity of these columns is to consider the effects of the end conditions on the deformed shape of the columns. Consider the deformed shape of the fixed-ended member (column B) illustrated in an exaggerated way in Figure 7–5(b). The shape of the curve can be simply sketched with a high degree of accuracy by noting that a fixed-ended condition of the type illustrated causes the tangent to the member to remain vertical at each end. Under the buckling load, the member would begin bowing as indicated, with the curvature beginning immediately outside the connection. In order for the curve to be continuous, as it must be, the resultant curve must be similar to that illustrated. Of critical importance is that the member must undergo a change in curvature. Evidently, points of inflection must exist at two locations where the sense of the curvature changes. The location of these points can be estimated fairly accurately. In this case they are $L_1/4$ from each end, where L_1 is the actual length of the column. Note that the shape of the column between those two points of inflection is similar to that of a pin-ended column. This is sensible, since both pin-ended connections and points of inflection are analogous. It follows that this portion of the column behaves as if it were a pin-ended column of a length equal to the distance between the points of inflection, in this case one-half the actual length of the column, or $L_1/2$. This distance is called the *effective length* (L_e) of the fixed-ended column. The buckling load of the whole column is controlled by this portion of the column. The buckling load of this portion is given by $P_B = \pi^2 EI/L_e^2$, where L_e is the distance between the points of inflection. Consequently, the buckling load for the column in terms of its original length is $P_B = \pi^2 EI/(L_1/2)^2 = 4\pi^2 EI/L_1$. Since the initial buckling load for a pin-ended column of the same actual length is $P_A = \pi^2 EI/L_1^2$, the effect of fixing both ends of the column is to increase its load-carrying capacity by a factor of 4. This is a substantial increase that is equivalent to that caused by halving the length of the column.

This process can be repeated for other end conditions. Deformed shapes are sketched and locations of inflection points are determined. Effective lengths are next determined. Critical buckling loads are then given by $P = \pi^2 EI/L_e^2$. The effective length of the column with one end pinned and the other fixed is $L_c = 0.7L_1$. Its buckling load is consequently $P_c = \pi^2 EI/(1/0.7L)^2 = 2\pi^2 EI/L_1^2$, or twice that of a column with pins on both ends. For the flagpole column, the deformed shape of the actual column can be seen to be one-half the shape analogous to that of a pin-ended column [see Figure 7–5(d)]. Its effective length is thus $2L_1$. Consequently, $P_D = \pi^2 EI/(2L_1)^2 = \frac{1}{4}\pi^2 EI/L_1^2$, or one-fourth of that for a pin-ended column of the same length.

The concept of effective length is thus very useful in analyzing columns with different end conditions, since it provides a shortcut for making predictions about their load-carrying capacities. The numerical value that modifies the actual length (L) is called the *k factor* of the column. Thus, $k = 1.0$ for a pin-ended column. Hence, $L_e = kL = 1.0L$ and $P_c = \pi^2 EI/(1.0L)^2$. Also, $k = 0.5$ for a fixed-end column, thus $L_e = kL = 0.5L$ and $P_c = \pi^2 EI/(0.5L^2) = 4\pi^2 EI/L^2$.

Quite often a column has different end conditions with respect to one axis than another (e.g., it may be pin-ended with respect to one axis and fixed with respect to the other). Consequently, care must be taken to couple the correct effective length with the appropriate moment of inertia or radius of gyration. Thus,

$$P_{cr_x} = \frac{\pi^2 EI_x}{(kL_x)^2} \quad \text{and} \quad P_{cr_y} = \frac{\pi^2 EI_y}{(kL_y)^2}$$

$$f_{cr_x} = \frac{\pi^2 E}{(kL_x/r_x)^2} \quad \text{and} \quad f_{cr_y} = \frac{\pi^2 E}{(kL_y/r_y)^2}$$

As in one of the examples previously discussed, the critical buckling load for the entire column is governed by the smaller of P_{cr_x} and P_{cr_y}.

The effects of imperfect end conditions in field applications are often taken roughly into account by simply modifying the effective length of a member. If a column is intended to have fixed ends but the actual field connection is such that only partial restraint is obtained and some rotations occur, for example, it is evident that the effective length of the column lies between $0.5L$ and $1.0L$. The more nearly full restraint is obtained, the closer is the effective length to $0.5L$. The more it rotates, the closer the effective length is to $1.0L$. Values such as $0.6L$ to $0.7L$ are often used.

In the case of frames, only partial restraint is often obtained due to the rotation of end joints (see Chapter 9). The result of this end rotation is to increase the effective lengths of members. When the end rotation is coupled with translation of the joint in space, the effective member length can be longer than the physical length of the column and can constitute a serious design problem.

Bracing.   To reduce column lengths and increase their load-carrying capacities, columns are frequently braced at one or more points along their length (see Figure 7–6). The bracing can actually be part of the structural framework for the rest of the building, which also serves other functions.

Figure 7–6(b) illustrates a pin-ended column braced at its midheight. When the member buckles, it will deform into an S shape as illustrated. Since the shape of the member between the bracing and the point of inflection is analogous to that of a pin-ended column, the effective length of the column is equal to this distance. The length of the column shown has thus been effectively halved, which increases its load-carrying capacity by a factor of 4: $P = \pi^2 EI/L_e^2 = \pi^2 EI/(L_1/2)^2 = 4\pi^2 EI/L_1^2$.

If the bracing were placed two-thirds of the way up from the bottom, the member would again deform into a modified S shape. Its effective length would then be $\frac{2}{3}L$, or $\frac{1}{3}L$. It is evident that the longer unbraced portion would buckle prior to the shorter portion. Consequently, the critical load for the column would be $P = \pi^2 EI/L_e^2 = \pi^2 EI/[(\frac{2}{3})L_1^2] = (\frac{9}{4})(\pi^2 EI/L_1^2)$. Clearly, bracing the member at this point is not as effective in increasing the load-carrying capacity of the column as is midheight bracing.

Note that a column can be braced about one axis but not the other. The column will have a tendency to buckle in the direction associated with the highest slenderness ratio. Any column must be checked for buckling about both axes (using appropriate combinations of I and L_e or kL values) by calculating P_{cr_x} and P_{cr_y} values or comparable critical stresses. The smaller of the loads is the critical load at which the column initially buckles.

◆ ◆   **EXAMPLE**

Consider the column shown in Figure 7–7. Assume that the overall height of the column is $L = 180$ in. and the bracing is at midheight. (a) If the narrow dimension $b = 1$ in. and the deep dimension $d = 4$ in., what

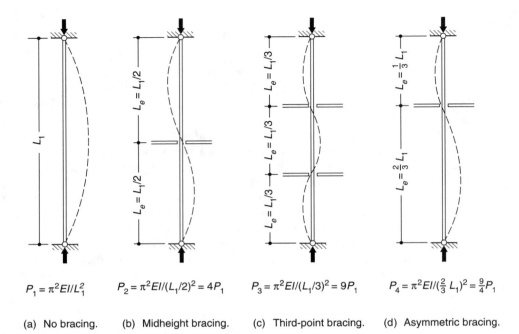

$$P_1 = \pi^2 EI/L_1^2 \qquad P_2 = \pi^2 EI/(L_1/2)^2 = 4P_1 \qquad P_3 = \pi^2 EI/(L_1/3)^2 = 9P_1 \qquad P_4 = \pi^2 EI/(\tfrac{2}{3}L_1)^2 = \tfrac{9}{4}P_1$$

(a) No bracing.   (b) Midheight bracing.   (c) Third-point bracing.   (d) Asymmetric bracing.

FIGURE 7–6 Effects of lateral bracing on column buckling. Bracing a column changes its buckling mode and consequently its effective length. The more a column is braced, the shorter its effective length becomes and the greater the load that is required to cause buckling. If bracing is used, it is usually more effective when placed symmetrically.

is the load which causes buckling? (b) Repeat for a column with an identical area with dimensions $b = 1.75$ in. and $d = 2.28$ in.

Solution: (a) Determine $I_x = bd^3/12 = (1)(4^3)/12 = 5.33$ in.^{4} and $I_y = db^3/12 = (4)(1^3)/12 = 0.33$ in.^{4}. Note that $L_{e_x} = L = 180$ and $L_{e_y} = (L/2) = 180/2 = 90$. Hence, $P_{cr_x} = \pi^2 EI_x/L_{e_x}^2 = \pi^2(29.6 \times 10^6)(5.33)/180^2 = 48{,}060$ lb and $P_{cr_y} = \pi^2 EI_y/L_{e_y}^2 = \pi^2(29.6 \times 10^6)(0.33)/(90)^2 = 12{,}015$ lb. Since $12{,}015 < 48{,}060$, the column buckles at $P_{cr_y} = 12{,}015$ lb about its weak axis in the plane of the bracing and in an S-shaped buckling mode. It is in no danger of buckling out of the plane of the bracing. (b) Determine $I_x = bd^3/12 = (1.75)(2.28^3)/12 = 1.72$ in.^{4} and $I_y = db^3/12 = (2.28) \times (1.75^3)/12 = 1.02$ in.^{4} Note that $L_{e_x} = L = 180$ and $L_{e_y} = (L/2) = 90$. (c) Determine critical buckling loads. $P_{cr_x} = \pi^2 EI_x/L_{e_x}^2 = \pi^2(29.6 \times 10^6)(1.72)/180^2 = 15{,}500$ lb and $P_{cr_y} = \pi^2 EI_y/L_{e_y}^2 = \pi^2(29.6 \times (1.02)/(90)^2 = 36{,}750$ lb. Since $15{,}500 < 36{,}750$, the column buckles at $P_{cr_x} = 15{,}500$ lb about its strong axis out of the plane of the bracing in a simple curve. It will not buckle in an S shape since this would require a higher buckling load than that associated with out of plane bracing. ◆

Actual Versus Ideal Column Strengths. When columns are actually tested, there is usually a difference found between actual buckling loads and theoretical predictions. This is particularly true for columns of lengths near the transition between short- and long-column behavior. Reasons for this include such factors as minor accidental eccentricity in the column loading, initial

FIGURE 7–7 Column bracing in one plane only. When a column is braced in only one plane, it can potentially buckle in two modes. The column will buckle in the mode associated with the higher slenderness ratio (*L/r*).

$$r_x = \sqrt{I_x/A}$$
$$r_x = \sqrt{I_y/A}$$
$$P_{cr_x} = \pi^2 E I_x / L_{e_x}^2$$
$$P_{cr_y} = \pi^2 E I_y / L_{e_y}^2$$

(column buckles at lowest P_{cr} value)

crookedness in the member, initial stresses present before loading due to the fabrication process, nonhomogeneity in the material, and others. Bending stresses not accounted for in the Euler expression often exist. The result is that buckling loads are often slightly lower than predicted, particularly near the transition zone between short and long columns, where failure is often partly elastic and partly inelastic (crushing). For this reason a number of additional theoretical and empirical expressions have been developed to take into account this phenomenon. Expressions are available, for example, for more accurately predicting behavior in the *intermediate* range. A full exploration of these expressions, however, is beyond the scope of this book.

Eccentric Loads and Moments. Many columns are subjected not only to axial loads but to large bending moments as well (see Chapter 9). For short columns, ways of taking such moments into account have already been discussed in Section 7–3–1. The moment is simply expressed as $M = Pe$, and combined stresses are considered. For long columns, the Euler expression does not take into account such additional considerations. Again expressions are available for situations of this type, but are beyond the scope of this book.

7–4   DESIGN OF COMPRESSION MEMBERS

7–4–1   General Design Principles

Sections.   A general column design objective is to support the design loading by using the smallest amount of material, or, alternatively, by supporting the greatest amount of load with a given amount of material. Whenever the buckling phenomenon enters in, it is evident by looking at the buckling curves discussed in the previous section that the full strength potential of the material used in the compressive member is not being exploited to the maximum degree possible.

As was previously noted, the primary factor of importance in connection with buckling is the *slenderness ratio (L/r)* of a column. A low slenderness ratio means that the column is not prone to buckling. High ratios are not desirable. The most efficient use of material can be achieved by either minimizing the column length or maximizing the value of the radius of gyration for a given amount of material. Either or both will reduce the slenderness ratio of a member, and hence increase its load-carrying capabilities for a given amount of material. Most design techniques hinge around one or the other of these operations. Determining the required cross-sectional shape for a column intended to carry a given load is a task that is conceptually straight-forward. In most cases the objective is to find a cross section that provides the necessary r_x or r_y values by using the smallest amount of material in cross section as possible. The problem is similar to that of designing beams, where the objective is to find a section that provides the greatest moment of inertia for the smallest amount of material. In column design, the task is more complicated because of the need to consider radii of gyration about different axes. In general, however, an efficient column section is one that removes material as far from the centroidal axis of the column as is feasible. This, in turn, increases the moment of inertia I for the section for a given amount of material A. Consequently, the radius of gyration r is increased since $r = \sqrt{I/A}$. Increasing the r decreases the slenderness ratio L/r for a column, thus making it less susceptible to buckling. The techniques for optimizing moments of inertia discussed in Chapter 6 are also relevant in column design. Several cross sections that are based on this principle are illustrated in Figure 7–8.

FIGURE 7–8   Cross-sectional shapes for columns.

Bracing.   Column strengths may also be greatly improved by increasing the end restraints on a column. By changing from pinned to fixed connection, the load necessary to cause a member to buckle is greatly increased. It follows that if the intent is to support a specified load, a member with restrained ends will generally require less material volume to support the load than will one with unrestrained ends. The end conditions associated with the flagpole column illustrated in the right of Figure 7–5 are least desirable.

The choice of whether to use restrained ends, however, should be tempered by other considerations. Fixed joints are invariably more difficult and costly to make than pinned joints (this is particularly true when materials such as timber are used). If the joint were at the foundation, the foundation itself would have to be designed to provide restraint to rotation rather than simply receive axial forces. For relatively small columns, this usually does not require significant additional material or effort, but may do so as column sizes and loads increase.

One of the most common tools that the designer has available to increase the efficiency of compressive elements is that of bracing. The addition of bracing decreases the effective length of columns. The addition of bracing must be done with care, however, since quite often, if not done properly, no benefit is gained and even a loss is incurred due to the added material and effort expenditures in the bracing. Consider the columns shown in Figure 7–9. In these cases the addition of bracing does *not* increase the load-carrying capacity of any of the columns. As a result of either their symmetrical cross sections or relative I_x and I_y values, all would buckle in a mode associated

FIGURE 7–9   Ineffective use of bracing. Columns always buckle in the mode associated with the highest slenderness ratio (L/r). The columns shown will buckle as illustrated. The corresponding buckling loads relate to an unbraced or unsupported column length of L and are the same as if the columns were not braced at all. The bracing patterns shown are ineffective in increasing the load-carrying capability of the columns.

with their actual rather than braced lengths simply because of their higher slenderness ratios with respect to this direction. Buckling loads would be the same as if there were no bracing present at all. Evidently, if a symmetrical member is to be effectively braced, the bracing must be such as to reduce the slenderness ratios in all directions (by providing bracing in more than one plane).

A very effective type of bracing is illustrated in Figure 7–10(a). Here a symmetrical member is frequently braced in all directions at several points along its length. The ideal number of brace points is quite easy to determine. As previously discussed, for a member of a certain size and material, there exists a certain length that marks the transition between short- and long-column behavior. By putting in a sufficient number of brace points, it is possible to completely eliminate the possibility of buckling anywhere in the member. Consequently, the member could be sized for direct stresses only (i.e., $A = P/F_{\text{allowable}}$) and no premium (in terms of additional area) would be paid to prevent the possibility of buckling. The minimum number of brace points thus corresponds to making column lengths between brace points exactly equal to the transition length between short- and long-column behavior. Putting in more brace points than this does not accomplish anything more in terms of reducing required areas, because the column size is already governed by direct stresses.

In many situations it is not possible to use bracing in more than one plane. Columns are often used in walls, for example, where the wall can serve as lateral bracing in one plane but where no bracing can be provided in other planes for functional reasons. In situations of this type, nonsymmetrical members can often be usefully employed wherein the strong axis of the member is so organized to be associated with the possible out-of-braced-plane buckling mode and the weak axis with in-plane modes. When this is done, the properties of the column can be exactly related to the number and kind of brace points to achieve a high level of efficiency. This is done by creating a set of conditions such that the critical load associated with buckling about one axis is exactly equal to that associated with buckling about the other axis (i.e., $P_{cr_x} = P_{cr_y}$). Thus, $\pi^2 EI_x/L_{e_x}^2 = \pi^2 EI_y/L_{e_y}^2$; so $I_x/I_y = L_{e_x}^2/L_{e_y}^2$. Note that for a rectangular cross section, $I_x/I_y = (bd^3/12)/(db^3/12) = L_{e_x}^2/L_{e_y}^2$, or $d/b = L_{e_x}/L_{e_y}$. Hence, a column with a depth-to-width ratio of $3:1$ should have two symmetrically placed brace points (so that $L_{e_x} = 3L_{e_y}$).

When the proportion shown obtains, the member is equally likely to buckle in either direction. Evidently, either the member configuration (I_x and I_y) can be varied, or the effective member lengths (L_{e_x} and L_{e_y}) can be changed by bracing to achieve this proportion; or both may be varied simultaneously.

The general relationship $I_x/I_y = L_{e_x}^2/L_{e_y}^2$ can also be used to determine the appropriate number of brace points for a given column in which I_x/I_y is fixed. Instead of I_x/I_y ratios, use is often made of r_x/r_y ratios in actual practice. The concepts involved are similar except that now $f_{cr_x} = f_{cr_y}$ or $\pi^2 E/(L_x/r_x)^2 = \pi^2 E/(L_y/r_y)^2$. Hence, $r_x/r_y = L_x/L_y$.

Columns in a Building Context. The previous discussion tacitly assumed that there was no penalty involved in using as many brace points as necessary. On the other hand, the brace points themselves must be built. This, in turn, requires material volume. While bracing members can be quite small since the prevention of buckling requires little force, an expenditure of construction effort is still required to put them in place. If column design is placed in the context of a building, it is evident that trade-offs occur in which the objective of optimizing the complete column and bracing system rather than the column alone makes the most sense. Quite often it may be preferable to use fewer brace points and a slightly larger column.

(a) The load-carrying capacity of a symmetrical column can be increased to the maximum extent possible by putting in a sufficient number of brace points such that the effective length of the column is reduced to the point where short-column behavior obtains. Consequently, no portion of the column at all would be susceptible to buckling. The maximum load would be associated wtih crushing rather than buckling.

(b) When the plane of the bracing possible is fixed, the load-carrying capacity of a column of a given cross sectional area can be increased by varying the relative proportions of the cross section with the objective of making the column equally likely to buckle in any of its possible modes (i.e., making the slenderness ratios of the column similar in all directions). This occurs when the following ratios obtain:

$$I_x/I_y = (L_{e_x}/L_{e_y})^2 \text{ or } r_x/r_y = L_{e_x}/L_{e_y}$$

These ratios can be achieved by careful proportioning of the column cross section. When they are achieved,

$$P_{cr_x} = P_{cr_y}$$

FIGURE 7–10 Effective use of bracing.

317

Figure 7–11 illustrates a column in a wall of a simple industrial building. The wall is made by attaching vertical siding to horizontal elements, which in turn frame into the column. Clearly, either a greater or fewer number of horizontal elements (girts) could be used from those illustrated. Using more horizontal elements implies that the span of the siding, which functions as a vertical beam carrying wind loading, is reduced (and thus a lighter gage siding could be used). Similarly, the columns would be braced at more points on one plane. This, in turn, would influence the choice

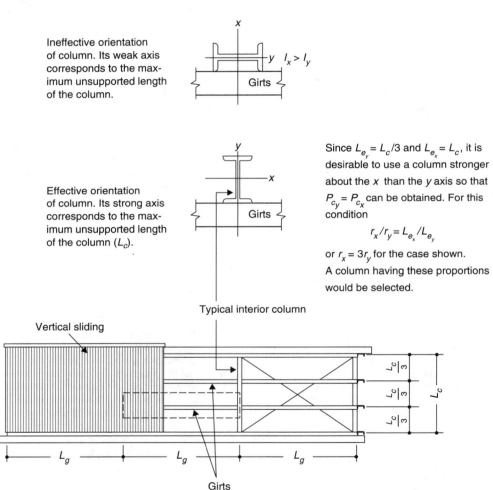

Ineffective orientation of column. Its weak axis corresponds to the maximum unsupported length of the column.

$I_x > I_y$

Girts

Effective orientation of column. Its strong axis corresponds to the maximum unsupported length of the column (L_c).

Girts

Since $L_{e_y} = L_c/3$ and $L_{e_x} = L_c$, it is desirable to use a column stronger about the x than the y axis so that $P_{c_y} = P_{c_x}$ can be obtained. For this condition

$$r_x/r_y = L_{e_x}/L_{e_y}$$

or $r_x = 3r_y$ for the case shown. A column having these proportions would be selected.

Typical interior column

Vertical sliding

Girts

L_g L_g L_g

$\frac{L_c}{3}$ $\frac{L_c}{3}$ $\frac{L_c}{3}$ L_c

The horizontal girts serve two functions: (1) To support the vertical siding which picks up wind loads. Consequently, the girts serve as beams having a span of L_g. The siding itself functions in beam fashion with a span of $L_c/3$. (2) To brace the column in one plane, thus reducing its effective length about the y axis to $L_c/3$. The effective length about the x axis remains L_c. The column itself carries both compressive loads from the roof and lateral forces from wind action transferred to it by the girts.

FIGURE 7–11   Small industrial building.

of the properties of the column itself. More horizontal elements are involved, however, and more construction difficulty. Using fewer horizontal elements increases the loads on the girts (hence their sizes), decreases the number of bracing points and increases the span of the siding, but tends to increase construction ease. Typically, the spacing of the horizontal elements is based on the optimum span for the most economic form of siding available. This, in turn, establishes where the column is braced. Column properties would be selected on the basis of these bracing points (i.e., an L_{e_x}/L_{e_y} ratio would be found and from this, an r_x/r_y ratio). A column with this r_x/r_y ratio would then be sized to carry the axial load involved. This example, it should be noted, implies that it is preferable to optimize the siding system rather than the column itself. This is often true in smaller buildings, but not necessarily always so. The larger the loads on the column, and the longer it is, the more important it is to pay attention to optimizing the column itself. There are invariably trade-offs involved, and each situation must be looked at individually.

7–4–2   Column Sizes

For columns made of elastic materials, design procedures are based on the Euler expression and crushing strengths with suitably incorporated factors of safety. Short columns may generally be designed on the basis of fixed allowable stress values. However, note that the concept of using a constant allowable stress value as a design basis is not applicable to long columns because of their sensitivity to length and specific section properties. The absolute value of the allowable stress that a column can experience depends on the length and properties of the column itself—variables that are in the actual allowable stress expressions for different materials. Design procedures for estimating column sizes are complicated since the allowable stress value cannot be known prior to selecting a column size; a frequently used design procedure is to estimate an allowable stress, size the column, use its dimensions to determine an appropriate allowable stress, and then check to see if the column is adequately sized for the specific conditions. The actual stress present is compared to the allowable stress calculated. If the actual exceeds the allowable, the process is repeated until the actual stress is less than the allowable stress. The following highlights some analysis and design approaches. Reference is made to other sources for a full treatment.[1]

7–4–3   Timber Columns

Allowable stress expressions for timber columns depend on their lengths. For *short columns* $F_{\text{allowable}} = F_{c\text{-max compression}}$, where the latter is adjusted for load duration, wet or dry conditions, and so on (see Section 6–4–2). *Intermediate-length columns* are defined as having an L/d ratio of greater than 11 but less than an empirically defined factor $\kappa = 0.67\sqrt{E/F_c}$. For intermediate-length columns, the allowable stress is $F'_c = F_c\{1 - (\frac{1}{3})[(L_e/d)/\kappa]^4\}$. *Long columns* are defined as having L/d ratios equal to or greater than κ but limited to 50. For a *long* timber column, the allowable stress can be obtained by dividing the critical buckling stress expression by a factor of safety: $F_{c\text{-allowable}} = \pi^2 E/(L_e/r)^2/(\text{safety factor})$. If the safety factor is taken as 2.73 and r values for rectangular sections $[r = \sqrt{I/A} = \sqrt{(bd^3/12)/bd}]$ are substituted, $F_{c\text{-allowable}} = 0.3E/(L_e/d)^2$.

---

[1] W. Scofield, *Modern Timber Engineering,* 3rd ed., Southern Pine Association, New Orleans, La., 1963; P.M. Ferguson, *Reinforced Concrete Fundamentals,* 3rd ed., John Wiley & Sons, Inc., New York, 1973; L. Beedle et al., *Structural Steel Design,* The Ronald Press Co., New York, 1964.

The *minimum* column dimension d would be used herein if the section is not square. End conditions are reflected through using the effective length L_e of the column ($L_e = kL$).

◆ ◆ **EXAMPLE**

Is a 4 × 4 in. (actual size) pin-ended timber column 10 ft (120 in.) high adequate to support an axial loading of 5000 lb? Assume that $E = 1.6 \times 10^6$ lb/in.^{2} and $F_{c\text{-max}} = 1500$ lb/in.^{2}

Solution:

Slenderness ratio:
$L/d = 120/4 = 30$ (which is greater than $\kappa = 0.67\sqrt{E/F_c} = 0.67\sqrt{1.6 \times 10^6/1500} = 22$, so the column is a *long* column).

Allowable stress possible on the column:
$$F_{\text{allowable}} = \frac{0.3E}{(L_e/d)^2} = \frac{0.3(1.6 \times 10^6)}{[1.0(120.0)/4.0]^2} = 533.3 \text{ lb/in.}^2$$

Actual stress:
$$f_{\text{actual}} = \frac{P}{A} = \frac{5000}{(4)(4)} = 312.5 \text{ lb/in.}^2$$

Since $f_{\text{actual}} = 312.5 < F_{c\text{-allowable}} = 533.3$ or $F_{c\text{-max compression}}$
$= 1500$ lb/in.^{2}, the column is adequately sized. ◆

7–4–4 Steel Columns

Ultimately, analysis and design expressions for steel columns are again based on the Euler expression, but they have been highly modified to reflect certain inelastic behaviors in steel members and, consequently, have an empirical basis as well. The Euler formula does not predict values for low slenderness ratios well, but it is more appropriate for larger ones. A variety of expressions for allowable stress values have been developed. For example, a typical allowable stress expression for the elastic design of *long columns* with slenderness ratios beyond a certain L_e/r (or kL/r) value takes the form $F_{\text{allowable}} = 12\pi^2 E/23(kL/r)^2$. This expression is obviously nothing more than the Euler critical stress expression with a factor of safety of (23/12). It is considered valid for columns when $kL/r > C_c$, where $C_c = (\sqrt{2\pi^2 E/F_y})/2$. The latter is derived empirically. Other more complicated expressions are used for shorter columns and more complicated loading and use situations. In general, kL/r ratios are commonly limited to 200 or less. End conditions are reflected through the k value.

A typical curve showing allowable stress values for steel members is shown in Figure 7–12. Practical steel design procedures recognize that columns are never perfectly straight and that small eccentricities occur.

An alternative ultimate strength approach for designing columns is based on the LRFD method (see Section 6–4–3).

◆ ◆ **EXAMPLE**

An unbraced pin-ended steel W 10 × 19 column 20 ft long carries a load of 15,000 lb. Assume A-36 steel and $r_x = 4.14$ in., $r_y = 2.14$ in., and $A = 5.62$ in.^{2} What is the maximum safe capacity of the member?

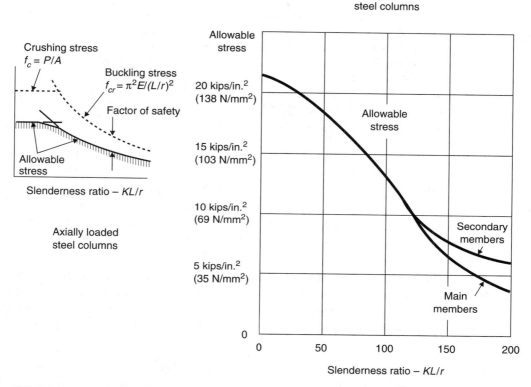

FIGURE 7-12   Typical allowable stress values for primary and secondary steel members in compression.

Solution:

Slenderness ratio:
$kL/r = (1.0)(20 \times 12)/2.14 = 112$. Since the column is unbraced, the minimum r is used and $k = 1.0$ since the column is pin-ended.

Allowable stress:
From Figure 7–12, $F_{\text{allowable}} = 11,300 \text{ lb/in.}^2$

Actual stress:
$$f = P/A = 15,000/5.62 = 2669 \text{ lb/in.}^2 < 11,300 \text{ lb/in.}^2$$

Hence, the member is adequately sized.

Maximum capacity:
$$P = F_{\text{allowable}} A = 63,506 \text{ lb}$$

◆

7–4–5 Reinforced Concrete Columns

Reinforced concrete columns are difficult to analyze and design because of the composite nature of the material, the complex state of stresses as a result of axial and bending loading, and the compressive axial load that may lead to buckling. So only general observations about reinforced concrete columns will be made herein. There are two primary kinds of reinforced concrete columns of interest: those that are spirally reinforced and usually round and those that are tied and usually rectangular in cross section. Both the spiral and the ties serve to contain the longitudinal reinforcement and prevent separation and buckling of the reinforcement itself. Spirally reinforced columns have a more desirable behavior near failure and in lateral loads than do those that are more simply tied, although the latter are usually cheaper and easier to construct. The different behaviors are reflected by the use of different ϕ values and other factors in *ultimate strength design* approaches commonly used to size columns. (See Section 6–4–4 for a general discussion of the ultimate strength design philosophy.)

Ductility. To ensure ductile behavior, the longitudinal reinforcing steel of concrete columns should not be less than 1% and not more than 8% of the gross area of the cross section. In practice, however, an upper limit of 4% makes the pouring of concrete easier, since the reinforcing steel is less dense.

Strength. In an axially loaded column, the applied load is shared between the concrete and the steel, which are expected to deform exactly the same amount since they are bonded together. The ultimate axial load-carrying capacity of a short column is normally taken to be $P_u = 0.85f'_c A_c + F_y A_s$, where A_c is the area of the concrete and A_s is the area of the steel (an *ultimate strength design* approach; see Chapter 6). The 0.85 factor reflects an uncertainty in the strength of concrete and the development of crushing zones. This expression does not reflect buckling phenomena or a bending moment. Reinforced concrete columns are almost invariably subject to bending as well as axial loads, as a result of loading conditions and connections with other members. For a particular column, an interaction curve showing the relative capacity of the column for different axial load and moment combinations may be developed (for a steel member, this curve would be a straight line since the material is linearly elastic). Axial load capacity is highest when the applied moment is zero (see the P versus M curve in Figure 7–8). Interestingly, moment capacity is highest when a small compressive load exists (since in it a smaller area of concrete is subject to tension). These curves depend on the precise layout of the cross section of a column. Tabular information provided by the American Concrete Institute or others is usually used to design columns in bending.

Long Columns/Buckling. The design of reinforced concrete columns, as given in the preceding paragraph, is based on the strength of the materials. The design process must be modified to include design for buckling only if the reinforced concrete column is defined as a long column. Short columns are not expected to buckle. The criteria for determining if a column is short or long include the slenderness ratio of the column, the type of its end supports, and its support against lateral movement. If there are elements in the structure other than the column that can provide the lateral support, the column is *braced* against lateral movement. Such elements are shear walls, elevator shafts, stairwells, and so on. A column is *unbraced* if this column and the other columns provide the lateral support of the building. Unbraced columns are more prone to buckling than braced columns, and this is quantified by establishing the appropriate checks. The bending moments for long columns are amplified according to the applicable codes and then the column is designed for strength criteria only.

QUESTIONS

7–1 An unbraced pin-ended square steel column has cross-sectional dimensions of 1.5 in. × 1.5 in. and is 20 ft long. What is the critical buckling load for this column? Assume that $E_s = 29.6 \times 10^6$ lb/in.^{2}
Answer: 2139 lb.

7–2 An unbraced pin-ended steel column has rectangular cross-sectional dimensions of 3 in. × 2 in. and is 25 ft long. What is the critical buckling load for this column? Assume that $E = 29.6 \times 10^6$ lb/in.^{2}

7–3 A pin-ended cylindrical steel column has a diameter of 20 mm and a length of 5 m. What is the critical buckling load for this column? Assume that $E_s = 204{,}000$ N/mm^2.
Answer: 632.5 N.

7–4 Assume that a pin-ended column of length L has a square cross section of dimensions $d_1 \times d_1$ and has a critical buckling load of P_1. What is the relative increase in load-carrying capacity if the cross-sectional dimensions of the column are doubled?

7–5 An unbraced steel column of rectangular cross section 1.5 in. × 2 in. and pinned at each end is subjected to an axial force. Assume that $F_y = 36{,}000$ lb/in.^{2} and $E = 29.6 \times 10^6$ lb/in.^{2} Find the transition point between short- and long-column behavior.

7–6 Compare the relative load-carrying capacity of a square column and a round column of equal lengths, similar end conditions, and identical cross-sectional areas. Which can carry the greater load? What is the ratio of the critical buckling loads found? Explain your answer in qualitative terms.

7–7 A pin-ended column of length L is to be braced about one axis at quarter points (i.e., there are three equally spaced bracing points). There is no bracing about the other axis. If a rectangular section of $b \times d$ dimensions is to be used, what is the most appropriate b/d ratio for maximizing the load-carrying capacity of the section? Assume that the dimension d corresponds to the strong axis of the section.

7–8 Using the same bracing and end conditions noted in Question 7–7, determine the most appropriate I_x/I_y ratio for a column having any cross-sectional shape. Also determine the most appropriate r_x/r_y ratio. Assume that I_x and r_x correspond to the strong axis of the section.

CHAPTER 8

Continuous Structures: Beams

8-1 INTRODUCTION

This chapter explores the analysis and design of beams that are continuous over several supports or have fixed ends (Figure 8–1). Mathematically, a statically indeterminate structure is one in which reactions, shears, and moments cannot be determined directly by applying the basic equations of statics ($\Sigma F_y = 0$, $\Sigma F_x = 0$, and $\Sigma M_o = 0$). Typically, there are more unknowns than there are equations available for solution. Another way of viewing this class of structures, which is of more intrinsic importance from a design viewpoint, is that in indeterminate structures the values of all reactions, shears, and moments are *dependent* on the physical characteristics of the cross section and the specific material used in the structure (and any variation with length), as well as the span and loading. This contrasts with statically determinate structures in which reactions, shears, and moments can be found through direct application of the basic equations of statics and, consequently, are *independent* of the shape of the cross section and the materials used (as well as any variations along the length of the member). Members having more than two points of support or with multiple fixed ends are typically indeterminate structures.

8-2 GENERAL PRINCIPLES

Two types of indeterminate structures are illustrated in Figure 8–2. The first [Figure 8–2(a)] is a continuous beam over three simple supports. Reactive forces are developed at each support. The

324

(a) Typical continuous beam structures.

Simple beams. A load on any one span causes curvatures and bending moments to develop in that span alone. No other span is affected. The only part of the total assembly playing a role in carrying the load is the member directly beneath the load.

Continuous beam. A load on any one span causes curvatures and bending moments to develop in all spans. Consequently all spans share in carrying the load on any one span. Member sizes can be smaller than those in a simply supported system since comparable design moments are smaller and rigidity greater.

Simple beams. Each beam deflects independently.

Continuous beams. Reverse curvatures are common. The system is typically stiffer (deflections are less) than in a simply supported system.

(b) General behavior of continuous beam structures.

FIGURE 8–1   Continuous versus simple beams and typical types of continuous beams.

magnitudes of these reactive forces cannot be found through the direct application of the basic equations of statics, since there are more unknown forces (R_A, R_B, and R_C) than there are independent equations ($\Sigma F_y = 0$ and $\Sigma M_o = 0$) that can be used to solve for these unknown reactions. The same is generally true for the fixed-ended beam illustrated in Figure 8–2(e). In this case there are four unknown reactions (R_A, R_B, M_A^F, and M_B^F) and fewer independent equations of statics ($\Sigma F_y = 0$ and $\Sigma M = 0$) available for use. Both of these beams are consequently termed *statically indeterminate*. Obviously, there is an added layer of difficulty involved in analyzing structures of this type.

Despite added analytical difficulties, however, indeterminate beams are frequently used in actual practice. One primary reason for this is that such structures generally tend to be more rigid under a given loading and span situation than do comparable determinate structures. Another reason for their extensive use is that the internal moments generated in the structure by the external loads are often smaller in magnitude than in comparable determinate structures. Consequently, member sizes can often be reduced. More efficient use is made of smaller amounts of

(a)

(e)

(b)

(f)

(c)

Effective length, L_e

Actual length

(g)

(h)

(d)

Actual length   Actual length

(i)

(a) Continuous beam over three supports.

(b) The beam is statically indeterminate, since there are three unknown reactions and only two independent equations of statics ($\Sigma F = 0$ and $\Sigma M = 0$).

(c) Deflected shape of beam. There are two points of inflection (where the beam undergoes a reversal in curvature) in this beam. These are also points of zero moment. The distance between points of zero moment is often called the "effective length" of the beam to create a direct comparison with a simply supported beam. The shorter the effective length, the smaller are the bending moments present. Consequently, the moments in the continuous beam are smaller than those in two comparable simply supported beams since its effective span length is shorter than its actual span length.

(d) In comparable simply supported statically determinate members, the effective length of a member is equal to its actual length.

(e) Fixed-ended beam.

(f) The beam is statically indeterminate, since there are four unknown reactions.

(g) Two points of inflection are developed in the beam. This makes its effective length much shorter than its actual length. Consequently the moments developed in the beam are smaller than those of a comparable simply supported beam. A fixed-ended beam is also far more rigid than a comparable simply supported beam.

(h) Deflections in a comparable simply supported beam are greater by a factor of four for this loading condition.

(i) The deflected shape of a simply supported beam can be transformed into that of a fixed-ended beam by applying rotational moments at each end. Doing this causes the midspan deflection of the member to decrease. The magnitudes of the rotational moments sufficient to twist the end tangents of the beam to a horizontal position correspond to the moments naturally developed as reactions in a fixed-ended beam.

326 **FIGURE 8–2** Behavior of simply supported versus continuous beams.

material. Disadvantages in structures of this type include their sensitivity to support settlements and thermal effects. Support settlements, for example, can cause undesirable bending moments to develop in continuous beams over several supports while not necessarily affecting a comparable series of simply supported beams.

8-2-1   Rigidity

The improved rigidity of beams having restrained ends or resting on several supports can be demonstrated through deflection studies. Using techniques discussed in Appendix 9, for example, it is possible to determine that the midspan deflection for a simply supported beam carrying a concentrated load at midspan is given by $\Delta = PL^3/48EI$ [see Figure 8–2(h)]. If the ends of the same beam were restrained by changing the nature of the support conditions to create fixed ends, the deflection at midspan would be given by $\Delta = PL^3/192EI$ [see Figure 8–2(g)]. Consequently, fixing the ends of the beam reduces maximum deflections by a factor of 4. This is an enormous difference. A careful look at the deflected shapes of the two members reveals the role of end fixity in increasing the rigidity of the structure under loadings [see Figure 8–2(h)]. Note that the deflection pattern associated with a fixed-ended beam can be obtained from that of a simply supported beam by applying a rotational moment at either end of the simply supported beam. The end of the beam can then be rotated until the tangent of the beam is exactly horizontal. Rotating the ends of the beam would, of course, cause the center of the beam to rise upward, thus causing the absolute midspan deflection of the member to decrease. The value of the moment corresponding to that needed to rotate the tangent of the beam to the horizontal corresponds to that naturally developed as a reaction, in this case, a fixed-ended moment, when the end of the member is initially restrained.

Similar observation could be made concerning the differences in rigidity between a beam resting on multiple supports as compared to a series of simply supported beams. The continuous structure is generally more rigid than its simply supported counterparts. In a design context this means that the continuous beam is often favored.

8-2-2   Force Distributions

The second reason why continuous or fixed-ended beams are frequently used in preference to simple beams is that the magnitudes of the internal shears and moments generated in the structure by the external force system are often smaller than those in simply supported beams. One way of visualizing why this is so is to think in terms of *effective* rather than actual beam lengths. With reference to the fixed-ended beam shown in Figure 8–2(e), for example, it is evident that the deflected shape of the beam between the two points of inflection (where the curvature of the beam changes sense) is quite similar to that of a simply supported beam of the type illustrated in Figure 8–2(h). The portion of the fixed-ended beam that is between the two points of inflection, which are also points of zero moment, can consequently be thought of as simply supported. The distance between the two points of inflection is termed the *effective length* of the fixed-ended member. The magnitude of the bending moment developed in this segment of the beam depends on this length as well as the value of the loading. The shorter the effective length, the smaller is the magnitude of the bending moment present, and vice versa. In a simply supported beam, the effective length of the beam is identical to its actual length. In a fixed-ended beam of identical actual length, the effective length is considerably less than the actual length. Thus, the midspan moment is smaller in the fixed-ended beam than in a comparable simply supported beam. It is evident, however, that bending moments are present in parts of the fixed-ended beam, at its ends, that are absent in the simply supported beam. This can be seen by looking at the deflected shapes of the two members and recalling that moments and beam curvatures are related. Fixing the ends of the beam changes not only the magnitude of the moments present in the structure but their distribution as well.

Thinking in terms of effective lengths is useful in analyzing any type of indeterminate structure. By sketching the probable deflected shape of a structure, the location of points of inflection can be estimated. Effective beam lengths can then be estimated. In the beam over three supports, illustrated in Figure 8–2(c), for example, points of inflection are developed as shown. The effective length of each span is less than the actual distance between support points. Consequently, moments in their middle portion of each span would be expected to be less than those present in two comparable simply supported beams whose effective lengths are identical to their actual lengths.

This way of looking at indeterminate structures is obviously similar to that described for columns in Chapter 7. It is important to note, however, that the points of inflection are induced by different types of loading. If compressive loads were applied to each end of the member over three supports illustrated in Figure 8–2(a), the member would certainly not buckle into a shape having two points of inflection, as illustrated in Figure 8–2(c), but would rather assume the shape of an *S*.

8–3 ANALYSIS OF INDETERMINATE BEAMS

8–3–1 Approximate Versus Exact Methods of Analysis

In the following sections we explore methods for determining reactions, shears, and moments in indeterminate structures. Over the years a number of different methods have been developed for analyzing indeterminate structures. Several elegant early techniques were based on "least work" theorems, such as that developed by Alberto Castigliano. This approach was based on an analysis of the internal elastic energy stored in various parts of a structure under a loading. The internal work performed can be shown to be the least possible necessary to maintain equilibrium in supporting the loading. "Deflection methods" of analysis were also introduced, in which sufficient supports were first conceptually removed to make the structure determinate and critical deflections were calculated. Forces required to push the structure back into its original shape were calculated. (This method is briefly illustrated in Appendix 10.) Another technique, called *moment distribution,* was introduced by Professor Hardy Cross. Based on successive cycles of computation that drew nearer and nearer to exact results, this technique was in wide use for many years. Most of these elegant approaches, however, have now been replaced by *matrix-displacement* techniques or various forms of *finite-element* techniques. These newer approaches, briefly discussed in Appendices 12, and 13, are particularly appropriate for use in a computer-based environment and have by now virtually replaced the older techniques noted here. The black-box character of these recent solution techniques, however, does little to help a student understand the characteristics of indeterminate structures and how better to design them. For this reason, the following discussion will focus more on approximate methods of analysis that convey a more physically based picture of how these complex structures work.

8-3-2   Approximate Methods of Analysis

While virtually all continuous beam analyses are now done via computer formulations, this section discusses a simplified method for determining the approximate values of reactions, shears, and moments in indeterminate structures as a way of understanding basic structural behaviors. The method is based on the concept of effective member lengths discussed in the preceding section. The method involves sketching the deflected shape of the structure, noting the location of points of inflection, and then using the condition that bending moments are known to be zero at points of inflection as a device for reducing the number of unknown reactions present. The accuracy of the method depends on the accuracy of the original sketch of the deflected shape of the structure. Experiments are useful. The method is primarily a conceptual way of understanding continuous beams rather than a practical analysis tool.

Consider the fixed-ended member illustrated in Figure 8–3(a). Through a careful sketch of the deflected shape, points of inflection can be estimated to be at the locations indicated. Since the internal moment is known to be zero at these points, the structure can be decomposed as illustrated in Figure 8–3(c). Each of these three pieces can now be treated as a statically determinate beam. The reactions for the center portion can be determined as indicated. These reactions then become loads on the cantilever elements shown. Vertical reactions and moments can then be found for these elements. Moment diagrams can also be drawn for each piece analyzed. The final moment diagram for the whole structure is a composite of individual diagrams.

The maximum bending moment developed in the structure, $M = wL^2/12$, occurs not at midspan but at the fixed ends. The midspan moment, $M = wL^2/24$, is only one-half of this value. The structure must be designed to carry these moments. A comparable simply supported beam has a midspan moment of $M = wL^2/8$. Consequently, fixing the ends of the member greatly reduces the maximum design moment as compared to the simply supported case. A substantial savings in materials is thus possible compared to the simply supported case because of these reduced design moments. It is interesting to observe that the sum of the absolute values of the positive and negative moments ($wL^2/12 + wL^2/24$) is equal to $wL^2/8$ (the same moment present at midspan in a simply supported beam carrying a uniformly distributed load). The moments the structure must be designed to carry at the ends and middle, however, are still those illustrated in Figure 8–3(d) ($wL^2/12$ and $wL^2/24$, respectively), and it is these moments that the beam would have to be sized to carry.

Figure 8–4 illustrates a similar analysis made for a beam with one end pinned and the other fixed. The approximate shape of the structure is sketched and the location of the point of inflection estimated. The structure is then decomposed into two determinate pieces. These pieces are analyzed and reactions, shears, and moments determined. The shear and moment diagrams for the whole structure are found by combining individual diagrams.

Figure 8–5 illustrates an analysis for a continuous beam over three supports. By carefully sketching the deflected shape of the structure under the loading shown, the member can be seen to have two points of inflection. These points are symmetrically located approximately $0.25L$ from the center support. The structure can then be decomposed for analytical purposes in the manner indicated in Figure 8–5(c). Each piece can then be treated as a determinate beam and appropriate reactions, shears, and moments found. The shear and moment diagrams for the actual structure are found by combining individual diagrams. With practice it is possible to sketch the moment diagrams of complex beams and from the sketches infer approximate values of moments.

(a) Statically indeterminate fixed-ended beam.

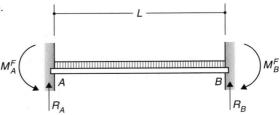

(b) Sketch of the deflected shape of the structure. Two points of inflection are developed at the approximate locations indicated. The locations of these points can be estimated from a consideration of the deflected shape of the structure or precisely calculated.

(c) The structure is decomposed into statically determinate pieces at the points of inflection. Moments for each statically determinate piece are calculated.

$$M_{\mathbb{C}} = wL_e^2/8 = w(0.6L)^2/8$$
$$\approx wL^2/24$$

$$M_B^F = (0.3wL)(0.2L)$$
$$+ (w)(0.2L)(0.2L)/2$$
$$\approx wL^2/12$$

(d) The moment diagram for the structure is a composite of the moment diagrams of the individual determinate pieces. The member must be designed to carry $wL^2/12$ and $wL^2/24$.

$M_{\mathbb{C}} \approx wL^2/24$

$M_T = wL^2/8$

$M_A^F \approx -wL^2/12$

$M_B^F \approx -wL^2/12$

FIGURE 8–3 Approximate analysis of a fixed-ended beam.

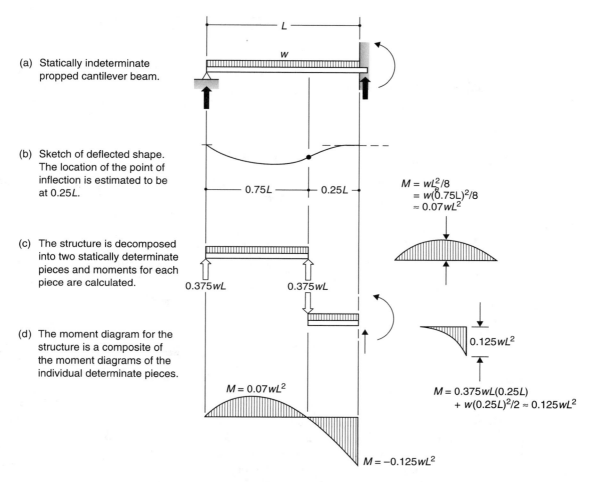

(a) Statically indeterminate propped cantilever beam.

(b) Sketch of deflected shape. The location of the point of inflection is estimated to be at 0.25L.

(c) The structure is decomposed into two statically determinate pieces and moments for each piece are calculated.

(d) The moment diagram for the structure is a composite of the moment diagrams of the individual determinate pieces.

$M = wL^2/8$
$= w(0.75L)^2/8$
$\approx 0.07wL^2$

$M = 0.375wL(0.25L)$
$\quad + w(0.25L)^2/2 \approx 0.125wL^2$

$M = 0.07wL^2$

$M = -0.125wL^2$

$0.125wL^2$

FIGURE 8–4   Approximate analysis of a propped cantilever beam.

8–3–3   Effects of Variations in Member Stiffness

In the opening of this chapter it was noted that one interpretation of why reactions, shears, and moments could not be found directly through application of the basic equations of statics was that these values are dependent on the exact geometrical cross section of the member used, its material characteristics, and any variation in either along the length of the structure. The analyses in the previous section were based on the assumption that the E and I of the member studied were constant along its length.

To study the effects of a member not having a constant E and I, it is useful to consider first two extreme cases of the fixed-ended beam analyzed in the previous section. The extreme cases involve assuming dramatic differences in the cross-sectional properties at different points in the beam. With respect to Figure 8–6(a), assume that at the ends of the member, either E or I (or

(a) Continuous beam.

(b) Sketch of deflected shape.

(c) Decomposition.

(d) Final shear and moment diagrams.

FIGURE 8–5 Approximate analysis of a beam continuous over three supports.

both) begin to be very small or approach zero. Both E and I, it will be recalled, are measures of the stiffness of the member. The modulus of elasticity, E, is a measure of stiffness as related to material. The smaller the value of E, the more flexible is the material (e.g., steel has a very high E and rubber has a very low E). The moment of inertia, I, is a measure of the amount and distribution of material at a cross section. The higher the I value, the stiffer is the section. The overall stiffness of a member at a cross section (i.e., its ability to resist deformations or rotations induced by the external load) depends on both parameters (EI). If either or both are low at a cross section, the stiffness of the member is low at that cross section.

When the whole member is loaded, the beam is more likely to undergo internal rotations at cross sections of lower stiffness than elsewhere. The capacity to resist rotation is smaller. If E and I actually approach zero at certain locations, the structure begins behaving (with respect to how it rotates) as if a pin connection were present. With respect to the fixed-ended beam, instead of points of inflection occurring at $0.2L$ from each end as they naturally did for a constant E and I member, the points of inflection occur at the locations of the drastically reduced E and I values. The deflected shape of the structure is influenced accordingly. By making the same type of analysis as was done for the beam with uniform cross section, the moment diagram illustrated in Figure 8–6(c) is obtained (this is obviously the same diagram as for a simply supported member). Alternatively, consider the behavior of the structure when it is assumed that the I or E value of the member becomes very small or approaches zero at the midpoint of the structure. Again, the

(a) Fixed-ended beam in which E or I approaches zero at each end of the beam.

(b) The reduced E or I at the ends reduces the capacity of the beam to resist rotations (induced by the loading) at these points. Consequently this causes points of inflection to be developed at these locations rather than further out toward the center as in a member with a constant E and I along its length.

(c) The changed location of the inflection points causes a change in the moment diagram. In this case the moment diagram is quite similar to that of a simply supported beam. A maximum moment of $wL^2/8$ is present.

(d) Fixed-ended beam in which E or I approaches zero at the center of the beam.

(e) The reduced E or I at the center causes a point of inflection to develop at this point.

(f) The member begins behaving quite like two cantilever beams, each of length $L/2$. The total moment diagram for the structure reflects this. Again a maximum moment of $wL^2/8$ is present.

(g) A fixed-ended beam with "haunches," or increased depths at each end.

(h) Since the beam is stiffer at either end than in the middle, the points of inflection tend to develop more toward the middle of the beam than they do in beams having a constant cross section.

(i) The movement of the points of inflection inward affects the moment diagram. Compared to a beam with a constant cross section, more moment is developed at the fixed ends and less at midspan. More moment was, so to speak, attracted to the ends by increasing member stiffnesses at these points. Note that the sum of the positive and negative moments remains $wL^2/8$. The total moment present has thus not been changed, only its distribution.

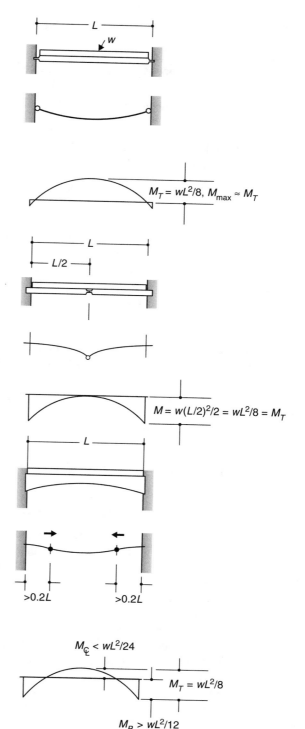

$M_T = wL^2/8, \; M_{max} \approx M_T$

$M = w(L/2)^2/2 = wL^2/8 = M_T$

$>0.2L \qquad >0.2L$

$M_{\mathbb{C}} < wL^2/24$

$M_T = wL^2/8$

$M_B > wL^2/12$

FIGURE 8–6 Effects of variations in member stiffness.

capacity of the structure to resist rotation is reduced at this point and the structure begins behaving as if a pin connection were present at this location. The resulting deflected shape and associated moment diagram are illustrated in Figure 8–6(e) and (f), respectively. Again note that the total moment present is $wL^2/8$.

Instead of extreme cases, consider the behavior of the structure if the ends are made stiffer than the central portion of the beam (often referred to as *haunching* the member). In sketching the deflected shape of the member, it is evident that by making the beam stiffer at the ends, the member is better able to resist rotation at these locations. The net effect is to cause the points of inflection to move more toward the center of the beam relative to their location in a beam with uniform cross section throughout. The exact location of these points can only be estimated at this stage. The net effect, however, of these points moving inward is to increase the magnitude of the moment present at the ends of the member and to reduce that present at the central portion of the member.

These examples generally illustrate why the internal moments in an indeterminate structure are dependent on the properties of the cross section and their variation along the length of the member. Note that the net effect of increasing the size of the member at a particular location (relative to other parts of the structure) was to increase the magnitude of the moment present at that point. Conversely, reducing the capacity of a member at a particular point resulted in a reduction in the moment present at the point. Moment was, so to speak, attracted by the stiffer portions of the member. This is a point of fundamental interest from a design viewpoint.

In all the variations just discussed, the sum of the positive and negative moments was always $wL^2/8$. The appearance of a constant total is of interest. The effect of end fixity and variations in E and I was to alter the way this total moment was distributed and carried by the beam, but the total moment associated with a simply supported beam remained present. The change in distribution, however, was advantageous since the actual moments the member should be sized to carry, of course, are the positive and negative moments themselves (each less than $wL^2/8$), which make up the total of $wL^2/8$.

8–3–4 Effects of Support Settlements

Continuous or fixed-ended beams are quite sensitive to support settlements. Support settlements can occur for a variety of reasons with the most common being consolidation of the soil beneath a support. The larger the load on the soil, the more likely is consolidation to occur. Rarely is the amount of settlement exactly the same beneath all support points on a structure. If this were so, the whole structure would simply translate vertically downward and consequently cause no distress in the structure. The more usual case of differential settlement, however, can potentially cause undesirable bending moments to develop in continuous and fixed-ended structures.

Consider the fixed-ended beam illustrated in Figure 8–7. The beam is not loaded with any external force. Assume that a differential settlement of an amount Δ occurs. When one support simply translates with respect to the other, the fixed-ended nature of the support still restrains the end of the beam from rotating. The net effect is that curvatures are developed in the beam. Associated with these curvatures are internal bending moments. Clearly, the greater the differential settlement, the greater are the internal bending moments developed in the structure. This behavior is in obvious contrast to that of a simply supported beam. As differential settlement occurs under a simply supported beam, the member simply follows along. Since the ends of the member

(a) Support settlements in a simply supported structure often cause no bending moments to develop in the structure since it simply rotates freely as it settles.

(b) Support settlements in a fixed-ended structure cause undesirable bending moments to be developed.

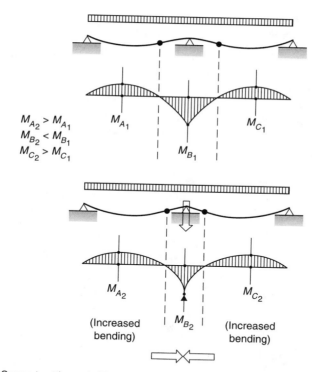

$M_{A_2} > M_{A_1}$
$M_{B_2} < M_{B_1}$
$M_{C_2} > M_{C_1}$

(c) Support settlements in continuous beams can cause increased bending moments to develop at different locations in the structure over those normally associated with the loading. Downward settlement of middle support causes points of inflection to move inward, thus increasing the positive moment present. The reaction at the beam ends also increases (that at the middle support decreases).

FIGURE 8–7   Effects of support settlements.

are unrestrained, the whole member simply rotates when the settlement occurs. The differential settlement does not cause curvature, hence bending moments, to develop in simply supported members. For this reason, simple support conditions are often preferable to rigid ones when problems with support settlement are anticipated.

Settlements also affect beams that are continuous over several supports. Consider the beam illustrated in Figure 8–7(c). If differential settlements of the type illustrated occurred, curvature and associated bending moments could potentially be induced in the beam. If settlements occur when the beam is fully loaded, the support settlement causes a change in the moment distribution present in the structure. The general effect of the center support settling relative to the two end supports, for example, is to cause the points of inflection to move inward toward the center support. This, in turn, increases the effective lengths of the end spans, thus causing an increase in the positive moment present in the member. Clearly, if the member is not sufficiently sized to carry this increased moment, the member could potentially fail or become seriously overstressed.

8–3–5 Effects of Partial-Loading Conditions

One of the more interesting aspects of the behavior of indeterminate structures under load is illustrated to the right in Figure 8–8. A typical indeterminate beam over four supports is shown carrying three different sets of loads. The structure is shown under full-loading conditions, in which all three spans of the structure are similarly loaded. Two different partial-loading conditions are illustrated in which one span is not loaded at all. These different conditions reflect different load patterns that might exist on the structure at one time or another. These figures also show the moments found from a rigorous analysis made using one of the methods discussed in Appendix 10 or 12.

When different locations on the structure are considered (e.g., at midspan to the left and over the first support), it is evident that each loading condition produces a different moment at each of the respective locations. An inspection of the moments associated with the three loadings shown reveals some seemingly curious results. The maximum midspan positive moment in the first span does *not* occur when the structure is fully loaded but rather under a partial-loading condition. Neither does the maximum negative moment over the first support occur when the structure is fully loaded but also rather under a partial-loading condition. In no case does the maximum moment at a point result from a full-loading condition. A partial-loading condition always produces the critical design moment. Similarly, no one partial-loading condition simultaneously produces the critical maximum moment at all locations.

The curvature of the member, hence the bending moment present, at a location is affected by loads placed *anywhere* on the structure. With respect to positive moments in the first span, for example, a load on span 1–2 causes a positive curvature and bending moment to develop. If span 3–4 is also loaded, the resultant effect is to further increase the curvature and, consequently, the positive moment in the first span. A more critical moment is thus produced than when the first span alone is loaded [see Figure 8–9(a)]. Note that loading the middle span, however, tends to cause the left span to rise upward. The effect of the rise is to decrease the curvature and bending moment in the first span. This loading condition thus produces a less critical moment than the partial-loading condition previously considered. Similar arguments could be made about other locations.

Beam with fixed ends: uniform loading

$$R=V=\frac{wL}{2}$$
$$M_{max}=\frac{wL^2}{12}$$
$$M_1=\frac{wL^2}{24}$$
$$\Delta=\frac{wL^4}{384EI}$$

Continuous beam—two equal spans: concentrated load at center of one span

$$R_1=V_1=\frac{13}{32}P \qquad M_{max}=\frac{13}{64}PL$$
$$R_2=V_2+V_3=\frac{11}{16}P \qquad M_1=\frac{3}{32}PL$$
$$R_3=V_3=\frac{3}{32}P$$
$$\Delta_{max}(0.480L\text{ from }R_1)=0.015\frac{PL^3}{EI}$$

Continuous beam—three equal spans: two adjacent spans uniformly loaded (highest moment over interior support)

$$R_1=0.383wL \qquad V_1=0.383wL \qquad M_1=0.0735wL^2$$
$$R_2=1.20wL \qquad V_2=0.617wL \qquad M_2=0.1167wL^2$$
$$R_3=0.450wL \qquad V_3=0.583wL \qquad M_3=0.0534wL^2$$
$$R_4=0.033wL \qquad V_4=0.417wL \qquad M_4=0.0333wL^2$$
$$\qquad\quad V_5=0.033wL$$
$$\Delta_{max}(0.430L\text{ from }R_1)=0.0059\frac{wL^4}{EI}$$

Beam with fixed ends: concentrated load

$$R=V=\frac{P}{2}$$
$$M_{max}=\frac{PL}{8}$$
$$\Delta=\frac{wL^3}{192EI}$$

Continuous beam—two equal spans: concentrated loading on one span

$$R_1=V_1=\frac{Pb}{4L^3}[4L^2-a(L+a)] \qquad M_{max}=\frac{Pab}{4L^3}[4L^2-a(L+a)]$$
$$R_3=V_3=\frac{Pab}{4L^3}(L+a) \qquad M_1=\frac{Pab}{4L^2}(L+a)$$
$$V_2=\frac{Pa}{4L^3}[4L^2+b(L+a)]$$

Continuous beam—three equal spans: end spans uniformly loaded

$$R_1=0.450wL \qquad V_1=0.450wL \qquad M_1=0.1013wL^2$$
$$R_2=0.550wL \qquad V_2=0.550wL \qquad M_2=0.050wL^2$$
$$R_3=0.550wL \qquad V_3=0.550wL \qquad M_3=0.1013wL^2$$
$$R_4=0.450wL \qquad V_4=0.450wL$$
$$\Delta_{max}(0.479L\text{ from }R_1\text{ or }R_4)=0.0099\frac{wL^4}{EI}$$

Beam fixed at one end and simply supported at other: concentrated load

$$R_1=V_1=\frac{5P}{16}$$
$$R_2=V_{2max}=\frac{11P}{16}$$
$$M_{max}=\frac{3PL}{16}$$
$$M_1=\frac{5PL}{32}$$
$$\Delta=0.0093\frac{PL^3}{EI}$$

Continuous beam—two equal spans: uniform loading on one span

$$R_1=V_1=\frac{7}{16}wL \qquad M_{max}=\frac{49}{512}wL^2$$
$$R_3=V_3=\frac{1}{16}wL \qquad M_1=\frac{1}{16}wL^2$$
$$V_2=\frac{9}{16}wL$$
$$\Delta_{max}(0.472L\text{ from }R_1)=0.0092\frac{wL^4}{EI}$$

Continuous beam—three equal spans: all spans loaded

$$R_1=0.400wL \qquad V_1=0.400wL \qquad M_1=0.080wL^2$$
$$R_2=1.10wL \qquad V_2=0.600wL \qquad M_2=0.100wL^2$$
$$R_3=1.10wL \qquad V_3=0.500wL \qquad M_3=0.025wL^2$$
$$R_4=0.400wL \qquad V_4=0.500wL \qquad M_4=0.100wL^2$$
$$\qquad\quad V_5=0.600wL \qquad M_5=0.080wL^2$$
$$\qquad\quad V_6=0.400wL$$
$$\Delta_{max}(0.466L\text{ from }R_1\text{ or }R_4)=0.0069\frac{wL^4}{EI}$$

FIGURE 8–8 Shears and bending moments in common continuous structures for different loading conditions.

(a) Loadings on span 1–2 and span 3–4 tend to increase the curvature at *A*. Increasing the curvature means that the moment in the beam is also increased. Therefore, loadings on both 1–2 and 3–4 contribute to the development of positive moment at *A*.

(b) Loading span 2–3 would cause a decrease in positive curvature at *A*, thus tending to decrease the positive moment there. Therefore, this span should not be loaded to develop maximum moment at *A*.

FIGURE 8–9 Critical loading conditions in continuous beams.

Loadings that produce maximum moments of the type discussed above are called *critical loading conditions*. There are several formal techniques for establishing what loading conditions are critical on a structure. Going into these techniques in detail, however, is beyond the scope of this book.

8–4 DESIGN OF INDETERMINATE BEAMS

8–4–1 Introduction

The process of designing a continuous beam is not unlike that of designing a simple beam. Once the value of the maximum moment that can be present under any loading is known, the process of determining the required member size at that point is straightforward. The process for doing this is identical to that already discussed in Section 6–4 in connection with simple beams. All the techniques for member sizing discussed there are appropriate for continuous beams as well. Principles concerning how best to optimally distribute material at a cross section are similarly applicable. This section, therefore, addresses only those general issues that are unique to the design of continuous beams.

8–4–2 Design Moments

Of particular importance in the design of continuous beams is to assure that the member is sized to account for the moments associated with all possible loading conditions. The discussion in Section 8–3–5 is particularly relevant here. There it was noted that the maximum moment that could be developed at any particular point in the structure rarely, if at all, resulted when the structure was fully loaded but typically occurred when the structure was only partially loaded. It should be noted, however, that both maximum positive and maximum negative moments conditions occur with full load on the span under consideration. The question of the effects of partial loads relates primarily to loading on adjacent spans. From a design viewpoint, it is therefore necessary to consider all the possible variants of the loading that might exist on a structure and to determine the moments produced by each of these loadings at all points in the structure. Some loadings will produce higher moments at certain locations than others. The size of the structure at any specific point would be based on the critical loading, which produces the maximum possible moment at that point. Other points would be based on maximum moments associated with other loads critical for those points. Consequently, under any one loading condition the structure would be somewhat oversized everywhere except where the critical moment associated with that loading condition exists.

In complex situations, determining appropriate design moments for the different critical points in a structure can obviously be tedious. For commonly encountered situations, appropriate design moments have been tabulated. For two or more approximately equal spans (the larger of the two adjacent spans not exceeding the smaller by more than 20%) carrying uniformly distributed loads in which the live load does not exceed the dead load by more than a factor of 3, the shears and moments listed in Table 8–1 are reasonable for rough design purposes. More rigorous analyses must be made for unusual situations.

While of obvious importance, the following discussions will not further consider the effects of partial loadings in detail and the actual need to design a structure for a variety of loading conditions. Rather, the discussion will focus on shaping the structure in response to its primary design loading condition. Quite often the effects of partial loadings in structures used in buildings are taken into account after the structure is initially shaped for its primary loading.

Table 8–1   TYPICAL DESIGN
MOMENTS

Positive moment	
End spans	
If discontinuous end is unrestrained	$\frac{1}{11}wL^2$
If discontinuous end is integral with the support	$\frac{1}{14}wL^2$
Interior spans	$\frac{1}{16}wL^2$
Negative moment at exterior face of first interior support	
Two spans	$\frac{1}{9}wL^2$
More than two spans	$\frac{1}{10}wL^2$
Negative moment at other faces of interior supports	$\frac{1}{11}wL^2$
Negative moment at face of all supports for (a) slabs with spans not exceeding 10 ft, and (b) beams and girders where ratio of sum of column stiffness to beam stiffness exceeds eight at each end of the span	$\frac{1}{12}wL^2$
Negative moment at interior faces of exterior supports for members built integrally with their supports	
Where the support is a spandrel beam or girder	$\frac{1}{24}wL^2$
Where the support is a column	$\frac{1}{16}wL^2$
Shear in end members at first interior support	$1.15\dfrac{wL}{2}$
Shear at all other supports	$\dfrac{wL}{2}$

8-4-3 Shaping Continuous Beams

The size of the cross section at a point of a continuous beam depends on the magnitude of the moment present at that point. There is a wide variation in the way moments are distributed in a continuous structure. The structure could be sized for the absolute maximum moment present anywhere in the structure and the same size simply used throughout [Figure 8–10(c)]. This is often done in building structures as a matter of construction convenience.

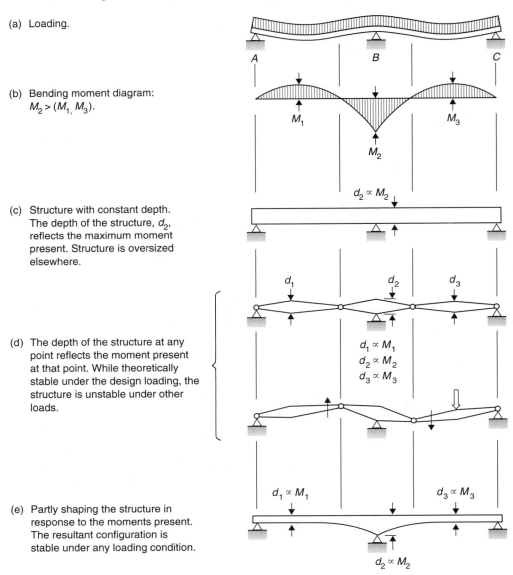

(a) Loading.

(b) Bending moment diagram:
$M_2 > (M_1, M_3)$.

(c) Structure with constant depth. The depth of the structure, d_2, reflects the maximum moment present. Structure is oversized elsewhere.

(d) The depth of the structure at any point reflects the moment present at that point. While theoretically stable under the design loading, the structure is unstable under other loads.

$d_1 \propto M_1$
$d_2 \propto M_2$
$d_3 \propto M_3$

(e) Partly shaping the structure in response to the moments present. The resultant configuration is stable under any loading condition.

$d_1 \propto M_1$

$d_3 \propto M_3$

$d_2 \propto M_2$

FIGURE 8–10 Alternative strategies for designing a continuous structure.

Alternatively, the size of the structure could be varied along its length in response to the moments actually present in the structure. Techniques for doing this have already been generally discussed in connection with simple beams (see Section 6–4–2). Shaping members is fairly frequently done in connection with highway bridge design when the possible material savings overshadow the added construction difficulties.

The issues involved in shaping a beam along its length are relatively straightforward, with one major exception. Consider the continuous beam illustrated in Figure 8–10. If the member depth were designed to be dependent on the magnitude of the moment present at a point and *no* deviations were allowed to this relation, a structure having roughly the configuration illustrated in Figure 8–10(d) would result. Clearly, where there are points of inflection, there is no moment in the structure, and its depth consequently can approach zero (if shear forces are ignored). Actually doing this, of course, is absurd. The resultant structure is not a configuration that is stable under any other than the exact loading condition illustrated. Any slight deviation in the loading (which is, of course, bound to occur) would cause immediate collapse. A reasonable alternative, however, is to design the structure to reflect maximum positive and negative moment values and simply ignore the points of inflection. When this is done, and the structure also designed for the shear forces present, a configuration of the general type illustrated in Figure 8–10(e) results. This configuration is frequently used as a practical structure, particularly in steel highway bridges.

Even if the effects of partial loadings are considered, the shape illustrated in Figure 8–10(e) is reasonably appropriate unless the live load/dead load ratio is very high. Figure 8–11 shows several examples of shaped beam and truss structures.

The *exact* shape of a member as it varies from points of maximum positive and negative moments depends on the choice of structure used. The exact optimum shape for a truss structure for a given moment variation differs from the optimum shape for a solid rectangular beam (see Chapters 4 and 6). Other beam cross sections (e.g., wide-flange shapes) would result in different variations of depth with moment. For this reason, the shapes sketched showing possible variations of depth with moment are diagrammatic only.

FIGURE 8–11   Common shapes for continuous structures in which the depth of the structure is partly shaped to reflect the bending moment present.

8-4-4 Use of Pinned Joints

Because of construction difficulties, it is often difficult to make a long continuous member out of one piece and it is desired to introduce pinned or different types of construction joints. Figure 8–12 illustrates the use of construction joints in a beam continuous over three spans but constructed of several pieces. To simplify the making of the joint and thus the connection between discrete pieces making up the total span, the joints are placed at or near points of inflection. Consequently, the joints need carry no moment and are sometimes designed as simple pinned connections. This type of connection is much easier to design and fabricate than rigid joints that can carry moment.

In the beam illustrated there are four points of inflection. Pinned construction joints, however, cannot be placed at each point of inflection, since this could result in a structure that would be unstable if the loading changed. Pinned construction joints can only be used when the resulting structural configuration is stable. For the beam illustrated in Figure 8–12(a), there are two basic ways of doing this. The first is by putting joints in the end spans, leaving a center span with two cantilever ends. The structure would be built by putting this center span in place first and then adding the end pieces. Alternatively, the joints could be placed in the middle span, leaving two stable beams with single cantilevers. The structure would be built by first putting in place the two end members and then adding the center piece. In either case the structure is converted into an assembly of statically determinate structures which function together in a way that *reflects* the behavior of a continuous member.

The advantage of using pinned construction joints occurs when the behavior of a continuous member can be exactly reflected. Pinned construction joints are most effectively used when the design loading, in this case a uniformly distributed load over the full structure, is expected to remain the primary loading. If loading conditions change from primary design loadings, these structures would still behave as assemblies of determinate structures but would *not* reflect the behavior of a continuous member and thus would not possess the implied advantages. For this reason, rigid rather than pinned construction joints are often used.

The general technique illustrated in Figure 8–12(e) is often coupled with a shaping of the structure in response to the extreme positive and negative moments present [Figure 8–12(f)]. Many large bridge structures reflect this general approach. In structures of this type the dead load typically is the primary design load and far exceeds in magnitude the variable live load.

8-4-5 Controlling Moment Distributions

The moments developed in a continuous and fixed-ended member can be affected to a significant degree by decisions made by the designer. This can occur in several ways. One way is through simply paying careful attention to the spans and loadings involved. Often, by not using identical span lengths, the moment distribution can be affected in an advantageous way. As discussed in Section 6–4, the use of cantilevers on the ends of beams is often desirable, particularly as a device for reducing positive moments on end spans. Deflections are also reduced by using end cantilevers.

Another way of controlling moment distributions in an advantageous way is through the use of construction joints. In the preceding section the use of such joints at the locations of point of inflection was discussed. Obviously, pinned construction joints could be put anywhere and automatically cause a point of zero bending moment to develop at that point in the structure rather

(a) Loading.

(b) Moment diagram.

(c) Use of construction joints (typically pinned connections) at each point of inflection. The resultant structure is unstable when partially loaded. Rigid construction joints capable of carrying some moment could be used to achieve stability. Otherwise, one of the options shown below must be adopted.

(d) Use of construction joints in end span only. The resultant configuration is stable under any loading. The joints facilitate construction. The center span would be put in place followed by the end spans.

(e) Use of construction in middle span. Again the resultant structure is stable under any loading. The end spans would be put in place first followed by the middle span.

(f) Use of construction joints in middle span coupled with shaping of structure to reflect moments present.

FIGURE 8–12   Use of construction joints in continuous members. Construction joints often facilitate construction. Creating a condition of zero moment by design at points of inflection models the behavior of a continuous member by a series of statically determinate members.

than where they would naturally occur. By locating such pin connections carefully, it is possible to reduce design moments.

Consider the fixed-ended beam previously analyzed (Figure 8–13). The moments naturally developed are $wL^2/12$ at the beam ends and $wL^2/24$ at the beam midspan. Points of inflection occur naturally at $0.21L$ from each end. While the maximum design moment of $wL^2/12$ is considerably less than the $wL^2/8$ associated with a comparable simply supported span, it is possible to reduce the design moment to an even smaller value by inserting pin connections at points nearer the ends than where the inflection points naturally develop. Doing this would increase the effective span of the midsection (increasing the positive moment) and decrease the effective length of the end cantilever portions (decreasing the negative moment). Indeed, the maximum positive moment can be made exactly equal to the maximum negative moment by placing the pin connections at $0.15L$. As before, the total moment (the absolute sum of maximum positive and negative moments) remains $wL^2/8$. By forcing the positive and negative moments to become equal, design moments are reduced to $wL^2/16$ for each. This maximum design moment is considerably less than that associated with the unaltered fixed-ended member. Member sizes are reduced.

Insertion of pins at locations other than inflections points does, however, have other consequences. One is that there is no longer a smooth curve between regions of positive and negative moments as occurs at a natural point of inflection or when a pin is located exactly at such a point. Rather, a discontinuity is developed due to different end rotations of the midspan and cantilever portions of the member. If the magnitude of this discontinuity is large, it could potentially cause problems if the beam is used in a building context. If a roof area was directly over the beam, for example, the sharp discontinuity could cause cracking, hence leaking, in the roof. This is typically not a problem when such discontinuities are not present and the reversal in curvature is smooth.

Another example of locating pins to control moments is illustrated in Figure 8–13(c). By carefully locating pins, positive and negative moments can be made approximately equal, thus minimizing the maximum design moment present. Again, discontinuities in curvatures occur at pin locations when they are moved from the natural points of inflection.

8–4–6 Continuous Beams Made of Reinforced Concrete

Reinforced concrete is a particularly suitable medium with which to construct continuous beams. Continuity is achieved by the way the reinforcing is arranged.

Figure 8–14 illustrates the reinforcing pattern for a two-span continuous beam. Reinforcing steel is put into regions where tension stresses would normally develop. The amount of steel used at a particular location depends on the magnitude of the moment present.

Continuous beams can also be post-tensioned or prestressed. Figure 8–14(d) illustrates how a post-tensioning cable would be draped to be effective for the type of moments present. Post-tensioning is frequently done. It is, however, difficult to prestress a continuous beam. The nature of the prestressing process is such that getting reverse curvatures in the prestressing strands is difficult. Since prestressing is most normally done in a factory circumstance (although not absolutely necessary), there is the added difficulty of transportation (i.e., a beam to be used over three supports would have to be transported with similar support conditions to keep moments in undesirable locations from developing). Prestressed beams are more normally used in simple support conditions.

(a) Fixed-ended beam. Deflected shape and moments developed naturally.

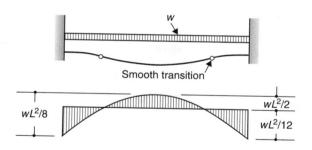

Smooth transition

$wL^2/8$

$wL^2/2$

$wL^2/12$

(b) By putting in pinned connections (points of known zero moment) at locations other than where the points would naturally develop, the maximum design moment in the structure can be reduced from $wL^2/12$ to $wL^2/16$. Material savings can therefore be accomplished.

A consequence of not locating the pinned connections at the locations where points of inflection would naturally develop is that a discontinuity in the defected shape of the member develops. This can be a disadvantage.

Construction joint (pin connection)

Angular discontinuity— angle of tangent to end of center portion does not equal that of the end of the cantilever

0.15L   0.7L   0.15L

w

0.35wL   0.35wL

$\dfrac{wL^2}{8}$

$wL^2/16$

$wL^2/16$

(c) Moments in structures continuous over several supports can also be controlled by carefully locating pinned connections. Again discontinuities in the deflected shape of the member would develop at the pins. By carefully locating construction joints (or pinned connections) and varying span lengths and overhangs, maximum positive and negative moments throughout the member can be made approximately equal.

FIGURE 8–13 Controlling moment distributions by controlling the location of construction joints (pinned connections).

(a) Loading.

(b) Moment diagram.

(c) Reinforced concrete beam.
Reinforcing steel is placed in
tension regions.

(d) Post-tensioned beam. Cable is
draped to reflect moments
present.

FIGURE 8–14 Use of reinforced concrete for continuous members.

QUESTIONS

8–1 Investigate several multiple-span steel girder highway bridges in your local area, preferably including one that uses shaped elements. Make careful sketches of the shapes and the locations of any construction joints of the type discussed in Section 8–4–4. Discuss your findings.

8–2 A beam that is pinned on one end and fixed at the other end carries a concentrated load of P at midspan ($x = L/2$). Using an approximate method of analysis, estimate the reactions, shears, and moments present in the structure.

8–3 Using the expressions suggested in Section 8–4–2, determine the design moments for a three-span beam that is continuous over four supports (ends are integral with column supports). Determine the critical design positive and negative moments for each span. Assume that the structure carries a uniformly distributed load of 300 lb/ft and that each span is 30 ft.

8–4 Consider the two-span continuous beam illustrated in Figure 8–5. How would you expect the moment diagram to change if the right support began settling vertically downward with respect to the other two supports?

8–5 Using a computer-based structural analysis program, determine reactions, shears and bending moments for a continuous beam with two spans of equal 50 foot lengths and carrying a uniformly distributed load of 1000 lb/ft. over the whole structure. Note: You will probably have to specify a trial member size. Use the same member size for both beams.

8–6 Using a computer-based structural analysis program, determine reactions, shears, and bending moments for a three span continuous beam of equal 50 foot lengths for each segment and carrying a uniformly distributed load of 1000 lb/ft over the whole structure.

8–7 Repeat Question 8–6, but use a member size for the middle beam segment that has at least three times the moment of inertia of the two end segments. Compare your results to those found in Question 8–6. Discuss.

CHAPTER 9

Continuous Structures: Rigid Frames

9–1 INTRODUCTION

A *rigid frame* structure is one made up of linear elements, typically beams and columns, that are connected to one another at their ends with joints that do not allow any relative rotations to occur between the ends of the attached members, although the joints themselves may rotate as a unit. Members are essentially continuous through the joints. As with continuous beams, rigid frame structures are statically indeterminate.

Many rigid frame structures resemble in appearance simpler post-and-beam systems but are radically different in structural behavior, owing to the joint rigidity. The joint rigidity can be sufficient to enable a framed structure to carry significant lateral loads, something a simpler post-and-beam system cannot do without additional bracing elements. Variants of rigid frame structures have been in use for a long time. A common table, for example, typically derives its stability from the rigid joints that are used to connect the legs to the table top. The traditional knee-braced timber structure can also be thought of as a type of rigid frame structure. Still, the rigid frame as a widely used structural device in major buildings is a relatively recent phenomenon. The development of the steel rigid frame in cities such as Chicago during the latter part of the nineteenth and early part of the twentieth centuries is a major event in the history of structures. The related movement made possible by the introduction of the rigid frame of separating and differentiating enclosure surfaces from the supporting structural skeleton also marks a major turning point in the history of architecture. This movement was a marked departure from

348

traditional building practices which made extensive use of dual functioning elements, such as the exterior load-bearing wall, that served simultaneously as both structure and enclosure.

9–2 GENERAL PRINCIPLES

A useful way to understand how a simple framed structure works is to compare and contrast its behavior under load with a post-and-beam structure that is identical in all respects except that members in the post-and-beam structure are not rigidly connected as they are in the framed structure (see Figure 9–1).

Vertical Loads.   A vertical load on a post-and-beam structure is picked up by the horizontal beam and is transferred by bending to the columns, which in turn carry the load to the ground. The beam is typically simply supported and merely rests on top of the columns. Consequently, as the vertical load causes bending to develop in the beam, the ends of the beam rotate on the tops of the columns. The angle formed between the beam and a column thus changes slightly with increasing loads on the beam. The columns do not in any way restrain the ends of the beam from rotating. No moment is transferred to the columns since the beam rotates freely. The columns carry only axial forces.

When a rigid frame structure is subjected to a vertical load, the load is again picked up by the beam and is eventually transferred through the columns to the ground. The load again tends to cause the ends of the beam to rotate. In the frame, however, the column tops and beam ends are rigidly connected. Free rotation at the end of the beam cannot occur. The joint is such that the column tends to prevent or restrain the beam end from rotating. This has several important consequences. One is that the beam now behaves more like a fixed-ended beam than a simply supported one. Coupled with this are many of the advantages of fixed-ended members discussed in Chapter 8 (e.g., increased rigidity, decreased deflections, and decreased internal bending moments). On the other hand, the fact that the column top is offering restraint to rotation means that the column must be picking up bending moments in addition to axial forces, thus complicating its design.

The rigid joint does not actually provide full end fixity for either the beam or the column. As the load tends to cause the end of the beam to rotate, the connected top of the column rotates as well. The whole joint between the column and the beam will rotate as a unit. While the whole joint rotates, however, the joint rigidity causes the members to retain their initial angular relationship to one another (e.g., if the members are initially at 90° to one another, they will remain so). The amount of the rotation that occurs depends on the *relative stiffnesses* of the beam and the column. The stiffer the column relative to the beam, the less total rotation occurs. *Some* rotation, however, invariably occurs. Thus, the end condition of the beam actually lies somewhere between a fully fixed-ended condition (in which the joint offers full restraint and no rotations occur at all) and a pin connection (in which the member is completely free to rotate). The same is true for the column. Each element enjoys some, but not all, of the advantages of full fixity.

From a member-design viewpoint, the behavior just described generally means that beams in a rigid frame system carrying vertical loads can be designed to be somewhat smaller than those in a comparable post-and-beam system (since moments are reduced), while the columns may need to be somewhat larger than their post-and-beam counterparts (since they pick up both

One-story steel frame

One-story reinforced concrete frame

Gabled steel frame

Multistory steel frame

(a) Typical rigid frame structures in steel and concrete.

Post-and-beam structure
(beam simply rests on top of column)

Rigid frame structure
(beam and column are rigidly joined)

The angle formed between column and tangent to the end of the beam changes with changing loads.

The angle between the tangent to the end of the beam and the tangent to the end of the column remains fixed (in this case at 90°). The whole joint rotates as a unit.

Under lateral loads a post-and-beam structure will collapse unless special precautions are taken (e.g., using shear walls). A frame structure is stable under lateral loads. The beam restrains the top end of each column from freely rotating which would in turn lead to the collapse of the whole structure.

The angle formed between column and tangent to the end of the beam changes with changing loads.

The whole joint rotates as a unit.

The columns in a frame tend to restrain the ends of the beam from rotating freely. This tends to reduce the midspan deflection of the horizontal member in the frame. If the two systems shown are identical in all respects except the way the members are joined, the midspan deflection of the frame (Δ_F) will be less than that of the post-and-beam structure (Δ_P), i.e., $\Delta_F < \Delta_P$

(b) General behavior of rigid frame structures.

FIGURE 9–1 Types of rigid frame structures and differences between post-and-beam structures and rigid frame structures.

(a) The vertical load tends to cause the columns to want to splay outward.

(b) If one of the pinned connections is released, the whole frame would splay horizontally. The application of a horizontal force would tend to cause the structure to resume its original shape. The force required to push the frame exactly back to its original location equals the horizontal thrust normally developed at the same location.

FIGURE 9–2   Horizontal thrusts in rigid frame structures carrying vertical loads.

axial loads and moments, whereas the columns in a post-and-beam system pick up only axial forces). Relative column sizes may be further affected when buckling is considered since the column in the framed structure has some end restraint, whereas the column in a post-and-beam system has none.

Another way that frames are uniquely different from comparable post-and-beam structures in carrying vertical loads that is intimately related to the presence of the moments in the columns discussed before is that frames typically develop horizontal as well as vertical reactions at the ground supports. The presence of these forces can most easily be visualized by imagining the deflected shape the structure would assume if the bases of the columns were not pin-connected to the ground foundation and allowed to freely translate horizontally (see Figure 9–2). The columns would naturally tend to splay outward. The application of horizontal forces that are inwardly directed at the column bases would cause the bases of the columns to tend to resume their original location. The amount of horizontal force that would cause the columns to be forced back into their exact original location equals the amount of horizontal thrust that the frame naturally exerts on the foundation when the column bases are normally attached to the foundation. As discussed later in this chapter, the magnitudes of the moments in the columns and those of the horizontal thrusts are directly related.

The foundations for a frame must be designed to carry the horizontal thrusts generated by the vertical loads. No such horizontal thrusts develop in post-and-beam structures carrying vertical loads. Foundations can consequently be simpler in post-and-beam systems than in frames.

Horizontal Loads.   Although the differences in behavior under vertical loads between frame structures and post-and-beam structures are pronounced, the differences with respect to horizontal or lateral loads are enormous. A post-and-beam structure is largely incapable of resisting significant lateral forces. What lateral force resistance such a structure does have stems largely from the large dead weight of the structure when stone or masonry is used or from the presence of some other element, such as an enclosure wall, that provides a bracing function. Column ends in timber structures might be sunk into the ground and thus provide a measure of lateral resistance by virtue of the end fixity achieved. By and large, however, most post-and-beam structures are not suited to carrying high lateral forces of the type associated with earthquakes and cyclones.

A rigid frame structure, on the other hand, is well capable of carrying lateral forces if designed properly. By virtue of the presence of a rigid connection, the beams restrain the columns from freely rotating in a way that would lead to the total collapse of the structure. The joints, however, do rotate (to a limited extent) as whole units. The stiffness of the beam contributes to the lateral-load-carrying resistance of a frame. It also serves to transfer part of the lateral load from one column to the other.

The action of a lateral load on a frame produces bending, shear, and axial forces in all members. Bending moments induced by wind loads are often the highest near the rigid joints. Consequently, members are either made larger or specially reinforced at joints when lateral forces are high.

Rigid frames are applicable to both large and small buildings. Many high-rise buildings use rigid frames to carry both vertical and lateral loads. The higher the building, however, the larger become the forces and moments developed in individual members. The lower columns in a high-rise structure in particular are subjected to very large moments and axial forces because of the huge lateral loads involved. A point is often reached where it becomes unfeasible to design members for these forces and moments and other bracing systems (e.g., diagonals or shear walls) are introduced to help carry the lateral loads and thus reduce forces and moments in the frames. Even in a lower building, supplementary bracing systems are typically used whenever possible, simply because carrying lateral loads by frame action alone is relatively inefficient.

9–3   ANALYSIS OF RIGID FRAMES

9–3–1   Methods of Analysis

Computer-Based Approaches.   As with continuous beams, rigid frame structures are statically indeterminate and these reactions, shears, and moments cannot be determined directly through the application of the basic equations of statics ($\Sigma F_x = 0$, $\Sigma F_y = 0$, and $\Sigma M_o = 0$) alone. There are typically more unknowns than equations. This implies that reactions, shears, and moments are dependent on the precise characteristics of the structure itself, including the relative stiffnesses of beams and columns, as well as the overall geometry of the whole structure and its loading condition.

In current practice, virtually all analyses of rigid frame structures is done with computer-based analysis programs. Users can input the geometry of overall configurations, specify member types and support conditions (pinned, fixed, etc.), and specify different types of vertical and horizontal loading patterns. Analysis results include axial forces, shears, bending moments, deflections of joints and members, and other information. Good programs can treat not only two-dimensional frames but complex three-dimensional configurations as well. The matrix displacement techniques, discussed in Appendix 12, frequently form the basis for these computer-based formulations. Finite element techniques, discussed in Appendix 13, are used as well.

Approximate Methods of Analysis.   Despite the widespread and correct use of computer-based analysis programs, it remains useful to look at different kinds of approximate methods of analysis that have historically been associated with hand calculations. In this day and age, this is done not so much for their use as practical analysis tools, but because they tend to give the analyst a better sense of how one of these structures is behaving, and how forces and moments are generally distributed throughout the structure.

The analytical methods discussed next are based on many simplifying assumptions and yield approximate results only. The approximate methods discussed yield results that are extremely useful during preliminary design stages to determine an initial set of member sizes and properties. These estimates are then used in more exact analyses made during design development stages, since some member-size estimates must be available before an exact analysis can take place.

An effective method of analysis is based on a procedure that assumes the locations of points of zero internal moment (points of inflection). These locations are initially estimated by looking at the deflected shape of the structure. This is the same basic technique described in Chapter 8 in connection with the approximate analysis of beams.

Single-Bay Frames: Lateral Loads.   Two simple rigid frames subjected to lateral loads will be analyzed by approximate methods in this section. The first is a single-bay frame with rigid connections between the beam and the columns and pin connections at the column bases. The second is identical except that it has fixed rather than pinned connections at the column bases. In both cases it is assumed that the lateral load carried by the structure can be characterized as a point force acting at the top joint. The exact type and location of the lateral forces carried by a frame in a real building depend on what type of force is being considered (wind or earthquake). An analysis should be made for the building considered to determine exactly how to model the load. A simple point load will be assumed in the following examples.

Figure 9–3 shows the reactions for the first frame. There are four unknown reactions (R_{A_H}, R_{A_V}, R_{D_H}, R_{D_V}) and only three equations of statics ($\Sigma F_x = 0$, $\Sigma F_y = 0$, and $\Sigma M_o = 0$) available for solution. Consequently, the frame is statically indeterminate to one degree. In this particular frame it is still possible to determine the vertical reactions, R_{A_V} and R_{D_V}, by simply summing the moments of the external and reactive forces around either of the pin connections (locations of known zero moment resistance). For the *whole* structure shown in Figure 9–3(a):

$$\Sigma M_A = 0: \quad -Ph + R_{A_V}(0) + R_{A_H}(0) + R_{D_V}(L) + R_{D_H}(0) = 0$$
$$\text{so } R_{D_V} = Ph/L \uparrow$$
$$\Sigma F_y = 0: \quad -R_{A_V} + R_{D_V} = 0; \quad \text{or} \quad -R_{A_V} + Ph/L = 0, \quad \text{so} \quad R_{A_V} = Ph/L \downarrow$$
$$\Sigma F_x = 0: \quad +P - R_{A_H} - R_{D_H} = 0; \quad \text{or} \quad R_{A_H} + R_{D_H} = P$$

It is evident that the vertical reactive forces can be found only because of the particular condition that the two unknown horizontal reactions pass through the moment center selected. It is not possible to determine any further information by direct application of the equations of statics. It can be surmised that the horizontal reactions, R_{A_H} and R_{D_H}, are equal but this is an assumption only.

In order to get a complete solution to the problem, use can be made of the fact that a point of inflection develops in the beam when the frame carries a horizontal load. By sketching the probable deflected shape of the structure, the location of this point of inflection can be accurately estimated. In this case the point of inflection is estimated to be at midspan [see Figure 9–3(a)]. The knowledge that at points of inflection the internal moment in the structure is zero can be used to

(a) Deflected shape of frame.

(b) Free-body diagrams for parts of frame separated at points of inflection (points of known zero moment). Since the structure is separated at points of zero moment, no internal moments need be shown or considered.

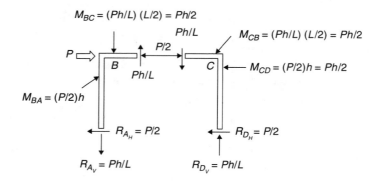

(c) Free-body diagram of individual beam, column, and joint elements. Since the structure is not separated at points of zero moment, the free-body diagrams must show internal moments.

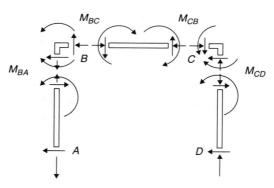

(d) Final moment diagram. Shear and axial forces are present in the members as well as the moment indicated.

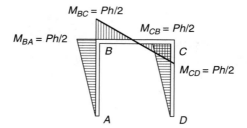

FIGURE 9–3 Simplified analysis of a single-bay rigid frame carrying a lateral load.

provide another independent equation which will lead to a complete solution. For analytical purposes, stipulating that the internal moment is zero at this point is equivalent to inserting a pin connection at that location. The resultant structure can thus be modeled as a statically determinate three-hinged assembly of the type discussed earlier (see Section 5–5–4). By decomposing the structure at the point of inflection into two separate assemblies, the horizontal reactions can be determined by considering the moment equilibrium for each piece [see Figure 9–3(b)]. Thus, for the *left* assembly, $\Sigma M_N = 0$: $P(0) + R_{A_V}(L/2) - R_{A_H}(h) = 0$. So $(Ph/L)(L/2) = R_{A_H}(h)$ and $R_{A_H} = P/2 \leftarrow$. By considering the horizontal force equilibrium of the whole structure, the remaining unknown reaction, R_{D_H}, can be found. For the whole structure $\Sigma F_x = 0$: $R_{A_H} + R_{D_H} = P$ (from before), so $P/2 + R_{D_H} = P$. Thus, $R_{D_H} = P/2 \leftarrow$.

All reactions are now known ($R_{A_H} = P/2$, $R_{A_V} = Ph/L$, $R_{D_H} = P/2$, $R_{D_V} = Ph/L$). Note that the assumption that the point of inflection in the beam was located at midspan is equivalent to assuming that the horizontal reactions are equal. Once the reactions are known, the shears V, moments M, and axial forces N in the structure can be found by considering each element in turn [see free-body diagrams in Figure 9–3(b)]. The typical designation system used is as follows: M_{xy} = moment in member $x-y$ at the end of the member that frames into joint x. Shears and axial forces are similarly denoted.

Shear forces and normal (or axial) forces are calculated by considering the translatory equilibrium of each section. In this case they can be determined by inspection. For example, $V_{BC} = Ph/L$ from $\Sigma F_v = 0$. Moments are calculated by multiplying the shear force present by the effective length of the member. For example, $M_{BC} = (Ph/L)(L/2) = Ph/2$. [Each member is thus treated like a cantilever beam with a concentrated load (in this case the shear force) at its end.] Results are shown in Figure 9–3. Note that the column on the right is in compression and the one on the left is in tension, but both experience similar bending moments. The center beam is in compression and experiences a positive moment on one end and a negative moment on the other, which in turn give the S shape to the member originally assumed.

The beam moments found above can also be determined by a slightly different procedure making use of another set of free-body diagrams. The free-body diagrams shown in Figure 9–3(c) indicate how the same structure can be broken down into individual beam, column, and joint elements. The concept of isolating joints in a frame, and considering their equilibrium, is similar to that used in the method of joints in truss analysis. The primary distinction is that in trusses the members were pinned together at joints, hence moments could not be developed and only translatory equilibrium needed to be considered. In the case of a frame, the member connections are rigid, hence internal moments are developed at member ends which must be reflected in the free-body diagrams of individual joints. Because of these moments, both translational and rotational equilibrium need to be considered for any individual joint. Using this type of free-body diagram, moments can be found as shown below.

As before, a moment is developed at the top of column $B-A$ due to the horizontal reaction. For column $B-A$: $M_{BA} = (P/2)h = Ph/2$. There is an equal and opposite moment acting on joint B. For rotational equilibrium for the joint to be maintained, a balancing moment must be developed in $B-C$. The beam provides this moment restraint. At joint B: $-M_{BA} + M_{BC} = 0$, so $M_{BC} = Ph/2$. Similar observations can be made about column $C-D$ and joint D. For column $C-D$, $M_{CD} = Ph/2$. At joint C: $-M_{CD} + M_{CB} = 0$, so $M_{CB} = Ph/2$.

The end moments found for the beam are clearly the same as those previously found. Figure 9–3(c) not only shows how the various beam, column, and joint elements are in moment equilibrium but shows how they are in equilibrium with respect to shear and axial forces as well.

Moment diagrams can now be drawn for each of the beams and columns in the frame. In order to plot moment diagrams, a sign convention other than the one used for horizontal members must be used since the notion of top and bottom surfaces is meaningless in a vertical member. Common practice for plotting moment diagrams for vertical members is to look at the member from the right and employ the usual convention (this is the same as turning the member 90° in a clockwise direction). An equivalent convention that is perhaps more generally useful since it is applicable to any member having any orientation is simply to plot the moment diagram on the compression face of the member and not to be concerned with whether the moment is called a positive one or a negative one.

A more complex type of frame is illustrated in Figure 9–4(a). This frame is identical to the one studied previously except that the column bases are fixed rather than pinned. Figure 9–4(a) shows the reactive forces and moments developed at the foundations. There are six unknown quantities (R_{A_H}, R_{A_V}, M_A^F, R_{D_H}, R_{D_V}, and M_D^F) and only three equations of statics available for use. Hence, the frame is statically indeterminate to the third degree. Consequently, three assumptions must be made if a static analysis is to be used. As before, a sketch of the probably deflected shape of the structure is made. As is evident, there are three points of inflection developed. One is in the midspan of the beam as before. Two others are near the midheights of the columns. They are not exactly at midheight since the top joints rotate slightly. If the joints simply translated horizontally without rotation, the points of inflection would have to be identically at midheight (by a symmetry argument). The slight rotation of the upper joints causes the point of inflection to rise somewhat to the location indicated in Figure 9–4(a).

Fixing the location of these three points of inflection makes a static analysis possible. The frame can be decomposed or separated at these points of zero moment in a manner similar to that previously described and each piece treated in turn (i.e., axial forces and shears can be found based on the knowledge that the net rotational moments around these points for any piece must be zero). This analysis is illustrated in Figure 9–4(b).

Note that if the frame is decomposed into two sections at the inflection points in the column, the upper part is quite analogous to the frame previously discussed (with pin-connected bases) except that column heights differ. The analysis technique is the same. This structure can then be imagined as simply resting on two vertical cantilever elements. The horizontal thrusts associated with the upper part produce moments in the lower elements. A final moment diagram is shown in Figure 9–4(d).

Note that the final moments in individual members are lower than in the pinned frame previously analyzed.

Single-Bay Frames: Vertical Loads. The general procedure for making an approximate analysis of a frame carrying vertical loads is much the same as the one described in the previous section for lateral loads. Consider the rigid frame shown in Figure 9–5(a), which has pinned connections at the column bases. The first step in the analysis is to sketch the probable deflected shape of the structure and to locate points of inflection [see Figure 9–5(a)].

It is somewhat more difficult to locate the inflection points associated with vertical loads than the ones associated with lateral loads. If the joints provided full fixity (and no end rotations occurred at all at beam ends), then the points of inflection would be at $0.21L$ from either end (see

(a) Deflected shape of frame.

$M_{BC} = (0.45Ph/L)(L/2)$
$= 0.225Ph$

$M_{CB} = (0.45Ph/L)(L/2)$
$= 0.225Ph$

$M_{CD} = (P/2)(0.45h)$
$= 0.225Ph$

(b) Free-body diagram for parts
of structure separated at points
of inflection (points of known
zero moment).

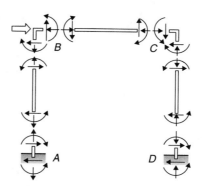

$M_D^F = (0.55h)(P/2)$
$= 0.275Ph$

(c) Free-body of individual beam column,
and joint elements. Each element must
be in a state of translatory and rotational
equilibrium.

(d) Final moment diagram. Shear and axial
forces are present in the members as well
as the moments indicated.

$M_{BC} = 0.225Ph$

$M_{CB} = 0.225Ph$

$M_{BA} = 0.225Ph$

$M_{CD} = 0.225Ph$

$M_A^F = 0.275Ph$ $M_D^F = 0.275Ph$

FIGURE 9–4 Simplified analysis of a single-bay rigid frame carrying a lateral load.

(a) Frame and loading. Inflection points are developed near both ends of the beams. Their locations are assumed to be as shown.

Location of points of inflection

(b) Free-body diagrams of parts of the frame separated at inflection points. Shears, moments, and axial forces are found in each piece by a statical analysis.

$M = w(0.8L)^2/8 = 0.08wL^2$

$M_{CB} = 0.4wL(0.1L) + w(0.1L)^2/2$
$= 0.045wL^2$

$0.4wL$

$0.045wL^2$

R_{A_H} R_{D_H}

$wL/2$ $wL/2$

$\Sigma M_C = 0$
$0.4wL(0.1L) + w(0.1L)^2/2$
$- R_{D_H}(h) = 0$
$R_{D_H} = 0.045wL^2/h$

(c) Final moment diagram.

(d) The moment present is proportional to the deviation of the structure from the funicular line for the loading.

$0.08wL^2$

$wL^2/8$

$0.045wL^2$

Proportional to moment

Funicular line for uniformly distributed loading (passes through inflection points)

FIGURE 9–5 Simplified analysis of a single-bay rigid frame carrying vertical loads.

Section 8–3). Since some rotations do occur, but the joint does not freely rotate, the actual end conditions lie somewhere between pinned connections and fully fixed connections; the inflection points in the beam thus lie somewhere between $0L$ and $0.21L$ from the joints. For beams and columns of normal stiffnesses, the inflection points are normally found about $0.1L$ from either end. As will be discussed more fully in Section 9–3–2, the precise location of the inflection points is very sensitive to the relative stiffnesses of the beams and columns.

If the inflection points are assumed to be at $0.1L$ from either end, the structure can be decomposed into three statically determinate elements and analyzed as illustrated in Figure 9–5(b). The final moment diagram obtained is shown in Figure 9–5(c).

As is evident, the vertical loads produce moments both in the beam and in the columns. Maximum moments in the beam normally occur at midspan but critical moments are present at end joints as well. Maximum column moments invariably occur at member ends.

9–3–2 Importance of Relative Beam and Column Stiffnesses

In any statically indeterminate structure, including a frame, the magnitudes of the internal forces and moments are, in the final analysis, dependent on the relative properties of the members themselves. None of the approximate analyses discussed thus far have reflected the importance of this fact. Implicit in the analyses, however, have been assumptions about the relative characteristics of the members used. Normal or typical stiffnesses were considered.

The importance of different member properties can be seen by looking at Figure 9–6. If it is initially assumed that one column is stiffer than the other (i.e., one has a higher relative I value), the stiffer column will end up taking a greater share of the horizontal load than the more flexible one. An assumption that horizontal reactions are equal is thus not tenable. Higher moments would also be developed in the stiffer member than in the more flexible one as a consequence of its taking a greater portion of the load.

Different relative stiffnesses between beams and columns also affects moments due to vertical loads. As Figure 9–7 illustrates, the location of the inflection points are affected by the relative stiffness of the beams and columns. The stiffer the column relative to the beam, the more it restrains the end of the beam from rotating. The consequence is that higher moments are developed in the column when it is very stiff relative to the beam than when the column is more flexible. Negative moments in the beam are also increased, whereas positive moments are decreased. When the beam is stiff relative to the column, converse phenomena occur.

Exact methods of analysis are available which take into account these effects. These analyses must be based on an assumed set of beam-and-column stiffnesses. The approximate analyses previously discussed are useful in providing these initial estimates.

◆ ◆ **EXAMPLE**

Crown Hall in Chicago, by Mies Van der Rohe (Figure 9–8 on page 362), is a well-known example of the use of exposed rigid frames. The horizontal members are considerably stiffer than the supporting columns, so it can be expected that relative stiffness issues are extremely important. Determine the bending moments present in a typical interior frame. All member properties, dimensions, etc., are estimated. The base connection is in actuality a complicated connection involving two pins, one at the base of each column and another just above it. This condition, however, can be approximately treated as a fixed connection with an unbraced column height of 19.5 ft. Use any available computer-based structural analysis program.

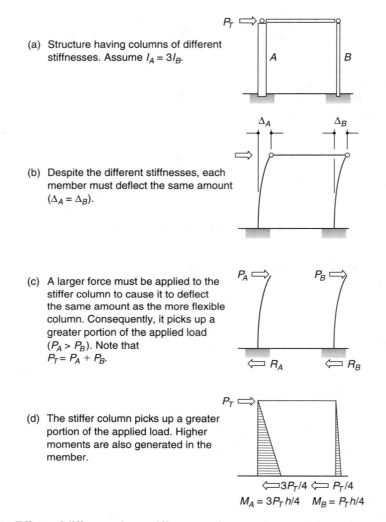

(a) Structure having columns of different stiffnesses. Assume $I_A = 3I_B$.

(b) Despite the different stiffnesses, each member must deflect the same amount $(\Delta_A = \Delta_B)$.

(c) A larger force must be applied to the stiffer column to cause it to deflect the same amount as the more flexible column. Consequently, it picks up a greater portion of the applied load $(P_A > P_B)$. Note that $P_T = P_A + P_B$.

(d) The stiffer column picks up a greater portion of the applied load. Higher moments are also generated in the member.

FIGURE 9–6 Effects of different column stiffnesses on forces and moments in a rigid structure.

Solution: See Figure 9–8.

Note: The moment distribution obtained illustrates the importance of relative beam to column stiffness considerations. The locations of the points of inflection are different than those previously estimated (which were based on other beam-to-column stiffness ratios). The moment values obtained are correspondingly quite different from those that would be obtained by using hand calculations. ◆

9–3–3 Sidesway

A phenomenon of particular interest in frames carrying vertical loads is that of *sidesway.* If a frame is not symmetrically shaped and loaded, the structure will sway (translate horizontally) to one side or the other. The reason for sidesway can be seen by inspecting Figure 9–9. Assume that

Statically determinate
structures

Frame structures with different relative
column and beam stiffnesses

(a)   (b)   (c)   (d)   (e)

(a) Three-hinged arch structure. Large negative moments are developed in the
     beam.

(b) Post-and-beam structure. Large positive moments are developed in the
     beam. The columns do not restrain the rotations of the beam ends at all.

(c) Frame with very flexible columns and an extremely stiff beam. The flexible
     columns do not provide significant restraint to the ends of the beam. The
     beam behaves similarly to a pin-ended one.

Zero line

M_T M_-

M_+

Beam moment diagram

(d) Frame with normal beam and column stiffness. The columns offer partial
     restraint to the ends of the beams. Some rotations occur. Negative moments
     increase and positive moments decrease.

(e) Frame with very stiff columns and a flexible beam. The columns offer
     almost full restraint to the ends of the more flexible beam.

(f) The sum of the positive and negative beam moments remains the same in
     each case. The location of the base line and hence of the design moments
     varies.

FIGURE 9–7   Effects of different relative beam and column stiffness on internal forces and moments in a
rigid frame structure. The moments generated in the frames by the vertical load vary with different locations
of the inflection points. The stiffer the section of a frame, the greater is the moment developed at the section.

the columns are very stiff and completely restrain the ends of the beam, which can then be modeled as a fixed-ended beam. Corresponding fixed-ended moments are shown in Figure 9–9(b).
Since the joints must be in rotational equilibrium, this means that the moments at the column
tops are the same magnitude as those in the adjacent beam. For equilibrium of the column, the
presence of a moment at the top implies the necessity of a horizontal thrust at the base of the
frame. The magnitude of this thrust at the base of a column is directly related to the magnitude of
the moment at the column top. Since the moments are unequal, this means that the thrusts are

(a) Crown Hall   (b) Results of structural analysis

FIGURE 9–8 The moment distribution illustrates the importance of relative stiffness considerations. The values obtained are quite different from that obtained by estimating points of inflection and using hand calculations.

also unequal. By looking at the overall equilibrium of the frame in the horizontal direction, however, it can be seen that the thrusts *must* be equal so that $\Sigma F_x = 0$ obtains, which in turn means that the moments at the column tops and beam ends must also be equal. The only way that such an equality can be naturally obtained is for the frame to sway to the left. As it sways to the left, there will be a tendency for the upper right joint to open up slightly, thus reducing the moment present (and the thrust of the column base), and for the upper left joint to close up slightly, thus increasing the moment present (and the thrust at the column base). Just enough sway will occur so that moment and horizontal thrust equality will be achieved.

9–3–4 Support Settlements

As was the case with continuous beams, rigid frames are quite sensitive to differential support settlements. Consider the rigid frame shown in Figure 9–10(a). Any type of differential support movement, either vertically or horizontally, will induce moments in the frame. The greater the differential settlements, the greater will be the moments induced. These moments can lead to failures in the design of the frame if not anticipated. For this reason, special care must be taken with the design of foundations for rigid frame structures to minimize this risk.

9–3–5 Effects of Partial-Loading Conditions

As was the case with continuous beams, the maximum moments developed in a frame often do not occur when the frame is fully loaded but only partially loaded. This, of course, complicates the analysis process enormously. The first problem is simply that of predicting which type of loading pattern produces the most critical moments. Only after this is done can an analysis take place. Usually, some variant of a checkerboard loading pattern over the whole frame produces

(a) A rigid frame that is not symmetrically loaded.

(b) Frame moments assuming that no joint rotation at all occurs.

$$M_B^F = (2/27)PL^2 \qquad M_C^F = (4/27)PL^2$$

(c) The assumption that no joint rotation at all occurs leads to the result that horizontal frame reactions at the foundation are unequal.

$M_B \neq M_C$

$$(R_{A_H} = 2PL^2/27h) \neq (4PL^2/27h = R_{B_H})$$

(d) From a consideration of the overall equilibrium of the frame in the horizontal direction, it is evident that the result found in (c) is not plausible. Horizontal reactions must be equal. This also implies that moments at the column tops must also be equal.

$M_B = M_C$

$R_{A_H} = R_{B_H}$

(e) The only way that the frame can naturally adjust itself so that moments at column tops are equal (so that horizontal reactions are equal) is to sway to the left. This has a tendency of closing up the upper left joint (and increasing the moments present) and opening up the upper right joint (and decreasing the moments present). The frame will sway until the moments present become equal.

FIGURE 9–9 Sidesway in rigid frames. The absence of complete symmetry in a frame or its loading leads to a horizontal sway in the structure.

(a) Single-bay frame. (b) Multistory frame.

FIGURE 9–10 Effects of support settlements on rigid frame structures. Curvatures, hence bending moments, are induced in a frame because of differential joint settlement.

maximum positive or negative moments at the location considered. There are several techniques for establishing exactly which loading conditions are most critical (e.g., the Miller-Breslau technique). Going into the problem of partial loadings in detail, however, is beyond the scope of this book.

9–3–6 Multistory Frames

As previously mentioned, virtually all analyses of rigid frame structures are currently done with computer-based analysis programs. This is particularly true for complex multi-story structures. These formulations allow shears, bending moments, and axial forces to be obtained for each member in a frame. The need to check different types of critical loading patterns is fully facilitated by the use of computer-based analysis programs. Nonetheless, it is still interesting to look at hand calculation techniques that were developed to analyze multistory frames because they tend to give the analyst a better sense of how forces and moments are generally distributed throughout the structure.

There are several approximate methods used to analyze multistory frames subjected to lateral forces. A time-honored approach called the *cantilever method* was first introduced in 1908. It involves making many of the same types of assumptions previously made, plus others. Generally, it assumes the following: (1) there is a point of inflection at the midspan of each beam in a complex frame; (2) there is a point of inflection at the midheight of each column; and (3) the magnitude of the axial force present in each column of a story is proportional to the horizontal distance of that column from the centroid of all the columns of the story under consideration.

These assumptions are diagrammatically illustrated in Figure 9–11. These illustrations also provide an insight into the behavior of a multistory frame under load. Moments are generated in

Wind acting against the face of the building creates overturning moments and sliding forces. Reactions developed at the base provide resisting forces and moments.

Lower-story columns: The wind force causes the columns to rack laterally. Curvatures and related internal forces and moments are developed in columns and beams.

Bending moments

A typical column is subjected to axial forces, shears, and bending moments. Beams are also subjected to similiar forces.

Columns in tension

Columns in compression

Distribution of column axial forces

Distribution of column bending moments

FIGURE 9–11 Multistory frames.

all members. The magnitude of these moments depend upon the magnitude of the resultant shear force V_L (the sum of the lateral loads above the floor considered). This shear force is balanced by resisting shear forces ($V_{C_1}, V_{C_2}, \ldots, V_{C_n}$) developed in the columns at the same level ($V_L = \Sigma V_{c_n}$). The moment in any column is the shear force in the column multiplied by its moment arm (one-half the column height). Moments in beams are generated to balance moments at column ends. Since the total shear force V_L is greater at lower floors than upper floors, bending moments in beams and columns are greater at lower rather than upper floors.

The magnitudes of the axial forces in the columns depend on the magnitude of the overturning moment M_L associated with the lateral loads above the section considered. Consequently, axial forces are greater at the base of the building where the overturning moment is the greatest; they tend to reduce in upper story columns.

The magnitudes of forces and moments in multistory frames that are due to vertical loads can be estimated in the same way as was illustrated for single bay rigid frames. Inflection points can be assumed at $0.1L$ from either end of the beam. This assumption has the effect of creating a statically determinate beam between the two inflection points that is supported by short cantilevers. Positive and negative moments can be found by statics.

Other, more exact methods of analysis that are computer oriented are now more commonly used to analyze multistory frames than the cantilever method (see Appendix 12). Nonetheless it still provides a useful way of conceptualizing the behavior of multistory structures.

9–3–7 Vierendeel Frames

The discussion thus far has dealt with frames that are used vertically. Frames can also be used horizontally, as illustrated by the *Vierendeel structure* (see Figure 9–12). This structure resembles a parallel chord truss with the diagonals removed and is often used in much the same way as a truss. The structure is used in buildings where the functional requirements present mitigate against the presence of diagonals. The structure is considerably less efficient, however, than a comparable structure having diagonals.

Vierendeel structures are analyzed in much the same way as previously described for vertical frames. Locations of inflection points are estimated and used to provide sufficient information to determine internal shears, moments, and axial forces.

The internal moments in elements tend to be the highest in members near the end of the structure and lower toward the middle. This distribution reflects the fact that the overall shear forces associated with the total loading which cause local bending moments and shears in specific members are highest toward the ends and decrease toward the middle. Axial forces in members are highest in middle top and bottom chord elements and decrease toward the ends. This distribution reflects that of the overall moment associated with the total loading. This pattern is similar to that present in parallel chord trusses.

The results of a finite-element analysis (see Section 6–3–9 and Appendix 13) for a typical Vierendeel structure are shown in Figure 9–13. The deformation analysis clearly shows the reverse curves developed in typical members. These reverse curves are associated with bending stresses that not only vary in magnitude but also change from tension to compression along the length of a member.

(a) Shear and moment diagrams for basic loading condition. The structure must carry this shear and moment.

(b) Determination of shears. Moments and axial forces in members.

(c) Bending moments in individual members depend on the magnitude of the external shearing force present in the structure. Moments are maximum in members toward the end of the structure (where the overall external shear force is the greatest) and decrease in interior members.

(d) Axial forces in upper and lower chords depend on the magnitude of the overall bending moment present in the structure. Axial forces consequently are maximum toward the middle of the structure.

(e) Diagram of member sizes as determined in response to the bending moments present in individual members.

FIGURE 9–12   Vierendeel structure: a special type of frame.

(a) Vierendeel structure

Loads at nodes (typical)

Rigid connection (typical)

Reaction

The finite-element analysis shows the complex deformed shape of the structure and the general stress distributions present.

Note the S-shaped deformation patterns in individual members.

(b) 1st principal stresses

Scale: 1st principal stresses

High   Low

FIGURE 9–13   Finite element analysis of a Vierendeel structure.

9–4 DESIGN OF RIGID FRAMES

9–4–1 Introduction

Designing a frame structure can be an involved process. One of the first questions to be asked is simply whether or not it makes sense to use frames at all. They are not, for example, particularly efficient types of structures to be used in situations where lateral loading conditions are high. Simply because frames can be designed to carry lateral loads does not mean they should be given preference over other approaches, such as structures using shear walls or diagonal bracing, that are better suited for carrying this type of loading. Frames make sense when the requirements of a building do not easily allow other solutions to be used.

When warranted, the general geometry and dimensions of the frame to be designed are often fixed in the building context and the design problem often becomes a more limited one of developing strategies for selection of connection types, selecting materials, and sizing members.

9–4–2   Selection of Frame Type

Frame structures are often described in terms of their relative degree of fixity, as characterized by the number and location of pinned and rigid joints throughout the structure. Several types of frames are illustrated in Figure 9–14. Different arrangements of pinned and fixed joints are desirable for different purposes. Minimizing design moments and increasing stiffness are common design objectives in selecting frame types. Other considerations include suitability for foundation conditions or construction ease.

With respect to design moments, notice that quite different moment magnitudes and distributions are present in the frames illustrated, which in turn says something about the relative sizes of members required. For example, the three-hinged structure shown in Figure 9–14 naturally

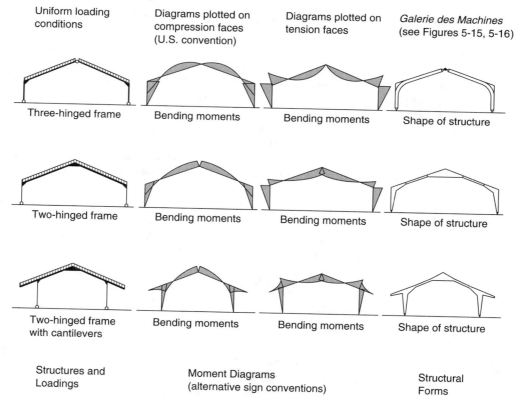

FIGURE 9–14   Different types of frame structures generally shaped in response to the bending moments present.

develops higher moments than its two-hinged counterpart. This in turn means that member sizes must be correspondingly larger. It can also be expected that deflections would be higher in the more flexible three-hinged structure than in its two-hinged counterpart. Moments can still be reduced, however, by using cantilevers as indicated.

The forces and moments developed in frames are particularly sensitive to member end conditions, as can be illustrated by a direct comparison of the four structures shown in Figure 9–15, which are identical except for the type of member connections present. Equivalent lateral loads produce significantly different forces and moments in the different structures.

Notice that no moments at all are generated in the trussed system, which indicates that member sizes could be quite small. Comparing the frame in Figure 9–15(d) with that in Figure 9–15(c) (the *table top* frame) reveals that while maximum moments are the same in the columns in both frames, the former has no moments developed in the beam at all, while the latter does. Differences also exist in member axial forces. From a design viewpoint these differences mean that the tabletop frame generally requires more total material to support the lateral load in space than does the first structure and is thus less preferable with regard to this criterion. Because of the need to assume full base fixity at the column, however, the first structure with pinned column tops requires more substantial foundations than does the tabletop frame with its pinned base connections. The maximum moments developed in the frame shown in Figure 9–15(b), which has rigid joints and fixed-base connections, are less than those developed in either of these two structures. It is interesting to note that the absolute sum of the positive and negative column moments in this fully fixed frame numerically equals the magnitude of the column moments present in the first two structures (members are, however, designed for either positive or negative moment values and not their sum). The same total moment is present in all cases, but its distribution is changed by the type of member end conditions present.

When all factors, including vertical loads, are considered, the fully rigid frame shown in Figure 9–15(b) usually displays the most advantages in terms of structural efficiency. In cases where the design of the foundation is a problem, however, an approach using pinned-base connections such as illustrated in Figure 9–15(c) may be the best overall solution. The moments induced by differential settlements in a frame having pinned-base connections are less than those induced in a fully rigid frame. Also, the foundation for a pinned-base frame need not be designed to provide moment resistance. Horizontal thrusts associated with vertical loads are also usually smaller in a pinned-base frame than in a fixed-base one. Still the advantages of full rigidity in terms of minimizing moments and reducing deflections often overshadow those advantages of a pinned-base frame. Each specific design must be evaluated in its own context to see which approach proves most desirable.

9–4–3 Design Moments

Once a frame type is selected, the frame may be analyzed and its members sized to carry the vertical and horizontal loadings that are present. The previous sections on analysis have discussed how to determine moments from either vertical or lateral loads. To determine *design moments,* it is necessary to superimpose moments generated by both types of loadings. Figure 9–16 illustrates this process for a simple rigid frame. In some instances the moments from the vertical and lateral loads are additive and in other cases they tend to negate each other. Critical moments occur when moments are additive. It should be remembered that lateral loads can typically come

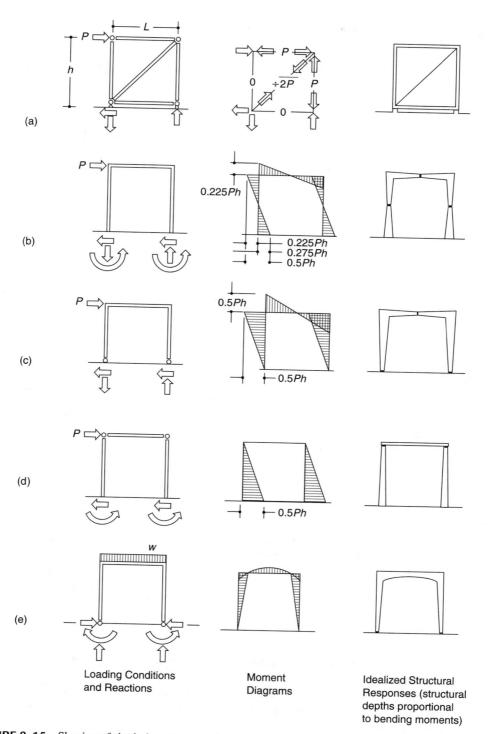

(a)

(b)

(c)

(d)

(e)

Loading Conditions
and Reactions

Moment
Diagrams

Idealized Structural
Responses (structural
depths proportional
to bending moments)

FIGURE 9–15   Shaping of single-bay structures in response to bending moments present and the effect of different end conditions.

371

(a) Moments due to lateral forces.

(b) Moments due to vertical forces.

(c) Moments in beam due to the simultaneous occurrence of both lateral and vertical forces (for lateral load from left only).

(d) A member intended to have a constant depth is sized in response to the maximum combined lateral and vertical load moment present.

FIGURE 9–16 Critical design moments in a single-bay rigid frame.

from either side; therefore, the subtractive cases are rarely of importance and all members are designed for additive effects.

In cases where the lateral load is very high relative to the vertical load, moments from the lateral forces will be dominant and maximum design moments in either beams or columns will usually occur at joints. When lateral loads are less dominant, the critical design moments in a beam occur at midspan or even at some other point. In columns critical moments almost invariably occur at joints.

The discussion above has not addressed the complicating problem of partial loadings potentially creating higher moments than primary or full loadings. An analysis could be made for each relevant loading, but this is often too exacting a task for preliminary design purposes and is not often initially done. In this connection the discussion in Section 8–4–2 on design moments in continuous beams is relevant. The approximate moments given in Table 8–1, which at least partly reflect the effects of partial loadings, are often used for frames as well as other continuous beams for preliminary design purposes. While of obvious importance, further consideration of the effects of partial loadings is beyond the scope of this book and the discussion will focus on designing frames in response to their primary loading conditions only.

Once the critical maximum moments and other internal shears and axial forces have been determined, then member sizing can take place. Two options are present for sizing a member. The first is to identify the maximum internal forces and moments present at any spot along the length of the member, size a member for these values, and then use a constant member size throughout. This would mean that the member would be oversized at every location but the critical one. The second general option is to shape the member in response to the variation in critical moments and forces that are present. These are the same options faced in the design of continuous beams (see Chapter 8). The first option of using constant-size members is an inefficient use of material in contrast to the second, but often preferred because of construction considerations. Member sizing for constant-depth members is discussed in Chapter 6. The implication of the second option, of shaping members, is discussed in the next section.

9–4–4   Shaping of Frames

Single-Bay Structures.   As discussed before in connection with the design of beams, members can be shaped in response to the way internal moments and forces are distributed within the member. In Figure 9–15, the frames are approximately shaped in response to the moments present for a single loading condition. In this section we look at shaping issues in greater detail with special reference to shaping for varying loading conditions. This discussion is in many ways simply a variant of the one on design moments presented in the previous section.

Consider the single-bay frame shown in Figure 9–17. This is the same frame analyzed in Section 9–3–1. If the member depth is designed to be dependent only on the magnitude of the moment present at a point (and thus temporarily ignoring other internal forces that are present), and no deviations were allowed to this relation, configurations of the type shown in Figure 9–17 would result for each type of loading condition considered. Since the type of moments generated by lateral loads are drastically different in distribution than those for vertical loads, resultant structural responses are also very different. It is important to follow through the implications of having this type of frame designed in response to one type of loading subjected to the other type (since both types would occur in a real building structure). The three-hinged structure designed in response to lateral loads can carry vertical loads as well. It is interesting to note that this structure is basically of the same type as the three-hinged arches discussed in Chapter 5. When vertical loads are applied to this three-hinged structure, moments of the type illustrated in Figure 9–17(c) result. The final structure could be designed for the combined effects of moments associated with both lateral and vertical loads. The only question present is one of whether or not the general strategy outlined above is a reasonable one leading to an efficient frame. By looking at the magnitudes of the moments due to the vertical loads in the three-hinged arch type of structure

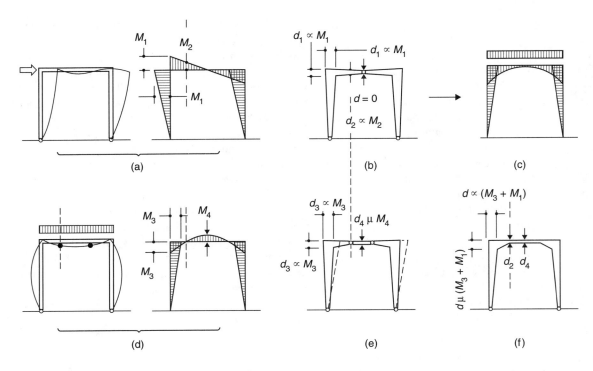

(a) Frame carrying lateral loading.

(b) Structural response to moments induced by lateral loads.

(c) Moments in the frame shown in (b) due to vertical load. These moments are higher than those in the frame shown in (d).

(d) Frame carrying vertical loading.

(e) Structural response to moments induced by vertical loading. Frame shown is an unstable four-hinged structure and cannot be used.

(f) Structural response to both lateral and vertical load requirements. The structure is shaped to meet critical requirements from both loading conditions but is optimum for neither.

FIGURE 9–17 Shaping frame members in response to moments from both lateral and vertical loads.

in comparison with those generated in the original two-hinged frame structure [see Figure 9–17(d)], the answer can be seen to be no. The insertion of a pin in the beam (dictated by the response to lateral loads) causes an unfavorable moment distribution to develop in the beam in that the moments generated are considerably higher than those present in the two-hinged frames. The consequence is that member sizes are probably larger than need be for low structures where lateral loads are small.

The alternative approach of using the response to vertical loads as the initial generator can be dismissed immediately because the structure (a four-hinged assembly) is clearly an unstable one.

An option that makes some sense is to shape critical parts of the structure in response to the positive and negative moment values present from either loading condition. A general configuration of the type shown in Figure 9–17(f) results. The configuration is optimum neither for the lateral-load condition nor for the vertical-load condition but works for the simultaneous presence of both loading types and fairly well for each individual type.

The frame shown in Figure 9–17(f) is characteristic of the compromise nature of the design of many frames, whether such a drastic shaping approach is taken or not. Often many frames are simply given additional local strengthening at the joints, which reflects the fact that moments are usually higher there than elsewhere. The general point to be remembered is that it is doubtful if there is any such thing as an optimum frame design when multiple loading conditions need to be considered.

Multistory Frames.   When multibay structures are considered, the same issues discussed in connection with single-bay structures arise (Figure 9–18). Again, resultant structures are characterized by a compromise approach that works for the presence of both lateral and vertical loading conditions but not optimally for either individual condition. Member shapes are exaggerated in the figure.

9–4–5   Member and Connection Design

Once design moments and forces are known, the process of sizing a member in a frame is like that of designing any member subjected to bending, shear, and axial forces—as has been described in Chapters 6 and 7.

Members in steel frames are often wide flanges. Shaped members can also be made using built-up sections. Moment-resisting joints are typically welded or bolted along opposite flanges to achieve rigidity (see the discussion in Chapter 16). Stiffening plate elements are typically used at rigid joints to keep web and flange elements from buckling due to the high compressive stresses accompanying the moments present (Figure 9–19).

Reinforced concrete frames typically use reinforcing along all faces due to the complex moment distributions associated with varying loadings. The largest amount of reinforcing steel typically occurs at rigid joints. Post-tensioning may be used effectively in horizontal members and to connect orthogonal vertical elements.

Timber frames are somewhat problematic because of the intrinsic difficulties in making moment-resisting joints out of timber. Common knee braces, however, provide an equivalent function in stabilizing timber structures. Base connections are typically pinned.

9–4–6   General Considerations

As mentioned earlier, special attention should be paid to whether or not a frame is actually the best structural solution possible for use in a given context. As Figure 9–15 indicates, an assembly using pinned connections and full diagonal bracing (a simple form of truss) is often quite preferable to any of the frame systems shown in terms of structural efficiency. Using a frame structure does not make sense if other approaches can be used.

(a) Structural response to lateral loads. This diagram is not meant to show what is necessarily a practical construction approach but rather an extreme design approach based on the criterion that structural depths should be proportional to moments present.

Moments in a typical bay

Possible practical building elements partly based on the design approach shown above.

(b) Structural response to vertical loads. This is clearly an impractical and even dangerous solution, since the shaping of members in response to moments results in an unstable structure.

Moments in a typical bay

(c) Structural response to both lateral and vertical load requirements. The structure is shaped to meet critical requirements from both loading conditions but is not necessarily optimum for either.

FIGURE 9-18 Shaping frame members in response to internal moments in a multistory structure.

(a) Rigid connection in steel.

(b) Rigid connection in reinforced concrete.

(c) Rigid connection in timber (knee-brace).

FIGURE 9-19   Typical types of rigid (moment-resisting) connections (see Chapter 16).

In many cases where a frame is still considered an appropriate or necessary structure because of its openness, it is possible to use a *braced-frame* approach wherein a basic frame is reinforced with diagonals in bays where the diagonals can be safely placed without interfering in building functions (see Chapter 14). Typical locations are around elevator shafts and other continuous vertical bays that are normally enclosed anyhow. Use of diagonal bracing greatly reduces the moments in the frame caused by lateral loads. Consequently, members can be reduced in size.

QUESTIONS

9-1 Find a frame building under construction in your local area. Draw a sketch of a typical beam-and-column connection.

9-2 Using an approximate method of analysis, analyze a single-bay frame of the type generally illustrated in Figure 9–3 that carries a horizontal load of 3000 lb acting at the upper left joint. Assume that $h = 12$ ft and $L = 22$ ft. Draw shear and moment diagrams. Indicate numerical values.
   Answer: $M_{max} = 18,000$ ft-lb and $V_{max} = 1500$ lb.

9-3 A single-bay frame of the type generally illustrated in Figure 9–4 carries a horizontal load of 5000 lb acting at the upper left joint. Assume that $h = 15$ ft and $L = 25$ ft. Draw shear and moment diagrams. Indicate numerical values. Use an approximate method of analysis.

9-4 Draw a sketch that diagrammatically illustrates possible member-size variations (along the lines of the sketches in Figure 9–15) for the frame analyzed in Question 9–2.

9-5 Consider the two single-bay structures in Figure 9–15(b) and (c), respectively. Assuming that both structures are identical in all respects, except for member end conditions, and carry identical loads, which would you expect to deflect more horizontally? Why?

9-6 A single-bay frame of the type illustrated in Figure 9–16 carries a horizontal load of 5000 lb acting to the right at the upper left joint. A downward uniformly distributed loading of 200 lb/ft is also present on its horizontal beam. What axial forces, shears, and bending moments should the beams and columns be designed to carry? Use an approximate method of analysis.

9–7 A fully fixed single-bay frame has a span of 50 ft and a height of 12 ft and carries a uniform loading of 1000 lb/ft on the horizontal beam. Using a computer-based structural analysis program available at your school, analyze the structure (shears and moments) for a situation where the moment of inertia of the beam is (a) equal to that of the columns, (b) twice that of the columns, and (c) three times that of the columns. Compare results. (Assume any I_c value for the columns that you wish, or use $I_c = 1200$ in.^{4}.)

CHAPTER 10

Plate and Grid Structures

10-1 INTRODUCTION

Plates are rigid planar structures typically made of monolithic material whose depths are small with respect to their other dimensions. A multidirectional dispersal of applied loads characterizes the way loads are carried to supports in plate structures. The advent of modern reinforced concrete has made the plate among the most common of all building elements. Plates can be supported along their entire boundaries or only at selected points (e.g. columns) or with some mixture of continuous and point supports. Support conditions can be simple or fixed. The variety of support conditions possible makes the plate a highly versatile structural element.

While strictly speaking, a plate is made of a relatively homogeneous solid material exhibiting similar properties in all directions, there are also several other types of structures whose general structural behavior is analogous to that of a plate (Figure 10–1). The *space frame* (actually a space truss), which is composed of short rigid elements triangulated in three dimensions and assembled to form a large rigid planar surface structure of relatively thin thickness, is one such structure. The *grid structure* is another. Plane grid structures are typically made up of a series of intersecting long, rigid linear elements such as beams or trusses, with parallel upper and lower chords. Joints at points of intersection are rigid. The basic shear and moment distributions in structures of these types are not unlike those present in comparably dimensioned monolithic plates. There are, however, many basic differences, which are explored later in this chapter.

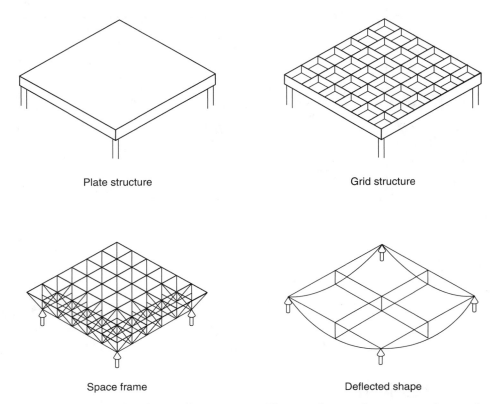

Plate structure

Grid structure

Space frame

Deflected shape

FIGURE 10-1 Plate, grid, and space-frame structures. The general types of curvatures and external moments induced in plate, grid, and space-frame structures are basically similar if loads and general dimensions are similar. The exact way in which each structure provides internal resisting moments and the specifics of behavior, however, are different.

10-2 GRID STRUCTURES

Consider the simple crossed-beam system supported on four sides shown in Figure 10–2(a). As long as both beams are exactly identical, the load will be equally dispersed along both beams (i.e., each beam will pick up one-half of the total load and transfer it to its supports). If the beams are not identical, a greater portion of the load will be carried by the stiffer member. If, for example, the beams were of unequal length, the shorter member would carry a greater percentage of the load than the longer member because it is stiffer. Both members would have to deflect equally at their intersection because they are connected. For both beams to deflect equally, it is necessary that a greater force be applied to the shorter beam than to the longer one to achieve the same deflection. Therefore, the shorter element picks up more of the applied load. The relative amount of load carried in mutually perpendicular directions in a grid system is dependent on the physical properties and dimensions of the grid elements.

The key to analyzing a grid structure of this type is to recognize that a state of deflection compatibility must exist at each point of connection in a crossed-beam system. This compatibility

(a) Basic structure.

(b) Each beam carries a portion of the total load.
$P_T = P_A + P_B$.

(c) P_A and P_B can be found by equating deflection expressions since $\Delta_A = \Delta_B$.

FIGURE 10-2   Simple two-way grid structure.

requirement assumes that the beams are rigidly connected such that both undergo an identical deflection due to a load. By equating deflection expressions appropriate for each beam, it is possible to determine the relative percentage of the load carried by each element. Let P_A be defined as the percentage of the total load (P_T) carried by member A and P_B be the load carried by member B. By equating deflection expressions for each member, we obtain

$$\Delta_A = \Delta_B \quad \text{so} \quad \frac{P_A L_A^3}{48 E_A I_A} = \frac{P_B L_B^3}{48 E_B I_B}$$

$$\frac{P_A}{P_B} = \left(\frac{L_B}{L_A}\right)^3 \left(\frac{E_A I_A}{E_B I_B}\right)$$

If the members are identical in all respects except their lengths, this expression becomes

$$\frac{P_A}{P_B} = \left(\frac{L_B}{L_A}\right)^3$$

For members of equal length it is evident that $P_A = P_B = P_T/2$. If $L_B = 2L_A$, then $P_A/P_B = (2L_A/L_A)^3 = 8$ and $P_A = 8P_B$. Thus, the shorter (more rigid) beam picks up eight times the load of the longer beam. Noting that $P_A + P_B = P_T$, it is evident that $P_A = 8P_T/9$, $P_B = P_T/9$. Associated beam moments are $M_A = P_A L_A/4 = (8P_T/9)/4 = 4P_T L_A/18$ and $M_B = P_B L_B/4 = (P_T/9)(2L_A)/4 = P_T L_A/18$. Thus, moments in the short span are four times as large as those in the long member.

The analysis of more complex grids with multiple crossed beams proceeds in a fashion similar to that just described. Deflections at the intersections of the various beams can be equated. An analytical difficulty arises, however, because of the fact that there are multiple points at which deflections must be compatible and that the interactive reaction forces between members at one point contribute to the deflections at another. Invariably, for a complex grid a number of equations are generated that must be solved simultaneously—a task for computer-based analysis systems (see Appendix 12).

Twisting

Twisting

(a) Interconnected one-way beams. The transverse member (*AC*) transfers a portion of the load from the center member to the end members, which are in turn subject to twisting. The torsional resistance of the end members increases the overall stiffness of the structure and helps carry the load.

(b) Interconnected two-way grid system. Twisting is developed in all members as a consequence of the way the structure deforms. The associated torsional resistance of members increases the stiffness of the grid.

FIGURE 10–3 Behavior of complex grid structures. Twisting is developed in all members as a consequence of the way the structure deforms. The associated torsional resistance of members increases the stiffness of the grid.

A study of the results of such analyses reveals what should be expected. If the cross members are of different lengths, the shorter, more rigid members pick up the predominate share of the applied load. The more rectangular the grid becomes, the less load is carried by the longer members. For very long, narrow bay dimensions, the longitudinal ribs can simply become nothing more than dead weight and are of limited value as structural elements, except as stiffeners.

Another aspect of the behavior of grids is evident in the one-way spanning system shown in Figure 10–3. As the center beam deflects downward under the action of the load, the transverse member transfers some of the load to the adjacent longitudinal elements. Just by looking at the geometry of the probable deflected shapes, it is possible to see that the center longitudinal member carries a greater portion of the load than do the outside members (the center member is bent more, which means that the internal moments are higher, which in turn means that the percentage of load supported is greater). All the grid elements, however, share in carrying the load. In a simple beam system, only the member beneath the load would carry the load.

Another interesting aspect of the one-way grid shown is the twisting induced in the exterior members by the transverse member. As the transverse member deflects, its ends tend to rotate. This tendency to rotate causes torsion to develop in the exterior members. At the same time these members provide a torsional resistance to the end rotations of the transverse member. The transverse member is, in effect, stiffened by the torsional restraint offered by the exterior members and has end conditions somewhere between a fixed end and a simply supported end. The center longitudinal member is also stiffened by the restraint offered by the transverse member, consequently reducing its deflections. The net effect is that a fractional part of the load is eventually transferred to the supports by a twisting action. All the grid elements participate more in carrying the load because of this twisting action. The stiffness of the whole grid is also thereby increased.

In a more complex grid both two-way action and twisting occur. All elements participate in carrying the loads to the supports through a combination of bending and twisting. Note that if the beams were simply crossed and nonrigidly attached at intersection points, the bending rotation of one member would not cause twisting in the other. The consequent loss in overall rigidity due to the loss in torsional resistance associated with the twisting action would cause greater deflections to occur in a nonrigidly connected system than in a rigidly interconnected grid.

10-3 PLATE STRUCTURES

10-3-1 One-Way Plate Structures

Uniform Loads. Plate structures behave in much the same way as the grid structures just described except that the various actions described take place continuously through the slabs rather than only at points of interconnection.

Assume that a simply supported one-way plate spanning between two walls carries a uniformly distributed load per unit area of w'. The plate can be *imagined* as a series of adjacent beam strips, each of *unit width,* that are interconnected along their lengths. The bending moments developed in the plate can then be expressed in terms of a *moment per unit width (m)* of plate corresponding to the strip width. This moment m is measured in ft-lb/ft or kN·m/m. Reactions are typically expressed for the strips in terms of a force per unit length.

The plate bends into a more or less uniform curvature between the line supports at either end; hence the moments developed in the different beam strips are generally similar, although moments in strips near midspan tend to be slightly higher than those near free edges. For a typical strip, $m = w'L^2/8$. Each unit width would be designed for this moment: in a reinforced concrete slab, for example, an amount of steel would be designed for a moment per foot or per meter of slab width.

Point Loads. Plates that carry concentrated loads are much more complex. They are, however, illustrative of the positive load-carrying action of plates. Consider the simple one-way plate carrying a point load shown in Figure 10-4. The plate can be *imagined* as a series of adjacent beam strips of unit width interconnected along their lengths. As an applied load is picked up by one beam strip, it tends to deflect downward. The interconnected adjacent strips, however, offer resistance to this tendency, thereby picking up part of the applied load. A series of shear forces are developed at the interface between adjacent strips. Twisting related to these shears is also caused in the adjacent strips. As beam strips farther and farther from the strip under the load are considered, twisting and shear forces are reduced since more and more of the load becomes transferred to the supports by the longitudinal action of the strips. Longitudinal curvatures also tend to decrease toward the edges of the plate. Internal moments must consequently also decrease. Figure 10-4 diagrammatically illustrates the way reactions and internal moments are distributed in the plate.

(a) Deflected shape of plate. Plate curvatures are greatest under the load.

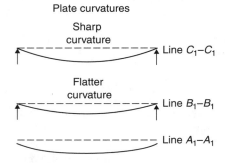

(b) From basic equilibrium considerations it is evident that the structure must provide a total internal resisting moment at a section which balances the external moment present at the same section. If the internal moments were assumed to be uniformly distributed, then the average moment per unit width of plate would be given by $m = Pa_1/4 \div a_2$.

(c) An inspection of the deflected shape of the plate indicates that the internal moments cannot be correctly assumed to be uniformly distributed but are greater where curvatures are sharp and smaller where the plate is flatter. Some internal moments are higher than the average value illustrated in (b) and some are lower. Their total sum of all moments per unit width, however, still must equal the applied moment.

FIGURE 10–4 One-way plate structure.

384

Slab span.
The slab in the transverse direction behaves like a plate continuous over several supports.

Primary span.
The load-carrying capacity of a one-way plate system can be increased by using longitudinal ribs.

FIGURE 10–5   One-way ribbed plates.

The sum of the reactions must total the applied load acting in the vertical direction, and the sum of the internal resisting moments distributed across the plate at a section must equal the total external applied moment. These observations follow from basic equilibrium considerations.

Assuming that the plate shown had a span of a_1 and a width of a_2, the internal moment per unit length in the plate at a transverse section at midspan would be the external moment divided by the plate width $[m = (Pa_1/4)/a_2]$ *if* it was assumed that the resisting moments were uniformly distributed across this section. As argued previously, however, these moments *cannot* be uniform but vary from a maximum at the middle of the plate to a minimum at each edge. Still, thinking in terms of average moments is a useful way of establishing an average reference line about which actual maximum moment values deviate to a greater or lesser degree. Note that using an average value for design purposes, however, is *not* conservative.

Ribbed Plates.   The common ribbed plate is a combined beam-slab system (Figure 10–5). If the connecting slab is relatively stiff, the whole assembly functions as a one-way plate rather than a series of parallel beams. For design purposes, however, it is still common to treat the structure as a series of parallel T beams in the longitudinal direction. The transverse slab is treated as a one-way plate continuous over the beams. Negative moments are developed in the slab over the beams.

10–3–2   Two-Way Plate Structures

Simple Plates on Columns.   Consider a plate that is simply supported on four columns [see Figure 10–6(a)]. The probable deflected shape of the structure is shown in Figure 10–6(b). The curvatures in the plate are highest in the plate strips nearest the free edges of the plate and less toward the middle. This implies that the internal moments in the plate generated to balance the external moments due to the applied forces are greater at the plate edges (with respect to the bending behavior of the plate between the columns) than are the moments in the middle. Since the plate is deformed into a doubly curved shape by the load, it is evident that moments are developed in multidirections rather than in one direction as is normally the case in a single curved element such as a beam.

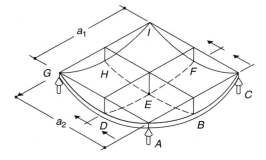

(a) Deflected shape of plate.

Unit width — internal moments are expressed in terms of moments per unit width of plate

m m

Bending in plate element at E

Bending in plate element at D

(b) Plate curvatures.

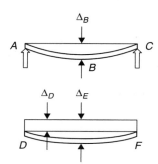

(c) Beam analogy (equivalent to looking at plate from the side). The total external moment along line D–E–F is equivalent to the analogous simple beam amount present.

$M_T = (w'a_1)(a_2)^2/8$

If $a_1 = a_2$, $M_T = w'a^3/8$

(d) The plate provides a total internal resisting moment that exactly balances the external moment present. The internal moment is actually distributed along line D–E–F. Maximum internal moments occur where plate curvatures are the greatest.

$m = 0.11$
$w'a^2$

$m = 0.15w'a^2$

$M_T = (w'a_1)(a_2)^2/8$
$= w'a^3/8$

Moment variation along line D–E–F

$m_{ave} = 0.125w'a^2$

FIGURE 10-6 Square plate simply supported on four columns (uniformly distributed load, w').

386

To find the magnitudes of the internal moments developed, the equilibrium of a section of the plate can be considered. Any segment of the plate can be considered, since it is fundamental that any portion of any structure be in equilibrium. If the moments need to be known along a line *D–E–F,* a section is passed through that line and the equilibrium of the left or right plate segment considered. In doing this it is convenient to view the plate from the side as illustrated in Figure 10–6(c), in which case the plate appears as a simply supported beam carrying a uniformly distributed load per unit length. If the width of the plate is denoted by a_1, the span a_2, and the *load per unit area* acting on the plate surface by w', then the uniformly distributed *load per unit length* that appears on the *analogous* simple beam is given by $w'a_1$. The reactions of the analogous beam on either end are simply the reactive forces in the columns (which by inspection must be $w'a_1a_2/4$). The external bending moment at midspan for this analogous structure is given by the simple beam moment in the form of $wL^2/8$ where w is expressed as a force per unit length. In the case of the plate, $w'a_1$ is analogous to w and a_2 to L. The *total* moment present is consequently $M_T = w'a_1a_2^2/8$ or $M_T = 0.125w'a_1a_2^2$, where w' is expressed as a *force per unit area.* This is the same result that would have been obtained by summing moments about the line *D-E-F,* a procedure described in Section 2–2–7. If the plate is square, $a_1 = a_2$ and $M_T = 0.125w'a^3$.

The simplified analysis above is a useful one since it is evident that the external applied moment along line *DEF* is, in total, equal to $0.125w'a^3$. The plate must, therefore, provide a total internal resisting moment of $0.125w'a^3$. In a beam, this moment would have been provided by a single discrete couple formed by the compressive and tension stress fields internally developed in the beam in response to the external moment. In a plate the total resisting moment is provided by a continuous line of resisting moments in couples across the width of the plate whose sum effect is to yield a total resisting moment of $0.125w'a^3$. The equivalent discrete moment in the analogous beam has been, so to speak, simply spread out across the width of the plate.

If the total resisting moment that the plate provides is known, the next step is to find how this moment is distributed across the section. *If* the resisting moment were assumed to be uniformly distributed across the section, the resisting *moment per unit of width* (m) would simply be the total moment divided by the width of the section (i.e., $m = 0.125w'a^3/a = 0.125w'a^2$, where m is the internal moment per unit width across the plate width at the section considered).

The argument made earlier, however, indicates that the total moment is *not* uniformly distributed but is greater at plate edges than in the middle. Quantitatively assessing the exact distribution, however, is fairly complex and beyond the scope of this book. It is obvious that maximum and minimum values vary about the average moment value of $m = 0.125w'a^2$ discussed before. Figure 10–6(d) shows the results of a more exact analysis. There it is seen that the maximum moment per unit width occurs at the plate edge ($m = 0.15w'a^2$) and the minimum at the center of the plate ($m = 0.11w'a^2$). Similar results would be obtained for an analysis about line *B–E–H,* since the structure is symmetrical.

Note that the maximum moment developed in the plate occurs at the free edge about an axis perpendicular to that edge. The moment about an axis parallel to the free edge at the same point is zero. At the plate midpoint, however, a moment of $m = 0.11w'a^2$ is developed about both axes.

The analysis discussed above highlights that maximum moments occur not at the midpoint of the plate, where one might normally expect them by virtue of a beam analogy, but at the midspan of the edges. The midpoint of this plate is, for example, a good place to put a hole in the plate if this must be done to accommodate some other building element.

Another interesting point is that this particular plate must provide the same *total* internal resisting moment as an analogous beam. When the plate is designed, it is therefore evident that the use of a plate will not necessarily result in the saving of material as compared to an analogous beam. The plate will, however, be shallower. The much heralded advantages of two-way plate action in terms of material savings are associated with other types of support conditions, not the one described and analyzed herein.

Plates Simply Supported on Continuous Edges.   Consider a plate similar to the one previously analyzed but supported continuously on all four edges by simple edge supports (e.g., walls) rather than being supported on columns. An inspection of the probable deflected shape of the structure reveals a radically different type of behavior under load. Maximum curvatures occur at the midpoint of the plate and decrease toward its edges. Internal moments can be expected to vary accordingly.

To find the magnitudes of these internal moments, a method of analysis similar to that used for the column-supported plate can be adopted. In this case, however, the first step of finding the plate reactions is not so easy. Considering the way the plate deflects, it can be seen that the reactions are not uniformly distributed but are at a maximum at the center of each line support and then decrease toward the corners [see Figure 10–7(b)]. A curious aspect of the plate reactions stems from the tendency of the corners of the plate to curl upward under the action of the vertical load. If the corners are to be restrained from curling upward, downward reactive forces must exist at the corners. The total sum of the upward nonuniformly distributed reactions and the downward corner reactions must total the value of the externally applied load acting downward—a fact obvious from basic equilibrium considerations. A quantitative assessment of the way the reactions vary is beyond the scope of this text, but their general form is illustrated in Figure 10–7(b).

By looking at the plate from the side and considering a beam analogy, it can be seen that the total external moment present along a midspan section is less than the moment existent in the previously analyzed plate on columns. The total moment in the plate on the columns was equivalent to the previously encountered $wL^2/8$ moment value, or in terms of the plate dimensions and unit area loads, $w'a^3/8$. This value is associated with concentrated reactions at either end of the structure. By looking at the derivation of the expression, i.e., $M_{L/2} = (wL/2)(L/2) - (wL/2)(L/4) = wL^2/8$, where the first term represents the effects of the end reactions, it can be seen that the dominant moment-producing effect is caused by the moments associated with the reactions and not the external loads. In the plate resting on four continuous supports, the comparable moment caused by the reactions must be less than that associated with point supports because a greater percentage of the reaction forces are nearer the moment center. Consequently, the net external midspan moment must also be reduced, since the moment from the load remains constant. Since external moments are reduced, internal resisting moments are also less. They are considerably reduced from those present in the plate supported on four columns. A shallower plate can therefore be used. The maximum positive plate moment per unit width in a square plate can be shown to be $m = +0.0479w'a^2$.

All in all, continuously supporting a plate is far more preferable to using point supports. When continuous supports are used, the true benefit of two-way action can be achieved.

Plates with Continuous Fixed-Edge Supports.   Figure 10–8 illustrates a plate similar to that analyzed above except that the edges are now completely fixed. The moments in the plate are

(a) Deflected shape of plate.

Corners tend to curl upward if not restrained

(b) Plate reactions. The downward forces shown on the corners keep the corners from curling up.

(c) Beam analogy (equivalent to looking at the plate from the side). The external moment developed is less than the comparable $wL^2/8$ for a simple beam because of the different reaction distribution. The total internal resisting moment is likewise smaller.

$M_T < wL^2/8$

(d) Plate moments.

m

M_T

FIGURE 10-7 Square plate simply supported along all edges (uniformly distributed load, w').

389

	Side Ratio	Bending Moments	
		$M_a = C_a wa^2$	$M_b = C_b wb^2$
	a/b	C_a	C_b
Simply supported on all four sides	1.0	+0.0479	+0.0479
	2.0	+0.0116	+0.1017
Fixed edges on all four sides	1.0	+0.0231 −0.0513	+0.0231 −0.0513
	2.0	+0.0039 −0.0143	+0.0412 −0.0829
Free corner (corner balcony)	1.0	+0.027 −0.050	+0.027 −0.050

Simply supported: Plate curvatures are the greatest in the short rather than the long direction. Moments are consequently greater in the short span direction than in the long span direction.

Plate with fully fixed edges.

FIGURE 10–8 Effects of different boundary conditions and bay proportions.

even further reduced by fixing the plate ends. This is a very advantageous type of support condition for plates. For a square plate, the maximum moments per unit width can be shown to be $m = +0.0231w'a^2$ and $m = -0.0513w'a^2$.

Bay Proportions: Effects on Moments. In the section on analysis of grids it was noted that the stiffer portion of a grid structure, which is often the short-span direction, usually carries the greatest percentage of the applied load. The same phenomenon is true in rigid planar structures.

Consider the rectangular plate (continuously supported) shown in Figure 10–8. Only the plate strips in the short direction are experiencing significant curvatures. The longitudinal strips are bent less. The implication is that only the strips in the short direction are providing internal moment resistance and are participating significantly in carrying the applied load. The long span strips are almost simply riding along.

The more rectangular a plate becomes, the more it behaves as a one-way rather than a two-way system. It is as if the plate were supported only along its long parallel edges. Consequently, none of the advantages associated with the two-way action of continuously supported plates are present.

If the *length/width bay dimensions* of a plate exceed a ratio of about 1.5, the plate essentially behaves as a one-way rather than as a two-way system.

Design Moments. The effects of different support conditions and bay proportions for plates with uniform loadings (e.g., w' in lb/ft^2) may be reflected directly by using bending moment expressions in the form $m_a = Cw'a_a^2$ and $m_b = Cw'a_b^2$, where a and b are plate dimensions and C represents a constant reflecting the type of support conditions present. A number of cases have been solved through more advanced analysis techniques and results as presented in Figure 10–8.

Plate on Beams Supported by Columns.   Figure 10–9(a) illustrates a variant of the first plate analyzed in which a plate is supported by continuous beams, which are in turn supported by columns. This is an interesting type of structure finding wide application in buildings. Assuming that the plate is merely simply supported on the beams gives the plate a set of end conditions somewhere between the situation where the plate is supported only by columns and the situation where the plate is supported by continuous edge supports. If the beams are extremely stiff, the support conditions of the plate approach those of continuous edge supports and similar moments are developed in the plate. If the beams are very flexible, however, little edge support is provided and the plate behaves more as if it were simply resting on four columns. Higher plate moments are accordingly developed than in the previous case. The relative stiffnesses of the edge beams therefore crucially affect the magnitude of the moments developed in the plate.

An interesting facet of this type of structure can be seen by passing a transverse section through midspan. By basic equilibrium considerations, it can be seen that the plate and beam structure must provide an internal resisting moment that exactly balances the external moment at the section. As was the case before when four point supports were used, the moment of interest is $0.125w'a^3$. If the beams were highly flexible ($I_b \rightarrow 0$), the sum of the internal moments that are developed in the plate is also equal to $0.125w'a^3$, as described before. The beams therefore would not provide any of the moment resistance. If, on the other hand, it were somehow possible to have the plate of minimum stiffness ($I_p \rightarrow 0$) and not capable of providing moment resistance, the beams would *have* to provide the entire resistance. Each of the two beams would therefore develop a moment of $0.125w'a^3/2$. The real situation lies between these extremes. The point herein is that the structure must provide a fixed requisite moment resistance, but the exact way in which this occurs is dependent on the nature of the structure used. Moments are never dispensed with, but merely redistributed.

The consequence of using stiffer beams is that plate moments are reduced and the plate can be made shallower. Alternatively, a stiffer plate can be used and the beams reduced in depth or eliminated (the plate, however, must be made thicker than in the previous case).

Other Types of Plates.   There are, of course, a wide variety of other plate types not yet considered. Because of the importance of end conditions, each type of plate must be treated separately. The reader is referred to more advanced texts on the subject. *Yield line* theory is a particularly interesting technique for reinforced concrete.

A good way of getting at least a general feeling for the way any plate behaves is to sketch its deflected shape, something that with practice can be done for virtually any type of plate (see Figure 10–10). These sketches will at least identify regions of critical positive and negative moment and thus will be useful in many situations (such as the preliminary design of reinforced concrete plates, where it is necessary to know whether reinforcing steel goes on the top or bottom of the plate).

Comparisons among Plates, Grids, and Space Frames.   As mentioned earlier, the general types of curvatures and moments induced in plates, grids, or planar space frames of comparable dimensions and carrying equivalent loads are similar. The exact way each structure provides

(a) Plate on walls. This is a favorable support condition for plates.

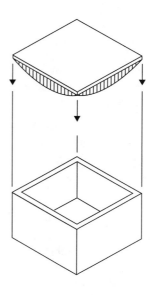

(b) Two-way beam and slab system. Plate on beams. If the beams are very stiff, the plate behaves as if it were supported on walls. If the beams are highly flexible, then the plate behaves as if it were supported on four columns.

(c) The total internal resisting moment provided by the beam and slab system must equal the total applied external moment.

$$M_T = w'a^3/8$$

FIGURE 10–9 Two-way beam-and-slab system.

FIGURE 10–10   Unusual support conditions. The basic behavior of plates having unusual support conditions can be at least qualitatively understood by drawing and studying the probable deflected shape of the structure (i.e., noting regions of tension and compression).

balancing internal moments, however, differs. In a plate structure the internal moment is provided by a continuous line of couples formed by the compression and tension forces developed in the upper and lower surfaces of the plate. In a grid the resisting couples are concentrated in the beams. In comparison to the moments developed in a plate (normally expressed in terms of a moment per unit length), the moment in a grid beam is very *approximately* given by the beam spacing times the average moment per unit length at that location (all the equivalent plate moments in a region are, so to speak, concentrated in a single beam). This approximation, however, can lead to unconservative results in coarse-grained grids, since grids and plates differ in many significant ways (particularly the relative contribution of the torsional stiffness of elements in carrying the applied loads). The approximation described above improves as the grid mesh becomes finer and finer (it begins to approach a continuous plate surface).

Thus, in a grid structure with beam members spaced s_1 apart, the average moments per unit plate width m present at the section may be considered collected into a moment $M_1 = m(s_1)$. The grid beam would then be designed for this bending moment as described in Chapter 6. A similar situation exists for space frame structures except that the resisting couples are provided by a trusslike, rather than a beamlike, fashion. Thus, in a space frame structure of depth d_1 and bar spacing s_1, the average moments per unit plate width m present at the section may be considered collected into a moment $M_1 = m(s_1)$, which is in turn balanced by a resisting moment formed by the tension and compression forces in the upper and lower bars acting over the depth of the structure. The bar forces themselves can be found by noting that $T_1 = C_1 = M_1/d_1$.

Since these relations exist, the general moment distributions discussed earlier in connection with plates can also be used to describe approximately the behavior of grids and planar space frames.

10–4   DESIGN OF TWO-WAY SYSTEMS: GENERAL OBJECTIVES FOR PLATE, GRID, AND SPACE-FRAME STRUCTURES

The process of sizing members for the shears and moments present in a two-way structure is the same as for any member in bending. There are, however, several steps that can be taken which initially minimize the bending present. There are also other critical variables which affect the design of a plate structure and influence the appropriateness of a system selected. These factors will be considered in the following section.

Support Conditions. A primary design objective is always to minimize the bending moments present in a structure. An effective way of doing this in rigid planar structures is to operate on the support conditions. (As discussed in the previous section, moments in rigid planar structures are critically dependent on support conditions.)

Generally speaking, a design that provides as much continuous support to a rigid planar structure as possible will be one in which moments in the structure are minimized. Structural depths can thereby be reduced. Thus, continuous edge supports are preferable to column supports. Fixed supports also result in smaller plate moments than simple supports (see Figure 10–8).

Techniques such as using overhangs described for reducing moments in beams are also applicable to planar structures in bending. Cantilevering a portion of the structure tends to reduce the maximum design moment present.

When the support system is basically repetitive in nature (e.g., a series of column bays), the use of a continuous rigid structure leads to lower design moments than does the use of a series of discrete, simply supported plates. The use of a continuous surface causes the portion of the plate over a single bay to behave more like a plate with fixed ends than does a simply supported one (see Figure 10–11).

Bay Proportions: Effect on Choice of Structure. As noted in the section on analyzing rigid planar structures, the less square or more rectangular a supporting bay becomes, the less the supported planar structure behaves like a two-way system and the more it behaves like a one-way system acting in the short-span direction. From a design viewpoint, the consequence of this phenomenon is that bays should be designed to be as dimensionally symmetrical as possible if two-way action is desired. Only if bay dimensions form a ratio of between approximately $1:1$ and $1:1.5$ does two-way action obtain.

(a) Simply supported plates.   (b) Continuous plates.

FIGURE 10–11 Plates on a column grid. A continuous plate surface is generally preferable to a series of simply supported plates in that design moments are reduced and rigidity increased by the continuity.

Using what appears to be a two-way structure, such as a space frame, over a long rectangular bay does not really accomplish very much. The structure will behave like a one-way system in the short direction. Members in the short-span direction would carry most of the load. Longitudinal members would simply ride along contributing little, except adding some stiffening. Therefore, a system deliberately designed and intended to be a one-way spanning system may as well be used. Less total material could be used to support the load in space.

Types of Loads: Effect on Choice of Structure.   A fundamental reason for using a rigid planar structure is quite often a functional one. These structures can provide usable horizontal floor planes. As such, the loads they typically carry are usually uniformly distributed. When this is the case, either plates, grids with small meshes, or space frames can be used relatively efficiently. These same structures are, however, relatively inefficient when called upon to support large concentrated loads. Surface structures work best supporting surface loads. Large concentrated loads can, however, be fairly effectively carried by coarse-grained grid structures in which the crossed beams intersect beneath the concentrated loads.

An additional point is that many current, commercially available types of space frame structures, such as those that are typically made of cold-formed light steel elements, are better suited to roof rather than to floor loads, since roof loads tend to be somewhat lighter. These structures do not work particularly well for floor loads. This is not a consequence of the basic structural approach but of the specific way they are constructed.

Span Range.   There is a wide variation in spans possible. Rigid plates made of reinforced concrete can economically span anywhere from 15 to 60 ft (4.5 to 18 m) or so. Grids and space frames can effectively span higher distances, depending on exactly how they are made. Commercially available space frames, for example, can easily span up to 100 ft (30 m), depending on the member sizes and support conditions used. Much higher spans are even possible with specially designed structures.

For short spans of the type often encountered in buildings [e.g., 15 to 30 ft (4.5 to 9 m)], the construction complexities of grids and space frames often render them less attractive than simple reinforced concrete plates. In Chapter 14 we discuss the influence of span in more detail.

10–5   DESIGN OF REINFORCED CONCRETE PLATES

Plate Moments and Placement of Reinforcing Steel.   The thickness of a reinforced concrete plate and the amount and location of reinforcing steel used in a constant-depth plate or slab is critically dependent on the magnitude and distribution of moments in the plate. Figure 10–12(a) illustrates the deformations present in continuous plate resting on columns. Reinforcing steel must be placed in all tension regions. This requirement results in a placement of reinforcing steel of the type illustrated in Figure 10–12(b). Since moments are continuous, reinforcing steel must be closely spaced. It is thus common to use a series of parallel bars. Since moments are multidirectional, mutually perpendicular sets of bars are used. These bars can be deformed as shown so that the steel is properly located in tension regions or discontinuous shorter linear pieces that are lapped can be similarly placed.

While the design moments in the plate (on which plate thicknesses and steel sizes would depend) can be found from techniques discussed in the section on analysis, some characteristics

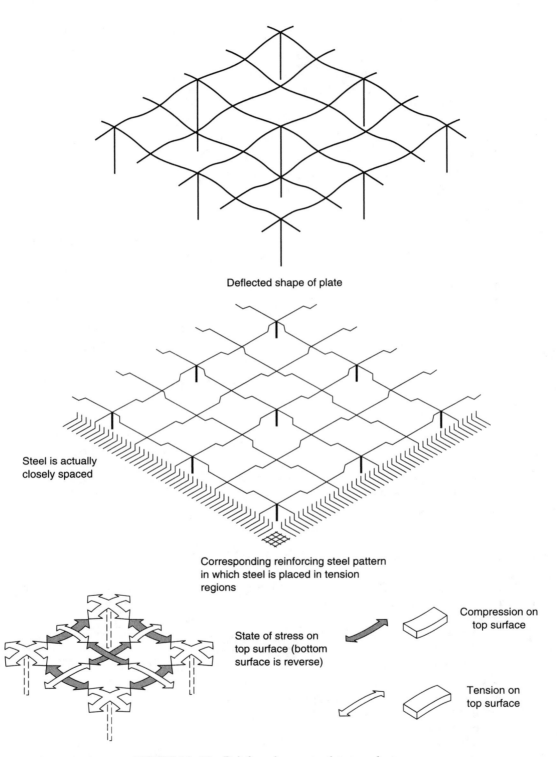

Deflected shape of plate

Steel is actually
closely spaced

Corresponding reinforcing steel pattern
in which steel is placed in tension
regions

State of stress on
top surface (bottom
surface is reverse)

Compression on
top surface

Tension on
top surface

FIGURE 10–12   Reinforced concrete plate on columns.

FIGURE 10–13   Column and middle strips. Column strips generally carry larger moments than middle strips and require greater amounts of steel.

peculiar to reinforced concrete cause a slightly different design approach to be taken. As noted previously, the total (positive plus negative) moments in a slab supported on columns is given by $M_T = w'a^3/8 = 0.125w'a^3$. It would therefore be thought that the total amount of steel needed would be in response to this value. If a more detailed study of the *plastic behavior* of the plate is made, however, it can be seen that designing for the $0.125w'a^3$ moment is more conservative than necessary. (See Section 6–4 for a discussion of the idea of plastic behavior in members.)

Practically, continuous reinforced concrete plates are designed such that the total design moment M_T (sum of all positive and negative moments) is divided throughout the slab on a highly empirical basis. In U.S. practice, the slab is first divided into column and middle strips (see Figure 10–13). Moments per unit width are assumed constant across each strip instead of varying continuously as theory suggests. The *total moment* is then defined as $M_T = wL_2L_1^2/8$, where w is the loading in lb/ft^2 (kN/m^2), L_1 is the direction considered, and L_2 is the clear panel width at right angles. For a continuous slab interior bay extending in both directions, this moment is empirically split as follows: total negative design moment $= (0.65)M_T$ and total positive design moment $= (0.35)M_T$. Then 75% of the negative design moment is apportioned to the column strip and 25% to the middle strip. Also, 60% of the total positive design moment is apportioned to the column strip and 40% to the middle strip. Many factors and assumptions that are beyond the scope of this book underlie this empirically based design approach. The following example is intended to convey only the spirit of the approach used, not to represent actual design practice.

◆ ◆   **EXAMPLE**

A 20 × 20-ft two-way interior bay flat slab supports a live loading of 80 lb/ft^2 and has a dead load of 90 lb/ft^2. Determine the design moments. Use an ultimate strength design approach.

Solution:

Total moments:

$$\text{loading:} \quad w = 1.4DL + 1.7LL = 1.4(90) + 1.7(80) = 262 \text{ lb/ft}^2$$

$$\text{total moment:} \quad M_{U_T} = \frac{wL_2L_1^2}{8} = \frac{262(20)(20)^2}{8} = 262{,}000 \text{ ft-lb}$$

$$\text{negative design moment} = 0.65M_T = 0.65(262{,}000) = 170{,}300 \text{ ft-lb}$$

$$\text{positive design moment} = 0.35(276{,}000) = 91{,}700 \text{ ft-lb}$$

Column strip:

$$\text{negative moment} = 0.75(170{,}300) = 127{,}725 \text{ ft-lb}$$

$$\text{positive moment} = 0.60(91{,}700) = 55{,}020 \text{ ft-lb}$$

Since the strip width is $20/2 = 10$, the

$$\text{design negative moment per unit width} = \frac{127{,}725}{10} = 12{,}772.5 \text{ ft-lb/ft}$$

$$\text{design positive moment per unit width} = \frac{55{,}020}{10} = 5502 \text{ ft-lb/ft}$$

Middle strip:

$$\text{negative moment} = 0.25(170{,}300) = 42{,}575 \text{ ft-lb}$$

$$\text{design negative moment per unit width} = \frac{42{,}575}{10} = 4257.5 \text{ ft-lb/ft}$$

$$\text{positive moment} = 0.40(91{,}700) = 36{,}680 \text{ ft-lb/ft}$$

$$\text{design positive moment per unit width} = \frac{36{,}680}{10} = 3668 \text{ ft-lb/ft}$$

The maximum design moments are negative and occur over the top of the columns ($m = 12{,}772.5$ ft-lb/ft), while midspan positive moments are relatively small ($m = 3668$ ft-lb/ft) by contrast. Reinforcing steel would be designed on a unit width basis in response to the column and middle strip moments found above. ◆

Effects of Span. For low-span ranges [e.g., about 15 to 22 ft (5 to 7 m)], common building loads result in moments that can be handled by relatively thin plates [e.g., on the order of 5 to 10 in. (13 to 26 cm)]. As spans increase, moments become greater and plate thicknesses must increase. A consequence of using thicker plates, however, is that the dead weight of the structure also dramatically increases. For this reason, plates are often hollowed out to reduce the dead load while at the same time maintaining an appreciable structural depth. One such system, called a *waffle slab,* is shown in Figure 10–14.

Another approach to increased spans is to use what is commonly referred to as a *two-way beam-and-slab system* (see Figure 10–14). Since the beams are relatively stiff and form a continuous edge support for the plate, the plate can be made relatively thin because of the favorable support conditions, which decrease the moments present in the plate.

Both the waffle and two-way beam-and-slab systems can span relatively long distances. A system exhibiting desirable properties of both systems is obtained by not hollowing out the

(a) Two-way beam and slab.

(d) Waffle slab.

(b) Plan view. The continuous edge support provided to the slab by the beams gives the slab a favorable support condition, whereby plate moments are reduced.

(e) The overall spanning capacity of a waffle slab can be increased by not hollowing out lines between columns. Two-way beam-and-slab action is thus obtained.

(c) Shear is not a major problem in this type of system because of the presence of the beams, which have a large shear capacity.

(f) To increase the shear capacity of the structure, the plate is not hollowed adjacent to the column heads.

FIGURE 10–14   Two-way beam-and-slab systems and waffle systems.

waffle slab between columns. A surrounding stiff-beam system is thereby created. Spans longer than that associated with the basic waffle slab are possible. The systems can be post-tensioned to even further increase their span capabilities. These systems are discussed more in detail in Chapters 11 and 14, to which the reader is referred.

Plate Thicknesses. L/d ratios for estimating slab thicknesses are approximately given by the following: two-way flat slabs, $L/d = 33$–40; two-way beam and slab systems, $L/d = 45$–55; waffle slabs, $L/d = 28$–30; one-way slabs, $L/d = 24$–36; and one-way ribbed slabs, $L/d = 24$–36. Reinforced concrete beams, by contrast, typically vary from $L/d = 16$ to $L/d = 26$.

Effects of Shear Forces. Although the discussion has thus far dealt exclusively with bending in plates, shear is also present and is often the dominant factor influencing the design of the plate.

Shear forces are highest in plates on columns or other discrete supports. A punch-through type of failure can occur in plates around such points because of the high shear stresses present. The entire reactive force in a column, for example, must be distributed in the form of shear forces in the plate around the interface of the column and plate.

The plate area resisting the external shear can be found by considering potential shear failure lines. A reinforced concrete plate, for example, tends to fail in a manner illustrated in Figure 10–15. The diagonal crack pattern is caused by diagonal tension cracks associated with the shear stresses present (see Section 6–4–4). The area of plate providing the resistance to punch-through failure is therefore this same crack surface. Note that the extent of this surface depends critically on the thickness of the plate and the circumference of the column. Punch-through shear failures are most common in either thin plates or those supported on pointed or small columns. The approximate magnitude of the shear stresses present is given by $f_v = V/A_p$, where A_p is the plate area in shear.

The punch-through type of failure potentially possible because of high shear forces is often a crucial design issue. The magnitude of the shear stresses present depends directly on the magnitude of the shear force and the plate area in shear. The latter depends on the thickness of the plate and the length of failure plane possible (which depends on the size of the support). If shear stresses are too high, the design options are to use special steel reinforcement in the overstressed regions (called *shear heads*) or to increase the plate area in shear.

Increasing the plate area in shear can be easily done by increasing the plate thickness. This may prove uneconomical to do for the whole plate if not needed for moment considerations. The plate can be locally thickened at critical points, however, through the use of drop panels (see Figure 10–15). Alternatively, the plate area in shear can be increased by increasing the support size. This can also be done locally through the use of column capitals. The larger the capital, the greater is the plate area in shear. Column capitals can be any shape, but due to the natural tendency to fail in diagonal shear, capitals are often given a sloped shape (simply because material below the 45° line is inactive).

Both drop panels and column capitals can be simultaneously used. The shear capacity of such a system is quite high and is used in special cases where loads are particularly high (e.g., warehouses).

Reinforced concrete slabs that do not use column capitals are usually referred to simply as *plates*. Those using capitals and drop panels are usually referred to as *flat slabs*.

Shear can also be a problem in waffle slabs but can be handled quite easily. The area adjacent to a column top is simply not hollowed out. A built-in column capital is thus created (see

(a) Column with drop panel.

(b) Column with drop panel and capital.

(c) The plate area in shear can be increased (thus decreasing shear stresses) by using a drop panel to increase locally the plate thickness.

(d) Column capitals. The use of column capitals increases the length of the failure plane, thus increasing the area of the plate in shear. Material below the diagonal shear failure plane is inactive and can be eliminated.

(e) Drop panels and capitals. Both drop panels and capitals can be used simultaneously to increase the shear capacity of the structure in cases where shear forces are extremely high.

(f) Insetting columns. At free edges of plates the shear capacity of the system is reduced because of the reduced length of the plate thickness in shear. Insetting the column by the amount shown increases the shear capacity of the system. This type of edge condition is commonly used in plate structures.

(g) Characteristic failure mode. A punch-through type of failure can result from excessively high shear forces.

FIGURE 10–15 Designing for shear in reinforced concrete plates.

Figure 10–14). In a two-way beam-and-slab system, the beams framing into the columns pick up most of the shear. Since their areas are relatively large and reinforcement is easy, shear is usually not a great problem in this type of system (see Figure 10–14).

Effects of Lateral Loads. Plates or slabs cast monolithically with columns naturally tend to form frame structures capable of carrying lateral loads. Their capacity to carry lateral loads depends to a great extent on the thickness of the horizontal structure at the column interfaces (deep structures have larger possible moment arms for increased resistance). A thin plate-and-column system can carry lateral loads, but its capacity is limited and thus its use is restricted to relatively low buildings. The use of column capitals or drop panels increases the system capacity. Waffles and two-way beam-and-slab systems can support substantial lateral loads. The two-way beam-and-slab system forms a natural frame system and is often used where lateral load-carrying capacity is important. The reader is referred to Chapters 11 and 14 for a more in-depth coverage of this topic.

Special Plates and Grids. Plate-and-grid structures may be shaped in a variety of ways to reflect variations in the internal force states present within them, albeit doing so may or may not be economic. As *idealized* forms, however, they are invariably worth attention. Figure 10–16(b) shows a simply supported plate structure resting on top of a surrounding simply supported beam structure. Both the plate and the beams have been shaped to better reflect the variation in bending moments present within them (depths are proportional to moments). Obviously the structure is not stable with respect to lateral forces. Figure 10–16(c) shows a variable-depth plate-and-beam structure that is continuous throughout and capable of carrying both vertical and lateral forces. Figure 10–16(d) shows a constant-depth grid structure in which the widths of grid elements are varied to match the bending moments present. Figure 10–16(e) shows a variable-depth structure similar to Figure 10–16(b) in which beam widths are held constant and depths allowed to vary. Figure 10–16(f) shows a continuous grid structure in which beam widths are held constant and depths allowed to vary to match the bending moments present.

These different shapes only generally reflect variations in internal force states, since compromises and judgments must be made to make the shapes viable or sensible. The discussions in Section 6–4–2 and Section 8–4–3 on the shaping of beams and frames, respectively, are highly relevant here.

A final special form of plate is shown in Figure 10–16(g). A detailed analysis of the elastic stress distributions present in a plate reveals the presence of lines of *principal stress*. These lines, often called *isostatics,* are directions along which the torsional shear stresses are zero. Some designers have devised plates that are ribbed in a manner intended to reflect these isostatic lines. These structures are, of course, expensive to construct, but their designers claim that these expenses are not excessive and that material savings compensate for any added construction cost. These structures are undoubtedly interesting but are curious from the viewpoint of classical theory in that they represent the physical manifestation of a model of a stress distribution in an elastic material that is actually constructed using an inelastic material (concrete). That the ribs are indeed lines of principal stress is not argued, but a self-fulfilling prophecy may be present in placing stiffer ribs along these lines.

(a) Two-way, constant-depth, flat-plate system.

(b) Simply supported plate and supporting beam structure (shaped to reflect bending moment variations due to vertical loadings).

(c) Plate structure continuous with supporting rigid frame structure (shaped in response to both vertical and lateral loads).

(d) Constant-depth grid structure (beam widths varied to reflect bending moment variations due to vertical loadings).

(e) Simply supported grid structure (constant beam widths and variable depths that reflect bending moment variations due to vertical loadings).

(f) Grid structure continuous with supporting rigid frame structure (shaped in response to both vertical and lateral loads).

(g) Continuous plate structure with ribs reflecting isostatic lines.

FIGURE 10–16   Special types of plate-and-grid structures.

10–6 SPACE-FRAME STRUCTURES

Forces in Members. Space-frame structures are typically made up of rigid linear members arranged in repeating geometric units to form a thin horizontally spanning structure. They are particularly suitable for uniformly distributed loads, but do not handle large concentrated loads well. Although typically called space frames, these structures are better characterized as *space trusses.*

As argued in Section 10–3, the general moment distributions discussed for plate structures are broadly relevant to space frames as well. Assume that the depth of the structure is d_1. To find the forces in a pair of upper and lower bar members spaced s_1 apart, the moments per unit width m may be considered collected into a moment $M_1 = m(s_1)$. Then the bar forces become $T_1 = C_1 = M_1/d_1$, since $M_1 = T_1d_1 = C_1d_1$. Increasing depths decreases forces, and vice versa. Members may be sized from these forces. Results are highly approximate. More exact forces may be obtained through more formal structural analysis techniques such as the matrix displacement method (see Appendix 12).

In addition to moments, shear forces around vertical supports cause forces to develop in members. High forces are developed in members in and around points of high shear concentration (e.g., column tops). Consequently, these members may have to be specially designed (Figure 10–17). Alternatively, increasing the number of elements picking up the shear force (by effectively increasing the size of the column top via brackets) decreases the forces present in individual members.

The importance of support conditions and general bay proportions should be recalled (Section 10–3). The common use of space frames on point supports (e.g., corner columns) is among the least desirable ways of supporting space frames.

Forms and Member Design Attitudes. An almost bewildering array of geometric units may be used to form the basic repetitive unit, ranging from simple tetrahedrons to any of a number of other forms derived from the Platonic and Archimedean polyhedral forms. A discussion of these forms is beyond the scope of this book. Some general comments, however, may be made.

The modules themselves may assume a wide variety of geometries and still work structurally. The more fine-grained the assembly, the lower are the member forces. Deeper modules reduce member forces in upper and lower planes.

The basic design problem is frequently less structural in concern and more about the relationship between geometry and construction—in particular, how to devise connections for attaching members in complex geometries. The choice of geometry is consequently often as dependent on construction attitudes or possibilities toward member shapes and connections as anything else. Nonetheless, major structural issues arise. Some simple modules, such as the rectangular gridlike system shown to the upper left in Figure 10–18, are particularly easy to fabricate. Since it has no spatial diagonals connecting opposite corners, however, these modules do not transmit very well the twisting or torsional forces normally present in plates or well-designed grids (the planar elements simply twist). As argued earlier, these forces are positive in nature and both stiffen the overall assembly and help transfer forces from one module to another. Adding diagonals as shown stiffens the structure.

In general, the more nodes are interconnected spatially (as in the tetrahedron), the stiffer are the resulting frameworks. The hexagonal unit shown in Figure 10–18 is thus problematic. In

(a) The large reaction force at a column must be transferred into the structure via members framing into the top of the column. Slender members may be prone to buckling.

(b) Axial forces in members may be reduced by increasing the number of members that distribute the reactive force into the structure. This is done by increasing the bearing area of the support, either by subframing or by using special rigid arms.

$$M = m_{ave} \times spacing$$

m = moment/unit length

$$M = Cd = Td$$

$$M = Cd = Td$$

Homogeneous Plate Structure

Space Frame Structure

(c) Variation in bending moments along a midsection of a simply supported homogeneous plate structure. Moments are expressed in terms of m (moment per unit length) along the section.

(d) In a space-frame structure, the bending moments are carried by the couples formed by axial forces in the upper and lower bars. For structures with many closely spaced bars, each pair of bars carries a moment corresponding approximately to their contributory areas ($M = m \times spacing = Cd = Td$, where m is the average moment present at the location considered). The forces developed in the upper and lower bars varies similarly to the moment distribution in a homogeneous plate.

FIGURE 10–17 Forces in space-frame structures.

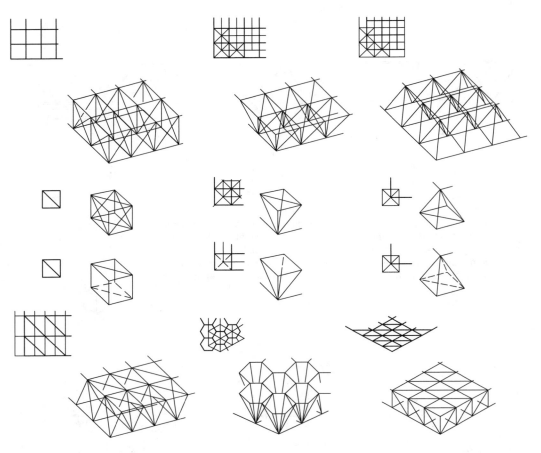

(a) Typical space-frame structures based on the use of repetitive modules. Variants shown use added bracing elements or rigid diaphragms in lieu of bars.

Constant member spacing and variable member size.

Constant member size and variable member spacing.

(b) Layered systems using continuous chords. The two structures shown (simply supported on four corners) are optimized to match the variation in bending moments present.

FIGURE 10–18 Types of space-frame structures.

addition, members in upper and lower planes naturally do not line up linearly. This, in turn, means that the tension and compression forces naturally developed in these members do not have a clearly organized straight element to receive them. Forces are split up at odd angles, which generally leads to higher forces than in straight members.

The varying moment distributions that were discussed earlier suggest that forces in individual members vary as well when repetitive geometries are used (a repetitious structure does *not* mean that all members are subjected to the same forces). For example, in a plate simply supported at the corners, maximum member forces are developed along the edges and reduce toward midspan no matter what module type is used. Since forces vary, the use of a repetitive module with constant-size members would necessarily imply that the individual members must be sized on the basis of the worst-case force condition, with consequent inefficiencies for members with less critical forces. Alternatively, member sizes may be varied in response to forces present. The latter is interesting but difficult to do because of the complex geometries.

Space frames need not be made of individual modules, but by planes of crossed linear members. The latter would not necessarily have to be spaced uniformly (Figure 10–18). Since the forces in members are dependent on both the moment present and the member spacings, it is not impossible to envision a spacing such that forces in upper and lower chord members are held reasonably constant.

10–7   FOLDED-PLATE STRUCTURES

The stiffness of a plate structure can be dramatically increased by not using a planar surface at all (ribbed or otherwise), but by radically deforming the whole plate surface in a way such that structural depths are greatly increased. The result is a form of plate with a unique cross section which can be envisioned as a series of thin, deep elements joined together along their boundaries (see Figure 10–19). Structures of this type, commonly called *folded plates,* are typically used as roofs and hence primarily carry uniformly distributed loads which impinge on the surfaces of the individual plates. A characteristic of folded-plate structures is that individual plate elements are long with respect to their width. An underlying design principle is that of moving as much material as possible away from the middle plane of the structure. Thin, deep members reflect this principle and have a high load-carrying capacity, but only if lateral buckling of the compression zone can be prevented. (See the diagram illustrating lateral buckling in Figure 6–13.) By arranging

(a) The stiffness and load-carrying capacity of a one-way plate can be dramatically increased by folding it.

(b) Typical folded-plate cross section

FIGURE 10–19   Folded-plate structures.

individual plates as illustrated in Figure 10–19, the compression zone in each individual plate is inherently braced by the adjacent plate. Lateral buckling is thus not a problem, and the full potential load-carrying capacity of the plates can be realized. The angle formed between adjacent plates must be relatively sharp for this bracing action to occur.

The actual way typical surface loads are carried to supports in folded plate structures is best envisioned by considering two types of beam action—longitudinal and transverse (Figures 10–20 and 10–21). First consider the transverse action. In the same way that one plate braces another against possible buckling in the latter's out-of-plane direction, it can also be regarded as providing a continuous edge support for the adjacent plate. An individual plate in a continuing series of folded plates can consequently be thought of as a one-way slab whose span is the width of the plate. Surface loads are transferred to adjacent folds through *transverse beam action*. If a rigid connection between plate elements is used, a typical transverse strip behaves like a continuous beam supported at several points (the folds). Once the surface loads are carried to the folds, they are transferred through the *longitudinal beam action* of the plates acting in their own deep planes to the supports (i.e., the reactions of the transverse beam strips have components in the in-plane direction of each of the adjacent plates at a fold). For preliminary design purposes the structure can thus be treated as a series of beams of unique cross section in the long direction and one-way slabs in the transverse direction.

It is crucial that the angle formed between plates be maintained constant. A transverse splaying can occur, which will substantially reduce the load-carrying capacity of the structure. This phenomenon can also occur in end plates of a continuous series of plates. To prevent this transverse splaying, stiffener plates are often used at the ends of folded plate structures and, in very long span structures, at interim locations. These stiffeners not only prevent splaying but also provide additional lateral braces for individual plates. If no such stiffeners are used, the rigidity of the joints between plates must be relied on to prevent this splaying. In this case, relatively high bending moments are produced in the transverse direction at the joints which typically require that the thickness of the plate be increased beyond what would be required in a structure using stiffeners.

FIGURE 10–20 Longitudinal action of folded-plate structures. A long folded-plate structure braced by transverse stiffeners behaves basically like a deep beam of unique cross section.

(a) A typical unrestrained transverse section of
a folded plate naturally tends to splay outwards.
Using tie-rods or, preferably, stiffening diaphragms
prevents this splaying.

Stiffening
diaphragms

Transverse plate strips are
designed as continuous beams
supported at fold points.

(b) Stiffener locations: stiffeners should be placed at
either end of a folded-plate structure and, if possible,
in the midregions also. The more that stiffeners are
used, the better will be the overall structural
performance of the plate.

FIGURE 10–21   Transverse action of folded-plate structures.

The general load-carrying actions described above assume that all the plates deflect similarly under load. This is generally true for interior plates. It is highly important that the plates be made to deflect equally, since not doing so would detrimentally affect the structure in the transverse direction. Unequal plate deflections would be equivalent in effect to unequal support settlements in a continuous beam (see Section 8–3–3) and produce undesirable bending moments in the transverse direction. End plates often deflect more than interior plates. Thus, they are often stiffened (see Figures 10–21 and 10–22) by the addition of boundary beams or special end plates. The stiffening plates discussed earlier also serve to equalize plate deflections.

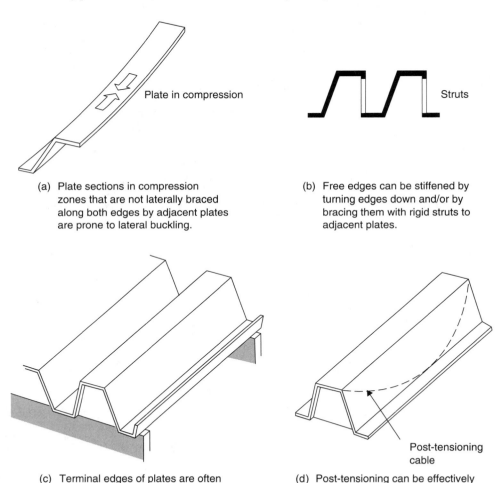

Plate in compression

Struts

(a) Plate sections in compression zones that are not laterally braced along both edges by adjacent plates are prone to lateral buckling.

(b) Free edges can be stiffened by turning edges down and/or by bracing them with rigid struts to adjacent plates.

(c) Terminal edges of plates are often stopped in the tension zone. Even so, the free edge can lack stiffness. Free edges are often turned or otherwise locally stiffened.

(d) Post-tensioning can be effectively used in reinforced concrete plates. The depth of the plates allows a post-tensioned cable to be deeply draped for efficient action.

Post-tensioning cable

FIGURE 10–22 Special conditions.

The efficiency of a folded-plate structure can be increased by placing as much material as possible away from the neutral axis in a way similar to that which was done in beam design. Consequently, plates of the type shown in Figure 10–20 tend to be more efficient than the type shown in Figure 10–19(a). When reinforced concrete is used, the use of a flattened area at the base of a plate allows plenty of room for the placement of tension-reinforcing steel.

Care must be taken to assure that individual plates self-brace each other to prevent lateral buckling. The open configuration shown in Figure 10–22(a), although in a sense a folded plate, is not very efficient, since the top plate is in compression and not laterally braced on one edge. The edge can, however, be locally stiffened.

Anytime a folded plate terminates, special attention should be paid to stiffening the free edge. Terminating a plate in the compression zone as just described is particularly undesirable. Many plates, therefore, are terminated so that the free edge is in the tension rather than compression zone (see Figure 10–22). Even these edges, however, should be stiffened to prevent undesirable deflections.

Folded plate structures can be made out of virtually any material. Reinforced concrete is a widely used material. By specially reinforcing the separating joint, adjoining plates can be rigidly connected along their edges. Reinforced concrete folded plates can also be post-tensioned to further increase their spanning capabilities (see Figure 10–22).

Steel is also used for folded plates, albeit less frequently than concrete. Rigid joints between adjacent plates can be obtained by welding or other special connections.

Wood, most usually in the form of plywood sheets, is extensively used. Rigid joints between adjacent plates are hard to achieve, however, and special care should be devoted to preventing lateral splaying of plates by using stiffening diaphragms or some other mechanism.

QUESTIONS

10–1 With respect to the *crossed-beam system* shown in Figure 10–2, if $L_B = 4L_A$, what part of the total load P is carried by beam A? By beam B? Assume that both beams have identical section properties and have the same end conditions.

Answer: $P_A = 64P_B$; $P_A = 64P/65$ and $P_B = P/65$.

10–2 For the simple crossed-beam system shown in Figure 10–2, draw a graph indicating the relative percentage of the load carried by each crossed beam as the relative lengths of the members vary. Repeat for the bending moments present in each member.

10–3 What are the maximum positive moments present in a square plate that is simply supported at its corners by four columns and that carries a uniformly distributed load of 80 lb/ft^2? Assume that the plate is 6 in. thick and measures 15 ft by 15 ft. Assume that the unit weight of reinforced concrete is 150 lb/ft^3.

Answer: 5231 ft-lb/ft.

10–4 Build a simple folded cardboard model of the folded plate illustrated in Figure 10–21. Do not include transverse stiffeners. Load the model with large flat weights at midspan. Note the behavior of the structure under load and measure the load that causes collapse. Cut out cardboard stiffeners that exactly fit into the end of the original plate configuration and glue them into place. Again load the structure and measure the load required to cause failure. Cut out additional stiffeners and place them in the interior of the structure (e.g., at third points) and repeat. Discuss.

10–5 A 60 × 60-ft homogeneous plate carries a live plus dead load of 100 lb/ft². Consequently, it has a bending moment of $m = 0.11wa^2 = 0.11(100)(60 \times 60) = 40,000$ ft-lb/ft at midspan. A bar system with a depth of 3 ft has members spaced 4.0 ft on center, has a similar self-weight and carries the same uniformly distributed loading. What is the *approximate* force present in a typical upper or lower chord bar member at midspan?

Answer: $T = C = 53,333$ lb.

10–6 What is the maximum negative bending moment developed in a 50 × 50-ft fully fixed plate that carries a load of 100 lb/ft?

Answer: $m = -12,825$ ft-lb/ft.

CHAPTER 11

Membrane and Net Structures

11-1 INTRODUCTION

A *membrane* is a thin flexible surface structure that carries loads primarily through the development of tension stresses. Net structures are conceptually similar, except their surfaces are made from cable net meshes. The soap bubble is the classic example used to illustrate both what a membrane is and how it behaves. Like their flexible-line counterparts, stretched surfaces tend to adapt their shapes to the way they are loaded. They are also very sensitive to the aerodynamic effects of wind, which can cause *fluttering* to occur (see the discussion of this phenomenon in Chapter 5). Consequently, most membranes that are used in buildings are stabilized in some way so that their basic shape is retained under a variety of loadings.

There are several basic ways of stabilizing a membrane or net surface. An inner rigid supporting framework, for example, could be used. Of special interest in this chapter, however, is stabilization through the prestressing of the surface. This can be accomplished through either the application of an external force which pulls the surface taut or through some sort of internal pressurization when the membrane is volume-enclosing.

Examples of prestressing though the application of an external force are some types of tents—an age-old type of structure. Many tents, however, do not have surfaces that are actually appreciably tensioned by supporting guy cables and thus tend to move under loads. Although capable of withstanding normal wind loads, for example, many tent surfaces flutter due to the aerodynamic effects of extreme winds and are not of direct value as permanent structures (although of obvious great value as temporary structures). It is possible, however, to sufficiently prestress a

413

Tent structure

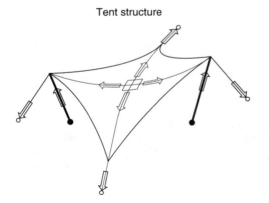

(a) Membrane prestressed or
    stretched by externally
    applied jacking forces.

Pneumatic structure

(b) Membrane prestressed
    air pressure.

FIGURE 11–1 Membrane structures.

fabric or net surface by external jacking forces or internal pressurization so that it remains completely taut under all anticipated loads (see Figure 11–1). Usually, such membranes are stressed in perpendicular directions all across their surfaces. Many roof structures of this type have been built.

The basic load-carrying mechanism in a membrane structure is one of tension. A membrane carrying a load normal to its surface tends to deform into a three-dimensional curve (depending on exact loading and support conditions) and carries the load by in-plane tension forces that are developed in the surface of the membrane. The load-carrying action is similar to that present in a crossed-cable system. In addition to the tension stresses, a type of tangential shearing stress is developed within the membrane structure which is associated with the twist normally present in the curved surface that also helps carry the applied load. The two-way tension field action and the tangential shearing action result, if the membrane is stabilized, in a surface structure that can carry loads in a funicular manner as long as the loads applied do not actually cause compressive stresses, which are manifested by folds in the membrane, to develop.

In line with the preceding, it follows that the fundamental principle underlying the design of membrane structures is simply that the surface must be maintained in a state of tension under any loading condition.

11–2 PNEUMATIC STRUCTURES

11–2–1 Background

Stabilizing a membrane through internal pressurization is possible when the membranes enclose a volume. A class of membranes typically called *pneumatic structures* obtain their stability in this way. Although pneumatic structures as applied to architecture are mostly of fairly recent origin, the basic technology of pneumatics has long been known to humans. The water skin, for example, is a type of pneumatic structure known for a long time. Bubbles have aroused people's curiosity for at least as long. The more immediate genesis of the pneumatic structures currently used in the building fields, however, undoubtedly lies in the balloons and airships that have graced our skies in the recent past.

Building applications of pneumatics are fairly recent. An English engineer by the name of William Lanchester attempted to apply the balloon principle in a patent for a field hospital in 1917. In 1922 the Oasis Theatre in Paris sported a pneumatic hollow roof structure that was rolled into place when it rained. A lot of research work on pneumatics occurred in World War II because of the military value of different types of pneumatic structures. Widespread use of air-supported structures began in 1946 with their application as *radomes,* which housed large radar antennae. The performance of these radomes in harsh arctic climates paved the way for commercial applications. Pneumatics are now part of our common building vocabulary.

There are several different types of membrane structures in use that obtain their stabilization through internal pressurization. The term *pneumatic structure* usually describes the particular subset of pressurized constructions that find applications in building. Most of these structures use air as the pressurization medium. Other gases (and even liquids), however, could potentially be used.

There are two primary classes of pneumatic structures—air-supported structures and air-inflated structures. An *air-supported structure* consists of a single membrane (enclosing a functionally useful space) which is supported by a small internal pressure differential. The internal volume of building air is consequently at a pressure higher than atmospheric. An *air-inflated structure* is supported by pressurized air contained within inflated building elements. The internal volume of building air remains at atmospheric pressure. Hybrid or combination approaches are also possible.

In both types of structures, the air pressure induces tensile stresses in the membrane. External forces acting on the membrane cause a relaxation of some of these tensile stresses. The internal pressure must be high enough under the action of any possible applied loading to prevent compressive stresses, which are manifested as folds, from appearing. Complete stability is achieved only when the whole membrane remains in tension. The high initial tension stress induced by the pressurization, however, must not exceed the allowable stress of the material.

The air-supported structure relies on the maintenance of an internal air pressure only slightly higher than atmospheric to maintain tension in its membrane [Figure 11–2(a)]. The actual internal pressure involved is rather small and usually causes no discomfort to building occupants. If the external loads were uniform, for example, an equal internal pressure would support the loads directly. The membrane would consequently serve merely as a separator. Since external loads are usually relatively small, the internal pressures required can be similarly small. The correct image of an air-supported structure is more one of a low-pressure air bag than of a high-pressure automobile tire.

An air-inflated structure has a different load-supporting mechanism [Figure 11–2(b)]. Pressurized air is used to inflate shapes (e.g., arches, walls, columns) used to form the building enclosure. There are two primary types of air-inflated structures in common use: the inflated rib structure and the dual-wall structure (Figure 11–3). A ribbed structure is made of a series of inflated tubes, usually arched, which form a space enclosure. Dual wall structures consist of a parallel membrane system. The space between the membranes is pressurized. The membranes are held together by connecting threads and diaphragms. Air-inflated structures generally tend to

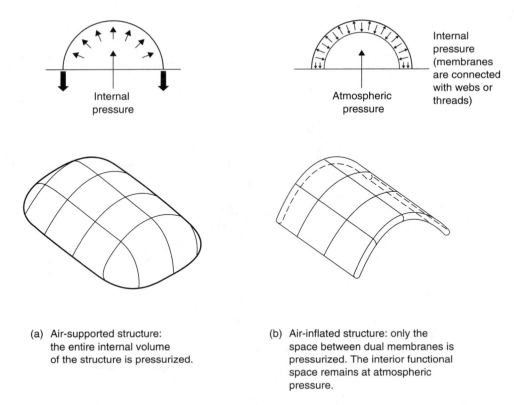

(a) Air-supported structure:
the entire internal volume
of the structure is pressurized.

(b) Air-inflated structure: only the
space between dual membranes is
pressurized. The interior functional
space remains at atmospheric
pressure.

FIGURE 11–2 Pneumatic structures: air-supported and air-inflated forms.

require a higher degree of pressurization to achieve stability than do air-supported structures. This is because the internal pressurization cannot be directly used to balance the external load but must be used to form shapes that carry loads in a more traditional manner. It is fairly obvious, for example, that a thin air-inflated plate structure of the type illustrated in Figure 11–4 is far more susceptible to collapse due to a type of folding or buckling in the top surface when inflation pressures are low than is a comparable air-supported membrane. Only by using a high internal pressure in the inflated plate can the load-carrying capacities of the systems be made equal.

All advantages, however, do not lie strictly with an air-supported structure. An inflated plate provides a certain degree of freedom in the design of the functional space it covers. Clearly, the air-supported system must come equipped with air locks and other paraphernalia in order that the space be usable. The air-supported system must also have an edge anchoring system that ties the membrane firmly to the ground and prevents leakage. The air-inflated plate can be used with simpler supports.

In general, air-supported structures are capable of greater spans than are air-inflated structures. Occasionally, hybrid structures are used that combine features of both air-supported and air-inflated systems. The spanning potential of air-supported structures are achieved, and the dual-wall system provides added insulation and safety against possible collapse.

(a) Dual-wall structure.

(b) Ribbed structure.

FIGURE 11–3 Air-inflated structures: ribbed and dual-wall.

Local   Snap-through
buckling   buckling

(a) Air-inflated structure: an overall folding type of failure can occur in some air-inflated plates. A high internal pressure prevents this type of failure.

(b) Air-supported structure: air-supported structures buckle differently. A local or snap-through mode can occur.

FIGURE 11–4 Plate forms: air-inflated and air-supported structures.

11-2-2 Air-Supported Structures

Types of External Loading Conditions. There are some unique conditions in connection with loads on pneumatic structures that are of special interest. Several types of loads can act on an air-supported structure. Snow can accumulate and cause a downward-acting load. If the structure is a spherical segment that is nearly a hemisphere, snow can accumulate only near the crown of the structure since it will slide off elsewhere. In low-profile sphere segments, snow can cover the whole roof. Rarely does snow accumulate to any great depth, however, because of the heat losses that normally occur through the membrane itself when the interior volume is heated.

Major concentrated loads, which induce very high local stresses, should be avoided at all costs and other structures selected when such forces exist. Minor concentrated loads such as a person walking on the roof, however, rarely cause much trouble.

Wind loads are a major problem. As previously discussed in Chapter 3, the forces due to wind on a shape such as a sphere are fairly complex and consist of both suction and tension forces. Figure 11–5 diagrams these forces. Whether or not a shell experiences simply pressure forces or both pressure and suction forces depends on the aspect angle defining the extent of the surface used.

Membrane Stresses Due to Internal Pressure. The in-plane forces in a membrane induced by an internal pressure are dependent on the dimensions and geometrical shape of the membrane as well as the magnitude of the internal pressure present.

The forces in a simple membrane shape are easy to determine. First consider a planar ring acted upon by an internal pressure per unit area p_r directed radially outwards (see Figure 11–6). The tension forces developed in the ring can be found by passing a section through the midline

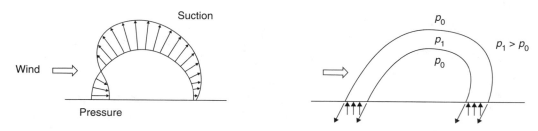

FIGURE 11-5 Effect of wind on a dual-walled pneumatic structure.

(a) Circular membrane of unit width carrying an internal pressure p_i. Tension forces in membrane: $T = p_r R$.

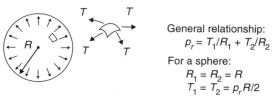

(b) Spherical membrane carrying an internal pressure of p_r.

General relationship:
$$p_r = T_1/R_1 + T_2/R_2$$
For a sphere:
$$R_1 = R_2 = R$$
$$T_1 = T_2 = p_r R/2$$

FIGURE 11-6 Membrane stresses.

of the ring and considering translatory equilibrium. The total translatory effect of the pressure p_r is simply the sum of the aligned components of the pressure forces acting on the surface in the direction considered. This total effect is exactly equivalent to the internal pressure acting over the projected area of the ring. The resisting total internal forces is simply given by $2T$, where T is the force developed in the ring. Consequently, $2T = p_r(2R)$, or $p_r = T/R$, or $T = p_rR$. If the shape is actually a surface curved in two directions, the analogous expression is given by $p_r = T_1/R_1 + T_2/R_2$, where r_1 and r_2 are the radii of curvatures involved and T_1 and T_2 are in-plane forces that are perpendicular to one another.

The general expression $p_r = T_1/R_1 + T_2/R_2$ is an invaluable one in analyzing membranes. For a cylindrical surface, $R_1 = R$ and $R_2 \to \infty$, hence $T = p_rR$. For a sphere, $R_1 = R_2 = R$ and consequently $T = p_r/R/2$. This is the internal force, expressed in terms of a *force per unit length of membrane*, in a spherical shape carrying an internal pressure p_r. Internal membrane forces can be converted to stresses by taking into account the membrane thickness (i.e., $f = T/tL$, where L is a unit length). These expressions will also be used later in the analysis of shells.

Internal Pressures Required.   The internal pressure required must be sufficient to keep the membrane surface from folding no matter what combination of applied loads exist. Different points on the surface of the sphere must be checked to find what loading combination produces a maximum radial component. The point on the surface having the largest of all radial components then becomes the value to be balanced by internal pressurization. The magnitude of the resultant pressurization, however, must be such that the tensile stresses anywhere in the membrane induced by the pressurization never exceed the allowable stress of the material fabric used. The stresses in the fabric under all possible loading conditions, including those due to internal pressurization, should be checked after an internal pressurization is decided upon since partial loadings may produce some unusual interactive effects.

By and large, the internal pressures required tend to be surprisingly small. Internal pressures on the order of only 100 mm of water pressure are not uncommon.

Support Conditions.   How an air-supported structure meets the ground is a critical design issue. There is, for example, the problem of ensuring an airtight seal. From a structural rather than detailing viewpoint, however, the dominant problem is that the structure exerts large uplift and, depending on the exact shape of the structure, horizontal forces on its supports.

Consider the air-supported structure shown in Figure 11–7. If it is simply space-enclosing, the structure exerts a total uplift force of p_rA_i, where A_i is the projected area of the structure (equivalent to the ground plane covered). Consequently, uplift forces of $T_v = p_rA_i/L$, where L is the circumference of the base ring and T_v is expressed in terms of a force per unit length of support, are developed at the support. Note that for a sphere segment, $T_v = p_r\pi\,(R \sin \phi)^2/2\pi R \sin \phi$ and $T = T_v/\sin \phi = p_rR/2$, as before. In addition, horizontal forces of $T_v/\tan \phi$ are also developed at the support. For low-profile shapes, the horizontal forces are inwardly directed. In some external load cases, other forces may be developed as well (e.g., uplift forces due to wind).

The foundation must be designed to resist both the vertical uplift and horizontal forces caused by the membrane in order to anchor it to the ground. For larger structures an often-used device for resisting these forces is some form of a base containment ring. For a low-profile structure, the horizontal components of the membrane reactions are inwardly directed. Hence, a containment ring would be in compression.

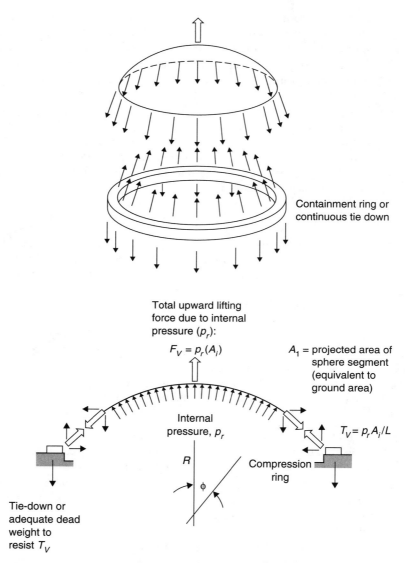

FIGURE 11–7 Support conditions. In low-profile structures, supports carry loads that are upwardly and inwardly directed. In high-profile structures, the loads are upwardly and outwardly directed (for 0 > 90°).

Containment rings for structures that are sphere segments are circular. For other membrane shapes the design objective of minimizing bending dictates that the containment ring shape be funicular for the loading. This may lead to unusually shaped rings if membrane shapes are unusual.

In very large span air-supported structures where a cable-net type of membrane must be used, the areas of junctions between the cables and the ring can be particular problematic because of the high concentrated loads involved. Special care must be taken to ensure that excessive local stresses are not developed at such points. Ring shapes may be affected if a system of primary and secondary cables are used, in which case ring loads can no longer be characterized as nearly uniform.

Profile.   One of the most interesting design problems associated with a pneumatic air-supported structure is deciding on the profile of the structure. Consider a sphere that has a radius R_M that is cut off to cover a ground area A_i (see Figure 11–8). Consider another sphere of a much larger

(a) High-profile structure.

(b) Low-profile structure.

(c) Effects of wind on a low-profile structure.

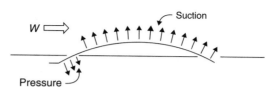

(d) Pressure forces due to wind can be eliminated entirely by using low-profile structures and embankments.

FIGURE 11–8   Profile considerations.

radius, R_N, that is also cut off such that it covers *exactly the same ground* area A_i. Assuming that each must have an internal pressurization of p in order to support the external loads, it is evident that for a given p the membrane stresses in the low-profile sphere segment of larger radius ($T_N = pR_N/2$) are much larger than those in the high-profile membrane with a smaller radius ($T_M = pR_M/2$) (i.e., since $R_N > R_M$, $T_N > T_M$). Since the choice of membrane is strongly affected by the magnitude of the force present, it would therefore seem that high-profile, small-radius sphere segments are preferable to low-profile, large-radius sphere segments. In addition, low-profile structures develop larger horizontal reactive forces and thus necessitate larger compression rings.

There are, however, trade-offs involved. One is that a larger building volume is enclosed in a high-profile structure in comparison with low-profile structures, and there is thus a greater demand placed on mechanical systems intended to ensure thermal comfort conditions for occupants.

Another trade-off is that the external forces due to wind effects can be utilized to advantage in low-profile structures. By cutting off the sphere segment at the point diagrammed in Figure 11–8(c), a condition can be created where the effect of wind is one of suction only. Pressure forces tending to cause folds to develop are thus avoided. Wind forces literally tend to hold up the roof rather than force it down. Design internal pressurization values are thus favorably affected.

There are examples of both high- and low-profile air-supported structures existent. Most very long span structures are low profile and use cable-net membranes. Small-span structures are more often high-profile structures.

11–2–3 Air-Inflated Structures

Structures using air-inflated elements carry external loads to the ground in a much more traditional way than do air-supported structures. Common elements, such as beams, columns or arches, are made rigid by high internal pressurization.

Consider the air-inflated beam shown in Figure 11–9 that is inflated with a pressure of p_r. Before a structure is loaded externally, uniform longitudinal tensile stresses exist along its length due to the pressure. Application of an external load tends to cause compression stresses to develop along the upper surface and tension stresses along the lower in much the same way as occurs in a beam made of a rigid material. These load-induced stresses interact with those caused by the pressurization. The consequence is that tensile stresses originally present along the upper surface are reduced and those along the lower surface increased. Clearly, the internal pressurization must be of such magnitude that no compressive stresses, which would be manifested as folds, are developed along the top surface. The resultant of the internal stress distribution and the resultant of the pressure force couple together to develop an internal resisting moment which balances the applied moment. The load-carrying mechanism is thus quite similar to a prestressed beam.

Other shapes also depend on internal pressure for rigidity. A double-walled sphere, for example, acts quite like a rigid thin shell. As such, it is particularly sensitive to buckling that might be induced by external loads.

The rigidity of all air-inflated structures largely depends on the degree of internal pressurization. Pressurization is usually higher in air-inflated than in air-supported structures.

(a) Air-inflated beam with internal pressure p_r.

(b) Free-body diagram of left portion of beam. Unloaded state.

Uniform internal membrane stresses

(c) Loaded state. Application of an external load tends to cause compressive stresses to develop on the upper surfaces and tension on the lower. These stresses interact with existing membrane stress. Upper surface stresses are relaxed and lower surface stresses increased. A couple is formed between the resultant of the pressure forces on the end of the cylinder to provide a resisting moment that balances the external applied moment.

FIGURE 11–9   Air-inflated beam: general load-carrying behavior.

11–2–4   Other Considerations

A common concern when pneumatic structures are used is what happens if the membrane is punctured. In this connection it is useful to compare two pneumatics, a common balloon and an air-supported structure.

When a balloon is punctured, it obviously seems to literally explode. In actuality, the puncture causes a crack to develop, which propagates very, very rapidly. One reason for the rapid crack propagation is that the very high degree of internal pressurization present in the balloon induces a very high state of stress in the membrane. A lot of energy is stored in the highly stressed membrane. As a crack begins to develop, all this stored energy is available to help the crack

(a) Due to the low internal pressures that are present, most inflated structures only gradually deflate after a puncture.

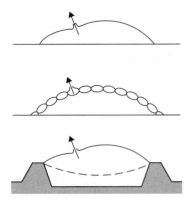

(b) A structure having cells that are inflated is less likely to collapse completely than the type of structure shown in (a).

(c) Structures can be designed to be viable even if fully deflated. In the case shown the structure begins working like a suspended cable surface when deflated.

FIGURE 11–10 Punctures in air-inflated structures.

propagate. In such structures, often called *high-energy systems,* crack propagation is consequently extremely rapid. In contrast, a typical air-supported building pneumatic is a *low-energy system.* Internal pressurization is relatively small, as are the stresses induced in the membrane, as compared to a balloon. There is relatively little energy stored in the membrane. Consequently, a crack initiated by a puncture does not propagate rapidly, since there is little stored energy in the membrane to help the crack propagate (Figure 11–10). Some tearing may occur, but the puncture effects remain essentially localized.

The relatively low pressure present in building pneumatics is also such that the pressure loss associated with holes is often not initially significant. The mechanical system used to inflate the structure often has sufficient capacity (or can be easily designed to have) to maintain the shape of the membrane even when minor punctures occur.

In any event, even a severely punctured roof will still tend to settle relatively gradually rather than instantaneously, thus allowing evacuation. Consternation will invariably be caused, but the danger is not as life-threatening as is often envisioned.

For complete safety in the event of a loss of pressure, pneumatics can be designed to act as suspended roofs (admittedly unstabilized ones). Supports are typically elevated so that clearance exists in the event of deflation.

Another important problem in connection with pneumatics is the choice of membrane material, since many tend to degrade with time due to the ultraviolet effects of the sun. This problem, however, is avoided by choosing material correctly.

11–3 ANALYSIS AND DESIGN OF NET AND TENT STRUCTURES

A detailed analysis of how prestressed membrane net and tent structures behave is fairly complex and beyond the scope of this book. Some of the important underlying principles, however, have already been covered in Chapter 5, since many prestressed membrane structures are basically crossed-cable systems. This section discusses a few of the more salient design problems.

11–3–1 Curvatures

For surfaces that obtain their stability through externally applied prestress forces, application of the design principle that surface tensions must be maintained generally means that prestress forces must be large and/or curvatures in surfaces must be maintained that are fairly sharp. Large flat areas in membranes are to be generally avoided since enormous prestressing forces would be required to maintain the areas when normal loads are applied to them. It will be recalled that as the sag of a cable approaches zero, cable thrusts increase indefinitely. Conversely, an indefinitely large prestress force is required to maintain a cable in a zero-sag configuration under an applied load. The same general phenomenon is true in stressed skin structures.

Flat areas can and must be avoided by paying close attention to the exact geometry of the shell surface. Models are often useful for these studies during preliminary design stages. Flat areas can generally be avoided by paying close attention to the geometry of the surface. Transition zones between positively and negatively curved surfaces can be particularly problematic and should be specially considered.

Curvatures can be assured by carefully controlling the placement of high points and low points. Two high points must always be separated by a low point, and vice versa. This principle is evident in the four-point structure shown in Figure 11–11(a). The two high points (A and C) are separated by a point that is relatively lower (B). The same point (B) is, however, high relative to the other two points (D and E). A continuous skin connecting points A, C, D, and E is therefore doubly curved. If the height differential between A and C and D and E is reasonable, the surface will have a relatively sharp curvature. Obviously, if all points are near the same level, the surface will be undesirably flat.

The same principle of separating highs with lows and vice versa can be applied to more complex or more extensive membranes, as is illustrated in Figure 11–11(b).

(a) Flat areas should be avoided in prestressed membranes. Prestressing must also be such that stretching occurs in opposite curvatures at any point. Careful placing of high and low points accomplishes these ends.

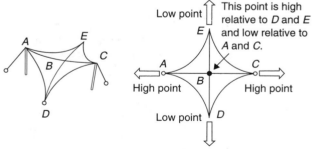

(b) Relative high and low points are deliberately introduced in a complex shape.

FIGURE 11–11 Curvatures in pretensioned membranes increase the stiffness of the surface and help prevent fluttering due to wind effects.

11-3-2 Support Conditions

Most prestressed membrane structures are usually supported by a series of discrete point supports. Primary high points are usually formed by using large compression masts. Masts of this type are designed basically as large columns that are almost invariably pin-ended. Primary low points are usually ground connections. Large horizontal and vertical uplift forces usually exist at ground foundations, since the prestressing force in the membrane is obtained by stretching the membrane, through a jacking procedure, between these tie-down points and high points. Since very high concentrated forces are present, the tie-down of ground connection points represents a major design problem.

The number and placement of support points generally determines the amount of force present in a mast or ground connection. The more supports, the less is the load present on any single point support. Care must be taken, however, not to use so many supports as to hinder the development of sufficient membrane curvatures.

An exception to the primary point-support type of condition for a membrane often occurs internally in the structure at the free edge of the prestressed membrane (see Figure 11–12). Edge cables are often used that stiffen the free edge and allow a more uniform tension field to be developed in the membrane itself (by essentially pulling all along the free edge of the surface). Forces in these edge cables are usually fairly high.

Since the local membrane stresses that would be generated where a surface drapes over a high point would be very great, eyelets of the type illustrated in Figure 11–12 are used to reduce membrane stresses by opening the surface at the point and using a cable ring. The membrane is

(a) Crossed cables with opposite curvatures are inherently resistant to wind-induced uplift or flutter. The cables are initially pretensioned. Vertical loads cause the tension in the upper cable to increase and those in the lower cable to decrease.

(b) Cable and arch structure: cables are pretensioned.

(c) Alternative ways of reducing forces in membranes around discrete point supports.

(d) Edge conditions in cable net structures.

FIGURE 11–12 Pretensioned membranes.

tied into the ring which distributes internal forces more evenly than a pure point support. The ring is, in turn, connected to the mast.

11-3-3   Form Finding

Finding the exact shape of a stretched skin or cable net structure is difficult, as is actually making the resulting doubly curved surface from real materials. In a complex skin structure consisting of various high and low points, determining the exact shape of the skin is a difficult problem. Final force distributions in the skin, of course, depend on the exact shape of the membrane. The problem of finding the exact shape of the membrane—typically called *form-finding*—is compounded when different prestressing forces are used in different directions. Even if the shape could be accurately determined, actually making it is also difficult. Since such surfaces are typically not developable, the use of naturally flat material sheets to make the surface poses problems. Usually, the surface is made of smaller nonuniformly shaped strips that are specially cut. Determining the shapes of these strips is a task unto itself. Analogous problems arise when a net of crossed cables are used such as would be needed for longer-span structures. The small grid shapes formed are, of course, not uniformly shaped squares or rectangles but highly variable shapes. Establishing individual cable lengths and cross-connection points is consequently a major task, as is devising an enclosure system to be supported by these cables.

Physical modeling was initially used for finding overall shapes, including elegant soap-film models, which exhibit equal surface tensions in all directions. Although the models were visually attractive, actually extracting geometric information for cutting panels or determining cable lengths remained problematic. Large models were often used. But in a real structure, the actual loads on the cables or fabrics and other movements present materially alter the curvatures present. Hence, computer-based formulations are now commonly used. The surface is often modeled as a pattern of elements, which are in turn given physical properties reflective of actual elements in the final structure. Constant stress levels, for example, may be set, and a corresponding form that yields this condition can be found in a process that necessarily takes into account the real biaxial deformation properties of the materials expected to be used (e.g., differences in stress-strain properties in warp and weft directions in fabrics must be considered). The computer programs must use complex nonlinear analyses, which take into account the displacements of the surface under loading. Various dynamic relaxation formulations are frequently used. Once the geometry of the system has been established, the geometry of panels for cutting or fabrication is extracted.

Widespread use is now made of sophisticated computer-based membrane analysis programs that do form-finding and various force and deformation analyses. In programs such as this, controlling high and low points and any other fixed geometry points must be input. Net parameters, including coarseness or fineness of the net and any prestress forces in the warp and weft directions, must be input. These programs then do complete non-linear analyses to obtain results.

11-3-4   Materials

Issues in the selection of a material fabric in a stretched-skin structure include both structural and use characteristics. Stretched skins are subjected to intense biaxial stress conditions. Common fabrics have different strength and stretch properties in the warp and weft directions that must be taken into account in the structural analysis and design process. Warp and weft differences are also evident in material creep properties. Differences must be taken into account in original form-finding and in fabric patterning to allow for ultimate differences in creep over time.

Commonly used fabrics include various types of PVC-coated polyester, Teflon-coated glass fiber, or silicone-coated glass fiber. In PVC-coated polyesters, the base polyester is strong but is subject to degradation over time. PVC is inexpensive, fire-resistant, and easily joined by radio-frequency welding. Surfaces easily discolor and retain dirt, however. Lifetimes are limited (around 10 years or so). Teflon coats improve degradation resistance but are easily abraded. Recently developed silicone-coated fabrics improve durability and can be joined by gluing. Initial costs, however, are quite high. Membranes may be reinforced with cable strands embedded in them. Various kinds of foils reinforced with glass fibers are also possible.

The multistrand cables typically used in net structures are made from spun high-strength steel. A primary design consideration is increasing corrosion resistance. Historically addressed by galvanizing, a variety of new technologies have evolved to achieve corrosion resistance, including approaches such as setting zinc powder in polyurethane coatings around elements during the spinning process. Many alternatives now exist. Values for strength and modulus of elasticity properties are tabulated elsewhere.

Cables must be terminated with full load-transfer details. Common approaches include the use of swaged-end terminations or hot-poured zinc fittings. Clamps are possible, but their use is commonly restricted to cross-cable connections.

QUESTIONS

11–1 A spherical balloon has a radius of 12 in. and a thickness of 0.05 in. The balloon is blown up with an internal pressure of 100 lb/in.^{2} What are the membrane stresses developed in the surface of the skin of the balloon?

11–2 How internally pressurized pneumatic structures meet the ground is a critical design and construction issue. Sketch at least one acceptable type of ground connection detail. Consult your local library.

11–3 Using literature from your library, sketch several different ways stretched-skin or cable-net structures are connected to cable masts.

11–4 How prestressed tent structures are tied down to the ground is a critical design and construction issue. Sketch several different ground-anchorage systems capable of carrying tension loads. Consult your local library.

CHAPTER 12
—
Shell Structures

12–1 INTRODUCTION

A *shell* is a thin, rigid, three-dimensional structural form taken by the enclosure of a volume bounded by a curved surface. A shell surface may assume virtually any shape. Common forms include rotational surfaces generated by the rotation of a curve about an axis (e.g., spherical, elliptical, conical, and parabolic surfaces); translational surfaces generated by sliding one plane curve over another plane curve (e.g., cylindrical and elliptic paraboloid surfaces); ruled surfaces generated by sliding the two ends of a line segment on two individual plane curves (e.g., conoids and hyperbolic paraboloid surfaces); and a wide variety of complex surfaces formed by various combinations of rotational, translational, and ruled surfaces (Figure 12–1). A shell can assume any of these forms. The shape used, however, need not be restricted to those easily described in mathematical terms. Free-form shapes may prove a viable solution to many structural problems. Construction considerations, however, may limit the range of form options.

Loads applied to shell surfaces are carried to the ground by the development of compressive, tensile, and shear stresses acting in the in-plane direction of the surface. The thinness of the surface does not allow the development of appreciable bending resistance. Thin shell structures are uniquely suited to carrying distributed loads and find wide application as roof structures in buildings. They are, however, unsuited to carrying concentrated loads. As a consequence of their carrying loads by in-plane forces (primarily tension and compression), shell structures can be very thin and still span great distances. Span/thickness ratios of 400 or 500 are not uncommon [e.g., 3 in. (8 cm) thicknesses are possible for domes spanning 100 to 125 ft (30 to 38 m)]. Shells of this

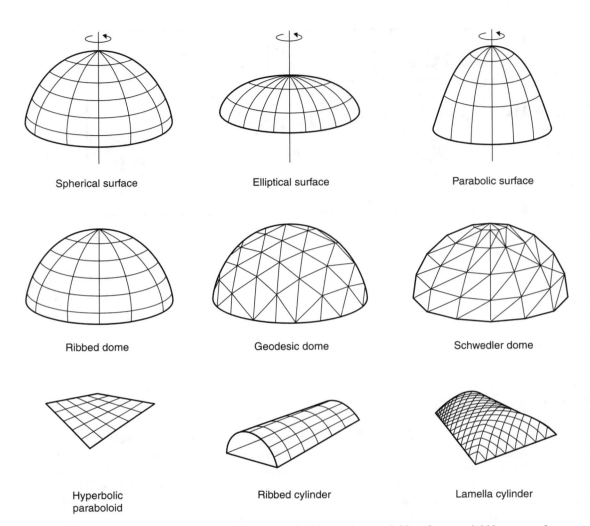

Spherical surface   Elliptical surface   Parabolic surface

Ribbed dome   Geodesic dome   Schwedler dome

Hyperbolic paraboloid   Ribbed cylinder   Lamella cylinder

FIGURE 12–1 Examples of different structures made of either continuous rigid surfaces or rigid bar networks.

thickness, however, are a relatively recent structural innovation made possible by the development of new materials such as reinforced concrete, which is uniquely appropriate for making shell surfaces. Older three-dimensional shapes, such as masonry domes, are considerably thicker relative to their span and cannot be exactly characterized as carrying loads by in-plane axial or shear stresses (more bending exists and final stresses are not uniform), even though an approximation of this type is good for conceptualizing the behavior of such structures. Terminating a shell surface is always problematic. In a dome, for example, the in-plane forces developed in the surface normally have outwardly directed components that must be absorbed by either a series of closely spaced buttresses or a tension ring.

Three-dimensional forms may also be made of assemblies of short, rigid bars. These structures are not, strictly speaking, shell structures, since they are not surface elements. Still their structural behavior can be conceptualized as being quite similar to continuous surface shells in which the stresses normally present in a continuous surface are concentrated into individual members. Structures of this type were first extensively used in the last century. The *Schwedler dome,* consisting of an irregular mesh of hinged bars, for example, was introduced by Schwedler in Berlin in 1863 when he designed a dome with a span of 132 ft (40 m). Other, more recent structures have bars placed on curves generated by the medians and parallels of surfaces of revolution. Some of the largest domes in the world follow this latter scheme.

To minimize the construction difficulties involved in having to use bars of different length to create the shell surface, some systems have been developed with the goal of using equal-length bars. The most widely publicized are the *geodesic domes* associated with Buckminster Fuller. Since the surface of a sphere is not developable, the number of identical repetitive patterns into which the surface can be divided is limited. The spherical icosahedron, for example, consists of 20 equilateral triangles. But the need to subdivide the surface further typically leads to bars of different lengths. The structural advantages often claimed for these forms are not necessarily greater than for other forms of reticulated domes.

Shapes other than surfaces of revolution can also be made using bar elements. These include typical ribbed barrel roofs and the *Lamella roof,* which is made of a skew grid of archlike forms composed of discrete elements. The latter form was developed largely in connection with wood as the building material, but concrete and steel have been used as well. Remarkably large spans can be obtained with Lamella systems.

12–2   SPHERICAL SHELL STRUCTURES

12–2–1   Introduction

This section considers a specific type of shell structure that is made from a portion of a spherical surface. Section 12–2–2 discusses in detail the kinds of in-plane forces developed within the surface of a spherical shell. Prior to this analysis, however, it is useful to look more broadly at how such a shell works and what kinds of forces are exerted on supporting elements. This is best done through a simplified example. *Il Palazzetto dello Sporto* by Pier Luigi Nervi, built in 1957, is studied.

◆ ◆   **EXAMPLE:**

Il Palazzetto dello Sporto
The dome of this structure apparently floats on top of a series of Y-shaped buttresses. The dome itself is composed of a series of highly reinforced, ferroconcrete elements used to make a closely spaced, ribbed surface. This surface is supported by the Y-shaped buttresses, which transfer forces developed within the surface of the shell to a massive *tension ring* (see Section 12–2–8) buried in the ground that contains the outward force components developed in the buttress, and transmits the vertical force components into the ground.

Determine the approximate force in a typical supporting buttress and in the surrounding tension ring. Use a highly simplified analysis that assumes a simple gravity loading condition and ignores variances induced by the open cupola on top of the structure or by the use of ribs. Assume that the combined dead load and vertical live load associated with the unit areas of the surface is given by $w_{DL+LL} = 80$ lb/ft².[1]

---

[1]This example is adapted from a classic older textbook, *Structure—An Architect's Approach,* by H. Seymour Howard, Jr., McGraw-Hill Book Company, New York, 1966.

Solution: First determine the approximate value of the total load (W) acting downward (weight of shell and live load). This value can be found by multiplying the surface area of the dome (A) by the load per unit area that acts upon it ($w_{DL+LL} = 80$ lb/ft^2). The surface area of a portion of a sphere from ϕ_1 to ϕ_2 is given in any reference book by $A = 2\pi R^2[\cos \phi_1 - \cos \phi_2]$. Alternatively, this same expression can be found by a simple area calculation, as follows (see Figure 12–2).

$$A = \int 2\pi a \, d\phi = \int 2\pi (R \sin \phi) \, d\phi = 2\pi R^2 [\cos \phi_1 - \cos \phi_2]$$
$$= 2\pi (159 \text{ ft})^2 [\cos 0° - \cos 38°] = 33{,}673 \text{ ft}^2$$
$$W = A \times w_{DL+LL} = (33{,}673 \text{ ft}^2)(80 \text{ lb/ft}^2) = 2{,}693{,}840 \text{ lb}$$

There are 36 buttresses present, so each buttress supports a downward load of $(2{,}693{,}840 \text{ lb})/36 = 74{,}829$ lb. This is the *vertical component* of the force developed in each buttress (see Figure 12–2). The total inclined force in the buttress is given by

$$F = 74{,}829 \text{ lb/sin } 38° = 121{,}542 \text{ lb}$$

This is the total force present in the lower stem of the Y. (Forces in the upper arms of the Y could be found by considering their angular orientation.)

Next, find the approximate force in the lower ring that serves to keep the buttress from spreading outwardly (the ring serves a function analogous to that of a tie-rod in an arch). As can be seen from Figure 12–2, the horizontal component of the force in the Y buttress acts outwardly. This outward force is resisted by forces developed in the ring that have inwardly directed components. If the ring is approximatedly modeled as a 36-sided polygon, then it is evident that

$$2T \sin \theta = 121{,}542 \cos \phi, \quad \text{or} \quad 2T \sin 5° = 121{,}542 \cos 38°$$
$$T = 549{,}455 \text{ lb}$$

This is the force developed in the ring as a consequence of the lateral spreading action of the buttresses. It is massive. A segmentally post-tensioned reinforced concrete ring was used in the actual structure to carry this force. The post-tensioning put the ring into an initial state of compression that counteracted the tension induced by the spreading action of the buttresses.

This simplified analysis has not addressed the distributed forces developed within the actual surface of the shell itself. These forces consist of *meridional* and *hoop* forces or stresses that act in the plane of the surface. Meridional forces act in the longitudinal direction (from the apex to where the shell terminates) and are discussed in Section 12–2–4. Hoop forces act in the circumferential or latitudinal direction and are discussed in Section 12–2–5. In the latter example, the tops of the buttresses collect the outwardly and downwardly directed components of the meridional forces and transfer them down to the surrounding tension ring. The approach shown above is a direct method for finding buttress and tension ring forces without first calculating distributed meridional forces. ◆

12–2–2 Membrane Action in Shell Surfaces

A good way to envision the behavior of any shell surface under the action of a load is to think of it as analogous to a membrane, a surface element so thin that only tension forces can be developed (see Chapter 11). A soap bubble and a thin sheet of rubber are examples of membranes. A membrane carrying a load normal to its surface deforms into a three-dimensional curve and carries the load by in-plane tension forces that are developed in the surface of the membrane. The load-carrying action is similar to that present in a crossed-cable system. The basic load-carrying mechanism of a rigid shell of a similar geometry is analogous to that produced in an inverted membrane. Of primary importance is the existence of two sets of internal forces in the surface of

(a) Area calculations

(b) Dome during construction.

(c)

(d)

The massive force T develops in the ring to resist the lateral spreading of the buttresses. A segmentally post-tensioned reinforced concrete ring was used. The post-tensioning put the ring into an initial state of compression, which, in turn, counteracted the tension induced by the outward thrust of the buttresses.

FIGURE 12–2 A highly approximate analysis of *Il Palazzeto del Sporto* by Pier Luigi Nervi. The dome was made of precast ferroconcrete elements supported by Y-shaped buttresses. A huge tension ring is buried in the ground.

a membrane that act in perpendicular directions. Also of importance is the existence of a type of tangential shearing stress which is developed within the membrane surface (which is associated with the twist normally present in the surface), which also helps carry the applied load.

12–2–3 Types of Forces in Spherical Shells

The existence of two sets of forces in separate directions within the shell surface tends to make the shell act in a fashion similar to a two-way plate structure. The shear forces between adjacent plate strips in a planar plate structure that were shown to contribute to the load-carrying capacity of the plate are present in shell structures as well.

These two characteristics, the development of shear forces and two sets of axial forces rather than one, characterize the difference between the structural behavior of a shell and that of a series of arch shapes of a similar general geometry that are rotated about a point to form a similar shape. In an arch no bending is present if the arch is funicularly shaped for the applied full-loading condition. If the loading is changed, however, to partial loading, substantial bending is developed in the arch.

In a shell in-plane forces in the meridional or longitudinal direction called *meridional forces* (see Figure 12–3) are induced under full loading that are not unlike those in the analogous arch. Under a partial-loading condition, however, the action of the shell differs remarkably from that of an analogous arch, in that no bending is developed because of the other set of forces that act in the hoop direction, which are also developed in the shell. These *hoop forces* act in the circumferential direction and perpendicularly to the meridional forces. The hoop forces restrain the out-of-plane movement of the meridional strips in the shell that is tended to be caused by the partial loading (bending under partial loading in an arch is accompanied by a movement of this type). In a shell the restraint offered by the hoop forces causes no bending to be developed in the meridional direction (or in the hoop direction for that matter). As a consequence, a shell can carry variations in loads by the development of in-plane stresses only. The plate shears mentioned earlier also contribute to this capacity.

The variations in load patterns involved, however, must be gradual transitions (e.g., a gentle change from full to partial loads) for bending not to be developed. Sharp discontinuities in load patterns (e.g., concentrated loads) do cause local bending to occur. Thus, any unusual forces in an arch cause bending that is propagated throughout the entire arch, while the effects of analogous forces in shells remain more localized.

The shell is thus a unique structure. It can be said to act funicularly for many different types of loads even if its shape is not exactly funicular. In the example discussed above, the funicular shape for an arch carrying a uniform load would be parabolic. A spherical shell which has a surface form that is not parabolic will also carry loads by in-plane forces. In this case, however, hoop forces will be set up even in the full-loading case, since the shape is not exactly funicular.

The meridional forces in a shell under full vertical loading are always compressive (by analogy with the action of an arch). The hoop forces, however, may be in either tension or compression, depending on the location in the shell considered (see Figure 12–3). In a semicircular shell, or simply one with a high rise, there is a tendency for lower meridional strips to deform in an outward direction. Hoop forces containing this movement are therefore in tension. Near the top of the same shell, the meridional strips tend to deform inwardly. Hoop forces resisting this movement are therefore in compression.

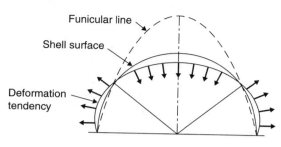

(a) Types of forces developed in a spherical shell.

(b) Relationships between the surface line of a spherical shell segment, the deformation tendency of the surface under a uniformly distributed loading, and the funicular line for the same loading.

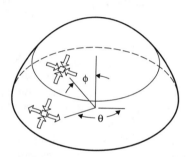

(c) Hoop forces are compressive in the upper zone of a sphere segment and tensile in the lower zone. Meridional forces are always compressive.

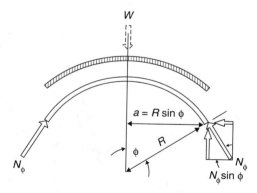

(d) Meridional forces acting in the plane of a shell.

(e) The sum of the vertical components of the in-plane meridional forces developed internally in the shell equals the external vertical live and dead load.

FIGURE 12–3 Meridional and hoop forces in spherical shells.

The stresses associated with meridional and hoop forces are generally fairly small for a uniform loading condition. Point loads, however, can cause very high stresses and should be avoided on shell surfaces.

Holes in shell surfaces of the type mentioned above are possible but should generally be avoided since they disrupt the continuity and hence efficiency of the shell surface. If holes are used, the shell must be specially reinforced around hole edges.

12-2-4   Meridional Forces in Spherical Shells

The internal forces and stresses in axisymmetric shells uniformly loaded can be found quite easily through application of the basic equations of equilibrium. A dome is analyzed in detail as an example.

Consider the dome segment illustrated at the bottom of Figure 12–3. Assume that the loading is a uniform gravity load distributed on the surface of the shell (e.g., the shell's own dead weight and insulative or protective coverings). If the total of all such loads acting downward is denoted as W and the meridional in-plane internal force per unit length present in the shell surface as N_ϕ, a consideration of equilibrium yields the following: $\Sigma F_Y = 0$: $W = (N_\phi \sin\phi)(2\pi a)$, where ϕ is the angle defining the shell cutoff and a is the instantaneous planar radius of the sphere at that point. The N_f forces in the shell are in-plane compressive forces developed in the shell at the horizontal section defined by ϕ. The vertical components of these forces (assumed uniform around the periphery of the shell) are simply $N_\phi \sin \phi$. Since the N_ϕ forces are expressed as a force per unit length (e.g., lb/ft or kN/m) along the section, the total upward force associated with all the continuous N_ϕ forces is simply the instantaneous circumference of the shell at that point (which is given by $2\pi a$) multiplied by $N_\phi \sin \phi$ (i.e., a total length times a force per unit length yields a total force). This upward force must be of a magnitude to exactly balance the downward force, hence the expression $W = N_\phi \sin \phi(2\pi a)$. This expression can be rewritten in terms of the actual radius of the sphere by noting that $a = R \sin \phi$. Thus, $W = N_\phi \sin \phi\, (2\pi R \sin \phi)$. Solving for N_ϕ, we obtain

$$N_\phi = \frac{W}{2\pi R \sin^2\phi}$$

If the total load acting downward (W) is determined, the internal forces in the shell can thus be found directly. Since these internal forces are expressed in terms of a force per unit length (e.g., lb/ft or lb/in.), actual internal stresses expressed in terms of a force per unit area (e.g., lb/in.^{2} or kN/mm^2) can be found by dividing by the shell thickness, or $f_\phi = N_\phi/t$. [This expression, seemingly a force divided by a thickness, may look odd for a stress measure (always force/area), but one part of the "area" is already reflected in the lb/ft definition of N_ϕ. For example, if $N_\phi = 1200$ lb/ft (or 100 lb/in.) and the shell thickness is 5 in., then $f_\phi = N_\phi/t = (100$ lb/in.)/(5 in.), or $(100$ lb)/(5 in.^{2}) $= 20$ lb/in.^{2}, which is still force/area. Occasionally the expression is written as $f_\phi = N_\phi/tL$, where L is the unit length.] Note that N_ϕ acts in the vertically oriented meridional direction, but the unit length is measured along the circumferential direction.

An expression can be easily derived that directly incorporates the load acting downward. If the load per unit area of shell surface acting downward is denoted by w, equilibrium in the vertical direction yields:

$\Sigma F_Y = 0$:

$$-\int_{\phi_1}^{\phi_2} w(2\pi R \sin \phi)R \, d\phi + N_\phi \sin \phi(2\pi R \sin \phi) = 0$$

where ϕ_1 and ϕ_2 define the segment of shell considered. The term on the left thus defines W. For $\phi_1 = 0$,

$$N_\phi = \frac{Rw}{1 + \cos \phi}$$

This expression is actually identical to $N_\phi = W/2\pi R \sin^2\phi$. Either expression defines the meridional forces present at a horizontal section.

12-2-5 Hoop Forces in Spherical Shells

Hoop forces that act in the circumferential or latitudinal direction are typically denoted as N_θ and also expressed in terms of a force per unit length, and can be found by considering equilibrium in the transverse direction. Alternatively, use can be made of the results of the membrane analysis discussed in Section 11–2. There it was found that the in-plane forces in a membrane that act perpendicularly to one another are related by the general expression $p_r = T_1/r_1 + T_2/r_2$. This expression is immensely valuable in the analysis of shells, since by using it the hoop forces (N_θ) can be related to the meridional forces (N_ϕ) that act in the longitudinal direction.

Since the load being studied actually acts downward rather than radially outward, however, the external force expression must be adjusted. The radial component of the downward load is given by the following: $p_r = w \cos \phi$. The expression relating hoop to meridional forces then becomes $w \cos \phi = N_\phi/r_1 + N_\theta/r_2$, or $N_\theta = r_2(w \cos \phi) - (r_2/r_1)N_\phi$. In a sphere, $r_1 = r_2 = R$, and substituting the expression previously found for N_ϕ, we have

$$N_\theta = Rw\left(-\frac{1}{1 + \cos \phi} + \cos \phi\right)$$

The preceding is a simple expression for hoop forces in terms of the radius (R) of the sphere and the downward load (w). Figure 12–4 illustrates hoop forces in shells. N_θ forces act in the circumferential direction (over a unit length in the meridional direction).

◆ ◆ **EXAMPLE**

Given a dome having a spherical radius of 100 ft (30.48 m) and a thickness of 4 in. (100 mm) that has an aspect angle of 45°, determine the meridional and hoop forces at the base of the shell for a loading of 100 lb/ft² (4788 N/m²).

Solution:

Meridional forces:

$$N_\phi = \frac{Rw}{1 + \cos \phi} = \frac{(100 \text{ ft})(100 \text{ lb/ft}^2)}{1 + 0.707} = 5858 \text{ lb/ft in compression}$$

$$= \frac{(30.48 \text{ m})(4788 \text{ N/m}^2)}{1.707} = 85,494 \text{ N/m}$$

Free-body diagram of shell
element at top: $\phi = 0°$

Free-body diagram of
shell element at $\phi = 90°$

Elevation

Meridional force

Hoop force

Elevation   Plan

(a) Rigid shell surface.
Elements in the surface
experience both
meridional and hoop
forces.

(b) At the top, all in-plane
forces must be in com-
pression for the element
to be in vertical equilibrium.

(c) The outward component
of the compressive
meridional force must be
balanced by tension
forces developed in the
hoop direction.

FIGURE 12–4 Hoop forces in spherical shells.

Meridional stresses:

$$f_\phi = \frac{N_\phi}{t} = \frac{(5858 \text{ lb/ft})/12 \text{ in./ft}}{4 \text{ in.}} = \frac{488 \text{ lb/in.}}{4 \text{ in.}} = 122 \text{ lb/in.}^2 \text{ in compression}$$

$$= \frac{85,494 \text{ N/m}}{(1000 \text{ mm/m})(100 \text{ mm})} = 0.85 \text{ N/mm}^2$$

Hoop forces:

$$N_\theta = Rw\left(-\frac{1}{1 + \cos \phi} + \cos \phi\right) = (100 \text{ ft})(100 \text{ lb/ft}^2)\left[-\left(\frac{1}{1.707}\right) + 0.707\right]$$

$$= 1212 \text{ lb/ft in compression}$$

$$= (30.48 \text{ m})(4788 \text{ N/m}^2)\left[-\left(\frac{1}{1.707}\right) + 0.707\right] = 17,684 \text{ N/m}$$

Hoop stresses:

$$f_\theta = \frac{N_\theta}{t} = \frac{1212 \text{ lb/ft}}{(12 \text{ in./ft})(4 \text{ in.})} = 25.3 \text{ lb/in.}^2 \text{ in compression}$$

$$= \frac{17,684 \text{ N/m}}{(1000 \text{ mm/m})(100 \text{ mm})} = 0.177 \text{ N/mm}^2$$

The stresses in the sphere at this point are thus extremely low. This is characteristic of most shell structures. ◆

12–2–6   Distribution of Forces

The distribution of meridional and hoop forces can be found by simply plotting the equations for the two forces (Figure 12–5). As is evident, the meridional forces are always in compression while the hoop forces undergo a transition at an angle of 51°49′ as measured from the perpendicular.

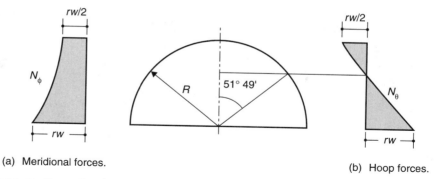

(a) Meridional forces.

(b) Hoop forces.

FIGURE 12–5   Stress distribution in a spherical dome carrying a uniformly distributed load along the surface of the sphere.

Shells cut off above this only develop compression stresses in their surfaces while deeper shells can develop tension stresses in the hoop direction. The magnitude of the stresses, however, always remains relatively low.

An interesting way of looking at the overall behavior of a dome-and-ring assembly is illustrated in Figure 12–6. As in other structures, the external moment at a section must be balanced by an internal resisting moment (in this case provided by a couple formed between the hoop and ring forces). Thinking of the structure in these terms also helps explain the development of tension hoop stresses in a dome.

12–2–7   Concentrated Forces

The reason why concentrated loads should be avoided on shells can readily be seen by analyzing the meridional forces present under such a loading. The general expression found before was $N_\phi = W/2\pi R \sin^2 \phi$, where W was the total load acting downward. For a shell carrying a concentrated load, P, the expression becomes $N_\phi = P/2\pi R \sin^2 \phi$. If the load is applied at $\phi = 0$ (the crown of the shell), a situation arises where directly beneath the load, the stresses become indefinitely large in the shell (i.e., as $\phi \to 0$, $\sin \phi \to 0$, and $N_\phi \to \infty$). Obviously, a failure would occur if the shell surface could offer no bending resistance and the load was truly characterized as a point force. In any event, such forces should be avoided on shell surfaces.

12–2–8   Support Conditions: Tension and Compression Rings

A major design consideration in a shell of revolution is the nature of the boundary or support conditions. In much the same way that buttresses or tie-rods must be used to contain the horizontal thrusts of arches, some device must be used to absorb the horizontal thrusts associated with the meridional in-plane forces at the lower edge of the shell. In a dome, for example, a circular buttress system could be used. Alternatively, a planar circular ring, called a *tension ring,* could be used to encircle the base of the dome and contain the outward components of the meridional forces (Figure 12–7). Since the latter are always in compression, their horizontal components are always outwardly directed at the shell base. The containment ring is, therefore, always in tension. If a hole were cut out of the shell at its crown, however, the same meridional force

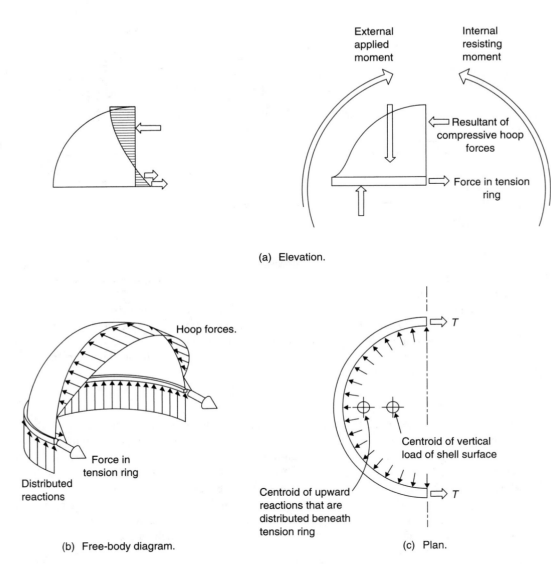

(a) Elevation.

(b) Free-body diagram.

(c) Plan.

FIGURE 12–6   Basic shell behavior.

components would be inwardly directed. A ring used to absorb these forces would, therefore, be in compression.

A tension ring is simply a planar ring against which the outward thrusts push, thus causing tension to develop in the ring. Consider the sum of the forces along any direction in a section cut through the ring as it sits on a horizontal plane. The horizontal components ($N_\phi \cos \phi$) of the meridional forces act outwardly along the circumferential length of the ring and produce a total outward thrust that is in turn balanced by the internal forces developed in the tension ring. This outward thrust can be shown to be equal to the unit outward thrust times the projected length

(a) Buttresses. The vertical and horizontal components of the meridional forces can be supported by buttresses. The buttresses must be capable of containing the large outward thrusts involved.

(b) Tension rings. A continuous tension ring can be used to contain the horizontal thrusts. Only downward forces are then exerted on the ground.

(c) If tension rings are used, they must be continuous around the shell base; otherwise, they are useless and severe stresses will develop in the shell.

(d) Shells using tension rings can be elevated on columns since below the ring only vertical forces need to be transmitted to the ground. Shells without tension rings would need a buttressing system.

FIGURE 12–7 Spherical shell support conditions.

over which they act (i.e., the diameter). Thus, $2T = (N_\phi \cos \phi) 2a$, or $T = (N_\phi \cos \phi)a$, where a is the radius of the tension ring ($a = R \sin \phi$). This expression follows from: $2T = \int (N_\phi \cos \phi)(a)(d\phi)$.

A tension ring completely absorbs all the horizontal thrusts involved. When resting on the ground, it also provides a continuous footing for transferring the vertical reaction components to the ground. Alternatively, the ring can be supported on other elements (e.g., columns), which then receive vertical loads only.

The use of a tension ring does, however, induce bending in the shell surface where the ring and shell intersect. These bending moments are largely due to deformation incompatibilities that exist between the ring and shell. Since the ring is always in tension, it always wants to expand outward. The hoop deformations in the shell, however, may be compressive (thus, the shell edge wants to deform inwardly), depending on the N_ϕ and N_θ forces. In any event it is highly unusual for the deformation tendencies to be exactly similar. Since the elements must be joined, the edge beam restricts the free movement of the shell surface, and thus bending is induced in the shell's edge. As mentioned before, however, this bending rapidly dies out in shells, so the bulk of the shell's surface is generally unaffected. The shell edge is locally stiffened and reinforced for bending (Figure 12–8).

Ideally, the supports should be such that they do not tend to cause any bending to be developed in the shell surface. Fixed edge conditions should be avoided if possible. One possible solution is illustrated in Figure 12–9(b), where the shell is pinned along its peripheral edge. Unlike

(a) In low-profile spherical shells, the in-plane membrane forces tend to cause the shell edge to contract inwardly. The ring containing the outward thrust of the meridional forces is in tension and thus tends to expand outwardly.

(b) The interconnected ring and shell edge restrain each other's free movement. This incompatibility induces bending moments in the shell at the edge. The bending moments, however, damp out rapidly in the shell.

(c) Shell edges are often thickened at the tension ring juncture to take care of the high local bending stresses.

FIGURE 12–8 Edge disturbances in spherical shells.

(a) Fixed-edge conditions induce undesirable bending in the shell surface.

(b) Pinned edges also tend to restrain the shell surface from free movement.

(c) Roller edges are desirable in that they allow movements to occur more freely but are very difficult to construct.

FIGURE 12–9   Shell support conditions.

the arch, however, the presence of hoop forces causes the shell to deform naturally in the out-of-plane direction. Restraining this deformation by a pinned connection would be equivalent to applying forces to the shell's edge, thus inducing bending. A peripheral roller support, as illustrated in Figure 12–9(c), is preferable since no restraint exists in the out-of-plane direction. Such supports are, however, extremely difficult to build for shells. In addition, slight angular changes due to movement still cause some bending to be induced (although less than in the case of fixed or pinned conditions).

For reasons of practical construction considerations, some bending is often allowed to develop at the shell edge for the sake of using easy-to-construct edge and foundation conditions. The shell is simply locally stiffened (usually by increasing its thickness) around the edge and specially reinforced for bending.

The problem with deformation incompatibilities can become a generator of design approaches intended to minimize undesirable consequences. One effective method is to utilize post-tensioning as a way of controlling deformations. A support ring normally in tension, for example, can be post-tensioned so that compressive forces (hence compressive deformations compatible with those in the shell in the hoop direction) initially exist in the ring. The outward thrusts of the dome would cause a relaxation of the compressive forces (and an increase in the tension in the post-tensioning wires). If the initial amount of post-tensioning is controlled, final ring deformations can be controlled and thus deformation incompatibilities with the shell minimized. The shell surface itself can also be post-tensioned in the hoop direction for added control of shell forces and deformations.

12–2–9   Other Considerations

There are a host of factors other than those already discussed that must be taken into account in the design of shells. Critical among these additional factors is the need to ensure that a shell does not fail prematurely and disastrously in a *buckling* or surface instability mode. When the curvature of the shell's surface is relatively flat, snap-through or local buckling can be a severe problem (see Figure 12–10). As with the analogous phenomenon in long columns, instability can occur at very low stress levels. It can be prevented by using surfaces of sharp curvature. The need to maintain sharp curvatures, however, effectively hampers the use of very large spans with

(a) Snap-through buckling. The whole shell can inwardly buckle due to external loads. Shells with flat curvatures are sensitive to this type of buckling. Increasing shell curvature reduces the possibility of this type of buckling.

(b) Local buckling. Rather than the whole shell snapping through, a local portion of the shell can buckle inwardly. Again sharp shell curvatures decrease the possibility of this type of buckling.

FIGURE 12–10 Buckling in thin shells.

low-profile shells, in which cases there is relatively little curvature present. The problem is also extremely severe in reticulated shells made of small rigid linear elements (e.g., geodesic domes). More advanced texts discuss the shell buckling problem and propose measures for predicting if instability is a problem in a given design context.

Another major concern is that shells must withstand loads other than those acting vertically. Figure 12–11 illustrates the stress trajectories in a spherical dome due to wind forces. Usually wind forces are not too critical in the design of shell structures. Earthquake forces that also act laterally, however, can pose extremely serious design problems. When such loadings are possible, special care must be taken with the design of the support conditions present.

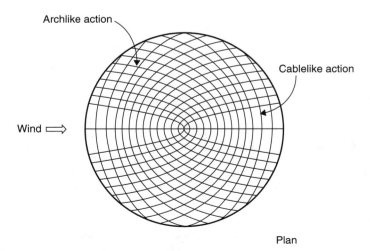

FIGURE 12–11 Stress trajectories in a spherical dome due to wind forces.

(a) Vaults: vaults are supported continuously along their longitudinal edges. Internal transverse forces are characterized by an archlike action.

(b) Short shell with stiff edge beams: the edge beams serve basically the same function as a wall in a vault if they are sufficiently stiff. An archlike action transfers surface loads to the beams, which carry the loads by bending to the supports.

(c) Long-barrel shells: if the shell does not have stiff edge beams, archlike action cannot develop in the transverse direction. Instead, loads are carried by a longitudinal bending action, which is similar to that present in beams.

FIGURE 12–12   Cylindrical shells.

12–3   CYLINDRICAL SHELLS

The behavior of structural forms that are defined by translational surfaces is critically influenced by the relative proportions of the shell and its support conditions.

Consider the cylindrical surface supported on walls illustrated in Figure 12–12(a). In this structure, commonly called a *vault,* the surface behaves much like a series of parallel arches as long as the supporting walls can provide the necessary reactions. If the surface is rigid (e.g., made out of reinforced concrete), the surface also exhibits plate action (i.e., shearing forces are developed between adjacent transverse strips), which is useful for carrying nonuniform loads. The same general type of action occurs when such a surface is supported on very stiff beams. The beams, in turn, transfer the loads to the supports by bending.

The behavior of a very short shell may differ appreciably from that just described if transverse end stiffeners are used. The surface loads may be transferred directly to the end stiffeners through longitudinal plate action.

As the shell structure becomes very much longer relative to its transverse span, a completely different type of action begins, particularly if edge beams are either not used or highly flexible ones are used. Any type of supporting edge beam, it should be noted, naturally tends to become more flexible as its length increases. The cylindrical surface will again *tend* to start behaving like an arch in the transverse direction. Flexible edge beams (or no edge beams) do not, however, provide any appreciable resistance to the horizontal thrusts involved. The consequence is that no arch-like action is ever actually exhibited in this direction. Indeed, if no edge beams are present, the longitudinal free edges tend to deflect inwardly rather than outward under a full loading. A different type of load-carrying mechanism must therefore be present. Structures of this type are called *barrel* shells. The principal action in a long cylindrical barrel shell is in the longitudinal rather than the transverse direction. A type of longitudinal bending occurs that is very analogous to that which occurs in either simple beams or folded plates. Compressive stresses in the longitudinal direction are developed near the crown of the curved surface and tension stresses in the lower part.

The analogy with folded plate structures is a useful one, since many of the same design principles are present. Transverse stiffeners, for example, are useful in increasing the load-carrying capacity of a barrel shell. The more that stiffeners are used, or if the barrel shell considered is one of a series of adjacent shells, the beamlike behavior becomes more pronounced and beam analysis techniques yield more accurate results. Barrel shells whose lengths are about three times (or more) their transverse spans exhibit this longitudinal type of behavior.

12–4 HYPERBOLIC PARABOLOID SHELLS

The behavior of shells having ruled surfaces may be envisioned by looking at the nature of the curvatures formed by the straightline generators. If the edge conditions are of the type which can offer restraint (foundations or very stiff edge beams), an archlike action will exist in regions of convex curvature and a cablelike action in regions of concave curvature. The presence of compression or tension forces in the surface depends on which action is present. When surfaces get very flat due to reduced curvatures, a plate action in which bending dominates may be present (necessitating increased plate thicknesses). If shell edges are not supported, a beam behavior may be present.

A ruled surface may be made by translating two ends of a straight line over two parallel but twisted straight lines. Interestingly enough, the shape formed can also be described as a translational surface generated by translating a concave parabola over a convex one. In this type of structure an archlike action will be present in the direction of convex curvature and a cablelike action in the perpendicular direction which is concavely curved. The stress field in the plate is thus compressive in one direction and tensile in the perpendicular direction. These directions are at 45° to the original straight-line generators.

Membrane forces are expressed on a unit width basis for the arch and cablelike actions noted, which are at 45° to the edges. Under a uniform loading, the force at the top of any arch or cable strip is $C_x = T_x = w_s L_x^2/8d_x$; where L_x is the span of the strip, d_x is its instantaneous height, and w_s is the load carried by the cable or arch strip. Since arch and cable strips cross one another, the normal distributed load w present at a point is half-shared between crossing strips. Hence, $w_s = w/2$ on a strip and $C_x = T_x = w L_x^2/16d_x$. Since d_x is small, this value can also be taken as the maximum force present in a strip of unit width [stresses can be found by noting that $f = C/t$, where C is a force per unit length and t is the plate thickness]. Thus, if C equals 6000 lb/ft or 500 lb/in., and t is 4 in., then $f = (500 \text{ lb/in.})/4 \text{ in.} = 125 \text{ lb/in.}^2$ Both L_x and d_x vary among adjacent strips because of the 45° strip orientation. By expressing d_x in terms of L_x, and L_x in terms of sides a and b for a hyperbolic paraboloid surface of maximum height h, the forces become

$C = -wab/2h$ and $T = wab/2h$, where h is the maximum rise present. Such an analysis also yields the seemingly curious result that C or T is a constant value in adjacent strips of any length throughout the shell (observe that when L_x is large, d_x is large, and vice versa, so that $C_x = T_x = wL_x^2/16d_x$ remains a constant value). Remarkably, the membrane force is more or less constant throughout the entire surface.

When the envisioned strips terminate at the edges of the plate, they exert forces vertically and horizontally. An arch strip meets a cable strip at a 90° angle, 45° to the shell edge. Vertical components balance each other. The components of the horizontal thrusts perpendicular to the shell edges also balance one another. There is, however, a resultant *edge shear force* directed along the edge of the plate. Edge forces along a unit length are approximately given by $F = wab/2h$. These edge shears accumulate along the length of the edge of the shell (a) against restraint points (e.g., a buttress) into large total edge forces: $F_{total} = wa^2b/2h$. Depending on the location of free and constrained points, these total edge forces may be in either tension or compression. Large edge beams may be required to carry these edge forces. These forces in turn bear against buttresses or other support conditions, and, in some cases, tend to cause them to splay outwards—as is the case in Figure 12–13(a). Tie-rods may be effectively used.

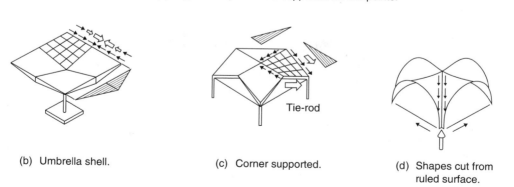

FIGURE 12–13 Hyperbolic paraboloid. The general nature of the forces in many shells can be ascertained by looking at the types of shell curvatures present. Concave curvatures generally indicate a type of cablelike action (a tension field) and convex curvatures an archlike action (a compression field).

Shell surfaces of many types may be made by aggregating simple hyperbolic shapes. Unusual forms may be formed by cutting the surface in other directions than along the straight-line generators, as shown in Figure 12–13(d).

QUESTIONS

12–1 A rigid shell having a spherical radius of 300 ft is cut off at an angle of $\phi = 51°49'$. Assume that the shell carries a distributed live load of 50 lb/ft^2. What are the in-plane forces in the shell at $\phi = 0°$? At $\phi = 51°49'$? What are the associated f_ϕ and f_θ stresses? Ignore the dead load of the shell itself.

12–2 A rigid reinforced concrete shell having a spherical radius of 200 ft is cut off at an angle of $\phi = 35°$. The shell thickness is 3 in. Assume that the unit weight of the shell material is 150 lb/ft^3 and that the shell carries a live load of 60 lb/ft^2. Draw force-distribution diagrams of the type illustrated in Figure 12–5. Indicate numerical values.

12–3 Assume that a tension ring is used in conjunction with the shell described in Question 12–2. What is the magnitude of the force developed in the ring?

Answer: $T = 1,660,063$ lb.

12–4 Assume a hyperbolic paraboloid surface is supported as shown in Figure 12–13, that $a = b = 50$ ft, $h = 20$, and that the live and dead loading is 60 lb/ft^2. Find the membrane forces in the surface and the maximum edge forces present. Note the location of the maximum edge forces.

PART III

PRINCIPLES OF STRUCTURAL DESIGN

The chapters in Part III discuss principles that are important in designing structures in a building context. The structural design process at this level is largely heuristic in nature and closely linked to the design of the remainder of the building.

Structural design activities may be classified into several broad categories that generally reflect the sequence in which design decisions are encountered: *First-order design* issues deal broadly with the relationship between structural fabric, design intent, and contextual or programmatic dictates. These issues normally hinge around the general type and organization of the structural system to be used in relation to the overall morphology of the building or other functional entity designed, including the way in which specific spaces are configured and defined by built elements. Of specific importance here is whether the structure to be designed is conceived of as a single large form or as some type of aggregation of smaller structural units or bays. Basic preconceived attitudes or images in relation to the general shaping and configuration of the structure come in at this level as well (e.g., frameworks versus shell or cable structures).

Second-order design issues deal with specific structural strategies in relation to the exact shape of the basic structural entity itself and the way this shape is formed by specific constituent structural elements. Choices of structural materials (steel, timber, reinforced concrete) are made at this level (if not already implicit in basic attitudes defined previously). Intrinsically related choices of specific structural systems are also made at this level (e.g., reinforced concrete flat plate versus two-way beam and slab systems; or steel systems based on rigid-frame action and beams to span horizontally versus those using diagonal bracing and trusses as horizontal spanning elements). Of importance here are the nature of the structural hierarchies present (levels, spacing of members), bay spans and proportions, and similar geometric characteristics, all of which are variable within certain limits imposed by first-order decisions.

Third-order design activities deal with specific member shaping and sizing. Associated with the choice of a framing pattern for a spatial entity in a given context and choice of materials are specific implications or even imperatives relating to the shape and sizes of constituent structural elements. Of initial importance here is the choice of member cross-sectional configuration: rectangular, square, round, hollow-tube, open box, and so on. Once the choice of member cross section is selected, actual member dimensions can subsequently be determined.

Many of the design activities discussed in Part II have focused on third-order design activities. A detailed knowledge of elements, however, is a necessary precursor for intelligently making the broader decisions entailed in first- and second-order activities, and for this reason a discussion of them has been presented first. In Part III we now look at the broader issues involved in first- and second-order activities, but assuming that the reader is thoroughly familiar with the analysis and design of specific elements. While it is convenient to discuss design issues at these three different levels, it is important to bear in mind that strong interdependencies exist. Certain structural systems may be structurally efficient and desirable when executed in certain materials, using certain member cross sections, and for certain span ranges. The same pattern might be completely impossible for other span ranges or material or cross-section choices. Hence the structural design process cannot really consist of a deterministic process that begins with a consideration of an overall form in the abstract and eventually results in the sizing of each elemental member through a series of independent design decisions at each of the three design levels. Nothing could be further from the truth. In reality, good designers typically deal with each of the three design levels at varying levels of engagement at all times as the overall design moves from a mental image to a fully developed design. The process is interactive and iterative. The structural system finally adopted is usually one that works well both in its own terms and with respect to other architectural objectives.

In Chapter 13 we discuss structural design considerations as they arise during the very early design phases of a building, where the designer is in the stages of establishing broad strategies and manipulating spaces within a building. Primary reference is in relation to *vertical* loadings. Chapter 14 continues this treatment, but focuses more on the effects of *lateral* loading conditions. Although the design principles that are presented seem quite simple, many only appear so because of their abstract presentation and actually embody far more involved concepts and choices than meet the eye. All are drawn from studies of real buildings. The reader is encouraged to identify real examples of the principles discussed.

In Chapter 15 we succinctly summarize different structural systems as classified by material. It is useful to review this chapter briefly first and to refer to it while reading Chapters 13 and 14. In Chapter 16 we focus on connection design.

CHAPTER 13

Structural Grids and Patterns: General Planning and Design

13-1 INTRODUCTION

In this chapter we address first-order design activities through a study of structural grids and other patterns. A study of existing buildings reveals the rather obvious fact that there are often strong and easily identifiable patterns present in the way buildings are functionally organized and in the structural systems used. The patterns formed by the structural configurations are intimately related to those of the functional organizations. Each affects the other. The adoption of a particular functional configuration for a building often determines to a large extent the structure used, and vice versa. For this reason the process of designing a structure is implicitly linked to the process of designing the overall building. Neither process can really exist without the other.

During very early design stages relatively little is initially known about the structure of a building. One way of interpreting design activities during this early stage is that the designer is manipulating the programmatic functions of the building with the objective of ordering them into a form such that when a physical building fabric is developed, the result will achieve the desired design goals or aspirations. During this process the designer often either adopts a pattern organization to give order to the building or encounters reasons that give rise to generalized patterns of both space usage and structure. The cellular nature of multiunit housing is an obvious example of the latter. The privacy requirements for individual dwelling units naturally lead to a repetitive pattern of space modules related to the size of a typical dwelling unit. In a typical building, the forces that give rise to patterns are often more a consequence of the functional programming requirements of the building or of construction considerations than of purely structural motivations. The fact that there are associated structural advantages to using certain patterns, however, is still a contributing factor, particularly in large-span or large-load situations.

In a particular context, issues relating to loading type, span, and the patterns of the support conditions interact to inform the selection and design of the structural system itself. This chapter considers these interactions, with particular emphasis on the effects of *vertical* loading conditions.

13–2   COMMON GRIDS

Many different types of structural patterns are possible. In most buildings there is usually a repetitive geometrical pattern or grid present both in the vertical support system, whether it is formed of load-bearing walls, columns, or some combination of the two, and in the horizontal spanning system.

The following sections focus on buildings of this type which are composed of repetitive bays or other forms of cellular units. The geometries and dimensions of individual units and the way these units aggregate in such buildings are invariably dependent on the programmatic requirements of the buildings. These same dimensions and geometries, in turn, strongly influence the types of structural systems most appropriate for use.

It is useful first to review briefly some basic characteristics of pattern types themselves. Obviously, many buildings (e.g., gymnasiums) are actually *single-cell* structures. Most buildings, however, are composed of a large number of *aggregated bays* or units.

Several common types of structural patterns are evident in the buildings illustrated in Figures 13–1 to 13–3. The first figure shows a housing scheme in which a serial aggregation pattern is used to arrange the basic units. The structural pattern for the vertical support system itself

FIGURE 13–1   Housing in Germany.

Ground floor

0   20   40

(a) Square column grid.

Exhibit

Library

Lecture

Long-span trusses

(b) Section.

(c) Plan.

FIGURE 13–2   Gund Hall, Harvard University, Cambridge, Massachusetts.

consists primarily of a series of parallel lines. The parallel lines could consist of a series of load-bearing walls or a column-and-beam system placed in the same pattern locations (the horizontal spanning system could be the same for either type of vertical support approach). It is the basic grid pattern that is of first importance.

A common square grid of discrete vertical support elements is illustrated in the plan shown in Figure 13–2. A two-way aggregation (staggered) approach is taken. In this plan the pattern is uniform throughout the building except near the left edge of the building and in the

FIGURE 13-3 Trenton Community Center, Trenton, New Jersey.

auditorium/lecture area. Grids are often altered in zones where something special occurs, such as an auditorium, or at boundaries. Some of the reasons for these alterations will be explored in later sections.

A more complex tartan grid of discrete vertical support elements is illustrated in the plan by Louis Kahn shown in Figure 13–3. This building is an often used example of how the structural pattern of a building can be related to and reinforce how a building is functionally zoned. In this building the basic pattern is again altered where a special event, the gymnasium, occurs.

Square or rectangular grids are common, but other geometries are frequently encountered as well. Systems that are based on any basic geometric pattern are common, especially when the overall shape of a building calls for an obvious nonorthogonal response (Figure 13–4). Note that a common shape, such as a septagonal plan, may be framed in significantly different ways.

In the following sections we explore issues that focus around the selection of appropriate grids and related structural types. Several general characteristics of basic structural hierachies are reviewed first to set the stage for the discussion.

(a) One-way radial beam-and-column system for a hexagonal or circular configuration.

(b) One-way circumferential beam-and-column system plan for hexagonal or circular configuration.

(c) Two-way flat-plate system (without beams) for a hexagonal or circular configuration.

(d) Three-dimensional shell or pneumatic structure for a circular configuration.

(e) Two-way slab-and-beam system for a triangular configuration.

(f) Two-way slab-and-beam system for a hexagonal pattern.

FIGURE 13–4   Influence of special building geometries on structural approach. Typical structures for circular, hexagonal, and triangular geometries.

13–3   GENERAL CHARACTERISTICS OF STRUCTURAL HIERARCHIES

13–3–1   One-Way Systems

Structures enclosing volumes may usefully be conceived in terms of *vertical support systems* and *horizontal spanning systems*. A great many horizontal spanning systems, particularly those in steel and timber, are made up of hierarchical assemblies of different kinds of members. Common post-and-beam systems, for example, are made up of a series of beam, decking, and column elements. Alternatively, trusses or frames may support the decking elements. It is helpful to define members according to different locations in a hierarchical arrangement (Figure 13–5). Placement of the lower-level members in a hierarchy typically defines the necessary location of vertical support locations. If the vertical support system is selected first, its type and geometry suggest something about the nature of the best hierarchical arrangement and appropriate horizontal spanning system. Usually, neither one dictates the design of the other, but they are interactively designed together.

One-level
spanning system

Two-level
spanning system

Two-level
spanning system

Three-level
spanning system

Relations between vertical
support systems and dif-
ferent types of two-, three-,
and four-level systems.

(a) Common types of one-way horizontal spanning systems
using hierarchical organizations.

(b) Three-level spanning system using widely spaced
trusses as primary collectors, more closely spaced
beams for the secondary framing system, and
decking for the surface-forming elements.

(c) Three-level spanning system using deep beams as
primary collectors, lighter beams for the secondary
framing system, and decking for the surface.

FIGURE 13–5 Typical one-way horizontal spanning systems.

Several simple hierarchies are illustrated in Figure 13–5. A simple *one-level hierarchy* can be made directly with simple surface-forming decking elements. Since reactions are line-forming, load-bearing wall support systems are uniquely appropriate for this kind of hierarchy.

A *two-level hierarchy* may be made to achieve longer spans. Individual structural elements are arranged so that shorter-span decking elements are carried by periodically spaced longer-span beams, trusses, or cables. Elements such as beams or trusses can be sized and shaped so that relatively large distances can be spanned. These elements are often referred to as *collectors,* since they gather loads from surface-forming elements. These collectors deliver concentrated forces to the vertical support system. If the collector members are widely spaced and have long spans, these concentrated forces are quite high and a columnar support system is normally dictated. If they are quite closely spaced and spans are low, and forces at the ends of members decrease accordingly, a load-bearing wall system and/or pilaster system may be the best choice for the vertical support system.

A *three-level hierarchy* involves introducing yet lower-level members. Lowest-level members are called *primary collectors,* and middle ones, *secondary collectors.* In systems of this type, the primary collectors invariably end up picking up large forces from the secondary system and delivering highly concentrated forces to the vertical support system. A columnar support system is almost invariably required. Hierarchies with greater than three levels are possible, of course, but rarely used except for very long span situations or other unique circumstances.

Short spans often may be made directly with one-level systems, whereas larger spans use two- or three-level systems. This principle is, of course, not universally applicable, since there are a number of special elements (such as prestressed concrete tees) that can very efficiently span large distances directly. The principle is more applicable to systems that use minor surface-forming elements (e.g., planks, decking) initially to pick up a uniformly distributed loading.

When minor surface-forming members are used, it is typical that they are all ubiquitous mass-produced elements. In a three-level system in steel, for example, the effective span of available decking usually determines the spacing of the secondary collectors. However, different kinds of decking are available for a range of possible spans. Secondary members are, in turn, typically off-the-shelf wide-flange elements. They are exactly sized and selected from a variety available for the specific spans and loadings involved. The primary collectors may, in turn, be off-the-shelf elements as well if spans and loads are small, but often they are specially designed. For longer spans and loadings, a specially shaped truss, plate girder, or cable would make sense. The spacing of these specially shaped forms would normally be dictated by larger building design issues (relation to functional spaces, etc.). The spacing of the secondary collectors, which is influenced in turn by the decking, often dictates the spacing of subelements in specially designed primary collectors. For example, the spacing of truss members (so that loads may come in at nodal points) or the locations of stiffeners in plate girders may well be dictated by the spacing of secondary collectors. Interestingly, the design of a three-level system normally proceeds with a simultaneous consideration of all three levels. Each affects the other. Working out an exact relationship can be surprisingly difficult due to the number of variables involved, particularly if some larger structural objective such as minimizing total volume is assumed.

While it is common to think in terms of hierarchies of orthogonally placed elements, the general ideas are applicable to other patterns as well. Just because a bay is square does not mean that the horizontal spanning system has to be organized in a parallel way. The grid could be twisted or otherwise manipulated.

Framing plans which use curved beams (as viewed from the top) call for special note, since their use is highly unusual and potentially problematic from a structural viewpoint. Detrimental torsional (or twisting) effects are induced in the curved members by vertically acting loads. The feasibility of using curved members for horizontal spanning elements is closely related to specific material choices. While it is not impossible to have curved members made of timber, for example, curving forms surely lend themselves more readily to the use of steel, and then advisably only in small-scale structures.

13–3–2   Two-Way Systems

The intrinsic nature of two-way systems and the extensive use of plates or slabs with multidirectional load-dispersal paths makes the notion of structural hierarchies less obvious for two-way systems than for one-way systems. In short-span systems, flat reinforced concrete plates have no beams at all. As spans increase, however, the need for two-way beam or ribbed systems to support flat plate elements becomes necessary. A critical characteristic of two-way systems is the invariable presence of square or nearly square support geometries rather than rectilinear patterns in both beams and vertical support systems (e.g., in the column or wall grids) so as to obtain true two-way action (see Chapter 10).

Figure 13–6 illustrates some typical hierarchies for two-way systems. When the surface forming elements are reinforced concrete plates, there are limits to the extent to which a flat plate may span (see Chapter 10). Spans may be increased by using column capitals to form a flat slab system, by a peripheral wall support, or by introducing beams around the periphery of a plate to form a two-way beam and slab system. Using a two-way ribbed "waffle" slab extends spanning capabilities. Extremely large spans between columns may be obtained by introducing a secondary beam system beneath a supported plate that runs between primary beams that span from column to column [Figure 13–6(f)]. These systems are often post-tensioned.

Two-way grid systems may be composed of beams of either reinforced concrete or steel and may in turn support other surface-forming substructures (flat or shaped). Reinforced concrete is a natural material for forming two-way grid structures. Steel plate-girder grids are possible but somewhat more difficult because of the need for making rigid intersecting joints. Similar grid systems may be made using steel trusses. The spacing of grid members depends largely on the nature of the supported substructure, but usually it is fairly generous (among other things, a coarse grid tends to reduce the number of difficult grid joints to be made). Some flat grid systems use one-way systems for the substructure planar modules that are supported by crossed members. This can lead to some peculiar pattern arrangements because it is not instrinsically obvious which way to orient the spanning directions of the modules, and, thus, random patterns can occur. The modular grid pattern inherently suggests the use of nondirectional two-way infill substructure modules.

Vertical support systems for horizontal grid structures may be either walls or columns, depending on functional needs and the spacing of grid elements. When grid elements are closely spaced [e.g., less than 5 ft (1.5 m)], walls are commonly used. In large structures with generous grid spacings [e.g., over 20 ft (6 m)], columnar rather than wall supports are suggested, with a column placed under each major horizontal grid element (a one-on-one relationship). In intermediate spacings, ring beams supported on periodically placed columns can be a good solution. Grids may effectively cantilever beyond inset wall or column lines to reduce the bending moments present.

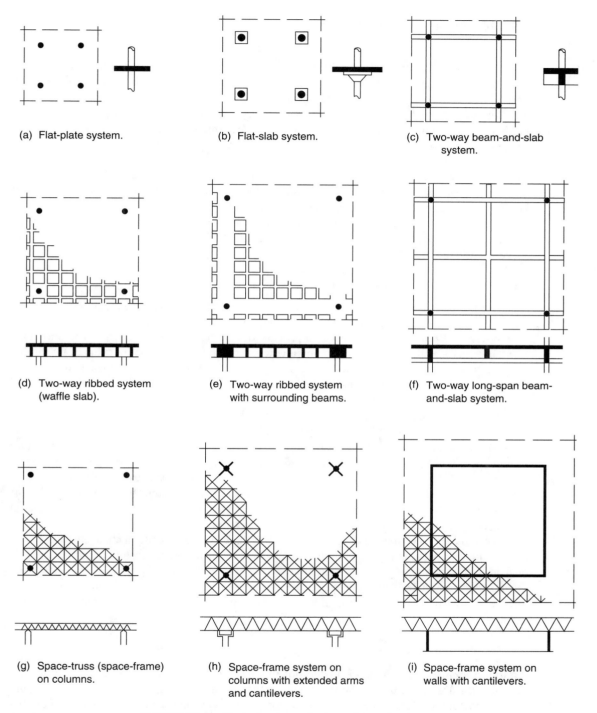

(a) Flat-plate system.

(b) Flat-slab system.

(c) Two-way beam-and-slab system.

(d) Two-way ribbed system (waffle slab).

(e) Two-way ribbed system with surrounding beams.

(f) Two-way long-span beam-and-slab system.

(g) Space-truss (space-frame) on columns.

(h) Space-frame system on columns with extended arms and cantilevers.

(i) Space-frame system on walls with cantilevers.

FIGURE 13–6 Typical two-way horizontal spanning systems.

Grid structures from crossed-folded plate elements may be made as well. Reinforced concrete systems can easily be made. Steel systems are possible but difficult because of the need for rigid joints at intersections. Spacings are usually fairly generous because of construction dictates.

Space-frame systems are inherently fine-grained systems in that individual members are normally spaced quite closely together, particularly when made of steel. Typically, they are long-span systems. Coarser grids may be obtained, however, simply by using larger members (connections may in turn become more difficult). Timber and even reinforced concrete may be used (the latter must be carefully designed and grid spacing becomes quite coarse). Space-frame systems are quite effectively supported with walls, a series of closely spaced columns, or on a ring beam system supported by columns. Cantilevers are useful in reducing design bending moments. Supporting space frames on four corner columns is indeed possible and often done, but it is among the less efficient support systems possible and leads to increased member sizes in the space frame itself.

13-3-3 Relation to Roof Shape

Thus far the discussion has focused on structures with flat horizontal spanning systems (e.g., floors). The basic idea of a structural hierarchy applies to other configurations as well (including roof systems). Roof shape is, however, a primary determinant of the framing organization utilized. Figure 13–7 illustrates in a diagrammatic way a number of common roof shapes for different plan forms. For most roof forms, there is invariably a number of different ways to structure the shape, so the diagrams are illustrative only.

There is usually a basic decision involved in structuring most volumetric shapes of whether to attempt to have the structure *only* coincident with the external envelope of the roof shape (and not have any structural members exist within the internal volume of the space itself) or to allow the structure to exist *within* the internal volume. An example of a *coincident system* is shown in Figure 13–7, where sloped members are used in a simple pyramidal form. Members are tied together at the crown and around the base periphery (the latter is needed to prevent outward spreading of the sloped members). By contrast, a crossed-truss system forming the same roof shape clearly passes through the interior space itself. This approach is often cumbersome and constructionally complex, but can sometimes be used to advantage.

When there is a change in the profile of a roof, there is also normally a change of some sort in the framing system at the same point (Figure 13–8). A change in roof profile might generate a change in the framing system, or alternatively, a change in the framing system necessitated by other factors might lead to a change in the profile of the roof shape. Frequently, the profile change necessitates the introduction of a vertical support line (e.g., walls or a column line) at the point of change.

13-3-4 Relations between Span Length and Structure Type

Common Spans. Span length is unquestionably a crucial determinant in selecting a structural response for a given situation. Some structural systems are quite appropriate for certain span ranges and not for others. To give a graphic sense of the scale and spanning capability of different systems, Figure 13–9 illustrates some typical economic span ranges for several one- and two-way systems. The *maximum* spans indicated do not represent maximum *possible* spans (since most of the systems indicated could be made to span farther than indicated) but represent spans

Geometry

Framing Alternatives

FIGURE 13–7 Relations between roof geometry and framing strategies.

FIGURE 13–8 Effects of changes in roof profiles. A line of vertical support is often introduced at profile transition points.

that are not to be considered unduly unusual, even though they are longer than typically encountered. The minimum limitations are intended to represent a system's lower feasibility range based on construction or economic considerations. There is obviously nothing sacred or fixed about the precise span figures shown. They are intended to give a feeling for relationships between structural systems and spans and nothing more. *More detailed span-range charts for specific materials are contained in Chapter 15.*

Underlying Principles Governing Span Lengths. The importance of the structural span is evident from noting that design moments for uniformly distributed loads are proportional to the square of the length of the span. Doubling a span length, for example, increases design moments by a factor of 4; quadrupling span lengths increases design moments by a factor of 16. Member sizes, of course, depend closely on the magnitude of the design moment present. The appropriateness of a particular structural option is dependent on this factor as well. For this reason it is useful to review briefly how different structural options provide an internal resisting moment to balance the external applied moment.

Figure 13–10 illustrates how several different structural options provide an internal resisting moment to balance the external applied moment. Note that in all cases the basic mechanism is the same. A couple is formed between compression and tension zones whose magnitude exactly equals the applied moment. For a given applied moment the magnitude of the internal forces developed in the compression and tension zones depends directly on the magnitude of the moment arm present. The deeper the structure, the greater the moment arm and the less are the tension and compression forces present.

The process of designing an appropriate structure for a given span range is directly linked to applying the principles discussed above. The sensitivity of the design moment to the span is critical. In low spans the design moments are low, and any of the basic structural options shown in Figure 13–9 are possible. As spans lengthen, however, design moments increase so rapidly that some of the options shown become less feasible. Constant-depth members such as beams, for example, are normally relatively shallow, and consequently increases in span lengths are linked with large increases in the magnitudes of the tensile and compressive stress fields which provide

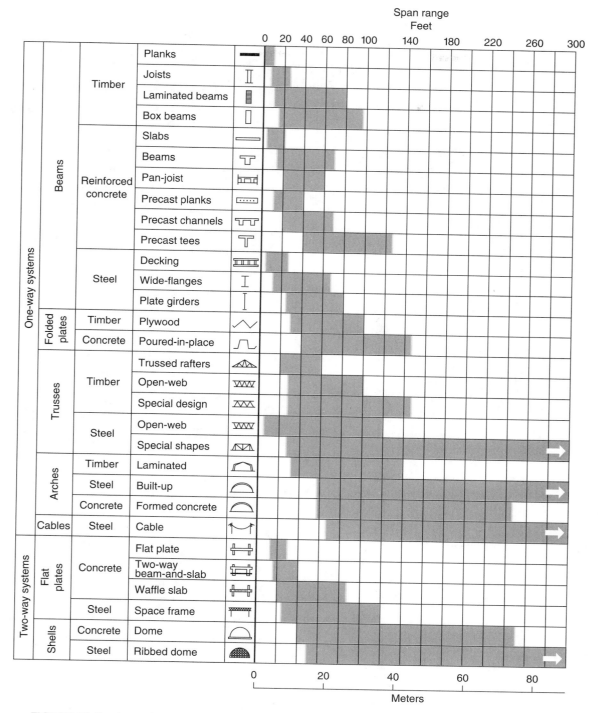

FIGURE 13–9 Approximate span ranges of different systems. See also more detailed charts in Chapter 15.

Structure	Basic Moment-carrying Mechanism	Free-body Diagrams with Respect to Rotational Forces		
		External Applied Moment	Part of Structure	Internal Resisting Moment
Truss			d	
Cable			d	
Arch			d	
Beam			d	
Plate on columns			d	
Plate on walls			d	
Dome			d	

FIGURE 13–10 Internal force couples that equilibrate external moments are developed in all structures. As the depth of the internal moment arm increases, the associated internal forces decrease, and vice versa.

464

the resisting couple. Since the depths of such members is inherently limited, these increases cannot entirely be controlled or compensated for by increasing the moment arm of the resisting couple or by other means (e.g., increasing flange areas). Consequently, members of this type are not capable of extremely large spans, since a point is reached where the internal compression and tension forces become too large to be handled efficiently. Deflection control also becomes a governing consideration. Obviously, if structural depths were *always* increased in response to the increased design moments associated with longer spans, internal forces could be kept at a reasonable level. This is essentially what the shaped truss, cable, or arch does. These structures are usually relatively deep and inherently provide a very large internal moment arm. The forces in the resisting couple can thus be fairly small with the structure still capable of providing a very large internal resisting moment. Large spans are thus possible.

Long-Span Structures.   In a curious way the selection of an appropriate structure for use in a given context becomes easier if the structural requirements, in terms of span, are very large. As noted above, a characteristic of appropriate long-span systems is that their structural depths are relatively large in comparison with their spans. A linked characteristic is that the structures are usually shaped in some way. Consequently, appropriate structural systems for long-span applications typically include shaped trusses, arches, cables, nets, pneumatics, and shells. Exceptions, to be sure, exist. There are many successful examples of long-span constant-depth trusses, space frames, and other structures. Rarely do these flat systems, however, match the efficiency of the simply conceived cable, arch, or shaped truss. Interestingly enough, the internal structural actions of these shaped structures are less complex than other elements, such as beams, which do not have long-span capabilities.

As a consequence of the geometry of common shaped structures, such structures are normally useful only for roofs in buildings or other situations where structural shapes can be allowed to vary. Rarely are such systems useful for providing the planar surfaces that are needed elsewhere in buildings for obvious functional reasons.

Intermediate- and Low-Span Systems.   As span or load-carrying requirements decrease in a building from the dramatic to the more commonplace, and if the structure must provide a rigid planar surface, the choice of structure becomes more difficult since more systems are possible in low- or intermediate-span ranges. There are a whole host of different systems made of different materials that are potentially applicable.

In the span ranges normally encountered in most buildings, it is evident from inspecting Figure 13–9 that a number of systems are potentially appropriate for use. For spans on the order of 16 to 20 ft (5 to 6 m), for example, either one- or two-way systems of all major types are potentially competitive. Which of the systems is most appropriate cannot easily be determined without a separate analysis consisting of designing alternatives for the specific span and load condition considered and making a cost analysis. Usually, the lightest or least involved construction type appropriate for a given span which is capable of carrying the design load is the most preferable. For example, in reinforced concrete, for a span of 20 ft (6 m) and for relatively light, uniformly distributed loads, the flat plate would probably prove the most preferable of all two-way concrete systems. The other reinforced concrete systems (e.g., waffle slabs) are possible but are more substantial and have higher span and load capacities by virtue of the way they are constructed than is needed. From a structural viewpoint there is no incentive to go to the trouble and expense of creating the special formwork required to construct these more complex systems when a simple flat plate would work just as well for the conditions at hand. With increases in span or load, however, the flat plate begins losing its viability and these other systems become more appropriate.

In low-span ranges, the deeper-shaped structures capable of very long spans are still structurally possible but are often not used because of construction considerations (reflected as high costs). A cable system could be used to span 15 ft (5 m), for example, but using such a system when a series of simple wooden joists would work just as well does not make good sense.

The versatility of the truss in terms of both its shape and the way it is made make it one of the few structural elements useful for the full range of short, intermediate, and long spans. Specific characteristics and geometries of trusses for these extreme span ranges, of course, vary. Short- and intermediate-span trusses are typically closely spaced and highly repetitive—as is common with typical bar joist systems. Often such elements are mass-produced. Long-span trusses are usually specially made and placed relatively far apart.

One- and Two-Way Systems. In low-span ranges [e.g., 15 to 35 ft (4.5 to 10.6 m)], a whole range of both one- and two-way systems may be appropriate. As spans begin to increase beyond a certain point around 50 to 60 ft (15 to 18 m), however, flat two-way concrete systems typically begin to lose some of their construction viability (although still possible) and one-way spanning elements are frequently found to be more appropriate. For roof systems carrying light distributed loads, closely spaced open-web steel joists are often highly efficient in this span range. Precast and prestressed reinforced concrete members are also extensively used.

As spans increase to 80 to 100 ft (24 to 30 m), systems are predominantly made of one-way elements. Steel is frequently used, although some prestressed concrete members can still very efficiently span this far. Of the flat two-way systems, the steel space frame has this span capability. It is typically most appropriate for lighter roof loads rather than floor loads. Specially designed two-way systems, such as a grid approach could, of course, be used. Such systems are, however, usually quite expensive.

13–3–5 Relations between Loading Type and Structure Type

Whether a loading is distributed or concentrated is a crucial factor in selecting an appropriate structural system for a given condition. There are a number of structural systems available that are particularly suited for light, uniformly distributed floor or roof loads. These structures are typically surface-forming in nature and are usually made up of a series of closely spaced similar elements or involve mass-produced components, such as wood joist systems, steel deck systems, long-span precast concrete planks, precast channels, open-web steel joists, and reinforced concrete flat plates.

When uniformly distributed floor loads are present, every effort should be made to make certain that the surface elements that first pick up the loads operate at their maximum efficiency. In such cases, the spacing of more specially designed members supporting these surface elements is often based on the most efficient span length for the supported surface elements rather than on some other criterion. The sizes and spacings of wide-flange members supporting a steel floor deck, for example, are often based on optimizing the decking used. The design process thus usually begins with the smallest and lightest (but most numerous) members first taking the load and proceeds to supporting beams, and then to the columns, instead of vice versa.

Surface-forming elements or systems are generally inappropriate when large concentrated loads are present. In most cases, members carrying large concentrated loads must be uniquely designed for the particular situation at hand. They are most often linear one-way spanning elements, including steel or timber trusses with unique bar configurations, plate girders, and post-tensioned reinforced concrete beams. Most of these structures are typically handcrafted. More attention should be paid to designing the structure in response to the force distributions within it.

13-3-6   Concentrated Versus Distributed Structures

When involved in the process of designing structures many other issues arise. One of the most interesting of these issues is whether it is better to use what may best be described as *concentrated* structures or to use *distributed* structures. The descriptive terms refer to alternative design strategies for a given loading condition. The first approach is characterized by designing a few very large members to carry the load and the second by designing a greater number of relatively smaller elements. Is it more efficient, for example, to carry a given load with one large column or with two slightly smaller ones? Or is it more efficient to use one large beam or two parallel smaller beams? On a more general scale, is it preferable to use a space frame (with many very small members dispersed throughout the system) or a series of more widely spaced trusses made of relatively larger elements? The basic choice of concentrated versus distributed structural strategies appears over and over again in many different situations.

As would be expected, there is no hard-and-fast answer to this question. It was noted earlier that surface-forming structures (which typically reflect a distributed element structural strategy) are best used when uniformly distributed loads are present and concentrated loads are absent. Similarly, discretized structures respond better to concentrated loads. These principles form one set of guidelines that are useful in formulating initial design strategies. Using distributed structures, such as space frames, in conditions where concentrated loads are present is one of the most typical of all faulty judgments made by novice designers. Curiously, such misuses are often made when the novice designer is attempting to use a system that *looks* structural.

The principles previously mentioned, however, do not help resolve questions where the type of load is not a variable and the issue is one of either using a single large member or multiple smaller ones to carry the load. There does seem to be evidence indicating that using a few larger elements to carry a given load is often preferable to using a number of smaller elements to carry the same load. This principle is primarily applicable to design situations, such as beam or column design, that involve manipulations with moments of inertia (which do not simply increase linearly with member dimension). In other situations, such as the design of tension members not involving moments of inertia, the principle is less applicable (often no differences exist in such situations).

13-3-7   Imposed Constraints: Fire Safety Requirements

A strong determinant of the structural system used in a building are the fire safety requirements imposed by building regulations. Codes typically classify buildings according to construction types, which can be roughly characterized as light, medium, and heavy, according to the construction's degree of fire resistivity. Light construction is typically wood-frame or unprotected metal framing. Medium construction typically uses masonry walls as load-bearing elements. Heavy construction is typically of reinforced concrete or protected steel framing.

The main influence of building regulations on the choice of structure is to place restrictions on the type of construction allowed in accordance with the degree of fire hazard present. High-hazard occupancies require substantially fire-resistant construction (typically necessitating reinforced concrete or protected steel structures), while less hazardous occupancies require less substantial construction types. In a similar vein, construction types are coupled with building heights. In low buildings, almost any type of construction is typically allowed unless a high-hazard occupancy is present. As heights increase, the construction used must have a greater degree of inherent fire safety. Buildings using masonry load-bearing walls are typically acceptable up to five or six stories, although much taller masonry structures have been built. Above this height reinforced concrete or protected steel structures are typical. It should be noted that any heavier type of construction suitable for more hazardous occupancies or taller buildings is allowable in less restrictive cases, but, of course, not vice versa. A single-family detached house can be built out of reinforced concrete but a high-rise office building cannot be built out of light wood framing. Using a heavier system when a lighter one is allowed, however, is usually not economical.

Coupled with construction types and heights are limitations placed on the maximum floor areas allowed in buildings between specially designed fire division walls. The intent of these walls is to separate the building into compartments and thus restrain the spread of a fire beginning in one compartment to another. In many cases, particularly in low- to medium-rise buildings, the load-bearing walls are designed to be coincident in location with required fire divisions so that the same masonry walls serve both functions. This has implications on where load-bearing walls are placed and often on the design and selection of horizontal spanning elements.

13-4 DESIGN ISSUES

13-4-1 Relation of Structure to Functional Spaces

Critical Programmatic Dimensions. Associated with any building are certain critical dimensions that define the minimum clear span for any structural system used. These critical dimensions may stem either from functional necessities (e.g., minimum clear spans for basketball courts or some other programmatic use), or simply from more subjective design intents. Assume that these critical programmatic dimensions are denoted as a_1 and a_2, which in turn define a minimum programmatic space. (There could well be several different such spaces, but for the moment, assume that only one type exists.)

The length of either a_1 or a_2 must obviously become the minimum clear span dimension for the structure. Elements in the vertical support system may not be placed any closer together than the minimum of these two distances. They can, however, be spaced farther apart, since a_1 and a_2 define minimum clear spans, not maximums.

Degree of Fit. A primary initial structural objective is invariably to determine an appropriate *degree of fit* that is possible or preferred between the pattern formed by the vertical support systems and the critical dimension a_1 or a_2. The selection of a degree of fit determines the magnitude of the horizontal span that the structural system must provide, and, consequently, has an important bearing on the final system selected for use.

Either one-on-one or looser fits are possible. In a one-on-one fit, the primary structural bay unit that is used repetitively corresponds directly with the space formed by a_1 and a_2. Alternatively, the structure selected may span over multiples of a_1 or a_2. (The span would thus be longer than minimally necessary.)

In more complex programmatic arrangements, any number of vertical support patterns and related horizontal spanning systems could possibly be fitted to a given arrangement (Figures 13–11 and 13–12). Consider the hypothetical building plan shown in Figure 13–12(a). Many radically different approaches reflecting different degrees of fit and different structural systems are possible and feasible. By looking at this diagram only, there is nothing a priori to suggest that one is preferable to another from a purely structural perspective, especially since critical information such as span magnitudes and loading conditions are not indicated. Clearly, resolution of which of the approaches diagrammed may ultimately prove most feasible depends on many of the issues discussed previously (Section 13–3), such as relations between span length and appropriate structure type. Obviously, functional and other considerations may affect the choice of type as well. Without such further consideration, any basis for choice at this level must relate to an almost intuitive assessment of the basic reasonableness of the various solutions. It is doubtful if solutions that are more chaotic or less orderly than others will prove feasible in the long run. It is possible and even probable that the solution indicated in Figure 13–12(h) would prove more difficult to construct and hence more costly to build than some of the other solutions (even though this actually depends on the scale of the building). Simple patterns usually prove superior to complex ones. As an aside, it is interesting to note that usually when a building can be framed in many different ways with no one solution clearly better than others, the building will probably never prove to be problematical (from a structural point of view) as the design develops, no matter what option is selected.

Other factors that might affect the degree of fit used are the foundation conditions present. Under some conditions building loads are best distributed over the entire site so that the load present at any discrete point is reduced. The structural implication is that a fine-grained grid system should be employed and one-on-one fits employed. If, on the other hand, unique conditions exist of the type where some site locations can carry enormous loads and other locations virtually no loads, it is obvious that the structural pattern should respond to these conditions by having vertical elements concentrated at high-capacity points and by using long-span horizontal elements to bridge over low-capacity points. A rough-grained pattern to the vertical support system often results.

Examples of both tight and loose relationships between the vertical support system, the horizontal support system, and critical functional dimensions are shown in Figure 13–13.

In general, one-on-one fits are considered preferable when critical functional distances are fairly large [e.g., a minimum of 15 to 30 ft (5 to 10 m)], since a structural objective is always to minimize bending and this is not done by using spans of unnecessary lengths. If distances are quite small [e.g., less than 10 ft (3 m) or so], one-on-one fits are usually desirable only when light timber systems are used (e.g., wood joists). Looser fits are desirable when materials such as steel or concrete are used. The point herein is simply that the structural order may be equal to or greater than critical functional dimensions, depending on exact span lengths and system capabilities.

13–4–2   Space-Forming Characteristics

A subjective consideration of unquestioned importance from a larger architectural viewpoint is that each of the systems illustrated has different spatial implications. The spaces formed by the bearing-wall system [Figure 13–14(a)] are one-directional (or linear) and have a strong planar quality which is imparted by the vertical and horizontal enclosure elements.

FIGURE 13–11 Basic pattern characteristics of vertical and horizontal elements of different planar structural systems. Spans shown are typical (see also Chapter 15).

Critical functional
dimensions: a_1 and a_2

(a) Basic functional
    modules.

Load-bearing wall

Eroded load-bearing wall

Framed system

One-way
spanning system

Two-way
spanning system

(b) Vertical and horizontal support systems.

(c) One-way system.

(d) One-way system.

(e) One-way system.

(f) Two-way system.

(g) Two-way flat-plate
    system.

(h) One-way system
    (undesirable random pattern).

FIGURE 13–12 Vertical support patterns. Most buildings can be fitted with many different types of structural patterns that correspond to different building configurations and functional needs.

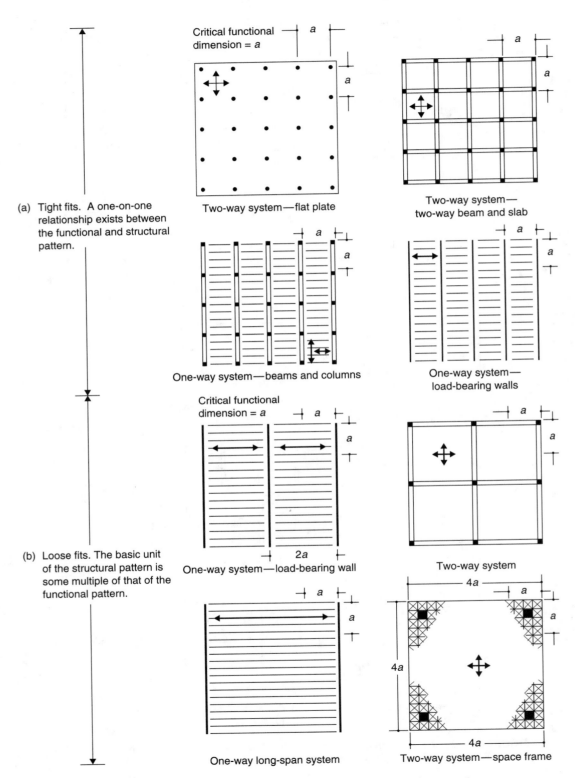

(a) Tight fits. A one-on-one relationship exists between the functional and structural pattern.

Critical functional dimension = a

Two-way system—flat plate

Two-way system— two-way beam and slab

One-way system—beams and columns

One-way system— load-bearing walls

(b) Loose fits. The basic unit of the structural pattern is some multiple of that of the functional pattern.

Critical functional dimension = a

One-way system—load-bearing wall

Two-way system

One-way long-span system

Two-way system—space frame

FIGURE 13–13 Types of fit possible between functional patterns and structural patterns.

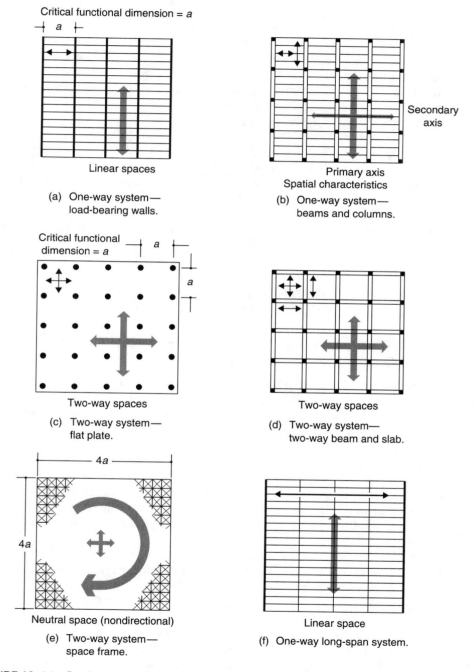

Critical functional dimension = a

Linear spaces

(a) One-way system—
load-bearing walls.

Primary axis
Spatial characteristics

Secondary axis

(b) One-way system—
beams and columns.

Critical functional dimension = a

Two-way spaces

(c) Two-way system—
flat plate.

Two-way spaces

(d) Two-way system—
two-way beam and slab.

$4a$

$4a$

Neutral space (nondirectional)

(e) Two-way system—
space frame.

Linear space

(f) One-way long-span system.

FIGURE 13–14 Spatial characteristics of different structural approaches.

473

The spaces formed by the beam-and-column system [Figure 13–14(b)] are also primarily one-directional, owing to the organization of the collector beams, but have in addition a secondary axis in the transverse direction. These characteristics are significantly influenced by the shape, spacing, and orientation of the columns. Rectangular columns with a long axis in the direction of the beams would further emphasize the linearity of the space, whereas placing the long axis in the other direction would emphasize the secondary axis more. Round columns are a neutral statement, and square columns are bidirectional.

The spaces formed by the flat-plate system [Figure 13–14(c)] are two-directional, since neither of the axes is dominant. The spaces formed are relatively neutral. Round columns or square columns do not alter this two-way directionality. Rectangular columns start causing one or the other axis to become more dominant. The spaces formed by the two-way beam-and-slab system [Figure 13–14(d)] are less neutral, with the beams even further emphasizing the two-way directionality of the spaces.

The space formed underneath a very large, completely neutral surface (such as a flat plane) is not directional. This assumes that any directionality that the support system might impart does not influence the observer. The space frame illustrated in Figure 13–14(e) would provide this type of space (the structural member spacing is sufficiently small as to impart little spatial influence).

While other structural arrangements may yield slightly different spatial properties, they are usually some variant or combination of the general types discussed previously.

13–4–3 One-Way Versus Two-Way Systems: Impact of Grid Geometry and Dimensions

Square Support Bays. The general considerations governing choices between one- and two-way systems were discussed in Section 13–3. It was noted that for two-way action to occur, an underlying vertical support grid of square or near-square dimensions was a virtual necessity. This is particularly true when the support system consists of a peripheral wall system. One-way systems would not take advantage of the support capability of walls parallel to the spanning elements and would thus require more structural depth and volume than a two-way system.

There are, however, some important nuances to these general observations. In particular, while square support grids are a necessary condition for two-way action to occur, the presence of a square support grid does not axiomatically mean that two-way systems are always preferred in such situations. Circumstances exist where one-way systems are more useful than a square support system.

When a support grid consists of a square grid of columns extending in *both* directions, continuity can be achieved in both directions and positive two-way action is easily obtained (Figure 13–15). When square grid modules form a long linear aggregation, however, the boundary conditions present preclude the development of continuity in both directions. A one-way system might prove equally feasible and efficient, if not more so.

Another issue is that of the absolute dimensions between support points. As seen from the discussion in Section 13–3–4 on span lengths, there are a wide variety of two-way structural systems available for use in low- and intermediate-span ranges [e.g., 15 to 40 ft (5 to 13 m)] and either type of system could potentially be used. When square bay dimensions are very long, however, one-way systems are often used for square grids simply because there are not many

Wall supports

(a) Wall supports—very effective use can be made of two-way action. One-way systems are usually less desirable, since the load-carrying capability of one set of walls cannot be utilized.

(b) Column supports—one- or two-way systems are possible.

(c) Two-way serial aggregations: when the square support grid extends in both directions, a two-way system is particularly appropriate.

(d) One-way serial aggregations: when a square support grid forms a linear pattern, one-way systems are often more appropriate than two-way systems.

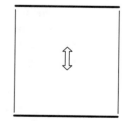

(e) Single-cell structures. In small bay systems, either one- or two-way systems are possible. When bay dimensions are very large, span limitations of available two-way systems often make one-way systems more appropriate for use.

FIGURE 13–15 Vertical support systems: Square patterns.

long-span two-way constructional systems available. For spans up to around 60 ft (18 m), there are still several two-way concrete systems commonly available. For longer spans there are fewer. For roofs in longer span ranges, the two-way steel space-frame system is useful but is generally not appropriate for heavier floor loads. Specially constructed two-way grid structures of either steel or reinforced concrete can be used but such systems are relatively expensive. Thus, for large square bays, a one-way approach is often used, since individual elements in the system can be designed easily to meet the unique load and span requirements. In practice, however, large square bays are not frequently encountered.

Rectangular Bays.   Whenever the support system is markedly rectangular, it is probable that a one-way horizontal spanning system would prove preferable to a two-way system. As discussed in Chapter 10, two-way structural action is not realized when the bay dimensions fall outside a range of 1:1 to 1:1.5 (the latter ratio is pushing reason).

   If a column-supported bay is rectangular and one-way spanning elements are to be used, the basic question is whether to arrange the spanning elements as indicated in Figure 13–16. In the first case shown in Figure 13–16, the long-span beams carry only uniformly distributed loads, while the short-span elements serve as collector beams carrying the reactions from the long-span members. The reverse is true of the second approach shown. There is nothing that suggests a priori that both approaches will require the same amount of structural material to support the same load in space or that structural depths will be the same. Indeed, it can be expected that one or the other approach would prove preferable with respect to either or both of these criteria for a given set of dimensions and loadings. The question of which way to arrange primary spanning elements is a highly interesting one from a theoretical viewpoint. Unfortunately, the question is not one that can easily be answered in the abstract. For a specific case, however, involving known dimensions, loads, and materials, the two framing approaches can be compared by designing them and then comparing resultant volumes and depths. For example, if $L_1 = 30$ ft (19 m) and $L_2 = 80$ ft (24 m) and reinforced concrete is to be used, a possible approach would be to use precast concrete single tees for the long-span direction (these elements are good primarily for distributed loads only) and two specially designed poured-in-place concrete beams for use as collectors in the shorter direction. If the alternative framing approach were used, it would be necessary to design and construct unique long-span collector beams (although smaller, prefabricated plank elements could be used in the short direction). The structural volumes and depths of those two systems could be evaluated after the members are sized. Costs could be assessed, as could

FIGURE 13–16   Vertical support systems: Rectangular patterns. One-way systems are usually preferred when the support system forms a rectangular pattern. Two-way structural action is not obtainable unless the ratio of long to short bay dimensions is less than about 1.5

other important considerations, such as the interaction of the structure with other building components. A statement of preferability could then be made depending on the relative importance assigned to the different criteria.

There is no hard and fast answer to which approach for framing rectangular bays is preferable. Often, but not always, the longer the absolute dimension of the long span (L_2) becomes, the more it is—in general—both desirable and necessary to opt for the first approach shown in Figure 13–16, in which the longest elements carry distributed loads only and do not act as collectors. The collector is kept as short as possible. When absolute dimensions are small (and thus collector depths are not excessive) and when both the collectors and the surface load-transfer elements can be off-the-shelf items instead of uniquely constructed ones, the other approach often proves preferable.

13–4–4   Effects of Local Geometrical Conditions

Corners.   There are numerous local geometrical conditions that may affect the choice of structure and whether a one- or two-way system is preferable. Whenever it is necessary to bend, distort, or do something else unusual to a structural grid because of an overall building geometry, there are certain to be structural implications. Even simply terminating a grid, for example, usually demands special end treatments.

Consider the plan shown in Figure 13–17(a), in which the whole building literally turns a corner. Under some circumstances, structuring the corner region can pose problems. Assume that the functional modules in the building are basically rectilinear, as illustrated in Figure 13–17(b). This is a very common pattern in many building types, such as housing, where each module would represent a dwelling unit. As is evident, this basic type of pattern lends itself well to a structural system that uses parallel beams or load-bearing walls along the depth of the building and a planar one-way system of some sort that spans horizontally between these elements. The only difficulty in using such a system is at the corner, where the one-way system cannot be oriented in two directions at once. It would thus be necessary to adopt an approach of the general type shown in Figure 13–17(b). While such an approach is obviously possible, it certainly lacks elegance. The basic difficulty, of course, is not really a structural one but one associated with the basic rectilinear pattern and the corner turning requirement. As a consequence, the structure most logical for the basic parts of the building becomes awkward at the corners.

Consider another type of functional pattern, which consists of aggregated squares [see Figure 13–17(c)]. In this case the basic pattern lends itself well to a two-way structural system supported by columns at grid intersection lines. In this case it is evident that no difficulty at all exists in structuring the corner region. The two-way system is naturally capable of turning corners because of its symmetry in both geometry and structural behavior. It would consequently seem that, whenever L-shaped conditions exist in a building, square rather than rectangular functional and structural grids should be used. A rule of this sort is somewhat simplistic, however, since square grids may not accommodate building functional requirements as well as rectangular grids (housing is a case in point). In addition, there are other structuring possibilities that may prove effective.

Several other ways a structural pattern can turn a corner are illustrated in Figure 13–17(d) and (e). Obviously, the axes of the basic grid can simply be *bent* around the corner in a radial fashion. While possible in a great many cases, building functional requirements may preclude

(a) Typical corner conditions.

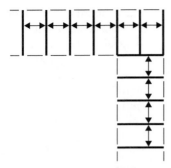

(b) One-way systems: turning corners with one-way systems is usually awkward.

(c) Two-way systems: turning corners with two-way systems usually presents no problem.

(d) Bent-axis approach.

(e) Transition structure.

FIGURE 13–17 Influence of building morphology on structural approach. Basic strategies for turning corners.

this approach in others. If a bent-axis system is adopted, one-way structural systems using prefabricated elements usually, but not always, prove difficult to use. There are construction difficulties involved in having to form a variable-length spanning surface in the bent region when materials such as steel or timber are used, since member lengths are not constant. A poured-in-place one-way reinforced concrete system using radial beams and simple one-way slabs, however, is quite appropriate. As will be discussed more in Chapters 14 and 15, however, span lengths are limited with this system. The two-way flat plate is another natural system for use in a bent-axis region. Again, spans are limited. In general, the bent-axis system is fairly difficult to structure when span distances between grid lines are large.

Another way of handling the corner condition is illustrated in Figure 13–17(e). In this case the primary system is simply terminated at either boundary of the corner and a *transition* structure is used. This transition structure invariably has two-way characteristics and often has a relatively small grain. As discussed in Section 13–4–9, one of the strategies in the meeting of patterns must be used at the intersection between the primary grid structure and the transition structure. The transition structure can be of the same materials as the parent structure, or it can be a different material altogether. This approach is somewhat of an overkill if the building is generally small and the absolute depth of the building is relatively shallow; it is simply not worth the trouble. In large buildings that are relatively deep, the transition-structure approach works quite well.

Slipped Units. Another commonly encountered building geometry involves units that are slipped with respect to one another. For buildings of this type, one-way structural systems usually prove more appropriate than two-way systems. One-way systems involving load-bearing walls, for example, can adapt to very small increments of slip [see Figure 13–18(a)]. If a beam-and-column system is used instead of load-bearing walls, the most preferable degree of slip

(a) For load-bearing wall systems, the amount of slip is easy to vary.

(b) For beam-and-column systems with uniformly spaced columns, the amount of slip is preferably equal to the spacing of the columns.

(c) Beam-and-column systems do allow flexibility in the amount of slip possible, since columns may be located anywhere along a beam line as long as spans and cantilevers are not excessive.

FIGURE 13–18 Some basic strategies for slipped-unit buildings.

corresponds to the normal repetitive distance between columns [see Figure 13–18(b)]. This same type of system does allow, however, for the fairly easy shifting of columns along the bearing line. Indeed, column spacings can be different along different bearing lines (particularly if beam spans are small), which makes this approach extremely versatile. This is not to say, of course, that such manipulations are at all desirable from a structural or constructional viewpoint. Still, such flexibility is occasionally highly important from a functional viewpoint. Two-way systems, other than the flat plate of limited span, do not really have this flexibility.

13–4–5   Varying Support Locations

It was pointed out in earlier chapters on beams and frames that manipulating support locations can potentially lead to improved structural efficiency by reducing the bending moments present. Some of these manipulations have strong implications on the structural patterning used. In many cases, once the structural pattern is fixed, such manipulations are impossible. A classic way of reducing design bending moments in beams or trusses, for example, is that of using end cantilevers (see Section 6–4–3). In the overall process of selecting a structural pattern in a building it might be quite possible to introduce cantilevers into the building. The rules of thumb of $\frac{1}{5}L$ and $\frac{1}{3}L$ discussed in Chapter 6 that define optimum cantilevers for homogeneous members, for example, often lead to absolute cantilever dimensions that serve quite well as overhangs covering circulation routes. The pattern implications of using cantilevers are, of course, significant (Figure 13–19). Other examples with continuous beams and frames could also be noted.

13–4–6   Nonuniform Grids

In situations where the pattern of the vertical support system is irregular, some structural systems are more attractive than others. Totally irregular grids make difficult the effective or economic use of systems involving a number of highly repetitive and typically off-site-produced, modular

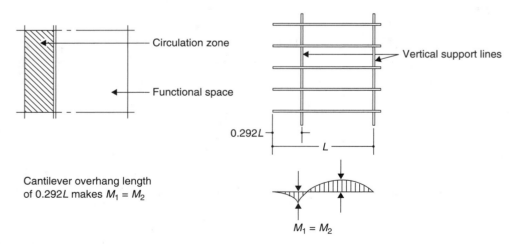

FIGURE 13–19   Optimizing support locations. In many cases a fit between the vertical support pattern and building use pattern can be achieved that works well from both structural and building use viewpoints.

FIGURE 13–20   For irregular grids, structural systems made on-site (e.g., poured-in-place concrete) are usually preferable to those utilizing relatively large off-site-produced elements.

units (e.g., precast concrete elements). For full advantage to be gained from the construction process possibilities inherent in such systems, they must be used in an almost brutally repetitive way. Poured-in-place concrete systems are usually preferable in cases involving pattern irregularities, since anomalies can be more easily handled (Figure 13–20).

Irregularity in the vertical support grid can most easily be accommodated when support points are relatively closely spaced. As horizontal spans become greater, so do the structural requirements for horizontal members. For maximum spans of around 16 to 20 ft (5 to 6 m), the reinforced concrete flat plate system, discussed in more detail in Chapter 15, can accommodate many irregularities in support placement. For longer spans, where this system is not appropriate, the rigid orthogonality associated with longer-span systems dictates a more orderly vertical support arrangement.

13–4–7   Accommodating Large Spaces

In most buildings the bulk of the functional requirements are handled through using generalized grids. In some situations, however, programmatic requirements exist that give rise to one or more special spaces that are very different in scale than other cases. An example is a school where there might be a large number of similar-size small spaces (classrooms) and a few very large spaces (gymnasiums, auditoriums, or cafeterias). Handling both types of spaces can present problems.

Figure 13–21 illustrates several basic ways of including a large volume in a more extensive cellular grid of smaller grain. A time-honored solution is to simply *separate* the two systems completely and connect them only along edges or with simple linkages of some sort. This allows the most appropriate structure to be chosen for each system independently of the other. A long-span, one-way, steel truss system could be selected for the large space, for example, and something else chosen for the smaller-grained system. The auditorium complex in the building shown later in Figure 13–24 is an example of how a large volume can be simply separated out and given its own structural system.

A completely opposite approach is also often used wherein the large space is *embedded* into the finer-grained system. Two situations are of interest here—one where the largest space is placed such that much of the finer-grained system is above the space and the second reverse case where the large space is located completely above the finer-grained system.

(a) Separation strategy: simply separating the large volume from the more general system allows efficient structural responses for each system to be developed independently.

(b) Embedment strategy — low placement of volume: placing the large volume at low levels requires the use of either large transfer members or long span members (where not otherwise required by functional considerations). Either alternative is usually structurally possible but economically dubious.

(c) Embedment strategy — roof-level placement of volume: placing the large space at roof level does not require the use of either large load-transfer members or a potentially uneconomical loose fit, as dictated by a low placement of the volume.

FIGURE 13–21 Strategies for accommodating large volumes in a small-grained system.

When the large space is embedded at a low level, a number of structural problems arise. There are two basic structural options available [see Figure 13–21(b)]. One is to use a one-on-one structural fit to the smaller-grained system combined with large transfer members to pick up the loads from the closely spaced vertical supports above the open span space and to carry them to the vertical supports at the edges of the large space. Such a strategy is used in the auditorium area in the building shown in Figure 13–24. The second basic option, the loose-fit approach, is to adopt the span of the larger space as the repetitively used dimension and use a series of large-span members everywhere. Both approaches are possible, but both have their problems. In the first case, the transfer members must carry very heavy loads and thus must be uniquely designed and constructed (i.e., off-the-shelf members will usually not work). These members are obviously problematic. The remainder of the structure in the fine-grained area can work quite well. The loose-fit alternative with long spans everywhere is inherently noneconomic. Spanning a large distance when a small one could be spanned instead usually does not lead to economic structures. Using special systems (e.g., precast and prestressed reinforced concrete tee shapes), designed specially for long spans, may tend to offset this inherent disadvantage somewhat, but it remains an influential factor.

Note that most of the difficulties mentioned here can be circumvented by placing the large-span space on top of the smaller grid system. Then the long-span elements carry roof loads only, which are relatively light, and any of a variety of systems could work. The design of the finer-grained system is not appreciably affected by the presence of the large space above it. A difficulty with this approach is not a structural one but a functional one, in that large spaces are usually more appropriately placed lower in a building because of access reasons—an important factor in view of the large number of people often using such a space.

13–4–8   Accommodating Special Conditions

Invariably, a host of special conditions arise in a building to which the structure must respond. These conditions usually represent particularized events related to building functions such as circulation (e.g., stairwells) or to building service systems (e.g., heating, ventilating, and air conditioning).

There are several basic strategies for accommodating building service elements that run horizontally. One is to use a one-way spanning system that naturally provides a space for parallel runs (see Figure 13–22). Except with trusses, service elements that run perpendicular to the spanning direction are obviously more difficult. It is possible to locally deform or penetrate the basic structural fabric to accommodate such instances. This is most often done when the elements to be accommodated are few in number and/or small in dimension. Most structural systems can be designed to accommodate minor penetrations in horizontal members. The *penetration* strategy can also be used to accommodate horizontal elements in two-way structural systems [see Figure 13–22(b)].

Some structural systems, such as trusses, can easily accommodate horizontal service elements, since they can simply pass between web members. Excepting such systems, it is generally true that whenever penetrations become numerous or large, the basic structural fabric can be compromised to the extent that the structure is more correctly characterized as a series of ad hoc solutions than as a system. When this occurs, it is usually preferable to switch to a different strategy for accommodating the special conditions.

Another strategy for accommodating horizontal service elements in either one- or two-way systems is simply to pass them beneath the primary structural system (leaving it intact) and either leave them exposed or enclose them with a dropped chase or ceiling. This approach is highly efficient from a construction viewpoint. Total building heights, however, are disadvantageously increased.

Most structural systems can be designed to accommodate minor penetrations for vertical service and functional elements without difficulty (Figure 13–23). More major penetrations, such as for stairways, must often be accompanied by special local framing. Still the basic structural pattern is not affected to any great degree.

One way of handling numerous vertical penetrations is to group the special functions into clusters and then to design the structure to accommodate this cluster. This is often done for vertical elements, in which case the elements are grouped into core units that fit into individual structural bays. The structure is simply eliminated or specially treated in this bay. The advantage of doing this is that the general structural fabric in other areas is undisturbed and can be designed to function efficiently in its own terms. This is a common approach in many high-rise structures.

Quite often the cluster approach does not work well with the functional requirements of the service elements. In many instances these elements have to be distributed throughout the building, as in the case of some types of heating, ventilating, and air-conditioning systems or laboratory piping systems. Under some conditions a structural system that provides spaces for locating

(a) One-way spanning systems easily accommodate service elements that run parallel to main members. Vertical service risers are often buried in walls or chases.

(b) Penetration approach: for minor service elements the basic structural fabric often can simply be penetrated.

(c) Passing of systems approach: when the horizontal service system is complex or contains large elements, an approach wherein structural and service elements are placed on nonconflicting planes is often very effective.

FIGURE 13–22 Accommodating horizontal service elements.

Plan

Plan

(a) Vertical service elements—penetration approach: for randomly distributed minor vertical elements the basic structural fabric can often be simply penetrated.

(b) Vertical service elements and special features— clustered passing approach: when vertical penetrating elements are large or complex, an approach wherein such elements are deliberately clustered into groups, which, in turn, bypass the basic structure is often utilized.

Plan—parallel beam strategy

Section—interstitial floor strategy

(c) Horizontal and vertical elements—provision of regular interstitial zones: it is possible to provide regularly spaced zones for vertical and/or horizontal service elements. Doing so is most appropriate in cases where the service elements must be distributed throughout the building and are relatively large or complex.

FIGURE 13-23   Strategies for accommodating building service systems and special features.

these elements at fixed intervals may prove effective. Such a system is shown in Figure 13–23(c). The interstitial spaces between the parallel beams and double columns is reserved for horizontal and vertical mechanical runs. The science center illustrated in Figures 13–24 and 13–25 has such interstitial spaces for mechanical service elements in the back part of the building where a double beam-and-column system is used. Mechanically intensive physics and chemistry laboratories are located in this part of the building. The front part of the building houses only libraries and offices, functions that are much less mechanically intensive. A single beam-and-column system without significant provisions made for mechanical equipment is accordingly used.

   A conceptual difficulty involved in using structural systems that provide fixed intervals for the provision of mechanical services is that there is nothing that a priori suggests that the rhythm of the mechanical system, in terms of where it is located to best provide its services, is at all the

(a) Basic structural patterns.

(b) Basic zones.

(c) Site plan.

FIGURE 13–24 Beam-and-column patterns: Science Center, Harvard University, Cambridge, Massachusetts (see also Figure 13–25).

same as that of the structural system. Forcing the mechanical system into a rigid pattern related to the structural system may not prove most efficient from the viewpoint of the overall building design, since the design of *both* the structural and mechanical systems might well be compromised. Whether this is true or not, however, depends on the specific building program involved as well as many other design variables.

Interstitial zones that provide service *layers* between floors can also be introduced if the intensity of service or flexibility demands so warrant. Service elements can be dropped from interstitial zones into floors below or rise to floors above. Changes and modifications can be made with minimum disruption to functional activities. A structural solution that takes advantage of the full depth of the interstitial zone is often, but not necessarily, employed [see Figure 13–23(c)].

In general, highly integrated and expensive approaches of the type described are justified only in cases when the mechanical system in a building is extremely complex and extensive, as might be the case in a hospital, where they can work well. In buildings of low mechanical intensity, such

FIGURE 13–25   Science Center, Harvard University, Cambridge, Massachusetts. The building is made with precast concrete elements. The part of the building housing laboratories uses a double beam-and-column system, which facilitates the distribution of mechanical services by providing regularly spaced interstitial zones between beams (see also Figure 13–24).

as churches, such integrated approaches are usually not economically justifiable, since distributed mechanical elements are few and small. The expensive interstitial spaces would thus simply not be utilized to the extent needed to justify their existence.

13–4–9   Meeting of Structural Grids

In many common cases more than one generalized structural pattern is used in a building. The reasons for this multiplicity of patterns vary. Quite often there is a wide variation in the programmatic requirements of the building such that a variety of minimum clear span dimensions exist. One or more standard functional patterns may be adopted to respond to this variation instead of seeking a single pattern that compromises the varying requirements present. In other cases physical constraints, such as nonuniform foundation conditions, may dictate using different structural grids in different areas. When more than one generalized structural pattern is used in a building, the way in which these patterns meet becomes a basic structural design issue. Intersection points always call for unique treatment or special elements.

Several structural patterns are used in the building illustrated in Figure 13–24 instead of just one generalized type. In the back part of the building, a double beam-and-column system is used, while in the front part a more traditional single beam-and-column system is employed. A third system, consisting of radiating arches, is used over the auditorium complex. Transitional structures of yet other types exist in the interstitial spaces between the different primary structural patterns. The exact reason for this multiplicity of systems stems largely from the different functional zones present in the building. The single-beam-and-column system houses traditional library and office spaces. The double-beam-and-column system houses laboratory spaces with complex mechanical demands. (The interstitial spaces between beams carry mechanical elements; see Figure 13–25.) The auditorium demands long spans. Special systems have been provided for each set of programmatic demands and have then been joined. The building does bring up the highly important structural design question of whether it is more preferable to attempt to find a single generalized pattern into which all the varied functional activities of a building fit, albeit occasionally with minor alterations or deformations, or, alternatively, to attempt to adopt specific structural systems in response to the specific conditions present, thus designing a building with multiple patterns. The buildings in Figures 13–2 and 13–3 represent the strategy of finding generalized patterns in which special spaces are accommodated, a strategy that clearly poses its own set of problems. Adopting multiple patterns, however, requires finding ways of rationally joining dissimilar systems.

Consider the two structural grid systems shown in Figure 13–26. If these two systems randomly intersected, it is evident that the structure in the region of the intersection cannot be characterized as typical of either general grid. If a beam were used along boundary line *B,* for example, the beam would be loaded in a way that is uniquely different from those present in either the grid to the left or right. It would therefore have to be designed differently. Additional columns may also be needed. While randomly intersecting grids are certainly possible, other strategies may prove preferable.

Figure 13–26 illustrates several basic approaches to pattern intersections. Other approaches exist as well. One basic approach illustrated in Figure 13–26(b) and (c) would be to use a strategy of alignment in which the smaller grid is designed as either directly related to, or as a subdivision of, the larger one. This alignment reduces the misfit between the systems and does not require additional vertical supports.

Another general approach is to use some sort of mediating system between the two general systems. One type of mediator would simply be a strip of space itself, in which case the whole problem is simply bypassed [see Figure 13–26(d)]. Another type of mediator would be a third structural system of some sort. This third system must necessarily reflect or be adaptable to the characteristics that are common to both of the general systems or be extremely flexible in some other way. A structural grid that is much smaller than either of the primary systems (but a logical subdivision of each), for example, is often used to join primary systems [see Figure 13–26(e)]. Smaller-grained systems of this sort are often, but need not be, made of different materials than the primary systems. The primary systems, for example, might be constructed of poured-in-place reinforced concrete, while the smaller-grained mediating system might be a light steel system. Mixing of materials in this controlled way is usually quite acceptable even in purely economic terms. Intermixing materials within primary systems, however, is usually more difficult. An advantage of using a small-grained mediating system is that the designer has greater freedom with placing the primary grids. Primary grid lines, for example, do not have to be aligned. The building illustrated

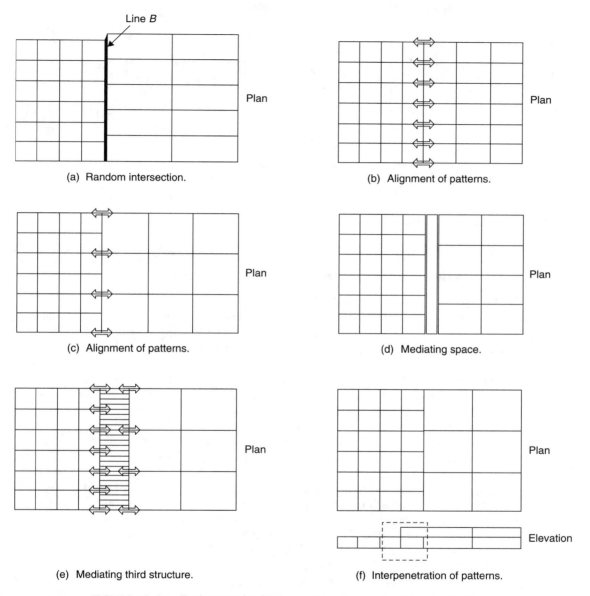

FIGURE 13-26 Basic strategies for the meeting of generalized structural patterns.

(a) Random intersection.

(b) Alignment of patterns.

(c) Alignment of patterns.

(d) Mediating space.

(e) Mediating third structure.

(f) Interpenetration of patterns.

Line *B*

Plan

Elevation

489

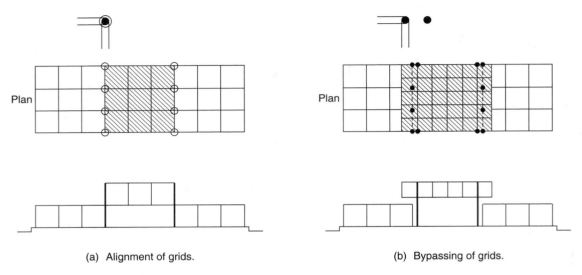

(a) Alignment of grids.   (b) Bypassing of grids.

FIGURE 13–27   Basic strategies for the layering of structural patterns.

in Figure 13–24 uses a small-grained mediating structure of the type described. Load-bearing walls are also often used as third element mediators, particularly when the primary systems are not aligned, as illustrated in Figure 13–26(a). A load-bearing wall line can be construed, however, as a continuous grid having an infinitesimal grid spacing and worked with accordingly.

Other approaches to intersecting patterns also exist; for example, an interpenetration strategy of the type illustrated in Figure 13–26(f) could be adopted as a variant of the basic alignment approach.

Pattern intersection can also be a problem with respect to using one grid on top of another. This situation quite often arises when it is desired to place a roof system having one grid geometry on top of an internal system having a different geometry. In such cases, a strategy of alignment is often used wherein vertical support points common to both systems are used [see Figure 13–27(a)]. An alignment system is used in the building illustrated in Figure 13–2. Occasionally, a bypassing type of approach is used wherein the vertical supports for the upper grid are maintained as different from those of the lower grid [see Figure 13–27(b)]. The systems are thus independent of one another. The former alignment strategy is commonly used when the overlapping grid patterns are fairly similar to one another. The latter bypassing strategy is frequently used when the upper structure (e.g., the roof) is a relatively long span as compared to the lower and of simple overall geometry, and has a different internal pattern than the lower structures. The bypassing structures need not necessarily be of the same material, although they can be. When the overlapping patterns are very similar, the same materials are often used. When they are very dissimilar, different materials are frequently used.

CHAPTER 14

Structural Systems: Design for Lateral Loadings

14-1 LATERAL FORCES: EFFECTS ON THE DESIGN OF STRUCTURES

14-1-1 Basic Design Issues: Low- and Medium-Rise Structures

Stability. In designing structural systems, the way lateral stability is achieved is of fundamental importance. The issue is important in buildings of any height. The way a structure resists lateral forces not only influences the design of vertical elements but the horizontal spanning elements as well.

The basic mechanisms for assuring lateral stability (shear walls, diagonal bracing, and frame action obtained through rigid joints) have already been discussed. All these mechanisms serve to create stiff shear planes capable of carrying lateral loads.

Of fundamental concern is that the structure must be organized such that sufficient lateral-load-carrying mechanisms exist to render the resultant assembly stable under any conceivable type of lateral loading condition. Some systems, such as two-way beam-and-slab frame constructions of reinforced concrete, normally inherently provide such mechanisms. Other systems, however, such as bar joists used with load-bearing masonry walls, do not, and special attention should be paid to their stability.

For common square or rectangular grids, the stability requirement usually means that frames, shear walls, or diagonal braces be placed in a series of mutually perpendicular planes placed throughout the building. Pattern implications are obviously present. The pattern illustrated in

Figure 14–1(f), for example, is obviously problematical with respect to loads acting perpendicular to the planes of the shear walls. Those illustrated in Figures 14–1(b)–(e) are intrinsically more viable.

In very early design stages it is often usually adequate to note only the basic lateral force resistance strategy and to identify its pattern implications. It is not always necessary to decide immediately whether a frame, shear wall, or diagonal bracing action will be used to carry the lateral loads. Appropriate locations of planes for these elements, however, must be provided. Further decisions are made as design development occurs.

(a) Lateral loads: forces can act in any direction.

(b) Lateral bracing mechanisms throughout plan (e.g., two-way beam-and-slab system).

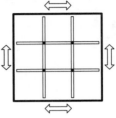

(c) Lateral bracing mechanisms around periphery only.

(d) Plan with symmetrically placed shear walls.

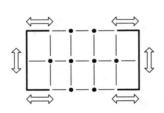

(e) Plan with end bracing.

(f) Plan with problematical shear wall arrangement in upper portion (for flooring systems not acting like rigid diaphragms).

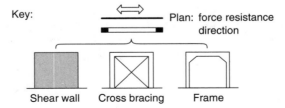

Key:

— Plan: force resistance direction

Shear wall Cross bracing Frame

Typical Lateral Resisting Mechanism

FIGURE 14–1 The lateral stability of any structure under any type of loading must be assured by the correct placement of lateral force-resisting mechanisms.

In low- or medium-rise structures, the adoption of any one of these approaches will provide sufficient lateral resistance. A sufficient number of shear planes must be used to ensure lateral stability. In some building types doing this is very easy. In housing, for example, the cellular nature of the building type lends itself well to using shear walls or diagonal bracing in the interface area between adjacent units. A frame could also be used in these locations but, as noted in Chapter 9, frames tend to be less efficient than shear walls or diagonal bracing as a lateral load-carrying device. In housing shear walls or diagonal bracing in the interfaces between units pose no functional problem and hence are preferably used. In many other building types, however, the barriers formed by shear walls or diagonal bracing systems create functional problems and cannot be freely used. Frames or a combination of frames and shear walls or diagonal bracing is consequently used. Intermediate- and low-rise office buildings, for example, quite often employ a basic frame throughout the building which is further stiffened by the placement of shear walls or diagonal bracing at building ends or around service cores. Usually, placing shear walls or diagonal bracing in these locations poses no functional problems.

In rectangular buildings the greatest problem with lateral forces is in the short direction of the building, although stability must be assured in both directions (see Figure 14–2). Sometimes one type of lateral load-carrying mechanism is used in one direction and another in the other direction (primarily for functional reasons). In simple steel buildings, for example, the more efficient mechanisms (e.g., shear walls or diagonal bracing) are often used in the shorter direction. Stability in the long direction is achieved either by similar means or by frame action (see Figure 14–3).

If shear planes are to be effectively used in conjunction with other vertical planes not having any significant ability to carry lateral loads, such as a pin-connected steel beam and column system, floor planes must be designed to serve as rigid horizontal *diaphragms* which act as thin horizontal beam elements spanning between shear planes (Figure 14–4). This diaphragm action serves to transfer lateral loads from interior non-load-carrying vertical planes to the load-carrying shear planes. When reinforced concrete systems are used, making floors serve as rigid

(a) Basic structure

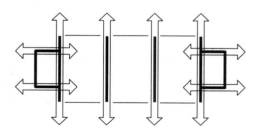

(b) When walls are used to achieve lateral stability in buildings, they should be organized along the short dimension of the building. Stability in the longitudinal direction is often achieved through transverse walls (stairway cores, etc.).

FIGURE 14–2   Organization of either shear planes or bearing walls, or both, in a low- to medium-rise structure.

(a) Basic structure.

(b) Lateral-load-carrying mechanisms: in the short direction, a bracing system is used and lateral loads are carried by truss action. In the long direction, lateral loads are carried by frame action. Loads in the short direction tend to be the most critical and the more efficient lateral-load-carrying mechanism is used in this direction.

FIGURE 14–3 Possible lateral-load resistance mechanisms in a simple steel structure.

diaphragms is typically no problem. With steel, special care should be taken to assure that diaphragm action does indeed occur. Depending on the spacing of the shear planes, it may be necessary to impart some lateral load-carrying capacity to interior vertical planes as well.

Anytime a structure is specially stiffened with shear walls or diagonal bracing systems, care should be taken to place these elements symmetrically. If this is not done, highly undesirable *torsional* effects can develop (see Figure 14–5) due to the fact that the center of rigidity of the building becomes noncoincident with the centroid of the applied lateral load. Placing elements symmetrically is particularly important in very tall buildings or when earthquake hazards are present. In either case, lateral loads capable of inducing high torsional forces are possible. Structures can be designed to resist these torsional effects, but a cost premium is paid.

Stability Approaches in Relation to Shape. The discussion thus far has centered on relatively simple building configurations. Real configurations are often quite complex, as illustrated in the series of diagrams shown in Figure 14–6, which are derived from real building examples. Drawing diagrams of the type shown is a good way of assessing the stability of real configurations consisting of complex assemblies of shear walls, rigid frames, and pin-connected elements.

Several approaches to simple configurations are shown in Figures 14–6(a)–(c). Figure 14–6(a) is a pin-connected structure with diagonal bracing in each of the end bays. Long low buildings of this type often need only bracing at ends. When longer bay assemblies are used,

(a) When the primary method of carrying horizontal forces in a tall structure is by shear walls, the horizontal floor planes are usually designed as rigid diaphragms (in which the floors act like deep thin beams in the horizontal direction) to carry forces from the building face to the shear walls.

(b) If the floors do not serve as diaphragms, interior frames must carry a major portion of the horizontal forces and many of the advantages of using shear walls are not obtained. Interior frames are usually less stiff than shear walls so they deflect more. Diaphragm action in the floors would prevent this.

No diaphragm action

Action with rigid floor diaphragms

FIGURE 14–4 Use of rigid floor diaphragms in framed buildings relying on shear walls to carry horizontal forces.

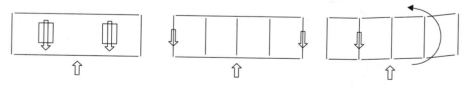

FIGURE 14–5 Use of shear planes in tall structures and effects of nonsymmetrical placement. When shear planes (walls or diagonally braced planes) are used to carry horizontal forces in a tall structure, the planes should be arranged symmetrically to avoid undesirable torsional effects.

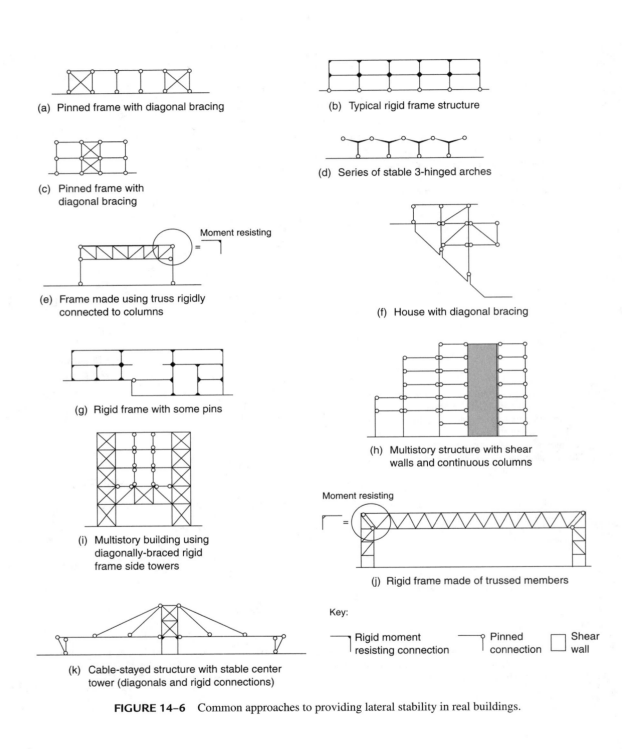

(a) Pinned frame with diagonal bracing

(b) Typical rigid frame structure

(c) Pinned frame with diagonal bracing

(d) Series of stable 3-hinged arches

Moment resisting

(e) Frame made using truss rigidly connected to columns

(f) House with diagonal bracing

(g) Rigid frame with some pins

(h) Multistory structure with shear walls and continuous columns

(i) Multistory building using diagonally-braced rigid frame side towers

Moment resisting

(j) Rigid frame made of trussed members

(k) Cable-stayed structure with stable center tower (diagonals and rigid connections)

Key:

Rigid moment resisting connection

Pinned connection

Shear wall

FIGURE 14–6 Common approaches to providing lateral stability in real buildings.

intermediate braced bays are also used. A simple rigid frame structure using moment resisting joints is shown in Figure 14–6(b). Base connections are pinned because of the frequent constructional difficulty of tying moment resisting base connections to foundations. In relatively low buildings, structural performance is not unduly affected even though there is some loss in stiffness (see Chapter 9). Figure 14–6(d) shows a low-rise building made up of inherently stable and interconnected three-hinged arch structures. Figure 14(e) shows how a horizontal spanning truss can be connected to the sides of columns to form a structure that in an overall way acts like a rigid frame in resisting lateral loads. The truss *must* be connected to each column face at two widely spaced points (the truss must have significant depth at its ends). This same general approach is evident in Figure 14–6(j).

There are many ways to stabilize a structure constructed on a slope. The structure in Figure 14–6(f) utilizes a stabilized central bay. Note that the large cantilevered space to the right is made by using pin-connected elements configured to form a simple trussed configuration.

Special building features, such as large interior spaces, may require that adjacent structural assemblies each have their own stability mechanisms as the example building shown in Figure 14–6(g) illustrates. Features such as cantilevers with their need for fixed or moment-resisting connections may naturally suggest that the larger structural assembly utilize rigid-frame action as well. Note that not all connections have to be designed to be moment resisting. Pin connections may be judiciously used.

Figure 14–6(k) shows one of many different types of cable-stayed structural configurations. Here the center tower, a combined rigid-frame/truss structure, also provides the primary lateral force resistance mechanism in the overall structure.

In smaller buildings of the type shown, the type and arrangement of stability devices is less critical than in larger buildings; although the earthquake design requirements discussed in Section 14–2 may impose strong requirements in some areas. As buildings get taller, there is an increasing necessity to have lateral-load resistance mechanisms that are clearly defined. As illustrated in Figures 14–6(h) and (i), core parts of a building (e.g., around elevators or stairs) frequently provide an excellent location for these mechanisms. For special buildings based on slender cores, as illustrated in Figure 14–6(i), the cores are necessarily clearly designed to resist lateral forces since they must ultimately carry all wind and earthquake forces acting on the structure. The center truss supports the floors above it to provide a large void area on ground level. Extremely tall multistory structures necessitate special consideration and are discussed separately in Section 14–1–2.

Influences on Member and Connection Design.   Of interest here is that the adoption of one or more of the lateral stability strategies discussed in preceding sections influences the design and/or selection of individual members and their connections.

Frame Action:

When securing lateral stability through frame action, it is preferable to use a structural system where necessary rigid joints can be readily obtained. Since carrying lateral forces via frame action induces severe bending moments in both beams and columns, member sizes are often larger than in a pin-connected system that relies on diagonal bracing or shear walls for stability. Recall that the rigid joint requirement means that beams and columns must be attached to one another so that no relative rotations occur between the attached members (although the joint may rotate as a unit). In steel members, this typically means that flanges are connected at tops and bottoms. In poured-in-place reinforced concrete, continuous steel placed in opposite faces of the member is necessary. In timber, knee braces or equivalent devices must be used.

Shear Walls and Diagonal Bracing:

When securing stability through shear walls or diagonal bracing, many members may be pin-connected, depending on the location of the bracing elements and whether or not floors act as rigid diaphragms. Diagonal bracing is commonly used in steel systems. Pin-connected members are relatively easy to make. Diagonal bracing is intrinsically less appropriate for reinforced concrete. Making pin-connected members in cast-in-place members is even more difficult than making pinned connections. The converse is true for precast members. Shear wall systems are intrinsically appropriate for cast-in-place reinforced concrete structures.

When shear walls or diagonal bracing elements are widely separated (e.g., several bays apart), fewer intermediate beam and column connections can be pinned and the floors must provide the structural function of transferring lateral loads to these elements. Consequently, floor planes must be designed as rigid diaphragms capable of carrying horizontal in-plane forces (in addition to their role in carrying normal, vertically acting dead and live loads). This requirement also has implications on specific details, such as how the decking is connected to underlying beams.

General Considerations—Member Orientation:

Use of frame action to achieve lateral stability suggests something about member orientation as well. Members should be organized so that their maximum bending resistance corresponds to the axes about which maximum bending occurs. In buildings with narrow dimensions that rely on frame-action for stability, this often suggests organizing their deepest dimensions parallel with the narrow direction so that the strong axis resists bending. On the other hand, if frame action is used in the long direction and combined with diagonal bracing in the short direction (Figure 14–3), in low buildings wide-flange elements are usually organized such that about their strong axis they function as part of the frame in the longitudinal direction, and about the weak axes they function as part of the diagonal bracing system in the short direction. Since the diagonal bracing acts in trusslike fashion, bending is minimum in a member in the short direction, so it is okay to have the weak axis oriented in this way. In the long direction, however, lateral loads are carried by frame action involving high bending in the members. Consequently, organizing the strong axis of the member in this direction makes sense.

When the narrow dimension of a steel building is very small relative to the building height (indicating a severe problem with lateral loads in the short direction) and the building is adequately braced in the long direction, a *combination* frame and diagonal bracing system can be used to carry loads in the short direction. In this event, wide-flange members are organized such that their strong-axes contribute to frame action in the short direction. The frame and diagonals supplement each other, yielding a total system of increased load-carrying capacity.

General Considerations—Effects of Member Characteristics:

The choice of a method for achieving lateral stability does not always precede the choice of a horizontal spanning system. In cases where the horizontal span is extremely long or loads are unique, the nature of the horizontal element may dictate the type of lateral stability approach used. If spans are on the order of 100 ft (33 m), for example, and precast single tees seem appropriate for the vertical loads, the provision of lateral stability through some other technique than joint rigidity is mandated, since the type and scale of the horizontal element, and the difficulty of getting rigid connections, make the idea of frame action unfeasible. In general, the longer the horizontal spans are, the less likely is frame action to be an appropriate mechanism for achieving lateral stability (Figure 14–7).

Often the unique characteristics of one structural element influence the selection of another. When masonry load-bearing walls are used in low-rise buildings, the walls serve as shear planes in resisting forces in the lateral direction. It is obviously best to organize them along the short

(a) Diagonal bracing (joints can be pin-connected)

(b) Frame action (joints must be rigid)

(c) Shear wall (joints can be pin-connected)

(d) Braced frame (a redundant system)

Simple connection—rigid connection not possible

Masonry pier

Plain masonry shear wall

Rigid connection easily possible

Reinforced concrete column

Reinforced concrete shear wall

Simple connection—rigid connection not possible

Long-span member (e.g., precast T)

Since rigid joints in this situation are difficult, lateral stability must be achieved by a shear plane (wall or diagonal bracing).

FIGURE 14–7   Common methods of resisting lateral forces: implications on connection type.

dimension of the building. Lateral stability along the long dimension can be achieved (depending on building height) through specially designed stair cores or interior walls placed transverse to bearing walls. The use of masonry walls implies that horizontal spanning elements should be simply supported since masonry walls, unless specially reinforced, cannot carry moments. Thus, attempting to use rigid connections at the end of horizontal elements (which would induce moments into the wall) would be counterproductive.

14-1-2 Multistory Construction

Strength Design. As buildings increase in height, the importance of responding to lateral forces caused by either wind or earthquakes becomes an increasingly important structural design consideration.

Of the basic approaches to stability, frame action is probably the least efficient way of achieving lateral stability and is preferably used only when lateral forces are not excessive—as in low- to medium-rise buildings. Typical steel-framed buildings that carry loads exclusively by frame action, for example, do so efficiently only up to 10 stories or so. After that a significant premium is paid in terms of excessive material used if a framed structure is used.

Even in low- to medium-rise structures where frame action may still be appropriate, there are differences in lateral-load-carrying capacities among the different types of framed systems possible. Steel systems are unique in that they can be designed to be responsive to virtually any situation. Reinforced concrete systems, on the other hand, must be used more carefully. Systems such as the flat plate and column assembly have a much smaller lateral-load-carrying capacity than other poured-in-place concrete systems. The flat-plate spanning element is uniquely suited to carrying the limited moments induced by relatively light floor loads and *not* the moments generated at the interfaces with columns by large lateral forces. The plate is too thin to carry such moments effectively. Systems with deeper horizontal members, such as the two-way beam-and-slab system or the waffle system, more effectively provide frame action in both directions. When flat plates are used, their lateral-load-carrying capacity is often supplemented by some other mechanism. In common rectangular apartment buildings, for example, which often use flat-plate construction, end walls are often turned into shear planes, which in turn largely carry the lateral loads. The flat-plate system can then be designed primarily in response to vertical loads. The enclosure around elevator cores is also often specially designed to serve this same function.

As heights increase from the low to intermediate range, it is preferable either to begin supplementing *any* type of frame system used with additional lateral bracing mechanisms, such as diagonal braces around elevator cores, or to adopt a radically different structural approach.

To get a feeling for what different types of structural approaches might be possible for *very* tall structures, it is useful to first briefly review some fundamental principles of the way a tall structure carries lateral loads. Most high-rise structures tend to be relatively tall and slender. Under the action of lateral forces they tend to act like vertical cantilever members. The lateral loads tend to produce an overturning moment which must be balanced by an internal resisting moment provided by the structure. This internal resisting moment is typically provided by couples formed between forces developed in vertical members (see Figure 14–8). If the building is very slender, the small moment arm present between the forces in the vertical members means that very high forces must be developed to provide the internal resisting moment. Buildings of similar heights with wider bases and generally less slender proportions could provide the same internal resisting

(a) Wind forces acting against the face of a tall building produce an overturning moment that must be balanced by an internal resisting moment provided by forces developed in column members. The structure acts much like a vertical cantilever beam.

(b) The magnitude of the forces developed in the columns are generally proportional to the moment arm separating the columns. Smaller column forces are developed in wider buildings than in those of more slender proportions.

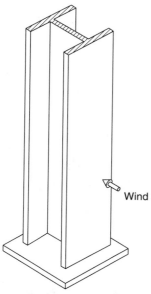

(c) For very tall structures, an efficient structure often results from conceiving of the building as a laterally loaded cantilever beam and distributing material to achieve a large moment of inertia.

Exterior columns carry axial forces caused by laterally acting forces (plus some gravity loads as well).
Interior columns carry only gravity loads.

(d) Many structures have been built on the principle described in (c). The structures must, however, be responsive to lateral forces in all directions. A tube type of structure results in which the exterior columns provide all the resisting moment to overturning lateral forces. Interior columns are designed to carry only gravity loads.

FIGURE 14–8 Very tall buildings can usefully be conceived of as vertical cantilever beams. **501**

moment with smaller forces developed in vertical members because of the increased size of the internal moment arm—obviously an advantageous consequence.

The view of a high-rise building as a vertical cantilever is useful in that in addition to implying something about appropriate building proportions, it also can help inform other design responses. In Chapter 6 it was noted that the most efficient use of material in bending is obtained by locating the greatest amount of material as far as practically possible from the neutral axis of the section. The overall moment of inertia of the section for a given amount of material is increased by doing this, as is the resistance to bending provided. The same principle held true for truss design. In a high-rise building of a given proportion, application of this same principle means that the greatest amount of material should be located in the outer, rather than the inner, vertical elements (see Figure 14–9). Many efficient high-rise structures are conceived in this way. The exterior column and beam assemblies are designed to provide a very stiff ring, or *tube,* capable of carrying lateral loads from any direction. Exterior columns are typically very closely spaced to one another. Spandrel beams are usually rigidly connected to columns to assure that the whole outer assembly acts in an integral way—like a stiff surface element. Although the outer frame assemblies can and do carry gravity loads and act like frames in the horizontal direction, their primary function is to carry forces generated by the overturning moments associated with lateral loads. Interior columns are designed to carry gravity loads only and are consequently typically smaller than exterior columns. Special attention must be paid to designing a floor system that will make the overall resultant structural assembly behave like a unit in carrying lateral loads. The stiffness of a tube of this type can be even further increased by the addition of large cross-bracing on the outside faces of the structure.

The configurations of some types of very tall buildings may ultimately involve a plan type that is long and narrow (e.g., as might be found in a residential highrise building where units are grouped around central corridors). Narrow plan shapes are intrinsically difficult to structure efficiently to carry lateral forces if used in a simple linear way. By deforming the overall plan configuration, however, the overall stiffness of the structure and its related ability to carry lateral loads can be dramatically increased (see Figure 14–10).

Deflection and Motion Control. The structural responses for multistory buildings discussed thus far have all been strength-oriented. Equally important, however, are deflection and motion considerations associated with the dynamic effects of winds. A typical tall building, for example, sways under the buffeting action of damping devices. This device, often called a *tuned mass damper,* is placed in the upper floors of a tall building. As motion begins to occur, the inertial tendency of the mass is to remain at rest. Hence, building movements cause the damping devices to accentuate and begin absorbing energy, thus damping out motions.

The use of damping devices of the type described above is usually restricted to very large buildings. They have, however, been successfully used in several situations. More commonly the stiffness of the structure is controlled. A very rough rule of thumb often used to limit both accelerations and deflections when dynamic analyses are not appropriate or feasible is to use a static wind-load analysis and limit maximum steady-state deflections to a particular value, say $h/500$, where h is the height of the building in feet, and to vary the stiffness of the structure until this criterion is met. This approach is much easier than a dynamic analysis but is dubious at best. Still the approach has historically proven useful if not always a sure bet.

(a) Frame.

(b) Braced frame.

(c) Suspended structure, reinforced concrete core.

(d) Tube structure. The exterior columns are closely spaced. Horizontal spandrel beams are rigidly connected to columns to form an exterior tube, which carries all lateral forces and some gravity forces. Interior columns carry only vertical forces.

(e) Trussed frame. The lateral stiffness of very tall structures can be markedly increased by superimposing major diagonal bracing members. Lateral forces are again taken by the exterior trusswork and frame. Interior columns carry only vertical forces.

FIGURE 14–9 Typical structural approaches in high-rise construction.

FIGURE 14–10 The plan configurations of buildings with narrow dimensions can usefully be shaped to provide overall structural configurations that are intrinsically resistant to lateral forces.

14–2   EARTHQUAKE DESIGN CONSIDERATIONS

14–2–1   General Principles

As discussed in Chapter 3, earthquakes tend to produce forces on structures that are *primarily* lateral in character, although some forces in other directions can develop as well. Most of the principles discussed in the preceding sections are therefore as applicable to the design of structures for earthquake resistance as they are for wind resistance. The extremely pronounced dynamic character of earthquake forces, however, makes the design problem even more complex. This section will briefly explore some of the primary issues involved and alternative strategies that are possible.

There are several basic types of hazards associated with earthquakes. These include *surface fault ruptures, ground shaking, ground failures,* and *tsunamis* (sea waves generated by earthquakes). While all these effects are important, this text will focus primarily on ground-shaking effects.

It is useful to review briefly the behavior of a structure subjected to an earthquake (also see Section 3–2–4). Figure 14–11 illustrates characteristic vibration modes for a tall building. As the figure illustrates, the ground acceleration can cause all floors to move in the same direction, or it can cause different floors to accelerate in different directions in a whiplash type of movement. The whiplash movement can occur because of the tendency for an elastic building to spring back to the vertical after its base has been initially translated and accelerated. Because of inertial tendencies, the upper mass of the building would lag behind the base movement. As the upper mass begins springing back to the vertical after the translation has occurred, it begins gaining momentum. Because of the momentum gained, the upper mass can actually swing past the vertical. If during this process the ground movement is changed such that accelerations and translations are reversed, very complex deformations can occur because of the inertial tendencies of the building masses to continue the movement already started, while at the same time countermovements are beginning. There is a lag as the effects of the reversed ground movement work their way up the building.

Associated with these complex accelerations are extremely high inertial forces, nonconstant winds. Even when winds are steady-state, however, a dynamic behavior is still present. As the wind blows against a building, the building bends over and slightly changes shape. The exact magnitude and distribution of wind forces thus also changes slightly. Increases or decreases in forces due to this phenomenon, coupled with any buffeting action of the wind that might be present, cause the building to oscillate. Typically there is an average deflection in the direction of the

(a) Possible ground movements—normally accelerations in the horizontal plane are the largest and most significant.

(c) Typical vibration modes for a tall building subjected to varying horizontal ground accelerations.

(b) Typical accelerogram data: North-south component of ground acceleration recorded for the 1940 El Centro, California, earthquake (recorded 4 mi. from the causative fault on deep alluvium).

FIGURE 14-11   Earthquake-induced motions in a multistory building.

wind force about which the building oscillates. The magnitude and frequency of these oscillations depend on both the characteristics of the impinging wind forces and the stiffness and the mass-distribution characteristics of the building itself.

These deflections and oscillations are highly important. Excessive deflections can impair the functioning of other building elements (e.g., building service systems) even though the structure itself is unharmed. Oscillations can cause extreme discomfort to building occupants. Human beings do not sense absolute deflections if they occur slowly, but they do sense the accelerations associated with rapid oscillations. A type of motion sickness can consequently occur. What constitutes an acceptable level of acceleration is not an easy criterion to establish rationally, although some values have been suggested by investigators. In addition, analyzing a building to predict what motions actually occur in a given circumstance is also difficult. The most common procedure is to model the structure as an assembly of springs (having elasticities derived from a study of the actual load-deformation characteristics of the structure) and concentrated masses representing building weights. The vibrations a model of this type undergoes when dynamically loaded can be used to predict the response of the real structure. Computer programs facilitate these kinds of analyses.

Thinking about a multistory structure as a spring-mass assembly is also useful in formulating design responses for how to deal with excessive motions or deflections. Clearly, one obvious way to control deflections is to increase the *stiffness* of the structure (not necessarily its strength) until wind-induced oscillations are held to an acceptable level. Increasing member sizes, using diagonal braces or other shear planes, and redistributing material placement are all ways of increasing stiffness.

Another way of controlling motions, particularly accelerations, is to build into the building physical *damping mechanisms* (these dampers are conceptually similar to door-closing devices that cause a door to close slowly and evenly when opened and released) or *friction connections*. Damping devices are typically installed at joints between beams and columns. As movements begin to occur, these devices absorb energy and damp the motion.

Excessive motions can also be controlled by installing a very large mass of material mounted on rollers and attached to the building structure with dashpot or that pose significant structural design problems. In addition to the high inertial forces normally expected, unique forces can also be induced in a structure because of unusual building proportions or features. Twisting, for example, can be induced because of nonsymmetrical placement of building masses. These effects will be explored in the following section.

14-2-2   General Design and Planning Considerations

Probably the single most important design principle with respect to ensuring that a building performs well during an earthquake is that of making certain that both the general masses present in the building (e.g., floors, roofs, etc.) and the stiffening lateral force-resisting mechanisms present in the building (e.g., shear walls, braced frames, etc.) are symmetrically located with respect to one another. Lateral forces associated with earthquakes are, of course, inertial in character and consequently related to the masses of different building elements. Nonsymmetrical placement of building masses and elements that resist the forces associated with these masses can lead to highly undesirable torsional effects in the building, which can be extremely destructive. This is the same issue that was generally addressed earlier in connection with wind forces (see Figure 14–5) but is of even more fundamental importance with respect to earthquake forces.

The principle noted earlier has significant implications for the overall building shape adopted, since both the mass distribution and placement of lateral force resistance mechanisms is strongly influenced by the shape of the building. An L-shaped building, for example, clearly has a nonsymmetrical mass distribution and normally a nonsymmetrical placement of stiffening elements as well. Destructive torsional forces develop in such shapes because of the reasons discussed above. Another way of understanding why the configuration is undesirable is to conceive of the building as made up of two separate masses (each leg of the L), each of which tends to vibrate in its own natural frequency. Since the stiffnesses of the two units differ, their natural periods also differ—a condition that sets up a deflection incompatibility at the interface of the two masses. The consequence is that failures often occur at interface locations. The problem can be somewhat alleviated by separating the building into symmetrical units connected by a *seismic joint,* which physically separates the masses and allows free vibratory movement to independently occur in each (the device is conceptually similar to an expansion joint).

From an earthquake-design viewpoint, preferred building shapes are those of simple plane geometry (e.g., squares, circles); L shapes, T shapes, H shapes, or other unusual shapes are invariably difficult to structure when earthquake hazards are present. Seismic joints can be used to advantage in most such configurations. Difficulties can arise, however, even in buildings that are seemingly symmetrical in plan if *stiffening* elements are nonsymmetrically placed. This is a condition that often arises when elevator cores or other natural stiffening elements are unusually located [see Figure 14–12(b)].

The structural U shapes of shear walls found in many common commercial buildings that are seemingly symmetrical (rectangular) are subject to undesirable torsion effects. Such buildings should preferably have their open faces where glass is normally present stiffened by the insertion of frames. Stiff roof diaphragms should also be used.

Some completely symmetrical buildings can be susceptible to torsion because of nonsymmetrical placements of occupancy loads—a condition that frequently arises in warehouses. This situation can be prevented somewhat by careful design.

The principle of imparting symmetrical stiffness and massing characteristics to a building also holds true for a building in its vertical dimensions as well as in plan. If the stiffness characteristics of different building elements change with building height, for example, nonsymmetries can develop that lead to destructive torsional effects at different levels of the building. Buildings with discontinuous shear walls can be particularly problematical.

There are other considerations that affect a building's sensitivity to earthquake movements. Buildings that are extremely elongated, for example, are preferably avoided even if they are symmetrically organized (Figure 14–13). The longer a building is in plan, the greater is the possibility that opposite ends of the building will be subjected to different relative ground movements that do not act in the same manner. This would tend to cause the building to be torn apart. Designing to prevent this tearing apart is very difficult. It is often necessary to separate extremely long buildings into series of adjacent volumes (through the use of seismic joints) that can move freely with respect to one another.

Another basic consideration is that tall slender buildings are less able to resist efficiently the overturning moments associated with earthquake forces than are lower, wider buildings (Figure 14–14).

Buildings that are constructed adjacent to one another should be adequately separated so that each can freely vibrate in its natural mode without touching the other. Otherwise, severe damage can occur because of *pounding* effects (Figure 14–15).

While forces associated with lateral movements are of primary design importance, vertically acting accelerations due to earthquake motions can also cause trouble. Cantilevers, for example, are particularly susceptible to failure because of vertical movements (see Figure 14–16). In such events, failure often also follows in interior members because of the moment redistributions that occur following the dropping off of cantilevers.

All the considerations noted above generally point to the fact that from the viewpoint of designing for earthquake resistance, buildings that are very symmetrically organized and of relatively compact proportions, and which have few or small overhangs or other protrusions are preferable to very nonsymmetrically organized buildings with exaggerated proportions. Other considerations, it should be noted, such as the specific site and soil conditions present, may also strongly affect the type of building configuration that is preferred.

(a) Symmetrical structures do not experience exceptionally high torsional forces and are hence preferred to nonsymmetrical structures.

(b) Structures that are nonsymmetrical because of either their basic configuration or the nonsymmetrical placement of lateral-load-resisting elements typically experience high torsional forces which are very destructive. Nonsymmetrically placed masses can also lead to similar torsional effects.

(c) Nonsymmetrical configurations with reentrant corners (e.g., L- or H-shaped buildings) are particularly susceptable to destructive torsional effects. Primary damage often occurs at the reentrant corners. Allowing separate building masses to vibrate independently by using seismic separator joints that allow free movement to occur generally improves structural performance.

(d) Buildings that are nonsymmetrical in the vertical direction also experience destructive torsional effects. Discontinuous shear walls are particularly problematic.

FIGURE 14–12   General planning considerations: symmetry versus nonsymmetry.

Seismic joint
(actually quite narrow)

High-damage
zone

(a) Not desirable.

(b) Preferred.

FIGURE 14–13   Elongated buildings are more susceptible to destructive forces associated with differences in ground movements along the length of the building than are more compact shapes. Long buildings can be subdivided by using seismic joints.

Possible overturning   High forces

Lower forces

(a) Not desirable.

(b) Preferred.

FIGURE 14–14   Relatively slender buildings are less able to resist efficiently the overturning moments caused by earthquakes than are shorter and more compact configurations.

Pounding

Clearance

(a) Small separation—not desirable.

(b) Large separation—preferred.

FIGURE 14–15   Adjacent buildings should be adequately separated so that buildings do not pound against each other during seismic events.

(a) Movements in cantilever induced by vertical accelerations: cantilevers can literally snap off due to moment failures associated with these movements.

(b) Failures of cantilevers often lead to other failures because of the moment redistributions that occur. In this example, midspan positive moments increase if the overhang is eliminated, which leads to a failure of the interior member.

FIGURE 14–16 Importance of the vertical components of earthquake ground motions.

14-2-3 General Characteristics of Earthquake-Resistant Structures

Structures that are *continuous* in nature and more or less uniformly distributed throughout a building generally perform well when subjected to earthquakes. The primary reason for this is that the earthquake resistance of a structure is significantly dependent on its ability to absorb the energy input associated with ground motions. Pin-connected structures, such as traditional post and beam assemblies, are far less capable of absorbing energy than are comparable continuous structures (e.g., frames with monolithic joints). The formation of plastic hinges in framed structures (which *must* precede their collapse; see Chapter 6) requires a significant energy input. Continuous structures, therefore, are quite effectively used in buildings in earthquake-hazard zones (Figure 14–17). Either steel or poured-in-place reinforced concrete framed structures designed to be ductile under earthquake forces can be successfully used. Precast concrete structures, with their lack of continuity at connections, are, by a similar token, more difficult to make successfully work, although they can be successfully used.

Even within the category of continuous structures, however, differences exist. Figure 14–18 illustrates the plans of two structures deriving their ability to carry lateral forces from frame action. The first structure, illustrated in Figure 14–18(a), with frames distributed throughout the structure, is generally preferable to that shown in Figure 14–18(b), which has frames around the periphery only. The first structure shown has a greater *redundancy,* and consequently has greater reserve strength than the second structure. Failure of relatively few members in the outer plane of the structure shown in Figure 14–18(b) may lead to total collapse, whereas many more mem-

(a) Frame.   (b) Post-and-beam assembly.

FIGURE 14–17 Continuous structures are generally preferable to pin-connected ones because the plastic hinges that necessarily form in continuous structures before collapse can occur absorb large amounts of energy.

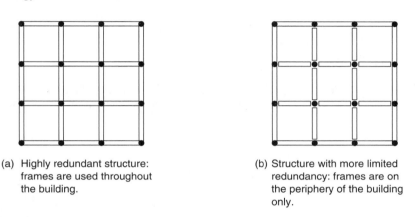

(a) Highly redundant structure: frames are used throughout the building.

(b) Structure with more limited redundancy: frames are on the periphery of the building only.

FIGURE 14–18 Redundant versus nonredundant structures: buildings with highly redundant structural systems in which multiple load paths exist for carrying earthquake forces to the ground usually perform better than less redundant structures during seismic events.

bers must fail in the more redundant structure. Generally, structures with redundancy are preferable to those without redundancy.

Another general characteristic of viable earthquake-resistant structures is that column-and-beam elements are generally coaxial. Offsets or nonaligned members often present extremely difficult design problems.

Earthquake-resistant structures also typically have floor and roof planes designed as rigid diaphragms capable of transmitting inertial forces to lateral-load-resisting elements through beam-like action (Figure 14–19).

Another aspect of earthquake-resistant structures is that they are designed such that horizontal elements which fail due to earthquake motions do so before any vertical members fail (Figure 14–20). Failure should never occur in vertical members first. The reason for this is simply a life-saving consideration. Horizontal elements in *continuous* structures (e.g., slabs or beams) rarely completely fall down even after experiencing extreme damage and when they do, the collapse is fairly localized. (This is not as true with pin-connected horizontal members.) When columns experience damage, however, complete collapse is imminent. The collapse of a column generally

(a) Typical diaphragm action: the horizontal plane acts like a beam in carrying earthquake-induced forces to shear walls or other lateral-load-carrying mechanisms.

(b) If diaphragms are improperly designed, failure can result in floor or roof planes.

FIGURE 14–19 Importance of rigid floor and roof elements: for earthquake-induced inertial forces to be transferred to lateral-load-carrying elements, floor and roof elements must be capable of acting like rigid diaphragms.

(a) Beam failure occurs first.

(b) Column failure occurs first (very undesirable).

FIGURE 14–20 Members should be designed such that failure occurs first in horizontal members rather than in vertical members (a "strong-column-weak-beam" strategy).

causes other portions of a structure to collapse as well. The effects of a single column collapsing can be extensive.

To assure that horizontal elements fail first, care is usually exercised in the design and general proportioning of beam-and-column elements. Extremely deep beams (e.g., spandrels) on light columns are generally best avoided, since experience indicates that such buildings often experience high damage in the light columns which have to pick up all the laterally acting forces by shear and bending. In contrast shear walls with a series of spaced small openings tend to perform somewhat better. Good engineering design, it should be noted, can make all types work adequately.

14-2-4 Materials

As noted before, fully continuous structures are desirable for use in earthquake-prone regions. Coupled with the idea of continuity is that of ductility. For energy absorption to take place, ductility is essential. Steel is a naturally ductile material and is consequently often used. Poured-in-place reinforced concrete can also be made to have a high degree of ductility by carefully controlling member proportions and the amount and placement of reinforcing steel. Reinforced concrete buildings of this type are often used in earthquake zones. Precast concrete structures, however, can be difficult to safely design in earthquake zones because of the difficulties involved in achieving a continuous and ductile structure. Such structures are also typically high-mass structures. The high mass contributes to the magnitude of the seismic forces developed and compounds the problem of their use.

Timber can be an extremely good material for use in earthquake regions. It is light in weight and capable of absorbing large amounts of energy when deformed and before collapse. Low-rise wood-framed structures are highly earthquake-resistant and perform well in earthquake regions.

Materials such as masonry, unless highly reinforced with steel, generally tend not to be suitable for use in earthquake regions. Masonry structures are highly massive but have little ductility. Masonry buildings frequently crack up when subjected to earthquake motions. Much of the damage that has occurred in cities during earthquakes has been because of the failure of older unreinforced masonry buildings. Masonry walls themselves often fail through the development of large *diagonal tension cracks* (recall that principal stresses in elements subjected to shear only act at 45° angles; see Chapter 6) that assume large *X* patterns. These cracks often initially develop at corners of windows or other openings. Another common failure is the collapse of floor systems due to horizontal beams pulling off of the masonry walls due to movements induced by the ground shaking. Tying walls and beams together helps prevent this kind of failure.

14-2-5 Stiffness Issues

Of primary importance in seismic design is the *natural period of vibration* of the building under consideration. It has already been noted in Chapter 3 that if the ground input motions have a similar frequency to that of the natural frequency of the building, then a resonance situation can begin to develop and high destructive forces can be generated. In any event, however, the forces that a building experiences are always directly related to its natural frequency even if resonance conditions do not occur. Forces specified in many building codes, for example, often assume the general form discussed in Section 3–3, which implies that "short"-period (high-stiffness) buildings must be designed for larger forces than "long"-period (low-stiffness) buildings (Figure 14–21). As will be discussed shortly, however, this is *not* the only factor that must be taken into account in choosing to opt for a relatively stiff building (e.g., one using reinforced concrete shear walls) or a relatively flexible (low-stiffness) one (e.g., a steel frame).

One important component of the decision has to do with the notion that for ground motions that are close to the natural frequency of the building itself, the structure will receive maximum

(a) Shear wall: a stiff structure with a short natural
period of vibration.

(b) Shear wall with small
openings: still a rela-
tively stiff structure with
a short natural period.

(c) Frame: a flexible structure with a long natural
period of vibration.

(d) Combination shear
wall/frame.

FIGURE 14–21 Different structural responses have widely varying natural periods of vibration, an important consideration in seismic design. The use of base isolation systems and other devices, however, can dramatically alter the structural response present (see Section 14–2–7).

punishment because of the tendency toward resonance. If the frequencies are different, however, the structure will experience lower seismic forces. (See the discussion on this point in Chapter 3.) A very stiff building should experience lower seismic forces when ground motions have a long period than a flexible building, and vice versa. It would therefore seem that the choice of relative stiffness should be made on the basis of the expected character of the ground motions that might be perceived by the building. The character of these motions, however, is highly diffi-cult to predict. The actual motions perceived by a building, it should be noted, are *strongly* influ-enced by the nature of the soil conditions present beneath the building and the interaction of the building with the soil. Still in certain circumstances, the general nature of expected ground mo-tions can be predicted to a greater or lesser degree.

Many designers generally advocate for all situations the use of fully flexible buildings in which a relatively flexible structure (e.g., a steel frame) is used. Such buildings are also normally designed such that no actual or potential stiffness is imparted by other building elements (e.g., partitions). Such nonstructural elements are detailed to allow the structure to move freely (a dif-ficult and sometimes nonfeasible task).

Briefly, the primary advantages of a full flexible approach appear to be that such buildings are especially suitable for sites where ground-motion periods are expected to be short. Ductility and continuity are also naturally easy to achieve because steel is typically used extensively. Dis-advantages occur when long-period sites are present and resonance situations can develop. Non-structural elements are also difficult to detail and often experience great damage if not designed properly when earthquakes do occur.

Stiff structures may have some advantages for long-period sites. Nonstructural elements are usually fairly easy to detail in stiff buildings, since structural movements are not large and dam-age to such elements is limited when minor earthquakes do occur. Stiff structures, on the other hand, are disadvantageous for short-period sites. For some materials the notion of high stiffness is also not generally compatible with the notion of ductility, which is important from an energy absorption viewpoint. (The presence of some ductility is important even in stiff structures.) By careful design, however, even apparently stiff structures (such as those made of reinforced concrete) can be made to be very ductile through the incorporation of appropriate amounts of steel in proper locations.

On some occasions, mixed systems are often advantageous. The mixed frame/shear wall system shown in Figure 14–21(d), for example, is often a good system in that for earthquakes of a low magnitude the stiff shear wall takes most of the forces involved, and the whole building responds stiffly, thus limiting nonstructural damage. The more ductile frame, however, provides a large measure of reserve capacity when high-magnitude earthquake forces are present.

14–2–6 Nonstructural Elements

Many nonstructural elements can significantly influence the dynamic behavior, and hence the seismic forces present, in a building. Depending on how such elements interact with the primary structure, they may alter the natural period of vibration of the structure, thus changing the forces present. They can also affect the distribution of lateral stiffness in a building, which can also have significant consequences.

One of two basic strategies is normally taken with respect to nonstructural elements (Figure 14–22). One is to carefully analyze all elements and include those that contribute to the stiffness of the primary structure in the analysis and design of the primary structure. Contributing elements would have to be carefully detailed to assure that they did indeed contribute to the building stiffness as expected. The second basic strategy is that noted earlier of preventing any of the nonstructural elements from contributing to the stiffness of the structure at all. This is done by attempting to detail connections such that gaps exist between the primary structure and nonstructural elements. The structure can then deform freely. Which of these two approaches is assumed is largely dependent on the attitude the designer takes toward the overall stiffness of the structure and whether flexibility is desired or not.

14–2–7 New Approaches: Base Isolation Systems and Other Techniques

In recent years there has been a spate of new developments in designing structures to perform well during seismic events. These approaches include the use of various base-isolation and damping systems, and careful manipulation of the stiffness of beam and column elements to

(a) Partition does not affect the stiffness of the building and is not susceptible to damage.

(b) Partition contributes to the stiffness of the building and is susceptible to damage unless carefully designed.

FIGURE 14–22 Nonstructural elements.

achieve improved performance and reduce damage during a seismic occurrence (including so-called "strong-column-weak-beam" approaches, see Figure 14–20). These manipulations allow designers to not only better control overall dynamic responses, but to better control where and how damage might occur.

Approaches include the use one type or another of system for seismic base isolation and passive energy dissipation. Systems of this type have been installed in buildings and bridges throughout the world. Here the basic idea is simple. The designer tries to avoid transmitting the shaking action into the structure in the first place by inserting an isolating device between the base of the building or bridge and its foundations. One of the most widely used approaches is passive base isolation. A layer of low stiffness layer is placed between the structure and its foundation.

There are many specific types of isolation systems used in practice. One widely used type uses elastomeric bearings of either natural rubber or neoprene. These bearings help decouple the building structure from the laterally-acting components of an earthquake's ground motion by introducing a layer with low horizontal stiffness between the structure and the foundation. This causes the fundamental frequency of the overall structure to change, and typically be lower than its frequency without the isolation devices, as well as being often lower than normal frequencies of the actual ground motion. In the first dynamic mode, a structure using an isolation system is more or less rigid above the isolation device, where most deformations occur. Higher modes can sometimes be problematic. Note that this kind of basic system does not necessarily absorb the earthquake energy, but rather alters the dynamics of the whole configuration. The addition of damping devices, however, can be beneficial and reduce the potential for any kind of resonant action. Fluid viscous dampers are often used.

Other kinds of isolation systems include the sliding system (in which the transfer of shear across the isolation interface is limited), friction-pendulum systems, and various kinds of active base isolation systems. This whole area is in a rapid state of change and development.

QUESTIONS

14–1 Identify at least one multistory building in your local area or one that is documented in the literature that uses shear walls for lateral stability. Draw a plan of the building and indicate diagrammatically the locations of these elements. Do they form a pattern capable of resisting loads in all directions? If not, what other load-carrying mechanisms are present to assure complete stability?

14–2 Repeat Question 14–1 using a framed building.

14–3 Repeat Question 14–1 for a diagonally braced building.

14–4 Review the literature and identify at least six different multistory buildings in different height ranges. The height range should vary from about 10 stories or less to some very tall buildings (e.g., the Hancock Building or World Trade Center). Identify the general type of structural system used in each case. Draw to the same scale a schematic diagram of the elevation of each building (emphasizing structural elements).

14–5 Review the literature and identify a major building that was specially designed for earthquake forces. Identify all structural and nonstructural design devices that were incorporated to reduce earthquake hazards. Record your findings with a series of annotated diagrams.

14–6 Review the literature and identify a major building that uses a *tuned mass damper* in its upper floors as a way of controlling lateral motions [consider, for example, the Citicorp Center building in New York (*Architectural Record,* Mid-August issue, 1976)]. Draw diagrams of how the device works.

CHAPTER 15

Structural Systems: Constructional Approaches

15–1 INTRODUCTION

This chapter provides a brief descriptive overview of many of the different structural systems found in common use. A highly useful way of characterizing these typical approaches is according to the nature of the primary material used in the structure. Three common materials, wood, reinforced concrete, and steel, will be addressed here. No attempt is made to do anything other than highlight basic characteristics of systems as grouped according to materials. Reference is made to preceding chapters on specific elements for analysis and design techniques.

The following sections also contain some *rule-of-thumb* information for determining approximate sizes of elements. Using rules of thumb is a time-honored way of initially sizing structures that at one time was the only way of utilizing empirical knowledge gained from observing built structures that performed successfully to inform the design of new structures (see Figure 15–1). They are still of interest for the same reason, but should be used with care. Since they were derived by looking at previously built structures their use in design tends to propagate the past state of the art rather than be forward-looking. As such, they inherently tend to preclude innovative structural solutions based on an understanding and application of the theory of structures.

(a) Arch bridge dimensions, according to Leon Battista Alberti.

(b) Determining the dimensions of a cupola, according to Carlo Fontana.

FIGURE 15–1 Early rules of thumb for sizing structures.

15–2 WOOD CONSTRUCTION

Primary Systems. Almost all constructional systems using timber as the base material can be characterized as being composed of linear one-way spanning elements. Hierarchical arrangements are typical. Figure 15–2 illustrates a sampling of the many different types of wood construction systems in common use. Many other systems are also possible and in use.

Light Framing. The familiar light joist system illustrated in Figure 15–2(a) is undoubtedly the most ubiquitous of all wood-framing systems used in current construction. The floor joist system is primarily useful for light occupancy loads which are uniformly distributed and for modest spans, conditions typically found in house construction. Joists are normally simply supported. Rarely are moment-resisting joists used since special connections are required. Usually, the transverse decking is not considered to act integrally with the joists unless special care is taken with connections.

The vertical support system is typically a load-bearing wall of either masonry or closely spaced wood elements (studs) sheathed in plywood. In the latter case, the lateral resistance of the whole structural assembly to horizontal forces is obtained by arranging plywood-sheathed walls to serve as shear planes. Structures of this type are typically restricted in height to three or four stories. This is not so much because of their theoretical load-carrying capacity as it is for fire-safety requirements stipulated in building codes.

Since each element is individually put in place on the job site, a great deal of flexibility is available in the use of the system and in how other building components are integrated with it.

Stressed-Skin Elements. *Stressed-skin members* are obviously related to the standard joist system [see Figure 15–2(b)]. In these elements, plywood sheathing is affixed to both sides of

(a) Light frame construction.

(b) Stressed-skin panels.

(c) Box beams.

(b) Heavy timber construction:
laminated beams.

(e) Heavy timber construction:
knee-braced frame.

(f) Trusses:
special designs.

FIGURE 15–2 Timber construction systems.

(g) Trusses: mass-produced "trussed rafters" for housing.

(h) Trusses: mass-produced open-web joists.

(i) Arches laminated timber members.

(j) Folded plates.

(k) Arch panels.

(l) Lamella construction.

FIGURE 15–2 *(continued)*

stringers in a way that assures that the sheathing will act integrally with the stringers in carrying bending. A form of plate is thus achieved.

The rigidity of the complete system is also increased by this integral action. Structural depths are consequently less than in standard joist systems. Stressed-skin elements are typically made off-site and put in place as modular units on the site. They are highly useful when they can be used in a highly repetitive way. They can be used in a variety of ways, including being made into long-span folded-plate systems.

Box Beams.   The built-up nature of plywood box beams [see Figure 15–2(c)] allows great latitude in the range of span and load conditions that they can be designed to meet. They are highly useful in long-span situations or where unique loading conditions are present. Box beams can efficiently span greater distances than can homogeneous or laminated beams.

Heavy Timber Construction.   Heavy timber beams with transverse planking historically preceded the lighter joist systems [see Figure 15–2(e)]. Laminated timber beams are now often used in lieu of homogeneous members. Such systems can have a much higher load-carrying capacity and span range than joist systems. With laminated beams, for example, relatively long spans are possible, since member depths can be increased almost at will. Elements of this type are normally simply supported, but rigid joints can be achieved through special connections.

The vertical support system is typically either masonry walls or timber columns. The lateral resistance of the whole structural assembly to horizontal forces is typically obtained by using walls as shear planes. Knee braces are also used to obtain lateral stability when columns are used. Gaining lateral stability through moment-resisting joints is possible in low structures but is not frequently done.

Trusses.   The timber truss is among the most versatile of all one-way spanning elements, since a wide variation is possible in the configuration and member properties used. Special hand-crafted trusses are specially suitable for unique load or span conditions. Mass-produced timber trusses, however, are also available. These are typically used in light-load and modest span situations. The *trussed rafter* illustrated in Figure 15–2(g), for example, is extensively used in roofs of single-family detached housing. The system shown in Figure 15–2(h) is analogous to the steel open-web bar joist and is useful in long-span situations (particularly for roofs).

Folded Plates and Arch Panels.   A variety of special flat- or curved-plate structures, which are typically one-way spanning elements useful for roofs, can be constructed from wood. Most involve the use of plywood. Figures 15–2(j) and (k) illustrate two examples of structures of this type.

Arches.   Standard arch forms can be made from timber. Laminated members are most often used. Almost any shape of arch can be made using laminated wood. Relatively long spans can be obtained. These structures are typically useful as roofs only. Most are either two- or three-hinged and not fixed.

Lamellas.   Lamella construction is a way of making extensive singly or doubly curved surfaces from short pieces of wood [see Figure 15–2(l)]. This interesting type of construction can be used to make long-span cylindrical surfaces or long-span domed structures. The system is very versatile and has found wide application in roof structures.

Member Sizes. Figure 15–3 illustrates *approximate* span ranges for different types of timber structures. As noted earlier, the "maximum" spans indicated on diagrams of this type represent not maximum possible spans but spans that are not to be considered unduly unusual even if they are longer than typically encountered. The minimum span limitations represent a system's lower-economic-feasibility span.

The figure also shows approximate depth ranges for the different spanning systems. One number represents the usual minimum depth system while the other, common maximums. An approximate depth of $L/20$ means, for example, that a member that spans 16 ft (4.9 m) should have a depth of about 16 ft (12 in./ft)/20 = 9.8, or 10 in. [(4.9 m)/20 = 0.24 m = 240 mm].

Timber columns typically have thickness to height (t/h) ratios that range from between 1:25 for relatively short and lightly loaded columns to around 1:10 for heavily loaded columns in multistory buildings. Walls made of timber elements have comparable t/h ratios, ranging from about 1:30 to 1:15.

Tables of the type shown in Figure 15–3 and the t/h ratios noted here should always be used with care and never as the only means for selecting and sizing a structure. Rule-of-thumb information should always be used only to develop a feeling for relationships among systems, spans, and depths, and nothing more.

15–3 REINFORCED CONCRETE CONSTRUCTION

Slabs and Beams. Among the simplest of all reinforced concrete spanning systems is the conventional one-way solid slab [Figure 15–4(a)]. The easy formwork is an attractive feature of this system. These constant-depth systems are particularly suitable for short spans. With longer spans, the dead weight of the solid slab becomes excessive and ribbed slabs become preferable [Figure 15–4(b)].

One-way beam systems with transverse one-way slabs can be used to span relatively long distances (particularly if the beams are post-tensioned) and carry heavy loads. Such systems are relatively deep. Beam spacing is usually determined on the basis of what is most reasonable for the transverse slab.

One-Way Pan Joist System. A one-way pan joist system is ribbed slab constructed by pouring concrete around special forms made of steel or fiberglass [Figure 15–4(c)]. Transverse beams of virtually any depth can easily be cast in place at the ends of pans so that the system can adapt to a variety of column grids. Longitudinal beams more substantial than the normal ribs can also be cast in easily by varying the pan spacing. The ribbed slab is more suitable for longer spans than a solid slab. With post-tensioning, very long spans can be obtained. The pan joist system tends to be too complex and hence uneconomical for short spans. The vertical support system can be either columns or load-bearing masonry walls.

The ribbed slab-and-column system is capable of considerable lateral-load resistance, since transverse and longitudinal beams are cast into the floor system monolithically with the columns. Frame action can thus be achieved in both directions.

Flat-Plate Construction. The flat plate is a two-way constant-depth reinforced concrete slab system [Figure 15–4(d)]. It is appropriate for use with light floor and roof loads and relatively short spans. It finds wide application in housing construction. Although a regular column grid is

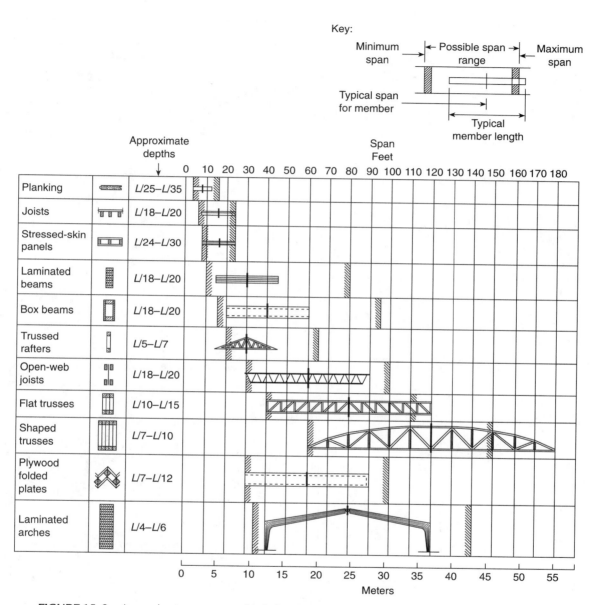

FIGURE 15–3 Approximate span ranges for timber systems. In order that typical sizes of different timber members can be relatively compared, the diagrams shown of the members are scaled to represent typical span lengths for each of the respective elements. The span lengths that are actually possible for each element are noted by the maximum and minimum span marks.

(a) One-way flat plate (poured in place).

(b) One-way beam-and-slab system (poured in place).

(c) One-way pan joist system (poured in place).

(d) Two-way flat plate (poured in place).

(e) Two-way flat slab (poured in place).

(f) Two-way beam-and-slab system (poured in place).

FIGURE 15–4 Reinforced concrete construction systems.

most appropriate, some flexibility is allowed in this respect. Indeed, flat plates are often used where the rigid orthogonality demanded by many other systems on the layout of the vertical supports is not desirable or possible. Spans are, however, limited in comparison with ribbed or beamed systems.

Lower floor-to-ceiling heights are possible with flat-plate construction than with many other systems. Relatively large amounts of reinforced steel, however, are typically required as a consequence of the thinness of the plates used. The governing design factor for flat plates is often the

(g) Two-way waffle slab (poured in place).

(h) Prestressed long-span planks (precast).

(i) Prestressed channels (precast).

(j) Prestressed single tees (precast).

(k) Beam-and-column system (precast).

(l) Housing system (precast walls and planks post-tensioned together).

FIGURE 15–4 *(continued)*

punch-through shear in the plate at the columns. Special steel reinforcement is often used at these points. At plate edges columns are also typically moved in from the free edge to ensure that the interface area between the slab and column remains as large as possible (see Chapter 10).

Lateral stability for the entire plate and column assembly can be a problem. Since the plate and columns are poured monolithically, joint rigidity is achieved which contributes to the lateral resistance of the structure and is sufficient for low buildings. Because of the thinness of the plate element, however, this resistance is limited. For tall structures, stability is often achieved through shear walls or stiff poured-in-place core elements in the building such as might be possible around elevators or stairways.

The simple formwork involved is an undoubted virtue of this system. The planar nature of the lower surface also facilitates the design and placement of other building components. The system is quite often used for apartment buildings and dormitories which are comprised of functional spaces that are of limited span and cellular in nature.

Flat-Slab Construction. The flat slab is a two-way reinforced concrete system similar to the flat plate except that the area of interface between the plate and columns is increased by the addition of drop panels and/or column capitals [Figure 15–4(e)]. The drop panels or column capitals serve to reduce the possibility of punch-through shear failure in the slab (see Chapter 10). The system is particularly appropriate for relatively heavy loading conditions (e.g., such as found in warehouses) and is suitable for spans larger than those possible with flat plates.

The capitals and drop panels also contribute to making the slab-and-column assembly more resistant to lateral loads than is the flat-plate system.

Two-Way Beam-and-Slab Construction. A two-way beam-and-slab system consists of a flat reinforced concrete plate with beams, monolithically cast in place, along the periphery of the plate [Figure 15–4(f)]. The system is good for medium spans and high loading conditions. Large concentrated loads can also be supported if carried directly by the beams. Columns are invariably used for the vertical support system. Since beams and columns are cast monolithically, and there is a substantial interface between these elements, the system naturally forms a frame in two directions. This provides an appreciable lateral-load-carrying capacity, and the system can consequently be used for multistory construction with ease.

The Waffle Slab. The waffle slab is a two-way, constant-depth reinforced concrete system having ribs in two directions [Figure 15–4(g)]. These ribs are formed by the use of special domed pans made of steel or fiberglass. The voids formed by the pans reduce the dead load weight of the structure. Waffle slabs are useful in longer-span situations than flat plates. These slabs can also be post-tensioned to increase their spans.

A thickness of concrete is usually left around column tops (by not using pans in these locations). This solid area serves the same function as drop panels or capitals in a flat slab. The possibility of shear failure is reduced and the moment-resisting capacity of the system is increased (and so is its lateral load-carrying capacity).

Both the span of the waffle system and its lateral load-carrying capacity can be increased by casting in place beams spanning between columns. This is done quite simply by eliminating the pans along these lines (or spacing them farther apart), adding appropriate reinforcing, and casting a full depth of concrete (see Chapter 10).

Curved Shapes. Virtually any singly or doubly curved shape (e.g., a cylinder, dome, etc.) can be made from reinforced concrete. Reinforcing typically consists of a mesh of light steel rods throughout the shell with special additional steel used in localized areas of high internal force. Post-tensioning is commonly used for special elements (e.g., tension rings in domes; see Chapter 12).

Precast Concrete Elements. Precast concrete elements are fabricated off-site and transported to the job. They are typically one-way spanning elements that are most often pretensioned (see

Section 6–4–4). A range of cross-sectional shapes are fabricated which are suitable for a wide variety of load and span conditions. They are most typically appropriate for uniformly distributed occupancy and roof loads and not for concentrated loads or unusually heavy distributed loads. These members are most often simply supported.

Moment connections are possible by using special connections but are difficult. Large cantilevers are also difficult and must be kept to a minimum. Precast elements are most successfully used when they can be used in a highly repetitive way. Several different types of precast members are discussed next (many other types are also available).

Precast Planks. Both short-span and long-span planks are available. Short-span planks are used in much the same way as timber planking is used, although appropriate spans are slightly longer. A poured-in-place concrete wearing surface is normally placed on top of the planks. They are often used in conjunction with precast reinforced concrete beams or with steel open-web joists. Long-span planks are available, which can typically span between 16 and 34 ft (5 to 11 m), depending on the exact width and depth of the element. These long-span planks are typically prestressed and also cored to reduce dead weights. A poured-in-place concrete wearing surface is placed on top of the planks. This concrete also forms a shear key between adjacent elements so that the resultant structure behaves like a one-way plate [see Figure 15–4(h)]. Precast planks are most appropriate for light occupancy or roof loads. They are invariably simply supported and are often used with load-bearing walls as the vertical support system (these walls must be either masonry or concrete, not wood stud). They are also frequently used with steel or reinforced concrete beams.

Channels and Double Tees. These are ribbed, one-way, precast, and prestressed elements that are suitable for longer spans than planks [Figure 15–4(i)]. They are appropriate for occupancy and roof loads. A poured-in-place concrete wearing surface is placed on top of adjacent members.

Single Tees. These are typically large, precast, and prestressed elements most suitable for relatively long spans. They are rarely used in short-span situations because of the difficulties in erecting them. They are invariably simply supported. They are suitable for fairly heavy occupancy and roof loads. They are, for example, quite often used in parking garages and other buildings having fairly large spans and heavier than usual loads [Figure 15–4(j)].

Special Building Systems. A whole host of systems are available for completely forming the entire shell of a building [Figure 15–4(l)]. Systems specially designed for housing are common. Approaches used to date usually fall into one of two categories: (1) those systems that employ off-site-produced linear or planar elements, such as walls or horizontal spanning systems that are assembled on-site (usually by a post-tensioning system) to form volumes; and (2) those systems in which volume-forming assemblies, such as complete boxes, are constructed off-site and then shipped to the site and aggregated.

Member Sizes. Figure 15–5 illustrates typical span ranges and depths for several typical reinforced concrete spanning systems. Reinforced concrete columns typically have thickness to height (t/h) ratios that range from $1:15$ for relatively short and lightly loaded columns to around $1:6$ for heavily loaded columns in multistory buildings. Reinforced concrete load-bearing walls have comparable t/h ratios ranging from about $1:22$ to $1:10$.

FIGURE 15-5 Approximate span ranges for reinforced concrete systems. In order that typical sizes of different members can be relatively compared, the diagrams shown of the members are scaled to represent typical span lengths for each of the respective elements. The span lengths that are actually possible for each element are noted by the maximum and minimum span marks.

15–4   STEEL CONSTRUCTION

Primary Systems.   Most heavy steel constructional systems are made up of linear one-way spanning elements. A variety of rolled steel sections (e.g., wide flange) are available in various sizes for use. This variety allows a remarkable flexibility in the design of beam-and-column elements. Although simple support connections are typically used when possible, for construction convenience, it is relatively easy to make moment-resisting joints. Frames thus formed are capable of resisting lateral loads. Lateral stability is also often achieved by the use of shear walls or diagonal bracing elements.

Beams.   Wide-flange shapes are commonly used as horizontal spanning elements [see Figure 15–6(a)]. The span range possible is rather wide. Members are usually simply supported unless frame action is needed for stability, in which case moment-resisting connections are used. Other shapes, such as channels, are occasionally used to carry bending but are usually limited to light loads and short spans.

Plate Girders.   Plate girders are special types of beams. The built-up nature of plate girders [Figure 15–6(d)] allows great latitude in the range of span and load conditions that they can be designed to meet. They are extremely useful when very high loads must be carried over medium spans. They are often used, for example, as major load-transfer elements carrying column loads over clear spans. For typically encountered distributed floor loads and span ranges, however, they are rarely used, since wide-flange elements are more appropriate and economical.

Composite Construction.   Many structural systems cannot be easily characterized according to material. The composite beam system illustrated in Figure 15–6(c) is fairly common. In this case the steel is first put in place and then concrete is cast around the shear connectors at the top of the steel beam. The shear connectors cause the steel and concrete to act integrally. A type of T section is thus formed with steel in the tension zone and concrete in the compression zone. If a concrete wearing deck is needed anyway, considerable economies can be achieved by this approach.

Trusses and Open-Web Joists.   An endless variety of truss configurations are of course possible. Potential load capacities and span ranges are enormous for uniquely designed or specially made trusses.

Open-web joists, which are mass-produced [Figure 15–6(b)], can be used for both floor and roof systems. They are often highly economical for intermediate to long-span situations in which relatively light, uniformly distributed loads are involved. The bar joist, for example, is frequently used as a long-span roofing element. Open-web joists are typically simply supported (although it is possible to devise rigid connections) and thus make no direct contribution to the lateral resistance of the whole assembly. Often wide-flange and open-web joists are used in the same system, with the former having moment-resisting joints so that frame action capable of resisting lateral forces can be obtained.

Special heavier-gage open-web joists are available for very long span situations. These are normally appropriate only for light, uniformly distributed roof loadings.

Arches.   Rigid arches of virtually any shape can be specially made from steel. Prefabricated arches are available for short to moderate spans. Specially designed arches have been used in

(a) Steel deck and beam floor system.

(b) Steel deck and open-web bar joist system.

(c) Composite steel and concrete floor system.

(d) Plate girders.

(e) Welded trusses: double-angle members.

(f) Welded trusses: tube members.

FIGURE 15–6 Steel construction.

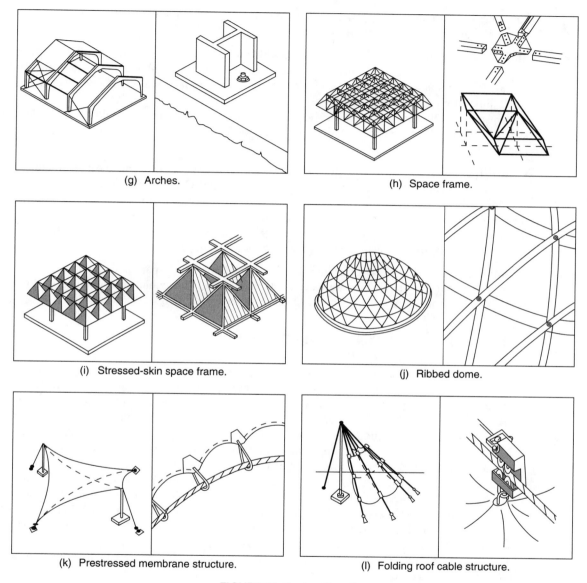

(g) Arches.

(h) Space frame.

(i) Stressed-skin space frame.

(j) Ribbed dome.

(k) Prestressed membrane structure.

(l) Folding roof cable structure.

FIGURE 15–6 *(continued)*

very long span situations [e.g., spans on the order of 300 ft (90 m) or more]. Steel arches can be made of solid sections or open-web sections.

Shells.   A whole variety of shell forms are possible using steel. The primary problem in using steel to achieve doubly curved surfaces is that of creating the shape by using line elements. In domes, for example, either ribbed or geodesic approaches are possible. Light steel decking of small dimensions is commonly used to form enclosure surfaces.

In some small-span situations, curved steel surfaces can be made by specially pressing steel sheets in a way similar to that done to create singly or doubly curved steel forms in automobile bodies.

Cable Structures.   Steel is really the only material extensively used to create cable structures. The forms that cable structures can assume vary enormously. Cables can be used to create permanent roofs whose enclosure surfaces are made by either rigid steel planar elements such as decking or by membrane surfaces. The former are usually singly curved shapes while the latter are doubly curved. Movable roofs are also possible using a cable system [see Figure 15–6(l)]. These movable roofs are usually temporary enclosures or semipermanent at best.

Member Sizes.   Figure 15–7 illustrates the span ranges and depth/span ratios for several common steel spanning systems. Structural steel columns typically have thickness to height (t/h) ratios that range from between 1:24 to 1:9, depending on column heights and loads.

15–5   FOUNDATIONS AND RETAINING WALLS

Foundation structures transfer forces from the building structure into the ground. Common types of foundations generally include the following: discrete spread footings associated with single columns, continuous spread footings associated with load-bearing walls, raft foundations (similar to other spread footings but larger and carrying multiple columns), various kinds of straight and battered bearing or friction pile systems, and different types of caissons. A detailed discussion of all important foundation types and conditions is far beyond the scope of this book. Nonetheless, some general observations can be made.

Spread footings distribute forces directly into the soil beneath. The area of the footing depends upon the magnitude of the loads carried and the allowable bearing pressure of the soil. Simple soil stress models assume that the pressure on the soil is evenly distributed. In actuality, theoretical and empirical studies from the field of *soil mechanics* indicate that stress distributions in the soil are far more complex than simple models indicate. Settlement mechanisms are similarly complex. Simple models can be used in many situations, but many situations warrant a more intensive study of the behavior of soil beneath a footing and the various kinds of structure–soil interactions that take place.

Piles are long column-like members that are driven into the soil and tied together at the top with a pile cap. Piles can either carry loads by frictional forces developed during driving, or by transferring loads directly from the building structure to an underlying bearing strata (e.g., a hard rock bed). In the latter cases, the piles simply pass through softer material. Caissons are typically larger versions of this general foundation class that can carry very large loads. They are made by a drilling rather than driving process. Concrete is typically poured into the drilled holes. Normally caissons extend downward to a bearing strata (a very stiff clay or rock) where they are

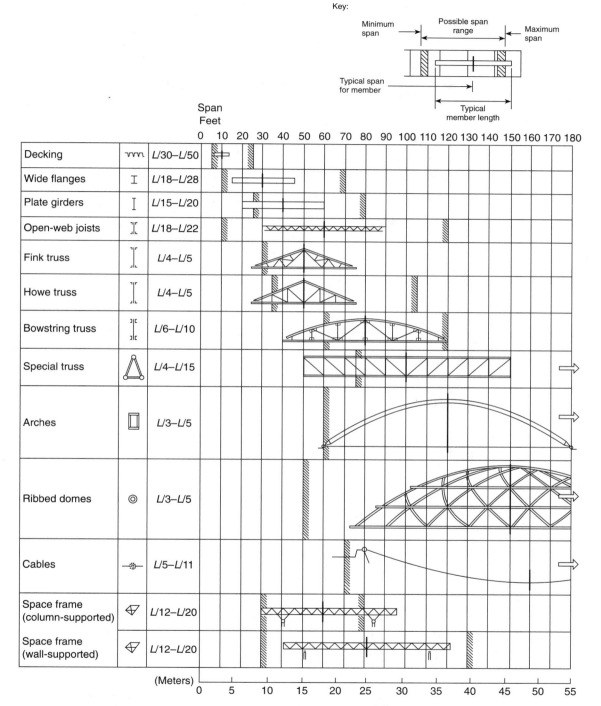

FIGURE 15–7 Approximate span ranges for steel systems. In order that typical sizes of different members can be relatively compared, the diagrams shown of the members are scaled to represent typical span lengths for each of the respective elements. The span lengths that are actually possible for each element are noted by the maximum and minimum span marks.

533

Commonly assumed bearing
stresses on soil ($f_{BG} = P/A$)

Deformation tendencies

Reinforcing
steel

Settlement caused by
lateral displacement

Heaving

Soil movement

Settlement of footings

Pressure bulb

$0.30p$
$0.20p$
$0.15p$
$0.10p$
$0.05p$

$0.02p$

Spread footings

Friction piles

Battered piles (good
for inclined loads)

Bearing piles

Bearing strata

Caissons

Bearing strata

Piles and Caissons

Active soil
pressure

$F_x = (1/2)K_A ph^2$

Lateral forces caused by soil pressures
on a typical retaining wall tend to cause
overturning

Reinforcing
steel placed
in tension
region

Typical reinforced concrete retaining wall

Retaining walls

Lateral soil
pressure

Soil
weight

Soil pressure

Deformation
tendencies

FIGURE 15–8 Typical foundation conditions. (Adapted from Daniel L. Schodek, *Structure in Sculpture*,
M.I.T. Press, 1993. Used with permission.)

belled out to distribute loads more evenly onto the bearing strata. Many different versions of both pile and caisson foundations exist.

Retaining walls are used to contain earth fill. Typical soils exert a lateral pressure on the interior face of a retaining wall that tends to cause the wall to either overturn and/or slide laterally. The amount of lateral force generated depends upon the type and weight of the soil present, its cohesion characteristics and water content, and other factors. A triangular stress distribution is often assumed in which the total lateral pressure increases with the square of the height of the wall. With this distribution, a lateral force factor of $F_x = (1/2)K_A ph^2$ is obtained. In this expression, K_A is an empirically derived coefficient (with values ranging typically from anywhere from 0.25 to 0.35) that depends on soil characteristics, p is the unit weight of the soil, and h is the height of the wall. Clearly the overturning moment is critically dependent on the height of the wall, h, which influences both the magnitude of the lateral force developed and the moment arm associated with overturning. The overturning force can obviously be resisted via a large heavy wall with a wide base (see the discussion on block overturning in Chapter 2). More sophisticated reinforced concrete retaining structures use an extended base with a toe and heel (see Figure 15–8). The dead weight of the soil above the heel portion helps stabilize the wall with respect to overturning and the toe helps extend the base width. The various forces cause tension and compression to develop at different points in the structure, which in turn dictate the location or placement of reinforcing steel. Clearly, the wall and the flat base must also be connected via reinforcing in the tension zones. In addition to this wall type, many other approaches, e.g., using counterforts (triangular walls placed perpendicularly to the retaining wall itself), are possible.

QUESTIONS

15–1 Obtain a set of working drawings for a structural steel building, preferably one in your local area that you can visit. Draw to scale vignettes of the type illustrated in Figure 15–6. A scale of ¾ in. = 1 ft is suggested for the connection detail drawing and a scale of ¼ in. = 1 ft is suggested for the overview.

15–2 Repeat Question 15–1, except use a building made of poured-in-place reinforced concrete.

15–3 Repeat Question 15–1, except use a building made of precast reinforced concrete elements.

15–4 Repeat Question 15–1, except use a building employing laminated timber elements.

15–5 Visit four different buildings that each have a different type of structural system and measure the dimensions of critical structural elements (e.g., beams, columns, trusses). Convert this information into rule-of-thumb type of information (e.g., L/d ratios).

CHAPTER 16

Structural Connections

16–1 INTRODUCTION

How structural members join or meet is often a very critical design issue and one that can under certain circumstances influence the choice of the basic structural system itself, particularly its patterns and materials. The strategies possible in joining structural elements are strongly dependent on the physical properties and geometries of the elements to be joined. The following section only highlights basic design considerations.

16–2 BASIC JOINT GEOMETRIES

In the joining of simple linear rigid members, most joints that are prevalently used employ a strategy of either *lapping* the basic elements, *deforming and interlocking* them or *butting* them. Monolithic joints, particularly in reinforced concrete, are also possible.

Most joints using one or another of these basic strategies also commonly make use of some type of *third-element connector*. Bolts, nails, and welds are typical third-element connectors. Third-element connectors may also involve the use of additional pieces (e.g., cover plates). The basic function of such connecting elements or assemblies is to aid in transferring the total load present at the joint from one element to another. A bolt connecting two lapped pieces, for example, transfers forces from one member to another through shear forces developed in the bolt itself. As will be discussed below, however, not all joints necessarily have to employ third-element connectors to serve this function. When used, the connecting elements or devices are typically smaller in terms of absolute dimensions than are the primary elements and are of higher relative strength (e.g., bolts connecting two lapped timber elements). If of the same relative strength, connectors are often of necessity larger so that loads can be transferred safely.

Figure 16–1(a) illustrates several *butt* joints. Third-element connectors are most often used with such joints. Joints can be made either pinned or rigid as discussed previously. In joints of this general type it is usual that either the vertical or horizontal element can be made continuous through the joint, but rarely both. This caveat obviously has significant structural implications, since if continuity is desired both vertically and horizontally, it is necessary to use special rigid joints with at least some of the elements. In steel construction, for example, it is typical to make columns continuous and to frame beams into column sides. If frame action is desired, rigid joints are then made. Butt joints can be advantageously used for unusual horizontal framing patterns. Figure 16–1(a) illustrates how many horizontal members can frame into the same point in a column by use of a third-element connector (the circular shelf). In such cases the column is invariably continuous and the beams discontinuous unless special rigid connections are made.

Figure 16–1(b) illustrates several *lapped* joints. This approach is frequently used in timber construction to achieve continuity. This joinery strategy lends itself well to one-way framing systems. Complex patterns of connected elements are difficult to handle with this type of joint.

Figure 16–1(c) illustrates several joints in which members are *deformed* in order to make the connection. The strategy shown to the right in Figure 16–1(c) is often used with materials that are easily moldable, such as reinforced concrete. Many precast concrete building systems employ such joints. Timber elements can also be deformed to make connections. The ancient mortise-and-tendon joint is such a connection. By and large, these joints employ either simple or pinned connections between elements. It is, however, possible to make rigid connections.

Joints made by deforming and interlocking basic elements sometimes do not need obvious third-element connectors, nor do those which are made by taking advantage of the moldability properties of certain materials (such as reinforced concrete). The latter is considered as a subclass of a deformation strategy. Sometimes the use of a deformed and interlocking strategy means that the member must be made larger at the joint in order to accommodate the deformations. In some cases this increase may imply that the remainder of the member is made relatively larger also so that a constant-size member can be used. Occasionally, third-element connectors are used internally in deformed joints (e.g., in poured-in-place concrete special reinforcing steel is often used at joints).

16–3   BASIC TYPES OF CONNECTORS

General Considerations.   The types of third-element connectors that are commonly used in making joints can be characterized as either *point* connectors (e.g., bolts, nails, rivets), line connectors (e.g., welds), or *surface* connectors (e.g., glued surfaces) (see Figure 16–2). The general type of connector used depends largely on the specific physical nature and geometry of the elements to be joined. The joining of large rigid surfaces, for example, generally calls for the use of distributed connectors. Joining two sheets of plywood via a lapping approach by using a single bolt, for example, is not feasible, since very large localized stresses would develop in the plywood around the bolt as it attempts to transfer loads from one sheet to the other. Bearing failures

Common types of butt joints   Typical additional
                                            connecting elements

(a) Butt joints. Most butt joints require the use of one
    or more additional connecting elements to effect
    a load transfer from one element to another.

Common types of lap joints   Typical additional
                                           connecting elements

(b) Lap joints. Lap joints also typically require the use of
    one or more connecting elements to effect a load
    transfer from one element to another.

(c) Deformed and/or interlocking joints. Supplementary
    pieces are also often used but less reliance is placed on
    the supplementary pieces to transfer loads.

FIGURE 16–1   Basic types of joints.

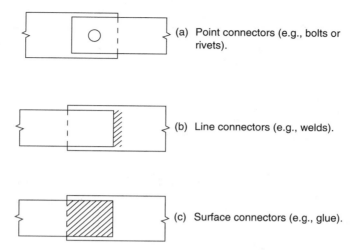

(a) Point connectors (e.g., bolts or rivets).

(b) Line connectors (e.g., welds).

(c) Surface connectors (e.g., glue).

FIGURE 16–2   Basic types of lap joint connectors.

would undoubtedly occur. A preferable approach would be to use a series of distributed smaller bolts such that the amount of load transferred by each bolt is relatively small. Alternatively, a lapped and glued joint is also possible, depending on the loads involved.

The general approach noted above of using a number of smaller distributed-point connectors (or line or surface connectors) is a useful one to consider for virtually any situation. While it is true that single point connectors can effectively be used in many situations (particularly those involving primary members having small dimensions), a distributed approach usually allows for reduced localized stress concentrations in the members joined, which is usually very advantageous or necessary.

Rigid Versus Pinned Joints.   The characteristics and importance of pinned and rigid joints have been discussed previously (Section 3–3–2). Single point connectors are, of course, clearly most appropriate for making pinned joints, while line and surface connectors lend themselves more to rigid joints. Point connectors, however, can be used to create rigid joints if at least two point connectors are used which are separated in space (e.g., at the top and the bottom of a member) so that a resisting internal moment can be developed. Forces developing in the separated point connections act over the involved moment arm and provide the resisting moment. The greater the separation in space, the smaller are the forces developed in the connectors for a given moment resistance (Figure 16–3).

For a rigid moment-resisting joint in steel, and in the case where the points of connection are separated a distance $d,$ the total tension or compression forces developed in the upper or lower points is given by $M = Td$ or $M = Cd$. The value of T or C obtained would then be used to determine the number of bolts or length of weld required along one of the upper or lower connection points. Thus, if $M = 48{,}000$ in.-lb and the depth of the section was $d = 12$ in., $T = C = M/d = 48{,}000/12 = 4000$ lb. Each weld line, as shown in Figure 16–3(b), would have to be designed to carry 4000 lb (see Section 16–3–2).

Undesirable type of
load transfer

Preferable type of
load transfer

Typical line or
surface connectors

(a) When surface elements are to be joined, it is usually best
to use either a surface or a line type of connector. Use of
single-point connectors leads to highly undesirable local
stresses in the surface elements at the point of connection.

Rigid joint

Pinned joint

Typical rigid connection

Typical pinned connection

(b) When pinned connections are required or desired, single
point connectors are most preferably used. Line and
surface connectors typically do not allow free rotation to
occur. When rigid joints are required or desired, either
multiple-point, line, or surface connections can be used.
Specific points of connection should be widely separated.

FIGURE 16–3   Selecting connector types.

Moment-resisting joints in reinforced concrete are easily made by using reinforcing steel on both faces of the attached members. Forces in the steel are again generally given by $M = Td = Cd$ for preliminary design purposes.

Moment-resisting joints in timber are difficult. The common knee brace, however, provides essentially the same function.

Line or surface connections can be used to approximate a pinned joint if localized in a region near the neutral axes of the connected members and if the extent of the joint is small relative to the size of the primary elements.

16–3–1   Bolts and Rivets

Simple lapped bolted joints rely on the shear capacity of the bolts to effect a load transfer between connected members. Many other types of bolted joints, however, do not depend on the shear capacity of the bolt at all for safety. Bolts are often tightened such that the frictional forces that develop between the compressed lapped plates that are joined are sufficient to effect a load transfer between elements. Obviously, bearing problems are reduced, as are other problematic phenomena. Care must be taken in field operations, however, to assure that bolts are adequately tightened. The following considers the simpler type of joints that rely only on the shear capacity of the bolts or rivets to transfer loads.

Bolts or rivets are usually used in situations involving lap joints. In a typical lap joint (see Figure 16–4) several types of failure are possible: a shear failure in the bolt, a tension failure in the reduced cross section of the loaded member, a crushing or bearing failure in the loaded member caused by excessively high bearing stresses at the interface with the bolt, a shear failure in the loaded member behind the bolt, and a tearing-out type of failure in the loaded member behind the bolt.

With respect to shear stresses, it is possible to assume reasonably that shearing stresses are uniformly distributed across the face of the bolt. This assumption is generally valid *if* the depth of the shearing area is small and the distance between shearing forces is also small. This is the type of condition that exists when a bolt is used to connect plates together. Such an approximation is not valid and would lead to unconservative answers in other situations involving large shearing areas and large distances between shear forces—the case in a common beam. If shear stresses can be assumed to be uniformly distributed, then they are simply given by $f_v = P/A$, where P is the applied load and A is the cross-sectional area of the bolt. The allowable load in shear for a bolt in the single shear state illustrated in Figure 16–4(a) is simply $P_v = AF_v$, where A is the cross-sectional area of the bolt and F_v is the allowable stress of the bolt in shear. Note that $P_v = (\pi d^2/4)F_v$.

◆ ◆ **EXAMPLE**

For a bolt in single shear, what bolt diameter is required if the shear force present, P_v, is 4000 lb (17,992 N)? Assume that $F_v = 14,000$ lb/in.^{2} (96.5 N/mm^2).

Solution:

Area required:

$$A = \frac{P_v}{F_v} = \frac{4000 \text{ lb}}{14,000 \text{ lb/in.}^2} = 0.285 \text{ in.}^2 = \frac{17,992}{96.5} = 184 \text{ mm}^2$$

Bolt in single shear

Bolt in double shear

(a) Bolted or riveted joint. Shear failure in bolt or rivet.

(b) Bearing failure in member due to excessively high bearing stresses at the interface between the bolt and the member.

(c) Tension failure in member at reduced cross section caused by bolt hole.

(d) Shear failure in plate due to insufficient plate thickness and/or end dimensions.

(e) Tearing failure due to insufficient plate thickness and/or end dimensions.

FIGURE 16–4 Types of failure in bolted or riveted joints.

Diameter required:

$$\frac{\pi d^2}{4} = 0.285 \text{ in.}^2 \quad \text{or} \quad d = 0.605 \text{ in.}$$

$$= 184 \text{ mm}^2 \quad \text{or} \quad d = 15.3 \text{ mm}$$

The nearest-stock-size bolt would be used. When a bolt is in the double-shear state illustrated in Figure 16–4(a), two shear planes are present and thus $P_v = 2(\pi d^2/4)F_v$. ◆

Bearing stresses can be found by simply $f_b = P/A_b$, where A_b is the area of the bolt and plate interface. A_b is usually taken as the projected area of the bolt, or $A = td$. Thus, $f_b = P/td$. Bearing stresses often control the design of a joint. Bearing stresses can evidently be reduced either by increasing the thickness of the plate present or by increasing the diameter of the bolt. If a 300-lb tension force is transmitted through a lap joint connecting two ½-in.-thick plywood members via a ¾-in.-diameter bolt in single shear, the bearing stresses developed in the plywood would be given by $f_b = P/td = (300)/(\frac{1}{2})(\frac{3}{4}) = 800 \text{ lb/in.}^2$ A typical allowable bearing stress would be on the order of 400 lb/in.², so the plywood is considerably overstressed and would probably crush around the bolt. Since the bolt itself is easily large enough, increasing plate thicknesses or using multiple bolts to increase the bearing area would be necessary.

The plates themselves must be carefully designed to accommodate bolts. The net area of the plate through a section rather than its gross area should be used in stress calculations. End distances must be made sufficiently large to prevent tear-out failures of the type illustrated from occurring. When multiple bolts are used, a kind of zigzag failure between closely spaced bolts may occur that must be guarded against (typically, by increasing spacings and plate thicknesses).

When multiple bolts are used in slender axially loaded members (e.g., truss members), they should be placed at centroids of members to prevent their being twisted. In larger members and when multiple bolts are necessitated, they are often arranged in a staggered pattern, with suitable distances between them to prevent the zigzag failure noted from occurring.

Other types of allowable loads for the connected elements can be found similarly simply by considering the area of the probable failure plane (A_p) and noting that $P_{max} = F_p A_p$, where F_p is the allowable stress for the material failure mode present.

When bolts are not symmetrically loaded, care must be taken to include in the load calculations any forces induced by the torque or twisting action of the imbalanced load (see F. L. Singer, *Strength of Materials,* 2d ed., Harper & Row, New York, 1962, Chap. 12).

16–3–2 Welded Joints

Welding is the joining of metals by fusion. High heat melts and fuses metal from a welding rod onto the plates being connected. A continuous and homogenous joint results. There are a huge number of different types of welded joints. Most are, however, a variant of either a butt weld or a fillet weld (see Figure 16–5).

The strength of a unit length of a butt weld in tension is simply equal to the allowable stress of the weld material in tension times the minimum thickness of the weld. For a specific thickness, the length of weld used is directly proportional to the load to be transmitted.

The strength of a fillet weld is dependent on the shear resistance of the weld since failure normally occurs at the throat of the weld. In a 45° weld with a leg thickness t, the shearing area through the throat is $A = Lt \sin 45°$, where L is the length of the weld. Thus, the strength of the

(a) Butt weld.

(b) Fillet weld.

(c) Fillet welds.

(c) Failure in a fillet weld typically occurs at the minimum cross section of the weld (at the "throat").

FIGURE 16–5 Welded joints.

weld is given by $P = AF_v = L(0.707t)(F_v)$. A common allowable stress is $F_v = 13,600$ lb/in.^{2} Thus, $P = 9600tL$. In terms of a $\frac{1}{16}$-in. weld 1 in. long, $P = (9600$ lb/in.$)(\frac{1}{16}$ in.$) = 600$ lb/in. Values such as this are useful for quickly estimating required weld lengths and thicknesses to carry given loads. A load of 4800 lb, for example, requires 8 in. of a $\frac{1}{16}$-in. weld, 4 in. of $\frac{1}{8}$-in. weld, or 2 in. of $\frac{1}{4}$-in. weld.

As with bolts, care must be taken to account for additional torque forces induced in weld joints by nonsymmetrically applied forces. Often, loads may look symmetrically applied and welds may look symmetrically placed, as when an angle member is welded to a plate, but the welds may be unequally loaded because the centroid of the member is nonsymmetrical and hence so is the applied load.

QUESTIONS

16–1 Examine and draw diagrams of several different types of structural joints found in buildings in your local area. Classify the joints as lapped, butt, or deformed (or a combination thereof). Are third element connectors present?

16–2 With respect to shear stresses alone, what is the required diameter for a bolt in single shear that transfers a shear force of 6000 lb between two plates? Assume that $F_v = 14,000$ lb/in.^{2}

Answer: $\frac{3}{4}$-in. diameter.

16–3 How many inches of ⅛-in. weld are necessary to transfer a shear force of 6000 lb from one plate to another? Assume that $F_v = 13,600$ lb/in.^{2}

   Answer: 5 in.

16–4 Will a bolt ½ in. in diameter used in double shear carry a force of 2000 lb? What is the shear stress present?

   Answer: Yes. $f_v = 5128$ lb/in.^{2}

16–5 Two ¼-in.-thick plywood sheets are joined by a ⅜-in. diameter bolt that transfers a shear force of 500 lb. Assume that the allowable stress in bearing for the plywood is 400 lb/in.^{2} Is the plywood overstressed in bearing?

   Answer: $f_{bg} = 533$-in. plywood (overstressed).

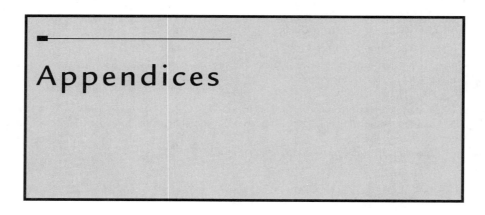

APPENDIX 1:   CONVERSIONS

In the SI system, the *newton* (N) is the basic unit of force. The weight of a 1-kg mass is taken as 9.807 N. Stresses are given in *pascal* (Pa); 1 Pa = 1 N/m² and 1 MPa = 1 N/mm². Note that: 1 lb = 4.448 N; 1 ft-lb = 1.356 N·m; 1 lb/ft² = 47.88 N/m² = 47.88 Pa; 1lb/in.²= 0.006895 N/mm². Also note that 1.0 kip = 1000 lb and 1 ksi = 1000 lb/in.²

APPENDIX 2:   NONCONCURRENT FORCE SYSTEMS

In many situations a varied series of forces act on a structure. Often the lines of action of these forces do not meet at a single point, hence they are called *nonconcurrent* forces. It is frequently useful to convert a complex set of nonconcurrent forces into a single *statically equivalent force* that produces translational and rotational effects on the structure that are the same as the original force set. Figure A–2–1 illustrates the process for finding a statically equivalent force.

APPENDIX 3:   CENTROIDS

The center of mass is that point which represents the mean position of matter in a body. The center of gravity of a body essentially represents the position of the resultant of the earth's

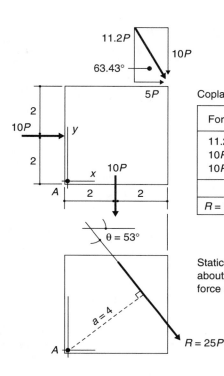

Coplanar nonparallel force system

Force	F_x	F_y	Moment of F_x	Moment of F_y
11.2P	5P	10P	(4)(5P) = 20P	(4)(10P) = 40P
10P	10P	0	(2)(10P) = 20P	0
10P	0	10P	0	(2)(10P) = 20P
	$\Sigma F_x = 15P$	$\Sigma F_y = 20P$	$\Sigma M_x = 40P$	$\Sigma M_y = 60P$
$R = [(15P)^2 + (20P)^2]^{1/2} = 25P$			$\Sigma M_A = 100P$	

(Reference point A)

Statically equivalent force system—a force R acting at a distance a about A produces an effect on the body equivalent to the original force system.

Resultant force = R = 25P
Resultant moment = R(a) = 100P
Moment arm of resultant force:
$a = \Sigma M_A/R = 100P/25P = 4.0$
$\theta = \tan^{-1} = \Sigma F_y/\Sigma F_x = 20P/15P = 53°$

FIGURE A–2–1 Nonparallel forces: finding statically equivalent force systems.

gravitational pull on a body and is thus that point in a body from or on which the body can be perfectly balanced or poised in equilibrium. Strictly speaking, the concept of center of gravity is applicable only to bodies having weight. The term *centroid* is used to describe the analogous point in a geometric form such as a line or area. The centroid of an area can be defined as that point at which the entire area may be conceived to be concentrated and have the same moment with respect to any axis as the original distributed area. With respect to this definition, it may be useful to visualize the geometric figure considered, such as a planar area, as a sheet of constant infinitesimal thickness which has a uniform mass per unit area. This makes the analogy with the center of gravity of a body more direct. Thus, the centroid of an area can be visualized as that point on which a geometric figure can be balanced. For a plane area in the *xy* plane and with respect to any arbitrary reference line, the coordinates of the centroid are

$$\bar{x} = \frac{\int_A x \, dA}{A} \qquad \bar{y} = \frac{\int_A y \, dA}{A}$$

$\bar{x}$ and $\bar{y}$ define the location of the centroid from the reference line. The algebraic sum of the moments of each elementary area unit with respect to a given point or line is equal to the moment of total area about the same point or line. The terms *x dA* and *y dA* are often referred to as the *first*

Centroid at point of symmetry

(a) Symmetrical section.

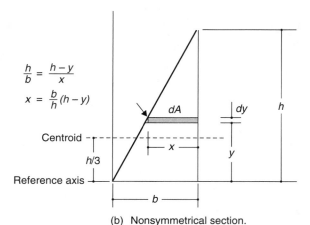

$$\frac{h}{b} = \frac{h-y}{x}$$

$$x = \frac{b}{h}(h-y)$$

Centroid

Reference axis

(b) Nonsymmetrical section.

FIGURE A–3–1   Centroids of geometric figures.

moments of the area about the reference line. If the reference axis used actually coincides with the centroidal axis (i.e., $\bar{x} = 0$, $\bar{y} = 0$), it follows that $\int_{A_c} x \, dA = 0$ and $\int_{A_c} y \, dA = 0$.

When an area is symmetrical with respect to an axis, the centroid invariably coincides with the axis of symmetry (see Figure A–3–1). This follows from the fact that the moments of the areas on opposite sides of the axis are equal in magnitude but opposite in sign. For areas having more than one axis of symmetry, the centroid must be a point that lies at the intersection of the axes of symmetry.

Determining the location of the centroid of an area is a straightforward process based on the use of the equations for $\bar{x}$ and $\bar{y}$. Any set of reference axes can be used to find the centroid of an area. The process for finding the centroid of a common figure, a triangle, will be illustrated. The base of the triangle is arbitrarily selected as a reference axis.

◆ ◆ **EXAMPLE**

Find the centroid for the triangle indicated in Figure A–3–1.

Solution: First set up the expression

$$\bar{y} = \frac{\int_A y \, dA}{A} = \frac{\int_A y \, dA}{\int dA} \quad \text{and} \quad dA = x \, dy = \frac{b}{h}(h-y)\,dy$$

Hence,

$$\bar{y} = \frac{\int_0^h y[(b/h)(h-y)]\,dy}{\int_0^h (b/h)(h-y)\,dy} = \frac{1}{3}h$$

◆

Many complex figures, commonly referred to as *composite areas,* can be considered as composed of simpler geometric shapes. If a given area can indeed be divided into parts (whose individual centroidal locations are known), the location of the centroid for the whole composite figure can be found without integration. This is done by obtaining the algebraic sum of the area moments of each individual part about a refence axis and dividing by the total area of the composite figure. This procedure follows from the definitions cited previously. Stated formally:

$$\bar{x} = \frac{\Sigma A_{x_i}}{A_T} \qquad \bar{y} = \frac{\Sigma A_{y_i}}{A_T}$$

These expressions are obviously similar in character to $\bar{x} = \int_A x \, dA/A$ and $\bar{y} = \int_A y \, dA/A$. An example of how this expression is applied is given in Chapter 6.

APPENDIX 4:   MOMENTS OF INERTIA

A–4–1   General Formulation

One of the most common expressions encountered in the analysis of structures is of the form $\int y^2 dA$. This expression is the *moment of inertia* (*I*) of the area. Examined by itself, it has little physical meaning. In the context of analyzing beams, columns, and other elements, however, it is of paramount importance as a general descriptor of the amount and way in which material in the element is organized or distributed with reference to the cross section.

The moment of inertia of an area with respect to an axis in the plane of the area can be defined as the sum of the products obtained by multiplying each element of the area by the square of its distance from this axis. Thus, the moments of inertia of an area with respect to the *x* and *y* axes are

$$I_x = \int_A y^2 \, dA \qquad I_y = \int_A x^2 \, dA$$

Strictly speaking, the name *moment of inertia* is misleading, since inertia is a property of physical bodies only. Since the preceding could be written as $I_x = \int_A y(y \, dA)$ and $I_y = \int_A x(x \, dA)$, the term *second moment of the area* is often considered preferable. The first moment of an area, as noted in the preceding section, is of the form $x \, dA$ or $y \, dA$; hence, multiplying this term by the distance again yields the second moment of the area. Although the first moment of an area about an axis can be either positive or negative, the second moment is always positive. The term *moment of inertia,* however, is widely used and is used here.

◆ ◆   **EXAMPLE**

Consider the rectangle shown in Figure A–4–1. Determine the moment of inertia, *I,* of the area with respect to its centroidal axis (which is, by inspection, midheight). Any other reference axis could be used, but selecting the centroidal axis is most meaningful in the context of analyzing beams or columns since the minimum *I* value for the section is obtained about this axis.

FIGURE A–4–1 Moment of inertia of a rectangle.

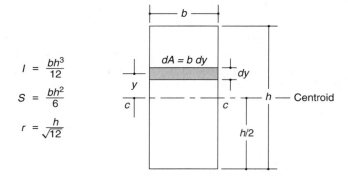

$$I = \frac{bh^3}{12}$$

$$S = \frac{bh^2}{6}$$

$$r = \frac{h}{\sqrt{12}}$$

Solution:

$$I_c = \int_A y^2 \, dA \quad \text{and} \quad dA = b \, dy$$

$$\therefore I_c = \int_{-h/2}^{+h/2} y^2 (b \, dy) = b \left[\frac{y^3}{3} \right]_{-h/2}^{+h/2}$$

$$\therefore I_c = \frac{bh^3}{12}$$

◆

For some shapes, such as circles, it is often more convenient to use polar coordinates rather than cartesian coordinates to find I values.

Figure A–4–2 gives moment of inertia values for many common geometric figures.

A–4–2 Parallel-Axis Theorem

If the moment of inertia of a figure with respect to its centroidal axis is known, the moment of inertia with respect to *any* parallel axis may be found quite easily. Doing this is a particularly useful tool in determining the moment of inertia of a composite area.

The area illustrated in Figure A–4–3 has a centroidal location c and a moment of inertia about its own axis of $\bar{I}$. The moment of inertia of this same area about a parallel axis located a constant distance d from the centroidal axis is given by $I_T = \int_A r^2 \, dA = \int_A (y + d)^2 \, dA = \int_A y^2 \, dA + 2d \int_A y \, dA + d^2 \int_A dA$. The first term, $\int_A y^2 \, dA$, in the expanded expression is the moment of inertia of the area about its own centroidal axis $\bar{I}$. The second term, $2d \int_A y \, dA$, is equal to zero since it involves $\int_A y \, dA$, which is simply the first moment of the area about its own centroidal axis (as noted in the discussion on centroids, this value is identically equal to zero when the reference axis corresponds to the centroid of a figure). The final term, $d^2 \int_A dA$, is more simply $d^2 A$, where A is the total area of the figure. The expression becomes $I_T = \bar{I} + Ad^2$. Thus, the moment of inertia for the area with respect to any axis in the same plane is equal to the moment of inertia of the area about its own axis plus a transfer term composed of the product of the square of the distance between axes and the area of the figure. This implies that

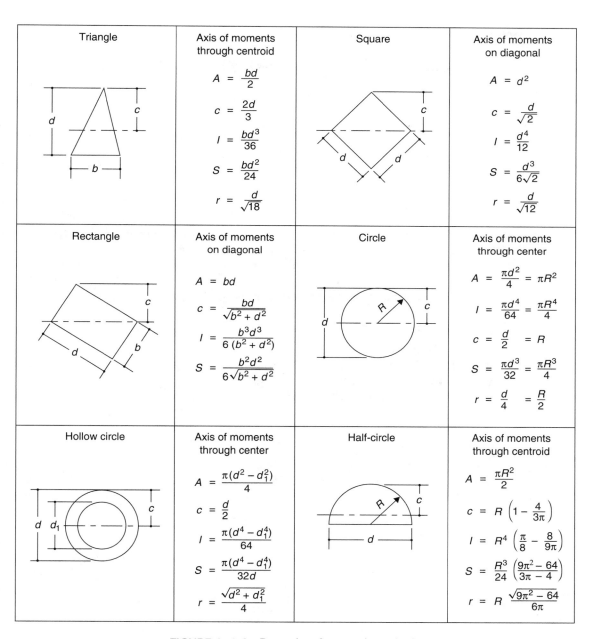

Triangle	Axis of moments through centroid	Square	Axis of moments on diagonal
	$A = \dfrac{bd}{2}$		$A = d^2$
	$c = \dfrac{2d}{3}$		$c = \dfrac{d}{\sqrt{2}}$
	$I = \dfrac{bd^3}{36}$		$I = \dfrac{d^4}{12}$
	$S = \dfrac{bd^2}{24}$		$S = \dfrac{d^3}{6\sqrt{2}}$
	$r = \dfrac{d}{\sqrt{18}}$		$r = \dfrac{d}{\sqrt{12}}$
Rectangle	Axis of moments on diagonal	Circle	Axis of moments through center
	$A = bd$		$A = \dfrac{\pi d^2}{4} = \pi R^2$
	$c = \dfrac{bd}{\sqrt{b^2 + d^2}}$		$I = \dfrac{\pi d^4}{64} = \dfrac{\pi R^4}{4}$
	$I = \dfrac{b^3 d^3}{6\,(b^2 + d^2)}$		$c = \dfrac{d}{2} = R$
	$S = \dfrac{b^2 d^2}{6\sqrt{b^2 + d^2}}$		$S = \dfrac{\pi d^3}{32} = \dfrac{\pi R^3}{4}$
			$r = \dfrac{d}{4} = \dfrac{R}{2}$
Hollow circle	Axis of moments through center	Half-circle	Axis of moments through centroid
	$A = \dfrac{\pi(d^2 - d_1^2)}{4}$		$A = \dfrac{\pi R^2}{2}$
	$c = \dfrac{d}{2}$		$c = R\left(1 - \dfrac{4}{3\pi}\right)$
	$I = \dfrac{\pi(d^4 - d_1^4)}{64}$		$I = R^4 \left(\dfrac{\pi}{8} - \dfrac{8}{9\pi}\right)$
	$S = \dfrac{\pi(d^4 - d_1^4)}{32d}$		$S = \dfrac{R^3}{24}\left(\dfrac{9\pi^2 - 64}{3\pi - 4}\right)$
	$r = \dfrac{\sqrt{d^2 + d_1^2}}{4}$		$r = R\,\dfrac{\sqrt{9\pi^2 - 64}}{6\pi}$

FIGURE A–4–2 Properties of geometric sections.

FIGURE A–4–3 Moment of inertia of an area about an axis located a distance d away from the centroid of the area.

$$I_T = \int_A r^2 \, dA = \int_A (y + d)^2 \, dA$$

$$= \int_A y^2 \, dA + 2d \int_A y \, dA + d^2 \int_A dA = \bar{I} + Ad^2$$

the minimum moment of inertia a figure can have is about its own centroidal axis. This is why the centroidal axis is often used as reference axis when applied to engineering calculations.

The only time the moments of inertia of individual areas forming a larger composite shape can be added directly is when their individual axes coincide with that of the larger composite shape. In such a situation $d = 0$ for each individual shape. Hence, $I = \Sigma \, (\bar{I} + Ad^2) = \Sigma \, (\bar{I})$.

A–4–3 Negative Areas

In many symmetrical shapes it is often convenient to decompose the figure into what are commonly termed positive and negative areas. A *positive area* adds to the actual area or figure and contributes positively to the moment of inertia of the figure, while a *negative area* produces converse effects. This is merely an alternative way of looking at what has been discussed just previously.

◆ ◆ **EXAMPLE**

Determine the moment of inertia of the cross-sectional shape shown in Figure A–4–4. Assume that $b_1 = 10$ in. (254 mm), $h_1 = 10$ in. (254 mm), $b_2 = 8$ in. (203.2 mm), and $h_2 = 6$ in. (152.4 mm). Note that $d_1 = d_2 = 0$, hence $I = \Sigma \, (\bar{I})$.

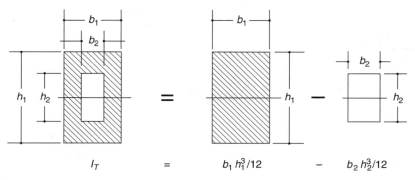

FIGURE A–4–4 Holes in symmetrical cross-sectional shapes can be treated as negative areas having negative moments of inertia.

Solution:

$$I_T = I_{positive} - I_{negative} = \frac{10 \text{ in.} \times (10 \text{ in.})^3}{12} - \frac{8 \text{ in.} \times (6 \text{ in.})^3}{12} = 689 \text{ in.}^4$$

$$= \frac{(254 \text{ mm}) \times (254 \text{ mm})^3}{12} - \frac{(203.2 \text{ mm}) \times (152.4 \text{ mm})^3}{12} = 286,900 \times 10^3 \text{ mm}^4$$

◆

APPENDIX 5: BENDING STRESSES IN BEAMS

As noted in Chapter 6, the effect of bending is to produce deformations in the beam fibers of the type illustrated in Figure A–5–1. It should be noted that while a plane of zero deformation and zero bending stresses (i.e., the *neutral axis*) is known to exist, its exact location is not known a priori. Finding the location of this plane is a necessary prerequisite to further analysis. This surface can be located by considering the equilibrium of the beam in the horizontal direction.

Assume that the maximum stress on a face a distance c from the neutral axis is designated f_{bmax}. The stress f_y at an arbitrary distance y from the neutral axis can be found through simple proportions [i.e., $f_y/y = f_{bmax}/c$ or $f_y = (y/c)(f_{bmax})$]. At a level defined by y, the force associated with the stresses f_y is simply $f_y\, dA$. The total force in the horizontal direction produced by the entire stress field is merely $\int f_y\, dA$. We also know that $\Sigma F_x = 0$. If there are no external horizontal forces acting on the beam, the total force produced by the tensile and compressive components of the whole stress field must total zero. Hence, $\int_A f_y\, dA = 0$. Expressing f_y in terms of the maximum stress, the outer fiber of the beam, we have $(f_{bmax}/c) \int_A y\, dA = 0$. Since (f_{bmax}/c) cannot be zero, it follows that $\int_A y\, dA = 0$. The quantity $\int_y dA$ is termed the *first moment* or *centroid* of the area of the beam with respect to the neutral axis (see Appendix 3). The quantity $\int_A y\, dA = 0$ defines the centroidal axis of a geometric figure and is readily calculable for any type of beam configuration. In the context of this analysis, the surfacing of the term $\int_A y\, dA = 0$ means that the neutral axis of a beam corresponds with the centroidal axis of the cross-sectional shape of the beam.

FIGURE A–5–1   Bending stresses in beams.

It was noted above that the sum of the elemental forces produced by the stresses in the horizontal direction had to equal zero from equilibrium considerations (i.e., $\Sigma F_x = 0$). Note that for $\Sigma M = 0$ the sum of the *moments* produced by these elemental forces about the neutral axis must equal the applied external moment. The moment of an elemental force about the neutral axis must equal the applied external moment. The moment of an elemental force about the neutral axis is simply $y(f_y \, dA)$ or $y(f_{bmax})(y/c) \, dA$. The sum of the moments of all these elemental forces becomes $(f_{bmax}/c) \int_A y^2 \, dA$. This, then, is the internal resisting moment, M_R, which identically equals the applied external moment, M_E. Thus, $M = (f_{bmax}/c) \int_A y^2 \, dA$. The term $\int_A y^2 \, dA$ is commonly called the *second moment* of an area when encountered in mathematics, and the *moment of inertia, I,* of an area in an engineering context. In general, it is a descriptor of the amount and way material in a beam is organized or distributed in a cross section (see Appendix 4).

The final expression relating the maximum bending stresses (f_{bmax}) to the properties of the cross section (defined by $I = \int_A y^2 \, dA$ evaluated about the neutral or centroidal axis of the cross section) and the moment M present at the section becomes $f_{bmax} = Mc/I$. The stress at any location y from the neutral axis is $f_y = My/I$.

APPENDIX 6:   SHEARING STRESSES IN BEAMS

This appendix derives relationships among the physical characteristics of a beam, the forces acting on the beam, and the shearing stresses that are developed in the beam as a consequence of these forces. *Horizontal shearing stresses* will be studied first.

Consider an infinitesimal element of a beam as illustrated in Figure A–6–1. As is typical in any beam, the bending moment, and consequently the bending stresses, will be larger at one section than the other. For equilibrium in the horizontal direction, a horizontal shear force must be developed as indicated in Figure A–6–1 to balance the difference in force produced by the action

FIGURE A–6–1   Horizontal shear stresses in beams.

of bending. If f_h represents the average shear stress over the differential area of length dx and width b, and if one expresses the bending forces in terms of the bending stresses acting on the beam, then equilibrium considerations in the horizontal direction yield the following:

$$\underbrace{f_h(b\ dx)}_{dH} = \underbrace{\int_{y_1}^{c}\left(\frac{M_2 y}{I}\right) dA}_{F_2} - \underbrace{\int_{y_1}^{c}\left(\frac{M_1 y}{I}\right) dA}_{F_1}$$

or, noting that $M_2 - M_1$ represents the differential change in moment between the distance dx and $dM/dx = V$ (the vertical shear force):

$$f_h = \frac{dM}{Ib\ dx}\int_{y_1}^{c} y\ dA \qquad \therefore \qquad f_h = \frac{V}{Ib}\int_{y_1}^{c} y\ dA$$

The integral $\int_{y_1}^{c} y\ dA$ is the first moment of the area *above the horizontal section considered* (and where the horizontal shear stresses in the expression above are located) with respect to the neutral axis of the beam. This integral is commonly denoted Q. Hence,

$$f_h = \frac{VQ}{Ib}$$

This is the general expression for horizontal shearing stress in a beam of any cross section. Note that the maximum shear stress occurs at the point where $\int_{y_1}^{c} y\ dA$ is maximum. This occurs when the horizontal section considered coincides with the neutral axis.

In a *rectangular beam,* the distribution of shearing stress can be found by setting up a general expression for the shear stress for a layer a distance y from the neutral axis. For a rectangular beam:

$$Q = \int_{y_1}^{c} y\ dA = \bar{y} A = \left[b\left(\frac{h}{2} - y\right)\right]\left[y + \frac{1}{2}\left(\frac{h}{2} - y\right)\right]$$

Thus,

$$f = \frac{VQ}{Ib} = \frac{V}{2I}(h^2/4 - y^2)$$

This relationship indicates that the shearing stress is parabolically distributed. As is evident, the maximum shear stress occurs at $y = 0$ (the neutral axis).

At any point in a beam, the horizontal shearing stress is accompanied by an equal vertical shearing stress f_v. This can be demonstrated in a variety of ways. A simple way is to look at the equilibrium of a typical element in a beam (see Figure A–6–1) subjected only to shear. By summing the moments of the forces produced by the stresses acting on the element, we find that $f_h(dx\ dz)\ dy - f_v(dy\ dz)(dx) = 0$ and $f_h = f_v$. It is this vertical shear stress that actually forms the resisting shear force, $V_R = \int f_v\ dA$, which equilibrates the external applied shear force, V_E. Since $f_h = f_v$, the distribution of the vertical shear on the face of a cross section is described for the horizontal shear stresses. This is the only way of finding the distribution of vertical shearing stresses in a beam.

APPENDIX 7: MOMENT-CURVATURE RELATIONS

This appendix explores the relation between the moment at a point and the curvature of the member at the same point. Consider an elemental portion of a member subject to bending (see Figure A–7–1). Assuming that initially plane sections in the member remain plane under the action of bending, the two adjacent planes bounding the element considered undergo a relative rotation ($d\theta$) because of the bending. The fibers at the top of the member are shortened and those at the bottom lengthened. The elongation of a typical fiber at a distance y from the neutral surface (the horizontal plane of zero deformation) may be found by considering the initial undistorted location of the two planes. The elongation is the arc of a circle having a radius y and subtended by the angle $d\theta$, or the elongation $= y\, d\theta$. If the original undeformed length of the element is a length dx and the strain (deformation per unit length) at y is ϵ_y, then $y\, d\theta = \epsilon_y\, dx$ or $\epsilon_y = y(d\theta/dx)$ or $(d\theta/dx) = \epsilon_y/y$.

From inspecting Figure A–7–1 it can also be seen that the radius of curvature, ρ, for the whole beam and dx are related through the expression $dx = \rho\, d\theta$, since the length dx at the middle surface is the arc of a circle of radius ρ and subtended by $d\theta$. Note that $(d\theta/dx) = 1/\rho$. Equating the two expressions for $d\theta/dx$: $1/\rho = \epsilon_y/y$ or $\epsilon_y = y/\rho$.

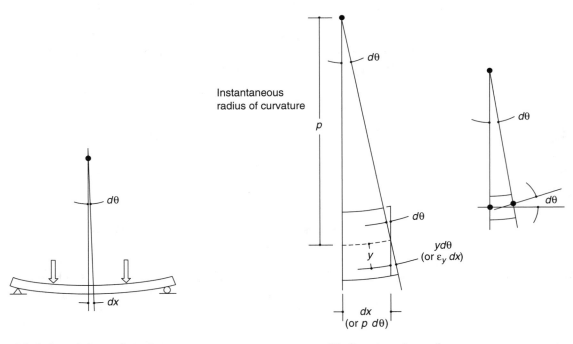

Instantaneous
radius of curvature

(a) Deflected shape of structure.

(b) Curvature at a section.

FIGURE A–7–1 Moment-curvature relation: $1/\rho = M/EI$.

The relation between stress and strain in a homogeneous elastic material is $E = f_y/\epsilon_y$. Alternatively, $\epsilon_y = (1/E)f_y$. From the study of bending stresses we know that $f_y = My/I$. Thus $\epsilon_y = (1/E)(My/I)$, or $y/\rho = (1/E)(My/I)$. Consequently, $1/\rho = M/EI$.

This is the *moment-curvature relationship*. The instantaneous radius of curvature (ρ) is directly dependent on the magnitude of the moment (M) in a member and inversely dependent on the product of the modulus of elasticity (E) and moment of inertia (I) for the member. Note that if $M = 0$, then $\rho \rightarrow \infty$, indicating that the member is straight (as it must obviously be under no moment). As the moment increases, the radius of curvature becomes smaller, indicating that the member is being more sharply curved or bowed under the action of the load.

APPENDIX 8: DEFLECTIONS

A–8–1 General Differential Equation

The expression $1/\rho = M/EI$ found in Appendix 7 may be alternatively expressed in terms of the deflection curve of the member. If the curve is defined by $y = y(x)$, then from basic calculus it is known that

$$\frac{1}{\rho} = \frac{(d^2y/dx^2)}{[1 + (dy/dx)^2]^{3/2}} \approx \frac{d^2y}{dx^2}$$

The expression dy/dx is the slope of the member at any point. For small deflections, the square of this term is negligible in comparison to other terms. Consequently,

$$\frac{d^2y}{dx^2} = \frac{M}{EI} \quad \text{or} \quad M = \left(\frac{d^2y}{dx^2}\right)EI$$

This is the basic differential equation for the deflection curve of a member subjected to bending.

A–8–2 Deflections: Double-Integration Method

The deflection of a beam at any point can be found by direct application of the result found above ($d^2y/dx^2 = M/EI$).

◆ ◆ EXAMPLE

Consider the cantilever beam illustrated in Figure A–8–1, and assume that it is desired to know the deflection at the end of the member. Assume that E and I are constant along the length of the beam.

Solution: The moment at x is given by $M_x = -wx^2/2$. Hence,

$$\frac{d^2y}{dx^2} = \frac{1}{EI}\left(-\frac{wx^2}{2}\right)$$

$$y_x = \frac{1}{EI}\left[-\frac{wx^4}{24} + \frac{wL^3x}{6} - \frac{wL^4}{8}\right]$$

FIGURE A–8–1 Deflections in a uniformly loaded cantilever beam.

This equation can be integrated once to yield

$$\frac{dy}{dx} = \frac{1}{EI}\left(-\frac{wx^3}{6} + C_1\right)$$

where C_1 is a constant of integration. It can be found by using the boundary condition that the slope of the beam, dy/dx, is zero at $x = L$. C_1 can be found to be $wL^3/6$. Thus,

$$\frac{dy}{dx} = \frac{1}{EI}\left(-\frac{wx^3}{6} + \frac{wL^3}{6}\right)$$

The latter is the equation for the slope of the beam at any point x. Integrating once more,

$$y = \frac{1}{EI}\left(-\frac{wx^4}{24} + \frac{wL^3x}{6} + C_2\right)$$

where C_2 is the second constant of integration, which can be found by noting that the deflection y at $x = L$ is zero. $C_2 = -wL^4/8$.

$$y = \frac{1}{EI}\left(-\frac{wx^4}{24} + \frac{wL^3x}{6} - \frac{wL^4}{8}\right)$$

This is the basic equation for the deflected shape of the member. The maximum deflection occurs at $x = 0$. Hence,

$$y_{max} = -\frac{wL^4}{8EI}$$

Note that the boundary conditions are extremely important and must be handled with care.

Deflections resultant from any loading condition on any type of member can be evaluated similarly. Also note that if E and I were not constant along the length of the member, they would also have to be expressed as a function of x. ◆

APPENDIX 9: MOMENT-AREA THEOREMS: SLOPES AND DEFLECTIONS

The *moment-area theorems* are a powerful tool in structural analysis. In Appendix 7 on moment-curvature relations, it was noted that with reference to Figure A–7–1 that $d\theta/dx = 1/\rho$ and that $1/\rho = M/EI$. Consequently, $d\theta/dx = M/EI$ or $d\theta = (M/EI)\,dx$.

With reference to Figure A–7–1, it can also be seen that $d\theta$ also represents the angular change between two points on the structure. Thus, the expression $d\theta = (M/EI)\,dx$ states that the change in slope in a distance dx is equal to $(M/EI)\,dx$. The total change in slope between two points A and B in a member then becomes

$$\theta_B - \theta_A = \int_A^B \left(\frac{M}{EI}\right) dx$$

This is the first of the moment-area theorems: *The change in slope between the tangents to the curve of the beam at two points is identical to the area under the M/EI diagram between those two points.*

The second moment-area theorem relates to deflections. For a structure undergoing the small deflections typically encountered in a real structure, the deviation ($d\Delta$) of one point on a structure with respect to the tangent drawn through another point x distance away is simply $d\Delta = x\,d\theta$. Combining $d\Delta = x\,d\theta$ with $d\theta = (M/EI)\,dx$, we obtain $d\Delta = (Mx/EI)\,dx$. The total change between two points A and B is given by

$$\Delta_B - \Delta_A = \int_A^B \left(\frac{Mx}{EI}\right) dx$$

Or, *the deviation of a tangent to the deflection curve at one point with respect to the tangent at another is identical to the first moment of the area of the M/EI diagram between the two points about the point at which the deviation is sought.*

◆ ◆ **EXAMPLE**

Consider the beam illustrated in Figure A–9–1. Find the slope and deflection at the end of the beam using the moment-area theorems.

Solution: The first step is to draw the moment diagram. The change in slope from A to B is given by

$$\theta_B - \theta_A = \int_A^B \left(\frac{M}{EI}\right) dx = \frac{1}{EI}\int_0^L (-Px)\,dx = -\frac{P}{EI}\left[\frac{x^2}{2}\right]_0^L$$

Since $\theta_B = 0$, $\theta_A = +PL^2/2EI$ (radians). In this case the angle found also represents the slope of the free end with respect to the horizontal, since $\theta_B = 0$. The deflection at the end can be found through application of the second moment-area theorem. Noting that the tangent of the member at B is horizontal, the expression for the deviation of point A with respect to the tangent through point B becomes coincidental with the absolute deflection of the beam with respect to the horizontal. Thus,

$$y_{max} = \Delta_B - \Delta_A = \int_A^B \left(\frac{M}{EI}\right) x\,dx = \frac{1}{EI}\int_0^L (-Px)\,x\,dx = -\frac{PL^3}{3EI}$$

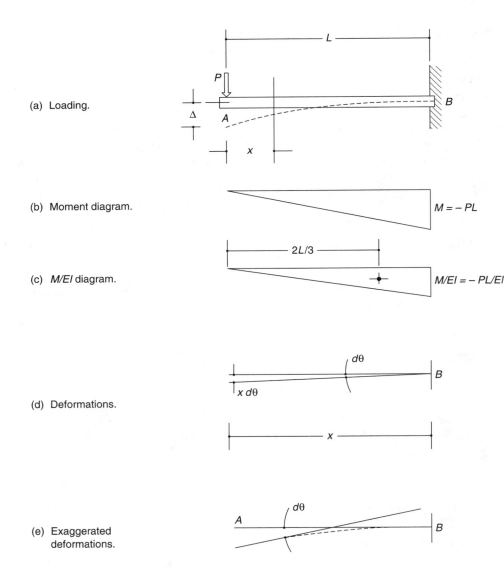

(a) Loading.

(b) Moment diagram.

(c) M/EI diagram.

(d) Deformations.

(e) Exaggerated deformations.

FIGURE A–9–1 Application of moment-area theorems.

Although moment-area expressions can be integrated directly as just illustrated, it is more common to evaluate the area and first moment of the M/EI diagram directly from the moment diagram. Thus,

$$\theta = \left(\frac{PL}{EI}\right)(L)\left(\frac{1}{2}\right) = \frac{PL^2}{2EI}$$

$$y_{max} = \Delta_B - \Delta_A = \left(\frac{PL}{EI}\right)(L)\left(\frac{1}{2}\right)\left(\frac{2L}{3}\right) = \frac{PL^3}{3EI}$$

This example is rather simple since it is known that θ_B is horizontal and Δ_B is zero.

◆

◆ ◆ **EXAMPLE**

Find the deflection of the member shown in Figure A–9–2 at midspan.

(a) Loading.

(b) M/EI diagram.

(c) Deformations.

FIGURE A–9–2 Application of moment-area theorems.

Solution: The moment diagram is first drawn. In this case it is evident that the slope of the beam is not zero at either support but must be zero at midspan because of symmetry. The deviation of point C from the tangent to the elastic curve at B is thus equivalent to the total deflection at B. Hence,

$$\Delta_{CB} = \underbrace{\left(\frac{PL}{4EI}\right)\left(\frac{L}{2}\right)\left(\frac{1}{2}\right)}_{\text{(M/EI) area}}\underbrace{\left(\frac{2}{3}\right)\left(\frac{L}{2}\right)}_{\substack{\text{moment arm} \\ \text{about } C}} = \frac{PL^3}{48EI} = \text{deflection at } b \; (y_b)$$

◆

For complex loadings when the beam slope at midspan is not zero, it is necessary to adopt the following general procedure (see Figure A–9–2). Δ_{CA} and Δ_{BA} are first calculated by moment-area theorems. Δ_B is next found by proportions. The beam deflection at B then becomes $y_b = \Delta_B - \Delta_{BA}$.

APPENDIX 10: OTHER METHODS OF ANALYZING INDETERMINATE STRUCTURES

Double-Integration Method. This section addresses a method of analysis that is frankly of little current practical importance as a structural analysis tool. It is, however, of interest in *conceptual* terms as a direct extension and application of some of the formulations previously discussed.

The double-integration method of analysis is based on the moment-curvature relation discussed in Appendix 7. In the example that follows, the moment present at the end of a fixed-ended beam is treated as an unknown in the basic differential equation (see Appendix 8) for the deflection curve of the member. Although the double-integration method of analysis demonstrated here is conceptually very elegant, its application becomes very cumbersome when symmetrical situations do not exist or if there are a large number of redundancies. For this reason, other methods of analysis are typically utilized.

◆ ◆ EXAMPLE

Consider the fixed-ended beam illustrated in Figure A–10–1. Find the moments developed at the supports using $EI(d^2y/dx^2) = M$.

Solution: For the fixed-ended beam, $EI(d^2y/dx^2) = M^F + wLx/2 - wx^2/2$. Integrating, $EI(dy/dx) = M^Fx + wLx^2/4 - wx^3/6 + C_1$. Since the slope of the beam is horizontal at the support, $dy/dx = 0$, where $x = 0$; consequently, $C_1 = 0$. Also, $dy/dx = 0$ at $x = L$. $0 = M^FL + wL^3/4 - wL^3/6$. Hence, $M^F = -wL^2/12$.

This is the moment developed at the support. Using this moment, the values of the moment present at other points in the beam can be found through equilibrium considerations. The moment at midspan, for example, can be shown to be $M = wL^2/24$. Note that in the preceding example, the moment of inertia, I, of the beam was assumed to be constant. If I were a variable, it would have to be expressed as a function of x and included in the integration. The moment found as a result would no longer be $M = -wL^2/12$, but a different value. This illustrates that moments in continuous beams are not independent of variations in member properties. Variations in the modulus of elasticity, E, would also affect results.

If it were desired to know the deflection at midspan of the member analyzed above, it is only necessary to make use of the moment found at the support.

$$EI\frac{dy}{dx} = -\frac{wL^2x}{12} + \frac{wLx^2}{4} - \frac{wx^3}{6}$$

$$EIy = -\frac{wL^2x^2}{24} + \frac{wLx^3}{12} - \frac{wx^4}{24} + C_2$$

Since $y = 0$ at $x = 0$, $C_2 = 0$.

$$EIy = -\frac{wL^2x^2}{24} + \frac{wLx^3}{12} - \frac{wx^4}{24}$$

By symmetry, the maximum deflection occurs at midspan.

$$\Delta = y_{max} = -\frac{wL^4}{384EI}$$

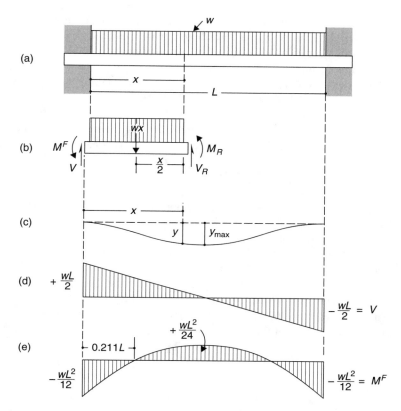

FIGURE A–10–1   Application of the double-integration method of analysis.   ◆

Deflection Method.   The deflection method of analysis is an older technique that involves isolating one (or more) of the redundant supports, conceptually removing the redundant support and allowing the structure to deflect freely (thereby making the structure statically determinate), determining the deflection at the support point, and calculating the magnitude of the force required to push the structure from its freely deformed condition *back* to its original state. The force required to reestablish the original shape of the structure is equivalent to the reaction normally developed at that point.

APPENDIX 11:   CRITICAL BUCKLING LOADS FOR COMPRESSION MEMBERS

This appendix derives the buckling load for a pin-ended column. The critical buckling load is defined to be that axial force that is just sufficient to hold the bar in a slightly deformed configuration. Under the load P the column deflects into a curved shape such that the lateral deflection at a point x from one end of the column is defined by the distance y.

The necessary condition that one end of the bar be able to move axially with respect to the other end in order that the lateral deflection may take place is assumed. The differential equation of the deflection curve is the same as that presented in Appendix 8: $EI\,(d^2y/dx^2) = M$.

The bending moment in the preceding expression is merely the moment of the force P times the deflection y at that point. Hence the bending moment is $M = -Py$. Thus, $EI\,(d^2y/dx^2) = -Py$. If we set $P/EI = k^2$, then $d^2y/dx^2 + k^2y = 0$.

This differential equation is readily solved by any one of several standard techniques discussed in textbooks on differential equations. We need merely find a function which when differentiated twice and added to itself (times a constant) is equal to zero. Evidently, either $\sin kx$ or $\cos kx$ possesses this property. These terms can be combined so as to form a solution to the equation above. Thus, $y = C \sin kx + D \cos kx$.

It is next necessary to determine the constants C and D. At the left end of the bar, $y = 0$ when $x = 0$. Substituting these values, we obtain: $0 = 0 + D$ or $D = 0$.

At the right end of the bar, $y = 0$ when $x = L$. Substituting these values in the expression for y with $D = 0$, we obtain: $0 = C \sin kL$.

Evidently, either $C = 0$ or $\sin kL = 0$. But if $C = 0$, then y is everywhere zero and we have only the trivial case of a straight bar, which is the configuration prior to the occurrence of buckling. Since we are not interested in this solution, we must then take $\sin kL = 0$.

For this to be true, we must have $kL = n\pi$ radians ($n = 1, 2, 3, \ldots$).

Substituting $k^2 = P/EI$ we find $(\sqrt{P/EI})L = n\pi$, or $P = n^2\pi^2 EI/L^2$.

The smallest value of this load P evidently occurs when $n = 1$. Then we have the *first mode of buckling*, where the critical load is given by

$$P_{cr} = \frac{\pi^2 EI}{L^2}$$

This is called *Euler's buckling load* for a pin-ended column. The deflection shape corresponding to this load is $y = C \sin \sqrt{P/EI}x$, or $y = C \sin \pi x/L$. Thus, the deflected shape is a sine curve.

The effects of other types of column end connections (e.g., fixed ends) on the buckling load of a column can be determined in a similar manner. The moment expressions, however, and boundary conditions used are different from those just presented.

APPENDIX 12: COMPUTER-BASED METHODS OF ANALYSIS: FORCE AND MATRIX-DISPLACEMENT TECHNIQUES

The use of computer-based methods of structural analysis and design are commonplace. Capabilities exist for the rapid analysis of most types of two and three-dimensional structural configurations. These techniques have virtually replaced most hand-calculation methods as a way of analyzing structures. The hand-calculation methods, however, remain valuable as a way of understanding how structures behave. Nonetheless, any designer must have a working knowledge of computer-based methods to be effective.

In computer-based approaches, there are typically many conventions. *Global geometries* are defined in terms of *nodes, node numbers,* and *node coordinates*. Structural topologies are defined in terms of *members, member numbers,* and *member properties.* Member incidences (which member end frames into what node) are also specified. Member characteristics are frequently defined in terms of *local geometries* related to each specific member. Support conditions (e.g., fixed, pinned, spring, specified displacements) can and must be specified for specific members, along with any special releases and/or constraints where one member frames into another. In most analysis environments, related "degrees of freedom" must be carefully defined. The loading environment must also be specified in terms of either global or local geometries. Various "cases" representing different loading conditions can be specified as well. In many programs, these conventions are quite evident and must be carefully specified. Some programs have graphical interfaces that speed the process, but by and large, the same parameters must be specified. Analysis outputs typically include reactions, axial forces, shear forces, bending moments, and torsional moments in each member. Also part of the output are typically nodal deflections and member deformations.

The above features are common in most analysis programs. Design-oriented programs may then use the obtained information to do stress and deformation checks for members in given materials, e.g., steel, in which specific member designs are analyzed. Many programs include databases, for example, of commonly available steel wide-flange members. Some programs seek to actually design (i.e., determine member sizes) as well.

There are many different types of approaches used in computer-based methods of analysis. For frameworks of one type or another, one method is generally called the *force* method. The more widely used approach, however, is termed the *displacement* method. Other methods of analysis include various finite-element techniques, discussed in Appendix 13.

In force methods, forces are the primary unknown values that are sought in the analysis. If a structure is statically determinate, these forces may be obtained through the laws of statics alone. Alternatively, *displacement* or *stiffness methods* may be used indistinguishably for both statically determinate and indeterminate structures in which nodal displacements are the primary unknowns. For any structure there are as many nodal displacements as there are externally applied nodal loads (including loads of zero magnitude). This observation leads to a powerful formulation of the problem relating nodal displacements with externally applied loads that requires the solution of a large number of simultaneous equations.

Matrix Force Method. An insight into the basic approach utilized in the matrix force method of analysis can best be gained by looking at the analysis of a simple truss structure by the joint equilibrium method discussed in Chapter 4. For any truss, a close inspection of the solution of member forces in trusses by the joint equilibrium methods reveals that the procedures could be reflected in a series of equations (two for each joint: $\Sigma F_x = 0$ and $\Sigma F_y = 0$) that could then be solved simultaneously instead of proceeding from one joint to another. For example, the two equations for a typical joint (B) in the truss shown in Figure A–12–1 are as follows. In the

FIGURE A–12–1 Force methods.

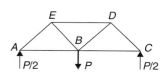

Truss (also see Figure 4–20)

Equilibrium of node *B*

y direction, $0.71F_{BE} + 0.71F_{BD} - P = 0$, and in the x direction, $F_{BC} + 0.71F_{BD} - 0.71F_{BE} - F_{BA} = 0$. Or, more fully including the unknown forces in all the members of the truss and defining P_1 and P_2 as external loads in the x and y directions, respectively, we have

$$P_1 = 0F_{AE} + 0F_{ED} + 1.0F_{BC} + 0.71F_{BD} - 0.71F_{BE} - 1.0F_{BA} + 0F_{DC}$$
$$P_2 = 0F_{AE} + 0F_{ED} + F_{BC} + 0.71F_{BD} + 0.71F_{BE} + 0F_{BA} + 0F_{DC}$$

The full system of equations for all joints can be defined in matrix form as $\{P\} = [S]\{F\}$, where $\{P\}$ is the vector of the externally applied loads on the joints, $[S]$ is the geometry or "direction cosine" matrix, and $\{F\}$ is the vector of the internal forces in the truss members. The matrix is a property of the geometry of the truss. The internal forces can be obtained by solving the equation $\{P\} = [S]\{F\}$ in the following form: $\{F\} = [S]^{-1}\{P\}$. However, for any truss with more than a few joints the solution of the series of equations is prohibitive by hand, but the approach lends itself quite well to computer formulations. For statically indeterminate trusses, there are more unknown forces than equilibrium equations; thus the size of the internal forces vector is larger than the size of the externally applied loads. This requires the employment of elaborate solution techniques. For these reasons, this approach is now rarely used.

Matrix Displacement (or Direct Stiffness Method). This widely used method of analysis is discussed in two parts. This section briefly characterizes the essential nature of the matrix-displacement approach by looking in detail at a simple two-member structural assembly. A more rigorous presentation for multi-member structures follows.

In the force formulation just presented and in most other techniques presented thus far, forces were considered as the primary unknown values. An alternative approach is to treat joint *displacements* rather than forces as the unknown values. This is a widely used formulation in many computer-based analysis programs. The following briefly presents some of the basic theory underlying these programs. In this approach, the different ways each joint may freely move are first examined. In Figure A–12–2, the joint A of the simple two-member truss is displaced to the position A' after the loads P_1 and P_2 are applied. The displacement from A to A' is X in the direction of the movement, or X_1 and X_2 in the horizontal and vertical directions, respectively. For these displacements to occur, the attached bars AB and AC must elongate or compress a certain amount, depending on the geometry of the truss. Assuming that the change of the geometry is

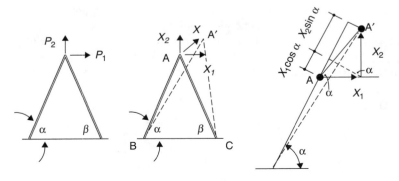

FIGURE A–12–2 Displacement method for two-member structure.

very small ("small displacement theory"), these deformations of the truss members are expressed in terms of X_1 and X_2: $\Delta L_{AB} = X_1 \cos \alpha + X_2 \sin \alpha$ and $\Delta L_{AC} = X_1 \cos \beta + X_2 \sin \beta$. Recall from the discussion in Section 2–7 that there is a relation between the internal force in an axially loaded member and its deformation, so $F_{AB} = (\Delta L_{AB}AE)/L_{AB}$ and $F_{AC} = (\Delta L_{AC}AE)/L_{AC}$, where A is the cross-sectional area of the members and E is the modulus of elasticity of their material. Finally, the joint A is in equilibrium, so the applied forces P_1 and P_2 and the internal forces F_{AB} and F_{AC} must be in equilibrium: $P_1 = F_{AB} \cos \alpha + F_{AC} \cos \beta$ and $P_2 = F_{AB} \sin \alpha + F_{AC} \sin \beta$. Substituting the elongations and internal forces, the applied loads P_1 and P_2 and the displacements X_1 and X_2 can be related as follows: $(k_{AB} \cos^2 \alpha + k_{AC} \cos^2 \beta) \times X_1 + (k_{AB} \cos \alpha \sin \alpha + k_{AC} \cos \beta \sin \beta) \times X_2 = P_1$ and $(k_{AB} \cos \alpha \sin \alpha + k_{AC} \cos \beta \sin \beta) \times X_1 + (k_{AB} \sin^2 \alpha + k_{AC} \sin^2 \beta) \times X_2 = P_2$, where $k_{AB} = AE/L_{AB}$ and $k_{AC} = AE/L_{AC}$. Or, in a matrix form,

$$\begin{bmatrix} K_{11} & K_{12} \\ K_{21} & K_{22} \end{bmatrix} \begin{Bmatrix} X_1 \\ X_2 \end{Bmatrix} = \begin{Bmatrix} P_1 \\ P_2 \end{Bmatrix}$$

After the displacements are calculated from the preceding system of equations, the deformation of the truss members and the internal forces are easily calculated. The same technique can be employed for larger trusses with more joints. However, this technique, which is described in more depth below, requires the solution of a system of many simultaneous equations that can be carried out by computers only.

The matrix displacement method does not distinguish between statically determinate and statically indeterminate trusses, since there are as many unknown displacements as there are externally applied loads on a truss. So indeterminate structures are handled as easily as determinate structures. Furthermore, three-dimensional forms may be analyzed similarly to two-dimensional forms. The effects of settlements of supports and similar phenomena may also be treated with ease. Because of these advantages, matrix displacement techniques have achieved almost universal usage in computer-based structural analysis.

Degrees of Freedom.   Essential to an in-depth understanding of displacement methods is an appreciation of the *degrees of freedom* that a structure possesses. At the node[1] level, there are as many degrees of freedom as there are different forces that can apply to that node to produce displacements. According to this definition, a two-dimensional truss joint has two degrees of freedom (horizontal and vertical translations). A two-dimensional beam node has three degrees of freedom (horizontal and vertical translations and rotation), since there are two forces and a moment that can apply to a beam node. Similarly, a three-dimensional truss has three degrees of freedom per node, while a three-dimensional frame has six degrees of freedom per node. Degrees of freedom can be either *free* or *constrained*. A free degree of freedom denotes that the node can move under the application of loads, whereas a constrained degree of freedom denotes that the displacement of the node in that direction is specified and independent of the applied loads. As a result, externally applied loads act on free degrees of freedom, producing

---

[1]The user defines the nodes on a structure so that the properties of the members between the nodes can be easily identified and calculated. Furthermore, the user can define nodes at points of interest where displacement and force information is sought. Nodes do not imply the presence of released degrees of freedom, such as hinges.

displacements, whereas the displacements are specified on constrained degrees of freedom, producing reactions. A completely fixed connection in the foundation has all degrees of freedom constrained. At the *structure level,* the term *degrees of freedom* is used to designate the total number of degrees of freedom corresponding to the nodes of the structure, representing the number of ways in which a structure may respond to a loading. Initially, all the degrees of freedom in a structure are free, but some are constrained after the supports are introduced (Figure A–12–3). Often, some degrees of freedom are released within the upper structure. The introduction of a hinge at the connection between a beam and a column results in two degrees of freedom at that node. The presence of the hinge prohibits application of a moment, thus eliminating the rotational degree of freedom from that node. Notice, however, that both the beam and the column will actually rotate at that node by different magnitudes and may be in different directions. These rotations will be determined from the equilibrium of each member after the nodal displacements are calculated, together with calculation of the rest of the rotations and displacements along each element.

The Loads-Displacements Matrix Equation. The basic structural concept underlying matrix-displacement methods involves examining a structure for the movements that can occur at each free degree of freedom. These displacements of the free degrees of freedom are the unknowns for the structural system to be determined prior to calculating any other quantities. Structural members are seen as constraints among the degrees of freedom (i.e., constraining the displacements). The deformations of the structural members should be consistent with the displacements of the nodes—thus a system of equations, the *compatibility equations,* are employed to express the member deformations as a function of the nodal displacements. A second set of equations, the *constitutive equations,* relate the member deformations with the internal forces in the structural members, engaging material properties as well as the geometry of the structural members. Finally, the *equilibrium equations* relate the internal forces with the externally applied forces at each degree of freedom. The compatibility equations, the constitutive

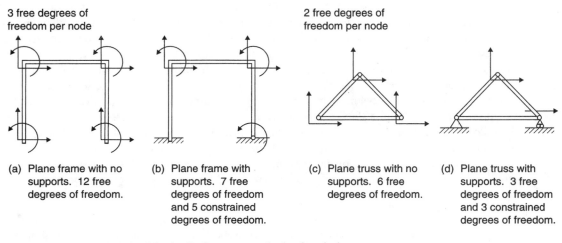

3 free degrees of
freedom per node

2 free degrees of
freedom per node

(a) Plane frame with no supports. 12 free degrees of freedom.

(b) Plane frame with supports. 7 free degrees of freedom and 5 constrained degrees of freedom.

(c) Plane truss with no supports. 6 free degrees of freedom.

(d) Plane truss with supports. 3 free degrees of freedom and 3 constrained degrees of freedom.

FIGURE A–12–3   Matrix displacement methods of analysis.

equations, and the equilibrium equations derive the equations that directly relate the externally applied loads with the displacements of the structure:

$$P_1 = K_{11}X_1 + K_{12}X_2 + \cdots + K_{1j}X_j + \cdots + K_{1n}K_n$$
$$P_2 = K_{21}X_1 + K_{22}X_2 + \cdots + K_{2j}X_j + \cdots + K_{2n}K_n$$
$$P_i = K_{i1}X_1 + K_{i2}X_2 + \cdots + K_{ij}X_j + \cdots + K_{in}X_n$$
$$P_n = K_{n1}X_1 + K_{n2}X_2 + \cdots + K_{nj}X_j + \cdots + K_{nn}X_n$$

or, in matrix form, $\{P\}_{n \times 1} = [K]_{n \times n}\{X\}_{n \times 1}$ P_i denotes the externally applied load on the free degree of freedom i, while X_j denotes the displacement of the node along the degree of freedom j. The stiffness matrix $[K]$ is always square. The stiffness coefficients K_{ij} denote the force in the direction of the ith degree of freedom due to a unit displacement in the direction of the jth degree of freedom. The coefficients K_{ij} are forces per unit displacement—hence their designation as *stiffness coefficients*. It can be shown, based on energy principles, that K_{ij} always equals K_{ji}, and as a result, the matrix $[K]$ is symmetrical. This property leads to the development of very efficient solution techniques for solving the equation $\{X\} = [K]^{-1}\{P\}$, which provides the displacements of the structure.[2] The internal forces of the structural members are then calculated on a member-by-member basis, employing the element's stiffness matrix to derive the forces in each element. Similarly, the reactions are calculated as the summation of forces on the degrees of freedom corresponding to the constraint degrees of freedom of the support.

Types of Analysis Programs. A multipurpose computer program with six degrees of freedom per node is able to provide the displacements and, subsequently, the member forces and reactions for any framework structure. Such a program would be appropriate for a three-dimensional frame with six degrees of freedom per each node (three translations and three rotations), but it would be difficult to use and possibly numerically unstable for structures that have less degrees of freedom per node, such as two-dimensional frames or trusses. As a result, specialized computer programs have been developed applicable for certain classes of structures.[3]

In *three-dimensional frames,* few assumptions are made; each free node is assumed to have six degrees of freedom. In *space trusses,* a node has three degrees of translatory freedom since connections are assumed pinned and the rotations that do occur do not influence forces found. In *plane frames,* all movements are assumed to occur in the plane of the frame (there are no loads applied out-of-plane and out-of-plane motions are considered negligible). As a result, there are two translatory and one rotational degrees of freedom per free node. A pinned support of a plane frame constrains the translatory degrees of freedom at that node, allowing a rotation only; hence one degree of freedom is present. A roller aligned with one of the axes constrains the free degrees of freedom present to two: one rotational and one translational. In *plane trusses,* each joint has two degrees of freedom only. In *grids,* all translations are assumed to take place out of the plane of the grid. At a free node, one translation and two rotations exist.

---

[2]For example, see Bathe, K.J., *Finite Element Procedures in Engineering Analysis,* Prentice Hall, Inc., Englewood Cliffs NJ, 1982.

[3]For example, see Wang, Chu-Kia and Salmon, Charles G., *Introductory Structural Analysis,* Prentice Hall, Inc., Englewood Cliffs, NJ, 1984.

For any computer-based analysis procedure, required inputs focus on all possible nodal movements via a specification of degrees of freedom for each node in a way compatible with the selected analysis procedure and assumptions. Computer-based programs are often called *PLANE TRUSS, PLANE FRAME, SPACE TRUSS,* or *SPACE FRAME* analysis programs or the like, depending on what assumptions of the type noted here have been built into the analysis techniques used. The analysis program type is matched with the characteristics of the structure analyzed. Thus three-dimensional *SPACE FRAME* programs may involve the fewest assumptions but are often cumbersome to use since so many freedom movements must be defined. Normally, they should not be used to solve plane frame or plane truss problems if more appropriate programs are available.

Inputs. Inputs in computer programs based on a displacement method follow very closely the assumptions and structure of the displacement method itself. Inputs are provided in the form of *geometry, materials,* and *applied loads.* The geometry of the structure is defined by the location of the nodes and the specifications of the free and constraint degrees of freedom per node. The structural members are often defined as connecting nodes in the form of *member incidences.* In addition, the properties of the cross section (area, moments of inertia) of the members are input in order to establish, together with the material properties, the relationship between deformation and internal forces. The information on the material and the cross-sectional properties makes a difference on the calculated displacements but does not change the internal forces for statically determinate structures. For indeterminate structures the relative stiffness of the structural members influences the distribution of forces in each member of the structure. Finally, the applied loads are specified. Loads applied on the nodes are usually specified by their magnitude and the corresponding degree of freedom. Loads acting along the members are converted to nodal loads prior to the analysis. Alternatively, many newer programs provide a graphic interface that allows the user to define interactively the geometry, materials, and applied loads.

Outputs. Outputs include the nodal displacements, the internal member forces (axial and shearing forces and moments), and the reactions at the supports (constrained degrees of freedom). Depending on the program, axial and shearing forces and moment values may or may not be provided along the length of the members. If not, these values may be calculated by equilibrium considerations for individual members with end forces (axial and shearing forces and moments) applied. Notice that the required material properties for input are limited to stiffness and do not normally include any strength information (i.e., there is no specification for a maximum allowable stress level). Similarly, the output of most analysis programs do not report the magnitude of stresses within the members. Analysis programs are not concerned with stress levels, which is the subject of the design process that follows the analysis.

Comments. A classic problem for the novice of using computer programs is that in order to analyze a structure, certain material and cross-sectional properties must be known a priori and entered as inputs. For example, for plane frame problems, the modulus of elasticity E, the cross-sectional area A, and the moment of inertia I of each member must be provided prior to the analysis. The approximate analysis techniques discussed earlier in the book may be used to estimate force and sizes to be used as a basis for E, I, and A estimates. Members should be designed on the basis of the analytical values obtained so that E, I, and A assumptions can be tested for reasonableness and the analysis process repeated if assumptions later prove to be far off. Another way is to input arbitrary initial values for E, I, and A and iterate a few analyses in order to define consistent values between input and output. For statically determinate structures the arbitary values of E, I, and A will affect the displacements only, but the internal forces will be accurate at the first cycle. For statically indeterminate structures the arbitrary values of E, I, and A will affect both the displacements and the internal forces.

Common analysis programs perform the analysis subject to a single set of loads. However, multiple loading patterns may have to be applied and maximum force and moment values extracted from each so that critical design values for each individual member may be determined. Members would consequently be sized on the basis of critical values, which collectively may correspond to no single loading condition. Analyses may have to be repeated using these member sizes.

Beyond the basics, displacement method computer programs can have more features, often desirable for more sophisticated problems. Such features include the input of loads along the members (for frames only) and the calculation of axial and shearing forces and moments along the members, the specification of "forced" displacements, the introduction of elastic foundations, the specification of the orientation of rollers (so that the horizontal and vertical displacements have a constant ratio), and the option for released degrees of freedom within the structure (such as the introduction of a hinge in a frame, etc.). At a different level, computer programs can handle nonlinear material properties and nonlinear geometrical deformations (buckling).

Cables. An interesting application of nonlinear materials is the analysis of cables (and tension shells) that can take tension loads but cannot take any compression loads. For small-size structures such an analysis can be done iteratively by adding and removing members so that all present members develop tension only and all members removed would develop compression only. For larger-size problems, such a manual process is quite tedious (and may not easily converge to a solution) and the computer program should be able to handle bilinear constitutive laws and solve the system of equations in an iterative process.

APPENDIX 13:   FINITE-ELEMENT TECHNIQUES

The matrix-displacement methods described briefly in Appendix 12 are suitable for complex frames, where the nodes are defined usually at the interconnection of the elements and the stiffness coefficients are conceptually convenient to define. For *continuum* problems, such as the analysis of thin-surface shells, *finite-element* techniques enjoy wide popularity. In a finite-element model, the continuum is replaced by a network or mesh of discrete pieces called *finite elements*. These elements are considered connected at specific points called nodes (typically at corners, but sometimes at edges). Loadings on surfaces are converted to nodal loadings. A structural model is then used to predict forces and displacements. The model used is often based on one or another of a variety of energy laws.

Finite-element models produce exact solutions under certain conditions, depending on the nature of the problem and the characteristics of the element employed. The structural analysis computer programs for trusses or frames are finite element programs, where the stiffness matrix is formulated according to an exact theory. However, for most problems, finite-element models only approximate the continuum, and other assumptions must necessarily be involved in the formulation of stiffness measures of displaced shapes. The use of an approximate displacement state is a fundamental part of most discrete finite element formulations for complex problems.

Briefly, one process is as follows: The continuum is divided up into a mesh (many shapes of elements are possible). An example is shown in Figure A–13–1. The number of elements used affects both the degree of analytical complexity and the quality of results. Small meshes may be used in critical places and coarser ones elsewhere. Each element is then assigned a displacement function that can be expressed in terms of displacements at designated nodes. Nodes are interconnected. A structural model, typically based on potential energy concepts, is used to analyze the structure (complementary energy models may be used as well). Minimization of potential energy for the mesh produces a stiffness model with nodal forces as known values and displacements as unknown values. Via matrix analysis a determination is made of nodal displacements, which in turn allows a determination of the displaced shape of each element and a subsequent calculation of stresses and strains.

Analysis programs have been developed for both framed members and two-dimensional field problems. Since the method is approximate, care must be used in matching necessary analysis assumptions with the reality of the structure and to avoid brute-force solutions. Dense meshes and more degrees of freedom per node than required can lead not only to huge computer requirements but also to numerical instabilities and wrong results. The distinction between plane-stress and plane-strain problems is crucial. Plane-stress formulations are typically used for problems such as the analysis of thin surface roof shells (since certain out-of-plane stress components are assumed nonexistent in the formulation). Plane-strain formulations are used for the analysis of massive dams (and the like where certain deformations may be assumed to have zero values). Furthermore, axisymmetric finite element formulations make axisymmetric problems easier to analyze.

Once principal stresses are found via a finite-element solution, many algorithms support safety checking of a structure via any of a variety of complex failure criteria that address stress interactions. Typical failure criteria include the following: the maximum von Mies stress criterion, the Mohr-Coulomb stress criterion, the maximum normal stress criterion, and the maximum shear stress criterion. The maximum von Mies stress criterion is based upon the energy associated with the change of shape of the material, and is very good for ductile materials. It is based on the premise that yielding in a ductile material occurs when the distortion energy per unit volume equals or exceeds that associated with a comparable volume when subjected to a simple tension test.

FIGURE A–13–1 Finite-element meshes. (Courtesy of Algor, Inc.)

The von Mies stress can be written in terms of three principal stresses in the following way: The maximum normal stress criterion (sometimes known as Coulomb's criterion) is more simply based on a comparison of maximum principal stresses to those in a simple tension specimen. The maximum shear stress criterion states that yielding begins when the maximum shear stress equals or exceeds that associated with yielding in a simple tension test. It is also useful for ductile materials. The Mohr-Coulomb theory is used largely for brittle materials and compares selected values to tensile specimens. The choice of criteria to be used depends very much on the type of material present and factors such as the rate of loading, temperature, and so forth. Rarely is a single theory appropriate for all conditions.

The above mentioned stress checks are commonly used in mechanical engineering situations, e.g., those involving objects with complex geometries and loading conditions, such as a ball joint, and in similar building design situations.

In some finite element analysis programs that are more directly targeted toward building applications and use beam/column elements, e.g., SAP2000, stress-checking can be done directly in relation to actual code provisions instead of the general failure criteria previously noted.

It must be emphasized that finite-element programs are not necessarily the end-all of structural analysis. Many novices often appear to believe that simply because one can imagine a mesh drawn on a surface, the difficulty ends there. As noted, care must be taken in formulating the problem properly, and results are always approximate and subject to interpretation. Often, many iterations are done to identify critical points so that a new and more appropriate mesh could be constructed. Finite-element techniques are used widely for nonlinear problems, with both material and geometrical nonlinearities. Furthermore, other approaches in finite elements have resulted in boundary finite elements that discretize the continuum or part of it, with fewer elements that extend to the boundaries, rather than many discrete elements. See other sources for a more complete description of finite-element techniques.[4]

---

[4]For example, see Gutkowski, Richard, *Structures,* Van Nostrand Reinhold Co., New York, 1981.

APPENDIX 14:   PROPERTIES

The tables here and in Appendix 15 show typical properties for members and materials.

Table A-14-1   MEMBER PROPERTIES[a]

Shape	Area (in.²)	Web Thickness (in.)	Axis X–X I_x (in.⁴)	Axis X–X S_x (in.³)	Axis X–X r_x (in.)	Axis Y–Y I_x (in.⁴)	Axis Y–Y S_x (in.³)	Axis Y–Y r_x (in.)	X–X S_x (mm³ × 10³)
W 36 × 280	82.32	0.885	18,819.3	1,031.2	15.12	1127.5	135.9	3.70	16,882
W 33 × 200	58.79	0.715	11,048.2	669.6	13.71	691.7	87.8	3.43	10,998
W 30 × 99	29.11	0.522	3,988.6	269.1	11.70	116.9	22.4	2.00	4,425
W 27 × 102	30.01	0.518	3,604.1	266.3	10.96	129.5	25.9	2.08	4,376
W 21 × 68	20.02	0.430	1,478.3	139.9	8.59	60.4	14.6	1.74	2,295
W 14 × 87	25.96	0.420	966.9	138.1	6.15	349.7	48.4	3.70	2,262
W 14 × 84	24.71	0.451	928.4	130.9	6.13	225.5	37.5	3.02	2,147
W 24 × 55	16.18	0.375	1140.7	109.7	8.40	44.0	10.7	1.65	1,868
W 14 × 74	21.76	0.450	796.8	112.3	6.05	133.5	26.5	2.48	1,836
W 18 × 60	17.64	0.416	984.0	107.8	7.47	47.1	12.5	1.63	1,764
W 16 × 50	14.70	0.380	655.4	80.7	6.68	34.8	9.8	1.54	1,324
W 16 × 36	10.59	0.299	446.3	56.3	6.49	22.1	6.3	1.45	926
W 8 × 31	9.12	0.288	109.7	27.4	3.47	37.0	9.20	2.01	449
W 12 × 27	7.97	0.240	204.1	34.1	5.06	16.6	5.10	1.44	733
W 10 × 21	6.19	0.240	106.3	21.5	4.14	9.7	3.40	1.25	352
W 8 × 24	7.06	0.245	82.5	20.8	3.42	18.2	5.6	1.61	341
W 8 × 17	5.00	0.230	56.4	14.1	3.36	6.72	2.60	1.16	231
C 9 × 15	4.39	0.413	50.7	11.3	3.40	1.90	1.00	0.67	185
C 6 × 13	3.81	0.437	17.3	5.8	2.13	1.10	0.65	0.53	95

[a]The beams in the table are arranged according to their relative S_x values in descending order of magnitude for the first entry in each grouping of members. Entries in each grouping are arranged in descending order of S_x for a group. The first entry in a group represents the lightest member and the member having the largest section modulus for all entries in the group. It is thus an efficient and often preferred member. W, wide-flange shape; C, channel shape; M, miscellaneous shape; B, light beam. Typical designation:

W 21 × 68 — weight per linear foot, lb
— nominal depth, in.
— shape designation

APPENDIX 15: TYPICAL MATERIAL PROPERTIES

Table A-15-1   ALLOWABLE STRESSES FOR STEEL[a]

ASTM grade	Yield stress (kips/in.^{2})	Allowable stress (kips/in.^{2})			
		Tension	Compression (no buckling)	Bending	Shear
A36	58	22	22	24	14.4
A572, A441	50	30	30	33	20

[a]Allowable stresses are in kips/in.^{2} (1 kip/in.^{2} = 1000 lb/in.^{2}). Values shown are based on U.S. practice: A36 steel, F_y = 36 kips/in.^{2}; bending, F_b = 0.66 F_y; shear, F_v = 0.40 F_y; compression in laterally supported beam flange, F_b = 0.66F_y; tension on gross area, F_i = 0.60 F_y; tension on net area, F_t = 0.60 F_y; other factors must be considered, so values are not to be used for actual allowable stress design purposes. For LFRD approaches, ultimate values are used.

Table A-15-2   ALLOWABLE STRESSES FOR TIMBER[a]

Type of Wood	Bending Stress f_b and Tension Parallel to Grain	Horizontal Shear	Compression	
			Perpendicular to the Grain	Parallel to the Grain
Lumber				
Douglas fir				
$E = 1.7 \times 10^6$ lb/in.^{2}	1200–2100	70–100	300–450	1000–1800
Southern pine				
$E = 1.7 \times 10^6$ lb/in.^{2}	1200–2800	85–160	260–455	900–2200
Glued-laminated timber: dry use				
Douglas fir				
$E = 1.8 \times 10^6$ lb/in.^{2}	1600–2600	165	375–450	1500
Southern pine				
$E = 1.8 \times 10^6$ lb/in.^{2}	1600–2600	140–200	375–450	700–1500
Glued-laminated timber: wet use reduction factors				
E: 0.83	0.80	0.88	0.67	0.73
Duration of loading factors				
Normal 1.00				
Permanent 0.90				
Two months (snow) 1.15				
Wind or earthquake 1.33				
Impact 2.00				

[a]Allowable stress values are in lb/in.^{2} (psi).

Table A–15–3 ULTIMATE STRENGTH STRESSES FOR CONCRETE[a]

Ultimate Concrete Strength, f'_c	E_c
3000	3.00×10^6
4000	3.60×10^6
5000	4.00×10^6

[a]Stress values are in lb/in.^{2} (psi).

Note: 1 lb/in.^{2} = 0.00689 N/mm^2: 1×10^6 lb/in.^{2} = 6.8948 kN/mm^2.

Index